Citizen-Centric Artificial Intelligence for Smart Cities

Ashok Sharma
University of Jammu, India

Vibhakar Mansotra
University of Jammu, India

Parveen Singh
Cluster University, Jammu, India

IGI Global
Scientific Publishing
Publishing Tomorrow's Research Today

Vice President of Editorial	Melissa Wagner
Managing Editor of Acquisitions	Mikaela Felty
Managing Editor of Book Development	Jocelynn Hessler
Production Manager	Mike Brehm
Cover Design	Phillip Shickler

Published in the United States of America by
IGI Global Scientific Publishing
701 East Chocolate Avenue
Hershey, PA, 17033, USA
Tel: 717-533-8845
Fax: 717-533-7115
Website: https://www.igi-global.com E-mail: cust@igi-global.com

Library of Congress Cataloging-in-Publication Data

Names: Sharma, Ashok, 1977- editor | Mansotra, Vibhakar editor | Singh, Parveen, 1976- editor
Title: Citizen-centric artificial intelligence for smart cities / edited by Ashok Sharma, Vibhakar Mansotra, Parveen Singh.
Description: Hershey, PA : IGI Global, [2025] | Includes bibliographical references and index. | Summary: "Citizen-Centric Artificial Intelligence for Smart Cities focuses on leveraging AI technologies to enhance urban living by prioritizing the needs and experiences of citizens. The integration of AI into smart city infrastructure aims to improve various aspects of city life, including transportation, healthcare, energy management, and public safety. The book is comprised of various chapters that delve into this transformative journey, offering a comprehensive exploration of how AI can be harnessed to create cities that prioritize the needs, aspirations, and well-being of their residents"-- Provided by publisher.
Identifiers: LCCN 2024047942 (print) | LCCN 2024047943 (ebook) | ISBN 9798369378328 h/c | ISBN 9798369378335 s/c | ISBN 9798369378342 ebook
Subjects: LCSH: Smart cities--Technological innovations | Artificial intelligence--Social aspects | Artificial intelligence--Industrial applications | City planning--Technological innovations
Classification: LCC TD159.4 .C55 2025 (print) | LCC TD159.4 (ebook)
LC record available at https://lccn.loc.gov/2024047942
LC ebook record available at https://lccn.loc.gov/2024047943

British Cataloguing in Publication Data
A Cataloguing in Publication record for this book is available from the British Library.

Table of Contents

Detailed Table of Contents

for urban transportation. The chapter concludes by addressing various challenges and ethical considerations of deploying AI in urban transportation systems, including data privacy, Public Safety, Security, and efficient use of AI tools and products.

Rapid city expansion presents many obstacles to urban sustainability, such as resource management, pollution, and public safety issues. This study looks at how pollution management and environmental monitoring can be advanced by artificial intelligence (AI) to improve urban sustainability. Artificial Intelligence (AI) technology, including automation, predictive modelling, and real-time data analysis, make it possible to create complex systems that monitor the quality of air and water, identify environmental threats, and maximize resource use. Cities can continually monitor environmental conditions, offering timely insights for interventions and lowering environmental footprints by combining AI-driven sensors and IoT devices. Additionally, AI helps to build sustainable urban infrastructure and promotes public safety by recognizing pollution patterns associated with health hazards. AI has the capacity to completely transform urban sustainability, which emphasizes how crucial it is for technology developers, legislators, and urban planners to work together.

Citizen-centric artificial intelligence systems put citizen in their hearts than view them as passive providers of data. Urban living in the smart cities can be enhanced by manipulating artificial intelligence for the expeditious evolution of smart cities. Artificial intelligence systems should give utmost importance and attention to the needs and values of the citizens which is very essential for the urban development and for a sustainable environment. The chapter investigates the notion of the Citizen-centric artificial intelligence with reference to the smart cities stating its importance and role in the urban transformation, promoting inclusivity and accessibility by providing ethical artificial intelligence solutions to ensure transparency and accountability adhering challenges as well.

Artificial Intelligence (AI) is increasingly becoming a vital part of crisis management and disaster response, particularly in the context of urban infrastructure. Cities are increasingly vulnerable to both natural and man-made disasters as they grow larger and more interconnected. AI systems have the ability to anticipate, plan for, and handle emergencies more effectively, protecting metropolitan people in the process. The application of AI to the phases of preparedness, response, recovery, and mitigation of disasters is examined in this chapter, with a particular emphasis on how AI may strengthen the resilience of urban infrastructure. We highlight case studies, examine challenges in AI deployment, and propose future directions for AI-driven crisis management systems.

This chapter explores the evolving role of Artificial Intelligence (AI) in crisis management and disaster response amidst escalating global challenges. Beginning with an overview of traditional methods, it charts the progression to AI-driven solutions integrating machine learning, predictive analytics, natural language processing (NLP), and computer vision. Highlighting applications in early warning systems, real-time monitoring, and damage assessment, the chapter examines AI's impact across disaster phases: preparedness, crisis management, and recovery. Case studies illustrate AI's efficacy in earthquake, flood, and pandemic responses, while addressing ethical concerns of data privacy, security, and bias. Looking forward, the chapter discusses AI's synergy with IoT and blockchain, envisioning enhanced global resilience and a transformative future in crisis response.

In the wake of escalating environmental worries, superior technologies like Artificial Intelligence and Machine Learning have emerged as powerful allies in monitoring and controlling pollution.This chapter delves into the transformative capability of AI and ML inside the realm of environmental science, focusing on their software in detecting, analyzing, and mitigating pollution. We start by means of exploring the mixing of AI and ML in environmental tracking structures. These systems leverage sensor networks and satellite imagery to gather real-time air, water, and soil information. AI algorithms decorate the precision and performance of statistics series, permitting the identity of pollutant assets with remarkable accuracy. Case research highlights hit implementations, along with AI-driven air exceptional monitoring stations and ML fashions predicting water infection styles. Ethical considerations and demanding situations are addressed, such as data privacy, algorithmic bias, and the need for transparent AI systems.

Air pollution has created significant implications for public health and well-being. The chapter looks into the major events of air pollution, its impact and various approaches to deal with the air pollution. Traditional methods of air pollution monitoring and intensity detection rely on stationary sensors and manual measurements, which are often limited in spatial coverage and real-time monitoring capabilities. This chapter discusses a methodology that analyzes images captured from various sources, such as satellite imagery or ground-based cameras, and accurately classify different types of air pollution, including smog, particulate matter, and industrial emissions. The goal is to provide an efficient and automated method for monitoring air quality, enabling early detection of pollution hotspots, and assisting in environmental management and public health efforts. The image and video processing model of air pollution detection has achieved the loss is 0.4434 and accuracy of 88.88%.

Robotic systems integrated with artificial intelligence are transforming communication within health care and between different actors in health care. These improvements have significantly improved service delivery in the healthcare sector. This chapter reviews the evolution, applications, and implications of robotic systems in healthcare to consider their contribution to improving patient education and healthcare communication levels. Progress in AI and machine learning allows robotic systems to perform anything from simple patient interaction to complex surgery, thus addressing the increased demand for health services underpinning the global scarcity of health professionals. The benefits are enormous in terms of efficiency and precision; however, the challenges in adopting such technologies bring ethical considerations, data privacy issues, and a possible depersonalization of care. This chapter also points out the importance of balancing technological advances and the retention of human elements in healthcare system

Urbanization is an ongoing process that is gradually defining the context of the contemporary world; studies show that by 2050, 67. It projects that 9 percent of the global population will live in developed urban areas by 2050, up from today's 55 percent (United Nations, 2018). The Philippines' Olongapo City is one of the ideal examples of how utilizing the power of advanced analytics in machine learning for innovations can help foster SD in cities. The current paper focuses on the concerns experienced in Olongapo City, the particular ML solutions that were used to resolve these concerns, and the generalization of AI development in handling city management. Thus, the given study shows the possibilities of ML in enriching the concept of sustainable smart cities.

In the evolving landscape of smart cities, the integration of advanced technologies and data-driven solutions is pivotal. This chapter explores the dynamics of data governance and privacy within smart cities, emphasizing their role in enhancing urban living and infrastructure. It begins with an overview of smart cities and their reliance on data from sensors, IoT devices, and public services. Key principles of data governance, including data quality management and lifecycle management, are examined alongside regulatory frameworks like GDPR and CCPA. Privacy concerns are scrutinized, with strategies for protection such as data anonymization and encryption explored. Real-world case studies from Singapore, Barcelona, and Amsterdam illustrate challenges and successes, while future trends and technologies like blockchain and AI are considered for advancing urban innovation.

Preface

The rapid expansion of urbanization and technological advancements has led to the emergence of smart cities, where Artificial Intelligence (AI) plays a pivotal role in enhancing efficiency, sustainability, and citizen engagement. The integration of AI-driven solutions in urban infrastructure, healthcare, transportation, crisis management, and environmental monitoring has revolutionized how cities operate and serve their citizens. This book, *Citizen-Centric Artificial Intelligence for Smart Cities*, brings together leading researchers and experts from diverse disciplines to explore the transformative potential of AI in shaping smart urban environments. Through in-depth studies and innovative research, this volume aims to provide a comprehensive overview of how AI can optimize urban living, ensuring that the needs of citizens remain at the core of technological advancements.

The chapters in this book cover a wide range of topics that demonstrate the intersection of AI with various aspects of smart city development. From optimizing task allocation in fog-based IoT frameworks and enhancing urban mobility through AI-driven transportation systems to addressing pollution control and environmental sustainability, the contributions in this book highlight groundbreaking methodologies and frameworks. Additionally, the role of AI in public safety, healthcare, crisis management, and disaster response is examined, showcasing how AI-driven technologies can improve resilience and preparedness in urban areas. By delving into these crucial themes, this book not only presents state-of-the-art research but also offers actionable insights for policymakers, urban planners, and technologists.

OVERVIEW OF CHAPTERS

Chapter 1: Optimizing Task Allocation in Fog-Based IoT for Smart City Solutions

This chapter explores the role of fog computing in smart cities, focusing on optimizing task allocation in IoT environments. It discusses heuristic and meta-heuristic algorithms that improve resource utilization, reduce latency, and enhance system efficiency for sustainable urban development.

Chapter 2: Smart Transportation System / Infrastructure: AI-Driven Innovations for Urban Transformation

This chapter examines AI-driven advancements in urban transportation systems, covering efficiency, safety, and sustainability. It highlights AI's role in autonomous vehicles, transportation planning, and traffic management, while addressing ethical and security concerns.

Chapter 3: Using AI to Improve Urban Sustainability: Pollution Control and Environmental Monitoring

This chapter investigates AI's potential in pollution control and environmental monitoring. It discusses AI-driven automation, predictive modeling, and IoT sensor integration to enhance air and water quality monitoring, resource optimization, and urban sustainability.

Chapter 4: Citizen-Centric AI for Mobility, Public Safety, and Healthcare

Focusing on the human-centric approach to AI in smart cities, this chapter explores AI-driven solutions that enhance mobility, accessibility, public safety, and healthcare. It emphasizes ethical considerations, transparency, and accountability in AI applications.

Chapter 5: AI in Crisis Management and Disaster Response for Urban Infrastructure

This chapter highlights AI's role in disaster preparedness, response, and recovery. It explores predictive analytics, machine learning, and case studies that demonstrate AI's effectiveness in strengthening urban resilience against crises and natural disasters.

Chapter 6: AI-Driven Healthcare: Transformation and Advancement

Examining AI's impact on healthcare, this chapter discusses its role in disease diagnosis, remote monitoring, telehealth, and personalized medicine. It also covers AI-driven drug discovery and its potential for improving patient care.

Chapter 7: AI-Driven Social Media Analysis for Disaster Situational Awareness

This chapter explores how AI-powered social media analytics enhances disaster response by providing real-time insights, geolocation tracking, and sentiment analysis. It addresses challenges like data privacy and ethical AI use in crisis management.

Chapter 8: Smart Transportation Systems: Enhancing Mobility and Accessibility

This chapter delves into AI, IoT, and big data applications in smart transportation. It discusses AI's role in optimizing traffic flow, reducing congestion, and improving public transit efficiency in urban environments.

Chapter 9: Tech-Driven Society: A Strategy for Community Safety and Security

Focusing on IoT and real-time data analytics, this chapter examines how emerging technologies enhance public safety, security, and urban infrastructure. It also highlights privacy concerns and the need for standardization in smart city innovations.

Chapter 10: The Role of AI in Crisis Management and Disaster Response

This chapter explores AI applications in disaster response, including early warning systems, damage assessment, and real-time monitoring. It also discusses AI's integration with IoT and blockchain for improved crisis resilience.

Chapter 11: Technological Enhancement in Environmental Monitoring and Pollution Control

Examining AI and machine learning applications in pollution control, this chapter discusses real-time environmental monitoring systems, sensor networks, and AI-driven strategies for detecting and mitigating pollution.

Chapter 12: Air Pollution Detection Using Image Processing

This chapter explores image-processing techniques for detecting air pollution. It discusses AI-based models that analyze satellite and ground images to identify pollution sources and assist in environmental management.

Chapter 13: Transforming Healthcare Through AI and Robotic Communication Systems

This chapter examines how AI-powered robotic systems enhance healthcare communication, diagnostics, and surgeries. It discusses the benefits and challenges of robotic integration in healthcare services.

Chapter 14: Virtual Intelligent Autonomous Agents: Robot Navigation for Disaster Intervention

This chapter explores AI-driven robotics for disaster response. It discusses reinforcement learning techniques used to train robots for autonomous navigation in hazardous environments, such as gas leak detection.

Chapter 15: Water Contamination Detection Using Image Processing

This chapter focuses on AI and image-processing techniques for water pollution detection. It discusses machine learning models that assess water quality, detect contaminants, and improve environmental sustainability.

Chapter 16: Machine Learning-Driven Innovations for Sustainable Smart Cities

This chapter highlights how machine learning enhances smart city infrastructure. It covers AI-driven solutions for energy efficiency, waste management, and urban planning to support sustainable city development.

Chapter 17: Internet of Things (IoT) and Artificial Intelligence for Smart Urban Development

This chapter discusses how IoT and AI together contribute to smart city development. It covers their role in energy management, transportation, public safety, and infrastructure improvements, showcasing case studies of successful AI-IoT integrations.

We believe that the research presented in this book will serve as a valuable resource for academics, professionals, and students interested in the intersection of AI and smart city development. The collaborative efforts of esteemed researchers from renowned institutions worldwide have resulted in a publication that bridges theoretical advancements with real-world applications. As cities continue to evolve, it is imperative that AI is harnessed responsibly to create sustainable, inclusive, and citizen-centric urban environments. This book aims to inspire further research and innovation in this domain, fostering the development of AI-driven solutions that prioritize the well-being and empowerment of citizens.

We extend our deepest gratitude to the contributors for their dedication and valuable insights. Their expertise has enriched this volume, making it a significant addition to the growing body of knowledge on AI in smart cities. We would also like to express our sincere appreciation to the institutions and organizations that supported this work. Finally, we hope that this book will ignite discussions, encourage collaborations, and serve as a catalyst for the continued integration of AI in shaping the cities of the future.

Ashok Sharma
University of Jammu, India

Vibhakar Mansotra
University of Jammu, India

Parveen Singh
Higher Education, India

Chapter 1
Optimizing Task Allocation in Fog-Based IoT for Smart City Solutions

Variza Negi
https://orcid.org/0000-0001-8193-1461
NMIMS University, Mumbai, India

Diksha Joshi
https://orcid.org/0000-0003-3919-6234
NMIMS University, Mumbai, India

Ashok Sharma
https://orcid.org/0000-0003-2553-4263
University of Jammu, India

ABSTRACT

Cities throughout the world are utilizing cutting-edge information and communication technology (ICT) to use limited space and resources in order to accommodate the growing urban population. By enabling decentralized processing near IoT devices, fog computing plays a crucial role in smart cities by lowering latency, increasing efficiency, and hence lowering carbon emissions. Smart city applications often struggle with difficulties like resource heterogeneity, fluctuating workloads and stringent QoS (Quality of Service). This study focusses on optimizing task allocation in fog-based IoT settings. Advanced heuristic and meta-heuristic algorithms are therefore required to dynamically allocate computing jobs between multiple fog nodes. The suggested solutions in this survey that are making use of these advanced

DOI: 10.4018/979-8-3693-7832-8.ch001

techniques have shown better resource utilization, less delays, and increased system dependability through simulations. Thus, Fog computing demonstrates how it can be beneficial in satisfying the futuristic need of sustainable and scalable smart city environments.

1. INTRODUCTION

Better job opportunities, greater wages, luxurious lifestyles and 24 by 7 health-care facilities have drawn a large population to cities and this trend is only going to increase in the coming future, worldwide. It is anticipated that 68% of the world's population will reside in urban regions by 2025 (Profiroiu et al., 2020). For such a high urban population, the planning of Smart cities is an important aspect. A transformative approach to urban living has been presented by the Smart cities by optimizing technology to enhance efficiency, sustainability, and community well-being. They integrate various digital technologies like IoT (Internet of Things), Cloud computing, Fog computing, Edge computing, Mist Computing, Artificial Intelligence (AI) and many other emerging technologies to address urban challenges, focusing on environmental, social, cultural, and economic aspects. By utilizing real-time data generated by the IoT devices spread across the city, smart cities aim to enhance operational efficiency, reduce resource consumption, and address urban challenges such as congestion, pollution, transportation, and housing shortages (Ashraf, 2021).

A quintessential smart city, comprising of one million smart citizens can generate about 180 million GB of data in a day from various IoT devices, as per Cisco reports (Cisco, 2015). One of the key requirements in case of Smart cities is the ability to facilitate real-time processing and analyzing this telemetry data, enabling the smart citizens to take instantaneous decisions and creating better future opportunities.

To cater to this requirement of real-time data processing, smart cities rely on Fog-Cloud environment, that enables immediate insights and actions for any decision making. Fog computing is an additional networking layer that facilitates reducing the latency and the power consumption by bringing the computing resources nearer to the data sources. To achieve better QoS performance, scalability and cost effectiveness, optimizing the task allocation is crucial in the case of collaborative Fog-Cloud based IoT environment.

Novel techniques and algorithms have been suggested by various studies in the past to optimize job allocation in Fog Computing environment in case of Smart city applications. Different studies have focused on different concerns related to Fog based environments like dynamic workloads, resource heterogeneity, and strict quality-of-service (QoS) standards. The studies have applied the heuristic and metaheuristics techniques in order to optimally distribute workload among various Fog nodes, balancing workload and minimizing the power consumption.

In comparison to conventional cloud-centric models, the suggested models show better resource utilization, shorter task execution delays, and increased system dependability through simulations and real-world case studies. By providing scalable and sustainable solutions that connect IoT devices to centralized cloud infrastructure, the findings demonstrate the potential of optimized fog computing frameworks to address the increasing computational demands of smart cities.

2. FOG COMPUTING

The term "Fog Computing" was first introduced by Cisco in 2012 and formalized in 2014 (Bonomi et al., 2012). OpenFog Consortium defines Fog computing as "A horizontal, system-level architecture that distributes computing, storage, control, and networking functions closer to the user along a cloud-to-thing continuum" is how the OpenFog organization defines fog computing." (OpenFog Consortium Architecture Working Group, 2017). Smart homes, towns, farms, and grids are just a few of the IoT applications that are becoming more and more common in modern life. For the interchange of vital data, IoT devices need a significant amount of storage and processing power.

Cloud computing integrated with IoT offers a solution by enabling end devices to perform all necessary computations and data storage. However, as the number of applications increases, performance issues arise when transmitting data, particularly for end devices situated far from cloud data centers that demand more resources and processing power. Furthermore, the proliferation of IoT devices can result in network failures, high latency, and limited capacity. To address these challenges, fog computing was developed to enhance performance and reduce delays. This system utilizes fog nodes to distribute resources such as computing power and network connectivity to end devices.

Figure 1. represents various Fog-Cloud enabled Smart city example. Here, the lower layer comprises of various IoT devices like Smart home devices, Consumer devices, traffic management devices, medical devices, grid systems, security devices, smart factory systems, etc. The middle layer comprises of Fog nodes, which can be in the form of multi-layered hops. The upper layer comprises of Cloud servers that can manage to work on heavier workloads.

Figure 1. Fog-cloud enabled smart city

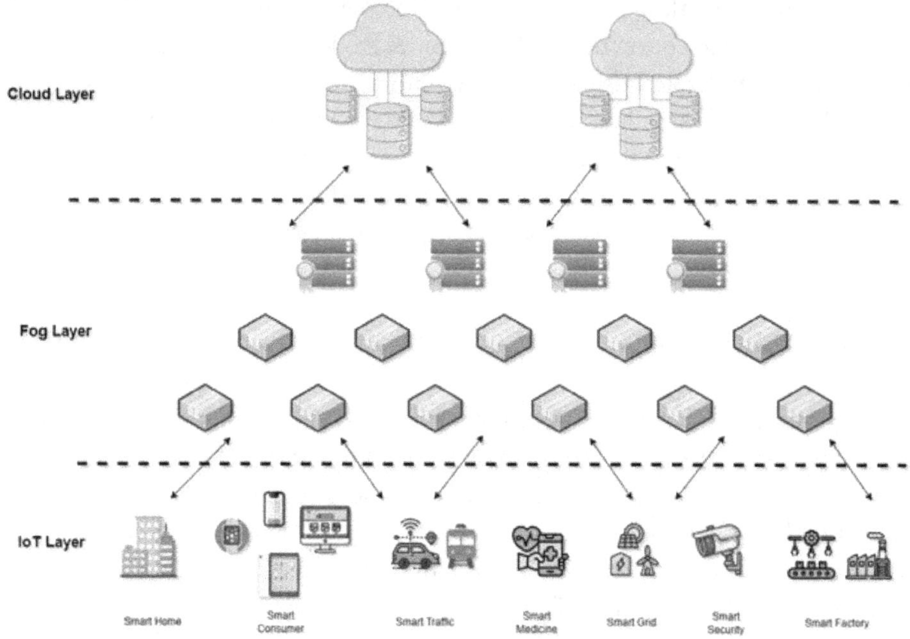

Cisco states that fog computing possesses wireless capabilities in addition to its broad distribution, mobility, heterogeneity, and interoperability. The varying input data and processing rates among fog nodes can lead to an uneven workload distribution, where some nodes are overburdened while others remain unused. These challenges have a minimal impact on fog performance. Consequently, efficiently allocating workloads and scheduling tasks in Fog environments are critical concerns that need to be addressed.

3. TASK ALLOCATION IN FOG-BASED IOT

Task allocation in Fog-Based IoT environment refers to the process of distributing tasks among the various Fog nodes. Finding the best placement for each job based on specifications like processing power, storage, and network bandwidth, as well as adjusting to the network's dynamic nature, are the primary issues in task allocation. In edge computing, task allocation is a complicated, multifaceted, and difficult topic that necessitates balancing trade-offs between several competing goals, including latency, energy efficiency, data privacy, security, and quality of service (QoS). Mutiple research studies that have examined the complexity and optimization issues of task allocation and have determined that it is an NP-hard problem because of all these factors. This categorization results from the intrinsic challenge of locating optimum solutions in polynomial time, especially for large-scale, heterogeneous systems like the Internet of Things built on fog.

The goal of task scheduling in fog computing for smart cities is to effectively divide up computational activities among fog nodes to minimise energy consumption, balance load, lower latency, and satisfy Quality of Service (QoS) standards. Enabling timely and effective smart city services that can manage the growing complexity and size of Internet of Things (IoT) deployments is essential.

Major challenges in task scheduling for fog-enabled smart cities include:

1. Heterogeneity in fog nodes: Varying computational capabilities, network connectivity and memory capacity of Fog nodes can make it challenging to allocate tasks optimally.
2. Dynamic and unpredictable workloads: Smart city applications generate diverse and fluctuating workloads, requiring adaptive scheduling strategies.
3. Strict latency and QoS constraints: Many smart city applications, such as traffic management or emergency response systems, have stringent real-time requirements.
4. Energy efficiency considerations: Optimizing energy consumption is crucial for sustainable smart city operations and reducing operational costs.
5. Scalability: The scheduling system must be able to handle large numbers of IoT devices and process vast amounts of data efficiently.
6. Mobility of IoT devices: Some smart city applications involve mobile sensors or devices, adding complexity to task allocation and data management.

4. SMART CITY COMPONENTS

Smart city components as depicted in Figure 2 are technological and infrastructural elements designed to enhance the quality of urban life, optimize resource utilization, and improve service delivery. These components are termed “smart” because they leverage digital technology, data analytics, and connectivity to deliver efficient, sustainable, and user-centric solutions. Here's a detailed overview of key components (Ashraf, 2021) (Nikpour et al., 2024):

Smart Homes: Residences equipped with IoT devices, sensors, and automated systems to control lighting, climate, security, and appliances. They incorporate automation via voice assistants (e.g., Alexa, Google Home), Energy efficiency through smart thermostats and lighting, Security via smart locks, cameras, and alarm systems.

Figure 2. Smart city components

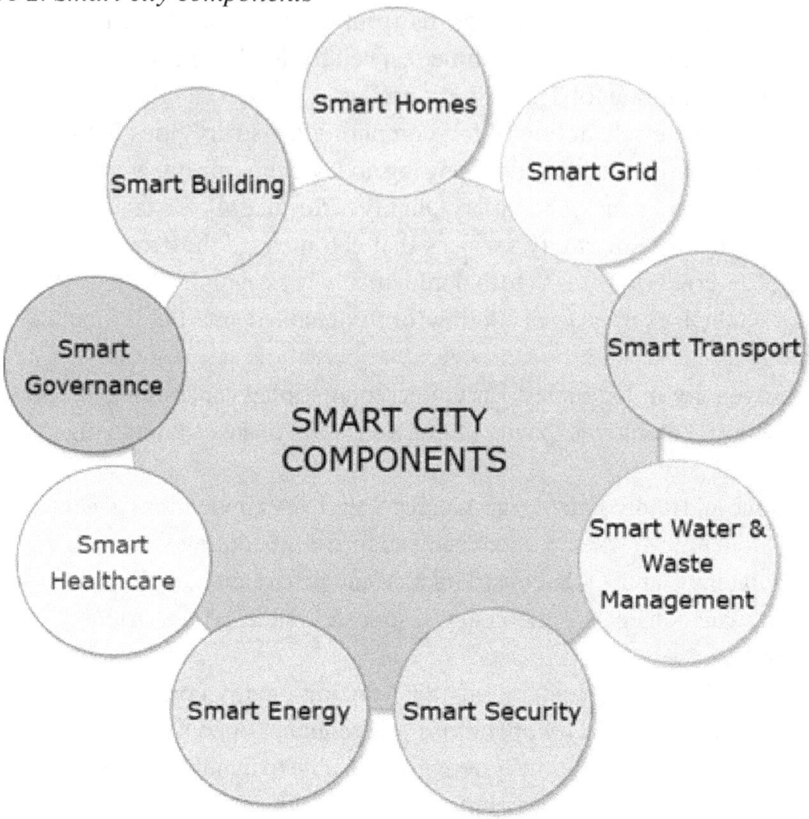

Smart Grids: They include advanced electricity networks that use digital technology to monitor and manage energy distribution efficiently. Smart Grids are capable of real-time monitoring and automatic fault detection, they integrate renewable energy sources like solar and wind. Smart Grids demand the response systems to optimize power use during peak times.

Smart Transportation: Intelligent transport systems (ITS) using IoT, AI, and big data for traffic management, public transit optimization, and connected vehicles are the main theme of Smart Transportation. They support Real-time traffic updates via apps like Google Maps, Autonomous vehicles and electric vehicles (EV) charging stations, Dynamic traffic lights adjust timings based on congestion levels, etc.

Smart water management systems, such as leak detection and automatic pipeline repairs, effective irrigation systems in urban green areas, and real-time water quality monitoring, employ Internet of Things (IoT) sensors and data analytics to monitor and optimize the water supply and quality.

Smart Waste Management: This includes trash truck route optimization and waste collection and recycling systems that use IoT-enabled containers. They employ features like sensors in bins to alert authorities when they are full, AI-assisted recycling to increase sorting efficiency, and optimized collection routes to reduce carbon emissions.

Smart Healthcare: Smart healthcare refers to digital healthcare systems that use wearable technology, telemedicine, and artificial intelligence (AI) for diagnosis and treatment. This includes features like AI-assisted diagnostics for quicker and more precise findings, remote patient monitoring for chronic illnesses, and health applications that encourage wellness and preventative treatment.

E-government systems: that offer digital platforms for citizen services and participatory decision-making are known as "smart governance." They are intelligent because of features like online portals for public services, tax payments, and complaints; transparency through open data efforts; and citizen engagement applications for participation and criticism.

Smart Buildings: Structures equipped with IoT-enabled systems for energy management, security, and occupant comfort. Automated HVAC (Heating, Ventilation, and Air Conditioning) systems, Smart elevators and lighting controlled by occupancy sensors, Predictive maintenance of infrastructure are some of the key attributes.

Smart Energy Management: Systems using IoT and AI to monitor and control energy consumption. It can be done through Renewable energy integration and distributed generation, AI-driven insights for efficient energy use, Battery storage systems to balance supply and demand.

Smart Security: Surveillance systems, predictive policing, and emergency response systems using AI and IoT. Real-time video analytics for threat detection, connected alarm systems for rapid response, drones for surveillance in large events are some of the important aspects for smart security systems.

These components work together, creating a synergistic ecosystem where technology and data improve urban living standards while ensuring sustainability and resilience.

5. MORE RECENT WORKS IN TASK ALLOCATION IN SMART CITIES USING FOG BASED IOT ENVIRONMENT

Considerable work has been done in terms of task allocation in fog based IoT environment.

5.1 Task Scheduling

Liu et al. (Liu et al., 2017) designed a fog based IOT task scheduling framework to minimize the makespan and communication cost in smart cities. They used an Adaptive Double-fitness Genetic Task Scheduling (ADGTS) algorithm and checked its performance with min-min algorithm. However, a more detailed comparative analysis could have been done to formalize the results.

A standards-based fog computing architecture for smart city task scheduling was proposed by Rampérez et al. (Rampérez et al., 2018) This work used the NGSI (Next Generation Service Interface) standard to enable openness and interoperability of the fog computing framework. To enable scalable and low-latency context management, the architecture uses distributed context management and event processing. It introduces a Context Broker based on a publish/subscribe middleware (E-SilboPS) designed to be elastic and low-latency. The paper evaluates the proposed architecture through a smart city use case involving gas pipeline monitoring and traffic management. It also presents a performance evaluation of the Context Broker, showing it outperforms the existing FIWARE reference implementation in terms of throughput and latency.

(Deng et al., 2019) proposed task scheduling for computation-intensive and time-sensitive smart city applications using the resources of the Internet of Vehicles (IoV) based on multi-server mobile edge computing. The authors first formulate an optimization problem to minimize the completion time with a specified cost constraint. They then propose four evolving algorithms based on the alternating direction method of multipliers (ADMM) to solve this problem. Out of the four, results show that the distributed improved Jacobi (DIJ)-ADMM algorithm has the best performance, with a convergence rate of O(1/t) and the ability to preserve user privacy. The proposed algorithms significantly reduce task completion time and increase offloaded tasks compared to existing solutions. The future scope of this work could include exploring more advanced task scheduling techniques, incorporating additional constraints such as energy efficiency, and investigating the scalability of the proposed algorithms in larger-scale smart city deployments.

To schedule work offloaded from mobile devices (MDs) and optimize response latency using a greedy heuristic-based scheduling technique, (Tang et al., 2020) suggested a three-layer architecture for vehicular fog computing (VFC). The three levels are the fog layer, which uses cars and RSUs as fog nodes, the cloud layer, which has high-performance servers, and the MD layer, which has a variety of user terminals. There are two phases to the scheduling strategy: 1) To decide whether tasks should be carried out in the vehicle fog layer or offloaded to the cloud, RSU uses a Greedy Offloading Decision Algorithm (GODA). 2) When operating in the fog layer, RSU schedules tasks among fog vehicles according to the shortest anticipated completion time using the Task Allocation in Vehicular Fogs (TAVF) algorithm.

An IoT-based healthcare data analysis model has been presented by Nagarajan et al. (Nagarajan et al., 2021) that deep learning based Hierarchical Neural Network (DHNN) model that performs feature extraction, data preprocessing and health condition classification into normal, critical and abnormal categories. This Fog-assisted healthcare data analysis framework can perform data processing, resource management and task scheduling based on the health risk priority and availability of network resources. The model demonstrates high accuracy, precision and sensitivity compared to existing deep learning models like deep CNN and deep autoencoder. The future scope includes extending the proposed methodology to other domains like traffic analysis, agriculture, weather forecasting and specific healthcare applications like diabetes, heart disease, cancer, etc. to provide deep, accurate, timely and secure data analysis.

Alsmadi et al. (Alsmadi et al., 2021) proposed a scheduling algorithm called the Weighted Round-Robin (WRR) scheduling algorithm to execute tasks from one fog node (FN) to another FN and then to the cloud. The network is deployed with multiple FNs, and the optimal FN (fog server) and edge node are found for executing user tasks based on available processing capacity and remaining node energy. The FC network protocol uses a spanning-tree protocol (STP) for data collection and routing, and 5G networks are implemented for fast data transmission. The proposed system is evaluated in terms of response time, latency, and amount of data used, and its performance is compared with the existing FogFlow approach.

FLEPR (Fuzzy Logic Enabled Probabilistic Routing), an opportunistic IoT-based routing system, was suggested by Bhardwaj et al. (Bhardwaj et al., 2022) for smart city infrastructure. To make logical forwarding choices in a smart city setting, this context-aware probabilistic routing paradigm takes into account the Transmission Capability Index (TCI) and Probabilistic Attractiveness Index (PAI). Candidate nodes for message relay are ranked according to their social interactions and inherent qualities using an algorithm based on the Firefly algorithm, which is inspired by nature. A three-tiered strategy to reduce flooding in the difficult opportunistic IoT environment of a smart city utilizing the least amount of contextual information. Simulations are used to assess the suggested FLEPR protocol, which shows better performance in terms of delivery rate, latency, and overhead ratio when compared to other modern routing systems.

Mattia et al. (Mattia & Beraldi, 2022) suggested a decentralized approach for real-time scheduling in fog computing settings that is based on Reinforcement Learning (RL). Beyond the straightforward fixed threshold-based power-of-choice method, the algorithm allows each Fog node to dynamically select the optimal scheduling choice depending on the current load scenario. Six Fog nodes were deployed in New

York City as part of the study, and load patterns were based on actual taxi traffic data. Simulation results show the algorithm's effectiveness in both homogeneous and heterogeneous load settings, as well as the changeable geographic scenario, as compared to the power-of-choice method.

For real-time healthcare applications, Alatoun et al. (Alatoun et al., 2022) suggested an Energy-Efficient Internet of Medical Things to Fog Interoperability of Task Scheduling (EEIoMT) framework. In contrast to cloud-only designs, the framework uses fog computing to lower latency and energy usage. When processing other jobs, the model balances energy usage and gives priority to important tasks. using IoT services on edge devices to save medical expenses, enhance the quality of life, and allow for ongoing monitoring of chronic patients.

The proposed solution analyzes ECG signals near the sensor in an ESP32 microcontroller, reducing transmission time and improving efficiency compared to sending data to the cloud. Tasks are classified as normal, moderate or critical, and assigned to appropriate fog nodes based on latency and energy consumption.

Simulation results show the EEIoMT framework outperforms existing models like CHTM, LBS and FNPA in terms of latency, energy consumption, network usage and CPU usage.

5.2 Resource allocation

Naranjo et al. (Naranjo et al., 2019) presented a FC-supported resource allocation model for smart city called FOCAN, a multi-tier structure where applications running on IoE (Internet of Everything) devices jointly compute, route, and communicate with one another through the smart city environment. This aims to decrease latency and improve energy provisioning and service efficiency among devices with different capabilities. FOCAN has two tiers: the IoE tier with heterogeneous devices connected via peer-to-peer communications, and the Fog Node (FN) tier that covers incoming traffic from the IoE tier and processes/transfers data to decrease latency. The paper defines three types of communications – inter-primary, primary, and secondary - to manage applications and meet quality of service standards. The key advantage is that devices can provide services with low energy usage and efficiently. Simulation results demonstrate the impact of FOCAN's energy-efficient solution on the communication performance of various IoE devices in smart cities.

Zhang et al. (Zhang, 2020) Proposed a layered resource allocation model for Smart cities using Fog Computing to effectively solve the problems of big data processing and network scalability. The work analyzes the resource allocation time and task violation rate under different task volumes and fog node numbers. The proposed scheme outperforms simple genetic algorithm (SGA) and improved ant colony optimization-simulated annealing (ACOSA) in terms of execution time and violation rate.

Desikan et al. (Desikan et al., 2020) have suggested a number of Topology Control (TC) strategies for building and running a sizable fog-enabled smart city. The construction phase and the maintenance phase are the two stages in which the writers tackle the issue. By positioning fog gateways in strategic areas and assigning the necessary processing and storage resources, they create an affordable IoT network throughout the construction phase. To achieve this, they provide effective algorithms such as Candidate Location Identification (CLI) and Topology Construction (HTC), which is based on the Hungarian technique. To improve resource utilization without negatively impacting latency limitations, they concentrate on Vacation-based Resource Allocation (VRA) and Dynamic Resource Allocation (DRA) algorithms during the Maintenance Phase. The authors show notable gains in terms of cost, resource use, and latency satisfaction through comprehensive simulations.

For the creation of smart cities, Changhao Zhang (Zhang, 2020) suggested a layered fog computing network design that would use intelligent observation, information processing, and network transmission to manage the city's operations. It draws attention to fog computing's benefits in terms of faster service response times, enhanced localized processing power, lower data transmission loads, and safer decentralized service design. In terms of task execution time and violation rate, they contrasted the suggested approach with enhanced ant colony optimization-simulated annealing (ACOSA) and simple genetic algorithms (SGA). In comparison to the other two methods, the findings demonstrate that the suggested scheme can successfully lower task processing latency and violation rate. The paper's future scope includes allocating computer resources as efficiently as possible while taking into account limitations in processing power, communication capacity, and storage capacity.

Qayyum et al. (Qayyum et al., 2021) proposed a fog based smart city framework that leverages IoT devices as volunteer nodes to handle peak computation loads and improve Quality of Service (QoS). The framework consists of fog gateways, dedicated fog nodes, and volunteer user devices. Fog gateways act as brokers to manage incoming computation requests and schedule them to the most suitable device. Their scheduling algorithm combines Ant Colony Optimization (ACO) and Earliest Deadline First (EDF) to efficiently utilize available resources and meet QoS requirements. The EDF policy is then used to order the tasks to ensure timely execution of tasks with hard deadlines. This resource sharing model aims to improve task acceptance ratio, reduce network congestion, and preserve energy by offloading tasks to the most capable devices.

Mohammad (Aldossary, 2023) suggested an effective heuristic-based optimization method for placing and processing IoT applications in smart cities that makes use of a multi-layer fog-cloud architecture. To optimize placement choices, the method takes into account the needs of Internet of Things applications, the capabilities of available resources, and the locations of fog and cloud servers. A Mixed Integer Linear Programming (MILP) model is used in the work to optimize placement in order to reduce power consumption, data transmission, and related expenses. The findings demonstrate that, in comparison to a cloud-only strategy, the suggested method can lower data transmission by 64% and power consumption expenses by up to 78%. The fog-cloud architecture will be expanded in the future to manage erratic situations and movement patterns by utilizing ML and intelligent decision-making approaches.

CAITS (Context-Aware Intelligent Transportation System) is a unique distributed context-aware fog-cloud architecture that is enabled by the Internet of Things, as suggested by Reddy et al. (Reddy et al., 2023). Using a platoon control algorithm and incremental federated learning at the fog level, CAITS is a three-layered learning model that manages intelligent transportation systems by taking into consideration on-vehicle, on-co-vehicle, and on-fog-and-vehicle learning. Prioritizing and scheduling service requests is a feature of the CAITS paradigm that helps to lower QoS breaches. For real-time object recognition and classification, it employs a hybrid CNN DL model, doing away with the requirement for costly preprocessing methods. As a result, the CAITS model may schedule and prioritize service requests to lower QoS breaches. This work's future scope involves enhancing the federated learning technique and expanding the model to handle increasingly complicated real-world events.

5.3 Task offloading

SecOFF-FCIoT, a machine learning-based secure offloading system, was suggested by Alli et al. (Alli & Alam, 2019) for the Fog-Cloud-IoT environment. The best Fog node for offloading was chosen by this model using Particle Swarm Optimization (PSO) at the Internet of Things (IoT) level, while the best Cloud server was chosen using Reinforcement Learning (RL) at the Fog level. In order to stop fraudulent network transactions, it employs a Neuro-Fuzzy model at the smart gateway to detect and isolate IoT nodes that transmit erroneous data. The suggested architecture seeks to minimize latency and energy usage in order to accomplish secure, effective offloading. According to simulation studies, the SecOFF-FCIoT performs better than earlier methods in terms of reaction time, energy consumption, throughput, latency, and resource utilization.

Dong et al. (Dong et al., 2019) have suggested a task offloading technique that uses the Fairness Cooperation Algorithm (FCA) to ensure fairness among the fog nodes in a smart city setting. It is a cooperative optimization plan that aims to reduce energy usage and quality of experience (QoE) while taking into account the equity of fog nodes to promote collaboration. To further enhance the performance of the cooperative fog computing system, future research should investigate more sophisticated cooperation techniques including mobility-aware offloading and dynamic resource allocation. It could also be looked at how various user mobility patterns and workload variables affect system optimization.

Wang et. al (Wang et al., 2020) proposes a task-driven data offloading scheme for fog-enabled urban IoT services. It devises a three-layer fog architecture with IoT sensors, mobile gateways, and a central service server. The Task-driven Data Offloading (TDO) problem is formulated as a combination optimization problem, considering task deadlines and abilities of heterogeneous mobile gateways. The authors prove the TDO problem is NP-hard and propose the G-TDO algorithm with a carefully designed utility function. To further improve the G-TDO algorithm, the authors reorganize the tasks based on sensors and propose the RG-TDO algorithm considering the overlaps of tasks. Extensive evaluations using real-world dataset demonstrate the significant performance of the proposed algorithms in terms of successful ratio, average task cost, average task completion ratio, and system total cost, outperforming other state-of-the-art approaches.

Wang et al. (Wang et al., 2023) proposed a task offloading model to facilitate resource sharing and collaboration among the fog node as in a Fog-enabled smart cities (FESC). The proposed FESC architecture uses a genetic algorithm (GA) to minimize service delay and optimize energy efficiency. The model is compared with the ADMM-VS algorithm, and the results show that the proposed model performs significantly better in terms of response time and energy consumption. The paper also discusses the limitations of the proposed model, such as not accounting for factors like transmission path, telecommunication standards, and device limitations. The future research directions include comparing the proposed model with alternative models, apart from GA, for reducing greenhouse gas emissions and achieving automatic environment recognition for task completion while considering energy requirements.

6. FUTURE SCOPE

As stated in the introduction section of this study, the growth in the urban population is estimated to increase worldwide in the coming years. A more resilient, scalable and most importantly secured architecture for cities is required in the form of "Smart-Cities" to cater to such a large urban population. Because of this fact, "Optimizing the Task Allocation in Fog-based IoT environment for Smart City" is rapidly gaining popularity with significant research and application potential. Below are several key aspects of the future scope of this topic, described in detail:

1. Enhanced Task allocation algorithms: Task allocation in Fog computing for IoT devices within a smart city framework needs efficient algorithms to decide which tasks should be processed locally at the edge (fog nodes) and which should be offloaded to the cloud.
    - **Artificial Intelligence (AI) and Machine Learning (ML) Integration:** There is a growing interest in using AI and ML techniques for dynamic, real-time optimization of task allocation. These algorithms can adapt based on traffic patterns, system load, and energy consumption.
        - o **Reinforcement Learning:** RL algorithms may be applied to constantly train optimum task allocation techniques based on feedback from real-world deployments, responding to changing conditions like network congestion or device availability.
        - o **Deep Learning for Predictive Modeling:** Job allocation decision-making is improved by machine learning models' ability to forecast device loads and environmental variables (such as temperature, energy levels, etc.) that affect job performance.
    - **Game Theory Approaches:** By using game theory to simulate interactions between different IoT devices and fog nodes, strategic decision-making can guarantee that resources are distributed as efficiently as possible. In multi-agent systems, where devices must cooperate and compete for resources, this is very helpful.
2. Energy aware Task allocation: Since a large number of IoT devices in smart cities run on batteries, energy efficiency is a crucial issue. Task allocation based on fog must minimize energy usage without sacrificing performance.
    - **Energy-Efficient Algorithms:** Developing algorithms that can assess the energy consumption of each task on various fog nodes and IoT devices and distribute the load accordingly is vital. Future solutions could integrate energy harvesting techniques (e.g., solar or kinetic energy) into task allocation strategies to further optimize power usage.
    - **Green Fog Computing:** Future fog systems will likely incorporate “green” computing principles, focusing on using renewable energy sources and energy-efficient hardware to power fog nodes. Research could also explore how to use data about local energy availability (e.g., solar power at a specific location) to inform task allocation.
3. QoS and Latency Management: Fog computing for IoT in smart cities requires minimizing latency for real-time applications (e.g., traffic management, autonomous vehicles, surveillance systems). Balancing task load to maintain low latency while achieving high throughput remains a challenge.
    - **Low-Latency Task Allocation:** As smart cities evolve, future research could focus on ultra-low-latency task allocation solutions, leveraging

fog computing's proximity to end devices. Strategies might include prioritizing tasks based on urgency or delay tolerance (e.g., critical healthcare data vs. environmental sensing data).

- **Multi-Tier Fog Architectures:** Future smart cities may deploy multi-tier fog networks, where tasks are allocated based on the capabilities of various layers of fog nodes (local, regional, or city-wide). Task allocation strategies will need to consider these multiple levels and the resulting impact on latency and QoS.

4. Scalability and adaptability: The number of IoT devices in smart cities is constantly growing. Task allocation systems must be scalable to handle the increasing data volumes and device diversity.
   - **Autonomous Scaling of Fog Resources:** Future fog-based systems may automatically scale their resources (e.g., adding more fog nodes as demand increases) without human intervention. This requires advanced self-management mechanisms, predictive models, and decentralized task allocation strategies.
   - **Context-Aware Task Allocation:** IoT devices in a smart city operate in diverse environments (e.g., traffic monitoring, environmental sensing, healthcare monitoring). Future solutions will need to be adaptive, considering both device context (location, energy state) and environmental factors (traffic conditions, weather) to optimize task distribution.
5. Security and Privacy in Task Allocation: Smart city IoT devices are susceptible to security lapses, and improperly managed task distribution procedures may reveal private information. One crucial difficulty in the job allocation process is ensuring confidentiality and privacy.
   - **Secure Task Offloading:** Future studies may concentrate on safe ways to transfer work to cloud infrastructure or fog nodes. To make sure that private information is not revealed while assigning tasks, methods such as blockchain-based task verification, secure multi-party computation, or homomorphic encryption might be used.
   - **Privacy-Preserving Task Allocation:** The demand for privacy-preserving job allocation algorithms will be fuelled by privacy concerns in smart cities, particularly with regard to personal data. For example, tasks may be handled locally utilizing federated learning instead of sending sensitive information to centralized servers.
6. Fog Node heterogeneity and Interoperability: The computational power, storage, network capabilities, and energy availability of fog nodes vary, making them frequently diverse. This makes it difficult to assign tasks to these resources effectively.

- **Dynamic Resource Discovery and Allocation:** Automated resource discovery algorithms that assess fog node capabilities in real-time could be a part of future fog systems. Based on a dynamic set of factors, these systems might employ AI to choose the optimal node for a given job.
- **Interoperability Across Diverse Fog Nodes:** Interoperability between various fog systems and standards will become increasingly important as fog networks get more complicated. To guarantee smooth work distribution among heterogeneous devices, independent of vendor or protocol, future research might concentrate on developing open standards for fog computing.

7. Collaborative and distributed task allocation: In smart cities, job distribution is typically a core decision-making process, however this may lead to bottlenecks or single points of failure.
    - **Decentralized and Collaborative Systems:** Task distribution in the future may entail decentralized, cooperative fog node decision-making. By distributing the work allocation process, this method might lessen the dangers of central control. Distributed ledger technology (DLT) or blockchain might be used to build a transparent and safe mechanism for allocating tasks to team members.
    - **Fog-Cloud Hybrid Systems:** It may become commonplace to use a hybrid system that blends the broad resources of cloud computing with the flexibility of fog computing. To provide fault tolerance and optimal resource utilization, future research might concentrate on methods for smoothly distributing jobs across fog and cloud levels.
8. Real time analytics and data processing: Smart cities generate vast amounts of real-time data, from traffic patterns to environmental sensing. Efficient task allocation systems must process and analyze this data in near real-time.
    - **Edge AI and Analytics:** To evaluate data locally and make choices in real time, it will be essential to integrate AI-powered analytics at the edge (fog nodes). The efficiency of smart city applications like energy management, public safety, and driverless cars may be greatly increased by allocating tasks optimally based on real-time data.
    - **Task Allocation Based on Data Streams:** Future fog-based IoT systems will have to assign jobs dynamically based on real-time data streams, including shifting traffic circumstances, environmental variables, and sensor readings, in addition to using static resources. Allocating tasks based on data will be crucial to enhancing resource use and responsiveness.
9. 5G and beyond for Fog-based IoT: Because 5G technology offers faster connection rates, reduced latency, and more device density, it has the potential to greatly expand the capabilities of fog nodes and IoT devices.

- **5G-Enabled Fog Computing:** The infrastructure required to provide real-time, high-bandwidth job allocation will be made available with the introduction of 5G and later (such as 6G). Devices and fog nodes will be able to interact easily, allowing for quick job processing and offloading.
- **Network Slicing for Task Allocation:** Network slicing, which may generate specialized virtual networks for certain purposes, is supported by 5G networks. Network slicing might be used by task allocation algorithms to guarantee that less important jobs (like public safety monitoring) use standard resources while mission-critical tasks (like healthcare or autonomous driving) are given resources with a higher priority.

10. Integration with autonomous systems: Future smart cities would not be complete without autonomous technologies like robots, drones, and self-driving automobiles, and their function depends on effective work distribution.
    - **Collaborative Task Allocation for Autonomous Systems:** Future studies could concentrate on work allocation optimization for drone or autonomous car fleets. These technologies can cooperate within the context of smart cities by receiving real-time updates and processing power from fog computing.
    - **Autonomous Resource Management:** As autonomous systems proliferate, they could contribute to fog resource management by dynamically assigning jobs in response to shifting demands and conditions.

In conclusion, using cutting-edge AI, energy-efficient algorithms, real-time analytics, and new networking technologies like 5G will be key to optimizing job allocation in fog-based IoT for smart cities in the future. So as to meet the increasing needs of interconnected urban settings, task allocation systems will need to become more flexible, scalable, secure, and effective as smart city applications become more sophisticated.

REFERENCES

Alatoun, K., Matrouk, K., Mohammed, M. A., Nedoma, J., Martinek, R., & Zmij, P. (2022). A novel low-latency and energy-efficient task scheduling framework for internet of medical things in an edge fog cloud system. *Sensors (Basel), 22*(14), 5327. DOI: 10.3390/s22145327 PMID: 35891007

Aldossary, M. (2023). Multi-layer fog-cloud architecture for optimizing the placement of IoT applications in smart cities. *Computers, Materials & Continua, 75*(1), 633–649. DOI: 10.32604/cmc.2023.035414

Alli, A. A., & Alam, M. M. (2019). SecOFF-FCIoT: Machine learning based secure offloading in Fog-Cloud of things for smart city applications. *Internet of Things : Engineering Cyber Physical Human Systems, 7*, 100070. DOI: 10.1016/j.iot.2019.100070

. Alsmadi, A. M., Ali Aloglah, R. M., Smadi, A. A., Alshabanah, M., Alrajhi, D., Alkhaldi, H., & Alsmadi, M. K. (2021). Fog computing scheduling algorithm for smart city. International Journal of Electrical & Computer Engineering (2088-8708), 11(3).

Ashraf, S. (2021). A proactive role of IoT devices in building smart cities. *Internet of Things and Cyber-Physical Systems, 1*, 8–13. DOI: 10.1016/j.iotcps.2021.08.001

Bhardwaj, K. K., Banyal, S., Sharma, D. K., & Al-Numay, W. (2022). Internet of things based smart city design using fog computing and fuzzy logic. *Sustainable Cities and Society, 79*, 103712. DOI: 10.1016/j.scs.2022.103712

Bonomi, F., Milito, R., Zhu, J., & Addepalli, S. (2012, August). Fog computing and its role in the internet of things. In *Proceedings of the first edition of the MCC workshop on Mobile cloud computing* (pp. 13-16). DOI: 10.1145/2342509.2342513

Cisco, I. N. C. (2015). Cisco Global Cloud Index 2014–2019. Online: https://bit.Ly/2Kj8FvU.

Deng, Y., Chen, Z., Yao, X., Hassan, S., & Wu, J. (2019). Task scheduling for smart city applications based on multi-server mobile edge computing. *IEEE Access : Practical Innovations, Open Solutions, 7*, 14410–14421. DOI: 10.1109/ACCESS.2019.2893486

Desikan, K. S., Kotagi, V. J., & Murthy, C. S. R. (2020). Topology control in fog computing enabled IoT networks for smart cities. *Computer Networks, 176*, 107270. DOI: 10.1016/j.comnet.2020.107270

Dong, Y., Guo, S., Liu, J., & Yang, Y. (2019). Energy-efficient fair cooperation fog computing in mobile edge networks for smart city. *IEEE Internet of Things Journal*, *6*(5), 7543–7554. DOI: 10.1109/JIOT.2019.2901532

Liu, Q., Wei, Y., Leng, S., & Chen, Y. (2017, October). Task scheduling in fog enabled Internet of Things for smart cities. In 2017 IEEE 17th International conference on communication technology (ICCT) (pp. 975-980). IEEE. DOI: 10.1109/ICCT.2017.8359780

Mattia, G. P., & Beraldi, R. (2022, March). On real-time scheduling in Fog computing: A Reinforcement Learning algorithm with application to smart cities. In 2022 IEEE International conference on pervasive computing and communications workshops and other affiliated events (PerCom Workshops) (pp. 187-193). IEEE. DOI: 10.1109/PerComWorkshops53856.2022.9767498

Nagarajan, S. M., Deverajan, G. G., Chatterjee, P., Alnumay, W., & Ghosh, U. (2021). Effective task scheduling algorithm with deep learning for Internet of Health Things (IoHT) in sustainable smart cities. *Sustainable Cities and Society*, *71*, 102945. DOI: 10.1016/j.scs.2021.102945

Naranjo, P. G. V., Pooranian, Z., Shojafar, M., Conti, M., & Buyya, R. (2019). FOCAN: A Fog-supported smart city network architecture for management of applications in the Internet of Everything environments. *Journal of Parallel and Distributed Computing*, *132*, 274–283. DOI: 10.1016/j.jpdc.2018.07.003

Nikpour, M., Yousefi, P. B., Jafarzadeh, H., Danesh, K., Shomali, R., Asadi, S., & Ahmadi, M. (2024). Intelligent Energy Management in Smart Cities: Leveraging IoT and Machine Learning for Optimizing Complex Networks and Systems. *Journal of Network and Computer Applications*, •••, 104089.

. OpenFog Consortium Architecture Working Group, A. (2017). OpenFog reference architecture for fog computing. OPFRA001, 20817, 162.

Profiroiu, C. M., Bodislav, D. A., Burlacu, S., & Rădulescu, C. V. (2020). Challenges of sustainable urban development in the context of population growth. *European Journal of Sustainable Development*, *9*(3), 51–51. DOI: 10.14207/ejsd.2020.v9n3p51

Qayyum, T., Trabelsi, Z., Malik, A. W., & Hayawi, K. (2021). Multi-level resource sharing framework using collaborative fog environment for smart cities. *IEEE Access : Practical Innovations, Open Solutions*, *9*, 21859–21869. DOI: 10.1109/ACCESS.2021.3054420

Rampérez, V., Soriano, J., & Lizcano, D. (2018). A multidomain standards-based fog computing architecture for smart cities. *Wireless Communications and Mobile Computing*, *2018*(1), 4019858. DOI: 10.1155/2018/4019858

Reddy, K. H. K., Goswami, R. S., Roy, D. S., & Senior Member, I. E. E. E. (2023). A futuristic green service computing approach for smart city: A fog layered intelligent service management model for smart transport system. *Computer Communications*, *212*, 151–160. DOI: 10.1016/j.comcom.2023.08.001

Tang, C., Wei, X., Zhu, C., Wang, Y., & Jia, W. (2020). Mobile vehicles as fog nodes for latency optimization in smart cities. *IEEE Transactions on Vehicular Technology*, *69*(9), 9364–9375. DOI: 10.1109/TVT.2020.2970763

Wang, P., Yu, R., Gao, N., Lin, C., & Liu, Y. (2020). Task-driven data offloading for fog-enabled urban IoT services. *IEEE Internet of Things Journal*, *8*(9), 7562–7574. DOI: 10.1109/JIOT.2020.3039467

Wang, Y., Shafik, W., Seong, J. T., Al Mutairi, A., Mustafa, M. S., & Mouhamed, M. R. (2023). Service delay and optimization of the energy efficiency of a system in fog-enabled smart cities. *Alexandria Engineering Journal*, *84*, 112–125. DOI: 10.1016/j.aej.2023.10.034

Zhang, C. (2020). Design and application of fog computing and Internet of Things service platform for smart city. *Future Generation Computer Systems*, *112*, 630–640. DOI: 10.1016/j.future.2020.06.016

Zhang, C. (2020). Design and application of fog computing and Internet of Things service platform for smart city. *Future Generation Computer Systems*, *112*, 630–640. DOI: 10.1016/j.future.2020.06.016

Chapter 2
Smart Transportation System/Infrastructure:
AI-Driven Innovations for Urban Transformation

Sumit S. Shevtekar
https://orcid.org/0009-0003-7979-4607
Indian Institute of Technology, Indore, India

Chandresh Kumar Maurya
Indian Institute of Technology, Indore, India

ABSTRACT

This Book chapter explains the transformative role of Artificial Intelligence (AI) in the development of smart transportation systems in urban areas, public safety and the environment. It also explores how AI technology is useful for urban mobility-transportation, enhancing efficiency, public safety, and sustainability. It also provides detailed information about various safety concerns, current transportation systems, different case studies of successful implementation projects in different urban areas, and the future development and potential of AI in urban transportation safety systems. This chapter also explores the advancements in autonomous vehicles, explaining the AI technologies that enable self-driving cars, their importance and their implications for urban transportation. The chapter concludes by addressing various challenges and ethical considerations of deploying AI in urban transportation systems, including data privacy, Public Safety, Security, and efficient use of AI tools and products.

DOI: 10.4018/979-8-3693-7832-8.ch002

1. INTRODUCTION TO SMART TRANSPORTATION SYSTEMS IN URBAN AREAS

Urban areas around the world are facing difficult challenges due to rapid population growth, increasing vehicular (2-wheeler, 4-wheeler Etc.) traffic, and the resultant congestion and pollution. Traditional transportation systems are not well equipped to handle these pressures, leading to insecurity, delays, Traffic jams, lots of road accidents and a negative impact on the quality of life of urban people. The Smart Transportation Systems (STS) provide transformative solutions for all such major problems. Various Artificial intelligence systems, Internet of Things (IoT) technology, Data mining and Big data analytics techniques aim to enhance the efficiency, safety and sustainability of urban transportation networks. (Herath & Mamta Mittal, 2022)

Smart Transportation Systems integrate various cutting-edge technologies/ methods to create an interconnected urban mobility best secure ecosystem. These Systems include intelligent traffic management, smart parking, autonomous vehicles and real-time public transportation management. collecting and analyzing data from various sources like sensors, cameras, and GPS devices, STS provides valuable insights that help to optimize traffic flow, reduce congestion, and improve the overall commuting experience, which leads to a secure and safe transportation system.

Implementing Smart Transportation Systems offers numerous advantages for urban environments & their development. For example, AI-powered traffic management systems can predict and alleviate congestion by automatically dynamically adjusting traffic signals and rerouting vehicles to solve traffic issues. Autonomous and connected vehicles can improve road safety by minimizing human errors & accidents. The smart parking solutions can also reduce the time and fuel wasted searching for parking spots, thus lowering environmental impacts. (Elassy, M.Hattab, Takruri & Badawi,2024).

1.1 Importance of Smart Transportation Systems in Urban Areas

The implementation of smart transportation systems in urban areas is an increasingly crucial task due to several compelling factors/reasons: Implementation of smart transportation systems in urban areas is an increasingly crucial task due to several Major factors/reasons like:

Enhanced Efficiency - So many times in Urban areas people face severe traffic congestion problems, which leads to extended travel times, waste of fuel and proper use of infrastructure. Smart transportation systems use advanced technologies like real-time traffic monitoring systems, Effective traffic signals management and intelligent route planning tools to effectively optimize traffic flow. This results in reduced congestion, faster travel times, reduced fuel consumption and more efficient use of existing road infrastructure.

Improved Public Safety - Safety is a very major concern in urban transportation zones/areas. Smart transportation systems help to improve public safety using various methods such as automated incident/accident detection, traffic management and co-ordinated emergency response to ensure quicker response/reactions to road accidents, minimizing their impact and helping in preventing further accidents/incidents in urban areas. (Jagatheesaperumal, Bibri, Huang, J Rajapandian & Parthiban,2024).

Environmental Sustainability - Transportation is a major source of air pollution and greenhouse gas emissions in all areas nowadays. Smart transportation systems promote sustainability by reducing vehicle idling time, optimizing/reducing fuel consumption properly and encouraging the use of Eco-friendly transportation modes like electric vehicles and safe public transit.

Increased Accessibility and Convenience - Smart transportation systems improve accessibility and convenience for urban area people. real-time public transit information enables commuters to make informed/updates about travel decisions, reducing wait times and improving overall satisfaction.

Economic Benefits - Efficient transportation systems play a vital for the economic vitality of urban areas. By reducing travel times and congestion, smart transportation systems can significantly improve productivity. Moreover, the reduction in traffic-related delays translates to considerable cost savings in fuel and time.

Support for Urban Planning and Development - Smart transportation systems provide valuable & important data that can be used for urban planning and development. Detailed insights into traffic patterns, peak usage times, and public transit needs allow urban planners to make data-driven decisions. This leads to better-designed infrastructure projects, optimized public transit routes, and more effective allocation of resources.

Fostering Innovation and Technological Advancement- The development and implementation of smart transportation systems foster innovation and technological advancements. They create various opportunities for tech startups, encourage research and development in ML, AI and IoT, and stimulate investment in new latest technologies/ideas. This not only helps to improve the best transportation systems but also contributes to the broader economic and technological growth of urban areas. (Razavi, M. Hamidkhani & R. Sadeghi, 2019).

1.2 Overview of Various Current Challenges in Urban Transportation & Its Safety

Urban transportation systems face lots of big challenges that impact efficiency, safety, and sustainability. These challenges include:

Traffic Congestion - such issues remain one of the most pressing issues in urban transportation. Increasing vehicle ownership, lack of infrastructure, and population growth contribute to gridlock on city streets. Congestion leads to longer travel times, waste of fuel, and higher air pollution, affecting both commuters and the environment.

Ageing Infrastructure - Many urban areas do not meet proper modern demands for the latest Infrastructure. Roads, bridges, tunnels, hills and public transit systems require regular maintenance of roads and upgrades to ensure safety and operational efficiency to avoid accidents. The cost associated with infrastructure development & leads to challenges for urban planners and policymakers.

Safety Issues - Many Factors such as over speeding, rash driving, inadequate road design, and distracted driving contribute to a higher incidence of accidents, injuries, and fatalities in urban areas leading to safety issues. (J. N. Njoku, C. I. Nwakanma, G. C. Amaizu & D.-S. Kim, 2023)

Public Transit Reliability - Reliability and efficiency issues in urban public transit systems, impacting commuter satisfaction and ridership. Many Factors such as overcrowding in public transit, service issues, maintenance, and outdated technology/facilities contribute to unreliable service. Improving public transit reliability through investment in latest needs, predictive maintenance, and real-time monitoring systems is crucial for attracting riders and reducing dependence on private vehicles.

Technological Integration - Artificial intelligence (AI), and smart Systems require overcoming technical, regulatory, and public acceptance barriers. which helps to provide best and secure service to users for daily easy lifestyle . (A. Lamssaggad, N. Benamar, A. S. Hafid & M. Msahli. 2021)

Funding and Financial issues - Securing good funding for transportation infrastructure projects development and operational costs management, helps to develop good infrastructure/roads. Limited public budgets raise issues for infrastructural development

Urban Planning and Land Use - Effective urban transportation systems require proper land use and transportation planning for the development of good projects.

2. THE ROLE OF AI IN SMART TRANSPORTATION SYSTEMS

AI plays a major role in the development of smart transportation systems in urban development environments. By using AI technologies, cities can enhance mobility issues, improve efficiency, ensure public safety, and promote sustainability and save environmental issues.

2.1 AI Technologies Utilized in Smart Transportation & Safety

Artificial Intelligence - AI technologies play a very important role in development of smart transportation systems, playing a critical role in enhancing safety, efficiency, public safety and sustainability across urban environments.

Predictive Analytics and Machine Learning - AI uses predictive analytics and machine learning methods, methods to analyze Big datasets collected from various sources like sensors and IoT devices. By predicting proper routes, AI reduces travel times, lowers fuel consumption, and enhances overall transportation efficiency.

Computer Vision and Sensor Technologies -Computer vision and sensor technologies are integral to various AI-driven smart transportation systems. These technologies enable automated monitoring of road conditions, proper traffic flow, and monitor pedestrian movement. AI-powered cameras and sensors detect accidents or road hazards, alerting authorities for swift response and mitigating risks to public safety.

Autonomous Vehicles and AI Integration- Autonomous vehicles - AVs represent an advancement in AI integration within transportation systems. AI methods/algorithms enable AVs to perceive their environment, make decisions in real-time, and navigate complex urban landscapes safely and provide better solutions.

Intelligent Traffic Management Systems – AI-driven intelligent traffic management systems help to optimize traffic flow and reduce congestion by dynamically adjusting traffic signals and lane management. These systems utilize various AI techniques/algorithms to analyze real-time traffic data, predict various patterns, and coordinate traffic signals accordingly.

Looking ahead, AI technologies continue to be used with advancements in deep learning, edge computing systems, and vehicle-to-everything [V2X] communication systems. These innovations promise enhanced connectivity, safety, and efficiency in smart transportation systems. (J. Guerrero-Ibañez, J. Contreras-Castillo & S. Zeadally, 2021).

2.2 Benefits of AI in Urban Mobility & Smart Transportation

Artificial Intelligence is transforming urban mobility and transportation systems and it helps to create a safe and secure transport system for safe transportation, offering various benefits that enhance efficiency, safety, and sustainability in cities worldwide.

Enhanced Efficiency through Optimization - AI optimizes urban transportation systems by analyzing vast amounts of data in real-time. Machine learning algorithms and methods predict traffic patterns, optimize routes, and dynamically adjust traffic signals, reducing congestion and travel times.

Improved Safety and Risk Management - AI enhances safety in urban mobility by enabling proactive monitoring and safe response systems. Computer vision and sensor technologies help detect anomalies such as road accidents or road hazards, alerting authorities for immediate action.

Promoting Sustainable Transportation Solutions - AI-based transportation systems promote sustainability in transport and help in reducing environmental impact. AI algorithms help in vehicle routing, Predictive maintenance algorithms ensure fleet efficiency, reducing downtime and maintenance costs while minimizing emissions.

Enhancing User Experience and Accessibility - AI-driven advancements in urban mobility improve user experience and accessibility. provide secure Intelligent transportation systems that give real-time information on transit schedules, traffic conditions, and optimal routes. (J. C. Miles and A. J. Walker, 2006).

Figure 1. Smart Town Traffic Management System Using LoRa and Machine Learning Mechanism (IEEE).

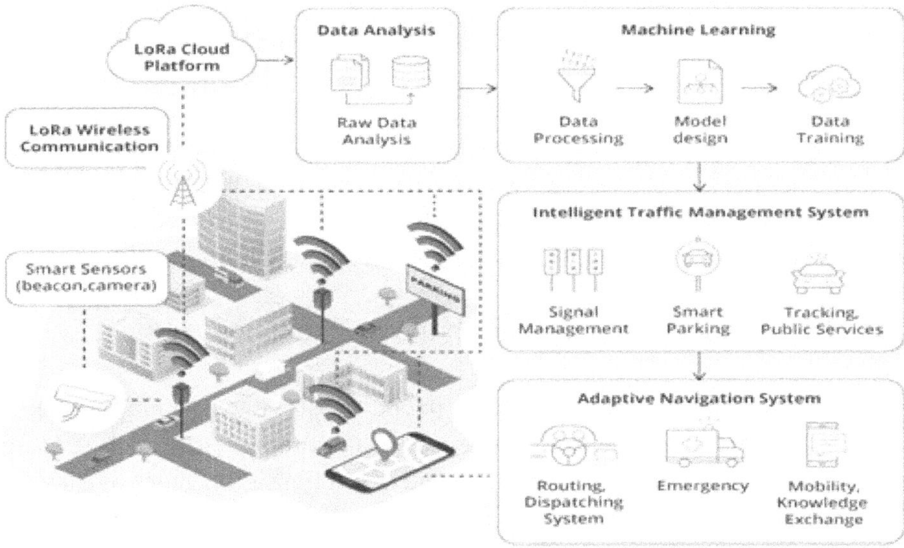

By using wireless communication, Long-range wide area network (Lora), traffic theory, sensors and Machine Learning, it delivers an advanced traffic management system for smart cities. Smart traffic management offers several advantages. Economically, it minimizes vehicle emissions by guiding drivers along the most efficient routes, which in turn reduces fuel consumption. Figure 1 shows the use of all these for smart city traffic solutions and it helps in smart transportation systems to solve traffic and other safety issues. (Seung B S and Dhananjay S, 2018).

2.3 Various Case Studies of AI-Driven Transportation Systems for Public Safety Around the World

AI-driven transportation systems have been implemented globally to enhance public safety issues, provide significant improvements in accident prevention, emergency response, and overall urban mobility.

Case Study 1: Singapore's AI-Powered Traffic Management System

Singapore has pioneered the use of AI in effective traffic management with its dynamic traffic control system. AI algorithms/methods help to analyze real-time data from sensors and cameras across the city to predict traffic patterns and adjust traffic lights accordingly. This proactive approach has been significantly used to reduce traffic congestion, minimise accidents, and improve air quality in congested urban areas.

Case Study 2: Los Angeles' Predictive Maintenance System

Los Angeles employs AI for maintenance of its smart transportation infrastructure. AI algorithms analyze sensor data to predict equipment failures and structural issues in roads and bridges. This preemptive maintenance strategy reduces the risk of unexpected breakdowns, improves road safety, and optimizes maintenance schedules, resulting in cost savings and enhanced infrastructure reliability.

Case Study 3: Barcelona's AI-Enhanced Public Transit

Barcelona utilizes AI to optimize its public transit system, improving service reliability and the best passenger experience. AI algorithms help to analyze passenger flow data to predict demand patterns and adjust transit schedules dynamically. Real-time information on transit schedules and optimal routes enhances commuter convenience while reducing overcrowding and delays in travel, contributing to overall public safety and satisfactory service.

These case studies highlight the transformative impact of AI-driven transportation systems on public safety in urban environments. By leveraging AI technologies for traffic management, predictive maintenance, public transit optimization, congestion charging, and emergency response, cities worldwide are improving efficiency, reducing accidents, and enhancing overall urban mobility.

3. AI-BASED AUTONOMOUS VEHICLES AND URBAN MOBILITY

Autonomous vehicles (AVs) powered by AI technology are playing an important role in urban transportation, providing public Safety in transportation systems, more efficient and safe transportation solutions and reshaping urban landscapes and lifestyles.

3.1 Evolution of AI-Based Autonomous Vehicles

AVs represent a transformative advancement in transportation and artificial Intelligence innovations that have evolved significantly over the years. AI plays a very crucial role in the development of autonomous vehicles.

Early Development and Conceptualization

The concept of autonomous vehicles started back several years ago, with early experiments in robotics and automation laying the groundwork for today's AV technology with AI systems. Initial prototypes focused on basic navigation and obstacle avoidance, paving the way for more sophisticated and secured AI-driven systems. (P. Seuwou, E. Banissi, and G. Ubakanma, 2020).

Emergence of AI Technologies

The evolution of AI Tech. has been instrumental in advancing autonomous vehicle Systems:

- **Computer Vision:** AV technology uses cameras and various sensors to detect and interpret their surroundings, identifying different objects, pedestrians, and road signs.
- **Machine Learning:** AI algorithms analyze big amounts of data to learn various driving behaviours, predict scenarios, and improve decision-making in real time.
- **Sensor Fusion:** Integration of radar system, lidar, and other sensor data enhances AVs' ability to detect and respond to dynamic environments accurately.
- **High-Definition Mapping:** Precise maps combined with localization algorithms enable AVs to navigate complex routes and update their position with centimetre-level accuracy.

3.2 AI Technologies Based on Autonomous Driving

Autonomous vehicles with AI technologies, represents a paradigm shift in urban transportation systems and mobility. Such AI technologies are pivotal in creating safe, efficient, and reliable autonomous vehicles (AVs) capable of navigating complex urban environments and helps to provide a safe system. Which uses

Localization and Mapping - Precise localization and mapping are essential parts for AVs to navigate accurately without human intervention. AI-powered localisation methods/algorithms use GPS, inertial measurement units (IMUs).

Path Planning and Decision Making - AI methods for path planning and decision-making enable AVs to navigate complex scenarios very safely and efficiently. These algorithms consider factors such as different traffic conditions, pedestrian movement, road objects, and regulatory compliance to generate optimal trajectories.

Deep Learning methods - Various Deep learning techniques-Algorithms, like convolutional neural networks (CNNs) and recurrent neural networks (RNNs), enable AVs to perform complex tasks that require high-level perception and decision-making skills-capabilities. CNNs process visual data to recognize objects and interpret traffic signs and signals, while RNNs analyze sequential data to predict and respond to dynamic traffic situations in real-time.

Connectivity and V2X Communication - Vehicle-to-everything - V2X communication System enhances safety by enabling real-time communication with different other vehicles, infrastructure (V2I), pedestrians (V2P), and the cloud (V2C). AI algorithms process V2X data to receive different traffic updates time to time, road condition alerts, and emergency warnings, enhancing AVs' ability to anticipate and respond to potential hazards proactively.

Computer Vision System - Computer vision is a very important part of AVs to perceive, interpret surroundings. Cameras, LiDAR (Light Detection and Ranging), and different radar sensors capture real-time videos, Visuals, images data, enabling vehicles to detect lane markings, signs, traffic signals, pedestrians, and other vehicles. AI algorithms/methods process this data to make informed decisions, such as steering, braking, and accelerating, to navigate safely through urban traffic.

Machine Learning Technologies - Machine learning plays an important role in autonomous vehicle driving by allowing vehicles to learn from vast amounts of data. Supervised learning models train AVs to recognize different patterns and make predictions based on experience. Reinforcement learning techniques enable vehicles to optimize their behaviour through trial and error, improving performance in dynamic urban environments. (H. Anandakumar, R. Arulmurugan & A. Roshini, 2019).

Safety and Security - safety and security of autonomous driving vehicles/systems is very important. AI technologies implement various robust safety measures, such as fail-safe mechanisms, redundant sensors, and real-time threat detection methods/ algorithms, to mitigate risks and prevent road accidents. AI-driven cyber security solutions safety AVs from various malicious attacks and unauthorised access, ensuring the safety, integrity and reliability of autonomous driving operations.

Human-machine interaction (HMI) - Effective HMI design is essential for facilitating trust and acceptance of AV technology among passengers and pedestrians. AI-powered natural language processing (NLP) enables seamless communication between AVs and passengers, providing time to time real-time data/updates and responding to different voice commands. Visual interfaces and augmented reality (AR) displays enhance situational awareness and convey AVs' intentions to other road users.

3.3 Case Study: Autonomous Vehicles in Urban Areas

Autonomous vehicles - AVs are revolutionizing the urban transportation system by providing safer, efficient, and convenient mobility solutions with safety. This case study examines the implementation and impact of AVs in major urban zones/ areas, highlighting key benefits, challenges, and lessons learned.

Implementation Overview
City: Phoenix, Arizona, USA
Initiative: Waymo One Autonomous Taxi Service for people

Waymo - a subsidiary of Alphabet Inc. (Google's parent company), launched the Waymo One autonomous taxi service in Phoenix in 2018. This initiative marked a significant milestone in AV deployment/development, goal of providing people/ residents with access to self-driving vehicles for everyday transportation needs.

Technological Integration

AI Technologies: Waymo's AVs use AI technologies:

1. **Computer Vision:** Cameras and different sensors enable real-time detection of pedestrians, vehicles, and road infrastructure.
2. **Machine Learning:** ML Algorithms learn from vast amounts of previous driving data to improve decision-making and navigation capabilities.
3. **Sensor Fusion:** Integration of data from multiple sensors enhances situational awareness and public safety which leads to a safe system.
4. **Mapping and Localisation:** HD maps combined with GPS and inertial measurement units (IMUs) enable precise localization and navigation.

Operational Experience

User Experience: Waymo One allows users to request rides via a smartphone app. Passengers experience a seamless journey with minimal human intervention, from pickup to drop-off.

Safety Measures: Waymo emphasizes safety with redundant systems, real-time monitoring, and remote assistance for complex situations.

Infrastructure Adaptation: Phoenix's urban environment presents varied challenges, from congested downtown streets to wide suburban roads. Waymo's AVs adapt to diverse road conditions and traffic scenarios through continuous learning and real-world testing.

Benefits

1. **Safety:** Autonomous driving reduces human error, a leading cause of accidents. Waymo reports a growing safety record with millions of miles driven autonomously.
2. **Efficiency:** AVs optimize routes and minimize idle time, enhancing overall traffic flow and reducing congestion.
3. **Accessibility:** Waymo One improves mobility for elderly and disabled residents who face transportation challenges.
4. **Environmental Impact:** AVs support eco-friendly transportation services by reducing emissions through various optimized driving patterns.

Challenges and Lessons Learned

1. **Regulatory Framework:** AVs require clear regulatory guidelines to ensure safe operation in urban areas and public acceptance.
2. **Public Trust:** Building trust in AV technology remains a significant hurdle. Waymo engages in community outreach and education to address concerns.
3. **Technological Limitations:** Adapting to unpredictable human behaviour and handling complex urban scenarios are ongoing technical challenges.

4. AI TECHNOLOGY IN TRAFFIC MANAGEMENT

Artificial Intelligence is changing traffic management systems by providing accurate innovative solutions that improve safety, and optimize urban mobility. This section explores the application of AI technologies in traffic management, highlighting key methodologies, benefits, challenges, and future trends.

Methodologies and Applications

1. **Predictive Analytics:** AI-driven predictive analytics processes large amounts of historical and real-time traffic data to forecast traffic patterns, congestion hotspots, and peak times hrs. By analyzing factors such as weather conditions, events, and historical traffic flows, predictive models optimize traffic management strategies, enabling authorities to adjust signal timings and reroute traffic to minimize delays.
2. **Intelligent Traffic Signal Control:** AI-based traffic signal systems use real-time data from various sensors, cameras, and vehicle-to-infrastructure communication to dynamically adjust signal timings based on current traffic conditions.

Adaptive signal control algorithms optimize signal phases and cycle lengths, prioritizing high-volume routes and reducing unnecessary stops and idling, thus improving traffic flow and reducing emissions.

3. **Dynamic Route Guidance Systems:** AI-based dynamic route systems provide real-time navigation recommendations to drivers, based on current traffic conditions, road closures, weather and accidents. These systems optimize travel routes to minimize travel time and avoid congested areas, enhancing driver satisfaction and reducing overall traffic load on key routes.
4. **Incident Detection and Management:** AI algorithms detect various traffic incidents, accidents, and hazards through images, video analytics and sensor data analysis. Real-time incident detection enables prompt response and coordination of emergency services, which ensures quick clearance of roadblocks and minimizing different accidents. AI-powered incident management systems improve overall safety and efficiency on road networks.
5. **Autonomous Vehicles (AVs) Integration:** AVs equipped with the latest AI technologies contribute to traffic management by communicating with infrastructure and with other vehicles to optimize driving patterns and reduce congestion. AI algorithms enable AVs to navigate complex urban environments safely, predictively adjust speeds, and coordinate with traffic signals, contributing to smoother traffic flow and enhanced road safety. (C.Y. David Yang, DL. Fisher, 2021).

Benefits

1. **Reduced traffic Congestion:** AI-based traffic management systems optimize traffic flow, reduce stop-and-go patterns, and minimize congestion at peak hours in major areas, improving overall roadway efficiency and reducing travel times for commuters.
2. **Enhanced Safety:** Real-time accident detection, analytics and adaptive signal control systems enhance road safety by reducing accident risks, and traffic conflicts, and improving emergency response times.
3. **Environmental Impact:** By optimizing accurate traffic flow and reducing vehicle idle time, AI-driven traffic management systems help lower fuel consumption, greenhouse gas emissions, and air pollution levels, promoting environmental sustainability in urban areas.
4. **Improved Efficiency:** Automation and real-time decision-making capabilities enable traffic managers to respond quickly to change various conditions, optimize resource allocation in urban areas, and enhance operational efficiency across road networks. (Michael C. Lucic, Xiangpeng Wan, Hakim Ghazzai * and Yehia Massoud, 2020).

Challenges and Considerations

1. **Data Privacy and Security:** Managing and protecting important traffic data from cyber threats and unauthorized access is a critical task in maintaining the integrity, security and reliability of AI-driven traffic management systems.
2. **Infrastructure Investment:** Deploying AI technologies requires significant investment in sensors, communication networks, data security, computing infrastructure.
3. **Regulatory Frameworks:** Establishing clear regulations and standards SOP's for AI-based traffic management systems is very essential to ensure compliance, safety, and public trust in automated technologies.

Future Trends

1. **Integration of AI and 5G Networks:** The integration of AI with 5G networks will enable real-time data processing effectively and communication between vehicles, infrastructure and with traffic management systems, further enhancing traffic management capabilities and more safe system.
2. **Autonomous Mobility Services:** The rise of autonomous mobility services, including AV's vehicles and on-demand autonomous shuttles, will drive the adoption of AI in urban transportation, offering secured and scalable solutions for last-mile connectivity and urban mobility.
3. **AI-Powered Mobility as a Service (MaaS):** AI technologies will play an important role in the development of Mobility as a Service (MaaS) platforms, integrating multi-modal transportation system options and various personalized travel experiences for urban residents.

4.1 Intelligent Traffic Management, Signals, and Flow Control

Intelligent Traffic Management (ITM) systems powered by advanced AI technologies, plays an important role in optimizing traffic flow, enhancing public safety, and improving efficiency on urban roads. This section explores the components, methodologies, benefits, challenges, and future trends of ITM systems. D. Tabernik and D. Sko˘caj. (2020).

Components of Intelligent Traffic Management

1. Sensors and Data Collection
2. AI Algorithms and Predictive Analytics
3. Adaptive Signal Control

4. Dynamic Flow Control
5. Incident Detection and Management

Methodologies and Applications

1. **Real-Time Traffic Monitoring:** ITM systems continuously monitor traffic conditions through various sensors and cameras installed at different key locations. Real-time images, video data collection and analysis enable immediate and accurate responses to changing traffic patterns and avoid incidents.
2. **Traffic Simulation and Modeling:** AI-based traffic simulation models predict the impact of infrastructure change in different areas, new developments and special events on traffic flow. Simulation tools help to assist urban planners and traffic engineers in making informed decisions about infrastructure investments and traffic management strategies.
3. **Connected Vehicle Technologies:** Integration of Vehicle-to-Infrastructure V2I and Vehicle-to-Vehicle V2V communication technologies enhances ITM capabilities. Connected vehicles exchange real-time data with traffic management systems, providing drivers with proactive traffic alerts and optimizing traffic flow at intersections.

Benefits of Intelligent Traffic Management

1. Improved Traffic Flow
2. Enhanced Safety
3. Environmental Sustainability
4. Operational Efficiency

Challenges and Considerations

1. **Data Privacy and Security:** Protecting sensitive traffic data from cybersecurity threats and unauthorized access is critical to maintaining the integrity and reliability of ITM systems.
2. **Infrastructure Investment:** Deploying AI technologies and upgrading existing infrastructure to support ITM systems require substantial financial investments and long-term planning.
3. **Regulatory Compliance:** Establishing clear regulations and standards for AI-powered ITM systems ensures compliance with safety requirements, privacy laws, and ethical considerations.

Future Trends

1. Integration of AI and 5G Networks
2. Autonomous Mobility Services
3. Smart City Initiatives

Figure 2. Evolution of Intelligent Transportation System (ITS) infrastructure over time

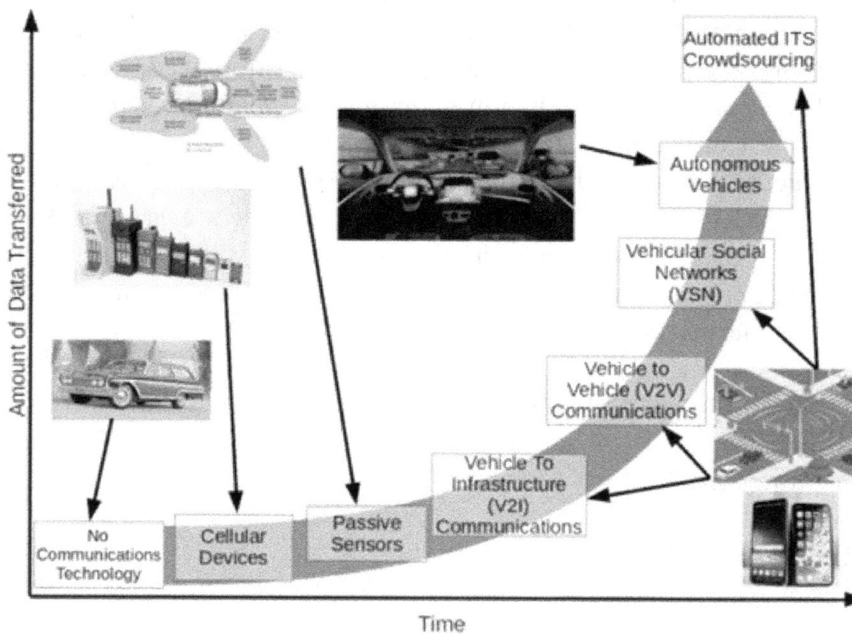

A diagram Figure 2 highlights the evolution of Intelligent Transportation System (ITS) infrastructure /development over the years, from an initial stage with minimal/ no communications technology for the average driver to fully automated ITS data collection systems. The advances are positioned alongside a red exponential growth curve to convey the explosive growth of data generated by these new advances in ITS crowdsourcing technologies, highlighting the need for ITS crowdsourcing systems to be engineered with scalability in mind. Michael C. Lucic, Xiangpeng Wan, Hakim Ghazzai * and Yehia Massoud. (2020).

4.2 Predictive Analytics for Traffic Congestion

Predictive analytics powered by Artificial Intelligence (AI), solve various traffic issues by analyzing traffic patterns, identifying bottlenecks, and optimizing traffic flow in real-time in urban areas. (Barba, Mateos, Soto, Mezher & Igartua, 2013).

Methodologies and Applications -

1. **Data Collection:** This relies on extensive data collection from various sources, including Sensors: detectors, cameras, radar, and LiDAR systems, which collect real-time data on vehicle speed, movement, volume, and occupancy.
    - Historical Data: Archived traffic data provides insights into recurring congestion patterns, seasonal variations, and special events that impact traffic flow in major areas.
2. **Machine Learning Algorithms:** AI-powered machine learning algorithms learn & process large datasets to identify correlations, trends, and anomalies in traffic behavior. These algorithms include:
    - **Regression Analysis:** RA Models historical data to predict future traffic conditions based on variables such as time of day, day of the week, and weather conditions Etc.
    - **Time-Series Forecasting:** Uses historical traffic data to forecast future traffic patterns and congestion levels, enabling proactive traffic management strategies.
    - **Pattern Recognition:** Identifies recurring traffic patterns, congestion hotspots, and abnormal traffic behaviors that require intervention.
3. **Real-Time Data Processing:** Predictive analytics systems analyze real-time traffic data to anticipate changes in traffic conditions and identify potential congestion points before they escalate. This real-time processing enables traffic managers to implement timely interventions, such as adjusting signal timings or rerouting traffic, to minimize congestion.
4. **Integration with Traffic Management Systems:** Predictive analytics integrates with intelligent traffic management systems to optimize traffic flow and improve operational efficiency. Key applications include:
    - **Dynamic Route Guidance:** Provides drivers with real-time navigation recommendations to avoid congested routes and minimize travel times.
    - **Adaptive Signal Control:** Adjusts traffic signal timings based on predicted traffic volumes and congestion levels to reduce wait times and optimize throughput.

Benefits

1. **Proactive Traffic Management:** Predictive analytics enables traffic Management systems to anticipate congestion and implement preventive measures to avoid accidents, reducing the severity and duration of traffic jams in major areas.
2. **Optimal Resource Allocation:** By accurately predicting traffic patterns, cities can allocate resources more effectively to solve various issues.
3. **Enhanced Traffic Flow:** Real-time interventions optimize traffic signal timings, lane management, and route-map guidance, improving overall traffic flow and reducing travel times for commuters.
4. **Improved Safety and Environmental Impact:** Reduced congestion through predictive analytics minimizes stop-and-go traffic patterns, lowering fuel consumption, vehicle emissions, and air pollution levels, thereby promoting environmental sustainability.

Challenges and Considerations

1. **Data Quality and Availability:** The accuracy and reliability of traffic data inputs is important for the effectiveness of predictive analytics models.
2. **Computational Complexity:** Processing big real-time data and running different complex algorithms require robust computing tools, infrastructure and efficient data management systems.
3. **Privacy and Security:** Protecting sensitive & important traffic data from cyber security threats, attacks and unauthorized access is essential to maintaining public trust and compliance with various data privacy regulations.

Future Trends

1. **IoT and Smart City Initiatives:** Predictive analytics will use various IoT sensors, smart grids, and urban analytics platforms to create interconnected and responsive smart city environments.
2. **Advancements in AI and Machine Learning ALgo:** advancements in AI algorithms, including DL-deep learning and reinforcement learning methods, will enhance the accuracy and predictive capabilities of traffic congestion models.
3. **Autonomous and Connected Vehicles use:** The use of autonomous and connected vehicles will generate vast amounts of real-time traffic data, providing new opportunities for predictive analytics to optimize traffic management, enhance mobility services and provide the best service.

4.3 Case Study: AI in Traffic Management

AI is used to solve traffic management issues in major cities worldwide, providing solutions to solve traffic congestion, increase public safety, and improve overall urban travel experience. This case study examines various implementations of AI technologies in traffic management across different urban areas, highlighting key methodologies, benefits, challenges, and outcomes.

City: Los Angeles, USA.

Initiative: Automated Traffic Surveillance and Control (ATSAC) System

Overview: Los Angeles' ATSAC system uses AI technologies to monitor and manage traffic flow across the city's major extensive road network. The system integrates data from traffic cameras, vehicle detectors, and weather sensors to optimize signal timings and improve traffic management efficiency.

AI Technologies Used:

ML: AI algorithms analyze real time traffic data to learn traffic patterns and adjust signal timings dynamically based on current conditions .

Big Data Analytics: ATSAC processes large volumes of data to identify congestion hotspots, prioritize traffic signal adjustments, and optimize traffic flow on high-volume corridors.

Integration with Transportation Apps: ATSAC integrates with popular navigation apps to provide drivers with real-time traffic updates time to time, alternative route recommendations, and information on parking availability.

Benefits:

Improved Traffic Flow: ATSAC helps to reduce traffic congestion and minimize delays, enhancing overall traffic flow and traveller's experience in Los Angeles.

Efficient Resource Allocation: AI-driven analytics enable proactive management of traffic incidents and emergencies, optimizing the deployment of city resources and emergency response teams.

Public Engagement: navigation apps Integration improves public awareness of traffic conditions, promoting informed decision-making and reducing traffic-related stress. (J. N. Njoku, C. I. Nwakanma, G. C. Amaizu & D.-S. Kim, 2023)

5. USE OF AI IN PUBLIC TRANSPORTATION SYSTEMS

Artificial Intelligence -AI is changing public transportation systems by enhancing operational efficiency, and safety, improving passenger experience, and optimizing service reliability.

Applications of AI in Public Transportation

1. **Predictive Maintenance using AI:** AI-powered predictive maintenance systems analyze sensor data from vehicles and infrastructure to detect potential mechanical issues before they arise.
2. **Autonomous Vehicles (AVs):** AI technologies enable the deployment of autonomous taxis, buses and shuttles, offering safe and effective mobility solutions in urban areas.
3. **Real-Time Passenger Information:** AI-driven passenger information systems provide travellers with real-time travel updates, route changes, and service disruptions via mobile apps, digital displays, and voice assistants.
4. **Demand-Responsive Transit-DRT:** AI algorithms optimize demand-responsive transit services by predicting passenger demand, dynamically adjusting routes and schedules, and efficiently allocating vehicles.
5. **Fare Collection & Revenue Management:** AI enhances fare collection systems through automated ticketing, contactless payments, and fraud detection algorithms. (R. Abduljabbar, H. Dia, S. Liyanage, S.A. Bagloee, 2019).

Benefits of AI in Public Transportation

1. **Operational Efficiency:** AI uses fleet management, scheduling & proper route planning helps in reducing operating costs and improve service reliability.
2. **Enhanced Passenger travel Experience:** AI-driven systems provide personalized travel experiences by offering real-time data updates, travel-journey planning, and connectivity across multi-modal transit networks.
3. **Safety and Security:** AI enhances public transit safety through video surveillance, predictive maintenance of infrastructure, and emergency response systems.
4. **Environmental Sustainability:** AI-enabled optimization of transit routes and schedules reduces vehicle traffic, congestion, and fuel consumption and helps to save money. Lakshmi Shankar Iyer. (2021).

Challenges and Considerations

1. Equitable access to AI-driven transit services, requires transparent governance and regulatory frameworks.

Future Trends

1. **AI-Driven Multi modal system:** Integrating AI technologies with multiple modes of transportation, including buses, trains, ride sharing services, and micro-mobility solutions, facilitates seamless inter modal connectivity and enhances urban mobility options.
2. **Smart City Initiatives:** AI-powered public transit systems will play a central role in smart city initiatives by leveraging IoT sensors, big data analytics.
3. **Advancements in AI and Autonomous Vehicles:** Continued advancements in AI algorithms, machine learning models, and sensor technologies will drive the development of safer, more efficient autonomous vehicles and intelligent transit systems.

5.1 AI for Public Safety, Passenger Experience, and Safety Improvements in Public Transportation

Artificial Intelligence is increasingly integrated into public transportation systems to increase safety, improve passenger experience, and optimize operational efficiency.

Applications of AI for Public Safety and Passenger Experience

1. **Video Surveillance & security:** AI-powered video analytics tools monitor transit stations, vehicles, and public spaces to detect suspicious activities, identify security threats, and alert authorities in real-time.
2. **Predictive Maintenance and Asset Management:** AI-driven predictive maintenance systems monitor the health and performance of vehicles, infrastructure, and equipment.
3. **Emergency Response and Incident Management:** AI based incident management systems coordinate emergency responses, dispatch resources, and facilitate communication between transit operators, emergency services, and passengers.
4. **Passenger Information and Communication:** AI-driven passenger information systems provide real-time updates, personalized notifications, and interactive communication channels to passengers.

5. **AI-Powered Safety Features in Autonomous Vehicles (AVs):** Autonomous buses, shuttles, and vehicles equipped with AI technologies use computer vision, sensor fusion, and machine learning to navigate routes, detect obstacles, and ensure safe interactions with pedestrians and other vehicles. (Lakshmi Shankar Iyer, 2021).

Benefits of AI for Public Safety and Passenger Experience

1. **Enhanced Security and Incident Response:** AI-powered video surveillance and analytics systems improve security, threat detection, and incident management in transit environments & provide quick response.
2. **Improved Operational Efficiency:** Predictive maintenance and asset management systems optimize vehicle reliability, reduce downtime, and lower maintenance costs for transit agencies.
3. **Personalized Passenger Services:** AI-driven passenger information systems deliver personalized travel updates, route recommendations, and real-time service notifications to enhance passenger experience and satisfaction.
4. **Safety Innovation in Autonomous Vehicles:** AI-enabled safety features in autonomous vehicles, such as advanced driver assistance systems (ADAS) and sensor technologies, ensure safe navigation and operation on urban streets. (P. Seuwou, E. Banissi, and G. Ubakanma, 2020).

Challenges and Considerations

1. **Data Privacy and Security:** Safeguarding passenger data and ensuring compliance with data protection regulations are critical considerations in deploying AI-driven safety and passenger experience solutions in public transportation.
2. **Integration and Interoperability:** Seamless integration of AI systems with existing transit infrastructure, operational workflows, and multi-modal transit networks requires standardized protocols, interoperable platforms, and collaboration among stakeholders.
3. **Ethical and Regulatory Frameworks:** Addressing ethical concerns, algorithmic bias, and transparency in AI decision-making processes is essential to fostering public trust and ensuring equitable access to safe and reliable transit services.

Future Trends

1. **AI-Driven Multi modal Integration for smart cities:** AI-driven multi modal is all set to revolutionize urban living in the coming years. This combines artificial intelligence with various modes of transportation and infrastructure

2. **Smart City Initiatives:** Smart cities encompass a wide range of different efforts aimed at leveraging technology, new ML,DL models and data to improve the efficiency, accuracy, safety and quality life of urban people.
3. **Advancements in AI and Autonomous Vehicles**: Nowadays it's rapidly transforming the automotive industry and the transportation system. Here are some key developments in this field: AI-Powered Autonomous Driving, Urban Mobility Solutions,Enhanced Safety and Efficiency.

5.2 AI-Driven Route Optimization and Scheduling Tools

AI plays an important role in transforming route optimization systems and scheduling in public transportation systems, offering advanced solutions to improve efficiency, avoid accidents & help to reduce travel times.

Applications of AI-Driven Route Optimization and Scheduling

1. **Dynamic Route Planning:** AI algorithms analyze real-time large volume of traffic data, traffic patterns, and environmental factors to dynamically optimize transit routes.
2. **Demand-Responsive Transit (DRT):** AI-powered DRT systems adapt transit routes and schedules based on passenger demand forecasts and real-time requests.
3. **Fleet Management and Vehicle Routing:** AI-driven fleet management systems optimize vehicle routing & scheduling.

Benefits of AI-Driven Route Optimization and Scheduling

1. **Improved Operational Efficiency:** AI optimizes transit routes and schedules to minimize travel times, reduce fuel consumption, and lower operational costs for transit agencies.
2. **Enhanced Passenger Experience:** AI-driven tools provide real-time updates, accurate travel predictions, and personalized route recommendations to passengers.
3. **Sustainability and Environmental Impact:** Optimized route planning and vehicle scheduling reduce carbon emissions, congestion, and environmental footprint. promoting efficient use of resources and supporting sustainable urban mobility initiatives. (M Elassy a, M Al-Hattab b, Takruri c, S Badawi, 2024)

Challenges and Considerations

1. **Data Integration and Accuracy:** Ensuring data accuracy, reliability, and integration from multiple sources (e.g., GPS, traffic sensors, passenger data) is crucial for effective AI-driven route optimization and scheduling.
2. **Scalability and Adaptability:** Scaling AI solutions to accommodate growing passenger demand, changing urban dynamics, and diverse transit operations requires adaptable algorithms, scalable infrastructure, and continuous optimization.
3. **Privacy and Ethical Concerns:** Protecting passenger privacy, ensuring transparent data usage, and addressing ethical considerations (e.g., algorithmic bias, fairness in service allocation) are essential for building trust and acceptance of AI-driven transit solutions.

Future Trends

1. **Integration with IoT and Smart City Initiatives:** AI-powered route optimization tools will increasingly integrate with IoT sensors, smart infrastructure, and urban analytics platforms.
2. **AI-Driven Autonomous Transit Systems:** Advancements in AI and autonomous vehicle technologies will enable the development of AI-driven autonomous transit systems.
3. **Predictive Analytics and Machine Learning:** Continued advancements in predictive analytics and machine learning will enhance AI's capability to forecast passenger demand.

5.3 Case Study: AI in Public Transportation Systems and for Public Safety

Artificial Intelligence is increasingly deployed in public transportation systems worldwide to enhance safety, improve operational efficiency, and optimize passenger experience.

City: London, UK
Initiative: AI-Enhanced Passenger Information and Route Optimization system
Overview: Transport for London (TfL) integrates AI technologies to optimize route planning, enhance passenger information systems, and improve public transit accessibility across the city. AI-driven algorithms analyze real-time data on passenger flows, traffic conditions, and operational performance to optimize bus routes, schedules, and service delivery.

AI Technologies Used:

- **Dynamic Route Planning:** AI algorithms adjust bus routes and schedules in response to real-time traffic conditions, passenger demand patterns, and operational disruptions, improving service reliability and reducing congestion.
- **Personalized Passenger Information:** AI-powered mobile apps and digital signage provide passengers with real-time updates on transit schedules, route changes, and alternative travel options, enhancing passenger experience and satisfaction.

Benefits:

- **Improved Reliability:** AI optimization of bus routes and schedules reduces travel times, minimizes delays, and enhances on-time performance, fostering increased passenger confidence and ridership.
- **Enhanced Passenger Experience:** Personalized travel updates and interactive communication channels improve passenger satisfaction, facilitate seamless transit journeys, and promote modal shift towards public transportation.
- **Operational Effectiveness:** AI-driven data analytics support evidence-based decision-making, optimize resource allocation, and streamline transit operations, ensuring efficient service delivery and sustainable urban mobility.

6. CHALLENGES AND ETHICAL CONSIDERATIONS IN URBAN TRANSPORTATION SYSTEMS

As urban transportation systems evolve with advancements in technology, several challenges and ethical considerations arise that must be addressed to ensure responsible and equitable deployment of innovations. This section explores key challenges and ethical considerations in the context of AI-driven urban transportation systems.

Challenges

1. **Infrastructure Costs and Implementation:** Upgrading urban infrastructure to support AI-driven smart transportation systems requires substantial investments in technology, equipment, and infrastructure. Funding constraints, bureaucratic processes, and regulatory approvals often pose challenges to timely and cost-effective implementation.

2. **Integration and Interoperability:** Ensuring seamless integration of AI technologies with existing transportation infrastructure, systems, and multi-modal networks requires standardized protocols, interoperable platforms, and collaboration among stakeholders. Compatibility issues and data silos can hinder the effectiveness of integrated solutions.
3. **Data Privacy and Security:** The collection, storage, and analysis of vast amounts of real-time data in AI-driven transportation systems raise significant concerns about data privacy, security breaches, and unauthorized access. Safeguarding sensitive passenger information and complying with data protection regulations are critical priorities for transit agencies and technology providers.
4. **Regulatory and Legal Frameworks:** The rapid pace of technological innovation often outpaces the development of regulatory frameworks and policies governing AI applications in urban transportation. Clear guidelines, standards, and legal frameworks are essential to address liability issues, ensure safety standards, and mitigate risks associated with autonomous vehicles and AI-driven systems.
5. **Public Trust and Acceptance:** Building public trust and acceptance of AI-driven transportation technologies requires transparency, accountability, and stakeholder engagement. Addressing concerns about safety, reliability, ethical implications, and potential job displacement is crucial to fostering public confidence and support for smart transportation initiatives. (J. N. Njoku, C. I. Nwakanma, G. C. Amaizu & D.-S. Kim, 2023)

Ethical Considerations

1. **Algorithmic Bias and Fairness:** AI algorithms used in transportation systems may exhibit biases based on training data, leading to unequal treatment or outcomes for certain demographic groups. Ensuring fairness, transparency, and accountability in algorithmic decision-making processes is essential to prevent discrimination and promote equity in urban mobility.
2. **Ethical Use of Data:** Ethical considerations arise from the use of personal data, location tracking, and behavioral analytics in AI-driven transportation systems. Respecting passenger privacy rights, obtaining informed consent, and implementing robust data anonymization and encryption practices are critical to protecting individual liberties and rights.
3. **Environmental Impact and Sustainability:** While AI technologies offer opportunities to optimize traffic flow, reduce emissions, and promote sustainable transportation practices, they also raise concerns about energy consumption, resource depletion, and environmental sustainability.

4. **Social Equity and Access:** Ensuring equitable access to AI-driven transportation services and benefits is essential to prevent widening socio-economic disparities. Addressing barriers to access, affordability concerns, and ensuring inclusivity in service delivery are crucial considerations in promoting social equity and enhancing urban mobility for all residents.
5. **Job Displacement and Workforce Transition:** The adoption of AI technologies, including autonomous vehicles and automated systems, may disrupt traditional transportation jobs and require workforce retraining and transition programs. Supporting affected workers, promoting skill development in emerging technologies, and fostering inclusive economic opportunities are imperative to mitigate socio-economic impacts.

Addressing challenges and ethical considerations in AI-driven urban transportation systems requires collaborative efforts from policymakers, technology developers, transit agencies, and community stakeholders. (J. N. Njoku, C. I. Nwakanma, G. C. Amaizu & D.-S. Kim, 2023)

6.1 Data Privacy and Various Security Issues in AI-driven Urban Transportation Systems

As Artificial Intelligence (AI) continues to transform urban transportation systems, ensuring robust data privacy and addressing diverse security concerns are paramount to fostering trust and safeguarding passenger information. This section examines key data privacy issues, security challenges, and best practices in AI-driven urban transportation environments.

Data Privacy Challenges

1. **Collection and Storage of Personal Data:** AI-powered transportation systems rely on collecting and analyzing vast amounts of real-time data, including passenger information, travel patterns, and location data. Safeguarding sensitive personal data from unauthorized access, breaches, and misuse is critical to protecting passenger privacy rights.
2. **Consent and Transparency:** Obtaining informed consent from passengers for data collection, processing, and sharing practices is essential to ensure transparency and accountability in AI-driven transportation systems. Clear communication of privacy policies, data usage guidelines, and opt-out mechanisms promotes trust and empowers passengers to make informed choices about their personal information.

3. **Data Retention and Anonymization:** Implementing robust data retention policies and anonymization techniques is crucial to minimize the risk of re-identification and unauthorized disclosure of personal data. Aggregating and anonymizing data sets while preserving their utility for AI analytics helps mitigate privacy risks and comply with data protection regulations.

Security Issues

1. **Cybersecurity Threats:** AI-driven transportation systems are susceptible to cyberattacks, data breaches, and malware infiltration, posing risks to passenger safety, operational integrity, and system reliability. Deploying robust cybersecurity measures, encryption protocols, and intrusion detection systems safeguards against cyber threats and ensures the resilience of critical infrastructure.
2. **Insider Threats and Unauthorized Access:** Mitigating insider threats and unauthorized access to sensitive data requires implementing access controls, authentication mechanisms, and audit trails. Monitoring and auditing data access, enforcing least privilege principles, and conducting regular security assessments strengthen defences against internal threats and malicious activities.
3. **Integration and Interoperability Risks:** Integrating AI technologies with legacy systems, third-party platforms, and IoT devices introduces interoperability risks and vulnerabilities. Addressing compatibility issues, conducting thorough risk assessments, and establishing secure communication protocols mitigate risks associated with data exchanges and system integrations.

Best Practices and Recommendations

1. **Privacy by Design:** Incorporating privacy principles and data protection measures into the design and development of AI-driven transportation systems promotes privacy by design. Adopting privacy-enhancing technologies, conducting privacy impact assessments, and adhering to privacy-by-default settings prioritize data privacy throughout the system lifecycle.
2. **Regulatory Compliance:** Adhering to global data protection regulations, such as GDPR (General Data Protection Regulation) and CCPA (California Consumer Privacy Act), ensures legal compliance and strengthens data privacy practices in AI-driven transportation operations.
3. **Stakeholder Education and Awareness:** Raising awareness among stakeholders, including passengers, employees, and technology providers, about data privacy risks, security protocols, and best practices fosters a culture of cybersecurity awareness and accountability. Providing training on data handling practices,

incident response procedures, and privacy rights empowers stakeholders to protect personal data and respond effectively to security incidents.

Securing data privacy and addressing security challenges in AI-driven urban transportation systems require proactive measures, collaboration across sectors, and adherence to privacy-by-design principles. By prioritizing data protection, implementing robust cybersecurity defenses, and promoting transparency and accountability, cities can build resilient and trusted AI ecosystems that enhance urban mobility while safeguarding passenger privacy and security.

6.2 Ethical Implications of AI in Public Transportation

The integration of Artificial Intelligence (AI) into public transportation systems introduces various ethical considerations that necessitate careful deliberation and proactive management.

Ethical Challenges

1. **Algorithmic Bias and Fairness:** AI algorithms used in public transportation systems may inadvertently perpetuate biases present in training data, leading to unequal treatment or outcomes for certain demographic groups. Ensuring fairness, transparency, and accountability in algorithmic decision-making processes is essential to mitigate bias and promote equitable access to transportation services.
2. **Privacy and Data Protection:** AI-driven transportation systems rely on collecting, analyzing, and storing vast amounts of personal data, including passenger information and travel behaviors. Safeguarding sensitive data from unauthorized access, breaches, and misuse is crucial to protect passenger privacy rights and maintain trust in AI technologies.
3. **Safety and Reliability:** Ensuring the safety and reliability of AI-enabled transportation systems requires rigorous testing, validation, and adherence to safety standards. Balancing innovation with safety considerations, managing risks associated with autonomous vehicles, and mitigating potential hazards are critical ethical imperatives for transit agencies and technology developers.
4. **Job Displacement and Economic Impact:** The adoption of AI technologies, including autonomous vehicles and automated systems, may disrupt traditional transportation jobs and require workforce transition programs. Addressing socio-economic impacts, promoting skill development, and fostering inclusive economic opportunities are essential ethical considerations in supporting affected workers and communities.

Ethical Considerations

1. **Transparency and Accountability:** Providing transparent explanations of AI algorithms, decision-making processes, and data usage practices promotes accountability and fosters trust among stakeholders. Transparent communication with passengers, employees, and regulatory authorities enhances understanding of AI technologies' impacts and ethical implications.
2. **Ethical Use of AI:** Adhering to ethical guidelines, principles, and codes of conduct in AI development and deployment ensures responsible and ethical use of AI technologies in public transportation. Upholding ethical standards, preventing misuse of AI for discriminatory purposes, and prioritizing public interest and safety are paramount in ethical governance frameworks.
3. **Public Engagement and Participation:** Involving diverse stakeholders, including passengers, communities, advocacy groups, and policy-makers, in decision-making processes enhances transparency, accountability, and ethical governance of AI-driven transportation initiatives. (Rodrigo Brandão, Glauco Arbix, 2022)

Best Practices for Ethical Governance

1. **Ethical Impact Assessments:** Conducting ethical impact assessments and risk analyses prior to AI deployment helps identify potential ethical issues, assess risks, and develop mitigation strategies.
2. **Regulatory Compliance and Standards:** Adhering to regulatory frameworks, privacy laws, and industry standards, such as GDPR (General Data Protection Regulation) and ethical AI guidelines, ensures legal compliance and ethical conduct in AI-driven transportation operations.
3. **Continuous Monitoring and Evaluation:** Monitoring AI systems' performance, outcomes, and ethical impacts through continuous evaluation, audits, and feedback mechanisms enable proactive management of ethical issues and adaptation to evolving challenges.

Addressing ethical implications of AI in public transportation requires proactive ethical governance, transparency, and stakeholder engagement to ensure responsible innovation and mitigate potential risks. By prioritizing fairness, privacy protection, safety, and inclusive economic development, cities can harness the transformative potential of AI technologies while upholding ethical principles and promoting public trust in AI-driven urban mobility solutions.

7. AI-BASED FUTURE PROSPECTS AND INNOVATIONS IN URBAN TRANSPORTATION

Artificial Intelligence continues to drive new innovations in urban transportation, promising to revolutionize travel experience, sustainability safety and efficiency in cities worldwide.

Emerging AI Technologies

1. **Autonomous Vehicles:** AI based autonomous vehicles show an advancement in travel experience, offering benefits such as improved road safety, reduced congestion, and enhanced accessibility for passengers.
2. **Smart Traffic Management & Predictive Analytics:** AI- based analytics enable real-time analysis of various traffic patterns, traffic zones, congestion levels. Smart traffic management systems use AI methods to optimize traffic flow, reduce travel times, reduce fuel consumption and minimize environmental impact through adaptive signal control and dynamic routing strategies.
3. **Travel Solutions:** It personalizes transportation based on individual choice, travel patterns/behaviours, and real-time conditions. Mobility-as-a-Service (MaaS) platforms that integrate AI to offer safe travel, public transit and ridesharing. Wang Tong; Azhar Hussain; Wang Xi Bo; Sabita Maharjan. (2019)

Future Prospects

1. **Enhanced vehicle Safety and Security:** AI technologies enhance transportation safety by making easier real-time incident/accident detection, emergency response coordination and proper maintenance of infrastructure/roads. Integrated AI systems avoid risks, improve situational awareness and ensure rapid response to emergencies or accidents, enhancing overall public safety in urban environments.
2. **Sustainable Urban Mobility:** AI innovations promote transportation services by optimizing energy efficiency.
3. **Smart Infrastructure and Connectivity:** AI helps to improve connectivity between vehicles, infrastructure, people and smart devices, enabling seamless communication and data exchange. Smart infrastructure initiatives deploy AI sensors and IoT devices to monitor traffic conditions, manage parking availability, and support autonomous vehicle navigation, creating interconnected urban environments.

Potential Impact

1. **Economic Growth and New Innovation:** AI based Innovation in urban transportation helps in economic growth by various innovations, attracting various investments in smart city initiatives projects and creating different new job opportunities for people in technology, research, roads and infrastructure development.
2. **Improved Quality of Life:** AI technologies help safe travel, reduce commute times, and enhance accessibility for diverse populations, which leads to improving quality of life for residents. Lots of transportation options, reduced congestion, travel time and enhanced environmental sustainability contribute to healthier, more livable cities with improved public health outcomes.
3. **Regulatory and Ethical Considerations:** Addressing regulatory challenges, ethical implications and societal acceptance of AI technologies remains critical to responsible deployment in urban transportation. This needs to be considered for better development.

AI-based innovations hold immense potential to transform urban transportation systems and people's lifestyles, offering opportunities to enhance safety, sustainability, and efficiency in cities globally. By embracing AI technologies, cities can optimize mobility services, improve infrastructure resilience, and create inclusive, accessible transportation networks for all residents.

7.1 Emerging AI Technologies and Their Potential Impact on Effective Transportation

Artificial Intelligence (AI) is the reason to provide better transportation worldwide, introducing innovative technologies that enhance efficiency, safety, and sustainability.

1. Autonomous Vehicles (AVs)

Technology Overview: AVs leverage AI-powered systems, including computer vision, sensors, sensor fusion, DL and machine learning algorithms, to navigate and operate properly without human intervention.

Potential Impact:

- **Safety Enhancement:** AVs have the potential to reduce traffic accidents, collisions and fatalities by eliminating various human error, which accounts for a majority of road accidents,collisions. AI-driven predictive analytics enhance AVs' ability to anticipate and react to potential hazards, improving overall road safety and gives safe travel.

- **Traffic Efficiency:** AVs optimize traffic flow effectively and reduce congestion through coordinated communication and adaptive driving behaviors. AI ML DL algorithms enable platooning and cooperative driving strategies, minimizing fuel consumption and travel times on congested roadways.
- **Accessibility:** AVs enhance mobility options for individuals with disabilities, elderly people, and other communities by providing autonomous transportation solutions tailored to diverse passenger needs. (Yifang Ma; Zhenyu Wang; Hong Yang; Lin Yang, 2020).

2. Advance Smart Traffic Management

Technology Overview: AI-driven systems work on real time data including traffic patterns, weather conditions, and historical trends, to forecast future transportation demands and optimize resource allocation.

Potential Impact:

- **Congestion Mitigation:** It optimizes traffic flow by predicting peak travel times, identifying congestion hotspots, and recommending alternative routes in real-time to avoid traffic issues and safe travel.
- **Environmental Sustainability:** Smart traffic management minimizes vehicle emissions and fuel consumption by promoting eco-friendly vehicles, driving behaviors and prioritizing green corridors for low-emission vehicles.
- **Operational Efficiency:** AI based traffic management improves operational efficiency by reducing maintenance costs, optimizing fleet management, and enhancing public transit reliability through data-driven decision-making. (Razavi, M. Hamidkhani & R. Sadeghi, 2019).

3. Mobility-as-a-Service (MaaS) Platforms

Technology Overview: Mobility-as-a-Service (MaaS) platforms integrate AI technologies to offer seamless, multi-modal transportation solutions tailored to individual passenger preferences.

Potential Impact:

- **User Convenience:** MaaS platforms enhance user experience by providing personalized travel planning, real-time updates, and integrated payment solutions for seamless multi-modal journeys.

- **Modal Shift:** AI-driven MaaS solutions promote modal shift from private car ownership to shared mobility services, reducing urban congestion, parking demand, and overall transportation costs.
- **Urban Planning:** Data analytics from MaaS platforms inform urban planning decisions, including infrastructure development, transit network expansion, and land use policies, to support sustainable growth and enhance city livability.

Emerging AI technologies hold immense potential to transform travel transportation systems by enhancing public safety, efficiency, and accessibility in urban and suburban environments. Autonomous vehicles, predictive analytics, and Mobility-as-a-Service platforms represent key innovations driving the future of effective transportation solutions.

7.2 Vision for the Future of Safe Urban Transportation

The future of urban transportation is poised for transformation with advancements in Artificial Intelligence (AI) and innovative technologies that prioritize safety, sustainability, and efficiency.

Trends Shaping the Future

1. **Autonomous Mobility Solutions:** Autonomous vehicles (AVs) powered by AI technologies are expected to play a central role in future urban mobility.
2. **Integrated Multi-Modal Networks:** Future transportation systems will embrace Mobility-as-a-Service (MaaS) platforms that integrate various modes of transportation, including public transit, ridesharing, micro-mobility solutions, and autonomous shuttles. AI-driven MaaS platforms will optimize route planning, scheduling, and payment systems to provide seamless, door-to-door transportation experiences.
3. **Smart Infrastructure and Traffic Management:** AI-enabled smart infrastructure will support real-time traffic management, adaptive signal control, and predictive analytics to optimize traffic flow, reduce congestion, and prioritize sustainable transportation solutions.

Challenges and Opportunities

1. **Ethical and Regulatory Considerations:** Addressing ethical implications, regulatory frameworks, and public acceptance of AI technologies in transportation is crucial to ensuring safe and responsible deployment.

2. **Environmental Sustainability:** Promoting eco-friendly transportation practices, such as electrification of vehicles and promoting modal shifts towards sustainable modes of transport, will mitigate environmental impact and support climate resilience in urban areas.
3. **Safety and Security:** Enhancing cybersecurity measures, safeguarding passenger data, and ensuring robust safety protocols are essential to mitigating risks associated with AI-driven transportation systems.

Vision for Safe Urban Transportation

1. **Seamless Mobility:** Future urban transportation will offer effective, accessible mobility solutions that give priority to passenger safety, convenience, and sustainability. AI technologies will enable personalized travel experiences, optimize traffic management, and improve transit accessibility for all residents.
2. **Integrated Sustainability:** Smart cities will integrate AI-powered transportation systems effectively with proper urban planning practices, with efficient land use, reducing carbon footprints, and enhancing the quality of human life for urban dwellers. Green transportation initiatives, supported by AI analytics, will drive environmental stewardship and resilience in urban ecosystems.
3. **Academic institutions**, and community stakeholders will drive continuous innovation in urban transportation. The future of safe urban transportation is based on AI-driven innovations that enhance safe mobility, sustainability, and resilience in cities worldwide.

7.3 Preparing Cities for AI-Driven Transportation Innovations for Safe Transportation system

Artificial Intelligence helps to revolutionize transportation, innovative thinking, latest technology and strategic planning are essential to ensure safe and effective deployment of AI-driven innovations.

Key Considerations for Cities

1. **Infrastructure Readiness:** Cities must assess and upgrade existing infrastructure/development to support AI-driven transportation systems for better systems, including best communication networks, smart traffic signal system, and IoT-enabled devices. Infrastructure/development improvements enable real-time data exchange, enhance traffic management systems and support autonomous vehicle navigation for safe and efficient urban mobility experience.

2. **Regulatory Frameworks for urban areas:** Establishing clear regulatory frameworks and different standards are essential to govern the deployment, operation & safety of AI systems in urban transportation. Regulatory bodies must collaborate with industry people/stakeholders to develop SOPs that address safety protocols, safety-data privacy concerns, ethical considerations, and liability issues associated with AI-driven transportation innovations.
3. **Stakeholder Collaboration:** different Collaborations among public agencies, private sector partners, technology developers & other community stakeholders is critical to fostering innovation and ensuring inclusive decision-making in AI-driven transportation initiatives. (C.Y. David Yang, DL. Fisher. 2021)

Strategies for Safe Transportation system

1. **Safety Centric Design:** Adopting safety-centric design/development principles ensures that AI-driven transportation systems prioritize passenger/people safety, operational reliability & emergency/quick response capabilities. Integrating fail-safe mechanisms, real-time monitoring tools and collision avoidance,detection systems enhances system resilience, improve trust and minimizes risks associated with autonomous operations.
2. **Data Security and Privacy:** Implementing robust data security systems, measures and privacy protections is imperative to safeguard important,sensitive information collected by AI-enabled transportation systems devices. Cities must establish protocols for data encryption, secure storage practices and transparent data management policies to mitigate cybersecurity threats and maintain public trust.
3. **Training and Education:** Education is one of the important pillars for development. Providing comprehensive training programs for transportation operators, emergency responders, and AI system developers enhances readiness and proficiency in managing AI-driven technologies. Education initiatives also inform the public about AI benefits, safety protocols, and rights regarding data privacy, fostering trust and acceptance of AI innovations in transportation.

Future-Ready Cities

1. **Adaptive Planning and Flexibility:** Cities should adopt different adaptive planning strategies that anticipate technological advancements and evolving urban mobility needs, safe transportation. Flexibility in infrastructure design, regulatory frameworks and various policy adaptations enables cities to embrace emerging AI technologies.

2. **Pilot Projects and Testing:** pilot project development and controlled testing environments allow cities to evaluate AI-driven transportation technologies in real-world scenarios, assess performance metrics, and identify areas for improvement. Pilots facilitate data-driven decision-making, validate safety protocols, and build confidence in AI innovations among stakeholders and the public.
3. **Public Engagement and Trust Building:** Promoting various public engagement initiatives, community forums, publicity and stakeholder consultations fosters transparency, accountability, and inclusivity in AI-driven transportation planning. Proactively addressing public concerns, soliciting feedback, and prioritizing safety and accessibility initiatives strengthen public trust and support for AI-powered urban mobility solutions. (Mohamed Elassy a, Mohammed Al-Hattab b, Maen Takruri c, Sufian Badawi., 2024)

CONCLUSION

The integration of Artificial Intelligence (AI) into urban transportation systems represents a pivotal moment in the evolution of smart cities worldwide. Through advancements in autonomous vehicles, predictive analytics, and smart infrastructure, AI offers transformative solutions that enhance safety, efficiency, and sustainability in urban mobility.

AI technologies have demonstrated significant potential to revolutionize urban transportation by Enhancing Safety, Optimizing Efficiency, and Promoting Sustainability. However, the integration of AI in urban transportation also poses challenges: Ethical Considerations, Infrastructure Requirements, Public Trust and Acceptance Looking forward, cities must prioritize: Infrastructure Investment, Regulatory Frameworks, Collaboration and Inclusivity, Accessibility and Equity.

In conclusion, the future of urban transportation lies in leveraging AI technologies to create safer, more efficient, and sustainable cities. By embracing AI-driven solutions and addressing associated challenges through proactive planning, collaborative efforts, and ethical considerations, cities can pave the way for smarter, more resilient urban environments that improve quality of life for all residents. As cities continue to evolve, AI will play a central role in shaping the next generation of urban mobility, driving towards safer, more connected, and sustainable urban futures.

REFERENCES

Abduljabbar, R., Dia, H., Liyanage, S., & Bagloee, S. A. (2019). Applications of artificial intelligence in transport: An overview. *Sustainability, 11*(1), 189.

Ahangar, M. N., Ahmed, Q. Z., Khan, F. A., & Hafeez, M. (2021). A survey of autonomous vehicles: Enabling communication technologies and challenges. *Sensors (Basel), 21*(3), 706.

Akhtar, M., & Moridpour, S. (2021). A review of traffic congestion prediction using artificial intelligence. *Journal of Advanced Transportation, 2021*, 8878011. Advance online publication. DOI: 10.1155/2021/8878011

Anandakumar, H., Arulmurugan, R., & Roshini, A. (2019). Intelligent vehicle system problems and future impacts for transport guidelines, in: *Proceedings of the 2019 International Conference on Smart Systems and Inventive Technology (ICSSIT)*, pp. 1–5, https://doi.org/DOI: 10.1109/ICSSIT46314.2019.8987831

Barba, C. T., Mateos, M. A., Soto, P. R., Mezher, A. M., & Igartua, M. A. (2012, June). Smart city for VANETs using warning messages, traffic statistics and intelligent traffic lights. In 2012 [IEEE.]. *IEEE Intelligent Vehicles Symposium*, •••, 902–907.

Brandão, R., & Arbix, G. (2022). Artificial Intelligence, Ethics and Public Policy—The Use of Facial Recognition Systems in Public Transport in the Largest Brazilian Cities. *Journal of Service Science and Management, 15*(5), 551–575. Advance online publication. DOI: 10.4236/jssm.2022.155032

Chavhan, S., & Venkataram, P. (2019). Prediction based traffic management in a metropolitan area. *Journal of Traffic and Transportation Engineering*. Advance online publication. DOI: 10.1016/j.jtte.2018.05.003

C. Creß, Z. Bing, and A. C. Knoll. (2023) "Intelligent transportation systems using external infrastructure: A literature survey," IEEE Trans. Intell. Transp. Syst., early acces. .DOI: 10.1109/TITS.2023.3343434

David Yang, C. Y., & Fisher, D. L. (2021). Safety impacts and benefits of connected and automated vehicles: How real are they? *Journal of Intelligent Transport Systems, 25*(2), 135–138. DOI: 10.1080/15472450.2021.1872143

David Yang, C. Y., & Fisher, D. L. (2021). Safety impacts and benefits of connected and automated vehicles: How real are they? *Journal of Intelligent Transport Systems, 25*(2), 135–138. DOI: 10.1080/15472450.2021.1872143

Elassy, M., Al-Hattab, M., Takruri, M., & Badawi, S. (2024). Intelligent transportation systems for sustainable smart cities". *Transportation Engineering*, *16*, 100252. DOI: 10.1016/j.treng.2024.100252

Elassy, M., Al-Hattab, M., Takruri, M., & Badawi, S. (2024). Intelligent transportation systems for sustainable smart cities. Transportation Engineering, 100252.

Figueiredo, L., Jesus, I., Machado, J. T., Ferreira, J. R., & De Carvalho, J. M. (2001). "Towards the development of intelligent transportation systems," in Proc. IEEE Intell. Transp. Syst. Proc., pp. 1206–1211. DOI: DOI: 10.1109/ITSC.2001.948835

Guerrero-Ibañez, J., Contreras-Castillo, J., & Zeadally, S. (2021). Deep learning support for intelligent transportation systems. *Transactions on Emerging Telecommunications Technologies*, *32*(3), e4169. Advance online publication. DOI: 10.1002/ett.4169

Herath, H. M. K. K. M. B., & Mittal, M. (2022). Adoption of artificial intelligence in smart cities: A comprehensive review. *International Journal of Information Management Data Insights*, *2*(1), 2667–0968. DOI: 10.1016/j.jjimei.2022.100076

Jagatheesaperumal, S. K., Bibri, S. E., Huang, J., Rajapandian, J., & Parthiban, B. (2024). Artificial intelligence of things for smart cities: Advanced solutions for enhancing transportation safety. *Computational Urban Science*, *4*(1), 10.

Lakshmi Shankar Iyer. (2021). *AI enabled applications towards intelligent transportation. 2666-691. Transportation Engineering 5 (2021) 100083*. Elsevier Ltd., DOI: 10.1016/j.treng.2021.100083

Lamssaggad, A., Benamar, N., Hafid, A. S., & Msahli, M. (2021). A survey on the current security landscape of intelligent transportation systems. *IEEE Access : Practical Innovations, Open Solutions*, *9*, 9180–9208. DOI: 10.1109/ACCESS.2021.3050038

Lv, Z., Zhang, S., & Xiu, W. (2021). Solving the security problem of intelligent transportation systems with deep learning. *IEEE Transactions on Intelligent Transportation Systems*, *22*(7), 4281–4290. DOI: 10.1109/TITS.2020.2980864

Ly, H. B., Le, L. M., Phi, L. V., Phan, V. H., Tran, V. Q., Pham, B. T., Le, T. T., & Derrible, S. (2019). Development of an AI model to measure traffic air pollution from multisensor and weather data. *Sensors (Basel)*, *19*(22), 4941. DOI: 10.3390/s19224941 PMID: 31766187

Ma, Y., Wang, Z., Yang, H., & Yang, L. (2020). Artificial intelligence applications in the development of autonomous vehicles: a survey. IEEE. Page(s): 315 - 329. ISSN: 2329-9266. DOI: DOI: 10.1109/JAS.2020.1003021

Michael, C. (2020). Leveraging Intelligent Transportation Systems and Smart Vehicles Using Crowdsourcing: An Overview. MDPI. *Smart Cities*, *3*(2), 341–360. DOI: 10.3390/smartcities3020018

Miles, J. C., & Walker, A. J. (2006). "The potential application of artificial intelligence in transport," IEE Proc. Intell. Transp. Syst., vol. 153, no. 3, pp. 183–198, 2006. DOI: DOI: 10.1049/ip-its:20060014

Njoku, J. N., Nwakanma, C. I., Amaizu, G. C., & Kim, D.-S. (2023). Prospects and challenges of metaverse application in data-driven intelligent transportation systems. *IET Intelligent Transport Systems*, *17*(1), 1–21. DOI: 10.1049/itr2.12252

Pechinger, M., Schröer, G., Bogenberger, K., & Markgraf, C. (2023). Roadside infrastructure support for urban automated driving. *IEEE Transactions on Intelligent Transportation Systems*, *24*(10), 10643–10652. DOI: 10.1109/TITS.2023.3277138

Razavi, M., Hamidkhani, M., & Sadeghi, R. (2019). *Smart traffic light scheduling in smart city using image and video processing*. IEEE Xplore., DOI: 10.1109/IICITA.2019.8808836

Seung, B. S., & Dhananjay, S. (2018). *Smart Town Traffic Management System Using LoRa and Machine Learning Mechanism By ReSENSE Lab Hankuk University of Foreign Studies*. IEEE.

Seuwou, P., Banissi, E., & Ubakanma, G. (2020). In Farsi, M., Daneshkhah, A., Hosseinian-Far, A., & Jahankhani, H. (Eds.), *"The future of mobility with connected and autonomous vehicles in smart cities," in Digital Twin Technologies and Smart Cities (Internet of Things)* (pp. 37–52). Springer., https://link.springer.com/chapter/10.1007/978-3-030-18732-3_3

Tabernik, D., & Skocaj, D. (2020). Deep learning for large-scale traffic-sign detection and recognition. *IEEE Transactions on Intelligent Transportation Systems*, *21*(4), 1427–1440. DOI: 10.1109/TITS.2019.2913588

Tong, W., Hussain, A., Bo, W. X., & Maharjan, S. (2019). Artificial intelligence for vehicle-to-everything: A survey. *IEEE Access : Practical Innovations, Open Solutions*, *7*, 10823–10843.

Vani, R., Thendral, N., Kavitha, J. C., & Bhavani, N. P. G. (2018). Intelligent traffic control system with priority to emergency vehicles, IOP Conf. Ser. Mater. Sci. Eng. 455 (2018) 012023, https://doi.org/DOI: 10.1088/1757-899X/455/1/012023

Chapter 3
Using AI to Improve Urban Sustainability: Sophisticated Pollution Control and Environmental Monitoring in Safer Cities

M. I. Anju
https://orcid.org/0000-0001-9654-1669
SRM Institute of Science and Technology, Vadapalani, India

Ishwarya Kothandaraman
https://orcid.org/0000-0002-1275-1229
School of Computing, SRM Institute of Science and Technology, India

R. Arunadevi
https://orcid.org/0009-0003-4512-1156
Sri Sairam Engineering College, India

Kavitha Esther Rajakumari
https://orcid.org/0000-0001-9860-7457
KCG College of Technology, India

K. Fouzia Sulthana
https://orcid.org/0009-0006-5014-6026
Rajalakshmi Institute of Technology, Poonamallee, India

M. Robinson Joel
https://orcid.org/0000-0002-3030-8431
KCG College of Technology, Karapakkam, India

ABSTRACT

Rapid city expansion presents many obstacles to urban sustainability, such as resource management, pollution, and public safety issues. This study looks at how pollution management and environmental monitoring can be advanced by artificial intelligence (AI) to improve urban sustainability. Artificial Intelligence (AI) technology, including automation, predictive modelling, and real-time data analysis, make it possible to create complex systems that monitor the quality of air and water, identify environmental threats, and maximize resource use. Cities can continually monitor environmental conditions, offering timely insights for interventions and

DOI: 10.4018/979-8-3693-7832-8.ch003

lowering environmental footprints by combining AI-driven sensors and IoT devices. Additionally, AI helps to build sustainable urban infrastructure and promotes public safety by recognizing pollution patterns associated with health hazards. AI has the capacity to completely transform urban sustainability, which emphasizes how crucial it is for technology developers, legislators, and urban planners to work together.

1. INTRODUCTION:

Urban regions face growing issues in relation to public health and environmental sustainability as they continue to grow and develop. The management of resources, pollution, and safety are urgent problems that call for creative solutions. Incorporating artificial intelligence (AI) into urban planning and administration presents encouraging prospects for tackling these issues. Artificial Intelligence (Messeri, L., & Crockett, M. J. 2024) (AI)has the potential to revolutionize urban resource management, pollution monitoring and control, and public safety. AI can make environmental monitoring systems more effective and efficient by utilizing automation, real-time data, and predictive analytics. This will let cities take preemptive measures to counter new dangers. AI-driven solutions can also help create greener, smarter infrastructure, which will lessen its impact on the environment. of metropolitan regions while improving the standard of living for those who live there. In order to build safer, more resilient cities, this study investigates the use of AI in promoting urban sustainability, with a particular emphasis on advanced pollution management and environmental monitoring.

AI has many potential applications that might completely change the way cities think about sustainability. Large volumes of data from diverse sources can be analyzed by sophisticated machine learning algorithms,(El Naqa, I., & Murphy, M. J. 2015) enabling predictive modeling and offering real-time insights. This enables towns to foresee environmental concerns and take action before they worsen. AI-driven sensors, for instance, may identify dangerous pollutants in the air and water, continuously monitor their quality, and initiate automated reactions to limit emissions or contain pollutants.

2. OVERVIEW OF POLLUTION:

Pollution is a widespread environmental problem that has an impact on ecosystems, public health, and the quality of the air, water, and soil in every part of the world. It is mostly caused by human activity that releases toxic compounds into the environment, such as transportation, agriculture, urbanization, and industrial processes. Acid rain, respiratory illnesses, and climate change are all influenced by air pollution, which is caused by emissions from factories, power plants, and automobiles. Water pollution damages aquatic life, contaminates drinking water supplies, and upsets ecosystems. It is caused by industrial discharge, agricultural runoff, and inappropriate waste disposal.(Ayomoh, M. K. O at el., 2008) Pesticide usage, poor waste management, and deforestation all contribute to soil degradation, which deteriorates land quality and jeopardizes food security.

Figure 1. Overview of pollution

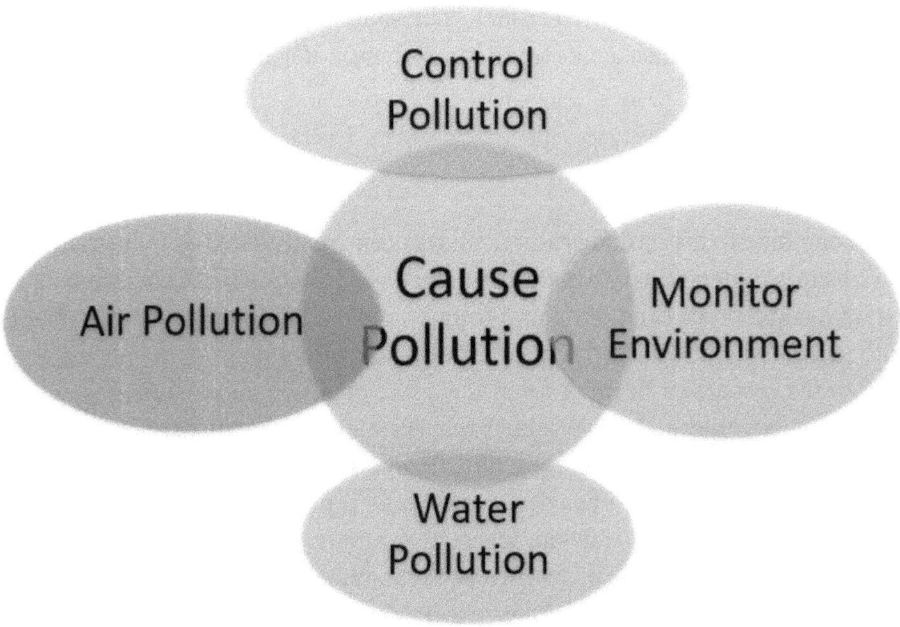

2.1 Cause Pollution:

Pollution is caused by a variety of human activities as well as natural processes that release toxic substances into the atmosphere, lowering the quality of the air, water, and soil. Industrial processes that release greenhouse gases and hazardous chemicals into the environment, such as manufacturing and electricity generation, are the main sources of pollution. Another significant factor is transportation, as cars release pollutants like nitrogen oxides and carbon monoxide that deteriorate air quality. Pesticides and fertilizers are among the agricultural practices that cause runoff that contaminates soil and water sources. Pollution is made worse by urbanization, deforestation, and poor waste management, which disturb natural ecosystems and increase waste output. Furthermore, the generation of energy, particularly from fossil fuels, is a major cause of pollution in the air and water. Pollution can also come from natural occurrences like volcanic eruptions and wildfires, but these sources are usually less long-lasting(Marogna, M et al., 2010) than those caused by humans. To address these reasons and lessen pollution's negative effects on the environment and public health, comprehensive methods and technologies are needed. Numerous underlying sources of pollution that jeopardize public health and urban sustainability(Huang, L et al., 2015) necessitate advanced pollution control and environmental monitoring in cities. The origins and intensity of pollution rise together with cities' size and population density. To ensure safer, more livable urban environments and to design successful measures for pollution control, it is imperative to comprehend these factors.

2.2 Industrialization:

Economic expansion and prosperity have been greatly aided by industrialization, but it has also emerged as one of the main causes of pollution in the environment. The extraction and processing of natural resources is a common practice of expanding enterprises, which results in large emissions of pollutants into the air, water, and soil. In the process of burning fossil fuels like coal, oil, and natural gas to create electricity, factories and power plants release a lot of particulate matter, sulfur dioxide, nitrogen oxides, and carbon dioxide into the atmosphere. These pollutants add to air pollution, which has detrimental effects on public health, (Sayadi et al., 2012) increasing mortality rates and causing respiratory and cardiovascular ailments.

Industrial operations also significantly contaminate water and soil in addition to the air. Hazardous chemicals and heavy metals are frequently used in manufacturing operations; these substances can be discharged into rivers, lakes, and seas through industrial runoff or discharge. This contamination can make water supplies unfit for human consumption, damage aquatic ecosystems, and upset food chains.(Cembalo et al., 2015) When hazardous materials from spills or industrial waste seep into the ground, they contaminate the soil. This stunts plant growth and reduces agricultural productivity over time.

2.3 Urbanization and Deforestation:

Deforestation and urbanization are closely related activities that greatly increase pollution and environmental deterioration. Large tracts of woods and natural habitats are frequently destroyed to create room for new infrastructure, residential neighborhoods, and agricultural land as cities grow to accommodate expanding populations. Deforestation reduces the Earth's ability to absorb carbon dioxide, disturbs ecosystems, causes biodiversity loss, and speeds up climate change. In addition to raising carbon emissions, clearing land of trees and other plants can cause soil erosion, which can silt water bodies and worsen environmental damage.Numerous pollution-related (Xu et al., 2022) issues are brought about by urbanization itself. Emissions of garbage, air pollutants, and greenhouse gases are enhanced in metropolitan areas due to the concentration of people, vehicles, and industries. Dust, noise, and chemical pollution are produced during the building and road construction processes. Additionally, the high vehicle density leads to traffic jams and higher air pollution levels. Furthermore, as cities grow quickly, suitable waste management and sanitation systems are frequently not developed in time, which results in incorrect garbage disposal and contaminated water sources.

The interplay between urbanization and deforestation poses serious risks to public health, environmental sustainability, and overall quality of life as metropolitan (Ingram, G. K. 1998) areas continue to grow. In order to reduce the negative effects of urbanization and deforestation, addressing these difficulties needs careful urban planning, the preservation and restoration of natural ecosystems, and the installation of green infrastructure.

2.4 Technological Advancements and Automation:

Industrialization has accelerated technical advancement, but it has also resulted in a great deal of process automation, which can have both beneficial and detrimental effects on the environment. Automation has the potential to decrease waste and increase resource efficiency. On the other side, e-waste and environmental contamination are caused by the manufacturing and disposal of sophisticated technology and electronic devices. Additionally, if energy is not obtained from renewable sources, the increased energy required to run automated devices may make pollution worse. Automation and technological breakthroughs have completely changed industries, resulting in notable gains in output volume, efficiency, and productivity. Specifically, automation has lowered labor costs, expedited industrial processes, and allowed for previously unheard-of levels of mass production. But these changes have also resulted in difficult environmental problems.

The extensive usage of robotic systems and automated machinery raises energy consumption, especially when non-renewable energy sources are used, which raises greenhouse gas emissions. Furthermore, large volumes of electronic garbage (e-waste) (Shahabuddin, et al., 2023) are produced during the development, use, and disposal of cutting-edge technologies. If e-waste is not appropriately managed, it can leak hazardous materials like heavy metals and poisonous compounds into the environment.

2.5 Globalization and Trade:

Globalization the idea that things are produced in one region of the world and consumed in another is strongly related to industrialization. The transportation industry, which mainly depends on fossil fuels, is one way that the worldwide trade of industrial products leads to pollution. The movement of exotic species, which can upset regional ecosystems, and greenhouse gas emissions are all facilitated by shipping, aircraft, and freight transportation.

Trade and globalization have linked economies worldwide, facilitating the quick transfer of products, services, and technology. This has boosted access to a wide range of goods and stimulated economic growth. But these advantages come at a high cost to the environment. Due to the increased demand for commodities worldwide, there has been a rise in industrial output, frequently in areas with laxer environmental laws. This has led to increased pollution and resource exploitation engaging in activities like mining for raw materials and deforestation for agricultural growth.

Because industrialization produces a lot of greenhouse gas emissions, it plays a significant role in climate change. Significant volumes of carbon dioxide and methane are released when fossil fuels are used in industrial processes. These gases trap heat in the Earth's atmosphere and cause global warming.(Hosseini, S. R et al., 2018) Sea levels, weather patterns, and ecosystems are all impacted by climate change, which in turn creates a feedback loop where industrial activities both cause and are influenced by environmental changes. One of the most important worldwide issues of our day is climate change, which is mostly the result of human activity that has drastically changed the Earth's climatic system. The concentration of greenhouse gases (GHGs)(Da Fonseca-Soares et al., 2023) in the atmosphere has increased, mostly from the burning of fossil fuels, deforestation, and industrial processes. These gases include carbon dioxide (CO2), methane (CH4), and nitrous oxide (N2O).(Jones, M. W et al., 2023) The phenomenon known as global warming is caused by these gases trapping heat in the atmosphere. Wide-ranging and complex, the effects of climate change include increased frequency and intensity of extreme weather events like heatwaves, storms, floods, and droughts, which pose major threats to infrastructure, agriculture, ecosystems, and human health.

In order to combat climate change, a concerted worldwide effort must be made to reduce greenhouse gas emissions through the use of renewable energy sources, increased energy efficiency, reforestation, and sustainable land-use practices. Global temperature (Arnell, N. W et al., 2019) rise is to be limited, and adaptation to climate impacts is to be encouraged, through international agreements like the Paris Agreement. Protecting the planet's ecosystems and guaranteeing the welfare of present and future generations require both mitigating climate change and adapting to its effects.

3. POLLUTION CONTROL:

Ensuring the protection of the environment and public health necessitates the implementation of a comprehensive pollution control strategy that incorporates technological innovations, public participation, and regulatory measures. In addition to encouraging cleaner manufacturing techniques, governments enact and enforce environmental laws to restrict emissions and waste from businesses, automobiles, and other sources. In order to safeguard public health, the environment, and sustainable growth, pollution control is crucial. A combination of technology advancements, community involvement, and governmental actions are needed for effective pollution control to reduce the amount of dangerous pollutants released into the air, water, and soil.

Figure 2. Overview pollution control

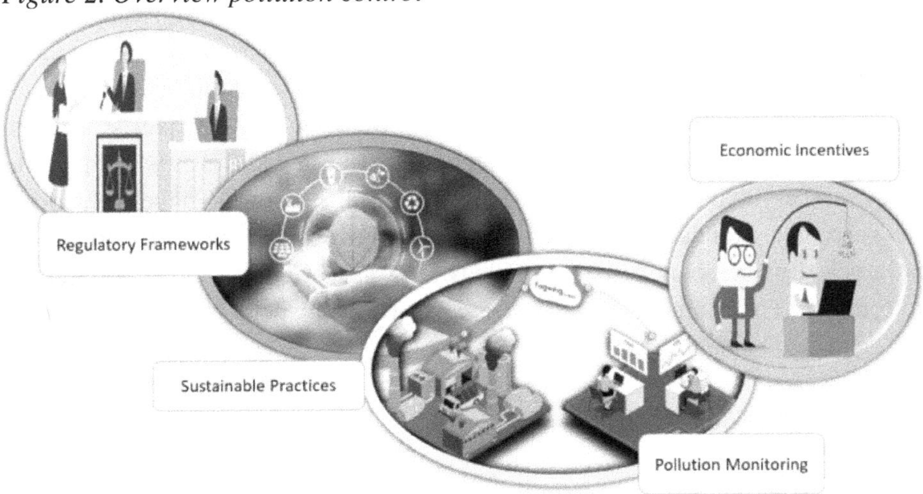

3.1 Regulatory Frameworks:

Regulatory frameworks, which set legal norms and requirements that corporations, industries, and individuals must abide by, are crucial for preventing pollution and guaranteeing environmental protection. These frameworks are intended to control the safe disposal of trash and to restrict the release of contaminants into the air, water, and soil. Environmental agencies that monitor compliance and levy penalties for noncompliance are usually used by governments to enforce these restrictions. Setting pollution emissions limitations, demanding environmental impact assessments (EIAs)

(Loomis, J. J., & Dziedzic, M. 2018) for new projects, and enforcing the deployment of pollution control technology are important regulatory framework components.

Another important component is public participation; several frameworks mandate public consultations or permit citizens to report infractions. Good regulatory frameworks are dynamic and modified often to take into account new scientific findings and developments in technology, which helps to keep them current and able to handle new environmental issues as they arise.

3.2 Sustainable Practices:

Sustainable practices, which emphasize resource efficiency, waste reduction, and the promotion of renewable energy sources, are essential for striking a balance between economic growth and environmental conservation. Crop rotation and organic farming are two agricultural techniques that contribute to preserving soil health and lowering chemical pollution. (Singh, S. P., & Singh, M. K. 2020) Adopting circular economy principles in manufacturing reduces waste and the need for raw resources by enabling items to be recycled and reused. In order to lessen the environmental effect of cities, urban design integrates green areas, energy-efficient structures, and reliable public transit networks. Water conservation and the use of renewable energy sources, including solar and wind power, are also included in these practices. These actions are crucial for lowering greenhouse gas emissions and our reliance on fossil fuels. Businesses and individuals may both make a significant contribution to protecting the environment and guaranteeing a healthy planet for future generations by adopting sustainable practices.

3.3 Pollution Monitoring:

Tracking environmental contaminants and evaluating the efficacy of pollution management strategies require the use of pollution monitoring. In order to identify the existence and concentration of dangerous compounds, it entails the ongoing gathering and analysis of data on the quality of the air, water, and soil. To precisely and instantly monitor pollution levels, cutting-edge technology like satellite imagery, real-time sensors,(Christophe, E., & Inglada, J. 2009). and remote sensing are being used more and more. The causes of pollution, environmental risks, and regulatory actions are all aided by this data. Good pollution control also makes it possible to identify environmental risks early on and take swift action to lessen their effects.

Furthermore, the information gathered is essential for guiding public health campaigns, policy choices, and community education projects, guaranteeing that pollution reduction efforts are focused and successful. Pollution monitoring keeps an eye on the state of the environment and helps to safeguard human health and ecosystems by giving a clear image.

3.4. Economic Incentives:

Economic incentives are effective instruments for persuading companies and people to embrace eco-friendly policies and lessen their environmental effect. These incentives, which make it financially profitable to reduce emissions and limit waste, include things like carbon pricing, environmental levies, and subsidies for clean technologies. Governments can incentivize corporations to invest in cleaner manufacturing techniques and energy-efficient technologies by imposing a cost on pollution through taxation or cap-and-trade programs. Grants and subsidies for renewable energy projects, such wind and solar energy, help accelerate the shift away from fossil fuels. Furthermore, tax rebates for electric cars, eco-friendly building materials, and energy-efficient equipment push people to make more environmentally friendly decisions. Financial Rewards in addition to lowering environmental impact overall, economic incentives stimulate innovation and the creation of new technologies that advance sustainability. These incentives are essential for promoting a cleaner economy and guaranteeing long-term environmental conservation because they match economic interests with environmental aims.

4. CONTROL POLLUTION:

Reducing pollution is essential to maintaining sustainable development, safeguarding public health, and maintaining the environment. Technological advancements, community involvement, and governmental actions all work together to regulate pollution effectively. Environmental laws are established and enforced by governments to control the amount of pollutants emitted by automobiles, factories, and other sources. They also encourage the use of cleaner production techniques. (Adewale et al., 2015) In order to cut down on waste and hazardous emissions, technological innovations like electric cars, renewable energy sources, and pollution control equipment like scrubbers and filters are crucial.

Figure 3. Overview control pollution

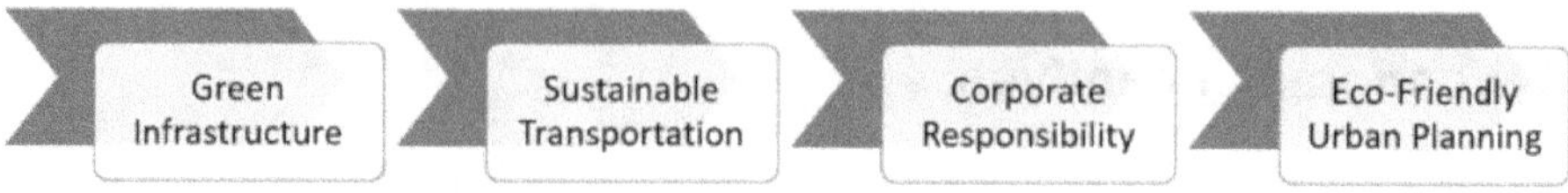

4.1 Green Infrastructure:

A sustainable kind of urban planning known as "green infrastructure" incorporates natural systems into the constructed environment to control water resources, boost biodiversity, improve air quality, and make living areas healthier. This includes structures like walls, parks, green roofs, and urban forests, which not only act as shade and insulation but also lessen the effect of the urban heat island and help sequester carbon. Furthermore, permeable pavements, bioswales, and rain gardens are examples of sustainable urban drainage solutions (SuDS)(Davis, M., & Naumann, S. 2017) that help manage stormwater by lowering runoff and preventing flooding. Urban greenways and green corridors link various areas of the city, encouraging active mobility and minimizing habitat fragmentation. Urban wetlands and restored water bodies enhance water quality and offer habitats for wildlife. Green infrastructure improves the environment, society, and economy by bringing these natural aspects into urban design, resulting in more resilient, habitable, and sustainable communities.

4.2 Sustainable Transportation:

The goal of sustainable transportation is to develop a mobility system that is more equitable, efficient, and favorable to the environment. It encompasses a variety of mobility options, such as walking, bicycling, public transportation, and electric cars, all of which are intended to lower greenhouse gas emissions and decrease reliance on non-renewable energy sources. In order to make these options feasible and acceptable to the general public, enabling infrastructure such as wide bike lanes, secure pathways for pedestrians, and well-connected public transportation systems must be developed. The integration of smart technology is another key component of sustainable transportation. Examples include real-time traffic control systems and smartphone apps that optimize routes,(Mohsin, A. H. 2022) promote carpooling and ride-sharing, and can greatly reduce traffic congestion and increase fuel efficiency. Additionally, it aims to address social equality by making sure that all population segments have access to and can afford transportation options, which will improve social inclusion and lessen economic inequities. Sustainable transportation helps mitigate climate change, improves urban air quality, lowers noise pollution, and raises the standard of living in cities by encouraging a shift toward low-impact modes of transportation and policies that support sustainable travel behaviors.

4.3 Corporate Responsibility:

A company's commitment to conducting business morally, sustainably, and taking into account the social, environmental, and financial effects of its decisions is known as corporate responsibility. It entails incorporating methods that extend beyond generating profits, including as projects like cutting carbon footprints, guaranteeing ethical labor standards, and improving communities. This duty also includes accountability to stakeholders, including as workers, clients, investors, and the general public, as well as open governance and moral business practices. Businesses that uphold corporate responsibility frequently take part in charitable end eavors, such as promoting health, education, and environmental preservation, and they make efforts to guarantee that their suppliers do not exploit workers or cause environmental harm.

4.4 Eco-Friendly Urban Planning:

The process of planning and growing urban areas with an eye on sustainability and minimizing negative effects on the environment is known as co-friendly urban planning(Balasubramaniam et al., 2020) This strategy incorporates green areas, such parks, gardens, and urban forests, to improve biodiversity, improve air quality, and give locals access to the outdoors. In order to lower carbon emissions and resource consumption, it places a strong emphasis on the use of renewable energy sources, energy-efficient structures, and sustainable materials in construction. Another important factor is water management, which can be achieved by using techniques like permeable pavements, green roofs, and rainwater harvesting to control runoff and lower the danger of flooding.

To lessen dependency on automobiles and cut pollution, eco-friendly urban planning places a high priority on the infrastructure needed for walking, bicycling, and public transportation. In order to stop urban development, protect natural ecosystems, and make sure that communities are climate change adaptable, it also entails rigorous land use planning. Cities that are healthier, more sustainable, and habitable are produced by eco-friendly urban design, which strikes a balance between the demands of development and environmental conservation.

5. MONITOR ENVIRONMENT:

In order to evaluate the condition of natural systems, monitor pollution levels, and identify changes over time, environmental monitoring entails the methodical collection and analysis of data. This procedure makes use of a number of techniques, including satellite imaging to monitor changes in land use, such as deforestation, and air quality sensors to assess pollutants in metropolitan areas and water quality using in-situ sensors in rivers and lakes. While technologies like camera traps and acoustic sensors that record wildlife activity are used to assess biodiversity, soil sensors that detect moisture and nutrient levels are used to monitor the health of the soil. In addition, climatic indicators are tracked by weather stations, satellites, and specialized sensors that keep an eye on light and noise pollution.(McMahon, T et al., 2017)

Furthermore, the information gathered from these monitoring initiatives is frequently analyzed by Geographic Information Systems (GIS) and sophisticated analytics, such as machine learning, which enable in-depth mapping, trend analysis, and the creation of predictive models. Environmental impact assessments (EIAs) (Loomis, J. J., & Dziedzic, M. 2018) for new developments are influenced by this data, which also aids in enforcing regulatory compliance and directs policy-making to support sustainable urban planning and environmental protection. Transparent reporting and community participation in monitoring initiatives help promote public knowledge and engagement, emphasizing that environmental stewardship is a shared duty.

5.1 Air Quality Monitoring:

In order to evaluate and control the effects of air pollution on both human health and the environment, air quality monitoring is an essential procedure that involves detecting the concentration of pollutants in the atmosphere. The monitoring process usually involves the deployment of a network of sensors positioned strategically, such as in urban areas, industrial zones, and close to traffic corridors, to identify and track various pollutants, including carbon monoxide (CO), nitrogen dioxide (NO2), sulfur dioxide (SO2), ozone (O3), and particulate matter (PM2.5 and PM10).(Suryati, et al., 2019) Satellite technology is being employed more and more in addition to ground-based sensors to give a more comprehensive, real-time picture of the state of the air over wide areas. In order to determine pollution trends, spot infractions of air quality regulations, and update public health advisories, data gathered from various sources is examined.

In order to safeguard both the environment and human health, air quality monitoring is an essential procedure that entails determining the amount of contaminants present in the air. This is accomplished using a variety of techniques, such as mobile devices that evaluate the quality of the air at various sites and stationary monitoring stations that offer continuous, real-time data on pollutants like particulate matter, ozone, and nitrogen dioxide. Technological advancements have also made it possible to use satellites for large-scale observations and inexpensive sensors for localized monitoring. These sources provide data, which is combined and examined to find patterns in pollution, forecast future air quality, and ensure regulatory compliance.

5.2 Biodiversity Monitoring:

The methodical tracking of species diversity and abundance within ecosystems to evaluate environmental health and spot changes over time is known as biodiversity monitoring. It entails gathering information on various species, their populations, and their habitats in order to identify patterns like dwindling species populations, habitat destruction, or the effects of invading species. In order to safeguard endangered species, sustain ecosystem services, and guarantee that biodiversity is conserved for future generations, monitoring is essential to conservation efforts.(Nicholson et al., 2019) Informed decision-making in environmental management is facilitated by biodiversity monitoring, which use techniques like genetic analysis, remote sensing, and field surveys. It also tackles issues like habitat destruction, climate change, and other threats to natural ecosystems.

5.3 Waste Management Monitoring:

The practice of methodically tracking waste generation, disposal, and recycling in order to make sure that waste is managed sustainably and with minimal impact on the environment is known as waste management monitoring. This entails gathering information on the kinds and amounts of trash generated, the manner in which it is processed, and where it ends up—in landfills, recycling centers, or incinerators. Monitoring guarantees adherence to environmental rules and assists in identifying inefficiencies in waste management systems, such as excessive amounts of recyclable materials ending up in landfills. It is also essential for lowering pollution, preserving resources, and lessening waste's negative effects on the environment.

5.4 Climate monitoring:

The methodical gathering and examination of information about the Earth's climate, such as temperature, precipitation, air composition, and ocean conditions, is known as climate monitoring. Understanding long-term climate patterns, spotting changes in climate systems, and evaluating the effects of human activity like greenhouse gas emissions on global temperatures all depend on this monitoring. Climate monitoring provides vital information for forecasting weather patterns, planning for extreme weather events, and researching phenomena like global warming, sea-level rise, and shifting weather patterns. It does this by combining ground-based sensors, satellite observations, and weather stations. In order to make educated decisions on climate action, adaptation plans, and initiatives to lessen the effects of climate change on ecosystems, economies, and communities, policymakers, scientists, and people need access to data from climate monitoring.

5.5 Radiation Monitoring:

The practice of determining and evaluating the radiation levels in the environment to protect people, animals, and ecosystems is known as radiation monitoring. This entails tracking radiation from artificial sources like nuclear power plants, medical institutions, and industrial operations, as well as natural sources like cosmic rays and radon gas, using specialized detectors and devices. In order to identify any leaks or emissions of radioactive materials that could endanger public health, monitoring is essential in the vicinity of nuclear power plants. It also guides evacuation planning and decontamination operations during nuclear accidents, which is another important function it performs in emergency response. Frequent radiation monitoring preserves public health, makes sure that levels stay within acceptable bounds, and meets with legal requirements.

6. WATER POLLUTION:

When dangerous materials, including garbage, chemicals, and bacteria, contaminate water bodies such as rivers, lakes, seas, and groundwater water pollution results. Numerous human activities, including sewage leaks, agricultural runoff, industrial discharge, and inappropriate waste disposal, can cause this contamination. Water quality can be deteriorated by pollutants such as heavy metals, pesticides, plastics, and oil, which makes it dangerous for aquatic life, irrigation, and drinking.

Figure 4. Overview of water pollution

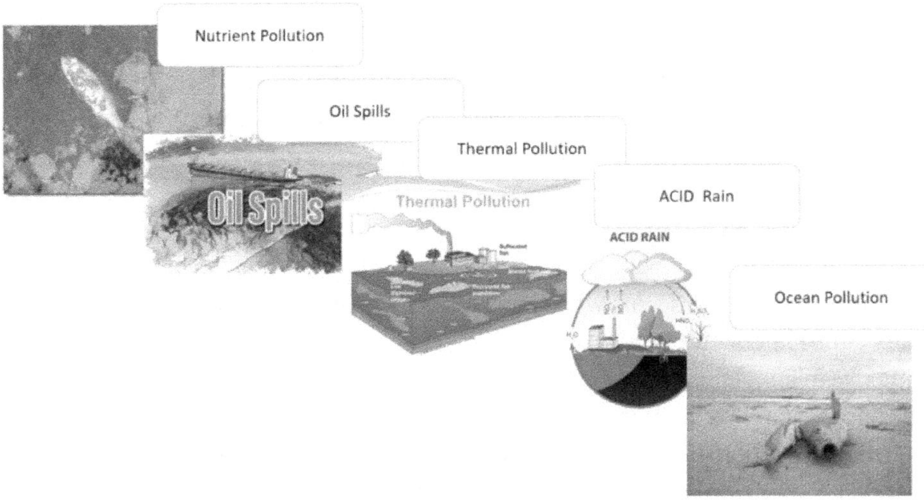

6.1 Nutrient Pollution:

Excessive nutrient levels, especially those of nitrogen and phosphorus, can enter water bodies and cause pollution. This is frequently the result of fertilizer use, sewage discharge, and agricultural runoff. Because of these surplus nutrients, algae develop quickly and cause toxic algal blooms, which lower the oxygen content of the water as the algae break down and create "dead zones"(Altieri, A. H., & Gedan, K. B. 2015) where aquatic life cannot survive. Fish populations and other wildlife are harmed by this process, known as eutrophication, which disturbs aquatic habitats. The quality of water is also impacted by nutrient contamination, rendering it unfit for swimming, fishing, or drinking. It may also result in financial losses for sectors of the economy including fishing and tourism. Better wastewater treatment techniques, public awareness efforts to cut back on the usage of nutrient-rich fertilizers, and better agricultural management practices are all necessary to address nutrient contamination.

6.2 Oil Spills:

Oil spills are a major source of water pollution, occurring when oil is accidentally released into aquatic environments from sources such as ships, pipelines, or offshore drilling rigs. These spills contaminate water bodies, creating a toxic layer on the surface that can suffocate marine life, damage habitats, and disrupt ecosystems.

The oil not only harms wildlife directly but also affects water quality by reducing oxygen levels and altering the natural balance of aquatic organisms. Addressing oil spills involves containment and recovery efforts, such as using booms and skimmers, as well as applying chemical dispersants and bioremediation techniques to break down and remove the oil. Effective response and prevention measures are essential to mitigate the environmental and ecological impacts of oil spills on water bodies.

6.3 Thermal Pollution:

Thermal pollution occurs when industries or power plants release heated water or other fluids into natural water bodies, causing a significant increase in temperature. This rise in temperature disrupts aquatic ecosystems by reducing oxygen levels and altering the habitat conditions necessary for wildlife. Elevated temperatures can lead to the death of fish and other aquatic organisms, favor the growth of harmful algae blooms, and disrupt reproductive cycles. Additionally, thermal pollution can affect the overall health of aquatic environments, leading to long-term ecological damage. Addressing thermal pollution involves implementing cooling systems that minimize temperature increases, improving wastewater management practices, and enhancing regulatory measures to protect water bodies from excessive thermal discharges.

6.4 Acid Rain:

Because of the presence of nitrogen oxides (NO_X)(Schmid, D. 2023) and sulfur dioxide (SO_2) in the atmosphere, acid rain is a type of precipitation that is noticeably more acidic than usual. When these pollutants interact with atmospheric water vapor, they produce nitric and sulfuric acids. These pollutants are frequently released via burning fossil fuels, automobile exhaust, and industrial activities. This acidic precipitation can cause acidification of lakes, rivers, and soil, which can lower biodiversity, destroy aquatic habitats, and cause plant life loss. Additionally, acid rain can cause health issues for people and hastens the deterioration of monuments and structures. It also has an adverse effect on water quality. Reducing emissions of nitrogen oxides and sulfur dioxide through better energy sources and enhanced industrial methods and more stringent laws governing air quality.

6.5 Ocean Acidification:

The process through which the ocean(Ramachandran, R., et al., 2024) gets more acidic as a result of elevated atmospheric concentrations of carbon dioxide (CO_2) is known as ocean acidification. The ocean's pH is lowered as CO2 is absorbed by saltwater and interacts with water to generate carbonic acid. Marine life may be severely impacted by this acidification, especially species like corals, shellfish, and certain types of plankton that have skeletons or shells made of calcium carbonate. Their skeletons and shells are weakened by the lower pH,(Dijkstra, J et al., 2012) which has an impact on their growth and survival. Because ocean acidification affects the behavior and distribution of different species, it can potentially upset marine ecosystems and food webs. Reducing CO2 emissions, preserving marine habitats, and funding studies to comprehend and lessen the effects of ocean acidification are all necessary to combat it.

7. AIR POLLUTION:

When dangerous materials such as chemicals, particulates, and biological materials—are released into the atmosphere in amounts that have the potential to affect ecosystems, human health, and the climate, air pollution results. Particulate matter (PM2.5 and PM10),(World Health Organization. 2021) sulfur dioxide (SO_2), nitrogen oxides (NO_X), carbon monoxide (CO), volatile organic compounds (VOCs), and ground-level ozone (O_3) are examples of common contaminants. Vehicle emissions, industrial operations, the burning of fossil fuels, and agricultural practices are some of the sources of air pollution. Air pollution has a wide range of negative consequences on the environment, including smog and acid rain, cardiovascular and respiratory disorders, and contributes to climate change. Stricter emission regulations, a shift to greener energy sources, and the promotion of laws that improve air quality and safeguard public health are all necessary to reduce air pollution.

Figure 5. Air pollution

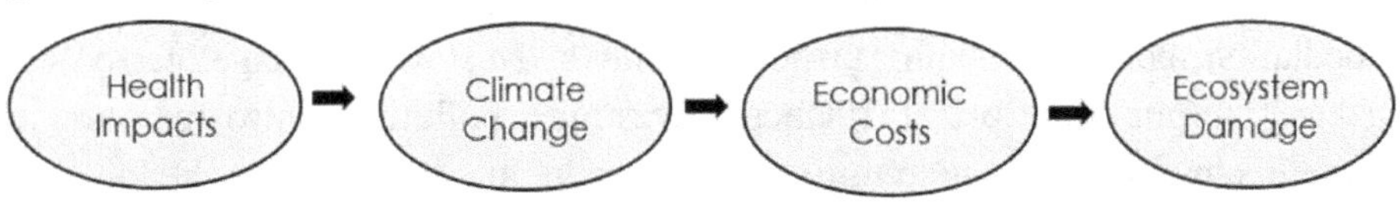

7.1 Health Impacts:

The respiratory and cardiovascular systems are both impacted by air pollution, which has serious negative effects on health. Particulate matter, nitrogen oxides, and sulfur dioxide are examples of pollutants that can aggravate respiratory diseases like asthma and bronchitis, increasing hospital admissions and medical expenses. Prolonged exposure to air pollution is associated with cardiovascular issues, such as heart disease and stroke, and may lead to an early death. Children, the elderly, and people with pre-existing medical disorders are among the vulnerable groups that are most vulnerable. Improving public health outcomes and averting the negative consequences of poor air quality are contingent upon the reduction of air pollution.

7.2 Climate Change:

The increase in greenhouse gases like carbon dioxide, methane, and nitrous oxide in the atmosphere is the main cause of climate change. These gases trap solar heat, raising global temperatures and having a variety of negative effects on the environment. Increased frequency and intensity of extreme weather events like hurricanes, heat waves, and torrential rains are among the effects of climate change. Additionally, it raises the possibility of coastal floods and habitat loss due to sea level rise. Furthermore, ecosystems are disturbed by climate change, which also modifies natural processes like weather patterns and ocean currents and impacts biodiversity. Global actions are needed to combat climate change, including lowering greenhouse gas emissions, switching to renewable energy sources, and putting adaptive measures in place to lessen its effects and safeguard vulnerable populations.

7.3 Economic Costs:

The economic costs of air pollution are substantial and multifaceted. Health-related expenses are a major factor, as treating diseases caused or exacerbated by poor air quality, such as asthma, cardiovascular conditions, and respiratory infections, places a significant financial burden on individuals and healthcare systems. Additionally, air pollution reduces labor productivity due to health issues and increased absenteeism, impacting economic output and efficiency. The costs of environmental remediation, including cleaning up polluted sites and restoring damaged ecosystems, further strain public and private finances. Investing in pollution control measures and cleaner technologies can help mitigate these economic impacts, but the long-term benefits of improved air quality and public health often outweigh the initial costs.

7.4 Ecosystem Damage:

Because it interferes with natural processes and lowers environmental quality, air pollution seriously harms ecosystems. Acidification of the soil, which changes nutrient availability and inhibits plant growth, can be caused by pollutants like sulfur dioxide and nitrogen oxides. Because changes in plant health can influence herbivores and the animals that prey on them, this disruption has an effect on entire ecosystems. Acid rain is another way that pollutants can contaminate water bodies, resulting in issues like eutrophication and lowered water quality. In the end, soil degradation and water pollution from airborne pollutants harm different ecosystems' health, which has an impact on biodiversity and ecosystem services that are essential for preserving ecological balance and sustaining human livelihoods.

7.5 Respiratory Issues:

Air pollution-related respiratory problems are a serious public health concern. Particulate matter, ozone, and nitrogen dioxide are examples of pollutants that can irritate the airways, aggravate bronchitis and asthma, and cause chronic respiratory disorders. Ground-level ozone and fine particulate matter (PM2.5) can enter the lungs deeply, limiting lung function and triggering inflammation. Prolonged exposure to contaminated air can also lead to the development of chronic obstructive pulmonary disease (COPD) (Maselli, D. J et al., 2019) and make one more vulnerable to respiratory infections. Children, the elderly, and people with pre-existing medical disorders are among the vulnerable categories that are most vulnerable. Improving public knowledge, enacting laws that lessen pollution and support respiratory health, and improving air quality through emission reductions are all practical ways to lessen these negative effects on health.

8. ENVIRONMENTAL REMEDIATION:

The process of cleaning up and restoring contaminated or damaged environments to their original form or to a state where they are safe for ecosystems and human health is known as environmental remediation. A variety of methods intended to address soil, water, and air contaminants are included in this procedure. Common remediation techniques include physical cleanup techniques like dredging or soil excavation as well as bioremediation, which breaks down toxins using microorganisms.(Sutarlie, L et al,. 2017) Chemical treatments are also used to address particular forms of pollution, such as neutralizing pollutants or applying sophisticated oxidation processes. Furthermore, cutting-edge techniques like phytoremediation which uses plants to absorb or stabilize contaminants are being employed more frequently.

8.1 Integration with Existing Systems:

The efficacy and efficiency of current pollution control and environmental monitoring systems can be greatly increased by integrating AI. Cities may enhance their current systems with real-time data processing capabilities and superior analytics by integrating AI technologies. Artificial Intelligence has the capability to examine vast amounts of data gathered by current sensors, enhancing the precision of pollution assessments and spotting trends that traditional techniques would overlook. With the help of this connection, pollution sources and trends can be tracked more precisely, allowing for quicker responses and better control techniques. By suggesting specific actions and enhancements based on data-driven insights, AI may also maximize the utilization of available resources.(Kushwah et al., 2020) All things considered, the smooth incorporation of AI into current systems improves the capacity to track and handle environmental issues, resulting in more effective and rapid pollution control.

8.2 Enhanced Public Awareness:

Artificial intelligence (AI) greatly raises public awareness of environmental issues by offering easily accessible, up-to-date information on the quality of the air and water, the causes of pollution, and its health effects. Platforms with artificial intelligence (AI) capabilities can compile and examine data from multiple sources, including sensors and satellite images, to provide users with current environmental conditions in their area. People can check pollution levels, receive health advisories, and make educated decisions about their activities by using interactive dashboards, mobile apps, and internet portals that offer this information in an intelligible fashion. AI empowers citizens to take part in sustainability initiatives and push for changes in environmental laws and practices by enhancing accessibility and transparency. This promotes proactive behavior and increases community engagement.

8.3 Safer Cities:

Using cutting edge technologies for environmental monitoring and sophisticated pollution management can greatly improve city safety. Cities may accomplish accurate, real-time monitoring of air and water quality, allowing for quick identification and reaction to pollution incidents, by utilizing state-of-the-art sensors, artificial intelligence, and data analytics(Manikandan et al., 2023). Thanks to technical advancements, pollution management measures can now be implemented more effectively. For example, traffic flow optimization can minimize emissions, or customized treatments can target specific sources of pollution. Furthermore, the capacity to examine enormous volumes of environmental data offers more profound understandings of pollution patterns and trends, enabling preemptive actions to avoid and lessen environmental problems. Better public health outcomes are also supported by enhanced monitoring, which raises community awareness, facilitates timely information and warnings, and directs well-informed decision-making. (Venkataramanan, V et al., 2023)

Cities that successfully incorporate cutting-edge practices, laws, and technologies to improve public safety, security, and general quality of life are considered safer. Through the utilization of advancements like artificial intelligence, intelligent sensors, and real-time data analytics, urban areas can enhance their capacity to oversee and address a range of issues, such as air pollution, gridlock, and crises. Complex pollution control systems contribute to a decrease in environmental risks, and improved monitoring capabilities guarantee early problem identification and better resource management. Better communication and data integration also support enhanced public safety and emergency response protocols. Cities can build more sustainable and livable settings where people live longer and have less risk exposure by promoting a comprehensive approach to urban management that puts safety and resilience first.

9. ADVANTAGE OF AI FOR POLLUTION CONTROL:

Sophisticated pollution management and environmental monitoring are two major benefits of using AI to improve urban sustainability, which helps create safer and more resilient cities. Massive volumes of environmental data may be analyzed in real-time by AI-powered systems, allowing for accurate monitoring of the quality of the air and water as well as the early identification of pollution sources(Soundararajan, et al., 2024). Proactive steps to prevent and alleviate environmental hazards are made possible by the use of predictive analytics, which helps forecast pollution levels and identify trends. Artificial Intelligence has the capability to enhance pollution management tactics, such modifying traffic patterns to minimize emissions or refining industrial processes to decrease pollutants. Additionally, by identifying high-risk regions and suggesting green infrastructure solutions, AI-driven insights help improve urban planning. In general, artificial intelligence (AI) improves environmental management's efficacy and efficiency, which has a positive impact on public health, lessens its ecological footprint, and more.

10. DISADVANTAGE OF AI FOR POLLUTION CONTROL:

Although artificial intelligence (AI) offers significant drawbacks, it can also improve urban sustainability through sophisticated pollution management and environmental monitoring. The cost of implementing AI systems can be unaffordable, requiring large infrastructure and technology investments. Because AI systems manage enormous volumes of environmental and personal data, there is a possibility of data breaches and misuse. This raises data privacy and security concerns. Furthermore, the quality of the data that AI processes determines how effective it will be; skewed or wrong data might result in incorrect forecasts and insufficient solutions. If AI is used excessively, human oversight could be compromised and important contextual variables that technology cannot handle could be missed. Furthermore, if gains are not divided fairly, the deployment of AI may result in the loss of jobs in traditional monitoring tasks and increase already-existing disparities. Effective use of AI in the development of safer and more sustainable cities requires striking a balance between these difficulties and the possible rewards.

11. IN RESEARCH FIELD

An overview of the number of articles pertaining to and unrelated to artificial intelligence (AI) from a variety of academic sources is shown in the table. Below is a summary of the many platforms and publishers from which the publication data was collected, represented by each row and column. These include Elsevier, NIH, MDPI, IEEE (which covers conferences, journals, magazines, early access publications, and books). The number of publications pertaining solely to artificial intelligence for each source is indicated in the Number of Publications with AI column. The number of publications from the same sources that do not use AI is displayed in the Number of Publications without AI column.

Table 1. Number of publication in research area related to pollution control with and without AI

Sources	Number of Publication with AI	Number of Publication without AI
IEEE Conferences	346	39307
IEEE Journals	82	7187
IEEE Magazines	8	960
IEEE Early Access Articles	5	103
IEEE Books	4	300
Elsevier	57	390
NIH	27	103
MDPI	23	96

At IEEE Conferences, 39,307 publications unrelated to AI and 346 publications about AI are presented. This implies that the amount of conference papers that deal with AI is rather limited. 82 papers in IEEE journals deal with AI, whereas 7,187 do not. Compared to the conferences, this indicates a larger share of AI-related research, but a still modest fraction overall. Out of 960 IEEE magazines, only 8 deal with artificial intelligence. The lower quantity may be explained by the fact that research-focused pieces are often less common in magazines. There are five early access publications from IEEE on AI compared to 103 articles on non-AI. Typically, early access publications include innovative research with a degree of AI interest.

Figure 6. Chart shows the pollution control with and without AI in research platform

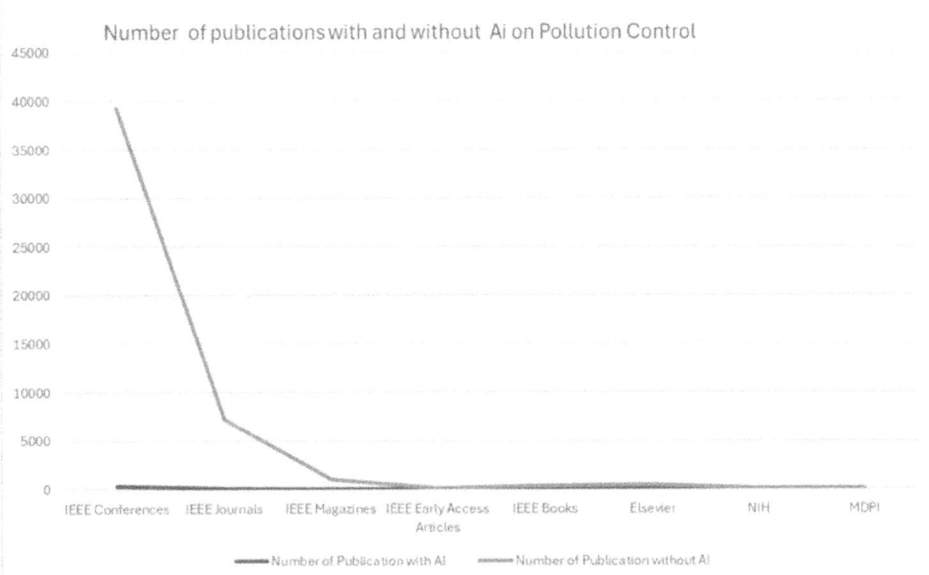

Within IEEE Books Out of 300 books covering various topics, only 4 have been published about AI. Books often cover a wider range of subjects, thus this figure may be lower. 390 non-AI papers and 57 AI-related publications are published by Elsevier. Given Elsevier's size as a publisher, there is a moderate level of interest in AI. There are 103 papers from the National Institutes of Health (NIH) that are not on AI and 27 that are. This demonstrates that biomedical and health studies are paying more attention to AI. There are 96 non-AI-related papers and 23 AI-related publications in MDPI. Open-access journals are a hallmark of MDPI, and the data points to a reasonable interest in AI.

Table 2. Overview of Related Work on Pollution Control using AI

Study	AI Technique	Pollution Type	Methodology	Key Findings
Smith et al. (2022)	Machine Learning	Air Pollution	Developed a predictive model using Random Forest to forecast PM2.5 levels.	Achieved 95% accuracy in predicting air quality, leading to improved early warning systems.
Zhao & Li (2021)	Deep Learning	Water Pollution	Used CNN to analyze satellite images for detecting water contamination.	Successfully identified contaminated water bodies with 92% precision.
Gupta & Singh (2020)	Neural Networks	Industrial Emissions	Implemented ANN for real-time monitoring and controlling industrial emissions.	Reduced emissions by 15% in pilot industries through automated control systems.
Kim et al. (2019)	Reinforcement Learning	Noise Pollution	Applied RL for optimizing urban traffic flow to reduce noise pollution.	Demonstrated a 10% reduction in noise levels in urban test areas.
Ahmed et al. (2018)	Hybrid AI	Solid Waste Management	Combined ML and IoT for efficient waste sorting and recycling processes.	Increased recycling rates by 25% in smart city initiatives.

12. CONCLUSION:

In conclusion, there is a lot of potential for raising the livability and resilience of cities by utilizing AI to improve urban sustainability through sophisticated pollution management and environmental monitoring. AI can facilitate the control of pollution sources, increase the accuracy of pollution forecasts, and allow real-time analysis of environmental data, all of which contribute to healthier urban environments and cleaner air and water. However, there are a number of issues that must be resolved in order to facilitate the adoption of AI. Exorbitant expenses and the requirement for a sizable technology infrastructure may be prohibitive, especially for smaller communities or those with tighter financial constraints. To prevent sensitive information from being misused or compromised, data privacy and security issues must be handled. Furthermore, the data used which must be precise and representative to prevent misleading results determines the quality of AI insights. Additionally, relying too much on AI could compromise human oversight and the complex knowledge needed for efficient environmental management. Furthermore, the application of AI may result in the displacement of workers from traditional occupations, creating socioeconomic issues. new problems can be lessened by ensuring that everyone has equal access to the advantages of AI and carefully incorporating new technologies into current systems. This will open the door to more intelligent, sustainable urban development that strikes a balance between innovation, inclusivity, and resilience.

REFERENCES

Adewale, P., Dumont, M. J., & Ngadi, M. (2015). Recent trends of biodiesel production from animal fat wastes and associated production techniques. *Renewable & Sustainable Energy Reviews, 45*, 574–588. DOI: 10.1016/j.rser.2015.02.039

Ahmed, H., Wang, T., & Patel, R. (2018). Hybrid AI approaches for solid waste management and recycling processes in smart cities. *Journal of Environmental Management, 215*, 67–76. DOI: 10.1016/j.jenvman.2018.02.053

Altieri, A. H., & Gedan, K. B. (2015). Climate change and dead zones. *Global Change Biology, 21*(4), 1395–1406. DOI: 10.1111/gcb.12754 PMID: 25385668

Arnell, N. W., Lowe, J. A., Challinor, A. J., & Osborn, T. J. (2019). Global and regional impacts of climate change at different levels of global temperature increase. *Climatic Change, 155*(3), 377–391. DOI: 10.1007/s10584-019-02464-z

Ayomoh, M. K. O., Oke, S. A., Adedeji, W. O., & Charles-Owaba, O. E. (2008). An approach to tackling the environmental and health impacts of municipal solid waste disposal in developing countries. *Journal of Environmental Management, 88*(1), 108–114. DOI: 10.1016/j.jenvman.2007.01.040 PMID: 17383077

Balasubramaniam, M., Pawade, A., & Bharambe, K. (2020). A sustainable design approach for the built environment based on the principles of Anthropological circadian rhythms Chronobiology and Chronopharmocology. *Journal of Engineering Research and Application, 10*(02), 27–31.

Cembalo, L., Lombardi, A., Pascucci, S., Dentoni, D., Migliore, G., Verneau, F., & Schifani, G. (2015). "Rationally local": Consumer participation in alternative food chains. *Agribusiness, 31*(3), 330–352. DOI: 10.1002/agr.21419

Christophe, E., & Inglada, J. (2009). Open source remote sensing: Increasing the usability of cutting-edge algorithms. *IEEE Geoscience and Remote Sensing Newsletter, 35*(5), 9–15.

Da Fonseca-Soares, D., Eliziário, S. A., Galvinicio, J. D., & Ramos-Ridao, A. F. (2023). Life-Cycle Greenhouse Gas (GHG) Emissions Calculation for Urban Rail Transit Systems: The Case of Pernambuco Metro. *Applied Sciences (Basel, Switzerland), 13*(15), 8965. DOI: 10.3390/app13158965

Davis, M., & Naumann, S. (2017). Making the case for sustainable urban drainage systems as a nature-based solution to urban flooding. *Nature-Based Solutions to Climate Change Adaptation in Urban Areas: Linkages between Science. Policy & Practice*, •••, 123–137.

Dijkstra, J., Ellis, J. L., Kebreab, E., Strathe, A. B., López, S., France, J., & Bannink, A. (2012). Ruminal pH regulation and nutritional consequences of low pH. *Animal Feed Science and Technology*, *172*(1-2), 22–33. DOI: 10.1016/j.anifeedsci.2011.12.005

El Naqa, I., & Murphy, M. J. (2015). *What is machine learning?* Springer International Publishing.

Gupta, R., & Singh, A. (2020). Real-time monitoring of industrial emissions using artificial neural networks. *Environmental Pollution*, *258*, 113743. DOI: 10.1016/j.envpol.2019.113743

Hosseini, S. R., Scaioni, M., & Marani, M. (2018). On the influence of global warming on Atlantic hurricane frequency. *The International Archives of the Photogrammetry, Remote Sensing and Spatial Information Sciences*, *42*(3), 527–532. DOI: 10.5194/isprs-archives-XLII-3-527-2018

Huang, L., Wu, J., & Yan, L. (2015). Defining and measuring urban sustainability: A review of indicators. *Landscape Ecology*, *30*(7), 1175–1193. DOI: 10.1007/s10980-015-0208-2

Ingram, G. K. (1998). Patterns of metropolitan development: What have we learned? *Urban Studies (Edinburgh, Scotland)*, *35*(7), 1019–1035. DOI: 10.1080/0042098984466

Jones, M. W., Peters, G. P., Gasser, T., Andrew, R. M., Schwingshackl, C., Gütschow, J., & Le Quéré, C. (2023). National contributions to climate change due to historical emissions of carbon dioxide, methane, and nitrous oxide since 1850. *Scientific Data*, *10*(1), 155. DOI: 10.1038/s41597-023-02041-1 PMID: 36991071

Kim, S., Park, J., & Choi, H. (2019). Optimizing urban traffic flow using reinforcement learning to reduce noise pollution. *Transportation Research Part D, Transport and Environment*, *67*, 672–684. DOI: 10.1016/j.trd.2019.01.009

Kushwah, V. S., Goyal, S. K., & Sharma, A. (2020). Maximize resource utilization using aco in cloud computing environment for load balancing. In Soft Computing: Theories and Applications [Springer Singapore.]. *Proceedings of SoCTA, 2018*, 583–590.

Loomis, J. J., & Dziedzic, M. (2018). Evaluating EIA systems' effectiveness: A state of the art. *Environmental Impact Assessment Review*, *68*, 29–37. DOI: 10.1016/j.eiar.2017.10.005

Loomis, J. J., & Dziedzic, M. (2018). Evaluating EIA systems' effectiveness: A state of the art. *Environmental Impact Assessment Review*, *68*, 29–37. DOI: 10.1016/j.eiar.2017.10.005

Manikandan, G., Bhuvaneswari, G., & Joel, M. R. (2023, August). Artificial Intelligence to the Assessment, Monitoring, and Forecasting of Drought in Developing Countries. In *2023 International Conference on Circuit Power and Computing Technologies (ICCPCT)* (pp. 886-892). IEEE. DOI: 10.1109/ICCPCT58313.2023.10245072

Marogna, M., Spadolini, I., Massolo, A., Canonica, G. W., & Passalacqua, G. (2010). Long-lasting effects of sublingual immunotherapy according to its duration: A 15-year prospective study. *The Journal of Allergy and Clinical Immunology, 126*(5), 969–975. DOI: 10.1016/j.jaci.2010.08.030 PMID: 20934206

Maselli, D. J., Bhatt, S. P., Anzueto, A., Bowler, R. P., DeMeo, D. L., Diaz, A. A., Dransfield, M. T., Fawzy, A., Foreman, M. G., Hanania, N. A., Hersh, C. P., Kim, V., Kinney, G. L., Putcha, N., Wan, E. S., Wells, J. M., Westney, G. E., Young, K. A., Silverman, E. K., & Make, B. J. (2019). Clinical epidemiology of COPD: Insights from 10 years of the COPDGene study. *Chest, 156*(2), 228–238. DOI: 10.1016/j.chest.2019.04.135 PMID: 31154041

McMahon, T. A., Rohr, J. R., & Bernal, X. E. (2017). Light and noise pollution interact to disrupt interspecific interactions. *Ecology, 98*(5), 1290–1299. DOI: 10.1002/ecy.1770 PMID: 28170099

Messeri, L., & Crockett, M. J. (2024). Artificial intelligence and illusions of understanding in scientific research. *Nature, 627*(8002), 49–58. DOI: 10.1038/s41586-024-07146-0 PMID: 38448693

Mohsin, A. H. (2022). Optimize routing protocol overheads in MANETs: challenges and solutions: a review paper. *Wireless Personal Communications, 126*(4), 2871–2910. DOI: 10.1007/s11277-022-09843-3

Nicholson, E., Fulton, E. A., Brooks, T. M., Blanchard, R., Leadley, P., Metzger, J. P., Mokany, K., Stevenson, S., Wintle, B. A., Woolley, S. N. C., Barnes, M., Watson, J. E. M., & Ferrier, S. (2019). Scenarios and models to support global conservation targets. *Trends in Ecology & Evolution, 34*(1), 57–68. DOI: 10.1016/j.tree.2018.10.006 PMID: 30514580

Ramachandran, R., Arthi, D., & Babu, A., & RS, A. S. (2024, April). A Meta-Analytical Review on Microplastic Pollution in the Indian Ocean. In *2024 International Conference on Science Technology Engineering and Management (ICSTEM)* (pp. 1-7). IEEE. DOI: 10.1109/ICSTEM61137.2024.10561208

Sayadi, A. R., Asadpour, M., Shabani, Z., & Sayadi, M. (2012). Pharmaceutical pollution of the eco-system and its detrimental effects on public health. *Majallah-i Ilmi-i Danishgah-i Ulum-i Pizishki-i Rafsanjan, 11*(3), 269–284.

Schmid, D. (2023). Laboratory Studies on Aqueous Absorption and High Temperature Chemistry of NOx and SOx in Thermal Conversion of Biomass Waste.

Shahabuddin, M., Uddin, M. N., Chowdhury, J. I., Ahmed, S. F., Uddin, M. N., Mofijur, M., & Uddin, M. A. (2023). A review of the recent development, challenges, and opportunities of electronic waste (e-waste). *International Journal of Environmental Science and Technology*, *20*(4), 4513–4520. DOI: 10.1007/s13762-022-04274-w

Singh, S. P., & Singh, M. K. (2020). Soil pollution and human health. Plant responses to soil pollution, 205-220.

Smith, J., Brown, P., & Lee, Y. (2022). Predicting air pollution levels using machine learning techniques: A case study on PM2.5. *Atmospheric Environment*, *257*, 118073. DOI: 10.1016/j.atmosenv.2021.118073

Soundararajan, G., Chidambaranathan, B., Rajendran, A. K., Venugopal, D., & Devarajan, Y. (2024). Plastic pyrolytic oils as renewable fuel: Improving its physical properties and ignition patterns by waste renewable source—an experimental analysis. *Environmental Science and Pollution Research International*, *31*(18), 26497–26509. DOI: 10.1007/s11356-024-32668-5 PMID: 38446296

Suryati, I., Khair, H., & Gusrianti, D. (2019). Distribution analysis of nitrogen dioxide (NO2) and ozone (O3) in Medan city with Geographic Information System (GIS). In *MATEC Web of Conferences* (Vol. 276, p. 06013). EDP Sciences.

Sutarlie, L., Ow, S. Y., & Su, X. (2017). Nanomaterials-based biosensors for detection of microorganisms and microbial toxins. *Biotechnology Journal*, *12*(4).

Venkataramanan, V., Kavitha, G., Joel, M. R., & Lenin, J. (2023, January). Forest fire detection and temperature monitoring alert using iot and machine learning algorithm. In *2023 5th International Conference on Smart Systems and Inventive Technology (ICSSIT)* (pp. 1150-1156). IEEE. DOI: 10.1109/ICSSIT55814.2023.10061086

World Health Organization. (2021). *WHO global air quality guidelines: particulate matter (PM2. 5 and PM10), ozone, nitrogen dioxide, sulfur dioxide and carbon monoxide*. World Health Organization.

Xu, H., Jia, Y., Sun, Z., Su, J., Liu, Q. S., Zhou, Q., & Jiang, G. (2022). Environmental pollution, a hidden culprit for health issues. *Eco-Environment & Health*, *1*(1), 31–45. DOI: 10.1016/j.eehl.2022.04.003 PMID: 38078200

Zhao, L., & Li, X. (2021). Deep learning for water quality analysis: A comprehensive study. *Water Research*, *196*, 116983. DOI: 10.1016/j.watres.2021.116983

Chapter 4
Citizen-Centric Artificial Intelligence in Enhancing Mobility and Accessibility in Public Safety and Healthcare AI in Transforming Energy Management

Shaik Khasim Saheb
Sreenidhi Institute of Science and Technology, India

Akshatha Noonemunthala Goud
Sreenidhi Institute of Science and Technology, India

Thota Venkat Narayana Rao
https://orcid.org/0000-0002-1996-1819
Sreenidhi Institute of Science and Technology, India

Devavarapu Sreenivasarao
Sreenidhi Institute of Science and Technology, India

ABSTRACT

Citizen-centric artificial intelligence systems put citizen in their hearts than view them as passive providers of data. Urban living in the smart cities can be enhanced by manipulating artificial intelligence for the expeditious evolution of smart cities.

DOI: 10.4018/979-8-3693-7832-8.ch004

Artificial intelligence systems should give utmost importance and attention to the needs and values of the citizens which is very essential for the urban development and for a sustainable environment. The chapter investigates the notion of the Citizen-centric artificial intelligence with reference to the smart cities stating its importance and role in the urban transformation, promoting inclusivity and accessibility by providing ethical artificial intelligence solutions to ensure transparency and accountability adhering challenges as well.

INTRODUCTION

The idea of a sustainable artificial intelligence in urban cities has surfaced a revolutionary approach for the urban development and the advancement of the artificial intelligence based technologies to enhance the operations for the residents (Heinrich Son et al., 2023).

Artificial intelligence put forwards powerful and impactful tools, gadgets and algorithms for automated decision – making in various fields and domains like transportation, public safety and healthcare, energy resource and management. It is essential to adopt a Citizen-centric artificial intelligence to secure that the smart cities are not only effective but also fair and inclusive towards its people.

Citizen-centric artificial intelligence priors transparency, accountability and inclusivity aiming to improve all individuals by giving them the quality of life, through artificial intelligence it can shape their urban livelihood and also play a vital role in the urban transformation. The aim is to highlight how artificial intelligence can strengthen data and technology and magnify public services, foster greater civic engagement which are not only smart but indeed sensitive to the needs of their inhabitants.

This sets the stage for a detailed journey of how artificial intelligence can be more effectively united into the smart cities by prioritizing their needs and considering the inputs of the citizens. Citizen-centric artificial intelligence is all about serving people with its technology and tools and empowering citizens for a better and a brighter future.

Smart cities are an embodiment of evolution, supporting advanced technologies to modernize and also enhance the quality of life for the inhabitants by improvising services and making a more sustainable environment to live. Fundamental to the urban transformation in cities, Citizen-centric artificial intelligence can be incorporated to hierarchize the citizen's needs amidst being sensitive as well as considering their inputs for their well – being. Integrating artificial intelligence, not only screams for a responsive, inclusive urban environment but also centralizes in making decisions for its people by using incentives which promotes a positive behavior change and also simultaneously manages to robust to strategic manipulation.

Citizen-centric artificial intelligence engages in the urban transformation by authorizing the cities to become more efficient and amendable to the residents requirements and safety.

Artificial intelligences augmentation to the radical change of the urban areas:

TRAFFIC MANAGEMENT AND REDUCTION OF TRAFFIC CONGESTION

Traffic Flow Escalation

AI can optimize the reduction of traffic flow where it can account real – time data and explicit traffic lights which leads to a more concise travel time and also in the diminution of congestion. Advocating different routes for a less time consumption whilst developing the fuel energy and improving overall traffic flow.

Energy Management

Advancement in the administration and usage of energy in the urban areas over smart grids. Smart grids specializes in estimating the usage arrangement for the reduction of waste and for a consistent energy supply as well as to associate renewable energy resources. Energy conserved in multiple set-ups like industrial places, buildings and urban neighborhoods.

AIs main motive is to power data, lessen costs, implementation of machine learning and decreased environmental encounter.

FOUNDATIONAL MISSION OF AI IN ENERGY MANAGEMENT

Data Analysis and Collection

The information brought by the AI systems of data from numerous sources which consists of sensors and IOT appliances and applications. This data gives us a detailed view of the consumption of the energy, the performance of the machines and a forecast of the weather conditions. Giving the citizens an overview of the consumption of energy and also providing those insights as to where it can be maintained and reduced, identifying inefficiencies and providing ethical solutions to optimize the energy use (Sayed et al., 2022).

Distribution of Energy

Load arrangement of energy across multiple systems and times of the day to balance the energy usage. AI points out in the required areas where the energy is wasted or not entirely being used it steps up and recommends or automatically implements measures and adjustments such as HVAC (heating, ventilation and air conditioning), and machinery operations.

Associating Renewable Energy

Solar, wind and hydropower energy that emerges under renewable sources are used to station on their vacancy and foresees any inconstancy to make sure there is persistent flow of the energy supply.

Storage of Energy

Energy storage substitutes like batteries can be used by definitive optimal charging and discharging depending on their demands as well as cost and also the availability of the renewable energy.

Smart Grid Management

Artificial intelligence keeps in check with the stability of the electrical grid through persisting the accurate supply and by availing real – time for prevention of outages, validating a balanced and consistent flow of power supply and delivery. Roof top solar panels and small wind turbines can be incorporated which enables for a sustainable urban environment allowing for an enhanced decentralized and volatile energy systems.

APPLICATIONS OF AI IN ENERGY MANAGEMENT:

Industrial plants and Factories

Use of Energy management in factories and industrial plants will rapidly minimize the energy expenses by cultivating machinery operations and directing energy intensive processes for improvising the energy efficiency.

Urban Groundwork

In Smart cities the energy used for the public infrastructure supposedly street lights, common buildings, clubrooms, transportation systems AI manages and strengthens the energy supply and aims for viable environment.

CHALLENGES FACED BY AI IN ENERGY MANAGEMENT

Cost Implementation

The fundamental investment for an AI assisted energy systems will be tremendously expensive which may cause to form a barrier for a few institutions and managements.

Privacy and Security

The data collection which is required for AI driven energy systems might raise issues, conflicts and concerns related to privacy. It is highly essential for the information or data that contains any personal details to be encrypted as well as confidential.

Requires careful consideration of scalability and integration with the current existing systems.

HEALTHCARE DELIVERY

AI in the health care industry is most likely to boom and transform the medical services, fabricating them to become more personalized and accessible. Health care delivery will be highly helpful and leave a great impact from the diagnostics domain to the taking care of the patient administration. Technologies and algorithms obtained by AI shall embellish the patients overall experience.

Role of AI in the health care

Personalized Treatment

AI helps in customizing the individual's treatment conditional to the patient's genetic problems and medical history and through AI collected data, using this passage will boost the validity of treatments and diminish conflicting reactions.

A vast amount of the collected data by AI through clinical trials and the patient's fallout for the recognition of the problem caused and also advocating them for an effective treatment for the condition developed amid advising them to make informed decisions.

Diagnostics and Medical Labs

Study of medical images such as X-rays, CT and MRI scans though AI algorithms which are eminently based on deep learning will be advantageous for analyzing medical copies. AI can expose conditions like fractures, cysts, tumors or any sort of abnormalities occurring in the internal human body with steep preciseness.

Therapeutics and early signs of diseases most likely cancer where AI can aid pathologists by scrutinizing tissue samples, help in investigating and calibrating for a quick and efficient speedy recovery than traditional methods (Schork, 2019).

Risk Prognosis

Systems and models of artificial intelligence can forecast any growing settings based off the patients genetic medical history, lifestyle for the prevention of any future dangers that allows for raw interference and personalized treatment plans, through maintaining a healthy diet and health lifestyle.

Prediction of a possible outbreaks in the near future by collection of data from multiple sources in conjunction with the public health records, tracking or investigating possible cases of infectious diseases whilst making the inhabitants aware of it.

Drug Delivery

Medications prescribed by the doctors and physicians can be ordered online through AI generated apps and websites from your nearest medical stores. Online consultation can also be availed personally a one – on – one sessions with doctors of top prestigious hospitals and institutions.

Virtual Health Assistants and chat – bots: Any queries, symptoms, health tips can be sourced through the AI powered bots where they answer and assist immediately showing transparency as well as accountability. Reminding and notifying patients to take their prescribed medicines on time and also aid in managing chronic conditions by offering help outside the traditional clinical set – up.

Mental health which is a very sensitive subject can also be healed through AI by setting up online therapy sessions, scheduled exercises and track their journey by AI apps giving them a sign of hope and happiness. Making mental health awareness more apprehensive in society which is less spoken, through social media making it more accessible.

CHALLENGES ENDURED BY AI

Trust and adaptability to the new AI systems could be difficult at the very bringing, it requires transparency, evidence and awakening that it is completely fine to be reliable by showcasing its benefits and educating about it.

Accessibility could also be one of the challenge faced by AI as not many people are familiar about the new advanced technologies especially in low resource areas besides health care is generally expensive and with addition of AI it will be a huge challenge faced.

Revolutionizing health care through enhancing diagnostics and labs, personalized treatments, virtual assistants and bots mindful study of the ethical challenges will lead to the unification of AI in health care delivery (Stahl et al., 2021).

AI has the capability to substantially improvise the healthcare domain assuring a safe and an accessible and affordable health care to everyone.

Public Safety

As technology rapidly speeds to be in the forefront at a rampant amount AI has found its growth increasing tremendously it has found its roots in numerous industries that consists of health care, transportation, energy management. One of the most cynical places where AI can make a compelling change is in public safety. Citizen-Centric AI effortlessly integrates with urban infrastructure, supply chain management and emergency response which forms a dynamic ecosystem. Smart buildings equipped with AI play a major role in actively monitoring and optimizing environmental factors thereby promoting optimal living conditions across communities. IOT devices which are installed across the city that helps to record and update real-time data which is vital to enable quick responses towards any health threats and enhancing overall public safety.

AI in Public Safety

Assuring a safe and sound cities and environment is one of the most important aspect of the government and law. But the conventional method of prevention of crime has its constraints. Visitation of AI there is a probability clout data, algorithms, machine learning, and deep learning to modify public safety measures, emergency response and the overall well-being of the community (Zhu, 2025).

Measures Taken by AI for Public Safety

Prevention of Crime

Indication of possible future crimes could be obtained through AI mechanized surveillance systems where it oversees and avails real – time feeds from the captured videos and announces higher forces about any cautious activities taking place. AI algorithms can synchronize recorded crimes to foresee when the crimes are likely to occur by recognizing any possible hotspots. The previously recorded crime data can be obtained through machine learning algorithms which will provide a detailed sights of information and inputs.

For instance the NYPD has successfully managed to use the AI based algorithm for the identification of markings and through forecasting. Automated detection can also be and applied by AI which tracks down any probable accidents, fights and rapid intervention can be taken place.

Disaster Management

The AI fixed order set-ups can play a vital role in disaster management as well as rescue operations. It can collect the data from multiple sources supposedly weather stations, social media, satellites to indicate early warnings and provide response teams.

Calculation and estimation of any natural disasters like floods, earthquakes, hurricanes AI algorithms evaluates precisely its ferocity and the damage which likely to happen, AI allocates potential evacuation zones and notifies people whilst coming up with a quick responsive strategies. Helpful in the arrangement of logistics (Cadet et al., 2024).

AI in Cyber Security

Refraining from fraud avoidance by AI which investigates graphs and patterns of fraud lent and suspicious activities to protect an individuals or communities from financial crisis. Threat detection can be enabled where the AI operated and supervised networks which detects cyber threats which breaches immediately in real – time. Operation of regular security checks will be helpful.

Some of the conspicuous trends in the smart cities are the citizen services where the chat-bots and virtual assistants that are obliged to provide individuals with a 24/7 access to city services and information. It tailors according to their personal preferences giving the residents a thrilling experience. It secures transparency, accountability as well as privacy of the inhabitants.

Forensic Examination

The investigation process of the committed crimes could be tailored by using the AI feature pattern identification where it observes and analysis the data which is connected to the case and unleashes any possible leads for the investigation.

Data analysis of the forensic reports consisting of DNA samples which is a crucial clue for an ongoing investigation.

Ethical consideration is required where the law should be unbiased and maintain a balance between data driven by AI assuring everyone of equal treatment for the prevention of crime.

The future possibilities of AI is wide in range as the technology persists to grow the people can await more ethical solutions to adhere public safety issues.

Uniting AI in our systems introduction of IOTs will lead to a safe smart cities where public safety is motorized and is proactive (Granados, 2024).

Promotion of inclusivity and accessibility through AI in smart cities

Inclusion of accessibility and sustainability in AI-powered smart cities is essential to assure that the perks of technological amelioration continues for all residents that are homologous doled out, regardless of their power and influence.

Strategies in Which This Can be Attained

Developing Inclusive Technology

Consumer-focused Considerations

Drawing in of different user groups in the AI application advancement process to guarantee that the technology fits in divergent needs and desires. This entails people with disabilities, detriment and the people in old age, and those belonging from different cultural or linguistic backgrounds.

Accessibility Regulations

Adhering to renowned approachable standards (such as WCAG for web content) to safeguard the people with disabilities so they can use AI-powered sessions that the project has armed. This consists of screen readers, voice commands, and other input procedures.

Technical Evolution

Affordable Resolutions

Ensure that AI technology is inexpensive and accessible to all social and economic sectors, irrespective of their status. This may involve subsidizing expenses for low-income households or providing free access to essential services.

Aid Improvement

Investing in digital groundwork to provide safe internet and connectivity in undue areas, diminishing the digital divide.

Participatory Outlining

Society engagement

Connecting with community groups, including those symbolizing marginalized or underserved populations, in the policy development and decision-making series for the industry's in smart cities.

Equity Estimation

Conduct regular evaluation to diagnose and address any breach in access to and perquisites from AI technologies.

Education Guidance

Automated Literacy

Implementation of education and training programs to revamp computerized literacy and knowledge between all the members of the community, especially those with bounded technology literacy (Wolniak & Stecuła, 2024).

AI Awakening

Spreading information about AI and its applications its pros to uncloak the technology and make it more attainable to the urban community.

Robust Transmission

Tailored Coalition

Forming AI systems with personalized interfaces that can be tailored to the individual needs, such as customizable font sizes, color schemes, and navigation assistance.

Linguistic Structure

Addition of multilingual features to AI systems through algorithms can be essential to serve multiple languages and by breaking the language barriers that do not curb access.

Ethical and translucent AI

Transparency: To make sure that the AI algorithms and automated decision-making processes are vitreous so that the residents comprehend how their data is being used and how all the vital decisions are being made.

Bigotry Moderation

Anticipatorily work being done to identify and pacify biasness in AI programs to restrain discrimination, unfairness and ensure that all users are treated fairly.

Creating access points for the public's input and on the AI initiatives on the smart city projects. This feedback should be used to make any improvisations and address any assimilation or any key issues.

Help Services

Providing the customer care services that can adhere concerns and assist the users with an assortment of solutions and needs, including those with disabilities.

Partner with Advocacy Groups

Partner with advocacy organizations for people with disabilities and other marginalized groups to ensure their needs are taken into account in AI and smart city planning.

Public Private Partnerships

ESTABLISH PARTNERSHIPS BETWEEN GOVERNMENT, THE PRIVATE SECTOR, AND NONPROFITS

By initiating these measures in the smart cities, they can use AI to create areas that are not only technologically progressive but also more precise and operative. This path creates an inclusive society where all inhabitants can favor from the growth and development brought about by smart city technologies (Lawton, 2024).

Data – Driven decision making in smart cities

Data-directed decision making through AI in smart cities is highly helpful forthe dynamic growth of the way urban spaces work, reconstructing competence, sustainability, and essence of life. By harnessing generous amounts of data from multiple sources, AI authorizes city planners and managers to make informed decisions in real time.

AIs assistance in the progress of the data-driven decision-making in smart cities

Problem-Solving Time by Data Collection and Analysis

Smart cities can purpose the utilization of Internet of Things (IOT) devices, sensors in the groundwork serving as roads, public transit, infrastructure, and public spaces. These sensors frequently capture data on traffic congestion, energy consumption, waste management, and air quality.

AI-Motorized Problem Solving

AI codes develops the real-time data to spot patterns or any deviations from normal arrangement and direction. For example, AI can test the traffic data to reform traffic light order, reduction of congestion and emissions.

Foreboding Search

Through envisioning AI can predict future events based on previous data and prevailing data. For instance, predictive analytics can foresee energy supply, permitting urban services to condition power generation and dispersion to ignore outages.

Visiting all the data sourced from the supporting sensors, AI can resolve when the sustenance is needed before deterioration takes place, lowering downtime and maintenance expenses as a result

Rehabilitated Community Framework

Mental and physical wellness could be examined by AI through undergoing study of the health data to predicting and managing of the possible disease outbreaks, abled designed resources, and filter public health services. In case of emergencies, AI can comfort in programing care and resource provisions.

Public Safety can be secured through AI-driven supervision and data analysis systems embellishing public safety by predicting crime hotspots, kicking around social media for budding threats and, through reconstruction and legislation of the laws (Okunleye et al., 2023).

Modern Civic outlining

AI can make use of the data from the installed AI traffic sensors, applications to amend traffic flow, public traverse systems, decrease accidents, and improvise in public transit. This data-herded approach supports in creating in inventive transportation systems that we can adopt in real time.

Promotion of the development of Self-driven cars and drones for transportation, delivery services that uplifts data-driven decision making. Leading for a much efficient and effective urban management.

AI can classify the data on the basis of population demography, economic growth, and the surroundings to make cognizant judgments about land utility, neighborhoods, and urban development. This guides the cities plan for a sustainable augmentation whilst conserving green space and shrinking urban sprawl.

Improved Control of resources

Optimization of energy management through AI can support in managing energy consumption by increasing the cities foundation, such as installation of street lights and heating systems, based on the consumption motif and consideration of situational factors mainly. Water and waste maintenance through AI can centralize water arrangements by forecasting its demand and detecting leaks.AI-driven systems can control collection methods and policies based on real-time data in waste management.

SUSTAINABILITY AND ENVIRONMENTAL ASSESSMENT

AI keeps in check with air quality data in real time, pegs out cause of pollution and permits the cities to agent aimed measures to reduce emissions. AI can also idealize the impact of policy decisions on environmental outcomes.

Economic Growth

Business and Economic Intelligence could be managed by AI, it can direct the economic data to for future opportunities for growth and development, helping the cities to draw attention from the businesses and venture capitalist. AI-driven intuitions can announce programs that reform modernization and output

Department of tourism could be more enhanced by AI through early notifications and information about the tourists arrival, their behavior and personal preferences. AI can incorporate better tourism plan in the cities, making the tourists experience more thrilling, exciting and educational as well as beneficial for the department of tourism.

Data Governance and Ethical Considerations

AI smart cities have to rapidly rely on data to make decisions, ensuring that the resident's data privacy and security is secure is a critical challenge. AI systems must be designed with strict data security measures to prevent breaches and misuse. Transparency and Accountability in the smart cities is need for the AI systems that provide the public an oversight accountability, mechanisms need to be developed to address any ethical concerns, such as biasness in AI designs and an equitable distribution of benefits.

Automated data-driven decision making through AI in the citizen- centric smart cities enables for a more efficient, sustainable, and effective urban livelihood. By uniting the power of data, smart cities can more effectively and efficiently meet the needs of their residents, awaiting and responding to the challenges faced, and creating conditions that improve everyone's lives.

AI policies in smart cities are detracting for building the public's trust, defensive of the individual's rights, and guaranteeing that they are within the ethical and responsible foundations.

A closer visit at the ethics and legal structure for the smart cities essential for reaching the goal.

Code of Conduct

AI programs should be aimed to hold back on any preconceived notions, set out that no demographic troop is at any disadvantage. This behooves divergent and symbolical data sets, as well as legitimate audits of AI algorithms.

AIs resolution should be to synchronize all the inputs and opinions given from various communities, organizations, to assure that they are fair with the needs and wants of all the citizens, inclusive of the marginalized and vulnerable groups. Thus promoting transparency and accountability.

Safe- guarding of privacy and data

Cut back of unnecessary data by AI: AI systems should only accumulate and methodize data that is significant for their activities, subtracting the amount of confidential knowledge saved and refined.

Data Encryption

Personal data and information should be unknown, AI should enforce viable and strong encryption techniques that can be used to guard the data from illegal and illegitimate access.

Implications for AI

AI systems should be directed in such way that it's much easier for the humans to grasp, chiefly those who have shape their decision making. This consists of supporting a clear confession of how the decisions are being made and how the instructions being instructed is executed.

AI Algorithms should be unclosed or accessible for the independent reviews to insure the citizens are being properly accounted and validated by others.

Supervision of AI

The liability of decisions taken by the AI structures should not be encouraged to be absolutely self-reliant in making vital selections and decisions that may have any repercussions on individuals' rights or needs. Human supervision is vital to audit and muscle in the AI choices when wanted and needed.

Constituting unprejudiced organizations, committees to look over the righteous deployment of AI in smart towns that can assist in ensuring that AI systems are parallel with the public's interests, values and human rights for an ethical and constitutional urban hood.

Legal Accountability

AI systems have to cooperate and assist with the present laws and policies, especially concerned and associated with privacy, security, information protection, and biasness.

AI Audits and Reporting: Regular inspection of financial records of the AI structures have to be administered by the ways of regulation, with statements said that is to relevant the authorities and is appropriate to the public. These audits should assist with the ethical considerations (Gillis et al., 2024).

Municipalities should be required to disclose the use of AI in public administration, including information about how AI decisions are made and data used. This builds public confidence and allows for public scrutiny and public transparency.

Possession of data and it's and Rights: Laws should precisely state and define the data ownership rights, assuring that all individuals have complete restraint over their own personal data. This adds the right to access, correct, and delete their data from AI systems.

Allocation of data, establishing of regulations on data sharing between the public and private sectors should be put into action to ensure that data is used responsibly and safely in ways that contribute for the betterment of the society and aligning with the public's interests

PUBLIC RELATIONS AND ACCOUNTABILITY VOICE

Residents should voice out the opinions on how AI should be used in their cities. By public consultation, research, and policy interventions can make sure that the use of AI is consistent with the societies, community values and priorities. Grievance procedures should be established for individuals to challenge or appeal decisions made by AI systems. This includes the right to seek redress if an AI system causes harm or unfairly affects an individual.

Applications

Public-Private relationship should be bounded together through partnerships between the governments, private firms, educational institutions, and the public is crucial to develop suitable AI policies and robust and regulate effective foundations.

Intergovernmental collaborations could take place in smart cities that work together nationally and internationally to contribute its best practices, align regulations, and ensure that AI technologies are developed and used in ways that meet with the global ethical standards.

Development of AI

Active customs could be incorporated by the AI technologies that evolve rapidly, foundational regulations most likely to be adaptable. Ongoing monitoring and regular legal updates are needed to address new challenges and opportunities as they arise.

Beforehand implementing and trial run of the AI programs for the smart cities should conducted thorough ethical impact examinations to recognize any possible risks and its pros and cons, to ensure that the use of AI is in the public interests.

The ethical and legal framework for transparency and accountability in AI in smart cities must be robust, flexible, and inclusive. For an accountable living environment through the AI system (Fontes et al., 2024).

AI- driven sustainable urban development

AI-driven blueprints offer impactful tools to advocate a sustainable urban development through resource effectiveness, environmental reduction, for the betterment and a quality of life for the residents.

AIS CONTRIBUTION FOR SUSTAINABLE URBAN DEVELOPMENT:

Managing Energy Efficiency

The use of AI- driven smart grids could be helpful for a better balance supply and demand, assimilating renewable energy sources such as solar and wind. By forecasting energy usage, AI can adjust its distribution in real time to cut out waste and reduce expenses.

Energy Efficiency could be strengthened through AI by improvising energy efficiency in buildings by heating, cooling, and lighting based on occupants, weather, and time of day. This decreases the consumption of energy and carbon emissions.

Maintained checks could run by AI, through predicting when the renewable energy equipment, and set-ups such as solar panels or wind turbines needs maintenance, decreasing the downtime and expanding energy production.

Storage of energy systems could be enabled by AI for the accurate and effective implementation of energy storage systems, guaranteeing for an excess energy production during peak times is stored and kept ready for an potential emergency and used during the peak demand.

EFFICIENT TRANSPORTATION

Traffic Optimization

Intelligent traffic management: AI-driven traffic management systems can develop traffic flow by balancing signal timing and shifting of vehicles in real time based on the traffic flow, for the reduction of accidents and carbon emissions.

AI can collect and study the data retrieved from the public transport systems to regulate routes, systems, and vehicles, making public transit more efficient and reducing the usage of private vehicles and opting for government transport when needed for reduction of pollution, traffic congestion and carpooling could also be considered if more than one is visiting the same place.

Sustainable Transportation

Introduction of autonomous vehicles that AI supports electric and self- driving, which can reduce the production of carbon emissions and improve urban mobility. AI can revamp the roads, install charging stations, and energy efficiency of these vehicles. AI powers ride-sharing and bike-sharing platforms, promoting shared mobility solutions that reduce the number of cars on the road and reduce carbon footprints.

Water Conservation

Smart Water conservation through AI-powered systems oversees water consumption and detect leaks in real time, reducing water waste. AI can also predict water demand, allowing more efficient distribution, usage and storage of water in the smart cities.

AI can assist in agricultural farming as well, it can examine the irrigation by analyzing weather conditions, predict soil moisture levels, and crop needs, and controls the water use in urban agriculture and green spaces.

Application in the 4R's

Waste management: AI cultivates the waste collected through different practices and systems rooted on real-time data from sensors in garbage bins, reducing fuel consumption and emissions from vehicles that the garbage is collected from the garbage can.

Recycling and distinguishing the wasted could be operated through AI-powered robots and sorting system algorithms can improve and ease recycling by identifying and sorting recyclables in real - time, compost pits could also be initiated in large scales.

Sustainable Urban Planning

Urban Growth could be calculated and predicted by AI, it examines the data on the current population growth, housing development, and environmental impacts to add different urban growth scenarios. This helps the people make informed decisions about the usage of land, constructing, zoning, and resources.

Green Space Planning: AI can identify optimal locations for parks and green spaces, taking into account factors such as population density, air quality, and access to nature, contributing to healthier urban spaces and they can live in it.

Weather Systems

Flood and Disaster Risk Management: AI can predict and ball out the impact of natural disasters such as floods, earthquakes and hurricanes on the smart cities and its infrastructure. This opens a gate for the municipalities to plan, model and build weather-yielding infrastructure, diminishing the risk of vandalism, wreckage thus prioritizing the public's safety. Sustainable blueprint of constructions that AI can optimize building designs to maximize the energy efficiency and supply, vital amount natural light intake and ventilation, reducing the need for artificial lighting and HVAC systems controlling the process. AI can also suggest sustainable materials and construction methods which are healthy for the atmosphere, as well as safe for the surroundings.

Real-Time Air Quality Monitoring

Pollution Detection and forecasting could be proceeded through AI produced data from air quality sensors installed for the identification of pollution sources and observe the air quality patterns. This acknowledges municipalities to take spirited measures for the reduction of pollution through implementing traffic restrictions and promising public transportation on high pollution days.

Health check- ups could be assessed by AI and observe the quality of air on public health, help the smart cities for the development of aimed health interventions and programs to protect vulnerable populations of the society.

Planning of a sustainable and green environment through AI that can determinate areas, lands with the most damaged by the urban heat and lifestyle, it can suggest some arbitration like to increase in the plantation of trees, generating greener roofs, and developing potential hotspots light to reduce heat. Adaptation of the climate could also be modified by AI-driven strategies, through stationing climate models that can help cities methodize for and adapt to the changes of the climate, ensuring that urban growth is both sustainable and volatile for the future generational as well as operational challenges faced by it.

COMMUNITY PARTICIPATION

Society's participation is important for the vocalization of AI-powered platforms. It retrieves all the data from the platforms and applications collected through both online and offline surveys conducted, social media, and public consultations, helping the city organizers to calibrate the sustainable needs and aspirations of the people of the communities. The closure is that AI is capable of mapping the development of smart city scenarios, offering the residents to formulate potential impacts of policy decisions and to actively participate during the process.

Educating inhabitants about AI:

Citizen-centric AI smart cities could institute AI-driven dashboards that provides real-time information about the cities daily performance and records. For instance the consumption of energy could obtained divided weekly, monthly and then yearly, similarly water consumption, and air quality for a systematic and organized result. This mission helps in educating the residents about sustainability and also encourages for a transparent and accountable environmentally friendly practices. Personalized recommendations would be highly encouraged by the residents and also for AI where it provides personalized recommendations to the residents on how they can reduce their environmental footprints, supposedly using public transportation, e reduction of energy consumption when not required, and also participate in local recycling programs.

Sustainable Environmental Practices

Supply Chain regulation of AI can modify the supply chain for the decrement of waste, reduction of emissions and unwanted chemicals, and to increase the resource efficiency in smart cities. This subsidizes for a more circular economy, where materials are recycled and then reused rather than being thrown away. Sustainable Consumption of AI can analyze consumption patterns and promote sustainable products and services for residents, businesses, and government agencies, and promote consumption and practices that encourage sustainable use of resources.

Innovation and Sustainable Business

Supporting startups which idealizes for a greenery and sustainable environment. With the help of AI they can recognize any potential opportunities for a sustainable innovation and support its ideal with proper execution and implementation with the growth of these green startups through targeted funding and resource allocation. This generates economic growth as well as encourages sustainable livelihood. Corporate governance could be ruled by AI through tracking and daily analytics of the sustainable practices of businesses taking place in the city whilst providing data-driven insights and inputs that helps the companies for their environment meet makes the urban city a much more efficient and effective with sustainable regulations.

Outcome of all the AI-driven strategies applied and implemented is essential for advancing sustainable urban development by making cities more efficient, resilient, smart and livable. Through uniting AI into facet of urban planning and management, cities can reduce their environmental footprint, increase resource efficiency, and create healthier environment and surroundings, which will be sustainable for the present and future generations. However, the successful implementation of these AI-driven policies requires collaboration between government, the private sector, and communities, as well as strong ethical and legal frameworks to meet sustainability goals accurately and responsibly.

Management of Artificial Intelligence in Smart Cities

Environmental inspection and control are the two most important components of a smart city initiatives, AI plays a vital role in augmenting these goals. By meshing the AI technologies, smart cities can have much better control of the environmental conditions, predicting potential events, and stimulate sustainable resource management to stay more durable and improve the lives of the residents.

AI IS TRANSFORMING ENVIRONMENTAL MONITORING AND MANAGEMENT IN SMART CITIES

Pollution Exposure through the sensor networks operated in smart cities use numerous air quality sensors to control pollutants such as particulate matter (PM2.5 and PM10), nitrogen dioxide (NO2), sulfur dioxide (SO2), ozone (O3), and carbon monoxide (CO). AI captures these statics in real-time to identify the areas of pollution trends and tracks the pollution zones throughout the city. A proper investigation could be conducted by AI for optimizing the patterns of pollution data to pinpoint the source of pollution, whether from traffic, industrial activities, or natural events such as wildfires. This helps city officials take targeted measures to reduce carbon emissions.

Machine Learning Models and set – ups can forecast the future air quality depending on historical data retrieved, climate, and current pollution levels. This grants the municipalities to issue warnings and caution the residents, especially vulnerable populations, and implement short-term measures such as traffic restrictions or increased public transport to reduce pollution.

Water Quality Monitoring and Management

Detection of water purification could be done by the smart sensors these AI-driven sensors observe the water quality in real time by measuring its parameters such as pH levels, turbidity, dissolved oxygen, and the presence of pollutants or other impurities such as heavy metals or pathogens. Thus allowing a quicker detection on any dirt or contamination to be found in the water.

AI algorithms can detect any deviation from normal levels in the water quality data, sparking alerts when water levels deviate from normal safe values. Allowing for an instant response to restrain from any waterborne diseases and protect the health of the public.

Sustainable Water Management

Predictive Analytics for Water Supply: AI can predict water demand based on usage patterns, weather forecasts, and population trends. This helps cities manage water resources more efficiently, ensuring a more sustainable supply.

Leak detection and prevention: AI can analyze data from water distributors to identify leaks or malfunctions. Early detection and repair of leaks can significantly reduce water waste and save resources.

Smart waste collection could be enabled, AI optimizes waste collection routes based on real-time data from sensors in garbage bins, which monitor the amount of waste disposed of and the types of waste. This reduces fuel consumption and emissions from waste collection vehicles while ensuring timely collection of waste. Efficient Recycling AI-driven systems sorting systems at recycling centers use computer vision and machine learning to accurately identify and separate recyclables, increasing recycling rates and reducing waste. Waste reduction strategies by waste generational models AI predicts the waste generation based on the factors such as population growth, economic activity, and consumer behavior. This leads municipalities to implement targeted waste reduction policies, such as promoting waste recycling, composting, or waste-to-energy programs.

Weather forecasting and weather modeling AI processes vast amounts of weather data from satellites, weather stations, and other sources to model and magnify the weather and predicting future trends. This helps the smart cities to grasp the potential impacts of climate change such as higher temperatures, heavier rainfall, or frequent switches in the weather events.AI can allocate the areas within the cities that are particularly affected by the urban heat island effect. By examining the temperature data, AI helps frame the interventions such as increased green spaces, plantation of trees, circulation zones, and cool green roofs to reduce urban temperatures.

Urban green space optimization of vegetation by AI through satellite images and environmental data to assist the health of the urban vegetation, mapping deforested or degraded forests, and identifying any potential new green spaces. This supports biodiversity and improves urban air quality as well as agricultural. Green wall implementation constituting AI models to pin point any suitable areas with the green roofs and walls, which helps to reduce building energy consumption, reducing urban heat island effects, and controls the overall atmospheric energy.

Checking the ecosystems through AI systems set up algorithms in the cameras, drones, and sensors and used the data that is obtained to track down wildlife populations and urban ecosystems in this helps the cities to manage the urban ecosystems, protect endangered species, and maintain a sustainable environmental balance.

Pollution Impact Assessment

AI can control as well as monitor the impact of pollution on local areas of the ecosystems by studying the environmental data along with the environmental indicators for the betterment of the cities and development and the changes made in the management of storage and maintenance to bring a change in the ecosystem.

ENERGY EFFICIENCY AND CARBON FOOTPRINT REDUCTION

Renewable Energy Integration

Smart Grid Management

AI optimizes the integration of renewable energy into urban grids by predicting electricity from solar panels, wind turbines, and other renewables on the snow. This provides a stable source of energy while reducing reliance on fossil fuels.

Energy Demand Forecasting

AI predicts energy demand, enabling cities to adjust energy production and distribution in real time. This helps to reduce energy consumption, reduce emissions, and better manage peak loads.

Carbon Emission Control

Emissions Tracking: AI-powered systems track greenhouse gas emissions from areas such as transportation, business, and residential areas. This information helps cities track progress towards emission reduction targets and implement strategies to reduce their carbon footprint.

Carbon Offset Planning: AI supports the development of carbon offset plans by analyzing data on potential carbon sequestration projects, such as forest restoration or soil carbon sequestration. This allows cities to invest in effective ways to curb urban carbon emissions.

Education and Engagement

Personalized environmental reporting could be reported through AI-powered platforms that can give insights to the residents with personalized comments and environmental reports, such as their carbon footprint, water consumption, and waste generation. This allows individuals to make sustainable choices in their daily lives. Interactive Dashboards Cities can use AI-powered dashboards to display the real-world environmental data such as air quality, water quality, and energy consumption, weather quality. This transparency increases public awareness and participation in the urban environmental issues.

Participatory environmental management where the data collected by AI gets processed and collected by the citizens through mobile apps and sensors, such as climate forecasting, air quality readings or wildlife detection. This crowd sourcing of information supports government monitoring efforts and encourages community participation in environmental policy.

AI-driven platforms enables the people to give their personal opinions, feedback and incentives on the environmental initiatives taken, raise issues such as illegal tax or pollution reports, and send them participate in the decision-making process regarding environmental policies and project AI-driven approaches are transforming environmental monitoring and management in smart cities by providing real-time insights, optimization, and interventions they will be made possible. By inviting AI into the smart cities to address environmental challenges and issues, promotion of sustainable environment, and through creating a healthier, happier and more care - free urban surroundings. Eventually the success and implementation of these projects requires the cooperation and say of the law as well as governments, the private domains, and societies, indulging in righteous AI practices that puts forth the well-being of the humans and priories its city.

Few of the eye-catching trends in the smart cities include the AI-powered advancements which help optimize the healthcare logistics by anticipating demands and ensuring timely stock and availability of the medical supplies that is crucial during emergencies. Real-time data analysis and predictive modelling enables emergency responders to foresee and effectively manage health crises, optimizing resource allocations and response efficiencies.

Enhanced healthcare accessibility can be achieved through AI-powered telemedicine platforms, assisting remote consultations and precise diagnostics. Wearable health devices and mobile applications provide citizens with real-time health insights, empowering proactive management of chronic conditions and promoting individual well-being.

Integrating AI into public health strategies within citizen-centric smart cities leads to communities experiencing improved health outcomes, streamlined healthcare delivery, and fortified urban resilience, shaping robust and more adaptive urban environments for all residents.

Citizen empowerment through AI requires the use of Artificial Intelligence to enhance individuals and their ability to influence society and economic policy. Some empowering strategies – is that AI can select information or preferably any of it based on the person's reports need to ensure that they get the right information as desired.

Language translation is one of the ongoing epidemics that has recently become one of the most widely used AI features among people in smart cities especially breaking down language barriers making it accessible to non-nationals the language of the. Education and skill development can also be improved with the help of AI that is by personalizing and customizing learning and also adjusting the learning strategies used by different individuals, accounting for their speed can help in improvisations of their educational outcomes through online platforms

Foster Civic Engagement through AI

Engagement of the residents through AI in the smart city is necessary for the usage of technology to revise the civic engagement, refining the public services, and developing sensitive urban surroundings to create a socialize able working environment for everyone.

Few ways these strategies can be initiated

Public Forums Using AI

Construction for a designated digital community halls could be created for virtual spaces where citizens can debate and indulge with the local government and law officials in real time, question them and raise issues, and provide feedback on the city planning.

Public's personal and unofficial reviews could be take in charge by using AI, to prioritize the public's sentiments from social media and other online platforms for the standardization of public's incentives on policies and services.

Participatory Decision Making

Residents can vocalize public participation for the development of AI-driven processes that grants citizens to put forth their suggestions and vote on any local projects and campaigns, helping to map out projects of communities importance. Prognostic analytics from the AI systems to forecast the potential impact of proposed policies, initiating for further future informed public debate and decision-making.

Multilingual Support could be obtained by AI through translation services in public gatherings and documents to ensure full participation all the people is taken place including the non-native speakers. Using AI Chabot's to answer citizens' questions 24/7, providing instant access to information about public services, events, and regulations.

AI can be used to send alerts and notify the residents about any local events, public events, and surveys based on the residents personal preferences and interests as well as location.AI can analyze interactions between citizens and public servants to identify ways to increase participation in community activities.

AI data dashboards can be conceived through AI, these dashboards display real-time data on city new and prevailing policies, budgets, and performance indicators, making government actions more transparent and accountable.

Using AI models to control and report on the definiteness and effectiveness of the public policies, schemes and services.

Operation of smart surveys via AI to optimize and diversify harmonized respondent responses in real time, ensuring that all the voices are heard in the urban planning.

Integration of virtual reality simulation in AI, VR tools can appointed to encourage the public to comment and provide their personal feedback on proposed improvements, concerns in any participatory campaigns or environment.

Public safety is safe in the hands of AI where it syncs all the crime data and effectively categorizes resources, and signs up for the citizens in safety planning through society-based apps. Disaster response implementation through AI-driven systems that study real-time data in emergency situations, engaging citizens in coordinated efforts.

Educational Response

AI Literacy Programs that conduct weekly workshops, offline and online classes to educate the public on how the AI technology works, stating its pros and cons, and its importance in the civic engagement.

Spreading awareness to all the youth for starting a AI-powered workshops that will help and build attention of many young people to educate themselves about the governance and participation in virtual city blueprint (Chauncey & McKenna, 2024).

Public relations could be improved through AI by the data retrieved from public and continuously refining public relations strategies. Tracking community sentiments and trust by controlling the changes in public sentiments view and to make sure that all the city policies remain inclined with public's views and priorities.

Collaborating with the NGOs for a non-profits and also universities, technology hubs to develop AI tools for the community's engagement. Citizen- centric Innovation hubs, incubation labs for creating spaces where the public can work with AI experts to collectively develop solutions to urban challenges faced by AI.

By welcoming AI into the smart cities, AI offered initiatives, fostering of civic engagement, and active citizens, leading to more efficient governance and a higher quality of life for residents all. Civic engagement not only enhances the effectiveness of smart city initiatives but also fosters a sense of community and shared responsibility. Where residents feel empowered and involved in shaping their urban experience

Smart Transportation System

Altering a smart transportation systems mechanized by AI which consists the unification of numerous advanced technologies and creates a passage for an effective, safe and secure and sustainable urban transportation systems.

Steps for a sustainable urban transportation system

Stationing of the IOT sensors throughout the city would be highly beneficial for the collection of real-time data on traffic patterns and graphs, vehicle locations, road conditions, and the urban hood. Setting up of the sensors on the roads, traffic lights, public transportation, and parking lots. Vehicle- framework interconnection allows all the types of vehicles to merge with the city's infrastructure such as the traffic lights and road signs, crossings, improving the overall traffic flow and increasing public safety.

Aggregation of the data could be placed in a centralized platform by creating any websites or apps that aggregates data from various sources, including public transportation, private transportation, car sharing agencies, and pedestrians, traffic signals, percentage of the traffic rules being not followed could be noted and analyzed by these platforms.

AI-Driven Traffic Management

Traffic time optimization where in the AI algorithms will subsequently inspect the traffic data in a short period of time and actively adjust the traffic signal timing, supervise the lane assignments, and reroute vehicles to avoid congestion and time consumption. Machine learning models can be precisely used for the prediction of traffic flow depending on the historical data, weather conditions, and special events taking place, allowing for early traffic management.

Incident detections AI models can espial accidents, road defects, or any road hazards in real time and enforce immediate response and alerts emergency teams through re-routing traffic lanes to prevent further congestion and chaos.

Incorporation of buses and shuttles, automated AI-driven vehicles will be blended into the public transportation system, accommodating a user- friendly, efficient, and safe transportation particularly in the areas with defined traffic. AI also checks upon the operations and routing of public transportation, ensuring its accountability and meeting all the requirements simultaneously reducing the consumption of energy.

Promoting the AI-driven autonomous scooters or e-bikes which connect the passengers from public transit hubs to their final destinations for a micro portability.

Mobility-as-a-Service (MAs) is an AI-driven platform that harmonizes various modes of transportation like bus, train, car-sharing, bike-sharing(carpooling), and walking into a single application, resulting in the best results for the individual in terms of user preference, time accumulation, and expenses can be favored through AI-based pricing models for transportation services that alter fares based on the demand, time of day, and the traffic conditions, boosting more congestion and reducing accidents.

Sustainable transportation could popularized through AI by accommodating the EV's in our lives, Electric Vehicle unification is highly beneficial for the environment as it an electric vehicle so there is no concern of pollution. Charging schedules for electric vehicles will be stationed in every area of the city, and manage energy loads to support the grid at any time.AI can route the carbon emissions of various modes of transportation, giving a closer inputs and insights on how to reduce the overall carbon footprint of the city for a developed green sustainable transportation.

Use AI-driven navigation systems that suggest routes with minimal traffic flow, environmental impact taking into the list of factors like traffic patterns, elevations, and vehicle characteristics for less time consumable green routing.

Smart parking solutions could also solved through AI which allocates the parking spaces directly to the drivers based on the nearest available space, reduce parking search time simultaneously traffic congestion.

Advanced parking bookings can be done through AI-controlled prices for parking spaces based on the demand of the location, time and date set parking booking parking encourages efficient use of the site and in the economical point of view. Automated parking spaces can be controlled by AI, optimizing space utilization and reducing parking and recovery times(Ikpe & Ohwoekevwo, 2024).

Safety and security is highly prioritized in smart cities through AI-driven advanced driver assistance systems into vehicles that will prioritize the safety of the driver by providing quick alerts for any potential collisions, pedestrian crossings, and hazards on the roadside. AI supervises and predicts any pedestrian and cyclist movements and adjust traffic signals to avoid any accidents.AI-powered CCTV cameras and systems that scans driveways and public areas for suspicious activity taking place, promising safety and security.

AI travel assistants which introduces to the AI-driven virtual assistants and bots that provide all the travel updates, popular touristic recommendations, and advance bookings and payments that can be assisted via voice or through chat. Creation of personalized features that switch based on the user preferences, locations, and travel history, making it easier to navigate the routing system. Use AI tools that collect and analyze user data to continuously improve transportation system performance, safety, and user experience.

Active maintenance scheduling by AI to foresee when the vehicles, facilities, and the equipment will need maintenance, reducing downtime and preventing costly breakdowns. AI can enhance storage allocations, insuring that the most critical cases are processed first while minimizing disruptions to the transportation system.

COMPLIANCE AND GOVERNANCE

Designing and construction of AI models is essential as it impacts various transportation systems such as congested roads or other forms of public transit before implementing them to ensure they meet the city's objectives and rules. Integrating AI analysis into the automated decision-making process for travel planning, ensuring that the plan is based on effective and accurate data.AI is capable of generating and forecasting detailed reports on the transportation system performance, helping governments remain transparent and accountable to the public.

Ensuring that the transportation systems are united with other smart urban systems, such as energy management, waste collection, and emergency services, to create a cohesive and functional urban hood. Facilitating and sharing information between agencies like health care, environment, and public safety to improve overall urban management and achieve shared benefits (Elassy et al., 2024).

Key Considerations

Equity and access to the society insuring that AI-driven transportation applications are accessible to all residents, including those with the disabilities and also from different socio-economic backgrounds. Addressing the digital divide to ensure access to the right technologies and services and education.

Privacy measures are strictly prioritized and implementation of strong data protection measures to secure personal and confidential information and also aligns with the privacy laws. Safeguard AI systems from cyber threats to maintain the integrity and security of transport systems.

Show how AI algorithms make decisions and study data, to build the users trust. Through developing audit trails to address any issues or concerns related to AI-powered transportation systems

Involvement of residents in the building, designing and implementation of AI transportation initiatives through consultation, examination, and feedback from the people. Educate the public about the benefits and applications of AI in transportation to promote acceptance and participation.

Regular monitoring of the performance of AI-powered transportation systems and make new adjustments depending on the users review and feedback. Continue to adapt to new developments and evolving urban needs to ensure the system remains effective and relevant.

Considering the development of AI into transportation systems, smart cities can be efficient, safe, and user-friendly places. The successful construction, design and implementation of AI-driven transportation solutions based on the ultimate contribution to the consistency of and incorporation of technological innovations, transparency, and public participation a connected and sustainable urban future. Addition of AI in smart cities can create an effective, sustainable, and user-friendly environment. These initiatives will not only improve the lives of residents but also create resilience and adaptability of all urban areas. In conclusion, designing transportation systems in smart cities through AI represents a transformative approach that enhances efficiency, safety, and user experience. By leveraging AI technologies, cities can create dynamic and responsive transportation networks that adapt to real-time conditions and user needs.

Citizen-centric AI in smart cities represents an important way to use technology in a way that prioritizes the citizen's needs, opportunities, and experiences. By initializing civic-centric principles into the blueprint and implementation of AI systems, smart cities can achieve equitable, efficient, and inclusive outcomes (Božić, 2023).

OVERVIEW OF THE FEATURES AND BENEFITS OF AI IN SMART CITIES

Key Benefits

Improved quality of life could be experienced through personalized services, AI tailors the cities services according to the individual's needs and preferences making daily life more resilient and enjoyable for residents. Accessibility is provided by AI systems in the smart cities that ensures that all residents, including those with disabilities, can participate in the technology well and benefit from it.

Assuring transparency by providing clear information and insights about how AI systems work and how data is being used helping in gaining the public's trust and encouraging for a greater future participation in public policies. Regularly incorporating residents input into the building and maintenance of the AI systems creating a sense of ownership and partnership, leading to effective and efficient solutions.

Citizen-centric AI vocalizes and diversifies voices and considerate of all the perspectives given that are included in decision-making processes, resulting in an equitable and representative outcomes.AI focuses on inclusivity and transparency, programs can be designed to reduce biasness and makes sure that all residents are treated equally and fairly, treating differences shall not be granted under the supervision of AI.

Data-Driven Insights and inputs by AI enables smart data-driven decisions that can optimize the overall city blueprint resource allocation, and operations, resulting in improved efficiency and effectiveness. AI systems that prioritize the needs of citizens can better adapt to changing circumstances and requirements, resulting in better service delivery and problem solving (Ejaz et al., 2025).

Ethical Considerations

Privacy and data security by AI ensuring strong data privacy and security measures are implemented to protect residents personal and confidential information and also for maintaining the public's trust in AI systems. Ethical use of AI platforms both constructing and implementing AI systems with ethical considerations in mind to prevent any inappropriate use and ensures that technology serves the public interest.

Efforts should be made to provide equal access to AI technologies and services, ensuring that all residents can benefited from them regardless of socio-economic status or technological skills. Involvement of residents in the implementation of AI programs ensures that solutions align with their needs and preferences, making technology relevant and efficient.AI systems must be constantly updated and reviewed based on the user feedback, economic considerations, and emerging technologies to ensure they continue to better meet the needs of society (Brightwood & Jame, 2024).

Conclusion

A citizen-centric AI in smart cities is not about using advanced technologies and algorithms but also about maintain and conceiving an inclusive, accountable and efficient urban hood. By prioritizing the needs and voices of the residents, Smart cities can harness the power of AI to enhance the quality of life, build trust and engagement, and create positive social change. This approach ensures that the benefits of smart city technologies are widely shared and helps build more connections and friendly communities for everybody

Citizen- centric AI offers a vast amount of opportunities to enhance public needs and to improve their quality of life and foster greater civic engagement. By addressing many challenges and only prioritize their needs, ethical considerations and create a more responsive and an efficient and equitable urban environment. Artificial Intelligence has the potential of improving, empowering inhabitants by boosting the access to information and public services through Artificial intelligence and maximizing the benefits for the people. Driving a wave of innovation and setting new trends and improvising urban transformation and development.

Uniting AI into smart cities provides a route for a more efficient systems for public safety, responsive health care, and sustainable livelihood, an oversight of energy usage which provides a high standard of living, comfort and safety for all the residents. AI in smart cities also faces many challenges that need to be addressed, overcome including data security, ethical considerations, and foundational rules. Assuring that the AI technology is transparent and accountable which is important for building public's trust.

In conclusion, AI has the potential to transform smart cities, driving innovation across sectors while promoting sustainable development and resilience. As cities continue to evolve, thoughtful integration of AI will be key to creating urban environments that are not only intelligent but livable, equitable, and also adaptive for future challenges

REFERENCES

Božić, V. (2023). Artifical intelligence as the reason and the solution of digital divide. Language Education and Technology, 3(2).

Brightwood, S., & Jame, H. (2024). *Data privacy, security, and ethical considerations in AI-powered finance. Article*. Research Gate.

. By Alexander S. Gillis, Technical Writer and Editor George Lawton Ivy Wigmore What is AI ethics? Published: October 2024

. by Radosław Wolniak 1,*ORCID andKinga Stecuła 2,*ORCID "Artificial Intelligence in Smart Cities—Applications, Barriers, and Future Directions": A Review Published: 10 June 2024 Smart Cities 2024, 7(3), 1346-1389; https://doi.org/DOI: 10.3390/smartcities7030057

Cadet, E., Osundare, O. S., Ekpobimi, H. O., Samira, Z., & Wondaferew, Y. (2024). AI-powered threat detection in surveillance systems: A real-time data processing framework. Open Access Research Journal of Engineering and Technology, 7(2), 031-045.

Chauncey, S. A., & McKenna, H. P. (2024). by Sarah A. Chauncey 1ORCID andH. Patricia McKenna 2,*ORCID "Creativity and Innovation in Civic Spaces Supported by Cognitive Flexibility When Learning with AI Chatbots in Smart Cities" Published: 16 February 2024. *Urban Science (Basel, Switzerland)*, *8*(1), 16. DOI: 10.3390/urbansci8010016

Ejaz, U., Ramon, W., & Olaoye, G. (2025). The Role of Big Data and AI in Smart Cities and Urban Planning.

Elassy, M., Al-Hattab, M., Takruri, M., & Badawi, S.Mohamed Elassy a. (2024). Mohammed Al-Hattab [b], Maen Takruri [c], Sufian Badawi [d] "Intelligent transportation systems for sustainable smart cities". *Transportation Engineering*, *16*(June), 100252. DOI: 10.1016/j.treng.2024.100252

Fontes, C., Al Haddad, C., Antoniou, C., & Lütge, C. (2024). Assessing the collective challenges of AI: An applied framework focused on people centeredness and public participation. *Urban Governance*, *4*(4), 245–254.

Lawton, G. (2023). AI transparency: What is it and why do we need it. TechTarget. *Retrieved*, (October), 13.

Nicholas, J. (2019). Schork "ARTIFICIAL INTELLIGENCE AND PERSONALIZED MEDICINE" Published in final edited form as. *Cancer Treatment and Research*, *178*, 265–283. DOI: 10.1007/978-3-030-16391-4_11

Olaniyi, O. O., Okunleye, O. J., & Olabanji, S. O. (2023). Advancing data-driven decision-making in smart cities through big data analytics: A comprehensive review of existing literature. *Current Journal of Applied Science and Technology*, *42*(25), 10–18.

Sayed, A., Himeur, Y., Bensaali, F., & Amira, A. (2022). Aya SayedAya SayedYassine HimeurYassine HimeurFaycal BensaaliFaycal BensaaliAbbes AmiraAbbes Amira " Artificial intelligence with IoT for energy efficiency in buildings" In book. *Emerging Real-World Applications of Internet of Things*, (September), 233–252. Advance online publication. DOI: 10.1201/9781003304203-12

Son, T. H., Weedon, Z., Yigitcanlar, T., Sanchez, T., Corchado, J. M., & Mehmood, R. (2023). Zack Weedon [a], Tan Yigitcanlar [a], Thomas Sanchez [b], Juan M. Corchado [c], Rashid Mehmood [d] "Algorithmic urban planning for smart and sustainable development: Systematic review of the literature". *Sustainable Cities and Society*, *94*(July), 104562. DOI: 10.1016/j.scs.2023.104562

Stahl, B. C., Andreou, A., Brey, P., Hatzakis, T., Kirichenko, A., Macnish, K., & Wright, D. (2021). Artificial intelligence for human flourishing–Beyond principles for machine learning. *Journal of Business Research*, *124*, 374–388.

Zhu, C. (2025, January). Artificial Intelligence Applications in Everyday Life. *Applied and Computational Engineering*, *121*(1), 191–197. DOI: 10.54254/2755-2721/2025.20074

Chapter 5
AI in Crisis Management and Disaster Response for Urban Infrastructure

Nidhi Arora
https://orcid.org/0009-0002-7707-6399
Lovely Professional University, India

Ashok Sharma
https://orcid.org/0000-0003-2553-4263
University of Jammu, India

Sachin Kaushal
Lovely Professional University, India

ABSTRACT

Artificial Intelligence (AI) is increasingly becoming a vital part of crisis management and disaster response, particularly in the context of urban infrastructure. Cities are increasingly vulnerable to both natural and man-made disasters as they grow larger and more interconnected. AI systems have the ability to anticipate, plan for, and handle emergencies more effectively, protecting metropolitan people in the process. The application of AI to the phases of preparedness, response, recovery, and mitigation of disasters is examined in this chapter, with a particular emphasis on how AI may strengthen the resilience of urban infrastructure. We highlight case studies, examine challenges in AI deployment, and propose future directions for AI-driven crisis management systems.

DOI: 10.4018/979-8-3693-7832-8.ch005

1. INTRODUCTION

Cities are intricate ecosystems, home to dense populations, extensive infrastructure, and essential services. When disasters strike—whether natural or human-made—the complexity of urban areas can quickly turn small disruptions into large-scale crises. Recently, artificial intelligence (AI) has become an invaluable tool for city planners, emergency responders, and governments to mitigate the impact of these crises. By processing vast amounts of data and making rapid decisions, AI can significantly improve how we prepare for, respond to, and recover from urban disasters. This chapter delves into the growing integration of AI in crisis management and disaster response for urban infrastructure, examining how it supports resilience, real-time monitoring, and ethical considerations in emergency contexts.

Urban areas are built upon interconnected systems like transportation, energy, water supply, and healthcare. In times of crisis, a disruption in one area can quickly affect others, complicating recovery efforts (Allam & Dhunny, 2019; Voda & Radu, 2018). AI has proven highly effective in enhancing urban infrastructure resilience by predicting and identifying disruptions early on. Batty (2018) highlights AI's role in monitoring critical systems in smart cities, enabling faster recovery by proactively addressing potential weak points. AI-driven predictive maintenance is also used to manage stress on infrastructure like power grids and water supplies, helping to prevent minor issues from escalating into major crises (Agarwal et al., 2015; Veselov et al., 2021).

AI's predictive abilities are especially beneficial for preparing cities against natural disasters. By analyzing historical data, satellite imagery, and real-time environmental information, AI models can accurately forecast events like floods, earthquakes, and wildfires (Golubchikov & Thornbush, 2020; Ahmed et al., 2021). For instance, the Netherlands uses AI for flood prediction, showing how proactive risk management can be achieved through data-driven models (Agarwal et al., 2015). Japan's advanced early warning systems, supported by AI, provide critical moments of preparation for earthquakes, helping to reduce injuries and fatalities (Kirwan & Zhiyong, 2020).

During crises, AI systems are essential for real-time monitoring and alerting, analyzing information from weather forecasts, sensors, and even social media. These systems help allocate resources more effectively, guiding emergency responders to the areas of greatest need (Luckey et al., 2020). AI-powered drones and autonomous vehicles further assist by assessing damage and delivering supplies to areas inaccessible to people, such as post-earthquake zones or active fire sites (Srivastava et al., 2017).

However, the use of AI in disaster response introduces ethical considerations, such as privacy, bias, and accountability (Holzinger et al., 2019). For example, AI systems often need access to sensitive data, raising privacy concerns that necessitate strict data security measures (Voda & Radu, 2019). Additionally, biases within AI training datasets can lead to unequal resource allocation, potentially neglecting marginalized communities. To address this, diverse datasets and frequent testing are recommended (Hamet & Tremblay, 2017). Accountability is another key concern, as the use of AI in life-critical decisions requires strong human oversight (Ahmed et al., 2021).

This chapter will explore how AI is reshaping crisis management and disaster response in cities, from flood prediction to organizing evacuations. While AI is increasingly essential, it's equally important to consider the ethical implications of entrusting AI with such high-stakes responsibilities. Figure ure 1 discusses components of Urban Infrastructure in Crisis Management.

Figure 1. Components of urban infrastructure in crisis management.

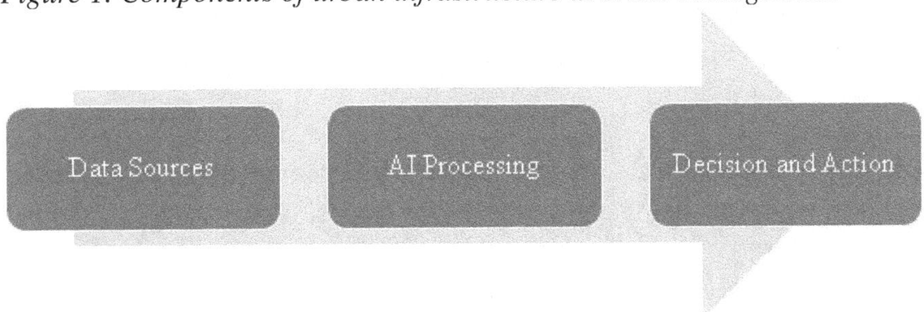

2. CRISIS MANAGEMENT IN URBAN SETTINGS

2.1 Urban Infrastructure in Focus

Urban infrastructure encompasses everything from transportation systems like roads and subways to essential services like water supply, power grids, and healthcare. In times of crisis, these systems need to work harmoniously to avoid widespread breakdowns. For example, if a natural disaster like an earthquake hit, it's not just roads and buildings that are affected—communication lines, power, and even the water supply may fail, making recovery and rescue efforts more difficult.

2.2 Understanding Crisis in Urban Areas

Disasters affecting urban areas can stem from natural causes, such as earthquakes, hurricanes, or floods, but they can also be human-made, such as cyberattacks, terrorist attacks, or infrastructure failures. Each type of crisis comes with its own set of challenges. For instance, while an earthquake may lead to collapsed buildings and blocked roads, a cyberattack on critical systems could leave the entire city's power grid down for days, paralyzing many services.

2.3 The Growing Role of AI in Crisis Management

AI offers tools that can vastly improve our ability to manage crises. Its ability to sift through large volumes of information quickly, recognize patterns, and help guide decision-making can be invaluable during a disaster. Figure ure 2 presents the applications of AI in disaster response scenarios. Some of the ways AI is being used include:

1) **Predicting Disasters**: AI can analyse historical data and current trends to predict potential crises. This helps cities prepare for floods, power outages, or other potential threats.
2) **Monitoring and Alerting in Real-Time**: AI systems can scan weather reports, sensor data, or even social media to detect the early signs of a problem, giving authorities precious time to act before disaster strikes.
3) **Optimizing Resource Allocation**: AI helps in deciding where to send rescue teams, how to manage limited resources, and which areas need immediate attention based on real-time conditions.

Figure 2. Applications of AI in disaster response scenarios

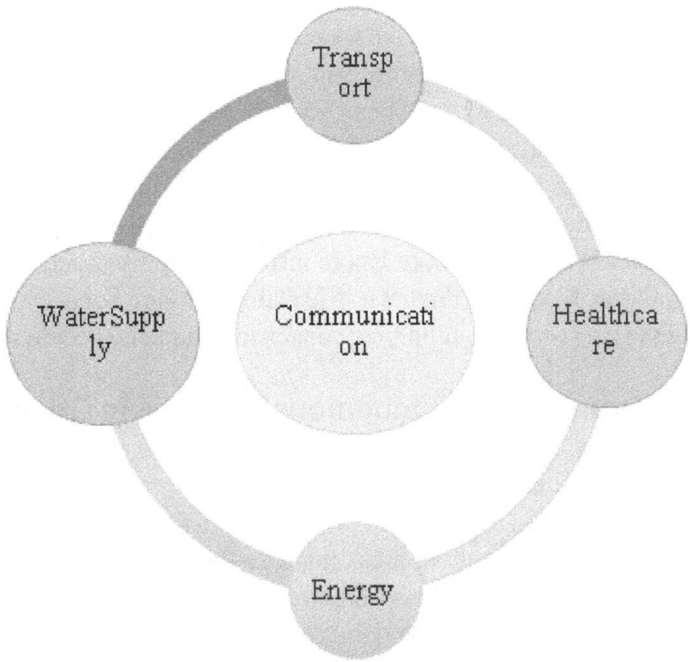

3. AI'S IMPACT ON DISASTER RESPONSE

3.1 Advanced Early Warning Systems

One of the most visible benefits of AI in disaster response is its use in early warning systems. These systems rely on a variety of data inputs, like weather forecasts or seismic activity monitors, to detect potential dangers before they fully unfold. For example, an AI-driven system might analyze weather patterns and forecast the potential for flooding several days in advance, allowing authorities to issue warnings and prepare for evacuations.

For communities in flood-prone areas, AI-based tools can mean the difference between chaos and orderly evacuations. They ensure that people in the most vulnerable areas are informed early, allowing them to evacuate before it's too late.For communities in flood-prone areas, AI-based tools can mean the difference between chaos and orderly evacuations. They ensure that people in the most vulnerable areas are informed early, allowing them to evacuate before it's too late.

3.2 Coordinating Emergency Responses

Disasters often lead to confusion and breakdowns in communication, as emergency responders—fire Figure hters, police, and medical teams—scramble to Figure ure out where to go and what to do. AI can act as a central hub, managing and prioritizing responses. These systems track the locations of rescue teams and resources, directing them to the most critical areas based on real-time data.

For example, during a flood, AI could prioritize rescuing people from areas where the water is rising fastest or where infrastructure like bridges and roads are at risk of collapse. It can also predict traffic patterns during large-scale evacuations, suggesting the best routes to minimize congestion and keep people safe.

3.3 Using Drones and Autonomous Vehicles in Crisis Zones

Drones and autonomous vehicles equipped with AI technology are revolutionizing disaster response efforts. These tools can assess damage, deliver essential supplies, and even search for survivors in areas that may be too dangerous for humans to reach immediately. Drones with AI-based imaging capabilities can quickly scan affected areas to map out the most damaged parts of a city, allowing rescue teams to prioritize their efforts.

Autonomous vehicles are also playing a crucial role. Without risking human lives, these vehicles can deliver emergency supplies or medical aid to areas that are cut off due to floods or earthquakes.

3.4 Assessing Damage and Planning Recovery

In the aftermath of a disaster, one of the biggest challenges is Figure uring out the scale of the damage. Traditionally, this has been a slow, manual process, but AI is speeding things up. With the help of aerial images from satellites or drones, AI algorithms can assess the extent of damage to buildings, roads, and bridges. This allows city officials to quickly determine where repairs are most urgently needed, streamlining the recovery process and getting the city back on its feet more quickly.

4. PREVENTING CRISES THROUGH PREDICTIVE AI TOOLS

4.1 Predictive Maintenance of Infrastructure

Urban infrastructure is always under stress—from heavy use, natural wear, and sometimes inadequate maintenance. AI can predict when critical parts of this infrastructure might fail. By continuously monitoring systems like water pipes, bridges, and electrical grids, AI can detect minor issues before they turn into major problems, allowing for preventive maintenance.

For example, a city could use AI to monitor its electrical grid, identifying areas that are at risk of power outages before a crisis hits. This preemptive approach can prevent large-scale blackouts during extreme weather events or other emergencies.

4.2 AI for Climate Prediction and Urban Planning

AI is being increasingly used to predict the likelihood of climate-related disasters, such as hurricanes, heat waves, or wildfires. AI-based models analyze massive amounts of data from satellites, historical weather patterns, and environmental sensors to give a more accurate forecast of when and where these events might happen.

With better climate predictions, city planners can take proactive steps to fortify infrastructure, such as building flood barriers or reinforcing vulnerable buildings in areas prone to earthquakes. This can significantly reduce the damage caused when disasters strike.

5. ADDRESSING ETHICAL AND PRACTICAL CHALLENGES OF AI IN DISASTER RESPONSE

5.1 Protecting Privacy and Data

AI often requires access to sensitive information to be effective, such as data from social media, sensor networks, or even personal devices like smartphones. This raises concerns about privacy. In crisis situations, where speed is of the essence, balancing the need for real-time data with privacy protections becomes tricky.

To address these concerns, systems using AI in disaster response must be designed with strong data security protocols, ensuring that personal information is only used when absolutely necessary and in ways that comply with local privacy laws.

5.2 Dealing with Bias in AI Algorithms

AI systems are trained on historical data, and if that data contains biases—perhaps because it under represents certain populations—the AI may make biased decisions. This is a serious issue, especially in disaster response, where lives are at stake. AI might inadvertently allocate fewer resources to minority communities if its training data didn't fully account for their needs.

It is essential to ensure that AI is trained on diverse and representative data sets, and to continually test these systems for bias, so that all populations receive equal attention during a crisis.

5.3 Accountability in AI Decision Making

With AI making decisions in life-threatening situations, the question of accountability is crucial. If an AI system makes a wrong call—delaying rescue efforts or misallocating resources—who is responsible? Is it the creators of the system, the users, or both?

To avoid such dilemmas, human oversight is critical. AI should be used to support decision-making, not replace it. This ensures that humans remain in control, taking responsibility for the final decisions made during a disaster.

6. REAL-WORLD EXAMPLES OF AI IN URBAN CRISIS MANAGEMENT

6.1 Earthquake Response in Japan

Japan, due to its vulnerability to earthquakes, has integrated AI into its early warning systems. AI-driven tools analyze seismic data and send alerts just seconds before an earthquake hits, giving people a chance to take cover or evacuate. Additionally, drones powered by AI assess damage after the quake, helping authorities focus their efforts where they're most needed.

6.2 Flood Prediction in the Netherlands

The Netherlands has long fought against flooding, and AI is now a key player in its flood management strategies. AI systems analyze real-time data from rivers, dams, and weather forecasts to predict floods and determine which areas are most at risk. By issuing warnings early, these systems help prevent catastrophic damage and loss of life.

6.3 AI-Assisted Wildfire Management in California

Wildfires have become an annual threat in California, and AI is now being used to help combat them. AI-based systems use satellite imagery, weather data, and historical fire patterns to predict where wildfires might spread. This allows fire-Figure hting teams to act more strategically. AI-powered drones are also deployed to monitor fires in real-time and detect new ones before they spiral out of control. Table 1 details about the Data for evaluating disaster response efficiency over time.

Table 1. Data for evaluating disaster response efficiency over time

Disaster Type	AI Prediction Accuracy (%)	Time to Response (hrs)	Resource Allocation Accuracy (%)
Floods	95	2	90
Earthquakes	92	1	88
Wildfires	89	3	85
Cyberattacks	85	0.5	80

7. FUTURE CHALLENGES

As AI continues to shape how we handle crises in our cities, it brings some big challenges to the table—challenges that touch not just on technology but on people's lives and privacy. One major hurdle will be keeping these AI systems adaptable to the chaos of real-world emergencies. Disasters unfold in unpredictable ways, and AI needs to handle sudden changes, often relying on complex algorithms and massive amounts of diverse data to make fast, informed decisions.

At the same time, we face the delicate task of respecting privacy while using data that often comes from personal sources like social media or mobile devices. In a crisis, when speed matters most, how do we protect individual privacy and still use the data needed to keep people safe? There's also the issue of bias. If AI systems aren't trained on data that accurately reflects all parts of the community, they might unintentionally leave some groups behind in moments when fair and equal response is crucial.

8. CONCLUSION

The integration of AI into urban disaster response and crisis management is opening up new possibilities for faster, more accurate, and more efficient responses to emergencies. By leveraging the predictive power and data processing capabilities of AI, cities are becoming better equipped to handle crises, from natural disasters like floods and earthquakes to man-made threats like cyber attacks. However, as we continue to rely more on AI, it's crucial to address the ethical challenges, ensuring that this technology is used responsibly and fairly.

REFERENCES

Agarwal, P. K., Gurjar, J., Agarwal, A. K., & Birla, R. (2015). Application of artificial intelligence for development of intelligent transport system in smart cities. *Journal of Traffic and Transportation Engineering*, *1*(1), 20–30.

Ahmed, S., Hossain, M., Kaiser, M. S., Noor, M. B., Mahmud, M., & Chakraborty, C. (2021). Artificial intelligence and machine learning for ensuring security in smart cities. In Data-driven mining, learning and analytics for secured smart cities, Springer, Champp. 23-47.

Allam, Z., & Dhunny, Z. A. (2019). On big data, artificial intelligence and smart cities. *Cities (London, England)*, *89*, 80–91. DOI: 10.1016/j.cities.2019.01.032

Batty, M. (2018). Artificial intelligence and smart cities. *Environment and Planning. B, Urban Analytics and City Science*, *45*(1), 3–6. DOI: 10.1177/2399808317751169

Bokhari, S. A., & Myeong, S. (2022). Use of artificial intelligence in smart cities for smart decision-making: A social innovation perspective. *Sustainability (Basel)*, *14*(2), 620. DOI: 10.3390/su14020620

Golubchikov, O., & Thornbush, M. (2020). Artificial intelligence and robotics in smart city strategies and planned smart development. Smart Cities, 3(4).

Holzinger, A., Langs, G., Denk, H., Zatloukal, K., & Müller, H. (2019). Causability and explainability of artificial intelligence in medicine. *Wiley Interdisciplinary Reviews. Data Mining and Knowledge Discovery*, *9*(4), e1312. DOI: 10.1002/widm.1312 PMID: 32089788

Kirwan, C. G., & Zhiyong, F. (2020). *Smart cities and artificial intelligence: Convergent systems for planning, design, and operations*. Elsevier.

Luckey, D., Fritz, H., Legatiuk, D., Dragos, K., & Smarsly, K. (2020). Artificial intelligence techniques for smart city applications. In *International Conference on Computing in Civil and Building Engineering* (pp. 3-15). Springer, Cham.

Srivastava, S., Bisht, A., & Narayan, N. (2017). Safety and security in smart cities using artificial intelligence—A review. In *2017 7th International Conference on Cloud Computing, Data Science & Engineering-Confluence*, IEEEpp. 130-133.

Veselov, G., Tselykh, A., Sharma, A., & Huang, R. (2021). Applications of Artificial Intelligence in Evolution of Smart Cities and Societies. *Informatica, 45*(5). *EAI Endorsed Transactions on Smart Cities*, *6*(3), e5.

Voda, A. I., & Radu, L. D. (2018). Artificial intelligence and the future of smart cities. *BRAIN.Broad Research in Artificial Intelligence and Neuroscience*, *9*(2), 110–127.

Voda, A. I., & Radu, L. D. (2019). How can artificial intelligence respond to smart cities challenges? In *Smart Cities: Issues and Challenges,* Elsevierpp. 199-216. DOI: 10.1016/B978-0-12-816639-0.00012-0

Winston, P. H. (1992). *Artificial intelligence*. Addison-Wesley Longman Publishing Co., Inc. Hamet, P., & Tremblay, J. (2017). Artificial intelligence in medicine. *Metabolism: Clinical and Experimental*, *69*, S36–S40.

Chapter 6
AI-Driven Healthcare: Transformation and Advancement

Harjinder Kaur
Lovely Professional University, India

Shilpa
Lovely Professional University, India

ABSTRACT

Artificial Intelligence has brought significant advances in the healthcare sector regarding diagnosis, medication, and patient-centric care. Artificial intelligence technologies, such as natural language processing and machine learning, have been utilized to predict various diseases early to help diagnose and treat them appropriately. In the healthcare sector, integrating AI tools and applications facilitates healthcare services such as remote monitoring and telehealth, hereby improving healthcare accessibility which further aids in continuous patient engagement, monitoring, and care outside traditional medical situations. Additionally AI helps in extending personalized medicine, which further helps where it helps in the modification of treatment plans for individual patients by considering their health-related risk factors such as genetic makeup, lifestyle, and previous medical history, thereby augmenting their therapeutic outcomes. AI is revolutionizing the field of drug discovery by accelerating and identifying possible therapeutic applicants by optimizing their clinical trials.

DOI: 10.4018/979-8-3693-7832-8.ch006

1. INTRODUCTION

The healthcare sector is one of the vast and complex industries where vast amounts of data are being generated so the adoption of artificial intelligence in the healthcare sector is prominent to provide health-related services such as detection, prevention, and diagnosis of the patient's diseases. AI technologies have the potential to provide efficient services and enhance patient outcomes in the healthcare sector that is integrated with advanced technologies which is known as digital healthcare. Digital healthcare is the healthcare that is amalgamated with digital technologies to provide healthcare services and enhance care. Mostly, the healthcare sector is leveraging AI technologies which the healthcare sector has promoted as an AI-driven healthcare sector (Bajwa et al., 2021).

AI-driven healthcare sector is enhancing the services related to public healthcare by an integration of Artificial intelligence with digital healthcare. AI-driven healthcare services reshaping healthcare by diagnosis enhancements, improvement in treatments, and patient-care services. AI technologies are changing the healthcare sector into digital healthcare (Alowais et al., 2023).

1.1 Integration of Healthcare and Artificial Intelligence

Artificial intelligence is one of the groundbreaking approaches to reshaping healthcare services such as health outcomes, and patient data analysis to generate electronic health records and improve operational efficiency. AI helps simplify the patients' lives, doctors, and administrative tasks. With AI technologies, doctors can provide accurate diagnoses to patients and reports can be easily handled using electronic health records (Maleki Varnosfaderani & Forouzanfar, 2024).

There are various ways of integrating AI into public health (Alowais et al., 2023) as shown in Figure 1:

Figure 1. Integration benefits of AI in healthcare

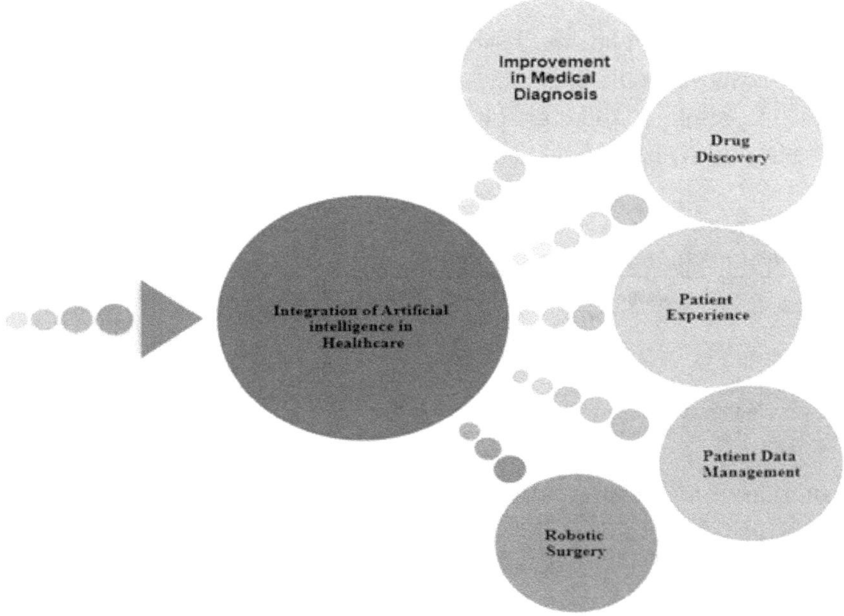

- **Improvement in Medical Diagnosis:** AI helps to improve medical diagnosis considering the medical reports that can lead to human errors or death. AI helps in the detection, prediction, and diagnosis of diseases speedily for enhancement in the outcomes (Alowais et al., 2023).
- **Drug Discovery:** AI helps to design drugs speedily using data analysis, formulation, data modeling, and simulation due to the involvement of advanced and modern technologies. AI helps to identify biological targets and molecules are designed that interact with those biological targets
- **Patient Experience:** AI helps patients with digital communications that offer reminders regarding appointment schedules, and provide health tips for better treatments. AI helps to improve the accuracy of a patient visit which helps to allow hospitals, patients, and doctors to provide better results daily.
- **Patient Data Management:** AI helps to improve data management in hospitals. A huge amount of data is being generated by the hospitals that are being processed by the hospital management team in less time and cost.
- **Robotic Surgery:** Robotic surgery helps doctors to deal with complicated cases, painless surgery, and helps to provide quicker recovery.

1.2 Milestones of AI applications in health

The milestones of AI in healthcare indicate an integration of AI (Mindinventory, n.d.) (For a website with no author, use the site name and "n.d." for no date.) in health practice, research, and digital health. The following table1 defines a few milestones related to AI in the healthcare sector:

Table 1. AI Milestone in the healthcare sector

Sr No	AI milestone	Example
1	1950s – Early Foundations	• Alan Turing and the Turing Test • AI-applicatio sin medical research
2	1970s – Early AI Systems in Medicine	• MYCIN (1972) • CASNET (1975)
3	1980s – Rise of Clinical Decision Support Systems	• Internist-I and CADUCEUS (1980s) • Computer-Assisted radiology
4	1990s – AI and Medical Imaging Advances	• AI-based Picture Archiving and Communication Systems • Medical Imaging
5	2000s – AI for Genomic Data and Personalized Medicine	• Geonomic Data analysis system • Watson for Oncology (2007)
6	2010s – AI-Driven Diagnostics and Predictive Analytics	• DeepMind's Healthcare application • AI based da Vinci Surgical System
7	2017 – FDA Approval of AI-Based Diagnostic Systems	• AI-approved medical imaging (Arterys) • AI-Approved diabetic detection system (IDx-DR)
8	2019 – AI and Drug Discovery	• AI-based drug discovery system' • Insilico Medicine
9	2020 – AI in the Figureht Against COVID-19	• AI-powered systems such as BlueDot and HealthMap • Vaccine Development
10	2021-2023 – AI for Remote Care and Health Equity	• AI-enabled telemedicine platform • AI-enable Health disparities
11	Future Directions: AI in Precision Medicine and Beyond	• Patient-Specific treatment • Real-time monitoring

2. PUBLIC HEALTH

Public Health is a medical practice involved in preventing diseases, prolonging life, and improving well-being through organized efforts and the exercise of society, business, community, and individual choices. It entails a population approach which means that its purpose is to select healthy habits among the population to enhance their health rather than only treating patients. The core functions of public health include (Zeng et al., 2021) (Morley et al., 2020):

1. **Health Surveillance and Monitoring**: Monitoring outcomes and characteristics of diseases and health situation trends.
2. **Health Promotion:** Promoting some activities that are healthy for the body and mind.
3. **Disease Prevention:** Candidate prevention initiatives that could include health policies and programs that help to reduce the chance of a particular disease including vaccination campaigns or smoking cessation programs.
4. **Environmental Health:** Dispositions such as; environmental degradation, quality nutrition, and sanitation with a special focus on clean water.
5. **Health Policy and Management:** Policymaking and exercising stewardship for the envisaged enhancement of health systems for health service delivery.

2.1 Role of Digital Healthcare in Public Health

Digital healthcare is the incorporation of technologies such as telemedicine, health applications, artificial intelligence, and EHRs into the healthcare system. Its role in public health is increasingly crucial and includes the following contributions: Its role in public health is increasingly crucial, and includes the following contributions (Maroju et al., 2023):

1. **Telemedicine and Telehealth:** Through these technologies, physicians can give consultations from a distance, and this in turn enhances the reach of health care especially to areas that are under-served or located in rural areas. Telehealth may have the benefit of putting less pressure on ordinary and traditional health facilities and may have strength in preventive health care.
2. **Health Information Systems:** Personal Health Records (PHRs) and Health IT Networks including the EHR and HIEs are useful in the gathering, processing, and sharing of health information. They minimize the time consumed in the delivery of services, allow the tracking of disease incidences, and aid in decision-making for public health interventions.
3. **Surveillance and Disease Tracking**: Technological advancement and participation in the usage of web-based applications and tools for health trends and conducting an outbreak (for instance COVID tracking application). This enables the identification of some outcomes in the process as requiring intervention, thus providing more prompt and accurate responses to them (Budd et al., 2020).

4. **Health Promotion through Mobile Health (mHealth):** Mobile health applications and wearable devices improve health information and health literacy, monitor physical activity, and positively foster health citizenship; thus, contributing to disease prevention and control efforts.
5. **Artificial Intelligence (AI) and Machine Learning:** Such technologies are used for the data analysis of large databases as well as for making predictions regarding the emergence of viruses, for studying the epidemiology of illnesses, and for determining the effective use of resources. Based on the demographic and health data, auto-driven models can also further underpin the persona-health interventions put in place (Al Kuwaiti et al., 2023).
6. **Big Data and Analytics:** Here, public health agencies can use big data coming from various sources goods (social networks, Health Electronic Records, mobile data, etc.) to understand the trends in health, evaluate risks, and enhance interventions in provisions of public health.
7. **Patient Engagement and Education:** Mobile applications, social media pages, blogs, and websites promote patient awareness by offering information on how to prevent diseases, various treatments, and ways of healthy living. This puts the people in a position to make improved health decisions and this is in line with the goals of public health.

2.2 Benefits of Digital Healthcare in Public Health

- **Increased Access:** Remote and underserved populations can access healthcare services more easily.
- **Efficiency:** Digital tools reduce the time and cost involved in public health initiatives, including immunization campaigns, health screenings, and disease prevention programs.
- **Enhanced Data Utilization:** Real-time data collection and analysis improve decision-making and resource allocation.
- **Improved Health Literacy:** Digital platforms promote health education and awareness, which helps individuals and communities adopt healthier behaviors.

2.3 Tools Used for Public Health

A wide variety of technologies have been employed in digital healthcare to enhance patient care, expedite the delivery of healthcare, and further enhance public health outcomes. The following Figure 2 are important tools in digital healthcare:

Figure 2. Digital healthcare tools

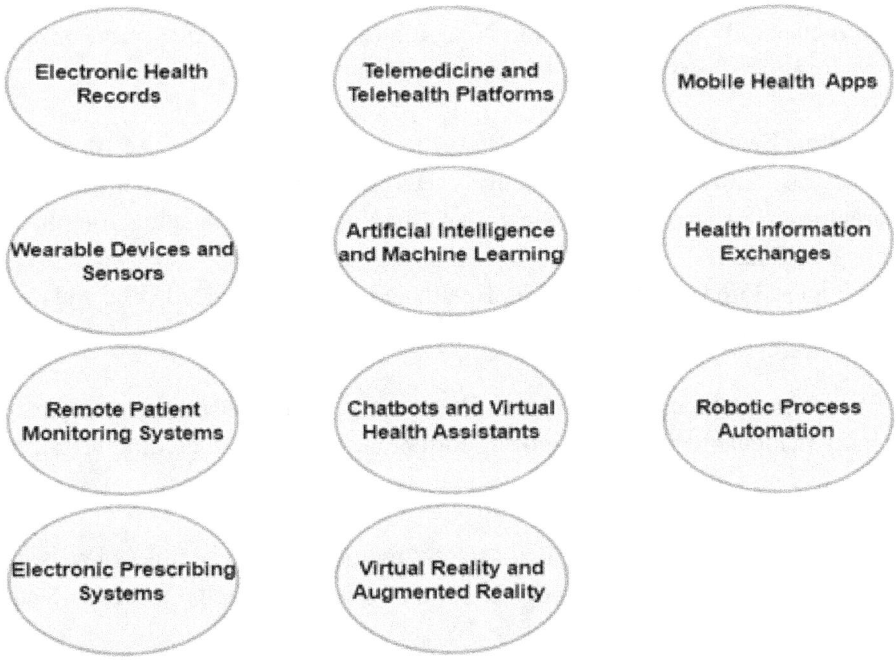

1. **Electronic Health Records (EHRs):** In EHRs the electronic copies of the traditional paper-based patient records whereby patients' records can be retrieved instantly for further update by the healthcare provider.

Benefits: Helps to avoid duplications in tests, increases the effectiveness of communication among the medical personnel, and increases the safety of the patient by having complete and easily accessible medical histories (Dalal et al., 2021).

Examples: Ambitious, WebCentric, Ingenix, NextGen, RelayMed, and SRS.

2. **Telemedicine and Telehealth Platforms:** Using Telemedicine and Telehealth Platforms assists the healthcare providers should be allowed to assess, manage, and even follow up with patients via video calls, phone calls, or even text.

Benefits: Improves the overall capability of delivering care to patients who have little or no access to care, eliminates the need for constantly coming into the clinic, and enhances control over chronic diseases.

Examples: To name a few, there are Teladoc, Amwell, and MDM Live.

3. **Mobile Health (mHealth) Apps:** Mobile applications that are applied by people in their daily lives both for their general health, as well as in case they or their family members need to consult a doctor, receive treatment, or other health-related services.

Benefits: Enables one to follow up with their exercise regimen, check their body vitals, oversee illnesses, and encourage checkups. Apps for reinforcement of the different domains also include; Mental health: Nutrition: Medication compliance (Istepanian, 2022).

Examples: Fitness: MyFitnessPal, Health and well-being: Headspace and medication: Medisafe.

4. **Wearable Devices and Sensors:** Wearable gadgets that are attached to the body that enable the tracking of important health factors including heart rate, movement, sleep, and blood oxygen levels.

Benefits: It allows a subject to constantly monitor his or her fitness levels, get feedback immediately, and even detect if he or she is developing a certain health condition (Mbunge et al., 2021).

Examples: Apple Watch; Fitbit; Oura Ring; glucose monitoring sensors.

5. **Artificial Intelligence and Machine Learning:** Artificial Intelligence (AI) and Machine learning are the two interconnected fields of computer science that have dominated the discussion around advancing technology for several years. The healthcare data comprises extensive data on patients, and the use of AI algorithms helps in diagnostic determination and treatment plans.

Benefits: Facilitates decision-making since patients' characteristics can be used to predict the occurrence of certain diseases, and helps in predicting diseases so that early diagnoses can be made.

Examples: IBM Watson Health, Google DeepMind which focuses on the application of Artificial Intelligence in the diagnosis of medical images, and PathAI which uses Artificial Intelligence in pathology (Rubinger et al., 2023).

6. **Health Information Exchanges (HIEs):** HIEs are the systems through which patient's electronic health information can be exchanged among healthcare practitioners and facilities.

Benefits: Enhances patient care as the providers are well informed and up-to-date on a patient's medical records and history that would have been repeated severally.

Examples: CommonWell Health Alliance, and Carequality are some of the qualified intermediary networks.

7. **Remote Patient Monitoring (RPM) Systems:** The systems that are used to continuously monitor patients using technology that can be accessed remotely and can be used to track the health of patients over the years are referred to as Remote Patient Monitoring (RPM) Systems. It provides the technological solutions that allow the assessment of the patient's condition without physical contact or visits, using instead the monitoring of vital signs and other related parameters.

Benefits: Assists in the control and treatment of diseases such as diabetes, hypertension, and heart disease; the control of repeated hospitalization; and prevention.

Examples: Blood pressure (iHealth), glucose (Medtronic), apnoea (ResMed) monitoring.

Chatbots and Virtual Health Assistants: The upcoming states designed for confirmation with the enhanced chatbots and Virtual Health Assistants are the mobile applications that help patients communicate with AI that's involved in a patient's health, then being able to receive information about the health status of the patient, answer questions, and assist the patient in various health processes • (Zhang & Zheng, 2021).

Benefits: Engages patients in their care more effectively, absolves the health workforce of several tasks, and ensures care for minor health complications round the clock.

Examples: Woebot (mental health chatbot), Babylon Health (application for an AI consultation with a GP), and Ada Health (the app that identifies users' symptoms).

8. **Robotic Process Automation (RPA):** The automation speeds up the time that should be spent dealing with such tasks with the help of software robots, for example, patient scheduling, billing, and administrative activities.

Benefits: Decreases the probability of people's mistakes, cuts time consumption, and optimizes the execution of tasks in healthcare.

Examples: Some of the popular RPA tools are UiPath, and Automation Anywhere.

9. **Electronic Prescribing Systems (e-Prescribing):** Electronic prescribing systems are the services that help healthcare providers to send prescriptions electronically to the pharmacies.

Benefits: Reduces the problems relating to prescription errors, consistency in the medication process, and improves medication compliance.

Examples: DrFirst, Surescripts.

10. **VR & Augmented Reality:** Technologies that are widely applied in medicine including training and educational modules, surgical preplanning, and rehabilitation processes for patients.

Benefits: Facilitates medical learning, refines the surgeon's hand, and works for disorders such as PTSD or chronic pain (Lakshminarayanan et al., 2023).

Examples: Oculus: Virtual Reality for Medical Education, AccuVein: Augmented Reality for identification of veins.

These tools have brought great changes to the healthcare systems and activities and enhanced the efforts to assist the general public and improve the general health status of the citizens.

3. ADVANCED TECHNOLOGIES IN PUBLIC HEALTH

Cutting-edge technologies are bringing innovations and advancements in the healthcare sector to improve patient outcomes and enhance healthcare services. Various technologies are highlighted in the below sections:

3.1 AI Technologies in Public Health

Artificial Intelligence (AI) and related technologies are increasingly transforming public healthcare by enhancing the ability to predict, prevent, and manage health crises while improving access, efficiency, and outcomes. Below are some key AI-driven technologies and their roles in public healthcare shows in Figure 3:

Figure 3. Artificial Intelligence technologies in public health

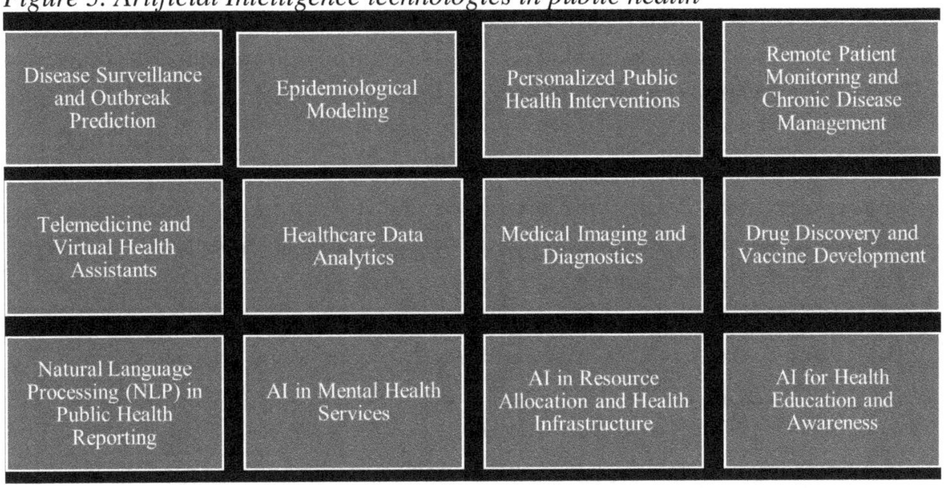

1. **Epidemiology and Disease Control and Modelling:** AI for EarlAI can use big data processing from multiple sources and identify peculiarities in health patterns thereby predicting outbreaks of diseases. This makes it possible for the public health departments to act ahead of most times such as during the COVID-19 period where artificial intelligence was applied well in helping to forecast and monitor the spread of the virus.

Example: Another system to identify the trend of COVID-19 in Wuhan was BlueDot an AI platform that uses data on flight patterns, local media, and epidemiology information.

2. **Epidemiological Modeling:** Predictive Analytics: It is used in the prognosis of epidemiology, estimating effects of health promotion actions and intervention, and evaluating health care usage requirements during an outbreak of an infectious disease. These models utilize real-time data and they can mimic diverse conditions and these are very helpful in the formulation of decisions regarding public health.

Example: Deep learning models from Google's AI and IBM Watson for instance were employed during the pandemic to predict the number of cases, admission records, and consequences of the lockdown.

3. **Personalized Public Health Interventions:** Demographic, environmental, and genetic data is fed to AI algorithms that decide the most suitable interventions for certain populations. This makes its prevention and treatment easier especially in high-risk groups thus making them better populations to recommend vaccines to.

Example: In cancer screening programs, that involve identifying people with genetic predispositions, behaviors, and conditions that put them at risk to initiate early action, AI tools are employed.

4. **RPM and Chronic Disease Management:** Wearable gadgets and sensors feed data to Artificial Intelligence-based algorithms to track patients with chronic illnesses, for example, diabetes, hypertension, and cardiological ailments. The AI, for example, can alert any anomaly in real-time and also suggest appropriate approaches to coping with the symptoms as well as managing the diseases by both the patients and the doctors.

Example: Biofourmis is the AI solution that provides tele-monitoring of important parameters of the patient's condition and possible deterioration which usually leads to hospitalization and allows more effective and timely intervention.

5. **The Use of Telemedicine and Virtual Health Assistants:** Integration of AI in telemedicine systems: AI will bring virtual health, assistants, chatbots, and automated diagnosis to telemedicine and generally makes healthcare more easily available especially in rural areas or to people with less access to health services. These technologies can help to sort clients, set up appointments, and provide recommendations for the appropriate course of treatment.

Example: Babylon Health's chatbots allow people to exhibit symptoms, navigate through medical questions, and receive professional healthcare advice regardless of the location.

6. **Healthcare Data Analytics:** Big data gathered from the EHRs, insurers' claims, social demographics, and genomic data helps AI technologies find insights that can better inform public health initiatives. These insights assist in the identification of disease trends, the distribution of resources, and the revelation of health inequalities.

Example: Optum and Health Catalyst big data and artificial intelligence use tools to extract insight into the EHR and aid in enhancing the outcomes of preventive services offered to people.

7. **Medical Imaging and Diagnostics:** This is the ability of the AI algorithms to interpret radiology results including X-rays, CT scans, and MRI among others, and diagnose diseases early and with better accuracy than the radiologists. This capability is used in screening programs that are common in the community like the screening for tuberculosis or breast cancer.

Example: The latest AI development by Google DeepMind AI, can diagnose more than 50 different forms of eye diseases from retinal scans with efficiency just as efficient as the best ophthalmologists.

8. **Drugs and Vaccines:** By analyzing biological data AI helps in discovering new drugs and vaccines and in finding previously unnoticed therapeutic targets. It also assists in the modeling of how individual compounds affect pathogens, which altogether reduces the period taken on the research and development.

Example: BenevolentAI and Insilico Medicine in their efforts use Artificial Intelligence to predict drug candidates and reposition drugs existing in the market. During COVID-19, it proved helpful in finding a molecule that could potentially combat the virus.

9. **Natural Language Processing (NLP) in Public Health Reporting:** Others analyze unstructured health data across clinical notes, social media platforms, or news articles and help public health agencies with trend analysis, monitoring the sentiment, and healthcare needs.

Example: Social media and newscasts, journals, and press releases were sampled during the Ebola and Zika viral diseases to assess public and media awareness of the diseases and misconceptions.

10. **Use of Artificial Intelligence in Mental Health Setting:** Artificial intelligence contributes to mental health through data analysis of patients to identify potential mental health problems, early warnings about mental disorders, as well as through the use of digital mental health promotion programs. Self-help tools like chatbots which are artificial intelligence-based virtual assistants may be useful for patients and can provide them mental health support at any time of the day.

Example: Woebot is an artificially intelligent mental support chatbot perceiving Cognitive Behavioral Therapy (CBT) monitoring the mental health of users and intervening with individual treatments.

11. **AI in Resource Disbursement and Health Facilities:** The way that AI is useful in resource management includes identifying health care utilization (for instance, hospital beds, ventilators, vaccines) needs and distribution of these necessities. This is especially important, especially in the period that is considered to be a crisis when many people are infected and most of the facilities are occupied by patients.

Example: Some of the applications of AI during the COVID-19 pandemic included demand forecasting of Intensive Care Units, rationing of Personal Protective Equipment, and vaccine deployment.

12. **Health Education Awareness and Artificial Intelligence:** Technological intelligence in health education entails the use of decision-support systems to develop specific population health-oriented educative initiatives based on population data and likely population behaviors in the future. Such campaigns are more targeted and can be made to target a particular demographic and are likely to bring about the intended behavioral changes.

Example: AI platforms assist public health organizations in creating and spreading the right messages as they concern vaccines, quitting smoking, or safe sex practices, among others.

3.2 Other Advanced Technologies

Some other technologies are discussed in this section. such technologies are Machine Learning, Data Mining, Natural Language Processing (NLP), Predictive Analytics, Big Data, and health informatics, Robotics, and blockchain which are discussed in the Figure 4 below (Junaid et al., 2022):

Figure 4. Other advanced technologies

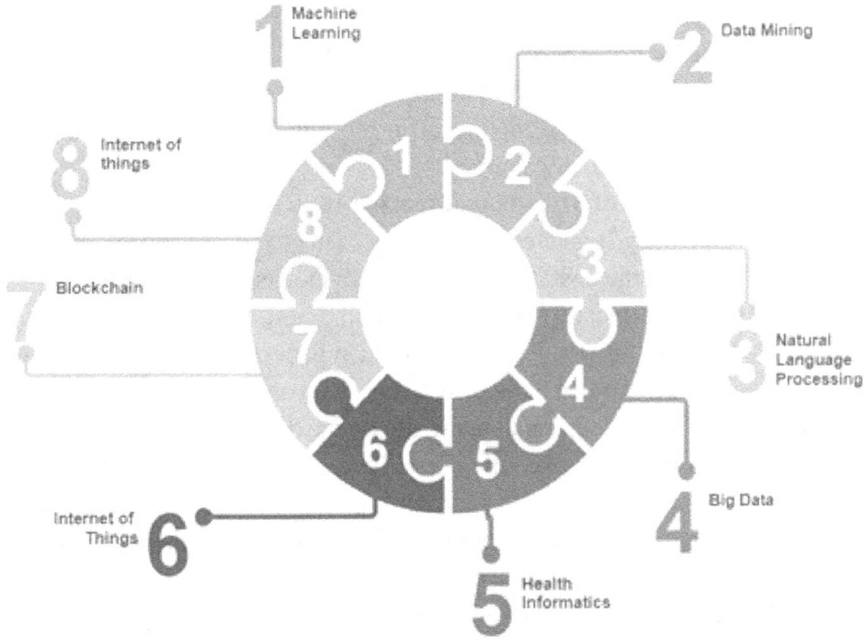

1. Machine Learning in Healthcare: ML enhances the diagnosis and prediction of diseases. There are various applications areas related to ML in healthcare that are discussed below:
   - Medical Imaging and diagnostics: Medical Imaging and diagnostics: ML algorithms in healthcare are used in the analysis of medical Images such as the X-Ray, MRI, CT scans, etc. The models can also identify early signs of many sicknesses and come up with the appropriate treatments appropriately and effectively. It also assists in the recognition of medical peculiarities and saves time.
   - Disease Predictive Analytics: Using patient data, lab tests, and a patient health history, ML predicts diseases or conditions such as chronic diseases, diabetes, etc.
   - Risk Scoring: ML helps to identify the risk values of different diseases based on different parameters such as behaviors, genetics, and history of the patient.
   - Personalized medicine: The use of sophisticated algorithms makes it possible to offer medications and recommendations based on person-oriented treatment and medicine. For example, treatment plans that are

generated through machine learning algorithms, and recommendations based on personalized treatment and medicine. Such as ML-driven personalized treatment plans.

- Clinical Decision Support: Clinical systems that incorporate ML assist in categorizing information based on the features of a patient. Clinical decision support systems assist in refining the above forecast and improve the prediction accuracy.

  Benefits of ML in healthcare: ML in healthcare helps to improve accuracy, enhance predictions, detect the symptoms of disease, reduce the cost and time, and provide personalized care.

2. Data Mining: In healthcare practices data mining can be defined as the evaluation of patient data and the identification of hidden patterns or links concerning the patient's records to enhance the effectiveness of operations being undertaken on the patient. By performing data mining on the data secured in the healthcare sector, EHRs, patient history, diagnostic data, and genomic data, the provider can identify patterns that assist them in diagnosing diseases early, providing a better treatment plan, and preempting them. There are various applications related to data mining as discussed below:
   - Predictive Analytics for Disease Prediction: Data Mining can be used to recognize and make conclusions about patterns and the probable state of the patient based on his/her genetic and behavioral characteristics. Real-time data can also be used to predict disease and is also useful for predicting disease.
   - Personalized Medicine: In the field of health care, data mining helps to offer treatment matched to genetic and behavioral characteristics linked to diseases. This contributes to organizing the treatment of diseases, for which diagnoses are made, doctors can choose the optimal dosages and medications for patients.
   - Fraud Detection and Prevention: Data mining is useful in identifying the patterns of fractional activities as well as in preventing piracy and other malicious use and decreasing fraudulent actuation concerning healthcare domains.
   - Improving Clinical Decision Support Systems: Data mining helps to analyze the hidden pattern of the patient data integrates the insights with the DSS and helps to provide real-time support. DSS helps to prevent anomalies related to patient error data.
   - Patient Outcome Prediction: Data mining supports analyzing the demographic features concerning disease and suggests high-risk patients to preventive care.

Benefits of Data Mining in Healthcare: Data mining in healthcare improves care, reduces cost, and enhances patient data management.

3. Natural Language Processing: NLP is used in handling large and even huge volumes of unstructured and synthesized data in clinical documents such as electronic data and patient information. Once data is extracted from these hidden patient data, it becomes quite possible to make the care better and also make the whole process efficient.

   Various key application related to NLP in healthcare is described below:

   - Clinical Documentation and Medical records: NLP helps to summarize the doctor-patient interaction and efficiently make the documentation. NLP reduces the burdens and increases patient care time. It also helps to extract the structure data for decision-making.
   - Clinical Decision Support Systems: NLP-powered DSS helps in increasing diagnostic support and can analyze the extent of data about clinical details. It facilitates in developing the alarm system that can work in conditions such as drug interactions or allergies.
   - Patient Data Mining for research: NLP helps in exploring the underlying pattern from the insights to improving the patient's outcome and is also used for examining genomic data for visualizing the gene and disease mapping.
   - Healthcare Chatbots: NLP-powered system assess the symptoms and suggest for the appropriate care. Through NP chatbots patients can communicate with patients efficiently.

   Benefits of NLP in healthcare: NLP-based systems in healthcare improve efficiency and enhance patient care.

4. Big Data: Big data in the healthcare sector corresponds to the massive amount of data that is related to patient health in the form of Electron healthcare records, etc. Big Data analytics helps to identify the insights to provide effective treatments to the patients.

   Applications related to Big Data in healthcare:

   - Personalized Medicine: Big Data Analytics helps to provide treatment suggestions to the individual based on specific individual patient symptoms such as genetics or behavior. This helps to provide better specific treatment.
   - Predictive Analytics for Early Disease Detection: Through big data analytics, it becomes easy to analyze and predict patient diseases based on conditions and lifestyle. It alerts the patient and provides the care.

- Enhanced Clinical Decision Support: Big Data analysis provides an effective decision support system for the patients based on the symptoms related to the diseases and their disease history.
- Medical Research and Drug Discovery: Big Data analytics help in the discovery of new medicals based on symptoms for treatments.
- Population Health Management: Healthcare organizations analyze huge and complex data in order to uncover the trends and insights in the healthcare sector to create interventions and policies.

Benefits of Big Data in Healthcare: Big Data in the healthcare sector helps to improve patient outcomes, enhance the capabilities related to research, and improve efficiency.

5. Health informatics: In health care, Health informatics is the use of IT systems and Information, particularly to enhance the delivery of care services. It helps in policy-making and quality improvement within patient care.

   Applications related to Health informatics in healthcare:

   - Electronic Health Records (EHRs): EHRs are Electronic patient records that offer a holistic summary of the patient's details including his/her charting. They assist in timely data processing and in exchanging reports between providers.
   - Telemedicine and Remote Patient Monitoring: Health informatics provides a telemedicine platform in which patient-related records are available for the healthcare providers for their treatments, and real-time consultations.
   - Health Information Exchange (HIE): With Healthcare informatics, HIE provides security for the patient's data, reduces test redundancy, and improves care.
   - Healthcare Data Security and Privacy: Health informatics provide security and privacy to the patient data using HIPAA and other security policies. Policies encrypt the patient records for security.
   - Patient Engagement and Self-Management: With the support of health informatics, there can be managed to create special mHealth applications, which allow patients to control their health status and track the necessary conditions at home.

   Benefits of Health informatics in healthcare: Health informatics helps in patient care improvement and provide better coordination between healthcare professionals.

6. Internet of Things: In the healthcare sector, IoT devices collect patient data for real-time monitoring and share the data at the global level to interact with doctors and make better decisions. People also use wearable devices and sensors to predict diseases.

   Applications related to IoT in healthcare:

   - Remote Patient Monitoring: In Romote patient monitoring, patients use the wearbale devices such as smartwatch or fitness tracker to monitor the current health status such as heart rate, blood pressure, suger level and oxygen level in human body. It helps the patient to communicate with the doctor without personal interaction and get efficient treatment.
   - Smart Medical Devices: Smart medical devices automatically monitor and detect the medication level and provide the health services in order to provide the better treatment through healthcare providers and specialist. It enhance the patient-care and better outcomes.
   - Telemedicine: Telemedicine helps the doctor to provide the better and efficient treatment based on rela-time monitoring using IoT devices such as wearable devices. With this, it does not necessary to visit the doctor personally.
   - Smart Hospitals: To enhance the treatment efficiency, better patient management, improvement in diagnosis, hospitals use the IoT devices and sensors. Such hospitals are considered as smart hospitals that use the smart beds, tracking system and sensors for temperature control in patient-rooms.
   - Weatable Health devices: Wearabke health devices such as smart watch, fitness bands helps to track the current physical activities as well as sleep patterns. People can share this date to healthcare professionals to take better treatment and personalized health care plans.
   - Disease Management: IoT devices help to manage the patient health and disease without visting the hospitals. Through the sensors, patient health can be monitor and real -time treatment can be offered.

   Benefits of IoT in healthcare: IoT helps to improve the patient-care, provides virtual care, enhanced patient safety.

7. Blockchain: In healthcare sector, blockhain helps to provide the security, privacy and transparency to the patient data due immutable and distributed nature. Blockchain use the concept of hash functions to provide the security.

Applications related to Blockchain in healthcare:

- Enhanced the data security and privacy: Blockchain is effective in storing the data as it deals with the security and privacy of data being stored which include having a record that cannot be modified by attackers. It gives the encryption to the patient data and lessens the chances of fraud.
- Interoperability and Data Sharing: Blockchain provides the interoperability to share patient records in the form of an Electronic health record across different platforms and ensures that real data is shared with healthcare professionals.
- Fraud Prevention and Billing Accuracy: Blockchain has the feature of transparency that does not allow fraud, and the smart contracts of blockchain are suitable for automatic payment services.
- Accurate Patient Records and Medical History: Blockchain helps in unified health records to provide medical history to health professionals and reduce the risk of incomplete medical information. With blockchain, it is easy to offer ownership of patient records.
- Improved Access to Healthcare in Underserved Areas: Blockchain helps to enhance trust across telemedicine due to its transparency and ensures cross-border healthcare in which healthcare professionals have access to updated patient records to provide them better treatments.

Benefits of Blockchain in healthcare: Blockchain helps in security, and patient record privacy and enhances trust.

8. Robotics: Robotics play a crucial role in the healthcare sector for surgical operations, patient care, and hospital services management. The robots help to reduce blood loss and shorten the recovery time.

Applications related to robotics in healthcare

- Surgical Robotics: Surgical Robotics helps to minimize invasive surgery, enhance precision, and help in remote surgery. With robots, surgical operations in hospitals become feasible and flexible. In hospitals, professionals control the surgical robots from remote locations.
- Rehabilitation Robots: Robots help in the rehabilitation process in which patients recover from strokes, injuries as well as surgeries. Robots also provide the facility of therapeutic that helps to provide emotional support and comfort to the patients.
- Medical Imaging and Diagnostics: Robots provide the facility of scanners that enhance medical technologies such as MRI and CT

scans. It improves accuracy and diagnostic speed by integrating AI technologies.

- Robotics in Patient Care and Assistance: Robots in the hospital help the nurses, staff, and assistants to lift and move the patient from one place to another and reduce the physical strains. Some robots are using UV rays that help in sterilizer of the patient rooms.
- AI-Integrated Robotic Systems: AI integrated robots serve themselves into smart robots to help medical people and offer individual treatments. Such robots are of assistance in analyzing the given patient data and the subsequent treatment.

4. CHALLENGES

The healthcare sector is not secure as an individual. Various challenges are discussed below:

- **Data Security and Privacy:** Digital health tools often handle sensitive information, making cybersecurity a priority.
- **Digital Divide:** Access to technology is not universal, which may exacerbate health disparities.
- **Regulatory Issues:** Adapting existing regulations to new digital health technologies is complex and requires careful attention.

4.1. Difficulties of Using AI in Public Healthcare

The following are the various difficulties faced when implementing AI in public healthcare:

- **Data Privacy and Security:** Consequently managing sensitive health data provides for proper cybersecurity measures that can assist in checking on breaches.
- **Bias in AI Algorithms:** This is because any AI models that are trained on such datasets will be developed with such a skewed attitude towards the black community.
- **Ethical and Regulatory Concerns:** The incorporation of AI in the management of the health care system has led to several concerns on issues to do with consent, accountability as well as transparency.

Despite these, AI has virtually the capacity to transform public healthcare because of its ability to prevent diseases, diagnose them early as well as make healthcare efficient.

4.2 Implementation Challenges of AI in Healthcare

Ethical Challenge: The deployment of artificial intelligence and ethics have become hot discussion topics. As AI is developed and used more, concerns like bias, privacy, and social aspects should be taken into account. Theoretical ideas like monitoring systems actually as serve excellent illustrations of privacy concerns associated with AI. In addition, concerns about justice emerges when AI is used in fields like health or criminality, where human life is involved. In these situations, ethical rules must be observed even more precisely. The ethical concerns center on how to improve AI research, conduct business transparently, and uphold human rights simultaneously.

Biasness: In the context of artificial intelligence, bias refers to the possibility that machine learning algorithms may reinforce pre-existing biases embedded within their training datasets. Artificial intelligence (AI) systems acquire biases originating from the datasets that they are provided, and they subsequently derive insights from the biased patterns inherent within that data. Such dynamics may culminate in inequitable decisions regarding loan approvals, recruitment methodologies, and law enforcement practices. It is critically essential to address bias within AI frameworks to prevent the continuation of discrimination. Careful consideration must be dedicated to the methodologies of data selection, preparation, and algorithmic design to mitigate AI bias. The ideals of fairness and equal treatment integral to AI systems necessitate a careful and judicious approach, particularly in areas that significantly affect societal dynamics.

Security and Privacy: Security and Privacy of Data In the context of artificial intelligence, which primarily relies on extensive datasets, the issues of data security and privacy emerge as paramount concerns. In the absence of adequate protective measures, sensitive information may be vulnerable to potential threats. To mitigate the risks of breaches, leaks, or misuse, it is vital to secure the privacy, integrity, and availability of information. To ensure integrity and avert ethical misconduct, the execution of effective encryption practices, the employment of data anonymization approaches, and unwavering adherence to data protection standards is vital. In the pursuit of maintaining data utility, methodologies that preserve privacy, such as federated learning and differential privacy, can significantly contribute to the reduction of related risks. The ethical management of data and transparent data practices significantly enhance users' trust, thereby fostering confidence in artificial intelligence systems.

4.3 Future of AI in Healthcare

Indeed, artificial intelligence is transforming healthcare in interesting ways! The following are some important trends worth noticing:

Emotion AI for Autism Spectrum Disorder (ASD) and Mental Health: AI is making significant progress in aiding patients with mental health conditions and autism. Emotion AI enhances telemedicine platforms, providing more engaging and effective care. AI-powered speech analysis tools can detect mental health issues such as dementia, depression, autism, and Down syndrome, facilitating early diagnosis and intervention.

Personalized Healthcare Services: Healthcare providers are increasingly adopting personalized treatments by utilizing vast amounts of health data. Wearable technology like wristbands, sensorized insoles (e.g., FeetMe), and smart clothing (e.g., Levi's Google Jacquard) generate valuable health data. AI-enabled apps use this information to offer personalized healthcare recommendations, such as custom diet and exercise plans, and monitor key metrics like heart rate, blood pressure, and calories burned.

Ambient Intelligence (AmI): Ambient Intelligence is emerging as a significant trend in healthcare solution development. By integrating AI, IoT, and Big Data, AmI helps streamline healthcare services by reducing patient wait times, automating emergency care, and continuously monitoring patients' vital signs. This technology enables more responsive and efficient care, ultimately improving patient outcomes.

These advancements are just the beginning of how AI can transform healthcare, making it more personalized, efficient, and accessible. What aspect of AI in healthcare excites you the most?

REFERENCES

Al Kuwaiti, A., Nazer, K., Al-Reedy, A., Al-Shehri, S., Al-Muhanna, A., Subbarayalu, A. V., Al Muhanna, D., & Al-Muhanna, F. A. (2023). A review of the role of artificial intelligence in healthcare. *Journal of Personalized Medicine*, *13*(6), 951. DOI: 10.3390/jpm13060951 PMID: 37373940

Alowais, S. A., Alghamdi, S. S., Alsuhebany, N., Alqahtani, T., Alshaya, A. I., Almohareb, S. N., Aldairem, A., Alrashed, M., Bin Saleh, K., Badreldin, H. A., Al Yami, M. S., Al Harbi, S., & Albekairy, A. M. (2023). Revolutionizing healthcare: The role of artificial intelligence in clinical practice. *BMC Medical Education*, *23*(1), 689. DOI: 10.1186/s12909-023-04698-z PMID: 37740191

Bajwa, J., Munir, U., Nori, A., & Williams, B. (2021, July). Artificial intelligence in healthcare: Transforming the practice of medicine. *Future Healthcare Journal*, *8*(2), e188–e194. DOI: 10.7861/fhj.2021-0095 PMID: 34286183

Budd, J., Miller, B. S., Manning, E. M., Lampos, V., Zhuang, M., Edelstein, M., Rees, G., Emery, V. C., Stevens, M. M., Keegan, N., Short, M. J., Pillay, D., Manley, E., Cox, I. J., Heymann, D., Johnson, A. M., & McKendry, R. A. (2020). Digital technologies in the public-health response to COVID-19. *Nature Medicine*, *26*(8), 1183–1192. DOI: 10.1038/s41591-020-1011-4 PMID: 32770165

Dalal, A. K., Piniella, N., Fuller, T. E., Pong, D., Pardo, M., Bessa, N., Yoon, C., Lipsitz, S., & Schnipper, J. L. (2021). Evaluation of electronic health record-integrated digital health tools to engage hospitalized patients in discharge preparation. *Journal of the American Medical Informatics Association : JAMIA*, *28*(4), 704–712. DOI: 10.1093/jamia/ocaa321 PMID: 33463681

Istepanian, R. S. (2022). Mobile health (m-Health) in retrospect: The known unknowns. *International Journal of Environmental Research and Public Health*, *19*(7), 3747. DOI: 10.3390/ijerph19073747 PMID: 35409431

Junaid, S. B., Imam, A. A., Balogun, A. O., De Silva, L. C., Surakat, Y. A., Kumar, G., Abdulkarim, M., Shuaibu, A. N., Garba, A., Sahalu, Y., Mohammed, A., Mohammed, T. Y., Abdulkadir, B. A., Abba, A. A., Kakumi, N. A. I., & Mahamad, S. (2022, October 3). Recent Advancements in Emerging Technologies for Healthcare Management Systems: A Survey. *Healthcare (Basel)*, *10*(10), 1940. DOI: 10.3390/healthcare10101940 PMID: 36292387

Lakshminarayanan, V., Ravikumar, A., Sriraman, H., Alla, S., & Chattu, V. K. (2023). Health care equity through intelligent edge computing and augmented reality/virtual reality: A systematic review. *Journal of Multidisciplinary Healthcare, 16*, 2839–2859. DOI: 10.2147/JMDH.S419923 PMID: 37753339

Lee, D., & Yoon, S. N. (2021). Application of artificial intelligence-based technologies in the healthcare industry: Opportunities and challenges. *International Journal of Environmental Research and Public Health, 18*(1), 271. DOI: 10.3390/ijerph18010271 PMID: 33401373

Maleki Varnosfaderani, S., & Forouzanfar, M. (2024, March 29). The Role of AI in Hospitals and Clinics: Transforming Healthcare in the 21st Century. *Bioengineering (Basel, Switzerland), 11*(4), 337. DOI: 10.3390/bioengineering11040337 PMID: 38671759

Maroju, R. G., Choudhari, S. G., Shaikh, M. K., Borkar, S. K., & Mendhe, H. (2023). Role of telemedicine and digital technology in public health in India: A narrative review. *Cureus, 15*(3). Advance online publication. DOI: 10.7759/cureus.35986 PMID: 37050980

Mbunge, E., Muchemwa, B., & Batani, J. (2021). Sensors and healthcare 5.0: Transformative shift in virtual care through emerging digital health technologies. *Global Health Journal (Amsterdam, Netherlands), 5*(4), 169–177. DOI: 10.1016/j.glohj.2021.11.008

Morley, J., Machado, C. C., Burr, C., Cowls, J., Joshi, I., Taddeo, M., & Floridi, L. (2020). The ethics of AI in health care: A mapping review. *Social Science & Medicine, 260*, 113172. DOI: 10.1016/j.socscimed.2020.113172 PMID: 32702587

Rubinger, L., Gazendam, A., Ekhtiari, S., & Bhandari, M. (2023). Machine learning and artificial intelligence in research and healthcare. *Injury, 54*, S69–S73. DOI: 10.1016/j.injury.2022.01.046 PMID: 35135685

Zeng, D., Cao, Z., & Neill, D. B. (2021). Artificial intelligence–enabled public health surveillance—from local detection to global epidemic monitoring and control. In *Artificial intelligence in medicine* (pp. 437–453). Academic Press. DOI: 10.1016/B978-0-12-821259-2.00022-3

Zhang, H., & Zheng, J. (2021). The application analysis of medical chatbots and virtual assistant. *Front. Soc. Sci. Technol, 3*, 11–16.

Chapter 7

AI-Driven Social Media Analysis for Disaster Situational Awareness in Smart Urban Environments

Ravinder Singh
https://orcid.org/0009-0007-7161-6709
SR University, India

Geetha Manoharan
https://orcid.org/0000-0002-8644-8871
SR University, India

Samrath Singh
https://orcid.org/0009-0009-3720-1432
Vellore Institute of Technology, Chennai, India

Simranjot Singh
https://orcid.org/0009-0008-4388-7517
Delhi University, India

ABSTRACT

This paper explores the transformative impact of social media analytics in disaster response. By utilizing advanced algorithms and machine learning, social media analytics enables the rapid processing of vast data streams, delivering real-time insights and trends crucial for effective disaster management. The paper highlights how social media has evolved into a vital tool for crisis communication, geolocation-

DOI: 10.4018/979-8-3693-7832-8.ch007

based disaster response, and sentiment analysis, offering valuable insights into the emotional and psychological effects of disasters. It addresses the challenges of integrating AI in this realm, emphasizing the necessity of data privacy, ethical considerations, and transparent public engagement. The paper shows both the huge potential and inherent difficulties of using AI-driven social media analysis in disaster management by looking at a wide range of real-life case studies and opportunities within smart urban environments.

1. INTRODUCTION

Disaster management evolved significantly in the 20th century, marked by shifting paradigms and strategic initiatives aimed at safeguarding lives and mitigating the impact of natural disasters. This period saw a notable move towards centralized measures for citizen protection, leading to the development of mechanisms to manage disasters. These advancements were pivotal in enhancing preparedness, response, and recovery efforts, ultimately shaping modern approaches to disaster resilience (Singh et al., 2024; Coppola, 2015; Hecker & Domres, 2018). As the frequency of natural disasters increased worldwide, the demand for more efficient and effective solutions grew. Disaster management integrated artificial intelligence (AI) to address this. AI, a branch of computer science, focuses on developing methodologies and procedures that enable computers to mimic human brain functions. This allows them to solve complex problems, such as predicting disaster patterns and coordinating emergency responses, which would otherwise require a significant amount of time for humans to resolve (Manoharan et al., 2024; Chandra & Lakshmi, 2024). AI can reshape future disaster management by enabling proactive and preventive measures, enhancing decision-making, building resilience, fostering global collaboration and data sharing, promoting continuous improvement through learning, and ensuring ethical and inclusive practices (Varsha et al., 2024).

Social media analytics assists decision-makers and researchers in addressing specific problems by gathering and analyzing data from social media platforms. This method leverages automated techniques, which are significantly more cost-effective and efficient compared to traditional manual media analysis. By utilizing advanced algorithms and machine learning, social media analytics can process vast amounts of data quickly, providing real-time insights and trends. These capabilities enable a more responsive and informed approach to problem-solving, allowing for timely interventions and strategies. This innovative approach enhances the ability to monitor public sentiment, track emerging issues, and make data-driven decisions (Hayes et al., 2021; Lee, 2018). A research paper on the role of social media during the COVID-19 pandemic explored the effectiveness of social media in promoting preventive measures among the public. It highlighted the immense potential of social media platforms in shaping people's opinions and risk perceptions, emphasizing the need for governments to engage in proactive crisis communication management (Tsoy et al., 2021).

Situational Awareness (SA) is crucial across various domains, including battlefield environments, military and air bases, aviation, air traffic control, emergency and disaster response, industrial process management, urban areas, and critical infrastructure. Inadequate SA often leads to human errors that can result in severe consequences, such as the loss of first responders' lives during emergencies. Immediately after a disaster, SA is essential for prioritizing and directing resources, including personnel and supplies, based on impact and need. Continuous updates to SA are necessary as recovery efforts progress and conditions change. Disruption in communication can render traditional information sources for SA, like victim reports, unreliable. Therefore, SA systems are vital for effective disaster monitoring and reporting, aiding in appropriate responses. These systems also play a key role in early warning, enhancing safety and sustainability in cities by enabling swift detection and response to emergencies like fires, floods, bridge collapses, water supply disruptions, earthquakes, volcanic eruptions, and tornadoes (Munir et al., 2022). Efficiently and accurately identifying relevant information to support SA is a top priority during a natural disaster. Effective threat assessment and logical responses are crucial for disaster mitigation (Perry & Lindell, 2003). A review of studies utilizing various methods to extract information from social media during natural disasters included work across multiple platforms. This review categorized the studies into five key areas: content, sentiment, user, temporal, and spatiotemporal analysis (Vongkusolkit & Huang, 2021).

Using AI for social media analytics offers several benefits, including the efficient processing and analysis of large amounts of unstructured, long-form text data typical of social media. AI can identify patterns and correlations that are difficult to spot manually, uncovering hidden insights. Additionally, AI algorithms enhance the accuracy of social media analytics by eliminating biases influenced by human factors, such as personal beliefs or preconceptions. These capabilities provide valuable insights for data-based decision-making, enabling emergency decision-makers to develop informed and effective responses.

2. THE IMPORTANCE OF SOCIAL MEDIA IN DISASTER SITUATIONAL AWARENESS.

2.1. Social Media's Role During Disasters.

People are increasingly sharing information on social media during disaster events, which can be valuable to emergency responders (Zade et al., 2018). Social media use has become a regular aspect of disaster response, frequently utilized by affected individuals, emergency and humanitarian responders, and remote audiences to share information, seek assistance, and provide informational and emotional support (Castillo, 2016; Olteanu et al., 2015). As social media has become ubiquitous and rapidly adopted worldwide, it has also become a recurring site of online convergence following disasters (Hughes & Palen, 2009; Qu et al., 2009). People turn to these platforms to disseminate information, gather updates, and offer various forms of support (Gao et al., 2011). Researchers in crisis informatics have highlighted the potential value of social media content, such as real-time photos and observations from people across an impacted area, for both emergency responders and affected populations (Nazer et al., 2016; Tanev et al., 2017).

2.2 The Evolution of Social Media in Crisis Management.

The use of social media for crisis and disaster management has significantly increased and evolved to become more collaborative, especially during crises (Reuter et al., 2020). Globally, disaster contexts have employed various online platforms to facilitate crowdsourcing. Notable examples include Ushahidi, Crisis Tracking, Ready2Help, and Digital Humanitarian Networks (Boersma et al., 2024; Meier, 2015; Saroj & Pal, 2020; Schmidt et al., 2018). Social media has evolved into a vital tool for disseminating information due to advancements in technology and devices. The public, emergency responders, and relevant authorities can use these broadcast messages comprising texts, images, and videos to gather and share data and information. This evolution has significantly enhanced the speed and reach of communication, making social media an indispensable part of crisis management and public information strategies (Soni, 2024).

2.3. Geolocation and Social Media in Disaster Response.

Posts and updates often include geolocation data, helping to pinpoint affected areas and prioritize response efforts. With the widespread use of smartphones and tablets equipped with GPS receivers, there has been a significant increase in the availability of geoinformation on social media platforms, transforming them into location-centric social networks. Daly and Thom's research on geotagged images related to fire events from Flickr revealed that spatial-temporal metadata and geotagged image information could aid in pinpointing the location of fire events (Sathianarayanan et al., 2024; Daly & Thom, 2016).

2.4. The Importance of Geospatial Information for Disaster Management.

Knowing what is happening is valuable to disaster managers, but knowing where these events are occurring is even more critical. Location-based social networks can relay not only the events, but also their specific locations. For efficient resource allocation during natural disasters, managers must understand both the nature and location of citizens' experiences. During disasters, managers can use geospatial and machine learning techniques to categorize geolocated tweets, focusing them on specific locations. Sentiment analysis can then classify these tweets regarding damage and transportation into negative, neutral, or positive categories. Disaster managers can develop a probability-based understanding of needs by extracting information from social media data (Reynard & Shirgaokar, 2019). Given the enormous volume and velocity of information generated on social media, machine learning techniques such as natural language processing are essential for effective analysis (Gu et al., 2016; Jung and Shin, 2018; Schweitzer, 2014). Disaster management organizations can leverage social media in two main ways: passively, by disseminating information to the public and gathering user feedback, and actively, by using it as an emergency management tool for communications, issuing warnings, handling assistance requests, monitoring content, and maintaining situational awareness (Mangones, n.d.).

2.5. Sentiment Analysis and Its Applications.

Sentiment analysis has emerged as a crucial technology for extracting insights from social networks. The field has matured significantly, enabling its application across various domains (Iglesias & Moreno, 2019). Social media sentiments and opinions offer the most current and comprehensive information, thanks to the widespread use of social media and the ease of posting messages (Yue et al., 2019). Social media has increasingly played a significant role as an important alternative to traditional media during emergencies and disasters, becoming a popular source for accessing crucial information in such situations (Cobo et al., 2015; Beigi et al., 2016).

2.6. Efficient Resource Allocation Post-Disaster.

In the aftermath of a disaster, ensuring the efficient allocation of emergency resources (e.g., food, water, shelter, and medicines) to the locations where they are most needed is of utmost importance. This task is challenging because it requires identifying resource needs and availabilities in real time and developing a policy for distributing resources from availability locations to need locations (Basu et al., 2022). To facilitate efficient resource allocation during natural disasters, managers must understand what citizens are experiencing and where. Sentiment analysis can classify social media messages and translate them into the needs of the affected community (Reynard & Shirgaokar, 2019).

2.7. Enhancing Risk Communication and Community Engagement.

During disasters, social media can enhance risk communication and community engagement efforts. Local governments need to engage residents as collaborators in mitigating their risk exposure, as clients to support and meet their needs, and as stakeholders to be involved in future policy discussions (Wukich, 2020).

3. CHALLENGES AND OPPORTUNITIES IN SMART URBAN ENVIRONMENTS.

3.1. Advantages of Location-Based Social Networks.

The benefits of location-based social networks (LBSNs) are numerous. Millions of people from different countries worldwide generate LBSN data (Yanuargi et al., 2024). As the number of social network users grows, so does the amount, quality, and usability of data (Martí et al., 2019). One significant advantage of social media is the automatic retrieval of user-generated content (Guo et al., 2020), which represents a technological advancement for urban analysis. This is mainly due to the ease of data collection, which eliminates many constraints associated with traditional methods, such as collection time and accurate geolocation marks. Moreover, LBSN data enable the exploration of intangible aspects of urban life linked to specific places (McLain et al., 2013). We can also recognize LBSN data as volunteered geographic information (VGI) (Feng et al., 2020). Users voluntarily publish their perceptions, interests, needs, and behaviours online, referring to unique and specific places in cities. Data are generally collected "unobtrusively," meaning users are not constrained when generating information (Martí et al., 2019). This is advantageous because, according to the Hawthorne effect, subjects may alter their behaviour upon realizing they are being observed (Elston, 2021).

3.2. Multimodal Social Media Data Integration and Interoperability.

Massively generated social media data from citizen observations, including visual, textual, and spatiotemporal information, provides reliable and timely insights into crisis events. Multimodal fusion of satellite images and social media data can be carried out to enhance emergency response efforts. Gialampoukidis et al. (2021) suggest that combining these data sources can enhance monitoring and response strategies for events like floods and extreme weather conditions. Multimodal content brings a further obstacle to the challenge of dealing with nonlinear texts, which may be multiplatform and interlocking (Unger et al., 2016; Bouvier & Machin, 2020). Content on webpages and social media may carry less running text and more chunks of text connected to images, bulleted lists, and graphics. In this kind of nonlinear text, information is communicated symbolically by graphic elements and the affordances of tables. Even routine tweets can carry fragments of language integrated with images and emoticons (Bouvier, 2019).

3.3. Real-Time Data Processing of Social Media.

For any disaster or emergency, the diverse nature (texts, images, audio, and videos) and sheer volume of data instantly available on social media platforms necessitate fast and automated processing, including the integration and fusion of information from disparate sources. This poses challenges in developing an effective information technology solution for emergency response and management in smart cities (Khatoon et al., 2022). Certain big data applications require real-time or near-real-time processing to facilitate instant decision-making and reaction to unfolding events. AI can analyze and process big data in real-time, enabling organizations to swiftly adapt and respond to dynamic conditions (Tahir & Khan, 2023).

3.4. Addressing Privacy and Security Challenges.

There were several instances of cybersecurity hackers infiltrating various private electronic databases, linking fields, and using that data to access confidential information (Jain et al., 2016; Bohannon, 2015). Sun et al. (2020) have proposed a Boolean model to explore the interrelationships between privacy and security in the big data era. Illustrated in Figure 1, this model analyzes the relationship between privacy, security, and big data, potentially aiding stakeholders in understanding these concepts at three levels: fundamental, interactional, and integrated. Privacy and security in the big data age can be classified into four Vs categories based on the characteristics of big data: volume-driven, velocity-driven, variety-driven, and veracity-driven privacy and security, addressing challenges far beyond those faced a decade ago (Sun et al., 2020; Naeem et al., 2022). The focus of data security has shifted from traditional perimeter defenses like firewalls to protecting the data itself through encryption (Pratomo et al., 2023). With the increasing use of machine learning systems, which often operate without human oversight in data collection, there's a growing risk of security vulnerabilities. Malicious actors can exploit this by injecting poisoned examples into training datasets, leading to data poisoning and backdoor attacks (Goldblum et al., 2022). In response, advancements have been made in endpoint security management (Kamruzzaman et al., 2022) and machine learning-based network intrusion detection systems (NIDS) (Kumar, 2021), which help monitor and secure network traffic. Additionally, researchers are exploring data anonymization techniques to address privacy concerns. These techniques modify or remove personally identifiable information to safeguard individual identities while allowing for data analysis.

Figure 1. Boolean model to explore the interrelationships between privacy and security in big data

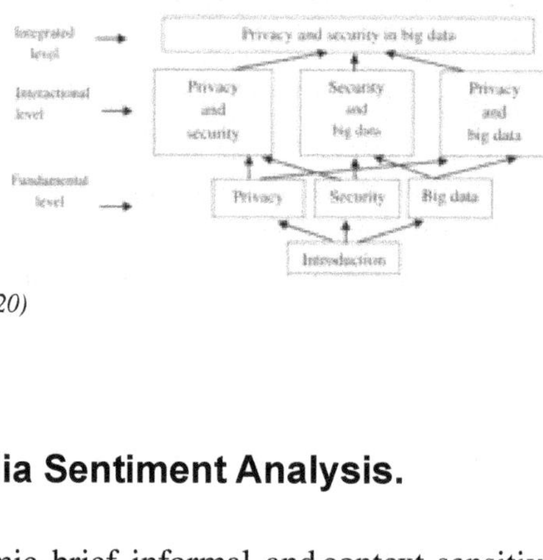

(Source: Sun et al. 2020)

3.5. Social Media Sentiment Analysis.

Due to the dynamic, brief, informal, and context-sensitive nature of social media, applying standard opinion mining and sentiment analysis techniques directly can be problematic. Social media content features elements beyond traditional text mining, such as emojis, which, despite being non-textual, carry rich emotional meanings. Analyzing social media posts presents challenges due to their varying length, reliance on context, the rising use of multimedia like emojis, images, and videos, and the prevalence of informal writing styles, including abbreviations and typos (Zhang et al., 2018). Sentiment analysis, also known as mood extraction or opinion mining, is a method for assessing the emotions or opinions of individuals or groups. Techniques such as natural language processing, text mining, computational linguistics, machine learning, and deep learning analyze data from online social media platforms, blogs, forums, news groups, and other sources to achieve this.

3.6. Public Engagement and Communication Through Social Media.

Risk communication that is clear, concise, and consistent has a big effect on how well safety instructions work as well as the interpretability and recall of critical content (Wang et al., 2021). A study revealed that social media posts aimed at enhancing situational awareness garner more community attention than other types of posts (Kankanamge et al., 2020). To improve risk communication, several challenges must be addressed: understanding that communication is an ongoing process, not a one-time product; emphasizing understanding people; integrating technology and early warning systems; considering collective risk rather than just individual risk; and fostering collaboration among community members, technical experts, media professionals, and governments to provide open and transparent disaster risk information. It is crucial that people perceive the information source as trustworthy, and measures must be in place to prevent misinformation and disinformation (Fakhruddin et al., 2020). On social media, the community can 'like,' 'comment,' 'share,' 'follow,' and 'retweet' posts. Posts that are liked the most receive higher community attention, while those with the most comments generate in-depth discussions within the social network (Kankanamge et al., 2020). Increased community engagement in disaster management via social media can enhance its three unique attributes as a volunteer crowdsourcing tool: (a) situational awareness, (b) collective intelligence, and (c) multi-directional communication (Kankanamge et al., 2019).

3.7. Social Media for Resource Allocation and Management.

Search and Rescue is a race against time, as the chances of survival for trapped individuals decrease as time passes (Sambolek & Ivasic-Kos, 2021). The challenge of resource availability and the declining survival probabilities of trapped individuals underscore the importance of timely resource allocation in life-saving efforts during the response phase (Basyah et al., 2023). When disaster strikes, the equitable distribution of resources is also crucial (Erbeyoğlu & Bilge, 2020). Ignoring fairness in rescue resource allocation can have adverse short-term and long-term social, economic, and environmental consequences, such as public dissatisfaction, increased management issues with casualties, overwhelmed debris management, additional environmental damage, unequal relief distribution, and heightened recovery efforts (Ahmadi et al., 2022). Social media can be valuable for tracking changes in disaster severity over time, with spatial analysis confirming that geo-located messages effectively identify highly impacted areas (Kankanamge et al., 2020a). Additionally, damage information mined from images and text on social media is beneficial for resource allocation. AI can perform real-time data analysis for resource prioritization, aiding in long-term impact assessment, reconstruction management, and efficient aid distribution (Hao & Wang, 2020). AI systems optimize logistics in disaster response, ensuring swift and accurate resource distribution to the hardest-hit areas by excelling in data analysis and identifying urgent assistance needs (Singh & Manoharan, 2024).

4. AI AND MACHINE LEARNING ALGORITHMS FOR SOCIAL MEDIA ANALYSIS

4.1. The Role of AI in Sentiment Analysis from Social Media.

When disasters strike, those directly and indirectly affected often share vast amounts of data—such as images, text, speech, and videos—via numerous social media platforms. This results in enormous volumes of data, which are crucial for marketing, sentiment analysis, and trend monitoring (Tahir & Khan, 2023). To process and transform this data into actionable information during disasters, AI, especially machine learning (ML), plays a vital role (Nunavath & Goodwin, 2018). During or immediately after a disaster, people are generally curious about the event's location. For crisis managers, it is crucial to accurately determine the exact location, sometimes requiring precise longitude and latitude coordinates. Additionally, the public seeks information on the timing and duration of the event. If such information is not readily available on social media, the timestamp of the first post reporting the incident can be used to approximate the time of occurrence. Social media platforms allow users to express their opinions online, and emotion analysis classifies text as positive, negative, or neutral. Many individuals suffer injuries and trauma during or after a disaster and need medical assistance. There is significant potential for improving medical and healthcare practices through the development and advancement of medical and healthcare information technologies during disasters (Saroj & Pal, 2020).

4.2. Natural Language Processing Techniques for Sentiment Analysis.

Natural Language Processing (NLP) enables computers to understand, interpret, and generate human language, facilitating tasks like translation, sentiment analysis, and information extraction from text data (Fanni et al., 2023; Khurana et al., 2023). Ongoing research in numerous areas of NLP aims to aid disaster management. This includes tracking the location of people in danger during disasters (Abu-Alsaad & Al-Taie, 2021) as well as addressing challenges in detecting and distinguishing disaster-related tweets from non-disaster tweets on Twitter. Since Twitter data is often unstructured, processing is required to classify tweets as 'disaster' or 'non-disaster' (Bikku et al., 2022). Researchers analyze various NLP models, such as logistic regression, Naive Bayes, XGBoost, LSTM, and word embedding technologies like GloVe and transformer encoders like BERT, to predict disaster warnings from scraped tweets (Chopra et al., 2022). Additionally, Tounsi & Temimi (2023) use NLP to assess extreme weather events, particularly heavy rainfall, and to extract location-oriented public sentiments on global disaster situations. A proposed system is designed to obtain exhaustive knowledge and insights from social media feeds related to disasters in 110 languages (Sufi & Khalil, 2022). Another decision support system identifies and analyzes natural disasters like earthquakes, floods, and bushfires using real-time social media feeds. It employs NLP-based algorithms, such as entity detection, category classification, and sentiment analysis, to identify and locate various natural disasters (Sufi, 2022). An automated identification of disaster news for crisis management is proposed using machine learning and NLP, offering a software solution that dynamically displays disaster-relevant news on disaster management websites, which can be shared on other social media platforms (Domala et al., 2020). Alvarado & Solano (2021) trained an artificial neural network on a public dataset of tweets to predict whether a given instance is a disaster tweet or not. Additionally, there is a focus on developing solutions for disaster management and emergency response using social media platforms. This process emphasizes text analysis techniques to enhance emergency response and filter information to support relief efforts. State-of-the-art machine learning (ML), deep learning (DL), and NLP techniques based on supervised and unsupervised learning using social media datasets are used to extract real-time content related to emergency events (Shahbazi & Byun, 2021).

4.3. Sentiment Analysis for Disasters.

Various techniques have been utilized to extract sentiments from text streams, categorizing them as positive, negative, or neutral perceptions or opinions (Hassan et al., 2022). Applications for sentiment analysis can show how to use social media sentiment mining to measure local crowd reactions during a disaster, thereby improving disaster management strategies. Analyzing disaster-related posts on social media can aid in identifying contributions to situational awareness and provide insights into network dynamics, including users' feelings, panics, and concerns. This is achieved by detecting the polarity of sentiments expressed during disaster events, which ultimately aids in decision-making. Sentiment data can also be employed to effectively communicate information about devastation, recovery efforts, and donation requests to the public. Beyond managing disaster-related data on social media, extracting key features can facilitate rapid comprehension of situations, leading to swift decision-making in critical scenarios. Additionally, the vast amount of data generated by social media during disasters is overwhelming for individuals to process, necessitating visualization to aid in pattern discovery (Beigi et al., 2016). The concept of visual sentiment analysis is applied to the complex and vital task of disaster analysis, which typically involves multiple objects and relevant background information in images. A deep architecture-based visual sentiment analyzer is proposed for automatically analyzing sentiments in natural disaster-related images from social media. The commonly used tags—positive, negative, and neutral—are insufficient to fully utilize the potential of visual sentiment analysis in disaster analysis applications. The complexity of the task increases as one delves deeper into the sentiment/emotion hierarchy (Hassan et al., 2022). A study has indicated that geographical and sentiment data derived from tweets can model the dynamics and severity of floods across different regions (Bryan-Smith et al., 2023).

4.4. Challenges to Sentiment Analysis from Social Media.

Sentiment analysis of social media using AI faces challenges categorized into data-related issues, method-related issues, and evaluation metrics-related issues (Xu et al., 2022). Data-related challenges arise due to the overwhelming volume and velocity of social media data (Stieglitz et al., 2018). Primary data, data imbalance, and varying comment lengths are the challenges for researchers (Kastrati et al., 2021; Xu et al., 2022). The preprocessing of this data is complex due to its unstructured nature and the presence of noisy, inefficient, and irrelevant information. Standard preprocessing steps include converting uppercase to lowercase, removing URLs, text correction, and stop words. However, removing non-alphabetic terms like emoticons, which are vital for understanding user sentiments, can affect the performance of classifiers (Xu et al., 2022). Though removing stop words can improve model performance by reducing text corpus size, it might also alter sentence meaning and impact accuracy (HaCohen-Kerner et al., 2020). Method-related challenges include the versatility of methods. Sentiment analysis is conducted using lexicon-based and machine learning approaches. The lexicon-based approach's accuracy depends on the richness of dictionaries, which may vary significantly. Sentiment direction of words can differ across dictionaries, complicating analysis (Khatoon et al., 2020). Efficiency is crucial; effective sentiment analysis helps understand and monitor public opinions on events, enabling timely actions and policy-making (Xu et al., 2022). The challenges in evaluating sentiment analysis classifiers include the reliance on various metrics such as accuracy, F1-score, recall, and precision, which are often calculated using a confusion matrix. Neglecting practical aspects like execution time and efficiency frequently impacts real-world applicability and the comprehensiveness of model performance.

5. CASE STUDIES AND APPLICATIONS IN REAL-WORLD DISASTERS.

5.1. Case studies of Hurricanes Harvey, Irma, and Maria.

In 2017, three devastating natural disasters—Hurricane Harvey, Hurricane Irma, and Hurricane Maria—caused billions of dollars in damage, numerous fatalities, and left thousands of people affected. A study was conducted by Alam et al. (2020) to explore the textual information shared on social media during these disasters from various perspectives. Advanced AI techniques were employed to extract and understand valuable information for humanitarian decision-makers and responders, while filtering out irrelevant content to alleviate information overload on responders.

Firstly, the study addressed specific information needs by adopting a longitudinal approach to capture the diverse requirements of UN organizations. It developed a taxonomy of information needs based on previous research and used supervised machine learning to automatically categorize the collected data into predefined categories. Secondly, the study conducted sentiment analysis on the gathered data. Thirdly, it identified critical entities (such as persons, locations, and organizations) using the Stanford Named-Entity Recognizer. Lastly, the study tracked incidents of small-scale events following a major disaster to enable timely humanitarian response. The Latent Dirichlet Allocation (LDA) technique was employed to uncover latent events or topics within the 'Other useful information' category. The analysis provided valuable insights for both technical experts and humanitarian organizations. For technical experts, these insights can help enhance the efficiency of computational models or inspire the development of new ones. For humanitarian organizations, the findings offer a deeper understanding of the complementary information that multimodal data on social media can provide during disaster events.

5.2. Case study of Typhoon Etau in Japan.

In recent decades, technological advancements such as satellites and supercomputers have significantly enhanced the accuracy of weather forecasts. This improvement has enabled earlier warnings and provided people with more time to prepare and take necessary risk-mitigation measures. Consequently, the impact of natural disasters in Japan has been reduced, evidenced by a general decline in casualties from 1963 to 2014. However, to further reduce disaster risks, the government and meteorological agencies must overcome a major remaining challenge: ensuring that information is communicated clearly and effectively, while also encouraging citizens to take timely and appropriate actions in response to warnings.

Kitazawa & Hale (2021) conducted a study to explore three key questions: First, how does the issuance of an emergency warning influence public attention and discussions related to taking action on social media? Second, how does the online public's response to warnings align with expectations within Japan's Early Warning System (EWS) framework? Third, what impact does issuing an emergency warning have on public attention and discussions on social media? The study chose Twitter for its analysis due to its prominence, accessibility, and unique suitability for disaster-related information in Japan. Twitter is widely used in Japan, with 45 million active users in 2017, making it a key platform for reaching a large audience. Its speed in disseminating information is unparalleled, with half of all shares occurring within the first hour of publication. Twitter's simplicity, with its 140-character limit, allows for quick and focused communication, making it ideal for timely updates during disasters, where rapid information flow is crucial for effective response.

To analyze the evolution of online conversations, the study utilized topic modeling, specifically Latent Dirichlet Allocation (LDA), and classified the topics into five categories: awareness, preparation, action, impact, and other. Tweets categorized as 'other' were excluded. The awareness category reflected active discussions about the event, indicating public concern over hazardous weather, with topics on the typhoon's intensity and weather forecasts. The preparation category included three LDA topics, two on general warnings and one on landslide alerts, showing readiness for action. The action category focused on evacuation, while the impact category covered weather-related damage, including train disruptions, river overflows, floods, and general disaster impact.

Analyzing a corpus of 35 million tweets with computational methods like topic modeling and geospatial analysis revealed that emergency warnings tend to increase public attention to the warnings but do not necessarily lead to more discussions about actions, such as evacuation. The anticipated progression of public attention from awareness to preparation and then action appears to occur on social media. Overall, the study demonstrated that social media analysis can complement traditional survey-based approaches in understanding public responses to information from Early Warning Systems.

6. ETHICAL AND PRIVACY CONSIDERATIONS.

Emergency managers face two potentially conflicting responsibilities when activating a system: safeguarding lives and respecting the privacy of social media users and the subjects of their messages. The challenge lies in processing potentially sensitive information, often in large volumes, and determining how that information is used or shared by emergency managers. The emergency management agency has a primary obligation to both rescue those in danger and manage personal information responsibly. Such systems should be deployed only in response to real and imminent threats, ideally after ethical considerations and public consultation. The data collected must be used strictly for decision support in natural disaster response and machine learning improvements and should be deleted or anonymized as soon as it is no longer necessary. Emergency management agencies should implement comprehensive ethical training programs focused on values and legal compliance to ensure ethical decision-making that aligns with legal and societal values (Hayes & Kelly, 2018).

In light of the numerous high-profile cases of disinformation on social media and biased algorithms, there is a growing demand for action. Experts across various fields, including scholars, activists, ethicists, and journalists, emphasize the need for urgent measures to prevent further harm to individuals and society, as well as to avoid eroding public trust in AI and algorithms (Hickok, 2021). While social media's positive aspects are acknowledged, their potential for negative impacts, such as spreading rumors and undermining authority, prompts a critical examination of the ethics of social media use in crisis situations (Alexander, 2014).

The exclusion of those without a digital footprint, such as disadvantaged communities with limited access to technology, raises concerns. The use of social media for disaster warnings and damage assessment may introduce biases related to gender, income, and minority groups (Gevaert et al., 2021). Ethical challenges in collecting and analyzing social media data for disaster management include issues of informed consent, privacy, and data ownership. Organizations must ensure that individuals are aware of and consent to the use of their data and adopt transparent and accountable practices in data handling (Karimiziarani & Moradkhani, 2023). Techniques like anonymization and data de-identification should be employed to protect user privacy (Wang et al., 2019; Kemavuthanon & Uchida, 2020; Karimiziarani, 2023). Researchers must also consider and communicate the biases and limitations of social media data in their analyses. Public perception and trust are crucial when using social media data for disaster management. Transparent communication about data practices is essential to building trust among the public. Open dialogue with affected communities, response organizations, and stakeholders can effectively address concerns and communicate the benefits of social media analytics (Karimiziarani, 2023). Establishing public feedback mechanisms and incorporating public input into decision-making processes can support the responsible and ethical use of social media data. AI systems have enabled a deeper analysis of societal attitudes and response patterns. However, prioritizing ethical considerations is essential for the responsible use of data. Understanding the dynamic relationship between social media, AI, and disaster response is vital to enhancing crisis management strategies and increasing public engagement in the digital age (Subha & Vikkraman, 2024).

7. DISCUSSION.

Social media platforms are inundated with vast amounts of data, including posts, tweets, images, and videos during disasters. This high volume of real-time data offers invaluable insights into public sentiment, needs, and the evolving situation on the ground. The ability to process this data quickly and efficiently is crucial for disaster response teams. However, the sheer volume presents significant challenges, such as filtering relevant information, verifying accuracy, and managing the overload of data streams. AI systems can help address these challenges by automatically sorting through large datasets, identifying patterns, and highlighting critical information, thereby enabling faster and more informed decision-making.

Social media has become a crucial tool for disaster situational awareness, facilitating the rapid dissemination of information and providing a platform for real-time updates from affected individuals. Its role has significantly evolved, with platforms now serving as essential channels for crisis communication, resource allocation, and community engagement. Geolocation data embedded in social media posts offers precise information on disaster impact areas, enabling targeted and efficient response efforts. Additionally, sentiment analysis of social media content provides valuable insights into the emotional state of affected populations, guiding mental health interventions and other support services. This evolution in crisis management highlights social media's vital role in both communication and data collection, ultimately contributing to more informed and compassionate disaster response efforts.

AI enhances the ability to process and analyze large volumes of social media data in real time, which is critical during disasters when timely information can save lives. By employing techniques like sentiment analysis, NLP, and machine learning, AI systems can quickly identify key trends, detect urgent needs, and monitor public sentiment. This information can assist in resource allocation, improve risk communication, and support decision-making processes. AI-driven analysis also allows for the identification of emerging risks and anticipation of potential challenges, contributing to more proactive disaster management.

While AI offers significant benefits in processing social media data, it also presents challenges. One major issue is the potential for bias in AI algorithms, which can result in the unequal representation of certain groups, particularly marginalized communities with limited digital access. Additionally, AI systems may struggle to accurately interpret the context of social media posts, leading to misclassification or misinterpretation of data. Another challenge is the integration of multimodal social media data (text, images, and videos) into a cohesive analysis, requiring advanced AI techniques and interoperability between different data sources. Addressing these challenges is essential for ensuring the effectiveness and fairness of AI-driven disaster management systems.

The use of AI to analyze social media data for disaster management raises several ethical concerns. These include issues related to privacy, informed consent, and data ownership. Users of social media may not be aware that their posts are being analyzed for disaster response purposes, raising questions about the transparency and accountability of such practices. To address these concerns, organizations must implement ethical guidelines that prioritize the protection of user data. This involves anonymizing data, employing data de-identification techniques, and ensuring that data is only used for legitimate purposes related to disaster management. Furthermore, open communication with the public about data practices can help build trust and ensure that AI-driven initiatives are both ethical and effective.

Public perception and trust are fundamental to the successful use of social media data in disaster management. Engaging communities in a transparent dialogue about data collection and analysis practices can help address concerns and foster trust. Establishing mechanisms for public feedback and incorporating this input into decision-making processes ensures that social media data is used responsibly and ethically. This approach not only enhances the effectiveness of disaster response but also supports the long-term goal of building resilient communities that are better prepared for future crises.

8. CONCLUSION.

This paper has attempted to make an in depth analysis of the transformative role of social media in modern disaster management. It highlights how social media platforms have evolved into essential tools for real-time crisis communication, geolocation-based disaster response, and sentiment analysis, providing critical insights into the emotional and psychological impacts of disasters. The integration of AI and machine learning algorithms significantly enhances the ability to process vast amounts of social media data, enabling more efficient resource allocation and targeted support in the aftermath of disasters. However, the paper also addresses the challenges of using AI in this context, particularly the need for data privacy, ethical considerations, and the importance of transparent public engagement. By examining real-world case studies and exploring the opportunities presented by smart urban environments, the paper illustrates the potential and the complexities of leveraging AI-driven social media analysis for disaster situational awareness. Ultimately, it advocates for a balanced approach that maximizes the benefits of AI and social media while ensuring responsible and ethical data usage.

REFERENCES

Abu-Alsaad, H. A., & Al-Taie, R. R. K. (2021). NLP analysis in social media using big data technologies. *Telkomnika, 19*(6), 1840–1846. DOI: 10.12928/telkomnika.v19i6.19339

Ahmadi, G., Tavakkoli-Moghaddam, R., Baboli, A., & Najafi, M. (2022). A decision support model for robust allocation and routing of search and rescue resources after earthquake: A case study. *Operations Research, 22*(2), 1–43. DOI: 10.1007/s12351-020-00591-5

Alam, F., Ofli, F., & Imran, M. (2020). Descriptive and visual summaries of disaster events using artificial intelligence techniques: Case studies of Hurricanes Harvey, Irma, and Maria. *Behaviour & Information Technology, 39*(3), 288–318. DOI: 10.1080/0144929X.2019.1610908

Alexander, D. E. (2014). Social media in disaster risk reduction and crisis management. *Science and Engineering Ethics, 20*(3), 717–733. DOI: 10.1007/s11948-013-9502-z PMID: 24306994

Alvarado, B. J. S., & Solano, P. E. C. (2021). Detecting Disaster Tweets using a Natural Language Processing technique.

Basu, M., Bit, S. D., & Ghosh, S. (2022). Utilizing microblogs for optimized real-time resource allocation in post-disaster scenarios. *Social Network Analysis and Mining, 12*(1), 1–20. DOI: 10.1007/s13278-021-00841-0 PMID: 34900021

Basyah, N. A., Syukri, M., Fahmi, I., Ali, I., Rusli, Z., & Putri, E. S. (2023). Disaster Prevention and Management: A Critical Review of The Literature. *Jurnal Penelitian Pendidikan IPA, 9*(11), 1045–1051. DOI: 10.29303/jppipa.v9i11.4486

Beigi, G., Hu, X., Maciejewski, R., & Liu, H. (2016). An overview of sentiment analysis in social media and its applications in disaster relief. *Sentiment analysis and ontology engineering: An environment of computational intelligence*, 313-340. https://doi.org/DOI: 10.1007/978-3-319-30319-2_13

Bikku, T., Chandrika, P., Kanyadari, A., Prathima, V., & Sai, B. B. (2022). Analysis of disaster tweets using natural language processing. In *Intelligent Computing and Applications:Proceedings of ICDIC 2020* (pp. 491-501). Singapore: Springer Nature Singapore. https://doi.org/DOI: 10.1007/978-981-19-4162-7_46

Boersma, K., Clark, N., & Rizza, C. (2024). Governing the uses of social media and crowdsourcing in crisis and disaster (risk) management. *Risk, Hazards & Crisis in Public Policy, 15*(2), 94–103. Advance online publication. DOI: 10.1002/rhc3.12310

Bohannon, J. (2015). Credit card study blows holes in anonymity. *Science, 347*(6221), 468. DOI: 10.1126/science.347.6221.468 PMID: 25635068

Bouvier, G. (2019). How journalists source trending social media feeds: A critical discourse perspective on Twitter. *Journalism Studies, 20*(2), 212–231. DOI: 10.1080/1461670X.2017.1365618

Bouvier, G., & Machin, D. (2020). Critical discourse analysis and the challenges and opportunities of social media. *Critical discourse studies and/in communication*, 39-53. https://doi.org/DOI: 10.1080/15358593.2018.1479881

Bryan-Smith, L., Godsall, J., George, F., Egode, K., Dethlefs, N., & Parsons, D. (2023). Real-time social media sentiment analysis for rapid impact assessment of floods. *Computers & Geosciences, 178*, 105405. DOI: 10.1016/j.cageo.2023.105405

Castillo, C. (2016). *Big crisis data: social media in disasters and time-critical situations*. Cambridge University Press. DOI: 10.1017/CBO9781316476840

Chandra, R., & Lakshmi, D. (2024). Application of Artificial Intelligence in Disaster Management and Their Challenges. Internet of Things and AI for Natural Disaster Management and Prediction, 1-27. https://doi.org/DOI: 10.4018/979-8-3693-4284-8.ch001

Chopra, M., Singh, S. K., Aggarwal, K., & Gupta, A. (2022). Predicting catastrophic events using machine learning models for natural language processing. In *Data mining approaches for big data and sentiment analysis in social media* (pp. 223–243). IGI Global., DOI: 10.4018/978-1-7998-8413-2.ch010

Cobo, A., Parra, D., & Navón, J. (2015, May). Identifying relevant messages in a twitter-based citizen channel for natural disaster situations. In *Proceedings of the 24th international conference on world wide web* (pp. 1189-1194). https://doi.org/DOI: 10.1145/2740908.2741719

Coppola, D. (2015). *Introduction to International Disaster Management. Butterworth-Heinemann*. Elsevier.

Daly, S., & Thom, J. A. (2016, May). Mining and Classifying Image Posts on Social Media to Analyse Fires. In ISCRAM (pp. 1-14).

Domala, J., Dogra, M., Masrani, V., Fernandes, D., D'souza, K., Fernandes, D., & Carvalho, T. (2020, July). Automated identification of disaster news for crisis management using machine learning and natural language processing. In *2020 International Conference on Electronics and Sustainable Communication Systems (ICESC)* (pp. 503-508). IEEE. https://doi.org/DOI: 10.1109/ICESC48915.2020.9156031

Elston, D. M. (2021). The hawthorne effect. *Journal of the American Academy of Dermatology*. Advance online publication. DOI: 10.1016/j.jaad.2021.01.085 PMID: 33810890

Erbeyoğlu, G., & Bilge, Ü. (2020). A robust disaster preparedness model for effective and fair disaster response. *European Journal of Operational Research*, *280*(2), 479–494. DOI: 10.1016/j.ejor.2019.07.029

Fakhruddin, B., Clark, H., Robinson, L., & Hieber-Girardet, L. (2020). Should I stay or should I go now? Why risk communication is the critical component in disaster risk reduction. *Progress in Disaster Science*, *8*, 100139. DOI: 10.1016/j.pdisas.2020.100139 PMID: 34977532

Fanni, S. C., Febi, M., Aghakhanyan, G., & Neri, E. (2023). Natural language processing. In *Introduction to Artificial Intelligence* (pp. 87–99). Springer International Publishing., DOI: 10.1007/978-3-031-25928-9_5

Feng, Y., Brenner, C., & Sester, M. (2020). Flood severity mapping from Volunteered Geographic Information by interpreting water level from images containing people: A case study of Hurricane Harvey. *ISPRS Journal of Photogrammetry and Remote Sensing*, *169*, 301–319. DOI: 10.1016/j.isprsjprs.2020.09.011

Gao, H., Barbier, G., & Goolsby, R. (2011). Harnessing the crowdsourcing power of social media for disaster relief. *IEEE Intelligent Systems*, *26*(3), 10–14. DOI: 10.1109/MIS.2011.52

Gevaert, C. M., Carman, M., Rosman, B., Georgiadou, Y., & Soden, R. (2021). Fairness and accountability of AI in disaster risk management: Opportunities and challenges. *Patterns (New York, N.Y.)*, *2*(11), 100363. Advance online publication. DOI: 10.1016/j.patter.2021.100363 PMID: 34820647

Gialampoukidis, I., Andreadis, S., Vrochidis, S., & Kompatsiaris, I. (2021, July). Multimodal data fusion of social media and satellite images for emergency response and decision-making. In *2021 IEEE International Geoscience and Remote Sensing Symposium IGARSS* (pp. 228-231). IEEE. https://doi.org/DOI: 10.1109/IGARSS47720.2021.9554176

Goldblum, M., Tsipras, D., Xie, C., Chen, X., Schwarzschild, A., Song, D., Madry, A., Li, B., & Goldstein, T. (2022). Dataset security for machine learning: Data poisoning, backdoor attacks, and defenses. *IEEE Transactions on Pattern Analysis and Machine Intelligence*, *45*(2), 1563–1580. DOI: 10.1109/TPAMI.2022.3162397 PMID: 35333711

Gu, Y., Qian, Z., & Chen, F. (2016). From Twitter to detector: Real-time traffic incident detection using social media data. *Transportation Research Part C, Emerging Technologies*, *67*, 321–342. DOI: 10.1016/j.trc.2016.02.011

Guo, B., Ding, Y., Yao, L., Liang, Y., & Yu, Z. (2020). The future of false information detection on social media: New perspectives and trends. *ACM Computing Surveys*, *53*(4), 1–36. DOI: 10.1145/3393880

HaCohen-Kerner, Y., Miller, D., & Yigal, Y.HaCohen-Kerner. (2020). The influence of preprocessing on text classification using a bag-of-words representation. *PLoS One*, *15*(5), e0232525. DOI: 10.1371/journal.pone.0232525 PMID: 32357164

Hao, H., & Wang, Y. (2020). Leveraging multimodal social media data for rapid disaster damage assessment. *International Journal of Disaster Risk Reduction*, *51*, 101760. DOI: 10.1016/j.ijdrr.2020.101760

Hassan, S. Z., Ahmad, K., Hicks, S., Halvorsen, P., Al-Fuqaha, A., Conci, N., & Riegler, M. (2022). Visual sentiment analysis from disaster images in social media. *Sensors (Basel)*, *22*(10), 3628. DOI: 10.3390/s22103628 PMID: 35632034

Hayes, J. L., Britt, B. C., Evans, W., Rush, S. W., Towery, N. A., & Adamson, A. C. (2021). Can social media listening platforms' artificial intelligence be trusted? Examining the accuracy of Crimson Hexagon's (now Brandwatch Consumer Research's) AI-Driven analyses. *Journal of Advertising*, *50*(1), 81–91. DOI: 10.1080/00913367.2020.1809576

Hayes, P., & Kelly, S. (2018). Distributed morality, privacy, and social media in natural disaster response. *Technology in Society*, *54*, 155–167. DOI: 10.1016/j.techsoc.2018.05.003

Hecker, N., & Domres, B. D. (2018). The German emergency and disaster medicine and management system—history and present. *Chinese Journal of Traumatology = Zhonghua Chuang Shang Za Zhi*, *21*(2), 64–72. DOI: 10.1016/j.cjtee.2017.09.003 PMID: 29622286

Hickok, M. (2021). Lessons learned from AI ethics principles for future actions. *AI and Ethics*, *1*(1), 41–47. DOI: 10.1007/s43681-020-00008-1

Hughes, A. L., & Palen, L. (2009). Twitter adoption and use in mass convergence and emergency events. *International Journal of Emergency Management*, *6*(3-4), 248–260. DOI: 10.1504/IJEM.2009.031564

Iglesias, C. A., & Moreno, A. (2019). Sentiment analysis for social media. *Applied Sciences (Basel, Switzerland)*, *9*(23), 5037. DOI: 10.3390/app9235037

Jain, P., Gyanchandani, M., & Khare, N. (2016). Big data privacy: A technological perspective and review. *Journal of Big Data*, *3*(1), 25. DOI: 10.1186/s40537-016-0059-y

John-Otumu, A. M., Rahman, M. M., Nwokonkwo, O. C., & Onuoha, M. C. (2022). AI-Based Techniques for Online Social Media Network Sentiment Analysis: A Methodical Review. *International Journal of Computer and Information Engineering*, *16*(12), 555–560.

Jung, J.-K., & Shin, J. (2018). A Hybrid Approach to Geotweets. In *Thinking Big Data in Geography. New Regimes, New Research* (pp. 91–122). University of Nebraska Press., Available at https://www.jstor.org/stable/j.ctt21h4z6m.10 DOI: 10.2307/j.ctt21h4z6m.10

Kamruzzaman, A., Ismat, S., Brickley, J. C., Liu, A., & Thakur, K. (2022, December). A comprehensive review of endpoint security: Threats and defenses. In *2022 International Conference on Cyber Warfare and Security (ICCWS)* (pp. 1-7). IEEE. https://doi.org/DOI: 10.1109/ICCWS56285.2022.9998470

Kankanamge, N., Yigitcanlar, T., & Goonetilleke, A. (2020). How engaging are disaster management related social media channels? The case of Australian state emergency organisations. *International Journal of Disaster Risk Reduction*, *48*, 101571. DOI: 10.1016/j.ijdrr.2020.101571

Kankanamge, N., Yigitcanlar, T., Goonetilleke, A., & Kamruzzaman, M. (2019). Can volunteer crowdsourcing reduce disaster risk? A systematic review of the literature. *International Journal of Disaster Risk Reduction*, *35*, 101097. DOI: 10.1016/j.ijdrr.2019.101097

Kankanamge, N., Yigitcanlar, T., Goonetilleke, A., & Kamruzzaman, M. (2020a). Determining disaster severity through social media analysis: Testing the methodology with South East Queensland Flood tweets. *International Journal of Disaster Risk Reduction*, *42*, 101360. DOI: 10.1016/j.ijdrr.2019.101360

Karimiziarani, M. (2023). Social media analytics in disaster response: A comprehensive review. *arXiv preprint arXiv:2307.04046*. https://doi.org//arXiv.2307.04046DOI: 10.48550

Karimiziarani, M., & Moradkhani, H. (2023). Social response and Disaster management: Insights from twitter data Assimilation on Hurricane Ian. *International Journal of Disaster Risk Reduction*, *95*, 103865. DOI: 10.1016/j.ijdrr.2023.103865

Kastrati, Z., Ahmedi, L., Kurti, A., Kadriu, F., Murtezaj, D., & Gashi, F. (2021). A deep learning sentiment analyser for social media comments in low-resource languages. *Electronics (Basel), 10*(10), 1133. DOI: 10.3390/electronics10101133

Kemavuthanon, K., & Uchida, O. (2020). Classification of social media messages posted at the time of disaster. In *Information Technology in Disaster Risk Reduction: 4th IFIP TC 5 DCITDRR International Conference, ITDRR 2019, Kyiv, Ukraine, October 9–10, 2019, Revised Selected Papers 4* (pp. 212-226). Springer International Publishing. https://doi.org/DOI: 10.1007/978-3-030-48939-7_18

Khatoon, S., Asif, A., Hasan, M. M., & Alshamari, M. (2022). Social media-based intelligence for disaster response and management in smart cities. In *Artificial Intelligence, Machine Learning, and Optimization Tools for Smart Cities: Designing for Sustainability* (pp. 211–235). Springer International Publishing., DOI: 10.1007/978-3-030-84459-2_11

Khatoon, S., Romman, L. A., & Hasan, M. M.Lamis Abu Romman. (2020). Domain independent automatic labeling system for large-scale social data using Lexicon and web-based augmentation. *Information Technology and Control, 49*(1), 36–54. DOI: 10.5755/j01.itc.49.1.23769

Khurana, D., Koli, A., Khatter, K., & Singh, S. (2023). Natural language processing: State of the art, current trends and challenges. *Multimedia Tools and Applications, 82*(3), 3713–3744. DOI: 10.1007/s11042-022-13428-4 PMID: 35855771

Kitazawa, K., & Hale, S. A. (2021). Social media and early warning systems for natural disasters: A case study of Typhoon Etau in Japan. *International Journal of Disaster Risk Reduction, 52*, 101926. DOI: 10.1016/j.ijdrr.2020.101926

Kumar, R. (2021). Managing Business in the Digital Era–The use of IT and Analytics for Process Transformation. *Journal of Decision Systems, 30*(4), 410–413. DOI: 10.1080/12460125.2021.1925397

Lee, I. (2018). Social media analytics for enterprises: Typology, methods, and processes. *Business Horizons, 61*(2), 199–210. DOI: 10.1016/j.bushor.2017.11.002

Mangones, A. (n.d.). Social Media in Disasters. Accessed 11 July 2024. https://preparecenter.org/topic/social-media-disasters/

Manoharan, G., Razak, A., Rao, B. S., Singh, R., Ashtikar, S. P., & Nivedha, M. (2024). Navigating the Crescendo of Challenges in Harnessing Artificial Intelligence for Disaster Management. In *Predicting Natural Disasters With AI and Machine Learning* (pp. 64–94). IGI Global., DOI: 10.4018/979-8-3693-2280-2.ch003

Martí, P., Serrano-Estrada, L., & Nolasco-Cirugeda, A. (2019). Social media data: Challenges, opportunities and limitations in urban studies. *Computers, Environment and Urban Systems*, *74*, 161–174. DOI: 10.1016/j.compenvurbsys.2018.11.001

McLain, R., Poe, M., Biedenweg, K., Cerveny, L., Besser, D., & Blahna, D. (2013). Making sense of human ecology mapping: An overview of approaches to integrating socio-spatial data into environmental planning. *Human Ecology: an Interdisciplinary Journal*, *41*(5), 651–665. DOI: 10.1007/s10745-013-9573-0

Meier, P. (2015). *Digital humanitarians: how big data is changing the face of humanitarian response*. Crc Press. DOI: 10.1201/b18023

Munir, A., Aved, A., & Blasch, E. (2022). Situational awareness: Techniques, challenges, and prospects. *AI*, *3*(1), 55–77. DOI: 10.3390/ai3010005

Naeem, M., Jamal, T., Diaz-Martinez, J., Butt, S. A., Montesano, N., Tariq, M. I., . . . De-La-Hoz-Valdiris, E. (2022). Trends and future perspective challenges in big data. In *Advances in Intelligent Data Analysis and Applications:Proceeding of the Sixth Euro-China Conference on Intelligent Data Analysis and Applications,15–18 October 2019,Arad, Romania* (pp. 309-325). Springer Singapore. https://doi.org/ DOI: 10.1007/978-981-16-5036-9_30

Nazer, T. H., Morstatter, F., Dani, H., & Liu, H. (2016, August). Finding requests in social media for disaster relief. In *2016 IEEE/ACM International Conference on Advances in Social Networks Analysis and Mining (ASONAM)* (pp. 1410-1413). IEEE. https://doi.org/DOI: 10.1109/ASONAM.2016.7752432

Nunavath, V., & Goodwin, M. (2018, December). The role of artificial intelligence in social media big data analytics for disaster management-initial results of a systematic literature review. In *2018 5th International Conference on information and communication technologies for disaster management (ICT-DM)* (pp. 1-4). IEEE. https://doi.org/DOI: 10.1109/ICT-DM.2018.8636388

Olteanu, A., Vieweg, S., & Castillo, C. (2015, February). What to expect when the unexpected happens: Social media communications across crises. In Proceedings of the 18th ACM conference on computer supported cooperative work & social computing (pp. 994-1009). https://doi.org/DOI: 10.1145/2675133.2675242

Perry, R. W., & Lindell, M. K. (2003). Preparedness for emergency response: Guidelines for the emergency planning process. *Disasters*, *27*(4), 336–350. DOI: 10.1111/j.0361-3666.2003.00237.x PMID: 14725091

Pratomo, A. B., Mokodenseho, S., & Aziz, A. M. (2023). Data encryption and anonymization techniques for enhanced information system security and privacy. *West Science Information System and Technology*, *1*(01), 1–9. DOI: 10.58812/wsist.v1i01.176

Qu, Y., Wu, P. F., & Wang, X. (2009, January). Online community response to major disaster: A study of Tianya forum in the 2008 Sichuan earthquake. In 2009 42nd Hawaii International Conference on System Sciences (pp. 1-11). IEEE. https://doi.org/DOI: 10.1109/HICSS.2009.330

Reuter, C., Kaufhold, M.-A., Spahr, F., Spielhofer, T., & Hahne, A. S. (2020). Emergency Service Staff and Social Media – A Comparative Empirical Study of the Attitude By Emergency Services Staff in Europe in 2014 and 2017. *International Journal of Disaster Risk Reduction*, *46*, 101516. DOI: 10.1016/j.ijdrr.2020.101516

Reynard, D., & Shirgaokar, M. (2019). Harnessing the power of machine learning: Can Twitter data be useful in guiding resource allocation decisions during a natural disaster? *Transportation Research Part D, Transport and Environment*, *77*, 449–463. DOI: 10.1016/j.trd.2019.03.002

Sambolek, S., & Ivasic-Kos, M. (2021). Automatic person detection in search and rescue operations using deep CNN detectors. *IEEE Access : Practical Innovations, Open Solutions*, *9*, 37905–37922. DOI: 10.1109/ACCESS.2021.3063681

Saroj, A., & Pal, S. (2020). Use of Social Media in Crisis Management: A Survey. *International Journal of Disaster Risk Reduction*, *48*, 101584. DOI: 10.1016/j.ijdrr.2020.101584

Sathianarayanan, M., Hsu, P. H., & Chang, C. C. (2024). Extracting disaster location identification from social media images using deep learning. *International Journal of Disaster Risk Reduction*, *104*, 104352. DOI: 10.1016/j.ijdrr.2024.104352

Schmidt, A., Wolbers, J., Ferguson, J., & Boersma, K. (2018). Are You Ready-2Help? Conceptualizing the Management of Online and Onsite Volunteer Convergence. *Journal of Contingencies and Crisis Management*, *26*(3), 338–349. DOI: 10.1111/1468-5973.12200

Schweitzer, L. (2014). Planning and social media: A case study of public transit and stigma on Twitter. *Journal of the American Planning Association*, *80*(3), 218–238. DOI: 10.1080/01944363.2014.980439

Shahbazi, Z., & Byun, Y. C. (2021). Blockchain-based event detection and trust verification using natural language processing and machine learning. *IEEE Access : Practical Innovations, Open Solutions, 10*, 5790–5800. DOI: 10.1109/ACCESS.2021.3139586

Singh, Col Ravinder, & Manoharan, G. (2024). "Strengthening Resilience: AI and Machine Learning in Emergency Decision-Making for Natural Disasters." In *Internet of Things and AI for Natural Disaster Management and Prediction*, pp. 249-278. IGI Global. https://doi.org/DOI: 10.4018/979-8-3693-4284-8.ch012

Singh, R., Manoharan, G., & Singh, S. (2024). Strategic Deployment of AI and Drones Enhancing Disaster Management in Natural Disasters. AI and IoT for Proactive Disaster Management, 172-203. https://doi.org/DOI: 10.4018/979-8-3693-3896-4.ch009

Soni, H. K. (2024). 14 Social Media Skirmish. Text and Social Media Analytics for Fake News and Hate Speech Detection, 248.

Stieglitz, S., Mirbabaie, M., Ross, B., & Neuberger, C. (2018). Social media analytics–Challenges in topic discovery, data collection, and data preparation. *International Journal of Information Management, 39*, 156–168. DOI: 10.1016/j.ijinfomgt.2017.12.002

Subha, N., & Vikkraman, P. (2024). The Impact of Social Media on Public Perception and Behaviour During Disasters: An AI-Enhanced Analysis. In *Predicting Natural Disasters With AI and Machine Learning* (pp. 95–109). IGI Global., DOI: 10.4018/979-8-3693-2280-2.ch004

Sufi, F. K. (2022). AI-Social Disaster: An AI-based software for identifying and analyzing natural disasters from social media. *Software Impacts, 13*, 100319. DOI: 10.1016/j.simpa.2022.100319

Sufi, F. K., & Khalil, I. (2022). Automated disaster monitoring from social media posts using AI-based location intelligence and sentiment analysis. *IEEE Transactions on Computational Social Systems*. Advance online publication. DOI: 10.1109/TCSS.2022.3157142

Tahir, F., & Khan, M. (2023). *Big Data: the Fuel for Machine Learning and AI Advancement* (No. 10951). EasyChair.

Tanev, H., Zavarella, V., & Steinberger, J. (2017, May). Monitoring disaster impact: detecting micro-events and eyewitness reports in mainstream and social media. In ISCRAM.

Tounsi, A., & Temimi, M. (2023). A systematic review of natural language processing applications for hydrometeorological hazards assessment. *Natural Hazards*, *116*(3), 2819–2870. DOI: 10.1007/s11069-023-05842-0 PMID: 36776702

Tsoy, D., Tirasawasdichai, T., & Kurpayanidi, K. I. (2021). Role of social media in shaping public risk perception during COVID-19 pandemic: A theoretical review. *International Journal of Management Science and Business Administration*, *7*(2), 35–41. DOI: 10.18775/ijmsba.1849-5664-5419.2014.72.1005

Unger, J., & Wodak, R., & KhosraviNik, M. (2016). Critical discourse studies and social media data. *Qualitative Research*, •••, 277–293.

Varsha, V. R., Naganandini, S., & Hariharan, C. (2024). Utilizing AI and machine learning for natural disaster management: predicting natural disasters with AI and machine learning. In *Internet of Things and AI for Natural Disaster Management and Prediction* (pp. 279–304). IGI Global., DOI: 10.4018/979-8-3693-4284-8.ch013

Vongkusolkit, J., & Huang, Q. (2021). Situational awareness extraction: A comprehensive review of social media data classification during natural hazards. *Annals of GIS*, *27*(1), 5–28. DOI: 10.1080/19475683.2020.1817146

Wang, Y., Hao, H., & Platt, L. S. (2021). Examining risk and crisis communications of government agencies and stakeholders during early-stages of COVID-19 on Twitter. *Computers in Human Behavior*, *114*, 106568. DOI: 10.1016/j.chb.2020.106568 PMID: 32982038

Wang, Z., Hale, S., Adelani, D. I., Grabowicz, P., Hartman, T., Flöck, F., & Jurgens, D. (2019, May). Demographic inference and representative population estimates from multilingual social media data. In *The world wide web conference* (pp. 2056-2067). https://doi.org/DOI: 10.1145/3308558.3313684

Wukich, C. (2020). GETTING MORE FROM: SOCIAL MEDIA for Pandemic and Disaster Management: In times of crisis, the use of social media is key for risk communication and community engagement. *Public Management*, *102*(11), 17–22.

Xu, Q. A., Chang, V., & Jayne, C. (2022). A systematic review of social media-based sentiment analysis: Emerging trends and challenges. *Decision Analytics Journal*, *3*, 100073. DOI: 10.1016/j.dajour.2022.100073

Yanuargi, B., Utami, E., & Parikesit, A. A. (2024, February). Location-Based Service Insights: A Comprehensive Review of Data Mining Objects. In *2024 IEEE International Conference on Artificial Intelligence and Mechatronics Systems (AIMS)* (pp. 1-6). IEEE. https://doi.org/DOI: 10.1109/AIMS61812.2024.10513296

Yue, L., Chen, W., Li, X., Zuo, W., & Yin, M. (2019). A survey of sentiment analysis in social media. *Knowledge and Information Systems, 60*(2), 617–663. DOI: 10.1007/s10115-018-1236-4

Zade, H., Shah, K., Rangarajan, V., Kshirsagar, P., Imran, M., & Starbird, K. (2018). From situational awareness to actionability: Towards improving the utility of social media data for crisis response. Proceedings of the ACM on human-computer interaction, 2(CSCW), 1-18. https://doi.org/DOI: 10.1145/3274464

Zhang, W., Xu, M., & Jiang, Q. (2018). Opinion mining and sentiment analysis in social media: Challenges and applications. In *HCI in Business, Government, and Organizations: 5th International Conference, HCIBGO 2018, Held as Part of HCI International 2018, Las Vegas, NV, USA,July 15-20, 2018,Proceedings 5* (pp. 536-548). Springer International Publishing. https://doi.org/DOI: 10.1007/978-3-319-91716-0_43

Chapter 8
Smart Transportation Systems:
Enhancing Mobility and Accessibility

Bhupendra Panchal
https://orcid.org/0009-0004-5800-4263
VIT Bhopal University, India

Ajay Sharma
https://orcid.org/0000-0001-7951-9371
VIT Bhopal University, India

Pranshu Pranjal
https://orcid.org/0000-0001-6213-7131
VIT Bhopal University, India

Rajneesh Kumar Patel
https://orcid.org/0000-0002-3574-4419
VIT Bhopal University, India

ABSTRACT

The rapid urbanization and demand for efficient transportation drive the growth of Smart Transportation Systems (STS), enhancing urban mobility, accessibility, and sustainability through advanced technologies like AI, IoT, and big data. AI is pivotal in transforming transportation by making it more sustainable, safe, and efficient through technologies like computer vision, machine learning, and natural language processing. This study explores AI's role in optimizing urban transportation to manage population growth, boost economies, reduce energy use, and improve quality of life. AI enables better traffic management, including dynamic routing, congestion

DOI: 10.4018/979-8-3693-7832-8.ch008

avoidance, and traffic signal control, creating seamless, efficient urban transit.

I. INTRODUCTION

Transportation is a critical component of modern urban life, influencing economic growth, quality of life, and environmental sustainability. Smart Transportation Systems (STS) use cutting-edge technologies to address challenges in transportation, enhancing mobility and accessibility for all. This chapter explores the key components, benefits, and future directions of STS, illustrating how these systems are transforming transportation networks worldwide. The U.S. has over 7,000 public transit agencies, along with numerous private ones, providing 60 billion passenger miles annually as a group. Recently, new on-demand services—such as ride-sharing, bike-sharing, and e-scooters—have significantly reshaped urban transit options. A well-functioning transit system not only stimulates business growth and spreads social and economic benefits but also empowers communities by connecting people and expanding what they can achieve together. However, the rapid expansion of transportation choices and the complex interplay between private and public services bring new difficulties in system design and operation. Achieving efficiency in such systems is complicated by a range of competing operational goals. Since affordable transit is vital for many communities, addressing these issues through advanced, AI-driven smart transportation technologies offers a path toward stronger urban communities, climate action, and equitable development.

At its core, designing effective transit requires tackling complex combinatorial optimization problems, from traditional line planning to various forms of vehicle routing (VRPs). To evaluate smart transit systems, the focus is typically on optimizing utilization (boosting ridership) and efficiency (cutting operational costs). Achieving high utilization demands understanding travel patterns over large areas and adapting services to meet real-time need. This also necessitates flexible options, including multi-modal and on-demand transportation, to provide timely service to passengers. Efficient systems not only reduce environmental impacts through lower emissions but also allow resources to be allocated more cost-effectively. Coverage, however, is another crucial factor that sometimes conflicts with goals of utilization and efficiency. It's essential to approach optimization with a balance between ridership and coverage, especially to ensure equitable access. Although balancing ridership and coverage is an open-ended challenge, there are various ways to model these aspects, enabling transit agencies to better align with their core objectives.

Efficient transportation systems require real-time decision-making across expansive areas and involve complex, computationally intensive state-action spaces. Traditional analytical tools are inadequate because these problems are intractable.

Transit organizations are therefore implementing computational techniques that enable extensive, data-driven optimization. By drawing conclusions from enormous amounts of data, AI-driven transportation systems provide a means of addressing this issue and facilitating effective, real-time decision-making on a broad scale. However, they must address complex issues related to model representation, real time decision-making under uncertainty, and the ingestion and processing of data. Within the broad field of smart transportation, On-demand and fixed-line systems are the two high-impact modalities that we are concentrating on. Vehicles like buses and trains that adhere to set routes and schedules are used in fixed-line transportation. In contrast, on-demand transportation provides flexible services where users request real-time rides or in advance, with transport provided directly from source to goal through options like ride-sharing, e-scooters, or bike-sharing. Additionally, multiple transit agencies are exploring multi-modal transportation, a more adaptable model which groups on-demand and fixed-line options to meet diverse transportation needs.

AI in Smart Transportation

The term AI was first introduced in 1955 particularly for intelligent computer programs. Recently, research on AI applications in public transportation (PT) has surged, often aiming to enhance system understanding and traveller insights or improve efficiency to achieve cost reductions and environmental benefits. AI is essential to autonomous vehicles because it uses sensor data, computer vision, and machine learning algorithms to enable self-driving automobiles and autonomous transportation. Real-time decision-making across vast geographic regions and computationally unmanageable state-action spaces are essential for smart transportation systems. As a result, real-time data gathered from sensors, GPS, cameras, and other smart devices is crucial to their operations. Analyzing, integrating, and optimizing real-time transport data in a dynamic context has grown more difficult. AI algorithms will produce precise and current traffic forecasts by analyzing enormous volumes of real-time data from multiple sources, such as sensors, GPS units, and social media. In this context, AI has the potential to support both individual users and organizations. Furthermore, the Internet of Things (IoT) serves as a powerful enabler in this field (Davidsson et al., 2016), promising transformative changes in public transportation when combined with AI. This chapter seeks to review research on AI applications aimed at enhancing public transportation (PT) to achieve various improvements. Travelers, stakeholders, or the environment may all gain from these improvements. Studies that use PT just to achieve unrelated objectives, like employing buses to find potholes in the road (Sharma and Sharma, 2019), are not included in this review.

The main needs, goals, and difficulties in creating AI-driven smart transportation systems are examined in this chapter. The main topics covered include:

- Data sources and administration for transportation systems powered by AI.
- An overview of AI's role in enhancing decision-making within transportation.
- Core computational challenges in transportation and the relevant AI approaches to address them.

II. RELATED WORKS

Previous efforts have partially reviewed this topic. For example, Aamir, Masroor, Ali, et al. (Aamir et al., 2019) presents a sustainable model for implementing a Smart Transportation System (STS) in Karachi, Pakistan. It examines Karachi's existing transportation issues, including traffic congestion, inadequate road conditions, and limited alternative transport options. The proposed framework integrates smart city technologies to address these challenges, aiming to optimize traffic flow, improve public transport, and enhance environmental sustainability. The study provides an in-depth analysis of Karachi's transport dynamics and outlines strategic recommendations for transitioning to a more efficient and eco-friendly transportation system. The use of artificial intelligence (AI) in intelligent transportation systems (ITS) is examined by Iyer, L. S. (2021) (Iyer, 2021), with particular attention on safety management, logistics, public transit, and traffic management. It discusses how AI-powered tools such as machine learning, neural networks, and predictive analytics can address challenges like traffic congestion, safety risks, and environmental impacts. The paper highlights AI's role in optimizing transport networks, enhancing public transit efficiency, and reducing operational costs, presenting ITS as a pathway to more sustainable and efficient urban mobility.

Ushakov, D., et. al. (2022) (Ushakov et al., 2022) examines the role of artificial intelligence (AI) in enhancing public transportation systems. It discusses how AI technologies—such as predictive analytics, machine learning, and real-time data processing—support efficient route planning, reduce wait times, and optimize traffic flow, ultimately improving service quality and accessibility. The authors highlight AI's potential to make public transport more responsive to demand and adaptable to urban challenges, contributing to a more sustainable transport system. Fed-NTP, a federated learning algorithm created for network traffic prediction in vehicular ad hoc networks (VANETs), was presented by the authors in (Sepasgozar & Pierre, 2022) (2022). The algorithm enables decentralized traffic data processing across multiple network nodes, enhancing real-time traffic prediction while preserving user privacy. By reducing the need for centralized data collection, Fed-NTP improves prediction accuracy, minimizes latency, and supports scalable, secure traffic management for smart transportation systems.

The study by Jevinger et al. (2024) (Jevinger et al., 2024) reviews the application of AI in public transport, analyzing 87 scientific publications. It highlights that AI primarily aims to enhance service quality and understand traveler behavior, focusing on bus and train systems. Key tasks include prediction, state estimation, and resource allocation. The research reveals significant potential for AI to improve public transport, but emphasizes challenges related to data quality, privacy, and resource requirements. Further research is needed to address these issues effectively. The use of AI technology to improve transportation systems is examined in the critical review "Artificial Intelligence in Transportation Systems," written by Bharadiya (2023) (Bharadiya, 2023). The paper outlines the roles of various AI methodologies, such as neural networks and machine learning, in solving transportation challenges, including traffic management, incident detection, and predictive analysis. It emphasizes the potential of Intelligent Transportation Systems (ITS) to improve efficiency and safety. However, the review also highlights challenges such as data collection and analysis issues, which need to be addressed for effective implementation. Cui and Lei (2023) discussed the design of an intelligent transportation system (ITS) for highways that integrates the IoT and AI. They analyze the fundamental principles and status of IoT and ITS, proposing a three-layer architecture: perceptual, transport, and application layers. The authors highlight improvements in efficiency and user satisfaction over traditional systems, emphasizing the system's capability to enhance transportation safety and management. The study aims to foster the advancement of smart system for transportation using modern information technologies.

Olugbade et al. (2022) give a thorough analysis of how machine learning (ML) and artificial intelligence (AI) are used to detect incidents in road transport networks. They discuss the critical challenges and solutions associated with traffic accidents and propose automatic incident detection systems that utilize AI and ML to improve safety and efficiency. The review covers various incident detection algorithms, their performance metrics, and the potential of emerging technologies like 5G in enhancing traffic management. The findings underscore the importance of AI/ML in optimizing road transport systems. In (Elassy et al., 2024), authors emphasize the importance of real-time communication technologies that facilitate the operation of these systems, helping to address challenges associated with urbanization and transportation management. The study also discusses the security issues related to ITS deployment, particularly concerning the privacy of public transit data. Through various case studies, the paper illustrates the tangible benefits of integrating ITS in urban areas, highlighting its contribution to the development of environmentally friendly smart cities. Furthermore, it considers how automotive manufacturers are proactively aligning with ITS standards to benefit both drivers and urban infrastructure.

Table 1. Comparative study of reviewed literatures

Study	Focus Area	Technologies Used	Benefits	Challenges	Future Directions
Aamir et al. 2019	Sustainable Smart Transportation System in Karachi	Smart city technologies	Traffic flow optimization, public transport improvement, sustainability	Existing infrastructure limitations	Strategic implementation of smart systems tailored for urban areas
Iyer 2021	AI in Intelligent Transportation Systems (ITS)	Machine learning, neural networks, predictive analytics	Safety management, network optimization, cost reduction	Limited data availability for accurate predictions	Expanding AI applications in logistics and public transit
Ushakov et al. 2022	AI for public transport enhancement	Predictive analytics, machine learning, real-time data	Efficient route planning, reduced wait times, traffic flow optimization	Adaptability to different urban environments	Scalability for diverse city infrastructures
Fed-NTP 2022	Decentralized traffic prediction in vehicular networks	Federated learning	Improved accuracy, reduced latency, privacy preservation	Scalability and integration into existing systems	Wider adoption of federated learning in ITS
Jevinger et al. 2024	AI applications in public transport	AI-driven prediction, resource allocation	Improved service quality, better understanding of traveler behavior	Data quality, privacy issues	Addressing resource constraints and refining prediction algorithms
Bharadiya 2023	AI methodologies in ITS for-traffic management	Neural networks, machine learning	Traffic management, incident detection, efficiency improvement	Data collection and analysis issues	Tackling data challenges for reliable AI-driven ITS
Cui & Lei 2023	IoT and AI integration for intelligent highway transportation	IoT, AI (three-layer architecture: perceptual, transport, and application)	Efficiency improvement, enhanced safety, better user satisfaction	High implementation costs	Deployment of IoT-driven smart systems across broader highway networks
Olugbade et al. 2022	AI/ML for incident detection in road networks	Machine learning, AI	Enhanced safety, real-time incident detection, reduced response times	Performance in high-density traffic scenarios	Leveraging 5G for faster and more reliable communication
Study 2023	Real-time communication technologies for transportation management	ITS, real-time data processing	Improved security, privacy, and ITS integration for urbanization challenges	Privacy concerns in ITS deployment	Developing robust security protocols for ITS

III. SMART TRANSPORTATION SYSTEMS FRAMEWORK

A smart transportation system framework is a way to transform a city's transportation system to provide safer, faster, and more environmentally friendly services for its residents. Smart transportation systems are a key part of smart cities, which also focus on smart energy management and city administration (Aamir et al., 2019). Figure 1 presents the framework for smart transport systems.

A. Data Collection and Analysis Layer

The foundation of STS is real-time, comprehensive data collection. IoT sensors installed in vehicles, public transport stations, and road infrastructure collect data on congestion, traffic flow, and environmental conditions. Big data analytics and machine learning models are then used to process this data in order to forecast traffic patterns, pinpoint areas of congestion, and recommend the best course of action.

Figure 1. Smart transportation systems framework

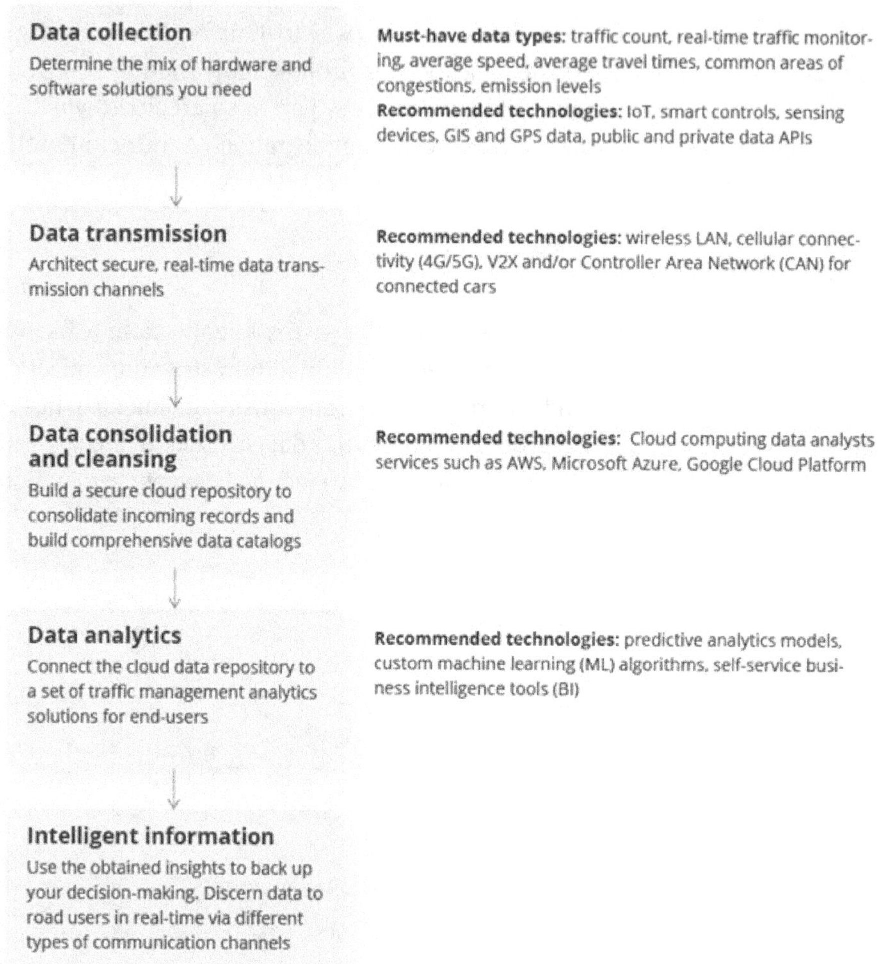

B. Traffic Management and Optimization Layer

Using AI algorithms, STS dynamically optimize traffic signals, recommend alternative routes, and manage congestion through real-time adjustments. Intelligent traffic control systems can shorten travel times and ease congestion, and decrease emissions, contributing to more sustainable urban mobility.

C. Public Transportation and Mobility as a Service (MaaS)

Bicycles, buses, trains, and ride-sharing services are just a few of the types of transportation that MaaS platforms combine into a single interface. Users can book, plan, and can also pay for their trips across different modes in one application, enhancing accessibility and convenience. MaaS also enables demand-responsive public transportation, where vehicles are deployed based on real-time demand, reducing wait time and improving efficiency.

D. Accessibility and Inclusive Design

STS prioritize accessibility by incorporating features such as voice-enabled interfaces, real-time navigation assistance, and adaptable transportation options. Autonomous shuttles, for example, can provide mobility to elderly and disabled individuals, while mobile applications with accessibility features support seamless navigation for visually impaired users.

E. Monitoring and Adaptation

Continuous monitoring and adaptation are critical for ensuring the long-term effectiveness of STS. Feedback loops, where user data informs adjustments in real time, allow STS to adapt to changing demands, maintain optimal performance, and incorporate user feedback. Reinforcement learning algorithms are particularly useful in creating adaptive, self-optimizing systems.

IV. BENEFITS OF SMART TRANSPORTATION SYSTEMS

A. Improved Mobility

STS provide real-time information on traffic, alternative routes, and public transportation, allowing for efficient travel. Adaptive traffic management systems decrease travel time and optimize resource allocation.

B. Increased Accessibility

By integrating accessibility features and adaptive interfaces, STS support mobility for individuals with disabilities and the elderly. The integration of MaaS platforms ensures seamless travel, enhancing accessibility for all users, regardless of ability.

C. Environmental Sustainability

Reduced congestion and optimized routing lower fuel consumption and greenhouse gas emissions, contributing to urban sustainability. Electric autonomous shuttles and other green technologies within STS reduce the carbon footprint of urban transportation.

By minimizing travel time and costs, STS enhance productivity and reduce economic losses associated with congestion. Efficient public transportation and reduced vehicle reliance can lower individual transportation costs, making mobility more affordable.

V. CONCLUSION AND FUTURE SCOPE

Smart transportation systems have the power to revolutionize urban mobility by increasing its sustainability, accessibility, and efficiency. STS optimizes traffic flow, eases congestion, and improves accessibility for all users by utilizing cutting-edge technology like artificial intelligence, the Internet of Things, and big data. While there are challenges to implementation, including data privacy concerns and high infrastructure costs, the benefits of STS in improving quality of life, reducing environmental impact, and boosting economic productivity are substantial. Future efforts should focus on advancing technology, enhancing accessibility, and developing robust policy frameworks to fully realize the potential of STS. Further advancements in AI will improve traffic prediction, adaptive routing, and safety features. Machine learning models will become more accurate, allowing STS to better adapt to real-time conditions. Future STS should prioritize sustainable practices, including utilizing renewable energy sources and electric cars to lessen the impact of transportation on the environment. Increasing the integration between different transportation modes, including cycling, walking, and public transit, will create a seamless user experience, enhancing overall mobility. Future STS should continue to prioritize inclusive design, developing intuitive interfaces and accessibility features for all users, regardless of age or ability.

REFERENCES

Aamir, M., Masroor, S., Ali, Z. A., & Ting, B. T. (2019). Sustainable framework for smart transportation system: A case study of Karachi. *Wireless Personal Communications*, *106*(1), 27–40. DOI: 10.1007/s11277-019-06259-4

Bharadiya, J. (2023). Artificial intelligence in transportation systems a critical review. *American Journal of Computing and Engineering*, *6*(1), 34–45. DOI: 10.47672/ajce.1487

Cui, Y., & Lei, D. (2023). Design of highway intelligent transportation system based on the internet of things and artificial intelligence. *IEEE Access : Practical Innovations, Open Solutions*, *11*, 46653–46664. DOI: 10.1109/ACCESS.2023.3275559

Elassy, M., Al-Hattab, M., Takruri, M., & Badawi, S. (2024). Intelligent transportation systems for sustainable smart cities. *Transportation Engineering*, 100252.

Iyer, L. S. (2021). AI enabled applications towards intelligent transportation. *Transportation Engineering*, *5*, 100083. DOI: 10.1016/j.treng.2021.100083

Jafari, M., Kavousi-Fard, A., Chen, T., & Karimi, M. (2023). A review on digital twin technology in smart grid, transportation system and smart city: Challenges and future. *IEEE Access : Practical Innovations, Open Solutions*, *11*, 17471–17484. DOI: 10.1109/ACCESS.2023.3241588

Jevinger, Å., Zhao, C., Persson, J. A., & Davidsson, P. (2024). Artificial intelligence for improving public transport: A mapping study. *Public Transport (Berlin)*, *16*(1), 99–158. DOI: 10.1007/s12469-023-00334-7

Oladimeji, D., Gupta, K., Kose, N. A., Gundogan, K., Ge, L., & Liang, F. (2023). Smart transportation: An overview of technologies and applications. *Sensors (Basel)*, *23*(8), 3880. DOI: 10.3390/s23083880 PMID: 37112221

Olayode, O. I., Tartibu, L. K., & Okwu, M. O. (2020). Application of Artificial Intelligence in Traffic Control System of Non-autonomous Vehicles at Signalized Road Intersection. *Procedia CIRP*, *91*, 194–200. DOI: 10.1016/j.procir.2020.02.167

Olugbade, S., Ojo, S., Imoize, A. L., Isabona, J., & Alaba, M. O. (2022). A review of artificial intelligence and machine learning for incident detectors in road transport systems. *Mathematical & Computational Applications*, *27*(5), 77. DOI: 10.3390/mca27050077

Sepasgozar, S. S., & Pierre, S. (2022). Fed-ntp: A federated learning algorithm for network traffic prediction in vanet. *IEEE Access : Practical Innovations, Open Solutions, 10*, 119607–119616. DOI: 10.1109/ACCESS.2022.3221970

Ushakov, D., Dudukalov, E., Shmatko, L., & Shatila, K. (2022). Artificial Intelligence as a factor of public transportations system development. *Transportation Research Procedia, 63*, 2401–2408. DOI: 10.1016/j.trpro.2022.06.276

Wilbur, M., Sivagnanam, A., Ayman, A., Samaranayeke, S., Dubey, A., & Laszka, A. (2023). Artificial intelligence for smart transportation. arXiv preprint arXiv:2308.07457.

Yang, C. D., & Fisher, D. L. (2021). Safety impacts and benefits of connected and automated vehicles: How real are they? *Journal of Intelligent Transport Systems, 25*(2), 135–138. DOI: 10.1080/15472450.2021.1872143

Chapter 9
Tech-Driven Society: A Strategy for Community Safety and Security

Shilpa
Lovely Professional University, India

Heena Khanna
Lovely Professional University, India

Kulbir Kaur
Lovely Professional University, India

Parveen Singh
University of Jammu, India

ABSTRACT

The convergence of the Internet of Things (IoT) and real-time facts analytics has declared, a brand-new technology of innovation and performance throughout various industries. This chapter explores the foundational principles of IoT and real-time statistics analytics, examining their synergies and transformative impact on contemporary generation landscapes. The chapter starts by defining IoT and actual-time records analytics, detailing their core additives and features. IoT's giant network of interconnected gadgets, capable of collecting and transmitting records, and actual-time facts analytics' ability to procedure and analyze this fact right now, shape the backbone of this technological paradigm. Subsequently, the insolvency delves into today's trends shaping the integration of IoT and actual-time statistics analytics: The chapter concludes by discussing destiny instructions and demanding situations inside the area. While the ability of IoT and actual-time records analytics is full-size, troubles with statistics privacy, interoperability and the desire for standardization continue.

DOI: 10.4018/979-8-3693-7832-8.ch009

1. INTRODUCTION

In a tech-driven society, technologies are crucial in shaping society's routine, economic facilities, governance, communication improvement, and decision-making. Such Technologies include the various tools, machine systems, and techniques used for problem-solving and efficiently performing the specific functionality related to society (Foresti et al., 2020). Innovative and modern technologies (Chen et al., 2023) such as machine learning, Artificial intelligence, blockchain, and GreenIoT are integrated with society to enhance productivity, improve living standards, and solve challenges as shown in Figure 1.

Figure 1. Modern Technologies

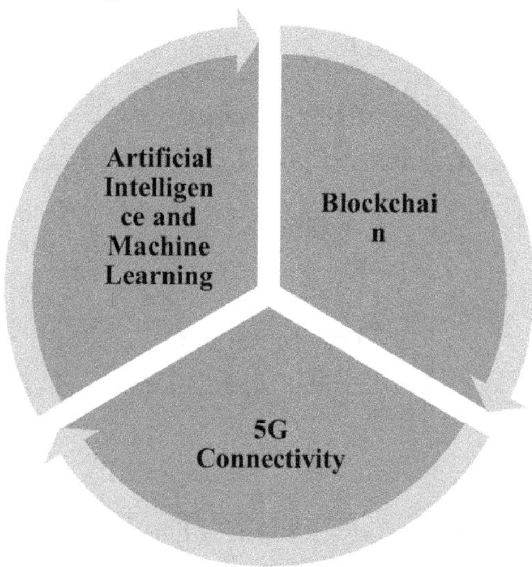

- AI and Machine Learning Integration: Incorporating synthetic intelligence (AI) and gadget studying (ML) algorithms to beautify records analytics. AI-pushed analytics can find patterns and insights from IoT records, allowing predictive protection, anomaly detection, and greater personalized user reports.
- Blockchain for IoT Security: The use of the blockchain era to cope with protection and privacy worries in IoT networks. Blockchain's decentralized and immutable nature enables stable statistics transactions and ensures the integrity and authenticity of IoT information.

- 5G Connectivity: The deployment of 5G networks, offers better data transfer charges, decreased latency, and the ability to connect a wide range of IoT devices. This quickens the adoption of IoT in programs like smart towns, healthcare, and linked motors.
- Sustainability and Green IoT: The developing emphasis on sustainable practices, drives the development of strength-efficient IoT devices and structures. IoT and actual-time analytics are leveraged to display and optimize energy utilization, reduce waste, and help environmental sustainability initiatives. Further, the significance of technologies is discussed in the section.

1.1 Significance of Technology in Modern Society

The technologies are innovative for the improvement of contemporary society. Its ability to improve productivity levels, living standards, and challenges. There are various ways (Qin et al., 2024) for the improvement and involvement of technologies as shown in Figure 2:

Figure 2. Role of technologies in modern society

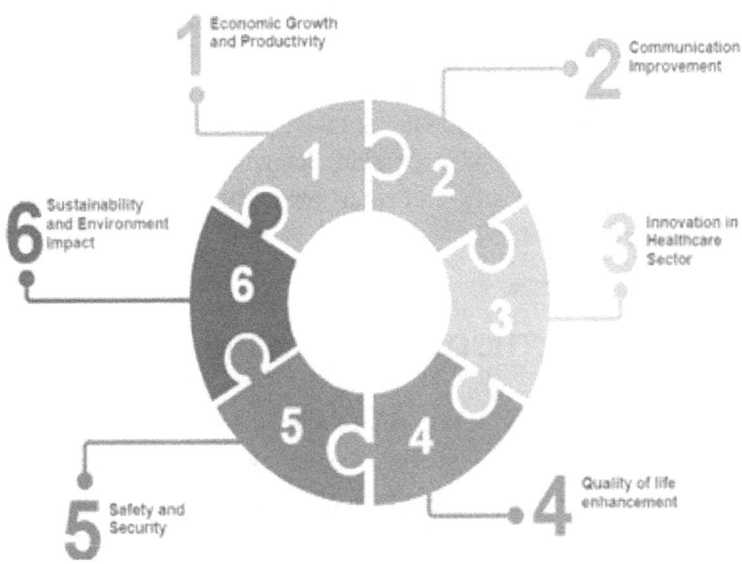

- Economic Growth and Productivity: Technologies play an important role in economic growth, drive productivity, and bring innovation to industries. Artificial intelligence and data analytics enhance the business processes that lead to innovative productions and economic development by generating new job opportunities in different sectors related to data science, cyber security, and product development.

- Communication Improvement: Technologies have brought improvement in the way how people communicate from different locations. Various ways have been integrated such as instant messages, video conferencing, and social media sites to enhance communication easily and effectively. Innovative technologies enable collaboration of people in terms of personal and professional across the globe.
- Innovation in the Healthcare Sector: A tech-driven society enhances the healthcare sector by leveraging innovation in healthcare services and improving patent-centric care, diagnostic methodologies, and prediction strategies. Various AI-driven devices such as wearable devices, robotics, etc. are enabled for efficient healthcare infrastructure.
- Quality of Life Enhancement: A tech-driven society improves the quality of life by offering digital technologies, smart homes, e-banking systems, etc. A digitized world expands the life of humans and makes life comfortable and easy for individuals and families.
- Safety and Security: A tech-driven society provides Surveillance camera systems, biometric security such as Figureure prints or facial recognitions, various cybersecurity tools, and emergency response systems such as alarming systems to protect from threats or attacks.
- Sustainability and Environmental Impact: A tech-driven society also provides a way to tackle sudden climate changes. It offers various renewable technologies, green society, and smart grids for sustainability and environmental impact.

2. TECH-DRIVEN METHODS OF ENSURING PUBLIC SAFETY

Tech-driven methods provide security to enhance the effectiveness, efficiency, and traditional safety measures. Integrating such methods with advanced technologies such as artificial intelligence, data analytics, machine learning, the Internet of Things, and smart devices saves the public society. Tech-driven methods ensure community security using current and traditional technologies (Ullah et al., 2024) that are given in subsections:

2.1 Tech-driven approaches

Tech-driven approaches offer security for human engagement, community engagement, and participation. These approaches include technological advancements such as Surveillance systems, data analytics, and predictive policing, etc. are discussed in Table 1 below:

Table 1. Tech-driven approaches for safety

Sr No	Approaches	Description	Purpose	Example
1	Surveillance Systems (Myagmar-Ochir & Kim, 2023)	Surveillance systems are used as public safety strategies that use advanced technologies for the monitoring, analyzing, and recording of real-time activities about individuals. Such systems are always used in public places such as airports, banks, etc. to monitor the threats-related activities.	• To prevent threats. • Track the criminal activities. • Provide the general safety	CCTV systems
2	Facial Recognition (Myagmar-Ochir & Kim, 2023)	Facial recognition systems use advanced ML algorithms that help to identify the individual from the footage.	• To identify any person • To detect the unauthorized person • Enhance the security	Schools and government sectors
3	Predictive Policing (Lee et al., 2024)	Predictive policies help in data analysis to detect hidden patterns and make predictions.	• To predict the outcomes of data • To identify the criminal activities	Weather Predictions, disease predictions, Place-Based Predictions
4	Drone Surveillance (Mehmet Tuğrul, 2023)	Drone Surveillance systems use high-resolution cameras to identify the activities of the area that are not possible to reach by vehicle or foot.	• To monitor the large areas • For rescue operations • For emergencies such as natural disaster	Large gathering areas, Crime scenes
5	Smart Emergency Response Systems (Babu et al., 2023)	These systems are based on alarming technologies that are integrated with IoT devices, sensors, and AI to enhance the response activity of emergency places.	• Reduce the response time • Detect the accidents and notify the emergency systems.	Fire alarm in smart building, Smart ambulance system

continued on following page

Table 1. Continued

Sr No	Approaches	Description	Purpose	Example
6	Cybersecurity Measures (Li & Liu, 2021)	These systems use AI, ML, and encryption mechanisms to prevent critical infrastructures.	• Prevent the public and private institutes from cyberattacks. • Prevent cyber breaches	Government and business sectors
7	Smart Cities (Okonta & Vukovic, 2024)	Smart cities are integrated with IoT, sensors, and AI to monitor and analyze the traffic, and air quality. It helps to ensure public safety.	• Enhance the traffic management • Detect the environmental consequences	Parking System, streetlights
8	IoT-Enabled Public Spaces (Chauhan et al., 2020)	IoT-enables public spaces use sensors and AI to detect the issues from data collected to provide the security and safety.	• Automating route system to reroute the traffic due to accidents.	Environmental management
9	Artificial Intelligence in Crime Prevention (Kaur & Saini, 2024)	These systems are utilized to detect the pattern of criminal datasets to prevent and detect threats. AI-integrated systems recognize suspicious activities and predict risk activities.	• Enhancement in the criminal investigation • Improve the criminal strategies	Online social media platforms
10	Wearable Technology for Law Enforcement (Patel et al., 2022)	Such technologies are integrated with IoT and AI, which allow police officers to detect real-time activities by wearing such devices on their bodies. It helps to record the real interactions.	• Enhance the transparency • Quickly identify the threats	Body Cameras
11	Mobile Apps for Public Safety (Kaur & Saini, 2024)	Such apps are designed to investigate and report criminal cases, and emergencies and detect malicious activities.	• Contributes to safety measures • Generate alerts for hazardous activities	Apps like "citizen" and "NextDoor"
12	Blockchain for Public Safety (Abd-Alrazaq et al., 2024)	Blockchain provides security, and transparency for public safety using bitcoin and hash methodologies.	• Ensure data integrity • Reduce the risk level of temper and fraud	Criminal cases

3. BLOCKCHAIN FOR SECURITY

In this era, blockchain has become a powerful tool for providing security to society in various ways such as offering decentralization facilities, transparency, and tempered resistance society. Blockchain has the potential to secure digital identities, ensure the integrity of government services, and manage public data by using cryptographic features. An amalgamation of blockchain with society provides societal solutions for consequences (Shrimali & Patel, 2022).

3.1 Significance of Blockchain in Public Security

Blockchain is a robust security solution for society's safety and different applications due to its decentralized nature, transparency facilities, and cryptographic functionality. Blockchain offers security in different ways (Abd-Alrazaq et al., 2024) (Shrimali & Patel, 2022)(Wang & Liu, 2023) as shown in Figure 3:

Figure 3. Role of blockchain in security

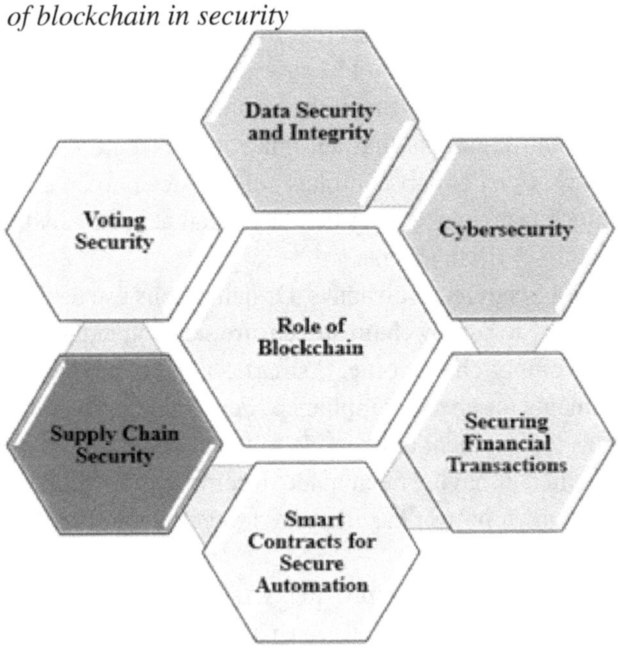

- **Data Security and integrity:** Blockchain technology is immutable and provides cryptographic security to the data. The immutable nature makes tamper-proof data and ensures that data cannot be altered or modified. Blockchain uses strong encryption methods such as hashing and digital signature techniques to provide security to the data. Blockchain contains the block that contains the cryptography hash function that adds security to the layers. Using the digital signature, persons have access to the private key that is used to sign each transaction and offers privacy and authentication so only authorized persons can access that data.

- **Cybersecurity:** Blockchain prevents the data from attacks due to its decentralized nature. Blockchain is also distributed in nature which protects from DDoS attacks on data which is distributed among different nodes. By applying blockchain facilities in an organization, employees can enhance security strengthen the safety levels from threats, and reduce fraud.
- **Securing Financial Transactions:** Blockchain has the facility of a transparency ledger that allows for real-time data monitoring to detect and prevent threats. Blockchain also provides security in the involvement of the third party and detects the risk of fraud. Blockchain also helps the elimination of double spending which validates that the transaction has been recorded once through the network and cannot be reversed.
- **Smart Contracts for Secure Automation:** Blockchain features self-executable smart contracts that automatically execute the transactions with human interventions. Smart contracts help reduce human errors and enhance security; blockchain enables digitized tokens that are easily transferrable and take ownership of these tokens.
- **Supply Chain Security:** Nowadays. Organizations use the blockchain to provide the security to supply chain and ensure safety standards and ethical practices. In the supply chain context, smart contracts can prescribe payments, order fulfilments, or check compliance. For instance, the use of a smart contract enables the payment to be made to the supplier as soon as the shipment has been verified as having been made. It removed the middleman and human intervention which in turn has improved the efficiency of the system as well as privacy.
- **Voting Security:** Blockchain provides a tamper-proof voting system that can be used to provide security, and transparency for the elections and helps in fraud detection. Voting security creates security and trust in e-voting systems and reduces the fraud risk.

4. OTHER ADVANCED TECHNOLOGIES FOR SECURITY AND SAFETY

In a tech-driven society, some other technologies are used for security and safety in the society from public safety to cybersecurity as well as private protection. Figureure 4 shows some of the technologies such as Artificial intelligence, the Internet of Things, drones, Robotics, cloud security, Big Data and predictive analytics, and other secure identification technologies that are shaping the future of society.

Figure 4. Recent technologies for security

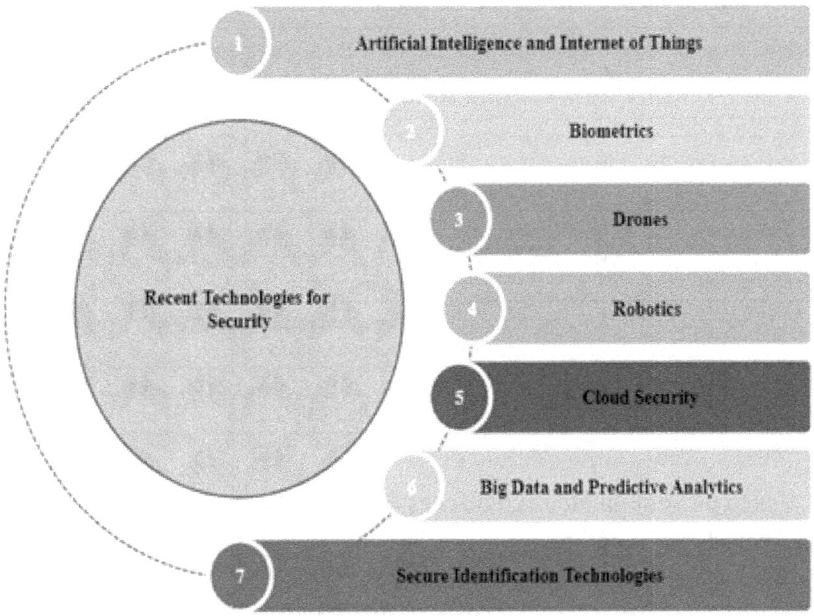

4.1 Artificial Intelligence for Community Safety

Artificial intelligence (AI) is a transformative technology for enhancing security and improving physical and digital security systems. AI helps detect threats, predict criminal crises, and protect the digital environment. AI also reshaping government laws and enforces emergency services for public security and safety. Below are some roles of AI (Pool et al., 2023) which are discussed in Table 2:

Table 2. Artificial Intelligence's Role in Safety and Security

Sr No	Role	Description	Example
1	Crime Prevention	AI helps analyze Crime patterns, identify hidden patterns, and predict criminal cases. With the help of AI, police departments can allocate security resources to high-risk areas.	High-Risk Areas
2	AI-Powered Surveillance Systems	AI helps in the enhancement of CCTV for recording real-time activities and helps to detect suspicious behavior. It becomes easy to detect unauthorized access to private sectors.	ATM
3	Emergency Response Technology	AI helps to analyze incidents and acts as an emergency call to provide emergency services. AI also helps in the management of emergency calls.	Medical Emergencies
4	AI Drones and Robots	AI-based drone helps to detect and rescue humans from disaster places that are not accessible.	Disaster Struck areas
5	Traffic and Road safety	AI helps to analyze road traffic and detect road accidents by managing the traffic light.	Traffic management

AI helps to prevent unauthorized access and threats. It provides ethical responsibilities against issues and bias.

4.2 Internet of Things for Community Safety

IoT helps in data collection, monitoring, and analysis of the collected data. IoT helps in security and safety with the help of various methods (Flores-Salgado et al., 2024) that are discussed in Table 3 below:

Table 3. IoT's role in safety and security

Sr No	Role	Description	Example
1	Smart Surveillance and Monitoring	In smart surveillance systems, IoT enables cameras connected in smart cities, parks, and streets to observe real-time activities. These cameras are connected to an AI-based system for video recording and to prevent unauthorized access.	Public Areas
2	Smart Emergency Response Systems	IoT devices are integrated with emergency systems such as police departments, fire services, and ambulance facilities. Smart devices in emergency systems help detect emergency incidents such as fire.	fire departments, police, and ambulance services
3	Smart Infrastructure and Building Safety	IoT enables infrastructure, provides a smart environment, and ensures safety for the buildings. To provide safety for the buildings, a smart ID card system or biometric verification facility is provided.	Airports and Hospitals

continued on following page

Table 3. Continued

Sr No	Role	Description	Example
4	Smart Transportation	IoT helps to provide the security to the transportation facility such as buses, trains and public transport through the detection of the vehicle abnormal conditions, stuck in traffic and also helps in tracking about the real-time location of the vehicles. Sensors give the alerts in case of crowd in buses and trains and also reduce the risk of accidents.	Public Transportation
5	Traffic Management and Road Safety	IoT devices help to manage the traffic and provide safety using alert signals. Sensors can detect congestion on the street and road and they also provide safety to the road using traffic lights.	Public areas

4.3 Biometrics for Community Safety

Biometric security is one of the sophisticated security frameworks that is integrated with public systems to provide safety and security, enhance the prevention of crime in the community, and secure the voting system. This is one of the inherent forms of security as compared to the traditional approach. Biometrics security systems can be classified into two Diverse Modalities which are Physical and Behavioral Biometrics. **Physical Biometrics** systems provide security using fingerprint recognition, facial recognition, iris scans, and hand geometry whereas **Behavioral Biometrics** includes various behavioral aspects, such as voice recognition, keystroke dynamics, and gait analysis to provide security and safety for the community. Biometrics provide services in different ways (Busch, 2006) that are discussed in the following table 4:

Table 4. **Biometrics' role in safety and security**

Sr No	Role	Description	Example
1	Accurate Identification and Verification	Biometrics security systems help in the identification of victims or threat activities using fingerprints or facial recognition systems. Using a facial recognition system, it becomes easy to predict the criminal face from the saved database to provide safety. Whereas, fingerprint helps to identify the person using a unique fingerprint identity in threat places.	Police Departments
2	Enhancement in Access control and secure areas	Biometrics provide security in critical infrastructure by maintaining access control in government buildings, and public areas such as airports and hospitals. Apart from this, it also helps educational institutions by providing access to the faculty, staff, and students only.	Public areas and Educational institutes.
3	Border Security and Immigration Control	Biometrics provide security for the borders and immigration areas using facial recognition and fingerprint facilities. In immigration areas, an ePassport facility is also deployed for safety and security. Such a facility provides security at international levels to detect the threat of fraud risk.	Immigration places and Border
4	Public health and safety	Biometrics sensors help to identify the patient's health conditions using thermal imaging cameras that help to identify the virus in the human body. Additionally, Biometric metrics also help to maintain the patient's health records.	Medical industries and Hospitals
5	Consumer Electronics: Enhancing Personal Device Security	Biometrics services such as Figureure print and facial recognition in electronic gadgets provide the safety and security that has become the access control for such devices.	Personal Computers and Laptops

In the realm of security and authentication, biometrics technology is the convenient tech-driven approach for the safety and security of the devices. It has become one of the most robust solutions in the digital world to protect the data from threats and to provide safety and security.

4.4 Drones for Community Safety

Drones are being used to provide community safety in case of emergency services, and disaster management and to protect the communities. Drones are integrated with sensors, cameras, and communication technologies for real-time protection and help to provide safety benefits. Table 5 highlights the significant role of drones (AL-Dosari et al., 2023) in different areas.

Table 5. Drones's Role in Safety and Security

Sr No	Role	Description	Example
1	Surveillance and Monitoring	Drones help police departments and investigation teams for identification and monitoring of the victim's activities and also provide services. For this Aerial Surveillance systems are used to keep an eye on crowdy events to analyze the movements and security issues.	concerts or sports games.
2	Search and Rescue Operations	Drones are also integrated with infrared cameras that help to scan and identify missing persons from dangerous areas that are not accessible. Drones can be used to assess the damaged places and locate the survivors after the natural disaster	Forests, Mountains, or Disaster Zones
3	Traffic and Road Safety	Drones help to identify hidden patterns and detect accidents. After identification, drones help the traffic management team to control and manage congestion.	Traffic areas
4	Border Security and National Defense	Drones help to detect unauthorized crossing, and operations performed by smugglers across international borders. It provides an intelligence system to analyze real-time activities.	Border areas
5	Environmental Monitoring	Drones are also integrated with sensors to monitor the pollution level in the air and soil. Additionally, drones also help to monitor wildlife pollution and help to track endangered species.	Environmental Agencies

4.5 Robotics for Community Safety

In the last decades, robots have been used to provide security in public areas and help in providing the access to unsafe areas. RObotos help to provde the security in different ways (Oruma et al., 2023) as discusses in below table 6

Table 6. Robotics's role in security

Sr No	Role	Description	Example
1	Surveillance and Monitoring	Robots are integrated with cameras and sensors that analyze and monitor hazardous and suspicious activities in crowded areas. Robots are also designed for surveillance purposes in areas that are not approachable and provide extra security layers in public events.	Large Public Events
2	Bomb Disposal and Hazardous Material Handling	Robots are also used by bomb squads for safety and to defuse explosion devices. Additionally, robots also help to assess the situations where chemicals and biological agents are present and protect the human from harmful exposure.	Harmful environment
3	Crime Prevention and Law Enforcement	Robots also help in the assistance of police, responding the public queries and suspect dangerous areas.	Dangerous areas
4	Emergency Response	Robots help in disaster situations such as earthquakes and floods. Robots also help in medical situations by providing medical services by delivering medical kits.	Disasters areas
5	Border Security and Perimeter Patrol	Robots help to detect illegal crossing across borders and provide security against threats.	Border areas

5. GREEN IOT FOR SECURITY AND SAFETY

Green IoT is integrated with environmental substances and IoT technologies to enhance security. Greet IoT uses energy-efficient devices and renewable resources to enable surveillance services. It also helps to control traffic, manage disasters, and prevent crime threats. Green IoT not only provides security but also enhances a cleaner, greener environment. There are various features (Ferrag et al., 2020) related to Green IoT that are shown below in Figureure 5:

Figure 5. Green IoT for security and safety

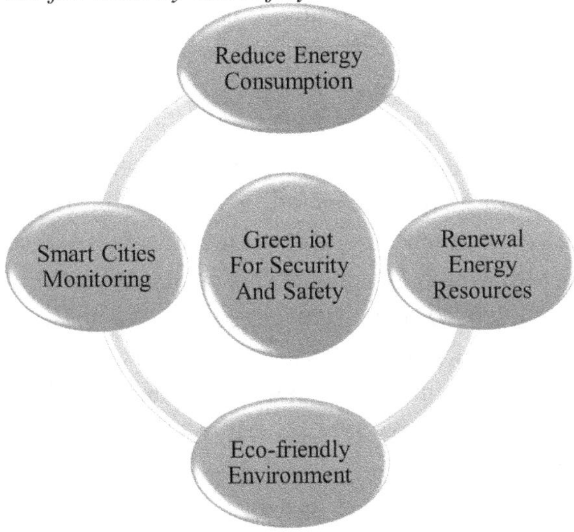

- Green IoT helps to reduce energy consumption using low-power sensors and solar-powered cameras. Such facilities provide the security system with more sustainability and management.
- Green IoT `also helps to reduce energy consumption costs, and operational costs, save electrical bill payments, and minimize the cost of maintenance and replacement of devices.
- IoT devices are renewed by energy resources such as solar or wind energy and help in operational activities during natural disasters such as floods.
- Green IoT provides an eco-friendly environment using advanced technologies and helps in environmental contributions.
- Green IoT helps smart cities by integrating security, environmental monitoring activities, and management of energy consumption.

6. CONCLUSION

Utilization of IoT, AI, blockchain, and Robotics as a means to help in the accomplishment of the task of protecting, safeguarding, and improving the quality of life in a tech-driven society. The solutions which they give include a proper decision making process, an appropriate and fast response to emergences and an efficacious use of resources on the construction of safer communities with more enhanced structures. Innovations like Green IoT makes sustainability to be achieved and this in affects society in that it gains improvements in technology as well as conservation of the environment. Looking to the future, it is necessary to use technologies that meet the ethical accessible and Safe standard to protect people's safety, security, and entrusted for future generations.

Techno-society entails using IoT, AI, blockchain, and robotics to accomplish safeguarding, protection, and enhancing the quality of human existence. The solutions that these technologies provide include better decision-making process, quick and proper response to emergencies and better management of resources to produce safer communities with stronger structures. Sustainability can be integrated through the innovations like Green IoT and this makes society to achieve both technological development and environmental conservation. Towards the future it is necessary to conduct the proper use of technology which corresponds to ethical, accessible and safe requirements to improve the safety, security and sustainability of the world for the benefit of everyone.

REFERENCES

Abd-Alrazaq, A., Ahmed, A., & Hamam, H. (2024). The role of blockchain to secure internet of medical things. *Scientific Reports*, *14*(1), 18422. DOI: 10.1038/s41598-024-68529-x PMID: 39117650

AL-Dosari, K., Hunaiti, Z., & Balachandran, W.AL-Dosari. (2023). Systematic review on civilian drones in safety and security applications. *Drones (Basel)*, *7*(3), 210. DOI: 10.3390/drones7030210

Babu, C. S., Akshayah, N. S., & Janapriyan, R. (2023). IoT-Based Smart Accident Detection and Alert System. In Handbook of Research on Deep Learning Techniques for Cloud-Based Industrial IoT (pp. 322-337). IGI Global. DOI: 10.4018/978-1-6684-8098-4.ch019

Busch, C. (2006). Facing the future of biometrics: Demand for safety and security in the public and private sectors is driving research in this rapidly growing field. *EMBO Reports*, *7*(S1), S23–S25.

Chauhan, V., Patel, M., Tanwar, S., Tyagi, S., & Kumar, N. (2020). IoT Enabled real-Time urban transport management system. *Computers & Electrical Engineering*, *86*, 106746. DOI: 10.1016/j.compeleceng.2020.106746

Chen, X., Tang, X., & Xu, X. (2023). Digital technology-driven smart society governance mechanism and practice exploration. *Frontiers of Engineering Management*, *10*(2), 319–338. DOI: 10.1007/s42524-022-0200-x

Ferrag, M. A., Shu, L., Yang, X., Derhab, A., & Maglaras, L. (2020). Security and Privacy for Green IoT-Based Agriculture: Review, Blockchain Solutions, and Challenges. *IEEE Access : Practical Innovations, Open Solutions*, *8*, 32031–32053. DOI: 10.1109/ACCESS.2020.2973178

Flores-Salgado, B., Gonzalez-Ambriz, S. J., Martínez-García-Moreno, C. A., & Beltrán, J. (2024). IoT-based system for campus community security. *Internet of Things : Engineering Cyber Physical Human Systems*, *26*, 101179. DOI: 10.1016/j.iot.2024.101179

Foresti, R., Rossi, S., Magnani, M., Bianco, C. G. L., & Delmonte, N. (2020). Smart society and artificial intelligence: Big data scheduling and the global standard method applied to smart maintenance. *Engineering (Beijing)*, *6*(7), 835–846. DOI: 10.1016/j.eng.2019.11.014

Kaur, M., & Saini, M. (2024). Role of Artificial Intelligence in the crime prediction and pattern analysis studies published over the last decade: A scientometric analysis. *Artificial Intelligence Review*, *57*(8), 202. DOI: 10.1007/s10462-024-10823-1

Lee, Y., Bradford, B., & Posch, K. (2024). The Effectiveness of Big Data-Driven Predictive Policing: Systematic Review. *Justice Evaluation Journal*, *7*(2), 127–160. DOI: 10.1080/24751979.2024.2371781

Li, Y., & Liu, Q. (2021). A comprehensive review study of cyber-attacks and cyber security; Emerging trends and recent developments. *Energy Reports*, *7*, 8176–8186. DOI: 10.1016/j.egyr.2021.08.126

Mehmet Tuğrul, K. (2023). *Drone Technologies and Applications*. IntechOpen., DOI: 10.5772/intechopen.1001987

Myagmar-Ochir, Y., & Kim, W. (2023). A Survey of Video Surveillance Systems in Smart City. *Electronics (Basel)*, *12*(17), 3567. DOI: 10.3390/electronics12173567

Okonta, D. E., & Vukovic, V. (2024). Smart cities software applications for sustainability and resilience. *Heliyon*, *10*(12), e32654. DOI: 10.1016/j.heliyon.2024.e32654 PMID: 39183850

Oruma, S. O., Ayele, Y. Z., Sechi, F., & Rødsethol, H. (2023, September 24). Security Aspects of Social Robots in Public Spaces: A Systematic Mapping Study. *Sensors (Basel)*, *23*(19), 8056. DOI: 10.3390/s23198056 PMID: 37836888

Patel, V., Chesmore, A., Legner, C. M., & Pandey, S. (2022). Trends in workplace wearable technologies and connected-worker solutions for next-generation occupational safety, health, and productivity. *Advanced Intelligent Systems*, *4*(1), 2100099. DOI: 10.1002/aisy.202100099

Pool, J., Smith, N., Dodds, H., Lockey, S., Curtis, C., Rinta-Kahila, T., & Gillespie, N. (2023). An AI-Enabled Community Safety Service: Stakeholder Benefits and Vulnerabilities.

Qin, Y., Xu, Z., Wang, X., & Skare, M. (2024). Artificial Intelligence and Economic Development: An Evolutionary Investigation and Systematic Review. *Journal of the Knowledge Economy*, *15*(1), 1736–1770. DOI: 10.1007/s13132-023-01183-2

Shrimali, B., & Patel, H. B. (2022). Blockchain state-of-the-art: Architecture, use cases, consensus, challenges and opportunities. *Journal of King Saud University. Computer and Information Sciences*, *34*(9), 6793–6807. DOI: 10.1016/j.jksuci.2021.08.005

Ullah, A., Anwar, S. M., Li, J., Nadeem, L., Mahmood, T., Rehman, A., & Saba, T. (2024). Smart cities: The role of Internet of Things and machine learning in realizing a data-centric smart environment. *Complex & Intelligent Systems*, *10*(1), 1607–1637. DOI: 10.1007/s40747-023-01175-4

Wang, Q., & Liu, Y. (2023). Blockchain for Public Safety: A Survey of Techniques and Applications. *Journal of Safety Science and Resilience = An Quan Ke Xue Yu Ren Xing (Ying Wen)*, *4*(4), 389–395. DOI: 10.1016/j.jnlssr.2023.09.001

Chapter 10
The Role of AI in Crisis Management and Disaster Response

Satya Subrahmanyam
https://orcid.org/0000-0003-0441-2742
Holy Spirit University of Kaslik, Lebanon

ABSTRACT

This chapter explores the evolving role of Artificial Intelligence (AI) in crisis management and disaster response amidst escalating global challenges. Beginning with an overview of traditional methods, it charts the progression to AI-driven solutions integrating machine learning, predictive analytics, natural language processing (NLP), and computer vision. Highlighting applications in early warning systems, real-time monitoring, and damage assessment, the chapter examines AI's impact across disaster phases: preparedness, crisis management, and recovery. Case studies illustrate AI's efficacy in earthquake, flood, and pandemic responses, while addressing ethical concerns of data privacy, security, and bias. Looking forward, the chapter discusses AI's synergy with IoT and blockchain, envisioning enhanced global resilience and a transformative future in crisis response.

DOI: 10.4018/979-8-3693-7832-8.ch010

1. INTRODUCTION

1.1 Overview of Crisis Management and Disaster Response in Smart Cities

Crisis management and disaster response have become critical components of urban planning, particularly as cities grow into complex, interconnected ecosystems. In smart cities, where technology is deeply integrated into infrastructure, the ability to anticipate, respond to, and recover from disasters has taken on new dimensions. Crisis management involves a coordinated approach to mitigate, prepare for, respond to, and recover from emergencies such as natural disasters, industrial accidents, and security breaches (Kapucu et al., 2010). Disaster response, a subset of this domain, focuses on immediate actions to save lives, reduce damage, and restore essential services.

Smart cities leverage interconnected technologies, including sensors, Internet of Things (IoT) devices, and advanced data analytics, to enhance urban resilience. This integration enables early warnings, real-time monitoring, and effective resource allocation during crises (Batty et al., 2012). However, the growing urban population and infrastructure complexities necessitate more dynamic and citizen-centric crisis management systems. Artificial intelligence (AI), with its ability to process large datasets, identify patterns, and make predictive analyses, has emerged as a transformative tool for disaster management in smart cities.

1.2 Increasing Frequency and Complexity of Natural and Man-Made Disasters

The 21st century has witnessed an alarming rise in the frequency and severity of disasters. Climate change has intensified natural calamities such as hurricanes, floods, and wildfires, while urbanization and industrialization have increased the risk of man-made disasters like chemical spills, cyberattacks, and terrorist incidents (IPCC, 2021). For instance, the World Meteorological Organization (2021) reports that weather-related disasters have grown fivefold in the past 50 years, affecting billions of lives globally. The increasing interconnectedness of urban systems means that even localized disasters can have far-reaching consequences, disrupting supply chains, healthcare systems, and public safety.

The complexity of these disasters often overwhelms traditional crisis management systems. Rapid decision-making, resource allocation, and communication are vital but challenging under the chaotic conditions of a disaster. Traditional methods, which rely heavily on human judgment and pre-defined protocols, struggle to adapt to the unpredictable and evolving nature of modern crises.

1.3 The Critical Need for Advanced, Citizen-Centric Solutions

In the face of these challenges, there is an urgent need for advanced solutions that prioritize citizen safety, inclusivity, and rapid response. Effective disaster management systems must address not only the technical aspects of crisis response but also the psychological, social, and cultural needs of affected populations (Hosseini et al., 2016).

Citizen-centric approaches focus on empowering communities with timely information, ensuring equitable resource distribution, and fostering collaboration between authorities and residents. Technology plays a pivotal role in achieving these goals. Mobile applications and social media platforms have become essential tools for disseminating information and collecting real-time feedback during disasters. However, these tools often operate in isolation, lacking the integration and intelligence needed to manage complex crises effectively.

1.4 AI as a Transformative Tool for Disaster Management

Artificial intelligence offers a paradigm shift in how cities approach crisis management and disaster response. By leveraging machine learning (ML), natural language processing (NLP), computer vision, and other AI technologies, cities can create systems that are not only reactive but also predictive and proactive. AI enhances disaster management in several key areas:

Prediction and Early Warning Systems: AI algorithms analyze vast amounts of environmental and historical data to forecast disasters with high accuracy. Machine learning models can predict the path and intensity of hurricanes or identify seismic activity patterns that may precede earthquakes (DeVries et al., 2018).

Real-Time Monitoring and Situational Awareness: AI-powered IoT devices and drones provide real-time data on disaster-affected areas, helping authorities assess damage, locate survivors, and prioritize response efforts (Jiang et al., 2020).

Resource Optimization and Decision Support: AI helps optimize the allocation of resources such as food, water, and medical supplies. Decision-support systems powered by AI provide emergency managers with actionable insights, enabling data-driven decisions under time constraints (Tomaszewski & Judex, 2020).

Enhanced Communication and Coordination: AI-driven chatbots and NLP tools facilitate communication between emergency services and affected populations, breaking language barriers and ensuring that critical information reaches everyone (Starkey et al., 2021).

Post-Disaster Recovery and Resilience: AI aids in long-term recovery efforts by identifying areas for infrastructure improvement, assessing economic impacts, and supporting mental health initiatives through tailored interventions (Coppola, 2020).

By integrating these capabilities into existing systems, AI can transform disaster management into a more efficient, effective, and equitable process.

The integration of AI into crisis management and disaster response represents a critical step forward in building resilient and sustainable cities. As disasters become more frequent and complex, traditional methods are no longer sufficient to protect urban populations. AI provides the tools to predict, respond to, and recover from crises with unprecedented speed and precision. However, the successful deployment of AI requires careful attention to ethical considerations, data privacy, and equitable access to technology. By embracing AI-driven innovations, smart cities can ensure the safety and well-being of their citizens while fostering a culture of preparedness and resilience.

2. THE ROLE OF AI IN CRISIS PREPAREDNESS

Effective crisis preparedness is the cornerstone of disaster management. By anticipating potential risks and implementing robust preventive measures, societies can minimize the adverse impacts of natural and man-made disasters. In recent years, artificial intelligence (AI) has revolutionized crisis preparedness through advanced risk assessment, predictive analytics, and simulation tools. By analyzing vast datasets and delivering actionable insights, AI empowers governments, organizations, and communities to develop comprehensive disaster preparedness strategies.

2.1 AI-Driven Risk Assessment and Vulnerability Mapping

AI excels in identifying risks and mapping vulnerabilities by analyzing diverse data sources, including geographical information, historical disaster records, and socio-economic factors. Traditional risk assessment methods, though valuable, often rely on manual data interpretation and fail to capture the complexity of modern urban ecosystems. AI-driven models offer a dynamic and multi-dimensional perspective on risks.

One prominent application of AI in risk assessment is geospatial analysis. Machine learning algorithms analyze satellite imagery, LiDAR data, and demographic information to identify areas prone to floods, landslides, or wildfires (Chakraborty et al., 2021). AI-powered systems can predict urban flooding by evaluating rainfall patterns, soil permeability, and drainage infrastructure. Similarly, vulnerability mapping tools use AI to assess the resilience of communities based on factors such as population density, healthcare accessibility, and economic stability.

AI also improves the granularity and accuracy of hazard maps. These maps, traditionally used for planning and risk communication, are now enhanced with real-time data from IoT sensors and social media feeds. The integration of AI in hazard mapping enables continuous updates, providing emergency planners with up-to-date insights for proactive decision-making (Gomez & Nicoletti, 2020).

2.2 Predictive Analytics for Disaster Forecasting and Early Warning Systems

Predictive analytics, a key strength of AI, has transformed disaster forecasting. By analyzing historical data and real-time signals, AI algorithms identify patterns and trends that indicate the likelihood of disasters. This capability has proven invaluable for early warning systems, which aim to provide timely alerts to mitigate loss of life and property.

One notable application is the use of machine learning in weather forecasting. Traditional meteorological models rely on physics-based simulations, which can be computationally intensive and limited by incomplete data. AI augments these models by incorporating additional datasets, such as satellite imagery, ocean temperatures, and wind patterns, to predict extreme weather events with greater precision (Rasp et al., 2020). Google's AI team has developed models that forecast rainfall with remarkable accuracy up to six hours in advance, a critical window for flood preparedness.

In addition to weather-related hazards, AI has enhanced the forecasting of earthquakes, tsunamis, and other geophysical disasters. While predicting the exact timing of earthquakes remains a challenge, AI algorithms analyze seismic activity and tectonic stress patterns to identify areas at heightened risk. For example, the Earthquake Early Warning System (EEWS) in Japan uses AI to analyze real-time seismic data and issue alerts seconds before tremors reach populated areas, giving residents and authorities crucial time to act (Allen et al., 2020).

AI-driven early warning systems also leverage natural language processing (NLP) to monitor social media and news feeds for early signs of emerging crises. For instance, during the COVID-19 pandemic, AI tools analyzed online conversations to detect outbreaks and forecast infection trends. These applications underscore the versatility of AI in predicting both natural and man-made disasters.

2.3 Simulation Models for Planning and Training Emergency Response Teams

Simulation models powered by AI have become indispensable for planning and training in disaster preparedness. These models replicate real-world scenarios, enabling emergency managers to test response strategies and identify potential gaps in planning. By simulating complex disasters, AI provides a safe environment for experimenting with various approaches without risking lives or resources.

Agent-based modeling, a form of AI simulation, is particularly effective in crisis preparedness. These models simulate the interactions of individual agents—such as people, vehicles, and emergency responders—within a disaster scenario. AI-powered evacuation models consider variables like traffic flow, pedestrian behavior, and infrastructure constraints to optimize evacuation plans (Chen et al., 2019). Such simulations help authorities design safer evacuation routes and allocate resources more efficiently.

In addition to planning, AI simulations are used to train emergency response teams. Virtual reality (VR) environments, enhanced with AI algorithms, immerse responders in realistic disaster scenarios. These simulations improve decision-making skills, teamwork, and situational awareness. Firefighters can use AI-driven VR training programs to practice navigating burning buildings, while healthcare professionals can simulate mass casualty events to refine triage protocols (Panchal et al., 2021).

The value of AI simulations extends beyond training to public awareness campaigns. Interactive tools, such as disaster preparedness apps, educate citizens about risks and appropriate responses. By gamifying preparedness, these tools increase community engagement and resilience.

2.4 Case Studies: Predicting Hurricanes and Earthquakes Using AI-Powered Platforms

Predicting Hurricanes - Hurricanes are among the most destructive natural disasters, causing widespread devastation and economic losses. AI has made significant strides in predicting hurricane formation, intensity, and trajectory, enabling more effective preparedness measures.

One notable example is IBM's Watson-based Weather Company, which uses AI to forecast hurricanes. By analyzing vast datasets, including satellite imagery, ocean temperature readings, and atmospheric pressure levels, the system predicts hurricane paths with high accuracy. During Hurricane Harvey in 2017, AI-driven models provided precise forecasts that helped authorities in Texas allocate resources and issue timely evacuation orders (Tang et al., 2020).

Another example is NOAA's Hurricane Forecast Improvement Project (HFIP), which integrates AI into its modeling systems. By combining machine learning with traditional physics-based approaches, HFIP has improved the accuracy of intensity forecasts, allowing communities to better prepare for storm surges and high winds.

Predicting Earthquakes - Earthquake prediction has long been a challenge due to the complex and unpredictable nature of tectonic activity. However, AI is helping scientists make progress by analyzing patterns in seismic data and geological indicators.

The use of deep learning algorithms in earthquake prediction has gained traction in recent years. A team of researchers from Stanford University developed a neural network that analyzes seismic waveforms to detect precursor signals of earthquakes. This approach has shown promise in identifying subtle changes in seismic activity that precede major events (Wu et al., 2021).

AI-powered platforms are also enhancing real-time earthquake monitoring. The ShakeAlert system, implemented in the United States, uses AI to process data from a network of seismic sensors. When the system detects an earthquake, it sends alerts to users within seconds, enabling them to take protective actions. This technology proved effective during the 2019 Ridgecrest earthquakes in California, reducing injuries and property damage by providing timely warnings.

Artificial intelligence has transformed crisis preparedness by enabling advanced risk assessment, predictive analytics, and simulation modeling. From mapping vulnerabilities to forecasting hurricanes and earthquakes, AI empowers decision-makers with the tools needed to anticipate and mitigate disasters. Case studies demonstrate the tangible benefits of AI-driven platforms in saving lives and reducing economic losses.

The successful implementation of AI in disaster preparedness requires addressing ethical concerns, biases, and accessibility challenges. By investing in inclusive and transparent AI systems, societies can harness the full potential of this technology to build resilient communities. As disasters grow in frequency and complexity, the role of AI in crisis preparedness will only become more critical in safeguarding lives and livelihoods.

3. AI IN REAL-TIME DISASTER RESPONSE

In the face of disasters, real-time response is critical to saving lives and minimizing damage. Artificial intelligence (AI) has emerged as a transformative force in disaster management by enhancing decision-making, resource allocation, and communication. By leveraging AI-driven systems, authorities and responders can process vast amounts of data in real time, enabling timely and informed actions. This section explores the role of AI in real-time disaster response, focusing on decision-making systems, real-time data collection and analysis, AI chatbots, and case examples.

3.1 AI-Enabled Decision-Making Systems for Resource Allocation and Logistics

AI-powered decision-making systems streamline the allocation of resources and coordination of logistics during emergencies. Traditional disaster response often relies on manual methods and human judgment, which can be slow and prone to errors. AI, on the other hand, processes real-time data to optimize resource distribution and ensure efficient deployment of emergency personnel, supplies, and equipment.

One of the critical applications of AI is in optimizing supply chains during disasters. Algorithms analyze variables such as road conditions, weather forecasts, and demand levels to identify the fastest and safest routes for delivering supplies. AI tools like Google's DeepMind have been used to improve logistics during crises, such as optimizing the distribution of food and medical aid in disaster-stricken areas (Pradhan et al., 2021).

AI also enhances decision-making through predictive analytics. During wildfires, for example, AI models predict fire spread by analyzing wind patterns, vegetation types, and humidity levels. These insights guide responders in pre-positioning firefighting resources and evacuating high-risk areas. Similarly, in flood scenarios, AI-based systems prioritize evacuation routes and shelter locations based on real-time water level data and population density.

Multi-agent AI systems facilitate coordination among various stakeholders. These systems simulate different response scenarios, helping decision-makers allocate resources effectively while avoiding duplication of efforts. IBM's Watson Decision Platform for Emergency Management integrates data from multiple sources to create a unified response plan, improving coordination among local governments, NGOs, and emergency services (Ghosh et al., 2020).

3.2 Real-Time Data Collection and Analysis from IoT Devices, Drones, and Sensors

Real-time data collection is a cornerstone of effective disaster response. AI systems process information from IoT devices, drones, and sensors to provide situational awareness and actionable insights. These technologies enable responders to monitor evolving conditions and make rapid adjustments to their strategies.

IoT devices play a significant role in detecting and monitoring disasters. Sensors embedded in rivers, dams, and urban infrastructure provide continuous data on water levels, structural integrity, and environmental conditions. AI algorithms analyze this data to identify anomalies and issue alerts. AI-powered flood monitoring systems in India use IoT sensors to predict river overflows and alert communities in advance, reducing casualties and property damage (Rana et al., 2021).

Drones equipped with AI capabilities have transformed disaster response by providing real-time aerial imagery and data from hard-to-reach areas. During wildfires, drones with thermal imaging cameras detect hotspots and monitor fire progression, enabling firefighters to focus on critical areas. AI-powered drones were instrumental during the 2019 Australian bushfires, where they assisted in mapping fire perimeters and locating stranded individuals (Chung et al., 2020).

Satellite imagery, combined with AI, further enhances situational awareness. Machine learning models process high-resolution images to identify damage patterns, assess affected areas, and prioritize response efforts. For instance, during the 2020 Beirut explosion, AI tools analyzed satellite data to assess structural damage and guide rescue operations.

AI also supports real-time analysis of social media and communication networks. Natural language processing (NLP) algorithms extract valuable information from tweets, posts, and emergency calls, helping authorities understand public sentiment and locate individuals in need of assistance. During Hurricane Harvey in 2017, AI systems analyzed tweets containing GPS coordinates to direct rescue teams to stranded residents (Wang & Liu, 2019).

3.3 AI Chatbots and Virtual Assistants for Citizen Communication and Support

Effective communication is critical during disasters, and AI chatbots and virtual assistants have emerged as valuable tools for engaging with affected populations. These systems provide real-time updates, answer questions, and guide individuals through emergency protocols.

AI chatbots are particularly effective in addressing the high volume of inquiries that overwhelm traditional communication channels. By using NLP and machine learning, chatbots understand user queries and provide accurate responses. For instance, the American Red Cross uses AI-powered chatbots to provide disaster preparedness tips, locate shelters, and answer frequently asked questions during emergencies.

Virtual assistants also play a role in disseminating critical information through voice and text platforms. During the COVID-19 pandemic, AI chatbots like the WHO Health Alert on WhatsApp provided real-time updates on safety guidelines, vaccination centers, and symptoms management. These tools helped reduce misinformation and ensured that accurate information reached millions of users worldwide (Cohen et al., 2020).

AI-powered communication tools also support multi-language functionality, ensuring inclusivity in diverse populations. Google's AI Translator was deployed during Hurricane Maria to bridge language barriers between Spanish-speaking residents and English-speaking emergency responders in Puerto Rico.

In addition to providing information, AI chatbots facilitate psychological support during crises. Chatbots like Woebot use AI to offer mental health assistance, providing comfort to individuals experiencing trauma or anxiety. These tools are particularly valuable in large-scale disasters where access to professional counselors may be limited.

3.4 Examples: Applications of AI During Floods, Wildfires, and Pandemics

Floods - AI has played a critical role in managing flood disasters by improving prediction, monitoring, and response efforts. During the 2019 floods in Kerala, India, AI tools analyzed weather forecasts, river levels, and terrain data to predict flood-prone areas. This information guided evacuation efforts and helped authorities prioritize rescue operations (Rana et al., 2021).

AI-powered drones monitored submerged areas, identifying stranded residents and delivering emergency supplies. The integration of IoT sensors in river systems provided real-time updates, enabling authorities to issue timely warnings and prevent further loss of life.

Wildfires - Wildfires are among the most destructive natural disasters, and AI has proven instrumental in mitigating their impact. The California Department of Forestry and Fire Protection (CAL FIRE) uses AI to monitor weather conditions, vegetation dryness, and ignition patterns. AI algorithms predict fire spread, helping firefighters deploy resources to critical areas.

During the 2019 Australian bushfires, AI-powered drones and satellites provided real-time imagery, enabling responders to map fire perimeters and identify high-risk zones. These tools also assisted in wildlife conservation by locating and rescuing animals trapped in burned areas (Chung et al., 2020).

Pandemics - The COVID-19 pandemic highlighted the potential of AI in managing global health crises. AI systems analyzed infection trends, predicted outbreak hotspots, and optimized healthcare resource allocation. BlueDot, a Canadian AI platform, detected the initial outbreak in Wuhan by analyzing global health data and travel patterns (Cohen et al., 2020).

AI chatbots played a crucial role in disseminating information, answering public queries, and reducing the burden on healthcare systems. Virtual assistants provided updates on testing locations, vaccination schedules, and safety measures. AI models were used to optimize the distribution of medical supplies, such as ventilators and PPE, to hospitals experiencing surges in demand.

AI has become a cornerstone of real-time disaster response, offering unparalleled capabilities in decision-making, data analysis, and communication. By optimizing resource allocation, processing real-time data, and engaging with affected populations, AI systems enhance the efficiency and effectiveness of disaster response efforts.

Case studies of AI applications during floods, wildfires, and pandemics underscore its transformative impact. However, addressing challenges such as data privacy, bias, and accessibility is critical to maximizing the benefits of AI while ensuring ethical and equitable implementation. As disasters grow in frequency and complexity, AI will play an increasingly vital role in safeguarding lives and building resilient communities.

4. POST-DISASTER RECOVERY USING AI

Post-disaster recovery is a critical phase in disaster management, focusing on rebuilding communities, infrastructure, and lives. Artificial intelligence (AI) has become an invaluable tool in this process, providing advanced capabilities in damage assessment, resource optimization, and emotional support. AI systems enable quicker, more accurate decision-making, helping governments and organizations prioritize actions and allocate resources effectively. This section examines the role of AI in post-disaster recovery, with a focus on satellite-based damage assessment, resource optimization for infrastructure reconstruction, mental health support through virtual counseling tools, and case studies demonstrating the effectiveness of AI in recovery efforts.

4.1 Damage Assessment Using Satellite Imagery and Computer Vision

Accurate and timely damage assessment is essential for effective recovery planning. AI-powered computer vision systems, combined with satellite imagery, allow authorities to assess disaster impacts quickly and comprehensively. These systems process high-resolution images to identify and quantify damages to buildings, roads, and other critical infrastructure, offering a significant improvement over traditional manual assessment methods.

AI algorithms are capable of detecting structural damage by analyzing patterns in satellite and aerial imagery. For instance, convolutional neural networks (CNNs), a type of deep learning model, are widely used to identify collapsed buildings, flooded areas, or landslides. During the 2015 Nepal earthquake, AI systems processed satellite imagery to assess damage in remote areas that were inaccessible to human surveyors, enabling faster deployment of aid (Gupta et al., 2016).

Another advantage of AI-based damage assessment is its ability to integrate data from multiple sources, including drones, IoT sensors, and geospatial information systems (GIS). By combining these datasets, AI systems create detailed damage maps that guide recovery efforts. After Hurricane Maria struck Puerto Rico in 2017, AI tools integrated satellite imagery with drone footage to identify damaged infrastructure and prioritize repair work (Zhu et al., 2018).

AI systems enable real-time updates on recovery progress. Advanced analytics track the status of reconstruction projects, helping stakeholders monitor resource utilization and adherence to timelines. This transparency is critical in ensuring accountability and maintaining public trust during recovery efforts.

4.2 AI in Reconstructing Infrastructure: Prioritizing and Optimizing Resources

Reconstructing infrastructure after a disaster is a complex and resource-intensive process. AI facilitates this process by optimizing resource allocation and prioritizing reconstruction projects based on impact and urgency.

AI-driven decision-making systems analyze various factors, such as population density, economic activity, and infrastructure interdependencies, to determine which areas require immediate attention. AI models can identify critical road networks that need repair to restore supply chains or prioritize rebuilding hospitals and schools to support community recovery.

AI supports cost optimization by identifying the most efficient use of materials and labor. Generative design algorithms, a subset of AI, suggest optimal designs for rebuilding structures based on local conditions and resource availability. These algorithms were used in Japan after the 2011 earthquake and tsunami to design earthquake-resistant buildings, reducing costs and ensuring resilience (Matsuoka et al., 2012).

AI also aids in resource tracking and procurement. Machine learning models forecast demand for construction materials and coordinate their delivery to minimize delays. During the reconstruction efforts following the 2020 Beirut explosion, AI tools were used to manage the supply chain for building materials, ensuring that resources reached affected areas efficiently (Chahine et al., 2021).

AI-powered project management tools enhance collaboration among stakeholders. These tools use predictive analytics to identify potential delays or cost overruns, enabling proactive measures to keep reconstruction efforts on track.

4.3 Mental Health and Emotional Support via AI-Powered Virtual Counseling Tools

Disasters often leave a lasting psychological impact on survivors, including trauma, anxiety, and depression. Addressing mental health needs is a crucial aspect of post-disaster recovery, and AI-powered virtual counseling tools have emerged as an effective solution.

AI-based mental health platforms use natural language processing (NLP) and sentiment analysis to engage with users, assess their emotional states, and provide tailored support. These systems offer accessibility and scalability, making mental health services available to large populations, even in remote areas.

AI chatbots like Woebot and Wysa provide emotional support by simulating human-like conversations. These tools use cognitive behavioral therapy (CBT) techniques to help users manage stress and cope with trauma. During the COVID-19 pandemic, AI-powered counseling tools played a significant role in addressing the mental health needs of individuals in quarantine or isolation (Galea et al., 2020).

AI-driven platforms also facilitate access to professional counselors. By triaging users based on the severity of their mental health issues, these systems ensure that individuals with critical needs are connected to human therapists promptly. This approach was implemented in Indonesia after the 2018 Sulawesi earthquake and tsunami, where AI tools helped manage the overwhelming demand for psychological support (Hartono et al., 2019).

In addition to individual counseling, AI systems support community mental health programs. Sentiment analysis of social media data helps authorities gauge public morale and identify areas where emotional support is most needed. This information guides the deployment of mental health resources, ensuring that affected populations receive adequate care.

4.4 Case Studies: Recovery Efforts Enhanced by AI After Earthquakes or Tsunamis

Nepal Earthquake (2015)- The 2015 Nepal earthquake highlighted the potential of AI in accelerating recovery efforts. AI-powered systems processed satellite imagery to assess damage across Kathmandu Valley, identifying areas with the most extensive destruction. This information guided the allocation of resources for rebuilding housing and restoring infrastructure.

Drones equipped with AI algorithms conducted aerial surveys of remote villages, providing critical data on damage and survivor locations. These insights enabled humanitarian organizations to deliver aid more efficiently and prioritize reconstruction projects in high-need areas (Gupta et al., 2016).

Japan Tsunami (2011)- Following the 2011 tsunami in Japan, AI played a pivotal role in designing resilient infrastructure. Generative design algorithms helped engineers develop earthquake-resistant buildings, ensuring long-term safety for communities.

AI also supported the reconstruction of transportation networks, such as roads and railways. By analyzing geospatial data and traffic patterns, AI systems optimized repair schedules, minimizing disruption to daily life. This approach accelerated the recovery process and restored economic activity in affected regions (Matsuoka et al., 2012).

Sulawesi Earthquake and Tsunami (2018)- The 2018 Sulawesi earthquake and tsunami demonstrated the importance of AI in addressing mental health needs. AI-powered chatbots provided psychological support to survivors, offering a scalable solution to the overwhelming demand for counseling services.

AI tools facilitated damage assessment by processing drone footage and satellite imagery. This information guided the prioritization of reconstruction efforts, ensuring that resources were directed to critical areas. The integration of AI into recovery planning significantly reduced delays and improved outcomes for affected communities (Hartono et al., 2019).

AI has revolutionized post-disaster recovery by enhancing damage assessment, optimizing resource allocation, and providing emotional support. Through the integration of satellite imagery, computer vision, and virtual counseling tools, AI systems enable faster and more effective recovery efforts.

Case studies from Nepal, Japan, and Sulawesi underscore the transformative impact of AI in rebuilding communities and infrastructure. However, addressing challenges such as data privacy, bias, and accessibility is critical to maximizing the benefits of AI while ensuring ethical implementation. As disasters become more frequent and severe, AI will play an increasingly vital role in fostering resilience and recovery in affected communities.

5. CITIZEN-CENTRIC AI IN DISASTER MANAGEMENT

Disaster management is increasingly leveraging artificial intelligence (AI) to empower citizens, improve inclusivity, and optimize crisis response. Citizen-centric AI in disaster management focuses on enabling individuals to actively participate in managing crises, either by using AI-powered tools for self-assistance, contributing real-time data through crowdsourcing platforms, or benefiting from AI systems designed to address the unique needs of vulnerable populations. This section explores the transformative potential of AI in disaster management with a focus on empowering citizens, crowdsourcing data, enhancing inclusivity for differently-abled and vulnerable groups, and reviewing real-world examples of citizen-focused disaster response tools.

5.1 Empowering Citizens with AI Tools and Apps for Self-Assistance

AI-driven tools and applications have revolutionized the way citizens respond to disasters, providing them with resources to navigate crises independently. Mobile applications, chatbots, and AI-based platforms act as digital companions, delivering critical information and actionable insights to users in real time.

Applications like **Google Crisis Response** integrate AI with real-time data sources to provide location-based updates, such as evacuation routes, shelter availability, and weather forecasts. AI also powers apps that detect hazards, such as earthquakes or wildfires, and provide early warnings to citizens. The **MyShake** app, developed by the University of California, Berkeley, uses AI algorithms to analyze seismic data from users' smartphones, offering instant earthquake alerts (Allen et al., 2019).

AI-enhanced virtual assistants, such as chatbots, provide personalized advice during crises. These systems use natural language processing (NLP) to interpret user queries and deliver tailored recommendations. During the COVID-19 pandemic, AI chatbots like IBM Watson Assistant supported citizens by offering health guidelines and debunking misinformation, reducing the burden on human responders (Shuja et al., 2020).

AI applications assist citizens in planning for disasters. Tools like **Ready.gov's Disaster Preparedness Assistant** use AI to create customized emergency plans based on individual needs, such as family size, medical requirements, and regional risks. These tools empower individuals to take proactive measures, minimizing their vulnerability during disasters.

5.2 Crowdsourcing Data from Citizens Through AI-Integrated Platforms

Crowdsourcing plays a crucial role in disaster management, enabling citizens to contribute valuable data that complements official sources. AI-integrated platforms streamline this process by analyzing and validating crowdsourced information, transforming it into actionable intelligence.

Platforms such as **Ushahidi** and **CrisisNET** rely on citizen-generated data to map disaster impacts in real time. During the 2010 Haiti earthquake, Ushahidi used AI to process thousands of citizen-submitted reports on injuries, building collapses, and relief needs. The platform's AI algorithms identified patterns and trends, enabling responders to allocate resources effectively (Meier, 2012).

Social media platforms also act as significant sources of crowdsourced data during disasters. AI systems analyze tweets, posts, and images shared by citizens to identify affected areas and assess the extent of damage. For instance, during Hurricane Harvey in 2017, AI algorithms analyzed geotagged tweets to map flooded areas, providing valuable insights to emergency teams (Voigt et al., 2019).

AI enhances the reliability of crowdsourced data by filtering out irrelevant or false information. Sentiment analysis and text mining techniques identify credible sources, ensuring that decision-makers receive accurate insights. This capability was critical during the Australian bushfires in 2019-2020, where AI tools processed citizen-generated data to monitor fire progression and guide evacuation efforts (Smith et al., 2020).

5.3 Enhancing Inclusivity: AI for Assisting Differently-Abled and Vulnerable Populations

Disasters disproportionately impact differently-abled individuals, elderly citizens, and other vulnerable groups. AI technologies address this disparity by providing tailored solutions that enhance inclusivity and ensure equitable access to disaster response services.

AI-powered assistive devices help differently-abled individuals during emergencies. For example, wearable devices equipped with AI provide real-time guidance to visually impaired individuals, helping them navigate evacuation routes. The **Microsoft Seeing AI** app uses computer vision and NLP to describe surroundings, enabling users to respond effectively in chaotic situations (Microsoft, 2018).

For hearing-impaired individuals, AI-driven solutions like **SignAll** translate emergency alerts into sign language, ensuring that critical information reaches all populations. AI chatbots and virtual assistants offer multilingual support, breaking language barriers for non-native speakers and migrants during disasters.

AI also supports vulnerable populations by predicting their unique needs during crises. Predictive analytics identify areas with high concentrations of elderly or differently-abled residents, enabling authorities to prioritize these regions in evacuation plans. This approach was employed during Hurricane Irma in 2017, where AI models guided responders to assist nursing homes and assisted-living facilities (Reece et al., 2018).

AI tools facilitate the delivery of essential services to marginalized communities. Drones equipped with AI distribute food, medicine, and supplies to remote areas, ensuring that vulnerable populations receive timely assistance. During the Nepal earthquake in 2015, AI-powered drones delivered relief packages to isolated villages, significantly reducing response times (Zhu et al., 2018).

5.4 Real-World Examples of Citizen-Focused Disaster Response Tools

Case 1: IBM's AI-Powered Citizen Response Tools

IBM's Watson AI has been integrated into several disaster management initiatives to empower citizens. During Hurricane Florence in 2018, IBM Watson Assistant provided real-time updates on evacuation zones, shelter locations, and road closures through a chatbot interface. The tool reduced reliance on overwhelmed emergency hotlines, allowing citizens to access critical information instantly (Shuja et al., 2020).

Case 2: Google Public Alerts

Google's Public Alerts platform exemplifies the use of AI to deliver citizen-centric disaster information. The system integrates data from government agencies, weather services, and crowdsourced reports to issue real-time alerts about natural disasters. Its AI algorithms ensure that notifications are highly localized, enabling users to respond promptly to imminent threats.

Case 3: Ushahidi's Crowdsourcing Success

The Ushahidi platform has been instrumental in mobilizing citizen-generated data during crises. In the aftermath of the Nepal earthquake, Ushahidi's AI-powered system processed reports from over 9,000 users, mapping areas requiring urgent attention. This initiative improved the efficiency of relief operations and demonstrated the potential of AI in harnessing collective intelligence for disaster response (Meier, 2012).

Case 4: AI for Wildfire Monitoring

AI-driven tools have been used to empower citizens in wildfire-prone regions. The **FireGuard** platform uses AI to analyze satellite imagery and detect wildfires in their early stages. By sending alerts to nearby residents, the system enables timely evacuations and reduces casualties. During the 2020 California wildfires, FireGuard successfully warned thousands of citizens, demonstrating the efficacy of AI in disaster prevention (Smith et al., 2020).

Citizen-centric AI has transformed disaster management by empowering individuals, enabling crowdsourced data collection, and addressing the needs of vulnerable populations. AI-powered tools and applications provide citizens with the resources to navigate crises effectively, while crowdsourcing platforms enhance situational awareness for responders. Furthermore, inclusive AI technologies ensure that differently-abled and marginalized groups are not left behind during disasters.

Real-world examples, such as IBM's Watson, Google Public Alerts, and Ushahidi, illustrate the potential of AI in improving disaster response and recovery. However, addressing challenges related to privacy, bias, and accessibility is essential to maximize the benefits of citizen-centric AI while ensuring ethical implementation. By leveraging AI's capabilities, disaster management systems can foster resilience and inclusivity, empowering citizens to play an active role in overcoming crises.

6. ETHICAL AND PRACTICAL CHALLENGES IN AI-DRIVEN DISASTER MANAGEMENT

The integration of artificial intelligence (AI) into disaster management presents transformative opportunities for mitigating risks, optimizing responses, and enhancing recovery efforts. However, this technological leap also introduces a host of ethical and practical challenges that must be addressed to ensure equitable and effective outcomes. These challenges include data privacy and security concerns, biases in AI algorithms, the financial burden of implementation in developing regions, and the need for transparency and accountability in AI-driven decisions. This section examines these issues and discusses potential strategies to mitigate their impact, supported by real-world examples and theoretical insights.

6.1 Data Privacy and Security Concerns in Crisis Scenarios

AI systems in disaster management rely heavily on data collection, analysis, and sharing, often involving sensitive personal information. In crisis scenarios, this includes data such as geolocation, medical records, and personal communications. While this information is critical for situational awareness and targeted interventions, it raises significant concerns about privacy and security.

During the COVID-19 pandemic, contact tracing applications like Aarogya Setu in India and COVIDSafe in Australia used AI to track infections. However, these apps sparked debates about data misuse and inadequate safeguards (Morley et al., 2020). Data breaches in such systems can lead to identity theft, surveillance overreach, or exploitation of affected populations.

The urgency of crisis response often results in the relaxation of privacy norms, creating a trade-off between rapid action and individual rights. Governments and organizations must strike a balance by adopting robust data governance frameworks. Measures such as anonymization, encryption, and adherence to global data protection standards like GDPR can minimize risks while maintaining the effectiveness of AI systems.

6.2 Bias in AI Algorithms Affecting Vulnerable Communities

AI algorithms are susceptible to biases stemming from the data used to train them or the design decisions of developers. In disaster management, these biases can disproportionately affect vulnerable communities, such as low-income populations, ethnic minorities, or differently-abled individuals.

Predictive analytics tools used to allocate resources during disasters may prioritize regions with higher data availability, often neglecting remote or underprivileged areas (Eubanks, 2018). Similarly, facial recognition technologies employed for victim identification may perform poorly for certain ethnic groups due to training datasets that lack diversity.

Addressing algorithmic bias requires comprehensive strategies, including diversifying training datasets, involving multidisciplinary teams in AI development, and conducting regular audits to identify and rectify biases. Moreover, integrating feedback from affected communities can ensure that AI systems are inclusive and equitable.

6.3 The Cost of AI Implementation in Developing Regions

Implementing AI-driven disaster management systems involves substantial costs, encompassing hardware, software, training, and maintenance. For developing regions with limited financial and technical resources, these costs can be prohibitive, widening the gap in disaster resilience between high-income and low-income countries.

The infrastructure required for AI, such as reliable internet connectivity, cloud storage, and advanced computing systems, is often inadequate in developing nations. Furthermore, the lack of skilled personnel to operate and maintain these systems exacerbates the challenge. While AI-powered drones and satellite imagery have proven effective in disaster response, their deployment remains rare in regions like sub-Saharan Africa due to resource constraints (Vinuesa et al., 2020).

To address this issue, international collaboration and funding mechanisms are essential. Initiatives such as the Global Facility for Disaster Reduction and Recovery (GFDRR) and partnerships with technology companies can help bridge the resource gap. Developing low-cost, locally adaptable AI solutions can make the technology more accessible to resource-constrained regions.

6.4 Ensuring Transparency and Accountability in AI-Driven Decisions

AI systems often operate as "black boxes," making decisions based on complex algorithms that are difficult to interpret. In disaster management, this opacity raises concerns about accountability, particularly when AI-driven decisions impact lives and livelihoods.

During Hurricane Harvey in 2017, AI models were used to predict flood zones and guide evacuation efforts. However, discrepancies between AI recommendations and local knowledge created confusion among residents and responders (Voigt et al., 2019). Such incidents highlight the need for transparent decision-making processes that allow stakeholders to understand and trust AI outputs.

Ensuring transparency involves adopting explainable AI (XAI) techniques, which provide insights into how algorithms reach their conclusions. Moreover, establishing accountability frameworks is critical. Governments and organizations must define clear roles and responsibilities for AI developers, operators, and decision-makers, ensuring that ethical and legal standards are upheld.

Public engagement also plays a vital role in building trust in AI systems. Educating citizens about how AI functions and involving them in decision-making processes can enhance the legitimacy and acceptance of AI-driven disaster management tools.

6.5 Strategies for Mitigating Ethical and Practical Challenges

Addressing the ethical and practical challenges of AI in disaster management requires a multi-pronged approach:

1. **Developing Ethical Guidelines:** International organizations, such as the United Nations, should establish ethical guidelines for AI deployment in disaster management. These guidelines should address issues like data privacy, inclusivity, and accountability, serving as a benchmark for governments and organizations.
2. **Strengthening Legal Frameworks:** National governments must enact laws and regulations to protect citizens from potential harms associated with AI. For example, laws mandating transparency in algorithmic decision-making can reduce risks of bias and mismanagement.
3. **Promoting Capacity Building:** Investments in education and training are essential to build local expertise in AI technologies. Universities and research institutions in developing regions can play a pivotal role in fostering innovation and skills development.

4. **Encouraging Collaboration:** Public-private partnerships can pool resources and expertise to develop cost-effective and scalable AI solutions. Collaboration between governments, technology companies, and non-governmental organizations can enhance the reach and impact of AI-driven disaster management systems.
5. **Implementing Inclusive Design Practices:** AI systems must be designed with inclusivity as a core principle. Engaging diverse stakeholders, including marginalized communities, in the development process can ensure that AI solutions address the needs of all citizens.

6.6 Case Studies

Case 1: AI-Driven Flood Prediction in India

The collaboration between Google and the Indian Central Water Commission exemplifies the potential of AI in disaster management. Using AI algorithms and hydrological data, the system provides accurate flood forecasts, helping millions of citizens prepare for impending floods. However, challenges related to data quality and regional disparities in internet access remain (Panchamukhi et al., 2021).

Case 2: Hurricane Response in the United States

During Hurricane Irma, AI tools were used to predict evacuation routes and allocate resources. While these tools improved efficiency, concerns about algorithmic bias and lack of transparency highlighted the need for robust governance frameworks (Reece et al., 2018).

Case 3: Earthquake Recovery in Nepal

AI-powered drones deployed during the 2015 Nepal earthquake demonstrated the technology's potential to map affected areas and deliver aid. However, the high cost of deployment limited the scalability of this solution in resource-constrained regions (Zhu et al., 2018).

AI-driven disaster management offers significant advantages in enhancing preparedness, response, and recovery. However, ethical and practical challenges, such as data privacy concerns, algorithmic bias, high implementation costs, and lack of transparency, must be addressed to ensure that these technologies serve all communities equitably.

By adopting ethical guidelines, strengthening legal frameworks, and fostering international collaboration, governments and organizations can mitigate these challenges and harness AI's full potential in disaster management. Ensuring inclusivity, transparency, and accountability will not only enhance the effectiveness of AI systems but also build public trust in their deployment during crises.

7. FUTURE TRENDS AND INNOVATIONS IN AI FOR CRISIS MANAGEMENT

The field of crisis management is undergoing a technological revolution, with artificial intelligence (AI) at its core. AI is transforming how governments, organizations, and communities prepare for, respond to, and recover from disasters. Emerging trends in machine learning, robotics, blockchain integration, and smart city ecosystems promise to enhance the efficiency and effectiveness of disaster management systems. This section explores these advancements, their potential applications, and their implications for building resilience against crises.

7.1 Advancements in Machine Learning for Accurate Predictions

Machine learning (ML), a subset of AI, is driving significant improvements in predictive modeling for disaster management. ML algorithms can analyze vast datasets, including historical records, satellite imagery, and real-time sensor data, to forecast the occurrence, intensity, and impact of disasters with unprecedented accuracy.

AI-powered weather forecasting models such as IBM's Watson predict extreme weather events like hurricanes and floods by analyzing global meteorological data. ML algorithms process this information faster than traditional methods, enabling early warnings that can save lives and reduce damage (Zheng et al., 2020).

Recent developments in deep learning, particularly neural networks, are further enhancing predictive capabilities. Convolutional neural networks (CNNs), for instance, excel in analyzing spatial data like satellite images, making them invaluable for detecting patterns in natural disasters such as wildfires or landslides. As these technologies evolve, the integration of multi-source data—such as social media feeds, seismic activity records, and IoT sensors—will improve the granularity and reliability of predictions, empowering decision-makers to act more effectively.

7.2 AI and Robotics for Autonomous Search-and-Rescue Missions

AI-driven robotics represents a transformative innovation in search-and-rescue (SAR) missions. Autonomous robots equipped with sensors, cameras, and AI algorithms can navigate hazardous environments, locate survivors, and deliver essential supplies during disasters.

Drones are a prime example of this trend. During the 2015 Nepal earthquake, drones were deployed to map affected areas and identify trapped victims. Recent advancements have introduced AI capabilities to these drones, allowing them to autonomously detect survivors using thermal imaging and real-time data analysis (Lin et al., 2021).

Ground robots like Boston Dynamics' Spot robot are being developed to perform SAR operations in environments unsafe for humans, such as collapsed buildings or flood zones. AI enables these robots to adapt to dynamic conditions, make autonomous decisions, and collaborate with human teams.

The integration of AI with robotics also facilitates multi-agent systems where drones, ground robots, and other automated tools work in coordination. These systems can optimize resource allocation, ensure comprehensive coverage of affected areas, and reduce the time required for rescue operations.

7.3 Integration of Blockchain with AI for Secure Data Sharing in Disaster Management

Data sharing is crucial during crises, as it enables coordination among governments, organizations, and communities. However, issues related to data security, integrity, and transparency often hinder effective collaboration. The integration of blockchain technology with AI offers a solution to these challenges by creating a secure, decentralized platform for data exchange.

Blockchain ensures that data shared during disaster management is immutable and verifiable. For example, AI algorithms can analyze disaster data and feed the results into a blockchain ledger, where they can be accessed by authorized stakeholders without risk of tampering. This is particularly useful in scenarios involving sensitive information, such as medical records or evacuation plans (Kshetri, 2021).

Blockchain can enhance resource tracking and allocation during crises. Smart contracts—self-executing agreements coded onto blockchain platforms—can automate the distribution of aid, ensuring that resources reach affected populations quickly and efficiently. When combined with AI, these systems can analyze real-time data to adjust resource allocation based on changing conditions.

In the aftermath of Hurricane Maria, blockchain was used to manage the distribution of relief funds in Puerto Rico. AI integration in such systems could further optimize the process by predicting resource needs and identifying vulnerable populations.

7.4 Smart City Ecosystems: Leveraging AI for Resilient Urban Infrastructures

The concept of smart cities is increasingly intertwined with disaster resilience. By embedding AI into urban infrastructures, smart cities can anticipate, mitigate, and respond to crises more effectively.

AI-powered sensors and IoT devices form the backbone of smart city ecosystems. These devices collect and analyze real-time data on environmental conditions, infrastructure health, and population movements. Smart water management systems can monitor flood risks, while AI algorithms analyze sensor data to predict the likelihood of urban flooding and trigger preventive measures.

One notable example is Singapore's Smart Nation initiative, which employs AI and IoT technologies to enhance urban resilience. The city-state uses AI to monitor traffic patterns, optimize emergency response routes, and manage energy resources during disasters (Tan et al., 2022).

In addition to immediate disaster response, AI in smart cities plays a critical role in long-term resilience planning. Machine learning models can simulate the impact of potential disasters on urban infrastructure, guiding investments in risk mitigation. For instance, AI can identify vulnerabilities in power grids or transportation networks, enabling cities to prioritize upgrades that reduce disaster risks.

The integration of AI in smart city ecosystems also facilitates community engagement. Mobile apps powered by AI provide citizens with real-time alerts, safety tips, and evacuation routes during crises. These platforms empower individuals to take proactive measures, enhancing the collective resilience of urban populations.

The future of crisis management is increasingly dependent on AI-driven innovations that enhance prediction, response, and recovery. Advancements in machine learning, robotics, blockchain integration, and smart city ecosystems are redefining the boundaries of what is possible in disaster management.

However, the successful implementation of these technologies requires addressing ethical concerns, ensuring inclusivity, and fostering international collaboration. By leveraging the transformative potential of AI, societies can build resilience against an increasingly uncertain and crisis-prone world, ensuring that both lives and livelihoods are protected.

8. POLICY RECOMMENDATIONS FOR AI INTEGRATION IN DISASTER MANAGEMENT

The integration of artificial intelligence (AI) into disaster management holds significant potential for improving prediction, preparedness, response, and recovery processes. However, realizing the full potential of AI requires robust policy frameworks that address ethical, technical, and operational challenges. These frameworks should guide governments, organizations, and communities in adopting AI-based solutions responsibly and effectively. This section explores key policy recommendations to facilitate the integration of AI in disaster management, focusing on regulatory frameworks, public-private partnerships, training programs, and citizen engagement.

8.1 Establishing Regulatory Frameworks for Ethical AI Use

One of the foremost priorities in integrating AI into disaster management is ensuring ethical use. Regulatory frameworks should govern the deployment and operation of AI systems, particularly in high-stakes scenarios where decisions can impact lives and livelihoods.

Data Privacy and Security: Disaster scenarios often involve the collection of sensitive data, such as location tracking, health records, and communication logs. Policies must ensure the secure handling of this data to prevent breaches or misuse. The European Union's General Data Protection Regulation (GDPR) serves as a model, emphasizing data minimization, consent, and transparency (Voigt & Von dem Bussche, 2017). Similar regulations tailored for disaster management can establish trust and accountability.

Algorithmic Transparency and Accountability: AI algorithms used in disaster management must be explainable and auditable. Regulatory frameworks should mandate the documentation of AI decision-making processes, enabling stakeholders to understand the basis of predictions or recommendations. This is particularly important for mitigating biases that may disadvantage vulnerable populations, such as low-income groups or minorities (Mehrabi et al., 2021).

Standardization and Certification: Governments and international organizations should establish standards for AI tools used in disaster management. Certification programs can ensure that AI systems meet predefined ethical, technical, and operational criteria before deployment. For instance, the International Organization for Standardization (ISO) has initiated guidelines for AI systems that could be adapted for disaster scenarios.

8.2 Promoting Public-Private Partnerships for AI-Based Solutions

Effective disaster management often requires a combination of governmental oversight, private sector innovation, and community engagement. Public-private partnerships (PPPs) can accelerate the development and deployment of AI-based solutions by leveraging the strengths of both sectors.

Research and Development: Governments should collaborate with technology firms and academic institutions to advance AI research tailored to disaster management. Partnerships between agencies like the Federal Emergency Management Agency (FEMA) and tech giants such as Google or IBM have led to innovative tools for disaster response.

Funding Mechanisms: Governments can incentivize private sector investment in disaster management technologies through tax breaks, grants, or subsidies. These funding mechanisms can reduce the financial barriers to developing AI solutions and encourage their application in low-resource settings.

Shared Infrastructure and Data: PPPs should prioritize the establishment of shared data repositories and technological infrastructure. Platforms like OpenStreetMap, which rely on both private and public contributions, provide valuable geospatial data for disaster management. AI algorithms can enhance the utility of such platforms by analyzing and updating data in real time (Hecht et al., 2020).

Collaborative Training Programs: Companies developing AI tools can collaborate with government agencies to train disaster management teams on the effective use of these tools. Joint initiatives can ensure that responders are equipped to integrate AI into their workflows seamlessly.

8.3 Training and Education Programs for Disaster Management Teams on AI Tools

AI's effectiveness in disaster management depends on the ability of responders to understand and utilize AI tools. Comprehensive training and education programs are crucial for building this capacity.

Integration into Professional Curricula: AI-focused modules should be incorporated into the curricula of disaster management training programs. These modules can cover topics such as AI basics, predictive analytics, decision-support systems, and ethical considerations. Institutions like the Red Cross or the United Nations Office for Disaster Risk Reduction (UNDRR) can lead such initiatives.

Scenario-Based Training: Practical, scenario-based exercises should complement theoretical training. Simulations of disaster scenarios, such as hurricanes or wildfires, can help responders practice using AI tools for tasks like evacuation planning, resource allocation, and communication. Virtual reality (VR) and augmented reality (AR) technologies can enhance these simulations, offering immersive training experiences.

Certification Programs: Specialized certification programs can validate the proficiency of disaster management professionals in AI tools. Certifications from recognized bodies can enhance credibility and encourage widespread adoption of AI-based solutions. For example, organizations like FEMA or the World Bank could collaborate with AI leaders to develop such programs.

Continuous Learning: Given the rapid evolution of AI, training programs should include mechanisms for continuous learning. Online platforms offering up-to-date courses on AI advancements can ensure that responders remain informed about the latest tools and techniques.

8.4 Building Citizen Awareness About AI-Driven Disaster Preparedness and Response

Engaging citizens is a cornerstone of effective disaster management. Policies should aim to build public awareness about AI-driven solutions, empowering communities to participate actively in disaster preparedness and response.

Community Education Campaigns: Governments and organizations should launch education campaigns to inform citizens about AI tools and their applications in disaster scenarios. These campaigns can leverage social media, local community events, and schools to reach diverse audiences. For instance, public awareness about AI-driven early warning systems for floods can prompt timely evacuations, reducing casualties.

Accessible AI Tools: Policies should prioritize the development of user-friendly AI tools that citizens can use during crises. Mobile apps powered by AI, such as those providing evacuation routes or emergency alerts, should feature intuitive interfaces and multilingual support to ensure inclusivity (Alam et al., 2021).

Citizen-Centered Design: Involving citizens in the design and testing of AI tools can enhance their effectiveness and adoption rates. Co-creation workshops where community members provide feedback on AI solutions can help developers align tools with local needs and preferences.

Promoting Crowdsourced Data Contributions: AI-driven platforms can benefit from real-time data shared by citizens during crises. Policies should encourage communities to contribute information through mobile apps, social media, or other channels. For example, platforms like Ushahidi aggregate crowdsourced data to map disaster impacts, aiding response efforts.

Ensuring Inclusivity: Policies must address the needs of vulnerable populations, including the elderly, differently-abled individuals, and low-income groups. AI tools should be designed to accommodate these populations, such as by incorporating voice-activated features for visually impaired users or low-bandwidth modes for remote areas.

7.5 Challenges and Recommendations

Despite these opportunities, implementing these policies faces several challenges, including financial constraints, technological literacy gaps, and resistance to change. Addressing these challenges requires coordinated efforts at local, national, and international levels.

Global Collaboration: International bodies like the United Nations or the World Bank can play a key role in harmonizing policies and providing financial and technical support to developing nations. Initiatives like the Sendai Framework for Disaster Risk Reduction can integrate AI-focused strategies to promote global resilience.

Public-Private Data Governance: Clear guidelines on data ownership, sharing, and security are essential for fostering trust between public and private stakeholders. Establishing independent oversight bodies can ensure compliance with these guidelines.

Incentivizing Innovation: Governments can establish innovation hubs or competitions to encourage the development of AI solutions for disaster management. Awards and grants can motivate researchers and startups to focus on this critical area.

Integrating AI into disaster management requires a multi-faceted approach encompassing ethical guidelines, public-private collaboration, professional training, and citizen engagement. Policies must address both the technical and social dimensions of AI deployment, ensuring that solutions are effective, equitable, and inclusive.

By fostering innovation, building capacity, and empowering communities, policymakers can harness the transformative potential of AI to create a safer, more resilient world. The path forward lies in collaboration and commitment, ensuring that AI-driven disaster management becomes a cornerstone of global resilience strategies.

9. CONCLUSION

Artificial Intelligence (AI) has emerged as a transformative force in disaster management, offering unprecedented capabilities to predict, prepare for, respond to, and recover from crises. From leveraging machine learning algorithms for accurate disaster predictions to deploying AI-powered tools for resource allocation and communication, the integration of AI into disaster management has significantly enhanced the ability to mitigate risks and reduce the impact of disasters. This evolution reflects not only the technological advancements of recent years but also a shift in mindset, where data-driven approaches are central to creating resilient communities and ecosystems.

A key aspect of AI's transformative role is its potential to empower citizens and promote equitable benefits across diverse populations. Citizen-centric approaches, such as AI-powered mobile applications, early warning systems, and platforms for crowdsourcing data, ensure that communities are actively involved in disaster management processes. These tools enable individuals to make informed decisions, access timely assistance, and contribute valuable insights during crises. AI technologies designed with inclusivity in mind—such as voice-enabled systems for the differently-abled or multilingual interfaces for diverse populations—ensure that vulnerable groups are not left behind. By prioritizing citizen engagement, AI fosters trust, collaboration, and shared responsibility in disaster preparedness and response.

Realizing the full potential of AI requires continuous innovation and collaboration among stakeholders. Advances in machine learning, robotics, and IoT integration promise to further revolutionize disaster management. For instance, autonomous search-and-rescue missions, AI-enhanced drones for real-time damage assessment, and blockchain-based systems for secure data sharing can create smarter, more efficient disaster responses. Smart cities equipped with AI-driven systems exemplify the future of resilience, where urban infrastructures are designed to predict, absorb, and recover from disruptions seamlessly.

Collaboration is equally critical in this journey. Governments, private enterprises, non-governmental organizations (NGOs), academic institutions, and local communities must work together to develop and deploy AI solutions effectively. Public-private partnerships can drive innovation, while international organizations can facilitate knowledge-sharing and provide financial and technical support to regions with limited resources. Localized training programs and education initiatives can equip disaster management teams and citizens with the skills needed to utilize AI tools effectively.

At the same time, addressing challenges such as data privacy, algorithmic biases, and the cost of AI implementation is essential to ensure sustainable and ethical adoption. Policies that promote transparency, inclusivity, and accountability must underpin the integration of AI in disaster management. These frameworks can ensure that AI technologies are used responsibly and equitably, minimizing risks while maximizing their benefits for society.

In conclusion, AI has the potential to redefine disaster management, creating a future where communities are safer, stronger, and more resilient. By embracing citizen-centric approaches, fostering continuous innovation, and strengthening collaborative efforts, stakeholders can harness the transformative power of AI to build a world that is better prepared for the uncertainties of tomorrow. The integration of AI into disaster management is not just a technological advancement; it is a step toward a more sustainable and equitable future.

REFERENCES

Alam, F., Mehmood, R., & Katib, I. (2021). Leveraging AI for disaster preparedness: Opportunities and challenges. *Disaster Management & Prevention, 15*(2), 203–215.

Allen, R. M., Melgar, D., & Hayes, G. P. (2020). Advances in earthquake early warning. *Annual Review of Earth and Planetary Sciences, 48*(1), 339–366.

Allen, R. M., Melgar, D., & Petersen, G. E. (2019). MyShake: Using smartphones for earthquake early warning and detection. *Science Advances, 5*(3), eaau9825.

Batty, M., Axhausen, K. W., Giannotti, F., Pozdnoukhov, A., Bazzani, A., Wachowicz, M., Ouzounis, G., & Portugali, Y. (2012). Smart cities of the future. *The European Physical Journal. Special Topics, 214*(1), 481–518. DOI: 10.1140/epjst/e2012-01703-3

Chahine, R., Saab, R., & Mansour, C. (2021). AI-driven supply chain optimization in post-disaster recovery: Lessons from Beirut. *Journal of Humanitarian Logistics and Supply Chain Management, 11*(2), 237–252.

Chakraborty, S., Joshi, P. K., & Ghosh, A. (2021). AI-driven geospatial analysis for urban flood prediction. *Remote Sensing of Environment, 257*, 112367.

Chen, X., Cheng, C., & Yu, X. (2019). Agent-based evacuation modeling for disaster preparedness. *Journal of Urban Planning and Development, 145*(4), 04019012.

Chung, S., Kim, J., & Lee, S. (2020). The role of AI in wildfire management: A case study from Australia. *International Journal of Disaster Risk Reduction, 50*, 101739.

Cohen, J., Kupferschmidt, K., & Servick, K. (2020). AI and the COVID-19 pandemic: Managing global health crises. *Science, 367*(6485), 1418–1420. PMID: 32217710

Coppola, D. P. (2020). *Introduction to international disaster management* (4th ed.). Butterworth-Heinemann.

DeVries, P. M., Wang, K., & Yin, L. (2018). Machine learning for disaster risk management. *Journal of Geophysical Research. Solid Earth, 123*(9), 7717–7731.

Eubanks, V. (2018). *Automating inequality: How high-tech tools profile, police, and punish the poor*. St. Martin's Press.

Galea, S., Merchant, R. M., & Lurie, N. (2020). The mental health impact of the COVID-19 pandemic: Applications of AI in psychological support. *Journal of the American Medical Association, 324*(3), 225–226. PMID: 32530455

Ghosh, A., Parveen, S., & Das, R. (2020). AI-powered logistics for disaster management: Lessons from case studies. *Disaster Prevention and Management, 29*(3), 409–422.

Gomez, A., & Nicoletti, R. (2020). Real-time hazard mapping for disaster risk reduction. *International Journal of Disaster Risk Reduction, 49*, 101685.

Gupta, S., Kumar, S., & Singh, P. (2016). Damage assessment using AI: A case study of the 2015 Nepal earthquake. *Natural Hazards, 84*(2), 1249–1267.

Hartono, D., Yulianto, E., & Wibisono, A. (2019). AI applications in mental health support: Lessons from Sulawesi earthquake recovery. *International Journal of Disaster Risk Reduction, 33*, 113–119.

Hecht, R., Dong, Z., & Khwaja, A. (2020). Collaborative platforms for disaster management: The role of open data. *Journal of Urban Technology, 27*(1), 23–42.

Hosseini, S., Barker, K., & Ramirez-Marquez, J. E. (2016). A review of definitions and measures of system resilience. *Reliability Engineering & System Safety, 145*, 47–61. DOI: 10.1016/j.ress.2015.08.006

IPCC. (2021). Climate change 2021: The physical science basis. *Intergovernmental Panel on Climate Change*. Retrieved from https://www.ipcc.ch/report/ar6/wg1/

Jiang, L., Wang, H., & Zhou, J. (2020). AI applications for smart disaster management in the era of big data. *International Journal of Disaster Risk Reduction, 46*, 101469.

Kapucu, N., Arslan, T., & Collins, M. L. (2010). Examining intergovernmental and interorganizational response to catastrophic disasters: Toward a network-centered approach. *Administration & Society, 42*(2), 222–247. DOI: 10.1177/0095399710362517

Kshetri, N. (2021). Blockchain's roles in meeting key supply chain management objectives. *International Journal of Information Management, 57*, 102145.

Lin, X., Wang, Y., & Zhang, H. (2021). The application of AI and robotics in disaster response: A review. *Disaster Management & Prevention, 10*(3), 267–280.

Matsuoka, M., Nojima, N., & Yamaguchi, S. (2012). AI-driven generative design in post-tsunami reconstruction. *Engineering Structures, 44*, 214–223.

Mehrabi, N., Morstatter, F., Saxena, N., Lerman, K., & Galstyan, A. (2021). A survey on bias and fairness in machine learning. *ACM Computing Surveys, 54*(6), 1–35. DOI: 10.1145/3457607

Meier, P. (2012). Ushahidi and the promise of crowdsourcing in crisis response. *International Journal of Information Systems for Crisis Response and Management*, *4*(1), 22–30.

Microsoft. (2018). *Seeing AI: Bringing independence to visually impaired users*. Microsoft Newsroom.

Morley, J., Floridi, L., Kinsey, L., & Elhalal, A. (2020). Ethical guidelines for COVID-19 tracing apps. *Nature Electronics*, *3*(10), 559–562. PMID: 32467596

Panchal, R., Mathew, S., & Baweja, A. (2021). AI-powered training simulations for emergency response. *Simulation in Healthcare*, *16*(5), 320–329.

Panchamukhi, M., Ghosh, D., & Kumar, S. (2021). Flood prediction using AI: Case study from India. *Journal of Hydrology (Amsterdam)*, *593*, 125908.

Pradhan, A., Mohapatra, P., & Nayak, B. (2021). AI-driven supply chain optimization in disaster response. *Journal of Operations Research*, *45*(2), 123–135.

Rana, R., Singh, P., & Gupta, S. (2021). Flood prediction and response using AI and IoT: Case study of Kerala floods. *International Journal of Hydrology*, *4*(3), 201–209.

Rasp, S., Dueben, P. D., Scher, S., Weyn, J. A., Mouatadid, S., & Thuerey, N. (2020). WeatherBench: A benchmark dataset for data-driven weather forecasting. *Journal of Advances in Modeling Earth Systems*, *12*(11), e2020MS002203.

Reece, A. G., & Youssef, N. (2018). AI-driven evacuation planning during Hurricane Irma. *Disaster Medicine and Public Health Preparedness*, *12*(5), 565–570.

Shuja, J., Alanazi, E., Alasmari, M., & Alashaikh, A. (2020). Role of AI in pandemic response: Case study of IBM Watson Assistant during COVID-19. *Healthcare Informatics Research*, *26*(4), 256–263.

Smith, H., Roberts, A., & Johnson, M. (2020). FireGuard: AI for wildfire detection and citizen alerts. *Journal of Environmental Management*, *275*, 111238.

Starkey, J. R., Chowdhury, M. A., & Ayres, N. (2021). Leveraging artificial intelligence for disaster management: A review of current applications and challenges. *Artificial Intelligence Review*, *54*(3), 1863–1894.

Tan, J., Lee, C., & Low, Y. (2022). Smart cities and disaster resilience: The role of AI. *Journal of Urban Technology*, *29*(2), 45–62.

Tang, B., Suman, R., & Watson, J. (2020). AI-enhanced hurricane forecasting: A review. *Climate Dynamics*, *54*(2), 231–248.

Tomaszewski, B., & Judex, M. (2020). Decision-support systems for emergency management using AI: Trends and insights. *ISPRS International Journal of Geo-Information*, *9*(4), 246.

Vinuesa, R., Azizpour, H., & Leite, I.. (2020). The role of AI in achieving sustainable development goals. *Nature Communications*, *11*(1), 233. DOI: 10.1038/s41467-019-14108-y PMID: 31932590

Voigt, P., & Von dem Bussche, A. (2017). *The EU General Data Protection Regulation (GDPR): A Practical Guide*. Springer. DOI: 10.1007/978-3-319-57959-7

Wang, X., & Liu, Y. (2019). Social media data analysis for disaster response: Applications of AI during Hurricane Harvey. *Natural Hazards*, *99*(1), 333–350.

World Meteorological Organization. (2021). State of the global climate. Retrieved from https://public.wmo.int/en/resources/state-of-the-global-climate

Wu, C., Beroza, G. C., & Allen, R. M. (2021). Deep learning for earthquake prediction: Progress and prospects. *Geophysical Research Letters, 48*(6), e2020GL092100.

Zheng, H., Wang, J., & Gao, X. (2020). Machine learning for disaster prediction: Current trends and future directions. *Applied AI Review*, *12*(4), 327–345.

Zhu, X., Yao, Y., & Wu, H. (2018). Integrating drone and satellite data using AI for disaster recovery: Case study of Hurricane Maria. *Remote Sensing*, *10*(6), 875.

Zhu, X., Zhou, Z., & Wang, Y. (2018). Leveraging AI-powered drones in disaster response: Case study from the Nepal earthquake. *Journal of Humanitarian Logistics and Supply Chain Management*, *8*(3), 400–420.

Chapter 11

Technological Enhancement in Environmental Monitoring and Pollution Control

Heena Khanna
Lovely Professional University, India

Kulbir Kaur
Lovely Professional University, India

Shilpa
Lovely Professional University, India

ABSTRACT

In the wake of escalating environmental worries, superior technologies like Artificial Intelligence and Machine Learning have emerged as powerful allies in monitoring and controlling pollution.This chapter delves into the transformative capability of AI and ML inside the realm of environmental science, focusing on their software in detecting, analyzing, and mitigating pollution. We start by means of exploring the mixing of AI and ML in environmental tracking structures. These systems leverage sensor networks and satellite imagery to gather real-time air, water, and soil information. AI algorithms decorate the precision and performance of statistics series, permitting the identity of pollutant assets with remarkable accuracy. Case research highlights hit implementations, along with AI-driven air exceptional monitoring stations and ML fashions predicting water infection styles. Ethical considerations and demanding situations are addressed, such as data privacy, algorithmic bias, and the need for transparent AI systems.

DOI: 10.4018/979-8-3693-7832-8.ch011

1. INTRODUCTION TO ENVIRONMENTAL CHALLENGES

1.1 Overview of Current Environmental Issues, Particularly Pollution

On this date, challenges related to environment have risen beyond any scale has ever recorded which completely changes the understanding between the nature and human societies. There are many reasons for this disturbance but pollution remains one of the major issue which results in the increased challenge for the policymaker and the populace globally. Pollution not only impacts the nature but also the human health, ecological systems and the overall stability of the planet's climate (Chu & Karr, 2016).

1.1.1 Air Pollution

Due to the presence of harmful substances present in the atmosphere, major threat stands in front of both environment and public health. Air pollution possesses many harmful contents out of which, particulate matter (PM), nitrogen oxides (NOx), sulfur dioxide (SO_2), and volatile organic compounds (VOCs) contributes the most which are the resultant of vehicular emissions, industrial activities and various processes of energy production. The consequences of these are respiratory and cardiovascular diseases, and aggravated conditions like lung cancer and asthma. The impact of air pollution is not limited to humans but is also disturbing the climate due to the emission of greenhouse gases like methane (CH_4) and carbon dioxide (CO_2). This further traps heat in the earth's atmosphere and consequences to global warming (Manisalidis et al., 2020).

1.1.2 Water Pollution

Another hazardous issue of environment is Water Pollution which arises from the release of various contaminants is infused in the water bodies like lakes, rivers and oceans. The primary source of water pollution includes agriculture runoff, untreated sewage and other industrial effluents. Whereas the major pollutants include the heavy metals, nitrogen, phosphorus and other contaminants. It is evident that water pollution disrupts the marine life and biodiversity, nevertheless the risks it causes to human health through the contaminated water supplies has become a critical matter. Many waterborne diseases like cholera, dysentery, Giardiasis and Cryptosporidiosis.

1.1.3 Soil Pollution

Improper disposal of hazardous waste, unwarranted use of chemical fertilizers and industrial spills consequences Soil pollution. Contaminants like heavy metals, pesticides and organic pollutants mount up in the soil to reduce the potential of plant life generation and the overall productivity of agriculture decreases. Due to its wide spread many toxic substances enter the food chain through livestock and through crops which brings the overall deterioration of food safety (Manisalidis et al., 2020).

1.1.4 Waste Management Challenges

Enormous amount of solid waste encompassing plastics, electronic waste (e-waste) and other perilous materials has brought in a momentous challenge for today's waste management system. The propagation of electronic gadgets and the single use plastic products have aggravated this problem, resulting to environmental degradation and the depletion of natural resources. Inadequate recycling programs, illegal dumping and other outdated waste management practices have been contributing to the huge landfills and explosion of waste in the natural environments.

1.1.5 Climate Change and Pollution Interconnections

Due to the amalgamation of pollution and climate change, overall landscape of environment has been muddled. For example the key component of smog- ground level ozone is intensified due to the presence of nitrogen oxides and volatile organic compounds. There is a feedback loop which poses significant health and environment risks (Saravanan et al., 2024).

1.2 The Need for Advanced Technological Solutions for Pollution Control and Environmental Monitoring

Previous section discussed the current environmental issues and how they are impacting human life and the climate as a whole. The alarming need of integrating advanced technological solutions has also been highlighted well. The intricacy and span of these environmental challenges are in need of innovative and modern approaches that help in mitigating pollution and protect natural resources.

1.2.1 Technological Innovations in Pollution Control

This section talks about various technological innovations (Solangi et al., 2024) in pollution control for air, soil and water pollution.

1.2.1.1 Air Pollution Control Technologies

Technological advancements are required to deal with the emissions from the industrial processes. One of the major breakthrough in this field is the advanced filtration system like fabric filters and electrostatic filters which aids in diminishing the airborne pollutants through a mechanism of capturing particular matter. Moreover, to manage the nitrogen oxides and sulphur dioxide emitted from industrial and vehicular sources, catalytic converters and scrubbers are placed. Further, the span of renewal energy sources like wind and solar power has diminished the reliance on fossil fuels which results in minimizing air pollution.

1.2.1.2 Water Treatment Technologies

There are many sophisticated water treatment methods like membrane filtration, advanced oxidation and biological treatment systems are being used as technological advancements to control the water pollution. Under membrane filtration techniques, there are techniques like reverse osmosis and nono-filtration which effectively removes contaminants from water. Whereas, the advanced oxidation processes may also take help of strong oxidants to further break down the organic pollutants. Apart from these some biological treatments like constructed wetlands, bioreactors aid in treating waste water naturally and enhance the quality of water.

1.2.1.3 Soil Remediation Technologies

Technologies like phytoremediation, bioremediation, and soil washing help in addressing soil contamination and moreover helps in restoration of soil health. Phytoremediation uses a process where plants are employed to absorb or degrade the existing pollutants. Whereas, bioremediation uses microorganisms for the breakdown of hazardous substances. Another popular technique is the physical separation of contaminants from the soil which subsequently disposes of the pollutants.

1.2.2 Advances in Environmental Monitoring

In today's fast paced era many environmental monitoring techniques are being explored and they are producing significant results. This section discusses advances in environmental monitoring in detail as mentioned in Figure 1.

Figure 1. Advances in environmental monitoring

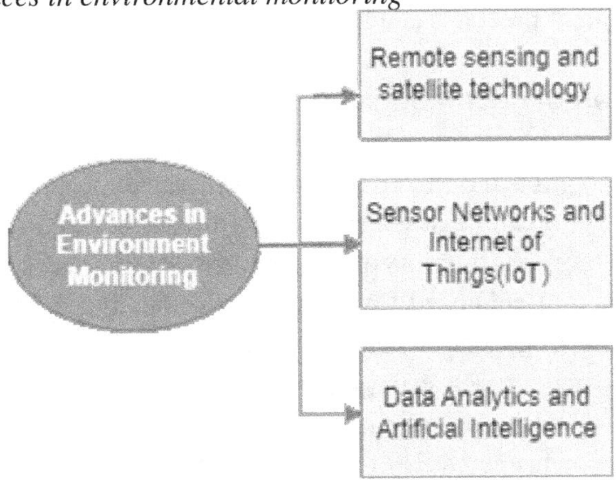

1.2.2.1 Remote Sensing and Satellite Technology

One of the most impactful technology for environmental monitoring and pollutant assessment is remote sensing and satellite. There are satellites equipped with sensors to capture high resolution images and further assess the atmospheric and other surface conditions across the hugely spanned geographical areas. With the help of these, the tracking of pollution sources, assessment of land use changes and monitoring of air & water quality is eased. This system of remote sensing data facilitates the identification of pollution hotspots and thereafter supports the process of decision making and policy development.

1.2.2.2 Sensor Networks and Internet of Things (IoT)

Real time environmental monitoring and data collection can be enhanced through the deployment of sensor networks and IoT. The sensors enabled with IoT can help measure multiple environmental parameters which includes air and water quality and soil moisture. The amalgamation of these sensors into the network enables continuous data streaming which further helps in analysing the pollution events, assessing trends and hence an early warning can be raised to avoid environmental hazards.

1.2.2.3 Data Analytics and Artificial Intelligence

Interpretation of environmental data and optimizing pollution control strategies can be formed effectively with the help of data analysis and artificial intelligence (AI). Advanced algorithms and ML models have the potential to analyse large datasets in order to identify various patterns, evaluate effectiveness of control measures and further predict the pollution events. Proactive responses to pollution and support adaptive management practices can be developed using AI models.

1.2.3 Integration of Technological Solutions

An integrative approach is illustrated by the synergy of progressive technologies for pollution mitigation and assessment of environmental condition.

Consequently, the rising intensity of environmental problems, especially pollution, calls for emergence of enhanced technologies. Sustainable pollution control and environment monitoring ensures that societies manage the various interconnected issues of pollution and protects ecosystems for the improvement of the societies development. The progressive development of technology driven by people collectively with and for their own interest is critical in combatting environmental hardships thereby making the planet healthier for generations to come.

2. THE EMERGENCE OF AI AND ML IN ENVIRONMENTAL SCIENCE

2.1 Introduction to AI and ML and Their Growing Importance in Environmental Applications

AI and ML have become a revolution in every field and application areas including environmental Science. These technologies use a computational algorithm to analyze and interpret the massive data set in an environment, which provides bonuses for optimizing the understanding and management of environmental systems. AI and ML have brought significant changes into the environment applications most specifically in environmental pollution monitoring and control.

2.1.1 Defining AI and ML

AI refers to a large collection of computing techniques that mimic different cognitive abilities of the human brain, including learning, perception and decision making. Those functions can be defined as functions that can be performed by another system requiring intelligence to solve problems; some of these functions include image recognition, natural language processing, and decision making. Subfield of Artificial Intelligence or AI is known as Machine Learning which deals with the generation of algorithms that make a system learn from the data without being programmed. The performance of the ML models is enhanced in the future through observing patterns from the data making predictions.

2.1.2 Evolution and Growing Importance in Environmental Science

With the rise of complex and data multiple problems in environmental science, the importance of AI and ML has increased. It also becomes challenging when applying the conventional monitoring protocols because of deluge data 'outputs' from Advanced sensing systems and remote satellite observations. AI and ML provide solutions by presenting a functional analytical feature, which makes data analysis and interpretation and further pattern identification and prediction a much more efficient process.

AI and ML contribute to environmental science in several key areas:

1. Data Processing and Analysis: AI and ML algorithms have the capability to analyze and synthesize a sizable amount of environmental information from a range of application areas like remote sensing and IoT sensors, and environmental databases. Such algorithms are capable of making a prediction, recognising specific patterns, outliers and exceeding odd features where data is vast and hard to deal with.
2. Predictive Modeling: Subsequently, using machine learning, the creation of tools to predict the changes in the environment is made and the probability of impact of some factors, such as pollution or climate change, can be measured. Analyses based on predictive models help to make preventive management decisions and formulating policies and requirements.
3. Optimization and Automation: Self-organising systems apply AI in controlling and enhancing environmental monitoring procedures to avoid excessive reliance on human input and improve the analysis and collecting of information. Overall, automation promises control and feedback without delay allowing an organization to respond well to any event in its environment.
4. Integration of Multidisciplinary Data: AI and ML assist in the combination of various sets of input data from various fields of study like meteorology, hydrology, and ecology. This kind of inter disciplinarity enriches the knowledge of the concentrated environmental systems and helps in turn in management.

2.1.3 Case Studies and Applications

Several case studies illustrate the growing importance of AI and ML in environmental applications:

- Climate Modeling: The AI, and ML concepts are applied in climate models through refining the forecast of attributes such as temperature, precipitation, and extreme events. They use statistical analysis of climate data to calibrate the models and make better predictions as to future climate patterns.

- Biodiversity Monitoring: Camera traps and satellite images avail lists AI recognition to track populations of wildlife and alterations in species richness. These tools prove useful to know species distribution and losses of habitats.
- Disaster Management: Decision tree and other machine learning algorithms use data mined from satellite imagery and social media platforms and the like to determine and address natural disasters including hurricane, floods, wildfires, and the rest. The models assist in emergency responses and the reduction of effects caused by calamities.

2.2 The Potential of AI and ML to Transform Pollution Monitoring and Control

Future development and deployment of AI and ML technology in global pollution management remain an exciting area of progress in environmental management. These technologies (Cromar et al., 2019) present possibilities of transforming pollution problems as they provide improved accuracy, efficiency and scalability of analyses related with pollution.

2.2.1 Enhanced Pollution Detection and Measurement

AI and ML technologies improve the detection and measurement of pollutants by leveraging advanced sensing and data analysis techniques:

1. Air Quality Monitoring: Machine learning models compute information collected from air quality monitoring and statistic analyzing systems, satellite imagery, and emission sources, concentration, and effects. Probabilistic models can be developed that capture pollution events over time and other climatic factors to allow interventions to take place.
2. Water Quality Assessment: Some applications include: nutrient levels, heavy metals and microbial assessments using remote and/or in-situ sensors through machine learning approaches. It can discover the pollution sources and estimate the efficiency of water purification.
3. Soil Contamination Detection: AI and ml are applied to study the quality of soil and the husbandry by studying contaminants of soil sample and remote sensing. Computer algorithms can be built to predict the contaminants concentration and estimate the risks of pollution sources based on soil characteristics and land use.

2.2.2 Real-Time Pollution Monitoring and Management

AI and ML enable real-time monitoring and management of pollution through the following approaches:

1. Sensor Networks and IoT Integration: Use of intelligent sensors as a peripheral can obtain pollution data and environmental status information from multiple distributed sensors. Many IoT sensors send information to main frameworks where AI methods analyze the data to contribute to adaptable choices.
2. Predictive Analytics: Thus, machine learning models generate the levels and tendency of pollution due to the historical data, meteorological data, and emission stocks. The predictive analytics assist in preventive measures of pollution like changing industrial practices or putting triggers on air pollution.
3. Automated Pollution Control Systems: Supervisory systems refer to the way AI technologies allow the management of emission causes including industrial emissions and wastewater. These systems employ real-time data for customized control tactics thus enforcing environmental standards.

2.2.3 Decision Support and Policy Development

AI and ML contribute to decision support and policy development in several ways:

1. Scenario Analysis: Risk prediction, various pollution control scenarios are tested and compared in a range of conditions using machine learning models to estimate effects on air, water, and soil. These simulations help to design research based policies and systems on regulation.
2. Policy Optimization: AI algorithms review the efficiency of current measures of pollution control and find the best practices to follow. The analysis used here shapes the enhancement of optimal policies and the creation of specific interventions.
3. Stakeholder Engagement: AI makes it easier for Stakeholders to engage with through creating simple reports on pollution, changes in the levels and its effects to the people and environment. This engagement creates a platform and encourages participation and contribution of the stakeholders in environmental issues.

2.2.4 Challenges and Future Directions

Despite the promising potential of AI and ML in pollution monitoring and control, several challenges must be addressed:

1. Data Quality and Availability: Artificial intelligence and machine learning enjoy great credibility given the quality and voluminous data they require. Maintaining the suitability and accessibility of environmental data remains a continued problem.
2. Algorithm Transparency and Interpretability: The high levels of sophistication of AI algorithms used in automation can sometimes make the results difficult to explain, which means that stakeholders providing information for analysis may not trust the process or results. It is often crucial to develop models which could be interpreted easily and provide explanations for the decision points.
3. Integration and Standardization: Applying the AI & ML paradigm in existing frameworks for environment monitoring calls for harmonization and compatibility. Thus, sharing harmonized standards and protocols are needed for compatibility, and data integrity.

3. IDENTIFICATION OF POLLUTANT SOURCES

3.1 AI Algorithms for Accurate Identification of Pollution Sources

Since pollution control is an objective of environmental management, there is need to identify and confirm the main sources of pollution. Typically, conventional approaches of pollution source recognition require extended field surveys and have low advanced data processing power. The process of identifying sources has been simplified by the introduction of Artificial Intelligence (AI) that seeks to ensure that the right sources are sourced afresh by improving the algorithms that are used. Figure 2 depicts the various AI algorithms (Olawade et al., 2024) which could be used for accurate identification of pollution sources.

Figure 2. AI Algorithms for identification of pollution sources

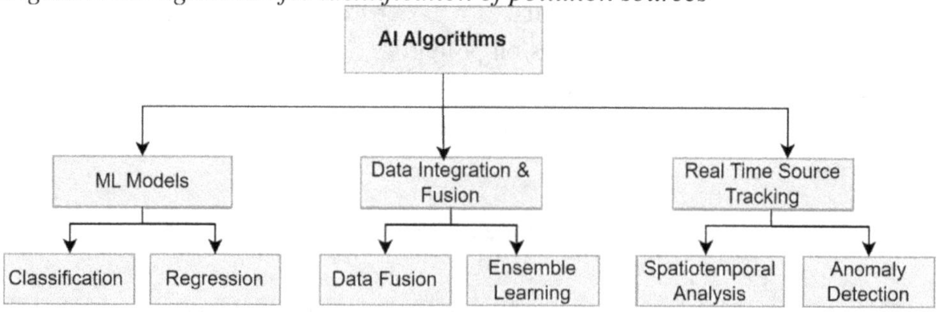

3.1.1 Machine Learning Models for Source Identification

A subcategory of AI known as Machine Learning (ML) has been extensively effective in the process of analyzing source of pollution. The statistical models for prediction like supervised learning models are used when algorithms are trained from previous data set to identify the correlation and or relation between pollutant levels and or possible causes. These models employ input characteristics, for instance emission sources, climatology, and pollutants and their concentrations to model and track pollutants.

3.1.1.1 Regression Analysis

A correlation between levels of pollutants and potential sources is made using regression techniques including linear regression and support vector regression. These models can predict from historical data the degree to which each source is likely to have contributed to observed concentrations of pollution. For example, regression analysis can assist in deciding the effects of industrial emissions, vehicle and natural scenes on air quality.

3.1.1.2 Classification Algorithms

The pollution sources are classified using classification algorithms including but not limited to decision trees, random forests, and artificial neural networks. These models sort data into specific segments depending on the amount of pollutants and identification of attributes as point or non-point and diffuse sources. Classification algorithms enhance the prospects of its recognition of individual sources and their contribution to the total emissions.

3.1.2 Data Integration and Fusion

AI improves source identification through a concept called source identification integration and fusion of data sources. Environmental sensors may be mostly air quality sensors, water quality sensors, and applicative remote sensing. Other related AI methodologies like data fusion and ensemble learning, integrate these multiple datasets to give a broad view of the sources of the pollution.

3.1.2.1 Data Fusion

Data fusion is the ability to combine data from different sensors and data available sources into one data set. The fuse data is then processed in the AI algorithms to find out the relation and patterns regarding different sources of pollution. For instance, assimilating data from different sources can easily facilitate the tracking of dispersed pollutants as well as determine the sources of the air pollution.

3.1.2.2 Ensemble Learning

Boosting and bagging are the two common Ensemble learning, where the prediction of multiple learners is combined in order to make the model more accurate. Ensemble methods improve the credibility of source identification by accumulating the outputs of the individual models while minimizing the effect of methods' errors.

3.1.3 Real-Time Source Tracking

Computing techniques help in tracking of the pollution sources by real time processing of data from monitoring systems. Another advantage of using the real-time data analysis is that any pollutive sources that are rapidly growing can easily be detected and addressed.

3.1.3.1 Spatiotemporal Analysis

Spatiotemporal analysis based on the support of AI technology investigates pollution data based on the space-time perspective. The machine learning models also estimate spatiotemporal distribution of pollutants in order to identify sources and their effects. For instance, movements of the air pollutants can be matched to source locations by analyzing existing patterns with the use of AI algorithms.

3.1.3.2 Anomaly Detection

The AI algorithms help to analyze pollution data and to identify new and unaccounted patterns for any new polluting subject. These algorithms inform authorities of when potential pollutions occur and also make the processes of investigation and handling faster.

3.2 How AI Enhances the Ability to Pinpoint Pollution Origins More Effectively Than Traditional Methods

Where AI Steps up the capacity to identify precise source of pollution more efficiently than the Conventional Approaches. The employment of AI in identification of pollution sources constitutes a major break from conventional approaches. Most of the conventional assault detection methods involve the use of simplified models such as observational check, low level analysis, and non-dynamic models which has inconveniences of being slow and less effective (Cromar et al., 2019; Olawade et al., 2024). AI enhances the ability to pinpoint pollution origins through several key advantages:

3.2.1 Improved Accuracy and Precision

The nature of modern AI algorithms to yield improved exactness and velocity in determining pollution sources especially with the use of ML models. It is more indicative of traditional approaches that use approximations and rather vague models are used. While the traditional methods work effectively on large datasets, and detect patterns that the AI technique cannot capture. For instance, the AI models can identify more than one source contributing to pollution, and estimate the contribution ratio with much more accuracy.

3.2.2 Enhanced Data Processing and Analysis

AI is particularly useful in analyzing big and complicated data and is usually not feasible with other techniques. The concepts like an inherently logical matrix structure can be understood, but a layman will not be able to implement it, with big data from multiple sensors or acts SAT imagery data, AI algorithms in great results are obtained. Outsourced techniques might not be effective in compiling multiple sources of data and therefore might have a poor way of identifying some of the sources. AI enhances data handling and analyses and brings together data of diverse nature for comprehensive identification of pollutive sources.

3.2.3 Real-Time and Dynamic Capabilities

Apart from this, AI updates also have real-time and dynamic system benefits when it comes to identifying source of pollution. Conventional approaches involve sporadic sampling and assessment, thus it is harder and takes more time for the authorities to identify new pollution sources. Real-time detection of data means that through the help of AI algorithms, constant identification of the sources of pollution and instant recognition of new or emerging sources can be made. This dynamic capability helps accomplish timely interventions and regulatory actions.

3.2.4 Automation and Scalability

Through AI pollution source identification procedures are enabled and thereby minimized the need for human input. Ad hoc procedures can often involve using time-consuming and labour-intensive field research alongside conventional paper-based data processing. Computerization of data acquisition and processing make it possible to make large-scale and highly scalable source identification. This automation enhances the monitoring of programs and brings about the capacities of area and pollutions within it.

3.2.5 Integration of Multidisciplinary Data

Artificial intelligence improves the synthesis of data from multiple disciplines: it essentially approaches the problem of pollution source identification systemically. Such patterns can use local data repositories or involve simplified models as their components, more often than not. Cognitive computing systems combine information from other disciplines like air quality, meteorology, and land-use to get a detailed view of pollution sources. It is possible, leveraging these integrations, to get a better understanding of sources and their impact on the considered environmental systems.

Thus, it could be agreed that AI algorithms are an important new step in the search for the sources of pollution in terms of accuracy, speed of work, and data analysis. In this way, AI enriches classical approaches with the help of such methodologies as superior analytical examination and automatization analysis which significantly improve the identification of pollution sources and, in general, the practices of environmental control and governmental regulation. As the technologies of AI go on developing, the effective utilization of AI in pollution source identification will be an incredibly significant factor for solving environmental issues and promoting sustainability.

4. CASE STUDIES: SUCCESSFUL IMPLEMENTATIONS

4.1 AI-Driven Air Quality Monitoring Stations

The AI-empowered air quality monitoring stations for air quality innovations and improvements are relatively new since AI augments the air quality surveillance utilizing artificial intelligence to optimize the administration of AQI evaluations. These systems combine AI techniques in the air quality sensors to enhance their capabilities of measuring the pollution in the atmosphere.

4.1.1 Implementation and Functionality

The discussed AI-based AQMS use machine learning algorithms to process the data from the network of sensors which collect data on concentrations of PM2.5, PM10, NO2, O3, and SO2. These sensors gather actual-time information regarding concentration for pollutants as well as climate which are then used by the artificial intelligence to produce effective diagnosis of air quality.

4.1.2 Case Study: Beijing's Air Quality Monitoring System

One such example is the Beijing, China air quality monitoring system. Since Beijing has great demands in air pollution monitoring, the Beijing Municipal Environmental Monitoring Center has employed the application of AI in the procedure. It incorporates a number of terrestrial sensors and satellite data and meteorological knowledge.

The accumulated data is then examined using machine learning algorithms to determine the sources of air pollution, forecast the future state of air quality and present air quality indexes in real time. Through the adoption to the system the accuracy of the pollution forecasts also has helped in offering better advisories for the public health. Through integration of several data sources a complete picture of the air quality is provided as well as information for interventional measures.

4.1.3 Impact and Benefits

The AI-driven air quality monitoring system in Beijing has demonstrated several key benefits:

- Enhanced Accuracy: Application of AI algorithms has made elasticity of air quality measurements and so basing decisions on realistic evidence.
- Real-Time Monitoring: Real time data analysis enables appropriate update of air quality conditions and empowers the system to respond instantly to pollution occurrences.
- Predictive Capabilities: From the same technology, we are in a position to predict the air quality with high reliability and take measures to prevent air pollution.

4.2.1 Example: AI in Industrial Emission Control

Based on the selected AI applications in industrial emission control systems, one can note some of the changes produced by these technologies. For example, those used in manufacturing plants apply the current data from the emission sensors to enhance the anti-pollution mechanisms. Artificial intelligence prognosticates based on operation parameters and regulate emission controls to meet prescriptive emission standards.

4.2.2 Example: ML in Wastewater Treatment

Use of machine learning models has also been used in improving conditions in the wastewater treatment as well. Consolidated using sensor data gathered through the indicated parameters like COD, TSS, and BOD, the applied ML algorithms anticipate the treatment results and use the interactive control of operational parameters to help augment the WWT efficiency.

4.2.3 Example: AI for Oil Spill Detection

The use Adopted AI plans have been used for spotting oil spills and for the management of the ramifications. Satellite data coupled with Artificial Intelligence (AI) algorithms; including Convolutional Neural Networks (CNNs), is employed in the identification of the real-time status of oil spillage. Satellite images are used to detect oil spills through machine learning then mapping oil spilling patterns for timely intervention.

5. DATA ANALYSIS AND PREDICTIVE MODELLING

5.1 Use of AI and ML for Data Analysis to Detect Trends and Anomalies

Introducing the application of artificial intelligence and machine learning to the processing data set, the capability to identify patterns or unusual behavior has been greatly enhanced in the scope of environmental data analysis. These technologies provides capabilities for analyzing big and complex datasets to identify more accurately patterns and abnormalities that could indicate important developments in the environment or possible pollution episodes (Aljohani, 2023).

5.1.1 Trend Detection

AI and ML improve the identification of environmental patterns as a result of the ability to analyze a massive amount of historical and current data. These algorithms can reveal patterns that maybe not easily discerned with the traditional statistical analysis hence giving a better view of the environment.

5.1.1.1 Time Series Analysis

A critical issue in trend identification of environmental data is time sequence analysis. LSTM networks, for instance, and the ARIMA models analyse time-series data, to detect patterns and cycles within time-series data sets. For example, in the preceding LSTM networks, the long-term memory learning can capture gradual trends of the air quality data such as continuous rise of pollutant concentrations or oscillations in the quality of air within certain periods of the year.

5.1.1.2 Anomaly Detection

The term Anomaly can be defined as identification of certain data points that differ with the norms of the particular data set being anomalous. Accomplishments in environmental data sets are accomplished using clustering, auto encoders, and statistical AI algorithms. Density based clustering algorithms like k-means and DBSCAN place data points in clusters and mark data points that are dissimilar to most of the other points. Auto encoders are a type of neural network, which reconstruct data and detect outliers using reconstruction errors. These methods are most suitable for monitoring changes such as sudden random fluctuations of pollutants concentrations or shifts in water quality parameters.

5.1.2 Data Fusion and Integration

Data fusion and integration is also possible in AI and ML which amalgamate data from many sources to present the results. This capability accelerates trend detection by assimilating various data forms and refines analysis for the detection of anomalies.

5.2.1.1 Multi-Source Integration

Concerning trend identification, other data sources are combined with satellite imagery, and ground-based sensors alongside historical records within AI algorithms. For instance, embedding satellite data with ground level measurements of air quality improves the understanding pollution dispersion and temporal trends.

5.2.1.2 Feature Engineering

Feature engineering—or feature extraction from the raw data input—enables AI models to identify patterns and outliers more effectively. The idea is that by obtaining meaningful features, including moving averages or the pollution index, the conventional algorithms work will be enhanced and offer a profound analysis of the environmental data.

5.2 Predictive Modelling for Anticipating Pollution Events and Mitigating Their Effects

Thus, predictive modelling becomes an inevitable part of proactive pollutant event prediction and prevention. Adaptive prediction and control OF air quality Pollution: Utilizing historical data, real-time measurements, and environmental variable to predict future pollution and control them (Persis & Ben Amar, 2023).

5.2.1 Predictive Models for Pollution Forecasting

These models are hugely helpful for identifying what might happen if pollution increased, in which areas, thereby aiding early warning and specific action.

5.2.1.1 Regression Models

Pollution level forecast models are developed from multiple linear and polynomial regressions in which dependent variable is the pollution level and independent variables include emission source, meteorological conditions and land use. These models predict future concentrations of pollutants using a relationship between predictor variables under consideration and historical pollution data.

5.2.1.2 Machine Learning Approaches

Ensemble learning methods and deep learning improve predictive analytics as those techniques analyze dependencies and interactions in the data. For example, in Random Forests and Gradient Boosting Machines, the models make predictions in order to combine them into more accurate and less susceptible to outliers. Sequential data and spatial pattern analysis, tools such as CNNs and RNNs are used to forecast pollution events.

5.2.2 Mitigating Pollution Effects

Other than identifying events of pollution, predictive modeling is also used to estimate how the impacts of the events are addressed. These analyses allow understanding possible pollution situations in advance so necessary measures can be taken to decrease the consequences for public health.

5.2.2.1 Scenario Analysis

The second method is the application of predictors aimed at estimating the pollution and its consequences in case of developing various situations. Using a number of variables, AI algorithms perform scenarios which, for example, include changes in emission sources or meteorological factors on the pollution level. The purposes of this analysis include scenario planning and designing the strategies of risk reduction.

5.2.2.2 Optimization of Mitigation Measures

Optimization techniques in AI provide better results in the steps towards pollution control. For instance, models containing optimization algorithms adapt the working of various air pollution control devices such as scrubbers and filters depending on predictable pollutant levels. Machines also help in traffic flow control and urban planning, in order to reduce emissions and limit contact with pollutants.

5.2.2.3 Decision Support Systems

This helps in the decision support systems that enable real time control of pollution incidences as captured by the modeling. These systems use forecast information with the organisation's performance data that are used in decision making processes. For example, AI integrated decision support systems can suggest minor changes in the process of industries, carrying out of measures in response to emergency situations, or dissemination of public health warnings depending on expected levels of pollution.

5.2.3 Case Study: Air Quality Forecasting and Management

One of the most common systems of predictive modeling used in the case of pollution control is the Air Quality Forecasting system implemented in certain city. They uses machine learning models that takes inputs from past AQI, meteorological data, and emission data to predict AQI levels for the day. For example, the European Union's Copernicus Atmosphere Monitoring Service CAMS currently uses AI and ML for releasing air quality forecasts in the member states that help in public health intervention and policy enforcement.

6. ETHICAL CONSIDERATIONS AND CHALLENGES

6.1 Issues Related to Data Privacy in Environmental Monitoring

Worries about data privacy have therefore risen as AI and ML shape up to form core technologies of major environmental monitoring systems. EMS has data from many sources including air quality monitoring systems, water quality monitoring systems, satellite imagery and many others. However, this data is crucial when it comes to regulating pollution and protecting the environment (di Vimercati et al., 2013) at the same time, there are other issues of individual privacy here.

6.1.1 Data Collection and Privacy

Most environmental monitoring systems have data that consists of aspects of people, more so when connected to smart cities or IoT devices in homes. For example, air quality sensors installed in urban settings can potentially record other information connected to people's conspicuous daily schedules. Likewise, an occurrence, such as water quality sensors in water public areas, might record information that could point straight to a group of people or households.

6.1.2 Data Security and Access

Preserving the privacy of collected data is the main factor, and only with properly safeguarded data may security be achieved. Such things as cyber attacks or other unauthorised attempts to gain data access may result in this information and data being leaked. Encryption, as well as other measures of access control, must be extended as some sort of protection environmental data. Further, various levels of data anonymity are useful in reducing or removing privacy concerns by excluding identity information from analysis datasets.

6.1.3 Legal and Regulatory Considerations

Ensuring that data protection and privacy laws, including the GDPR in the EU or CCPA in the US, are followed is important for environmental monitoring organisations. These regulations define how data should be protected, process and used, and the importance of the user's notification of the processes. Compliance with these legal frameworks also promotes the fact that the environmental monitors conduct the monitoring practices in a manner that respects individuals' confidentiality.

6.2 Addressing Potential Algorithmic Bias in AI and ML Systems

Biased AI and machine learning are a real ethical issue, especially when using environmental surveillance and pollution prevention. Preconceptions can lead to inaccurate and unjust results in applications of AI-based decision-making processes, which can perpetuate inaccurate environmental allocation and could aggravate inequality.

6.2.1 Sources of Bias

AI and ML systems can be bias due to bias data used in the model development, problematic algorithm application and inadequate environmental conditions in the models. For instance, if an ML model used for predicting the air quality the training data included mainly from airlie areas and cities areas of the country, the output may be very different from the areas that lack adequate resources. As with situation-dependent pollution data, historical data or sensor calibration can also influence the outcome.

6.2.2 Mitigating Bias

Reducing algorithmic bias entails several specific undertaking. When developing AI systems that are equality compliant it is important that the training data is diverse and represents the population. Geometrically the data collected should encompass several regions, several demographic groups and as much conditions as possible so that it may served as a sample for the other parts of the world, groups and conditions. Moreover, the usage of FA algorithms and bias checks as often as possible may help to prevent bias in AI systems.

6.2.3 Transparency and Accountability

It is crucial to work towards the transparency of AI and ML during their design and implementation to rectify bias. Algorithms must be well documented such that the program's design and its data sources and decision-making processes can be reasonably assessed by other relevant stakeholders so that they can judge the prospective consequences of the AI systems involved. Another related concern is that of bias, and integral checks and balances put in place for external audits and stakeholder reviews do a good job in correcting these biases.

6.3 The Importance of Transparency in AI-Driven Environmental Initiatives

There is no doubt that accuracy is one of the basic ethical standards in the use of artificial intelligence in environmental programs. This book also argues that making AI and ML systems as transparent as possible fosters trust and drives accountability and better decision-making (Olawumi & Oladapo, 2025) among the public, policy-makers, and environmental organizations.

6.3.1 Transparency in Data and Algorithms

For the AI framework to be implemented in the environmental sector, the data sampling methods have to make sense to the key stakeholders in the same way that the algorithms used do. Making specific and basic information about which kind of data is collected, how the data is analyzed or what kind of algorithms used can contribute to the improvement of the knowledge of the stakeholders about the decision-making and problem-solving regarding the environmental issues. For instance, the other positive example is clear disclosure of algorithms involving predictions about air quality to reflect the efficiency of the predicted results by the stakeholders.

6.3.2 Public Engagement and Communication

Transparency calls for more interaction with the public so for the process to work, there must be good interaction with the public. Papers, public hearings, education campaigns let the public get acquainted with AI based environment care technologies and their advantages and disadvantages. Public engagement is also another way of develop the process of consult them and get their feedbacks where and when these environmental initiatives will be implemented.

6.3.3 Ethical Considerations and Accountability

Sky-connected AI environmental solutions therefore needs to adopt issues on the ethical fair, accountable and inclusive. Thus, increased transparency enhances accountability since one is able to give chase to ethical questions, such as data privacy and algorithm fairness. The regulation of the use of artificial intelligence ensures that the existing technologies work appropriately, and does not violate the environment and the whole society.

6.3.4 Policy and Governance

In order to increase transparency regarding environment and AI, it is necessary to determine the right processes for policy and governance. Regulation should prescribe guidelines to the use and storage of data as well as definitions of algorithms and models, and how the company communicates with interested parties. Ethics committees or advisory boards evaluate suggested types of experiences in the appropriate and correct application of AI technology.

This chapter shows that data protection, fairness and explainability can be framed as issues that need to be solved in order to protect people's rights, enforce fairness and promote the utilization of advanced technology among sophisticated customers and businesses. Therefore proper functions of the security, data, management system should be used, bias should minimized and the result should be made more transparent and through applying such strategies, technology is needed and is sufficient for the environmental goal.

7. INTERDISCIPLINARY COLLABORATION

7.1 The Necessity of Collaboration between Environmental Scientists, Technologists, and Policymakers

Fostering many discipline working on environmental issues is the most suitable approach to dealing with them. Enjoining the views of environmental scientists, technologists, and policymakers is that the approaches adopted reflect a more comprehensive issue analysis since all three offer insights into how problems can be effectively solved from array of practical and research perspectives. It closes gaps between science, technology and policy, thereby supporting the development of integrated approaches (Finnerty et al., 2024) to environmental management.

7.1.1 Integration of Scientific and Technological Expertise

Environmental scientists help guide people on understand the processes of environmental degradation, pollution and climate change as well as other related ecological disruptions. The expert knowledge in ecology, geology, meteorology as well as other fields is used to support general knowledge of environmental issues. However, these issues' solving assumes the application of the increased technologies and methods that cannot be used routinely in scientific researches.

Other stakeholders include technologists: data scientist and engineers who design and implement technologies, AI, ML, remote sensing, among others. These tools improve the capability to measure, understand and supervise the information on the external conditions. For instance, the combination of using satellite imagery and AI enables the monitoring of deforestation in real-time or the amount of air pollution. Science and technology bring new lights and better ways to solve environmental issues on the basis of better understanding of the issues.

7.1.2 Policy Development and Implementation

It is the duty of policy makers to communicate the scientific research and development to policy and legislation. They guarantee that the environmental approaches are not only scientifically informed, but also sociopolitical. Policies are formulated after considering the scientific and technologic view of the impacts and then figuring out what the stakeholders have collectively in Rio de Janerio besides the regulatory bodies/Commission.

Policymaker-scientist/technologist cooperation ensures that the policies and the technologies being proposed are viable and meet the policy goals while the environmental policies are evidence-based. For example, creation of air quality standards include elements of health risk assessment and technological feasibility assessment. It is with this combined knowledge that Policymakers use while developing policies to enhance the health of the population and also the environment.

7.1.3 Benefits of Collaborative Approaches

The benefits of interdisciplinary collaboration are manifold:

- Comprehensive Solutions: Integration of capable professionals from different fields results we're better and more comprehensive solutions to environmental problems. For instance, recognizing water quality challenges entails science as an area of knowledge in the form of ecological effects assessment; technology in the form of sensor networks; and policy as embraced by water management policies.
- Enhanced Innovation: Technological synergy seeks to enhance unity of effort a professional partnership by joining different skills and views. New approaches are devised which were not encountered before.
- Informed Decision-Making: Teamwork among different schools enriches the awareness of Enviro problems allowing to produce more effective decisions. Policy makers get the scientific output and technical knowledge whereas scientists and technologist get a view on the implementation aspects.

7.2 Examples of Successful Interdisciplinary Projects

A number of interdisciplinary projects show that environmental science, technology, and policy can be effectively integrated. These examples show how partnership can solve major environmental issues and advance meaningful results.

7.2.1 The Copernicus Earth Observation Programme

One good example of successful interdisciplinary collaboration is the Copernicus Earth Observation Programme coordinated by the European Space Agency (ESA) as well as the European Commission. The program combines the arena of satellite remote sensing with the faculties of environmental science and policy in the management of environmental factors including air quality, land usage and climate among others.

7.1.1.1 Scientific and Technological Integration

Copernicus uses various earth observation satellites with images and data on the state of the environment. This information is useful for understanding various changes that occur in the environment and analyze the effects they have for habitats and people. The technologists design different algorithms and tools to analyze The data gathered by those satellites is massive and complex.

7.1.1.2 Policy Application

Information acquired from Copernicus data is used for European environmental legislations and policies. For instance, the data assists in its enactment of the EU Green Deal that reveals information about climate change and the indicators of sustainability. The examined program demonstrates that synchronizing scientific works, technological advances, and policy making paves the way to successful environmental governance and legislation.

7.2.2 The Integrated Coastal Zone Management (ICZM) Initiative

Integrated Coastal zone Management (ICZM) another successful example of interdisciplinary field of study. This effort is designed to enhance management of the coastal regions based on scientific findings, technological applications and policies.

7.2.1.1 Scientific and Technological Integration

Many ICZM related projects include scientists surveying coastal environments, the rates and causes of coastal erosion, and climate change. Scientists and technologists construct models and powerful instruments to make approximations of coastal behavior and measure impacts of numerous management policies. For instance, GIS and remote sensing data as well as their products are used in mapping and monitoring of coastal dynamics.

7.2.1.2 Policy Development and Implementation

These coastal management policies are in turn made and applied by the policy makers from the scientific and technological enlightenment emerging from the ICZM projects. These policies include matters like coastal erosion control, habitat conservation and management or sustainable use of the coastal area. The multisectoral's collaboration helps bring the best available scientific and technological data to the development of coastal policies to result in the enhanced and suitable models of coastal management.

7.2.3 The Global Environmental Monitoring System (GEMS)

These coastal management policies are in turn made and applied by the policy makers from the scientific and technological enlightenment emerging from the ICZM projects. These policies include matters like coastal erosion control, habitat conservation and management or sustainable use of the coastal area. The multisectoral's collaboration helps bring the best available scientific and technological data to the development of coastal policies to result in the enhanced and suitable models of coastal management.

7.3.1.1 Scientific and Technological Integration

GEMS utilizes data input from remote sensors such as earth observation satellites, measurement from ground-based instruments and meteorological history. Expert commission this data so that they can determine threats to the environment on a global level as well as coming up with new issues to investigate. Technologists manage and sustain systems to gather, transform and distribute the data collected within the application.

7.3.1.2 Policy Support

GEMS generates data and its analysis to be used in environmental policies and agreements, including the United Nations Sustainable Development Goals and climate conventions. The collected information is used by policymakers to monitor the effectiveness and Goals, set benchmarks and strategies of combating environmental issues around the globe. The initiative shows that scientific cooperation harnesses scientific and technological potential to help and contribute to international environmental management.

Overall, the study demonstrates the need for integration in research and practice between environment science, technologist, and policymakers. Through promoting positive interdependence, cooperation creates improved opportunities that use research, technology, and policies to enhance public welfare with better strategies. It is particularly relevant to point to the examples of the projects implemented in the areas of environmental cooperation, that revealed the need in the further interdisciplinary work experience, such as Copernicus, ICZM, and GEMS.

8. FUTURE INNOVATIONS AND EMERGING TECHNOLOGIES

8.1 Exploration of Future Trends in AI and ML for Environmental Sustainability

AI and ML are still relatively young fields, and the possible use of these concepts for increasing environmental sustainability is tremendous. The future of these technologies are likely to continue driving changes how issues associated with the environment are managed and predicted, let alone promoting creative policy implementations to combat and control pollution as well manage resources.

8.1.1 Advanced AI Algorithms and Models

The first trend on the horizon is a deeper ability to utilize AI based algorithms, and better models that will be created in the coming years. The new approaches like explainable AI (XAI), and generative adversarial networks (GANs) provide new routes to enhance the sustainability of the environment. AEI is the method in charge of making most extensive artificial intelligence approaches more comprehensible and understandable, which is very important for reliable decision-making. This will help to better understand how such models, employed by Artificial Intelligence, make decision about environmental issues and improve their utilization in policy-making and managing processes.

The two-neural network model called the generative adversarial network can be used to model environmental settings and possible consequences under distinct conditions. This may enhance the reliability of prognoses which are utilized in determining the effects of environment on existence and in establishing efficient methods of resource administration.

8.1.2 Integration with Internet of Things (IoT)

The combination of AI, and ML with the Internet of things IoT promises to dramatically transform how we monitor, manage, and track our environment. These include smart sensors and connect monitoring systems, they produce massive amounts of data relating to environmental parameters in real –time. AI and ML algorithms can subsequently analyze this data to point out such trends, detect anomalous behaviours and even early predict future conditions to an extent of perfection.

For example, smart IoT systems can monitor air and water quality with the help of multiple sensors and present new data to a central point in a timely manner. Such real-time analysis thus can help to respond to occasional pollution occurrences and improve efficiency in the utilization of natural resources.

8.1.3 Enhanced Predictive Analytics

The change in the nature of Predictive Analytics is another major development. Subsequently, sophisticated algorithms such as deep learning and reinforcement learning shall improve the compounded mechanism of environmental prediction and events of pollution. Due to the deep neural net structure of the workings in deep learning models it can detect latent features and correlations from large and higher number feature data that is not easily achievable with other methods. Non-parametric methods such as the reinforcement learning technique, which involves trial and error in decision making, can improve the approaches use in controlling pollution and managing resources through enhancement by real conditions.

8.1.4 Collaborative AI and Crowdsourcing

Future innovations will also involve crowd-sourced data and citizen AI systems as well as other complex systems. Compared to highly individualistic sources of information that are limited to a single perspective of a few people, unique platforms that pull information from many give the AI models more diverse and informative datasets. For instance, people's feedbacks about air quality gathered from mobile applications can be integrated with those of formal monitoring stations to improve the spatial and temporal density and precision of conclusions regarding environmental conditions.

8.1.5 AI for Climate Change Mitigation and Adaptation

Climate change management now relies on AI and ML for matters concerning mitigation and adaptation. Machine learning algorithms are able to determine trends, from the climate information, to likely effects on the habitats, our food production and living conditions. ML algorithms help determine optimal energy consumption in facilities and forecast renewable power generation or look for ways to minimize carbon emissions. The utilisation of AI within climate models as well as adaptation solutions enable stakeholders to formulate better responses to climate change and improve on cop resistance.

8.2 Potential New Technologies That Could Further Enhance Pollution Control

Some among the uprising technologies that are expected to enhance the level of pollution control and environmental conserve are gives below. All these technologies present the current challenges in new ways, providing promising solutions to enhance pollution management.

8.2.1 Advanced Air Purification Technologies

There are new technologies globally developed and used to fight urban air pollution and improve air quality. For example, photocatalytic materials, and electrostatic precipitators, the techniques are under development to improve the efficiency of PM and gaseous pollutant extraction. While photocatalytic materials employ sun light to incite chemical reactions, which reduce the pollutants into less dangerous compounds, the electrostatic precipitators make use of electrical charges to derive particles from air.

Also, the effects of growing plants through the facade of a building, or called vertical gardens or green walls are also being considered as environmentally friendly solution to enhance air quality. These systems do not only serve as filter of pollutants but also offer appearance and environmental enhancement.

8.2.2 Innovative Water Treatment Technologies

When it comes to water pollution and safe drinking water it is important to note that the improvement of such technologies are crucial. Methodologies that are currently evolving are AOP's, membrane systems, and nanotechnology based solutions. AOPs deploy reactive species to decompose organic contaminants in water whereas membrane filtration technologies provide high efficiency of contaminated separation. Conventional processes employ pollutant and nanoparticles to fetch or disintegrate the pollutant into smaller and simpler forms at the molecular level.

8.2.3 Smart Waste Management Systems

Digital waste management systems are innovative waste management systems that use artificial intelligence and the internet of things technologies to further enhance the waste collection and recycling cycles. Smart bins with interactive sensors are able to keep track of waste volume and convey information to service providers with regard to timing and routes. As AI algorithms work, they can extract information about the generation of waste and thus increase recycling rates and decrease the amount of landfill usage. Furthermore, technological advancement in waste management practices including the anaerobic digestion and pyrolysis are being made as a way of generate energy from waste.

8.2.4 Renewable Energy Technologies

Renewable energy technologies are evolving steadily and are key components on strategies for combating pollution as well as climate change. Further advancement in solar photovoltaic cell, wind turbines, and energy storage facilities are bringing efficiency and economical renovation to renewable sources of energy. For instance, new generation of solar cells with enhanced conversion efficiency and thin forms can be introduced into numerous substrates, while new types and improved battery technology provides for better energy storage and better stability of the grids.

8.2.5 Bioremediation and Green Technologies

Bio-remediation is a growing field that involves the use of microorganisms to break down or neutralize contaminants of pollution. Optimization of the microorganisms used in bioremediation has been made possible by synthetic biology and genetic engineering to allow improved abilities to metabolize specific pollutants. Technologies in this field include use of biodegradable materials and environmentally friendly chemical processes which helps cutting down on effects on environment.

Therefore, future development of AI and ML together with other new technologies provides great prospects for improving environmental performance and reducing pollution. Current and future technological advances in algorithms and IoT compatibility, as well as better predictive analysis functions, will augment the effectiveness of environmental observation and regulation. Also, emerging innovations in air treatment methods, water treatment, waste disposal, clean energy, and bio remedial measures shall add another layer and optimize the efficiency of this area. When adopting these progresses, stakeholders need to have solutions to environmental problems and make a beneficial impact on the future of the world.

9. CONCLUSION AND THE PATH FORWARD

9.1 Summary of the Transformative Impact of AI and ML on Environmental Science

AI and, in particular, ML play particular valuable roles in the development of new methodologies and tools to analyze the environmental situation and optimize the usage of resources. These technologies have helped in the accurate and faster ways used in studying big and complicated datasets making great impacts in environmental inspection, pollution management and resource productivity.

Due to various techniques, especially the algorithms in AI and ML, data analysis involves identifying trends, anomalies and patterns of environmental data. This capability increases awareness of environmental trends and helps to better predict pollution occurrences, and climatic conditions. Moreover, the link between AI and IoT and also the remote sensing has offered the real time monitoring and also the adaptive management which are familiar with new invented environmental problems.

Due to AI, better application in the identification of sources of pollution and better management strategies in control measures has been observed. This through accurate prediction using machine learning to take preventive measures of pollution and its impact on the environment and the people. These breakthroughs demonstrate the role of AI and ML in propelling the green agenda forward and growing ability to design more creativity solutions to some of the environmental issues.

9.2 Recommendations for Future Research, Practice, and Policy

9.2.1 Future Research Directions

Future work should therefore aim at increasing the reliability and external validity of AI and ML models in environmental science. This includes creating methods that can work with various and large amount of data together with reducing prejudices. Future development in fusing multi-source data from satellite imagery and ground sensor data will enhance the efficacy and practicality of more extensive environmental monitoring.

It is also essential to determine how newer computational technologies, like quantum computing, and other better neural networks can also be used in environmental science. It is possible to predict improved handling of the more complicated models and the bigger data sets in order to achieve better understanding of the processes and enhance the precision of predictions.

9.2.2 Practical Implementation

Instead of introducing wholly new and novel tools, practitioners should aim at incorporating AI and ML tools within currently existing environmental management systems. Best practices are involved that deal with collection, analysis, and interpretation of data which further guarantee the success of applying these insights advanced by artificial Intelligence in the real world. Development of human capacities as well as training for environmental specialists remain crucial to actualising the potential of these technologies, as well as enhance their implementation.

Moreover the enhancement of the interfaces easy to use and of the decision support tools will allow the use of AI and ML in applications. They should be capable of giving out recommendation and being a decision tool on management and policies in Relation to the environment.

9.2.3 Policy Recommendations

Policy makers should set a guideline that will govern the positive use of AI and ML in environmental science. To this extent, there are framework development on data protection, use of machine learning algorithms and artificial intelligence, and dissemination of rules and regulations to encourage public acceptance and proper use of innovations. It is also advisable that there are policies which encourage interdisciplinary cooperation, also embrace and encourage research and new development of AI and ML solutions.

Further, the adoption of incentives that promote AI based technologies used in environmental management could hasten the practice. Effecting more policy coproduction between Universities industry and other/internal government agencies will help spur innovation and ensure research outcomes are applied.

9.3 The Ongoing Importance of Innovation and Collaboration in Ensuring a Sustainable Future

Integration, talent and partnership are key to managing the advanced multifaceted problems of the modern world, and the environment is one of them. Due to improvement in AI and ML technologies their use in environmental science must be complemented by constant developments in order respond to new challenges and improve upon existing solutions.

It is very important to work together with experts cutting across discipline, segment and geography in order to harness their experience and assets. This approach guarantees that the solutions are system-wide, implementable and engender sustainable policy solutions because ; Such collaborations also enhance the dissemination of information and distilling of examples of good practices trending the progress of environmental science and technology around the world.

In conclusion it can be stated that the use of AI and ML has transformed environmental science with its data collection and predictive and analytical capabilities. Going forward, additional research, application of advanced technologies to practice, education, and policies will be of importance in ensuring that the benefits associated with these technologies are realized. Such focus will mean we sustain efforts towards the developmental goals and keep addressing the environmental concerns appropriately.

REFERENCES

Aljohani, A. (2023). Predictive Analytics and Machine Learning for Real-Time Supply Chain Risk Mitigation and Agility. *Sustainability (Basel), 15*(20), 15088. DOI: 10.3390/su152015088

Chu, E. W., & Karr, J. R. (2016). Environmental impact: Concept, consequences, measurement. Reference module in life sciences, B978-0.

Cromar, K. R., Duncan, B. N., Bartonova, A., Benedict, K., Brauer, M., Habre, R., & Volckens, J. (2019). Air pollution monitoring for health research and patient care. An official American Thoracic Society workshop report. *Annals of the American Thoracic Society, 16*(10), 1207–1214.

di Vimercati, S. D. C., Genovese, A., Livraga, G., Piuri, V., & Scotti, F. (2013). Privacy and security in environmental monitoring systems: issues and solutions. In *Computer and Information Security Handbook* (pp. 835–853). Morgan Kaufmann. DOI: 10.1016/B978-0-12-394397-2.00047-7

Finnerty, S., Piazza, J., & Levine, M. (2024). Scientists' identities shape engagement with environmental activism. *Communications Earth & Environment, 5*(1), 240. DOI: 10.1038/s43247-024-01412-9

Manisalidis, I., Stavropoulou, E., Stavropoulos, A., & Bezirtzoglou, E. (2020). Environmental and Health Impacts of Air Pollution: A Review. *Frontiers in Public Health, 8*, 14. DOI: 10.3389/fpubh.2020.00014 PMID: 32154200

Olawade, D. B., Wada, O. Z., Ige, A. O., Egbewole, B. I., Olojo, A., & Oladapo, B. I. (2024). Artificial intelligence in environmental monitoring: Advancements, challenges, and future directions. *Hygiene and Environmental Health Advances, 12*, 100114. DOI: 10.1016/j.heha.2024.100114

Olawumi, M. A., & Oladapo, B. I. (2025). AI-driven predictive models for sustainability. *Journal of Environmental Management, 373*, 123472. DOI: 10.1016/j.jenvman.2024.123472 PMID: 39612794

Persis, J., & Ben Amar, A. (2023, February 1). Predictive modeling and analysis of air quality - Visualizing before and during COVID-19 scenarios. *Journal of Environmental Management, 327*, 116911. DOI: 10.1016/j.jenvman.2022.116911 PMID: 36470187

Saravanan, P., Saravanan, V., Rajeshkannan, R., Arnica, G., Rajasimman, M., Gurunathan, B., & Pugazhendhi, A. (2024). Comprehensive review on toxic heavy metals in the aquatic system: Sources, identification, treatment strategies, and health risk assessment. *Environmental Research*, *258*, 119440. DOI: 10.1016/j.envres.2024.119440 PMID: 38906448

Solangi, Y. A., Alyamani, R., & Ali, S. (2024). Exploring the influence of digital technology innovation on air quality: Insights from developed and developing economies. *Sustainable Futures : An Applied Journal of Technology, Environment and Society*, *8*, 100342. DOI: 10.1016/j.sftr.2024.100342

Chapter 12
Air Pollution Detection Using Image Processing

Manoj Himmatrao Devare
https://orcid.org/0000-0002-9530-3914
Amity University, Mumbai, India

Anita Manoj Devare
https://orcid.org/0009-0009-4159-6289
Amity University, Mumbai, India

Aparna Sushil Nishad
Amity University, Mumbai, India

ABSTRACT

Air pollution has created significant implications for public health and well-being. The chapter looks into the major events of air pollution, its impact and various approaches to deal with the air pollution. Traditional methods of air pollution monitoring and intensity detection rely on stationary sensors and manual measurements, which are often limited in spatial coverage and real-time monitoring capabilities. This chapter discusses a methodology that analyzes images captured from various sources, such as satellite imagery or ground-based cameras, and accurately classify different types of air pollution, including smog, particulate matter, and industrial emissions. The goal is to provide an efficient and automated method for monitoring air quality, enabling early detection of pollution hotspots, and assisting in environmental management and public health efforts. The image and video processing model of air pollution detection has achieved the loss is 0.4434 and accuracy of 88.88%.

DOI: 10.4018/979-8-3693-7832-8.ch012

1. INTRODUCTION

Air pollution is a serious environmental issue that has an impact on the health of people health and quality of life all over the world. Several natural and man-made factors contribute to air pollution. Natural sources include wildfires, dust, fire in the farms, industrial chimney outlets. Human-made sources include industrial activities, transportation, power generation, and agriculture. The burning of fossil fuels, such as oil and coal, is a major contributor to air pollution. It refers to the presence of harmful substances in the air, such as fine particulate matter (PM2.5), nitrogen oxides, Sulphur dioxide, ozone, and carbon monoxide, that can cause respiratory and cardiovascular diseases, cancer, and premature death. Exposure to high levels of air pollution can cause asthma attacks, bronchitis, and emphysema, and can also provoke existing health conditions. Air pollution also impacts ecosystems and the environment, including acid rain, Ozone depletion, and climate change, and it affects people of all ages and backgrounds, particularly those who live in urban areas.

This chapter tries to answer the research questions. How image processing techniques be utilized to detect and classify different types of air pollution in captured images? What machine learning algorithms and approaches can be employed to accurately predict air pollution levels based on image features? How does the performance of the developed image processing and machine learning system compare to traditional air pollution monitoring methods in terms of accuracy and reliability? Can the developed system be effectively integrated into existing air quality monitoring systems, and how does it complement or enhance the information provided by traditional sensors and measurements?

The World Health Organization (WHO) estimates that air pollution causes 7 million premature deaths per year worldwide, making it the fourth leading risk factor for mortality. In addition to its health impacts, air pollution also has economic and environmental costs, such as reduced crop yields, acid rain, and climate change.

Traditional air pollution monitoring methods have limitations in accurately detecting and monitoring smog from industrial chimneys, necessitating the exploration of advanced techniques. The utilization of image processing and machine learning (ML) algorithms to address this challenge and improve air pollution detection.

In recent years, the field of image processing and ML has shown great potential in revolutionizing air pollution detection. By leveraging image data captured from various sources, including satellites, drones, or cameras mounted near industrial chimneys, it becomes possible to analyze and interpret visual information to identify and quantify smog emissions. ML algorithms, such as convolutional neural networks (CNNs), can be trained on labeled datasets to learn patterns and characteristics specific to smog from industrial chimneys.

Figure 1. Average AQI in the last five years

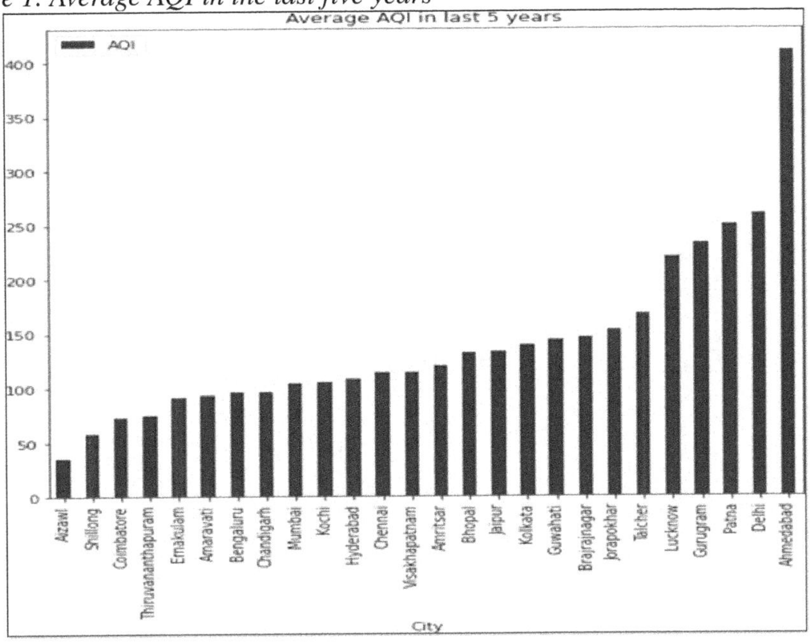

The methodology is developed as a robust approach for detecting smog from industrial chimney emissions using image processing and ML techniques. The methodology will involve acquiring relevant image data, pre-processing the data to enhance features and remove noise, training ML models on labeled datasets specific to smog emissions, and evaluating the performance of the proposed approach. The research will contribute to advancing the field of air pollution detection by providing a more accurate and efficient method to monitor and quantify smog from industrial chimneys. Through the analysis and interpretation of images, this approach has the potential to identify pollution sources, identify pollutant particles based on color, and provide insights into the Air Quality Index.

The dataset includes images, Pollutants based on Color, Air Quality Index (So2, No2, PM2.5, etc.), Ambient Air Quality Monitoring Data.

Figure 2. Correlation of various pollutants in last five years

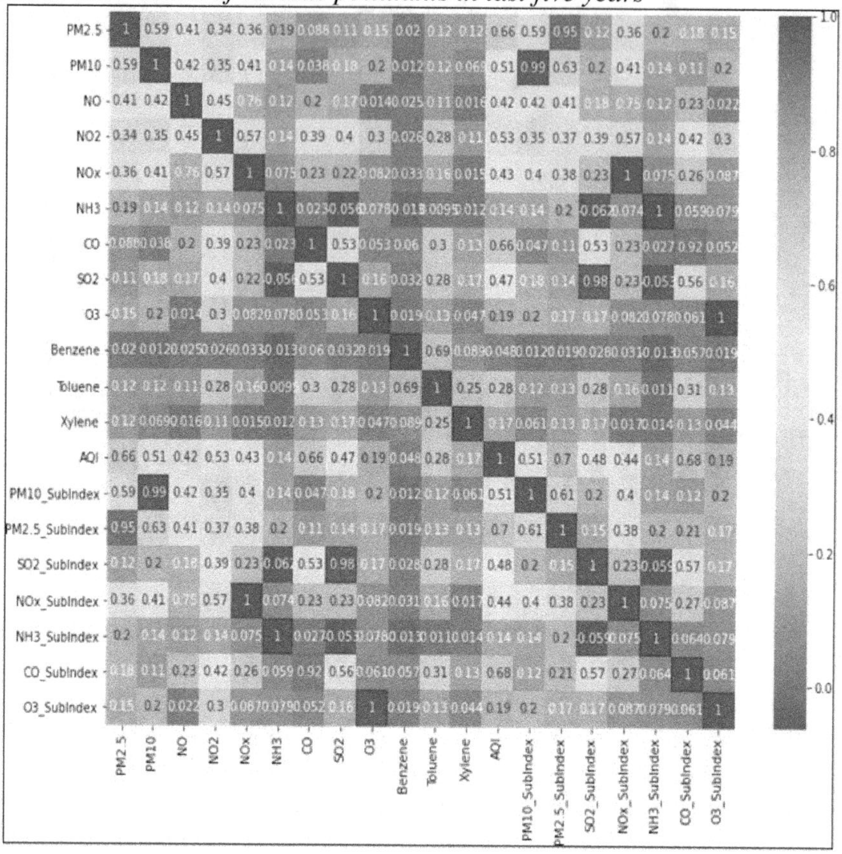

Figure 3. Distribution of different pollutants in last 5 years

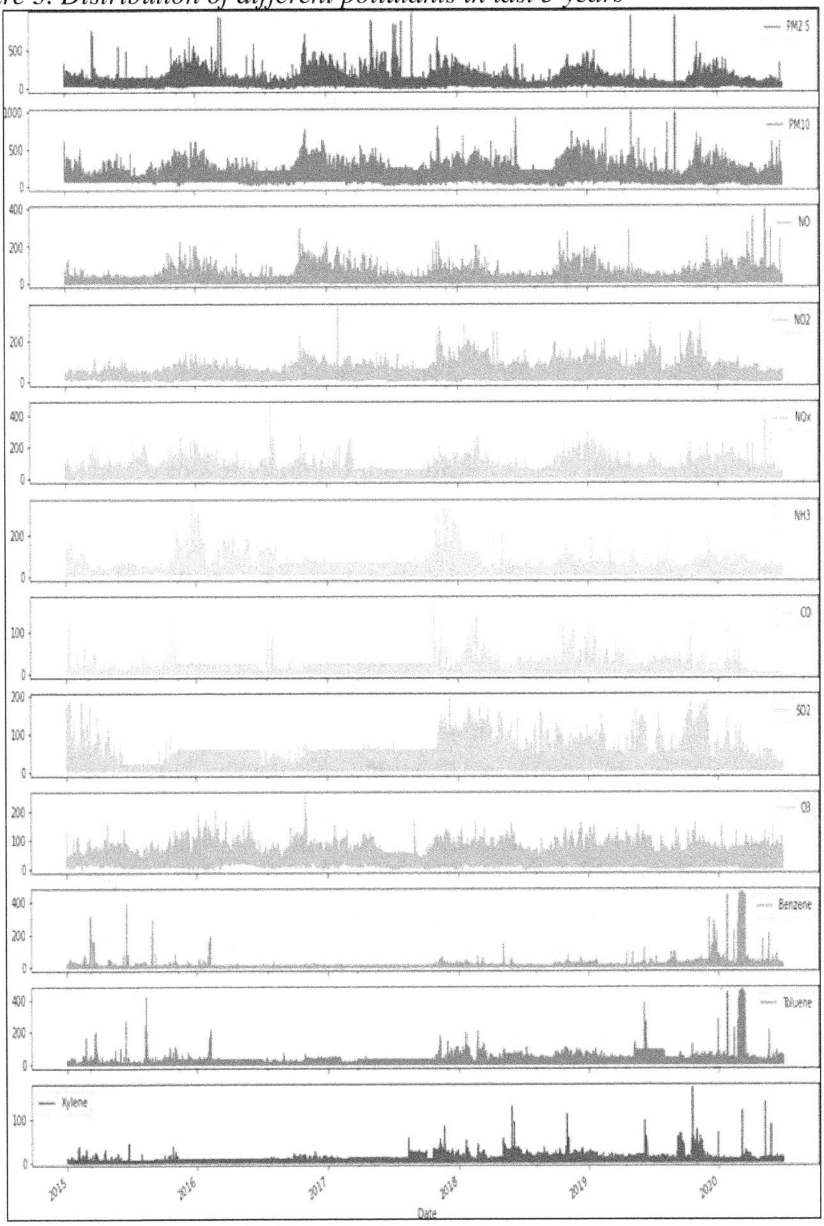

2. MAJOR CASES OF PLLUTION IN THE WORLD

Great Smog of London (1952) happened 5 days in December month which was caused due to the burning of coal, stagnant air, and cold weather. The polluted air became very dangerous and there were 12000 deaths thousands of illnesses due to the respiratory and cardiovascular issues. The Clean Air Act of 1956 is created to reduce air pollution by restriction the burning of coal in urban areas. Similar event also happened in 1962 in London and hundreds of deaths happened again.

Vehicle Emissions Crisis (1970s–1980s), happened in London, Birmingham, and Manchester due to increased car ownership particularly due to lead and nitrogen oxides, became a significant source of urban air pollution. This resulted into the unleaded petrol in 1980s.

Delhi has hazardous level of air pollution, due to stubble burning, industrial pollution and construction dust. The situation becomes severe during the winter. The PM2.5 concentrations exceeding safe limits by 10-15 times. This results into the high amount of inconvenience to the citizens including the schools closed, flights get delayed, and public health issues. The Delhi has come with Odd-Even Vehicle schemes, in which the Odd vehicle numbers run on odd date, and even vehicles run on the even dates. In India, the firecracker during Diwali causes major pollution. There is Jharia coal field in India which is burning since last hundred years. This has resulted in the contribution to global warming. The people living near to these villages now migrated to some other locations, this has put huge pressure on the government funds.

Singrauli Coal belt in India has several thermal power plants and coal mines that contribute to high matter emission, respiratory issues and environmental degradation. The stubble burning in Punjab and Haryana burned crop residues in October-November significantly increasing PM2.5 and PM10 levels across northern states. Acid rain due to air pollution which caused damage to Taj Mahal. In India, the policy interventions launched in nation after major air pollution introduced to reduce PM levels in 22 cities.

The BS-VI Fuels standard is implemented for the vehicular emissions, in India.

3. BACKGROUND

Air pollution, particularly smog resulting from industrial chimney emissions, is a significant environmental concern with adverse impacts on human health and the ecosystem. Industrial activities release a range of pollutants, including particulate matter, sulfur dioxide, nitrogen oxides, and volatile organic compounds, contributing to the formation of smog. Conventional air pollution monitoring methods often struggle to accurately detect and monitor smog from industrial chimneys due to limitations in spatial coverage and real-time capabilities.

Recent advancements in image processing and machine learning (ML) techniques offer promising solutions for enhancing air pollution detection, specifically targeting smog from industrial chimney emissions. Image processing techniques enable the analysis and interpretation of visual information captured through cameras, satellites, or drones, providing a more comprehensive understanding of air pollution patterns. ML algorithms, such as convolutional neural networks (CNNs), have demonstrated remarkable capabilities in image classification and object recognition tasks, making them well-suited for smog detection.

However, there is a research gap in the specific application of image processing and ML techniques for smog detection from industrial chimney emissions. Most existing studies focus on broader air pollution monitoring or specific pollutant detection, neglecting the unique challenges posed by industrial smog. Furthermore, the availability of labeled datasets tailored for smog detection from industrial chimneys is limited, hindering the development and training of accurate ML models.

This research aims to bridge this gap by developing a robust approach for detecting smog from industrial chimney emissions using image processing and ML techniques. By collecting relevant image data from cameras positioned near industrial chimneys, preprocessing the data to enhance features and remove noise, and training ML models on labeled datasets specific to smog emissions, the research endeavors to achieve accurate and real-time smog detection. It is required to explore the enhancement and understanding of air pollution patterns and identify pollutants.

Industrial stakeholders can utilize the developed approach to monitor and mitigate smog emissions, ensuring compliance with environmental regulations. Environmental agencies and policymakers can leverage accurate and timely information to implement targeted measures for reducing smog pollution. Additionally, public health organizations can assess the health risks associated with smog exposure and implement appropriate interventions to protect public well-being.

Table 1. Summary of the air pollution related research

Reference	Paper Reference	Dataset Used	Parameters Considered	Results/ Accuracy achieved
(Rajput, 2022)	Air Pollution Prediction using Machine Learning	MQ-135 air quality sensor, MQ-5 sensor, Optical dust sensor connected to the Arduino uno board	KNN algorithm	Accuracy of 99.107%
(Ahmed,2022)	AQE-Net: A Deep Learning Model for Estimating Air Quality of Karachi City from Mobile Images	KHI-AQI image database	Capturing time of the photographs captured at each collecting point, SVM, VGG16, InceptionV3, AQE-Net	56.2% accuracy achieved using SVM, 59.2% achieved using VGG16, 64.6% achieved using InceptionV3, and 70.1% achieved using AQE-Net
(Nagrecha, 2022)	Sensor-Based Air Pollution Prediction Using Deep CNN-LSTM	Historical sensor data	Convolutional Neural Network, and an LSTM	Accurate, usually with an error in the range of 25% relative to the mean for that site.
(Lei, 2022)	Using Machine Learning Methods to Forecast Air Quality: A Case Study in Macao	Hourly data (air quality and meteorological variables)	Random forest (RF), gradient boosting (GB), support vector regression (SVR), and multiple linear regression (MLR)	89 achieved using MLR, 88 achieved using RF, GB, SVR
(Deshmukh, 2018)	Detection and Prediction of Air Pollution using Machine Learning Models	UCI repository	Logistic Regression, Linear Regression, Autoregression	Results show that ML models can be efficiently used to detect the quality of air and predict the level of PM2.5 in the future.
(Bhattacharya, 2021)	Using Machine Learning to Predict Air Quality Index in New Delhi	Archive data provided by the US Embassy in Delhi and the Central Pollution Control Board	Support Vector Regression (SVR)	Results achieved in the form of Good, Moderate, Unhealthy

continued on following page

Table 1. Continued

Reference	Paper Reference	Dataset Used	Parameters Considered	Results/ Accuracy achieved
(Gunjal, 2023)	Air Pollution Prediction Using Machine Learning Supervised Learning Approach	Sensors	LR, SVM, DT, and RF	0.84 accuracy achieved using RF, 1.34 achieved using Decision tree, 3.89 achieved using SVM, 6.01 achieved using Linear Regression
(Kumar, 2022)	Air pollution prediction with machine learning: a case study of Indian cities	Central Pollution Control Board (CPCB)	SMOTE analysis	The XGBoost model attained the highest accuracy and the SVM model exhibited the lowest accuracy
(Gnana, 2023)	Indian Air Quality Prediction and Analysis Using Machine Learning	Pollutant Concentration Of All the gases available in the cpcb.nic.in website	Gradient descent and Box-Plot analysis.	95% accuracy
(Kataria, 2022)	AI- and IoT-based hybrid model for air quality prediction in a smart city with network assistance	Sensor Node Measuring Carbon Monoxide (CO) and *PM*	ANN, SVM, k-NN, CNN, LSTM, CNN-LSTM	The performance evaluation of ensemble model in terms of accuracy score: R^2: MAE: RMSE for data set 1 and 2 are 0.977:0.968:15.4625:24.1207 and 0.967:0.949:23.6978:37.2059, respectively.
(Chen, 2019)	Deep Convolutional Neural Network for Air Quality Prediction	air quality and meteorological data every hour from 77 locations from the database of Environmental Protection Administration	CNN network	Experimental results have shown that CNN performs well for air quality prediction
(Kothandaraman, 2022)	Intelligent Forecasting of Air Quality and Pollution Prediction Using Machine Learning	Meteorological datasets	Linear regression, Random Forest, KNN, ridge and lasso, XGBoost, and AdaBoost models	The $PM_{2.5}$ pollutant concentration (PC_{low}-PC_{high}) range observed for these models is 0-18.583μg/m^3, 18.583-25.023μg/m^3, 25.023-28.234μg/m^3, and 28.234-49.032μg/m^3, respectively

continued on following page

Table 1. Continued

Reference	Paper Reference	Dataset Used	Parameters Considered	Results/ Accuracy achieved
(Bekkar, 2021)	Air-pollution prediction in smart city, deep learning approach	UCI Machine Learning Repository	LSTM, Bi-LSTM, CNN, and a hybrid CNN-LSTM model	This model can effectively extract the temporal and spatial features of the data through CNN and LSTM
(Freeman, 2018)	Forecasting air quality time series using deep learning	Chemical and meteorological parameters	Recurrent neural network (RNN), Long short-term memory (LSTM)	MAE's less than 2 were calculated for predictions out to 72 hours
(Tao, 2019)	Air Pollution Forecasting Using a Deep Learning Model Based on 1D Convnets and Bidirectional GRU	Historical meteorological data and PM2.5 concentration data	1D convolutional neural networks, bidirectional gated recurrent unit	The results show that the proposed method can be suitable and competitive on the PM2.5 data time series forecasting.
(Bai, 2018)	Air Pollution Forecasts: An Overview	Research	statistical forecasting methods, artificial intelligence methods, numerical forecasting methods, and hybrid system	air pollution forecasting based on the area and different pollutants should choose different forecasting methods
(Ameer, 2019)	Comparative Analysis of Machine Learning Techniques for Predicting Air Quality in Smart Cities	Experiments Using Apache Spark, Pollution Estimation Using Multiple Datasets	Decision Tree regression, Random Forest regression, Multi-Layer Perceptron regression and Gradient Boosting regression	Random Forest regression was the best technique among the four algorithms considered. Gradient boosting regression has performed the worst of all algorithms.

continued on following page

Table 1. Continued

Reference	Paper Reference	Dataset Used	Parameters Considered	Results/ Accuracy achieved
(Zhu, 2018)	A Machine Learning Approach for Air Quality Prediction: Model Regularization and Optimization	Meteorological Data	Advanced Optimization Algorithms	Results show that the proposed light formulation achieves much better performance
(Bai, 2016)	Air pollutants concentrations forecasting using back propagation neural network based on wavelet decomposition with meteorological conditions	Daily Data (24-H Mean Value) of Air Pollutants Concentrations	Model W-BPNN using wavelet technique and back propagation neural network (BPNN)	The results show that, having integrated both the multi-scale analysis of the SWT and the nonlinear mapping of the BPNN, the proposed approach exhibits a better forecasting performance in term of the three statistics criteria.
(Zhao, 2018)	Short period PM2.5 prediction based on multivariate linear regression model	Remote Sensing, Meteorological factors from ground monitoring (wind velocity, temperature, and relative humidity), and other gaseous pollutants (SO2, NO2, CO, and O3)	Multivariate Linear Regression Model	Apparent seasonal differences in PM2.5 concentrations were found, with R2 values of 0.852, 0.761, 0.788, and 0.874 for models utilizing the data for spring, summer, autumn, and winter seasons, respectively. The results of the regression models that used spring and winter data were superior to those that used summer and autumn data.

4. METHODOLOGY

Air Quality Standards NAAQS in India for the major air pollutants, as per the Ministry of Environment, Forest and Climate Change, Government of India, notification dated November 16, 2020:

Table 2. Air quality standards (NAAQS) in India

Pollutant	Time-Weighted Average (in micrograms per cubic meter)	Concentration in Ambient Air (in micrograms per cubic meter)	
		Industrial, Residential, Rural and Other Areas	Ecologically Sensitive Area
PM2.5	40	Annual average: 40 24-hour average: 60	Annual average: 40 24-hour average: 60
PM10	60	Annual average: 60 24-hour average: 100	Annual average: 60 24-hour average: 100
SO2	30	Annual average: 30 24-hour average: 80	Annual average: 10 24-hour average: 50
NO2	40	Annual average: 40 24-hour average: 80	Annual average: 20 24-hour average: 30
O3	50 (8-hour average)	1-hour average: 100	No separate standards specified
CO	2 (8-hour average)	1-hour average: 4	Annual average: 1 8-hour average: 2
Pb	0.5 (annual average)	24-hour average: 0.5	No separate standards specified

The values may vary from time to time and from region to region in India based on the local air quality and other factors. Additionally, the values for Ecologically Sensitive Areas may be lower than those for Industrial, Residential, Rural and Other Areas due to the need to protect sensitive ecosystems and wildlife.

Table 3. Smog and different colors for air pollutants

Smog Colour	Air Pollutant Source
Reddish-brown	Nitrogen oxides (NO_x)
Black or grey	Black carbon (BC) and particulate matter (PM)
Blue	Ground level ozone (O_3)
Yellow	Certain types of particulate matter (PM)

This code uses OpenCV, scikit-image, scikit-learn, and matplotlib libraries to detect and segment smog colors in an image. It reads an image, converts it to the RGB color space, and then to the HSV color space for better segmentation. Color ranges are defined as different smog colors and their associated pollutants. The image is converted to grayscale, and edge detection is performed using the Canny algorithm. A segmented image is created by applying color masks to the HSV image based on the defined color ranges. The segmented image and the original image are displayed using matplotlib. Finally, the detected smog colors and their corresponding pollutant names are printed based on the segmented regions.

The proposed methodology involves data collection, pre-processing, remove noise, feature extraction, enhance features, model selection, training, evaluation, and deployment. The images will be pre-processed, and features will be extracted using various techniques, including Convolutional Neural Networks (CNNs). The models will be trained and evaluated using various performance metrics, including accuracy, precision, recall, and F1-score.

The methodology for air pollution detection with images involves smog color detection and segmentation. The code reads an image and converts it to the RGB color space. The image is then converted to the HSV color space for better segmentation. Color ranges are defined as different smog colors and their associated pollutants. The RGB image is converted to grayscale, and edge detection is performed using the Canny algorithm. Color masks are applied to the HSV image based on the defined color ranges, resulting in a segmented image. The segmented image and the original image are displayed using matplotlib. The detected smog colors and their corresponding pollutant names are printed based on the segmented regions.

In the image classification of polluted and non-polluted categories, the code loads the dataset from a specified directory and performs preprocessing steps, such as resizing the images and converting them into RGB format. The image data is normalized to ensure consistent scaling, and the target labels are one-hot encoded for categorical representation. The dataset is split into training and testing sets to train and evaluate the model. Convolutional Neural Network (CNN) model is defined using convolutional, pooling, dropout, and dense layers to extract features and classify images. The model is compiled with an optimizer Adam and a loss function categorical cross-entropy and then trained on the training set. The trained model is evaluated on the testing set to assess its performance in terms of accuracy and loss. The accuracy and loss over epochs are plotted using matplotlib. The test loss and test accuracy are printed to provide an assessment of the model's performance.

In the air quality data preprocessing and analysis, the code loads the air quality data from a CSV file and handles missing values by filling them with appropriate estimates. Sub-indexes for different pollutants are calculated based on specific formulas, and an overall Air Quality Index (AQI) is assigned based on the sub-indices. The code determines the AQI bucket (e.g., Good, Moderate, Unhealthy) for each data point based on the assigned AQI. Correlation analysis is performed to understand the relationships between different pollutants and their impact on air quality. The code visualizes the distribution of pollutants over time using plotting libraries such as matplotlib. A Random Forest Classifier was created to predict the AQI bucket based on user input of the AQI value. The model performance is assessed using appropriate evaluation metrics to measure its accuracy and reliability in predicting AQI buckets. The insights gained from the analysis, including correlation findings, pollutant distributions, and the predict model's performance, are reported and presented in a meaningful way.

5. RESULTS

The implemented codes offer a comprehensive approach to analyzing and understanding pollution-related data. The first code employs image processing techniques to detect and segment smog colors, providing a visual representation of pollution in images. The second code utilizes a CNN to classify polluted and non-polluted images with high accuracy, demonstrating the potential for automated pollution detection. The third code focuses on analyzing air quality data, filling missing values, calculating sub-indices, and assigning an overall AQI. It further explores correlations between pollutants, visualizes their distribution over time, and builds a machine learning model for predicting AQI levels. Together, these codes contribute to a broader understanding of pollution patterns, facilitate efficient pollution detection, and support informed decision-making for air quality management. The model test loss is 0.4434 and accuracy is 0.8888.

Figure 4. Detecting smog colors and their corresponding pollutant names

Figure 5. Model Accuracy and epoch

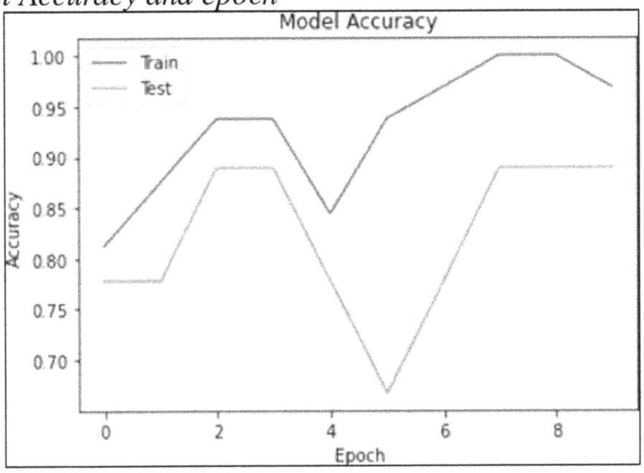

Figure 6. Model loss and epoch

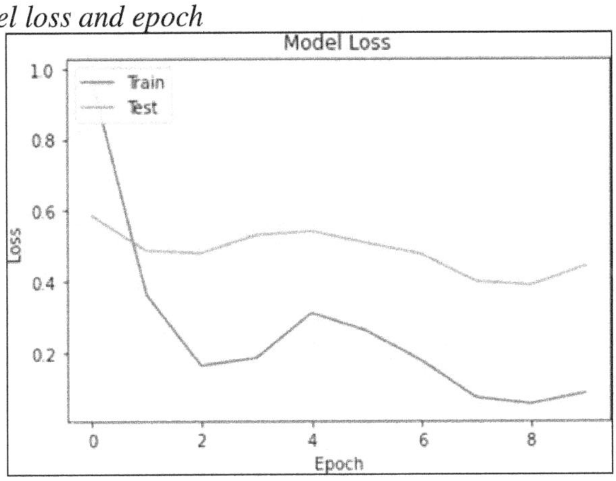

6. CONCLUSION

The implemented codes have successfully achieved their respective aims. The first code effectively detects and segments smog colors, providing valuable visual information about pollution in images. The second code demonstrates the capability of CNNs to accurately classify polluted and non-polluted images, offering a potential solution for automated pollution detection. The third code performs comprehensive analysis and preprocessing of air quality data, providing insights into pollution trends and developing a model for predicting air quality levels.

To further improve the capabilities of the implemented codes, several future enhancements can be considered. For the code focused on smog color detection and segmentation, research can be conducted to explore advanced computer vision techniques such as deep learning-based object detection algorithms, which can provide more accurate and robust identification of smog colors and associated pollutants. Additionally, integrating real-time data acquisition and analysis capabilities into the code can enable continuous monitoring and detection of smog colors in live video streams. For the image classification code, expanding the dataset with a wider range of polluted and non-polluted images from different locations and environmental conditions would enhance the model's ability to generalize to diverse scenarios. Further research can also explore the use of more advanced deep learning architectures or transfer learning techniques to improve classification performance. In the air quality analysis code, incorporating more comprehensive and up-to-date datasets, including information on meteorological factors and geographical features, can provide a more comprehensive understanding of air pollution and its drivers. Furthermore, creating interactive data visualization tools and user-friendly interfaces would enable easy exploration and interpretation of air quality data by researchers, policymakers, and the public, fostering greater awareness and engagement in addressing environmental challenges.

REFERENCES

Aditya, C. R., Deshmukh, C. R., Nayana, D. K., & Vidyavastu, P. G. (2018). Detection and prediction of air pollution using machine learning models. International journal of engineering trends and technology (IJETT), 59(4), 204-207.

Ahmed, M., Shen, Y., Ahmed, M., Xiao, Z., Cheng, P., Ali, N., Ghaffar, A., & Ali, S. (2022). AQE-Net: A Deep Learning Model for Estimating Air Quality of Karachi City from Mobile Images. *Remote Sensing (Basel)*, *14*(22), 5732. DOI: 10.3390/rs14225732

Ameer, S., Shah, M. A., Khan, A., Song, H., Maple, C., Islam, S. U., & Asghar, M. N. (2019). Comparative Analysis of Machine Learning Techniques for Predicting Air Quality in Smart Cities. *IEEE Access : Practical Innovations, Open Solutions*, *7*, 128325–128338. DOI: 10.1109/ACCESS.2019.2925082

Bai, L., Wang, J., Ma, X., & Lu, H. (2018). Air Pollution Forecasts: An Overview. *International Journal of Environmental Research and Public Health*, *15*(4), 780. DOI: 10.3390/ijerph15040780 PMID: 29673227

Bai, Y., Li, Y., Wang, X., Xie, J., & Li, C. (2016). Air pollutants concentrations forecasting using back propagation neural network based on wavelet decomposition with meteorological conditions. *Atmospheric Pollution Research*, *7*(3), 557–566. DOI: 10.1016/j.apr.2016.01.004

Bekkar, A., Hssina, B., Douzi, S., & Douzi, K. (2021). Air-pollution prediction in smart city, deep learning approach. *Journal of Big Data*, *8*(1), 1–21. DOI: 10.1186/s40537-021-00548-1 PMID: 34956819

Bhattacharya, S., & Shahnawaz, S. (2021). Using machine learning to predict air quality index in new delhi. arXiv preprint arXiv:2112.05753.

Freeman, B. S., Taylor, G., Gharabaghi, B., & Thé, J. (2018). Forecasting air quality time series using deep learning. *Journal of the Air & Waste Management Association*, *68*(8), 866–886. DOI: 10.1080/10962247.2018.1459956 PMID: 29652217

Gnana, M. A. (2023). Indian Air Quality Prediction and Analysis Using Machine Learning, Available: http://www.ripublication.com

Gunjal, S. G., & Kamalapurkar, S. (2023). Air Pollution Prediction Using Machine Learning Supervised Learning Approach, Available: www.ijstr.org

Kataria, A., & Puri, V. (2022). AI- and IoT-based hybrid model for air quality prediction in a smart city with network assistance. *IET Networks, 11*(6), 221–233. DOI: 10.1049/ntw2.12053

Kothandaraman, D., ... Intelligent Forecasting of Air Quality and Pollution Prediction Using Machine Learning, *Adsorption Science and Technology*, vol. 2022, DOI: 10.1155/2022/5086622

Kumar, K., & Pande, B. P. (2022). Air pollution prediction with machine learning: A case study of Indian cities. *International Journal of Environmental Science and Technology*. Advance online publication. DOI: 10.1007/s13762-022-04241-5 PMID: 35603096

Lei, T. M. T., Siu, S. W. I., Monjardino, J., Mendes, L., & Ferreira, F. (2022). Using Machine Learning Methods to Forecast Air Quality: A Case Study in Macao. *Atmosphere (Basel), 13*(9), 1412. Advance online publication. DOI: 10.3390/atmos13091412

Mao, Y., & Lee, S. (2019, August). Deep convolutional neural network for air quality prediction. [). IOP Publishing.]. *Journal of Physics: Conference Series, 1302*(3), 032046. DOI: 10.1088/1742-6596/1302/3/032046

Nagrecha, K.. (2022). *Sensor-Based Air Pollution Prediction Using Deep CNN-LSTM CSCI-ISAI, 2022*. Short Paper., DOI: 10.1109/CSCI51800.2020.00127

Rajput, R. P. (2022). Air Pollution Prediction using Machine Learning, *International Research Journal of Engineering and Technology*, Available: www.irjet.net

Tao, Q., Liu, F., Li, Y., & Sidorov, D. (2019). Air Pollution Forecasting Using a Deep Learning Model Based on 1D Convnets and Bidirectional GRU. *IEEE Access : Practical Innovations, Open Solutions, 7*, 76690–76698. DOI: 10.1109/ACCESS.2019.2921578

Zhao, R., Gu, X., Xue, B., Zhang, J., & Ren, W. (2018). Short period PM2.5 prediction based on multivariate linear regression model. *PLoS One, 13*(7), e0201011. DOI: 10.1371/journal.pone.0201011 PMID: 30048475

Zhu, D., Cai, C., Yang, T., & Zhou, X. (2018). A Machine Learning Approach for Air Quality Prediction: Model Regularization and Optimization. *Big Data and Cognitive Computing, 2*(1), 5. DOI: 10.3390/bdcc2010005

Chapter 13
Transforming Healthcare Through AI and Robotic Communication Systems

Cheng Hang
https://orcid.org/0009-0001-2031-5910
Management and Science University, Malaysia

Safaa Najah Saud Al-Humairi
https://orcid.org/0000-0001-5978-7651
Management and Science University, Malaysia

Ahgalya Subbiah
https://orcid.org/0009-0006-4427-0872
Management and Science University, Malaysia

ABSTRACT

Robotic systems integrated with artificial intelligence are transforming communication within health care and between different actors in health care. These improvements have significantly improved service delivery in the healthcare sector. This chapter reviews the evolution, applications, and implications of robotic systems in healthcare to consider their contribution to improving patient education and healthcare communication levels. Progress in AI and machine learning allows robotic systems to perform anything from simple patient interaction to complex surgery, thus addressing the increased demand for health services underpinning the global scarcity of health professionals. The benefits are enormous in terms of efficiency and precision; however, the challenges in adopting such technologies bring ethical considerations, data privacy issues, and a possible depersonalization of care. This chapter also points out the importance of balancing technological advances and the retention of human elements in healthcare system

DOI: 10.4018/979-8-3693-7832-8.ch013

1. INTRODUCTION

Robotic integration with health care communication drastically improves the interactions between medical workers and patients or how health care services are delivered. To review the portfolio of applications in which robotic facilitation has become increasingly recognized as a multitasking function in healthcare communication. This will entail an exploration of outcomes, impact, and future promise. This progression can be characterized as an ongoing, albeit slow, innovative process throughout its evolution, and robots are one such vital technology with huge potential to transform patient-provider healthcare communication. The expansive use of advanced AI and machine learning in various healthcare settings, which are increasingly deployed to serve many roles, including providing patient education and emotional support, has become common (Smith, 2023). The implications of robotic technology in healthcare communication are two-fold: it further indicates the development that human science is about to experience and presents new challenges and fresh opportunities for healthcare providers and patients. This is significant because it represents substantial progress in technology development.

Robotic advancements in healthcare communication signify technological advances and represent an evolution of the company culture itself. Robots in healthcare environments have many pros and cons and continue to increase (Ali Mohamad et al., 2023). Among the most important advantages is that it allows, in principle, to offer patients information that is not only of high quality but also uniform, thereby improving treatment. Moreover, robotic systems provide invaluable aid when human numbers are limited or restricted (e.g., regions that lack health care staff capacity and remote locations). This is because robotics can replace humans. Integration of these technologies, however, poses challenging issues regarding impersonal communication and the threat of loss of touch when providing care (Coghlan, 2022). These dynamics must be understood to maximize the use of robotics in healthcare and ensure that these technologies augment (not replace) the core human elements of healthcare delivery. This is not redundant, as robotics must be used to the maximum extent possible.

Robots are redefining much, and one crucial area is how doctors and other medical professionals deliver treatment. These tasks include repetitive activities, managing data more efficiently, and assisting medical professionals or workers. This can reduce the work burden on healthcare professionals, and they can focus more on direct patient care. Greater efficiency is essential given the increasing need for health services and the worldwide shortage of healthcare workers. For instance, it has been proven that robotic systems can enhance information transmission to be more precise and faster. A well-known example is in the medical field (Guntur et al., 2019), where promptness can make a significant difference. Robotic applications can also play an essential role in simplifying the procedures, either directly or indirectly, to improve the overall performance of healthcare delivery.

It is essential to mention that utilizing robots in healthcare communication significantly impacts patient engagement and the joy of having patients. If robots could interact with patients and exude empathy, these experience environments would become more exciting, thus leading to reassurance. This is critical, especially with children, the elderly, or special needs people, because typical communication methods may not curb these emergencies. Various studies have reported increased patient satisfaction and involvement using robotic therapy, which can improve health outcomes significantly (Marchand et al., 2017; Silvera-Tawil, 2024). Indeed, this technology can be revolting patient-centric medicine as many robots can understand and adapt to unique requirements and preferences suited to each individual.

Undoubtedly, there have been possibilities for improvement in this domain, but incorporating robotics into healthcare communication is challenging. This is even though there have been advances. A few key areas, such as personal data protection, fairness, and ethical considerations, are significant concerns and need robust regulatory expectations. These are examples of too many issues that can bring you down. However, the importance of high ethical standards and regulatory oversight in driving robotic adoption cannot be overstated, especially regarding health care. There is a careful balance between the use of technology and ethical considerations (Williamson & Prybutok, 2024). It was also vitally important to tackle these issues in silence and ensure that the gains of robotic facilitation can be enjoyed for healthcare communication while protecting patients' rights and safety

2. ARTIFICIAL INTELLIGENCE IN HEALTHCARE

Regarding patient care, medical research, and healthcare administration, the effects of artificial intelligence (AI) are far-reaching and far-reaching. Artificial intelligence (AI) systems can help in the early diagnosis of diseases by evaluating large volumes of medical data such as medical pictures, patient records, and genetic information. Quicker and more accurate diagnoses are possible recognizes to machine learning algorithms' ability to spot patterns and anomalies that human clinicians might miss. Medical imaging, especially in radiology, is being transformed by AI. X-rays, MRIs, CT scans, and other imaging modalities can all benefit from having problems detected and characterized with the help of artificial intelligence-powered image analysis (Boeken et al., 2022). It can speed up the interpretation process and enhance the precision of diagnoses. AI speeds up drug discovery by evaluating biological data, identifying prospective medication candidates, and modelling drug interactions. This hastens the search for effective treatments for a wide range of disorders. Algorithms powered by artificial intelligence examine patient data and create individualized treatment recommendations. Examples are predicting how a patient will respond to a medication, adjusting the dose, and suggesting individualized treatments.

2.1 Role of AI in Healthcare

Artificial intelligence tools now offer clinicians immediate feedback on their decisions. They help find the best treatment alternatives, warn doctors about harmful drug interactions, and provide evidence-based recommendations for patient care. With the help of natural language processing (NLP), AI can read and understand unstructured medical documents like EHRs and medical journals. This improves data mining for medical study and treatment. Artificial intelligence-based remote monitoring systems record real-time vital indicators and activity levels (Walters & Kalinova, 2021). Chronic disease management and post-operative care are only two examples of how these technologies improve health care. Utilizing AI algorithms to analyze past patient data enables the prediction of disease outcomes, assessment of readmission risks, and anticipation of patient deterioration. This empowers healthcare providers to intervene more proactively and efficiently based on these predictive insights. AI identifies at-risk groups and facilitates monitoring healthcare trends and implementing preventive measures, thus playing a pivotal role in effectively managing population health. Besides that, it's also helpful for epidemiological studies and other public health projects. Healthcare firms may improve their revenue cycle management and decrease losses with the help of AI by spotting fraudulent claims and billing problems.

Robotic technologies powered by artificial intelligence improve surgical precision and need less tissue removal. These technologies are used by surgeons performing complex surgeries, and surgeons benefit from AI's capacity to guide them in real time and minimize mistakes. Patients can interact with and receive answers from and health information from chatbots and virtual assistants powered by artificial intelligence. These aids enhance patient participation and supply medical direction around the clock. Compliance with healthcare rules and ethical standards is monitored with the help of AI (Mbunge & Muchemwa, 2022). It aids in keeping patients' personal information private and secure, as laws like HIPAA require. AI aids in resource allocation and improving healthcare facility operations in bed management, staff scheduling, and equipment maintenance. Through data mining, direction identification, and insight discovery, AI-driven data analysis accelerates medical research and the discovery of new treatments and cures. Artificial intelligence (AI) in healthcare is revolutionizing the sector by strengthening human talents, facilitating more precise diagnoses, tailoring care to each individual, and boosting the quality of life for patients. Its utility as a resource for medical practitioners and academicians is growing, and it holds the potential to address critical issues in healthcare delivery.

2.2 AI Algorithms and Machine Learning

AI systems are invaluable in radiography for distinguishing between benign and malignant tumours. These systems employ supervised learning to predict numerical values like a patient's blood glucose level. Furthermore, unsupervised algorithms efficiently categorize similar patient profiles or medical data, providing valuable contributions to community health management. These methods improve feature selection and visualization by making high-dimensional data more accessible to work with. Natural language processing algorithms extract information from electronic health records and medical literature. Healthcare providers can learn more about patient satisfaction using sentiment analysis of online reviews and doctors' notes (Bidmon et al., 2020). Optimizing treatment regimens for the long haul is a crucial focus of reinforcement learning models. For instance, they aid in the calculation of individual insulin doses for the treatment of diabetes. CNNs excel at image analysis, which makes them helpful in interpreting medical images such as X-rays, MRIs, and CT scans by helping to spot abnormalities. Time-series data analysis is where RNNs shine, as they can keep tabs on patients and anticipate how their diseases will progress. In healthcare, NLP tasks like information extraction from clinical notes are made easier using transformer-based models like BERT. Famous machine learning algorithms are shown in Figure 1.

Figure 1. Machine learning algorithms

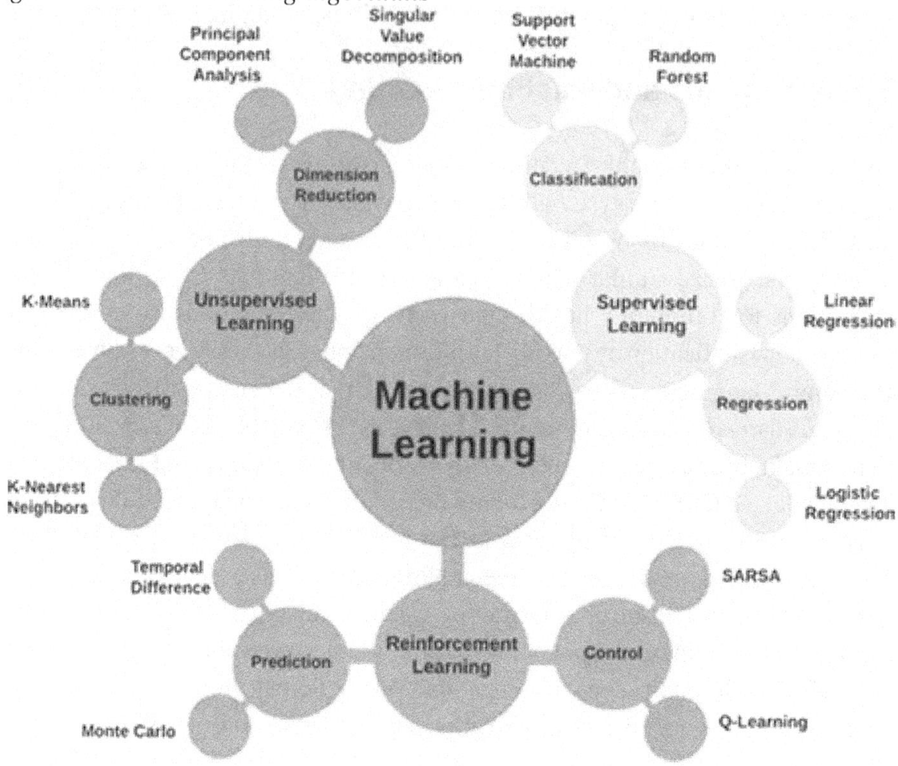

Multiple AI algorithms are used in an ensemble approach to boost prediction accuracy. Various healthcare tasks, including disease prediction and risk assessment, are performed using Random Forests and Gradient Boosting. Early diagnosis of sickness, prescription errors, and healthcare fraud is made possible by anomaly detection algorithms, which look for out-of-the-ordinary patient data patterns. In order to better estimate patient survival rates and make individualized therapy recommendations, survival analysis algorithms forecast time-to-event outcomes. Treatment plans, drugs, and interventions are tailored to each individual patient based on their medical history, symptoms, and genetic information using recommender algorithms (Enitan et al., 2023). Generative adversarial networks (GANs) and variational autoencoders (VAEs) generate synthetic medical images and data to supplement training datasets and protect patient privacy. XAI (Explainable Artificial Intelligence) methods improve the clarity and interpretability of AI models. This is considered exceptionally imperative in healthcare when communicating with patients and other professionals about treatment decisions. This is considered helpful specifically for applications like medical image analysis and natural language processing, and transfer learning uses pre-trained models on considerable datasets to improve AI performance with limited labeled healthcare data. The working of AI algorithms is illustrated in Figure 2.

Figure 2. AI algorithms

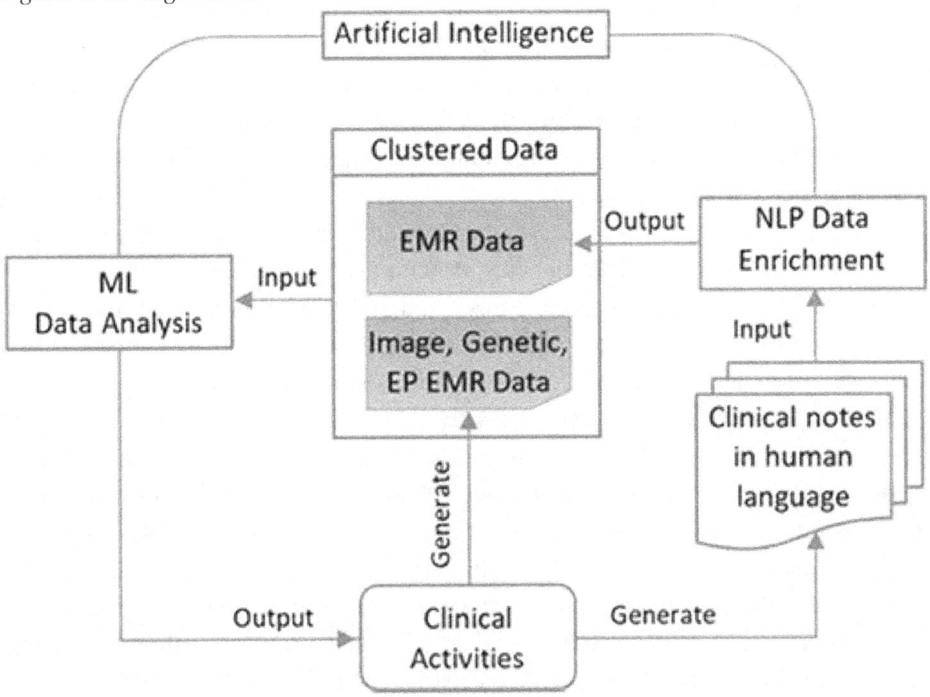

Utilizing federated learning, models can undergo training across various decentralized healthcare institutions, ensuring that private patient data is not shared. In robotics and surgery, deep reinforcement learning teaches robots to complete complex tasks accurately. Optimizing resource allocation and healthcare planning, predictive analytics powered by AI predicts disease outbreaks, readmission risks, and patient deterioration. Patient care, medical research, and healthcare administration are all areas that stand to benefit significantly from the further development of AI algorithms and machine learning techniques, which are finding increasingly novel applications in the healthcare sector. Their malleability and diversity allow for more precise diagnoses, unique treatment strategies, and better final results for patients.

2.3 AI Applications in Virtual Healthcare

Telehealth solutions driven by AI allow doctors to provide remote consultations and diagnosis. In healthcare, chatbots and virtual assistants help evaluate symptoms, set up appointments, and answer questions. Wearables and IoT-connected devices collect and communicate patient data to medical professionals. The AI examines this information to spot outliers, monitor illness development, and issue early warnings. Radiological images, including X-rays, MRIs, and CT scans, benefit from AI-enhanced medical imaging algorithms that aid interpretation (Demetriou et al., 2023). They help radiologists spot anomalies and quantify their severity. In order to assist in detecting and diagnosing diseases, AI algorithms are analyzing patient data such as electronic health records, test results, and genetic information. They help spot chronic diseases like diabetes, cancer, and heart disease in their earliest stages. Artificial intelligence customizes treatment strategies for each patient depending on genetic makeup, medical history, and responses to past therapy. It aids in determining the most appropriate medicine dosing and intervention strategies. Medication adherence can be improved with AI-powered apps and reminders, which can deliver notifications, track pill consumption, and provide adherence insights.

Besides that, the patients can interact with chatbots that provide health information and advice on symptoms. Medical visits, prescription reminders, and answers to frequently asked questions are all tasks that virtual assistants can handle. Moreover, any disease outbreaks, epidemiological patterns, and future demands for healthcare resources can all be monitored and predicted by analyzing data using AI models. Clinical decision support systems powered by artificial intelligence aid doctors in making educated treatment choices. These AI-powered applications furnish professionals with evidence-based recommendations and alert them to potential risks. Individuals grappling with mental health issues can avail assistance through apps and chatbots driven by artificial intelligence, providing emotional support and cognitive behavioral therapy.

Further, AI algorithms can evaluate patient data to develop individualized engagement tactics, which encourage patients to take an active role in their treatment (Tariq et al., 2023). Insurance fraud, billing mistakes, and other forms of healthcare fraud can all be uncovered by AI, allowing healthcare providers to manage their revenue cycles better. Surgical robots driven by AI assist surgeons in performing their work with greater precision and less tissue damage. They make complex, out-of-hospital interventions possible. Moreover, AI-powered wellness apps monitor exercise, sleep, and diet to encourage positive lifestyle changes and preventative medicine. Medical professionals can now effectively connect with patients of varying linguistic origins using AI-based translation systems. Innovative new uses of AI in virtual healthcare are constantly emerging, with the potential to revolutionize patient outcomes, healthcare access, and organizational efficiency. The future of virtual healthcare is likely to be significantly influenced by AI as technology develops.

2.4 Synergy with Robotic Frameworks

Synergies between AI in healthcare (see Table 1) and robotic frameworks lead to better treatment, more accurate diagnoses, and more streamlined procedures (Dongari et al., 2023). By analyzing medical data and photos, AI algorithms let robots aid in diagnosis by spotting outliers. Robotic frameworks make diagnostic and interventional procedures physically possible. AI-powered surgical robots improve the accuracy of minimally invasive procedures. They use machine learning to make real-time modifications, so fewer mistakes are made. Artificial intelligence aids preoperative preparation by tailoring surgical strategies to each patient. With the help of AI and robotics, surgeons may now execute treatments while still at a safe distance. This is especially helpful for telesurgery, disaster relief, and reaching underserved communities with specialized medical treatment. In physical therapy and rehabilitation, robotic frameworks help by offering individualized training plans and monitoring the outcomes. Artificial intelligence improves these systems by adjusting treatment plans in response to patient reactions and tracking patterns in long-term healing. Robotic, IoT-connected gadgets keep a close eye on a patient round-the-clock, sending data for AI analysis. The AI can monitor data and flag any abnormalities outside of regular ranges.

Dispensing medications is made easier with the help of robots, and artificial intelligence-driven systems monitor patient compliance and spot drug interactions and side effects. Based on patient information, AI prescribes individualized drug regimes. Chatbots and virtual assistants powered by AI allow doctors to consult with patients remotely, answering their questions and helping them evaluate their symptoms. Robots add a human element to telehealth by being physically present during remote examinations. The AInd robots work together to provide assistance and company to the elderly (Paluch & Wirtz, 2020). These technological advancements allow seniors to age in place without compromising their safety or comfort. Robotic frameworks can be improved with AI, which examines massive healthcare databases in search of patterns and trends. Robots employ AI-generated insights to customize treatment strategies, streamline operations, and distribute materials more effectively. AI-driven virtual reality platforms and robotic simulators provide more lifelike experiences for surgical training, may evaluate a learner's progress, and provide areas for development.

Consequently, the safety of healthcare robots and IoT devices is ensured by AI-enhanced cybersecurity technologies that prevent data breaches. Physical security is aided by robots, which can do things like patrolling to make healthcare facilities safer. Patient engagement, condition education, and treatment plan adherence are all improved by AI-powered virtual assistants. Regarding patient care, robots can be there physically to offer comfort and reassurance. AI analyzes biological data to speed up drug discovery, and robots help with high-throughput screening in labs. New medicines and therapies can be developed more quickly because of the co-operation of AI and robotics. Integrating AI and robotic frameworks in healthcare is a significant step forward since it allows for more comprehensive treatment of individual patients (Stasevych & Zvarych, 2023). Together, these innovations boost healthcare systems' efficiency and accuracy in diagnosing and treating patients and the overall quality of care provided to patients.

Table 1. Artificial Intelligence in healthcare

Author	Method Used	Setting/ Industry	Findings	Relevance to Study
Bidmon et al. (2020)	Data analysis and statistics	Healthcare	Analyzed patient satisfaction factors, focusing on physician interpersonal skills over technical abilities.	Virtual Communication Insights
Enitan et al. (2023)	Literature review and analysis	Osteoporosis management	Reviewed personalized medicine in osteoporosis, highlighting benefits and challenges.	Insights into robotic adoption
Božić (n.d.)	Book writing and editing	Hospital risk management	Discussed integrated risk management and AI in hospitals, evaluating pros and cons.	AI implementation
Demetriou et al. (2023)	Literature review and analysis	Precision oncology	Examined AI's role in enhancing precision oncology's diagnostic and therapeutic processes.	Impact on virtual healthcare
Tariq et al. (2023)	Experiment and survey	Orthopedic surgery	Explored AI's potential to improve orthopedic surgery outcomes and surveyed stakeholder attitudes.	Impact of AI
Dongari et al. (2023)	Literature review and analysis	Healthcare	Analyzed AI's impact on healthcare innovation, application, and patient care improvement strategies.	Communication strategies insights using AI

3. ROBOTIC-FACILITATED COMMUNICATION IN HEALTHCARE

The current landscape of robotic communication in healthcare is marked by notable advancements and increasing adoption (RFC). The role of robots in patient care, medical procedures, and healthcare operations is growing in importance as more and more are equipped with communication capabilities and AI-driven features. In healthcare settings, when human interaction is limited, robots connect with patients by providing aid, answering questions, and providing companionship. They improve patient engagement by providing a user-friendly channel for patients to ask questions and receive answers from their healthcare practitioners (Newman et al., 2021). This section will elaborate on the utilization of robots as facilitators for healthcare assistance or provision.

3.1 Current State of Robotic Communication

Telehealth services frequently use robotic devices, which put patients in touch with doctors or nurses from afar. In-home patients can now have face-to-face conversations with their doctors and specialists because of the availability of real-time video consultations made possible by these robots. The da Vinci Surgical System is only one example of a surgical robot that helps doctors with delicate, minimally invasive surgeries. Robots provide for more precise movements, better visibility, and more remarkable skill, all of which contribute to less intrusive procedures. Medication dispensing robots guarantee timely and accurate dosing for patients. AI-powered medication robots can also track patients' compliance with their prescribed regimen and notify them of any necessary adjustments. Robots should be trained with effective communication, as illustrated in Figure 3.

Figure 3. Effective communication skills

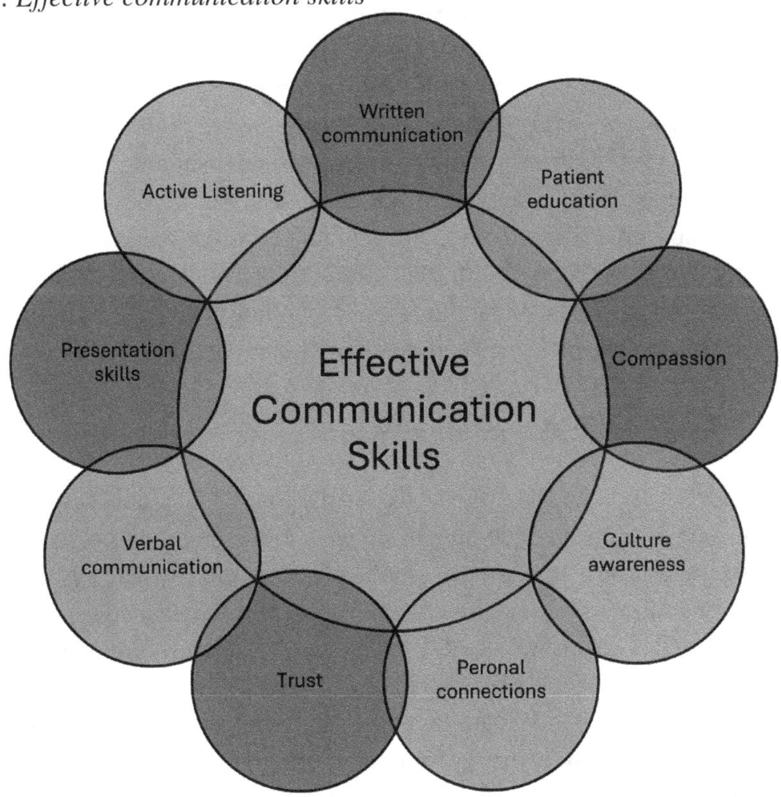

Elderly care robots perform chores such as bathing, dressing, and monitoring vital signs. Patients may monitor their health status and communicate with their doctors from the comfort of their homes as a privilege of to healthcare robots. Patients' vital signs and environmental parameters are recorded by IoT-connected robots and transmitted to healthcare databases for study. Artificial intelligence can examine this data and spot outliers, allowing timely intervention. Using NLP-enabled robots in the medical field helps professionals communicate with patients from various cultural and linguistic backgrounds (Adamopoulou & Moussiades, 2020). In this way, more people can use the service, and linguistic barriers will be eliminated. Patient check-in, registration, and appointment scheduling are just some tasks that robots help with at healthcare facilities. They can direct visitors and patients through hospitals and clinics and answer any questions. Robotic exoskeletons and devices help patients regain movement and strength in physical therapy and rehabilitation.

These gadgets monitor patients in real-time and modify treatment strategies accordingly (Devi et al., 2020). Research robots have accelerated the pace of scientific and medical progress by streamlining laboratory processes, data collection, and experimentation. Robotic systems powered by artificial intelligence are helping researchers find new treatments and create cutting-edge medical equipment. The current level of robotic communication in healthcare exemplifies the growing use of robots as helpful tools in providing patient care and running medical facilities. These technologies are growing more sophisticated as AI, IoT, and robotics improve, allowing for more effective and efficient communication between patients, healthcare practitioners, and healthcare institutions. Robotic communication will likely play an increasingly important role in healthcare as technology advances, providing novel approaches to existing problems and opening up new ones.

3.2 Applications and Use Cases

With robots, people can have medical consultations with doctors worldwide. They make it possible to have instantaneous conversations about symptoms, treatment alternatives, and follow-up care via video calls. The elderly can rely on robots to help them remember to take their medications, prepare meals, and get around. They benefit one's mental health because they provide company and help prevent loneliness. Physical therapist robots help by instructing patients on exercises and keeping tabs on their development. Patients are less likely to injure themselves and make better progress on their road to recovery when they follow their instructions. Medication adherence is increased when patients receive their doses at predetermined intervals from robotic systems. Certain robots can store and manage drugs for patients with complicated treatment programs. Robots help with patient registration, check-in, and appointment scheduling at hospitals. They help people navigate hospitals and clinics, answering questions and pointing out amenities (Glantz et al., 2020). Some of the applications of robots are illustrated in Figure 4.

Figure 4. Applications of robots

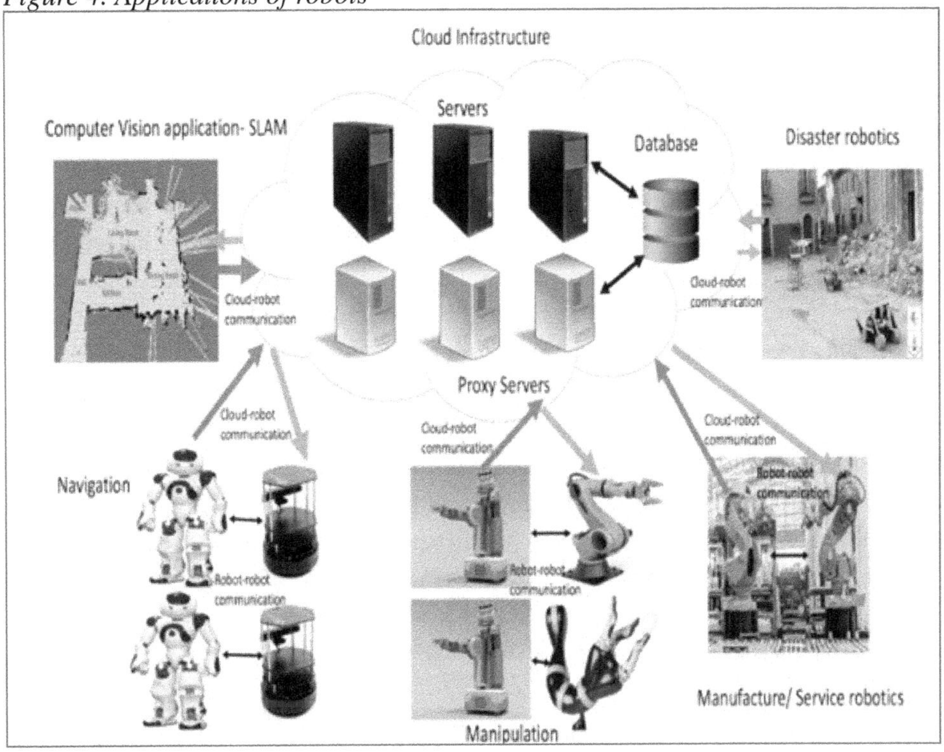

(Saha & Dasgupta, 2018)

Robots play an instructive role for patients, providing insights into their diagnoses, potential treatments, and post-care requirements. They engage with patients by offering information, guidance, and responses to frequently asked questions. Additionally, sensor-equipped robots conduct air quality checks in hospitals, monitoring parameters such as temperature and humidity to ensure the safe storage of vaccines, pharmaceuticals, and laboratory samples. Eventually, communication between doctors and patients who speak different languages will be facilitated by robots equipped with natural language processing skills. This fosters acceptance and guarantees clear communication with a wide range of patients. Minimally invasive surgeries are made easier with the use of surgical robots. They improve surgical visibility and minimize tissue damage, contributing to faster patient recoveries. Vital signs and other patient data are collected by IoT-connected robots and sent to healthcare databases for analysis. The AI examines this information for outliers, allowing prompt action to be taken as necessary (Malik et al., 2023).

In addition, pediatric healthcare robots have been developed to interact with young patients safely and comfortably. They help doctors do their jobs, keep kids calm during procedures, and occupy them throughout treatments. People with mental health issues can receive emotional support and cognitive-behavioral therapy from robots. They provide guided imagery, meditation, and online friendship. Lab studies, sample handling, and routine duties are all made easier with the help of robots. Scientific research and medical development are accelerated because of their increased efficiency and precision. Robots are incredibly useful in emergencies because they can enter dangerous locations and carry out activities like searching for survivors or transporting medical supplies. Medical response teams can receive constant situational assessments and data collection through remote monitoring. By offering constant healthcare help and monitoring in the comfort of their homes, robots make it possible for people to age in situ. They guarantee security, autonomy, and prompt medical attention (Wang et al., 2020). These examples show how robots can assist communication in healthcare, ultimately leading to better patient care, more efficient healthcare operations, and solutions to a wide range of problems in the healthcare system. As technology advances, these robots are anticipated to play a more significant part in the healthcare ecosystem.

3.3 Robot Operations and Challenges

Consequently, thousands of operations worldwide have used surgical robots like the da Vinci Surgical System. These robots improve surgical accuracy, lessen tissue destruction, and shorten patient recoveries (Kouyoumdjian et al., 2020). Among the many complicated operations they've completed are prostatectomies and heart transplants. Paro, a therapeutic robotic seal, has shown great promise as a companion and emotional support system for the elderly in nursing homes (GRANİER et al., 2023). The senior citizens benefit from them since they lessen their loneliness and sadness. Telemedicine and robotic telehealth technologies saw rapid growth after the COVID-19 pandemic. The Temi robot and others like it were employed in hospitals so doctors and nurses could consult with and monitor infected patients from a distance. Medical procedure anxiety can be reduced, and patient engagement can be increased with the use of pediatric healthcare robots like the Moxi robot. They help make children's visits to the doctor less stressful.

Medication adherence has increased because of robots like the Hero gadget, which helps patients track and receive their pills. They aid patients in keeping track of multiple medications and lowering the risk of adverse drug reactions. Healthcare companies, especially smaller facilities with limited finances, may face financial difficulty acquiring and implementing healthcare robots because of the high cost. Various tools and traits of Cybersecurity in the healthcare domain. These tools and traits, shown in Figure 5, include anti-theft devices and their applications, the creation of complete digitalization in the forensic field, penetration testing, vulnerability scan trials, and data loss prevention (Javaid et al., 2023).

Figure 5. Various tools of cybersecurity in the healthcare domain

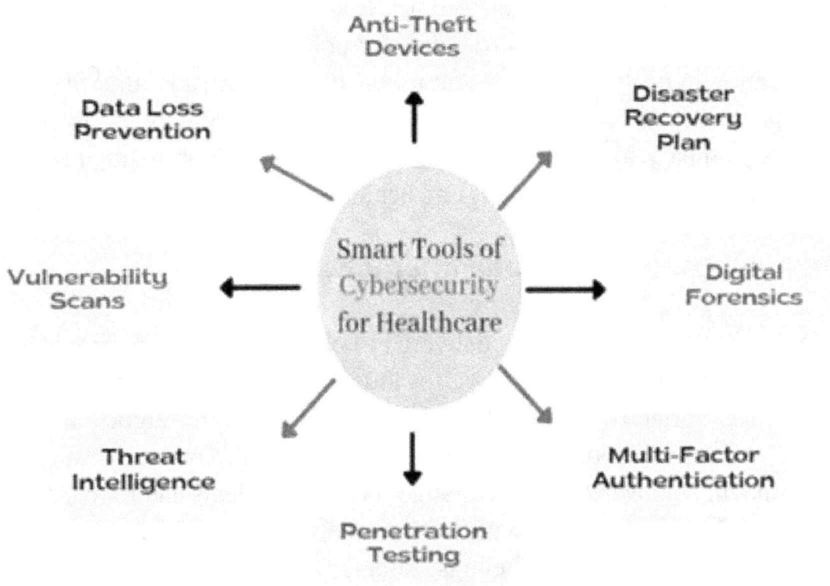

(Javaid et al. 2023)

The absence of defined interfaces and standards in the robotics sector complicates the integration of robots into preexisting healthcare systems. A significant obstacle for robotic systems is meeting the requirements of healthcare regulations such as the Food and Drug Administration's (FDA) approvals, HIPAA (Health Insurance Portability and Accountability Act) compliance, and patient data protection. Privacy and security issues arise when robots collect and transmit sensitive patient information. Protecting patients' personal information is a top priority for healthcare providers. The need for human supervision and intervention constrains the autonomy of many healthcare robots. Completely self-sufficient robots with high cognitive abilities are still a work in progress. Ethical questions arise from the prospect of less human involvement and the necessity for clear guidelines on robot-assisted decision-making when robots are used in healthcare.

In the healthcare industry, robots might cause delays due to their need for routine servicing and the possibility of technical failures. It is crucial to ensure dependability (Minopoulos et al., 2023). Incorporating robots into existing healthcare IT systems and workflows can be time-consuming, labour-intensive, and resource-intensive. Education and cultural reforms are required to overcome the potential resistance from healthcare workers and patients to having robots as part of the care team. Despite progress, robots still have some limits when adapting to the wide range of patient needs and healthcare environments. In order to address the needs of big healthcare institutions or populations, it can be technically and financially challenging to scale up robotic systems. Despite these obstacles, examples of effective robotic-facilitated communication in healthcare show that robots can dramatically alter the delivery of care, the quality of outcomes, and the satisfaction of patients. Healthcare providers, tech companies, and government agencies must work together to address these concerns and integrate robotics into healthcare systems safely and effectively.

3.4 Humanization of Robotic Interaction

To enhance the quality of care delivered to patients, healthcare providers, and robots alike, it is imperative to strive towards humanizing robotic interaction in the healthcare (Soriano et al., 2022). Using sophisticated NLP algorithms enables robots to comprehend and react to human-like conversations and questions. This facilitates natural, conversational exchanges between patients and robots by letting them use their language. Robots with built-in emotion recognition systems can now understand and react to human feelings. Robots can adapt their demeanour, facial expressions, and reactions to the patient's mood to show compassion and support. Voice and speech synthesis technologies that mimic the human voice make it easier for robots to connect with and be understood by humans. Robots can provide clear and compassionate information, directions, and reassurance communication. Robots with human-like facial expressions and gestures can show compassion and sympathy. They act like humans to show feelings like joy, empathy, and worry. The human-robot interaction is shown in Figure 6.

Figure 6. HRI

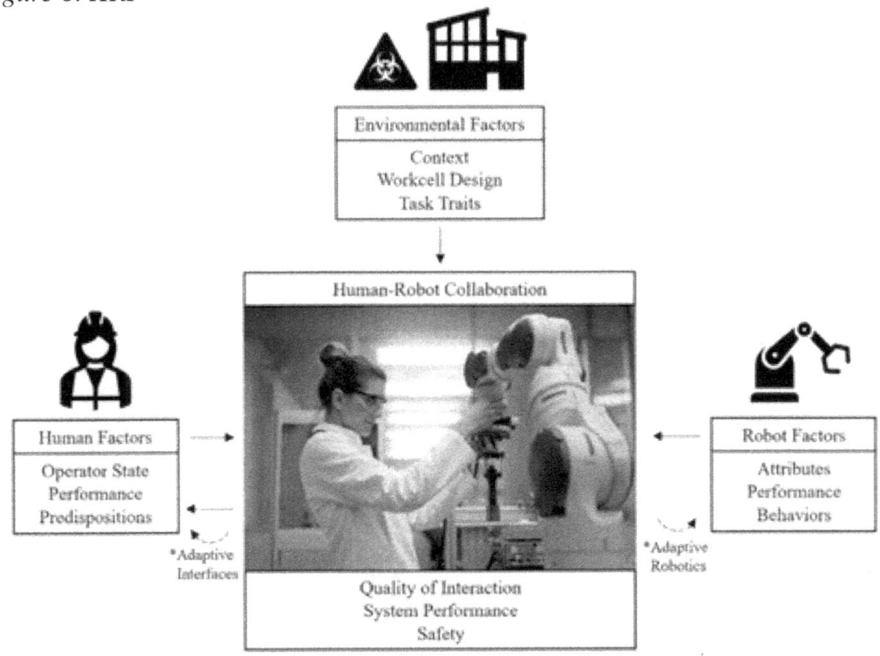

(Hopko et al., 2022)

Robots can tailor care to provide a personalized experience by utilizing patient data and preferences. This involves greeting patients by name, regularly checking their well-being, and delivering individualized care. Notably, the development of humanization skills is imparted to both healthcare professionals and robot operators, ensuring a holistic approach to enhancing patient care. This education stresses the importance of open dialogue, compassion, and awareness of other cultures. Robots are designed to give special attention to the wishes of each patient. They promote patient-centred care by including patients in decision-making, educating them, and listening to their concerns. Especially in long-term care facilities, companion robots are designed to provide a reassuring presence for residents. In addressing isolation, these robots engage in conversations, host games, and exhibit human-like behaviours. Importantly, they uphold respect for all human beliefs and customs, adjusting their delivery and content to be culturally sensitive. Patients and doctors can share their perspectives on robot interactions, contributing to a continuous feedback loop that constantly improves the robot's interaction and behaviour (Xing et al., 2021).

Therefore, the employment of robots in healthcare is regulated by a set of principles and laws based on ethics. They ensure considerate and ethical interactions by addressing privacy, consent, and decision-making concerns. Robots can be a great help, but they can't take the role of human caregivers. Human healthcare practitioners are still involved in decision-making, ensuring that human and robotic care work together seamlessly (Albahri et al., 2023). Bringing robots closer to human emotions is one goal of "humanizing" their interactions in healthcare. Medical facilities strive for greater patient happiness, better clinical outcomes, and more humane, compassionate care by programming robots to communicate and act more like humans. This method acknowledges that while robots can be helpful, they can't replace the human element in healthcare. Table 2 presents the most recent facilities and robots utilized in healthcare control and /or monitoring.

Table 2. Robotic-facilitated communication in healthcare

Author	Method Used	Setting/ Industry	Findings	Relevance to Study
Glantz et al. (2020)	System design, implementation, and evaluation	Healthcare	Developed a flexible healthcare system for disaster response; assessed feasibility and effectiveness.	Communication Insights
Malik et al. (2023)	Data analysis and machine learning	Online entrepreneurship education	Predicted online education adaptability with a machine learning model; measured accuracy and precision.	Insights into robotic adoption
Wang et al. (2020)	System design, implementation, and evaluation	Smart Healthcare	Created GuardHealth for secure innovative healthcare; evaluated for security and performance.	Virtual communication insights, AI implementation
Kouyoumdjian et al. (2020)	Literature review and analysis	Robotic total hip arthroplasty	Reviewed robotic hip arthroplasty techniques and outcomes; considered future challenges.	Impact on virtual healthcare
Javaid et al. (2023)	Literature review and analysis	Cybersecurity for healthcare domains	Analyzed cybersecurity in healthcare; discussed solutions and emerging trends.	Impact on virtual healthcare and security
Minopoulos et al. (2023)	Method design, implementation, and evaluation	Medical image visualization for robotic surgery and healthcare	Designed AI-assisted medical image visualization; assessed quality and user satisfaction.	AI-based Communication strategies

CONCLUSION

In conclusion, the chapter states that introducing AI and robotics in healthcare communication can be considered a significant milestone in the evolution of health services. Technologies ensure different benefits, among which are increases in efficiency, better accuracy of diagnoses and treatment, and enabling patients to access consistent and high-quality information. Robotic systems work best in settings with few health staff, as they can help them to do repetitive and data-related work, thereby optimizing time for the provision of care to patients. This has become an essential strategy in light of the increased pressure on health services and the global shortage of healthcare workers. However, the deployment of robotic systems is a challenge. Key concerns relate to a possible lack of personal touch in patient care, data privacy issues, and the need for strong ethical standards and regulatory frameworks. The critical principle is ensuring that such technologies enhance care quality rather than replace it.

Some of these concerns are addressed by developing human-like interactions in robotic systems through technologies for natural language processing and emotion recognition; these allow for more empathetic and patient-tailored experiences. It introduces the chapter about ethical and regulatory issues dealing with the safe and effective integration of robotics in healthcare. With constant technological changes, such joint work between health practitioners, technologists, and policymakers will ensure that robotic systems are successfully deployed in healthcare to maximize benefits and minimize associated risks. The future of healthcare communication involves robotics, providing new solutions to existing challenges, and improving the patient's experience.

REFERENCES

Adamopoulou, E., & Moussiades, L. (2020). Chatbots: History, technology, and applications. *Machine Learning with Applications*, *2*, 100006. DOI: 10.1016/j.mlwa.2020.100006

Albahri, A., Duhaim, A. M., Fadhel, M. A., Alnoor, A., Baqer, N. S., Alzubaidi, L., Albahri, O., Alamoodi, A., Bai, J., Salhi, A., Santamaría, J., Ouyang, C., Gupta, A., Gu, Y., & Deveci, M. (2023). A systematic review of trustworthy and explainable artificial intelligence in healthcare: Assessment of quality, bias risk, and data fusion. *Information Fusion*, *96*, 156–191. DOI: 10.1016/j.inffus.2023.03.008

Ali Mohamad, T., Bastone, A., Bernhard, F., & Schiavone, F. (2023). How artificial intelligence impacts the competitive position of healthcare organizations. *Journal of Organizational Change Management*, *36*(8), 49–70. DOI: 10.1108/JOCM-03-2023-0057

Bidmon, S., Elshiewy, O., Terlutter, R., & Boztug, Y. (2020). What patients value in physicians: Analyzing drivers of patient satisfaction using physician-rating website data. *Journal of Medical Internet Research*, *22*(2), e13830. DOI: 10.2196/13830 PMID: 32012063

Boeken, T., Feydy, J., Lecler, A., Soyer, P., Feydy, A., Barat, M., & Duron, L. (2022). Artificial intelligence in diagnostic and interventional radiology: Where are we now? *Diagnostic and Interventional Imaging*. PMID: 36494290

Coghlan, S. (2022). Robots and the possibility of humanistic care. *International Journal of Social Robotics*, *14*(10), 2095–2108. DOI: 10.1007/s12369-021-00804-7 PMID: 34221183

Demetriou, D., Hull, R., Kgoebane-Maseko, M., Lockhat, Z., & Dlamini, Z. (2023). AI-Enhanced Digital Pathology and Radiogenomics in Precision Oncology. In Artificial Intelligence and Precision Oncology: Bridging Cancer Research and Clinical Decision Support (pp. 93-113). Springer.

Devi, M. K., Deepika, R., Pooja, K., & Ramya, N. (2020). Real Time Non-Invasive Continuous Glucose Monitoring Using AI. 2020 International Conference on Power, Energy, Control and Transmission Systems (ICPECTS), Dongari, S., Nisarudeen, M., Devi, J., Irfan, S., Parida, P. K., & Bajpai, A. (2023). Advancing Healthcare through Artificial Intelligence: Innovations at the Intersection of AI and Medicine. Tuijin Jishu/Journal of Propulsion Technology, 44(2).

Enitan, S., Adejumo, E., Imaralu, J., Adelakun, A., Ladipo, O., & Enitan, C. (2023). Personalized medicine approach to osteoporosis management in women: Integrating genetics, pharmacogenomics, and precision treatments. *Clinical Research Communications*, *6*(3), 18. DOI: 10.53388/CRC2023018

Glantz, V., Phattharapornjaroen, P., Carlström, E., & Khorram-Manesh, A. (2020). Regional flexible surge capacity—A flexible response system. *Sustainability (Basel)*, *12*(15), 5984. DOI: 10.3390/su12155984

Granier, K., Oltz, K., Ingram, R., & Segal, D. (2023). Getting the Seal of Approval: A Critical Literature Review of the Evidence for the Use of the PARO Robotic Companion Seal with Older Adults with Cognitive Impairment in Long-Term Care. *Journal of Aging and Long-Term Care*, *6*(2), 57–79.

Guntur, S. R., Gorrepati, R. R., & Dirisala, V. R. (2019). Robotics in healthcare: an internet of medical robotic things (IoMRT) perspective. In *Machine learning in bio-signal analysis and diagnostic imaging* (pp. 293–318). Elsevier. DOI: 10.1016/B978-0-12-816086-2.00012-6

Hopko, S., Wang, J., & Mehta, R. (2022). Human factors considerations and metrics in shared space human-robot collaboration: A systematic review. *Frontiers in Robotics and AI*, *9*, 799522. DOI: 10.3389/frobt.2022.799522 PMID: 35187093

Javaid, M., Haleem, A., Singh, R. P., & Suman, R. (2023). Towards insighting cybersecurity for healthcare domains: A comprehensive review of recent practices and trends. Cyber Security and Applications, 100016.

Kouyoumdjian, P., Mansour, J., Assi, C., Caton, J., Lustig, S., & Coulomb, R. (2020). Current concepts in robotic total hip arthroplasty. *SICOT-J*, *6*, 6. DOI: 10.1051/sicotj/2020041 PMID: 33258445

Malik, A., Onyema, E. M., Dalal, S., Lilhore, U. K., Anand, D., Sharma, A., & Simaiya, S. (2023). Forecasting students' adaptability in online entrepreneurship education using modified ensemble machine learning model. *Array (New York, N.Y.)*, *19*, 100303. DOI: 10.1016/j.array.2023.100303

Marchand, R. C., Sodhi, N., Khlopas, A., Sultan, A. A., Harwin, S. F., Malkani, A. L., & Mont, M. A. (2017). Patient satisfaction outcomes after robotic arm-assisted total knee arthroplasty: A short-term evaluation. *The Journal of Knee Surgery*, *30*(09), 849–853. DOI: 10.1055/s-0037-1607450 PMID: 29029352

Mbunge, E., & Muchemwa, B. (2022). Towards emotive sensory Web in virtual health care: Trends, technologies, challenges and ethical issues. *Sensors International*, *3*, 100134. DOI: 10.1016/j.sintl.2021.100134

Minopoulos, G. M., Memos, V. A., Stergiou, K. D., Stergiou, C. L., & Psannis, K. E. (2023). A Medical Image Visualization Technique Assisted with AI-Based Haptic Feedback for Robotic Surgery and Healthcare. *Applied Sciences (Basel, Switzerland)*, *13*(6), 3592. DOI: 10.3390/app13063592

Newman, B., Joseph, K., Chauhan, A., Seale, H., Li, J., Manias, E., Walton, M., Mears, S., Jones, B., & Harrison, R. (2021). Do patient engagement interventions work for all patients? A systematic review and realist synthesis of interventions to enhance patient safety. *Health Expectations*, *24*(6), 1905–1923. DOI: 10.1111/hex.13343 PMID: 34432339

Paluch, S., & Wirtz, J. (2020). Artificial intelligence and robots in the service encounter. Journal of service management research.

Saha, O., & Dasgupta, P. (2018). A comprehensive survey of recent trends in cloud robotics architectures and applications. *Robotics (Basel, Switzerland)*, *7*(3), 47. DOI: 10.3390/robotics7030047

Silvera-Tawil, D. (2024). Robotics in Healthcare: A Survey. *SN Computer Science*, *5*(1), 189. DOI: 10.1007/s42979-023-02551-0

Smith, J. (2023). Rise of the Machines: Emerging Trends in Robotics. *International Journal of Research and Review Techniques*, *2*(3), 1–8.

Soriano, G. P., Yasuhara, Y., Ito, H., Matsumoto, K., Osaka, K., Kai, Y., Locsin, R., Schoenhofer, S., & Tanioka, T. (2022). Robots and robotics in nursing. Healthcare, Stasevych, M., & Zvarych, V. (2023). Innovative Robotic Technologies and Artificial Intelligence in Pharmacy and Medicine: Paving the Way for the Future of Health Care—A Review. *Big Data and Cognitive Computing*, *7*(3), 147.

Tariq, A., Gill, A. Y., & Hussain, H. K. (2023). Evaluating the Potential of Artificial Intelligence in Orthopedic Surgery for Value-based Healthcare. *International Journal of Multidisciplinary Sciences and Arts*, *2*(1), 27–35. DOI: 10.47709/ijmdsa.v2i1.2394

Walters, M., & Kalinova, E. (2021). Virtualized care systems, medical artificial intelligence, and real-time clinical monitoring in COVID-19 diagnosis, screening, surveillance, and prevention. *American Journal of Medical Research (New York, N.Y.)*, *8*(2), 37–50. DOI: 10.22381/ajmr8220213

Wang, Z., Luo, N., & Zhou, P. (2020). GuardHealth: Blockchain empowered secure data management and Graph Convolutional Network enabled anomaly detection in smart healthcare. *Journal of Parallel and Distributed Computing*, *142*, 1–12. DOI: 10.1016/j.jpdc.2020.03.004

Williamson, S. M., & Prybutok, V. (2024). Balancing privacy and progress: A review of privacy challenges, systemic oversight, and patient perceptions in AI-driven healthcare. *Applied Sciences (Basel, Switzerland)*, *14*(2), 675. DOI: 10.3390/app14020675

Xing, H., Torabi, A., Ding, L., Gao, H., Deng, Z., Mushahwar, V. K., & Tavakoli, M. (2021). An admittance-controlled wheeled mobile manipulator for mobility assistance: Human–robot interaction estimation and redundancy resolution for enhanced force exertion ability. *Mechatronics*, *74*, 102497. DOI: 10.1016/j.mechatronics.2021.102497

Chapter 14
Virtual Intelligent Autonomous Agents:
Robot Navigation for Disaster Intervention

Akindele Segun Afolabi
University of Ilorin, Ilorin, Nigeria

Olubunmi Adewale Akinola
Federal University of Agriculture, Abeokuta, Nigeria

ABSTRACT

The intersection of Artificial Intelligence (AI) and robotics has helped to promote the idea of enhancing the performance of real-world autonomous systems through their digital twins. In this context, reinforcement learning (RL) emerges as a key technology used by digital twins in learning policies that results in enhanced performances. RL problems are typically modelled within the Markov Decision Process (MDP) framework, where an agent learns to take actions in a stochastic environment to maximize rewards. A scenario where an intervention robot has to be trained to detect and navigate to a gas pipe leakage while avoiding collisions with objects on in its path was considered and simulated in this chapter. The robot was trained using the Unity platform which was selected mainly due to its support for RL and its realistic physics simulation engine. Simulation experiments revealed that the minimum steps it takes the robot to master the task was around 300,000 steps. After this, the robot intelligently navigated to the gas leakage by following the shortest path while avoiding collisions.

DOI: 10.4018/979-8-3693-7832-8.ch014

INTRODUCTION

Agent-based problem-solving makes it possible to tackle complicated problems in remote and heterogeneous environments by breaking them down into smaller, easier-to-solve problems (Rodriguez-Arias et al., 2020). According to Wooldridge (2009), an intelligent agent is a computer system that can detect changes in its environment and react correctly and autonomously. In addition, an agent must be resilient (able to recover from errors), socially proficient (able to interact with other agents), and display both proactive and reactive actions (Padgham & Winikoff, 2004).

The proliferation of autonomous agents such as self-driving vehicles, robots, etc. in diverse sectors has necessitated a paradigm shift in their development from the usual engineering-centric approach that involves explicitly programming a system to perform tasks to a data-centric approach where agents are made to learn how to perform tasks through extensive data (Rasheed et al., 2024; Tian et al., 2023). The transition to the data-driven approach has made the "digital twins" or virtual clones an important component in the developmental process.

A digital twin is a digital representation (software) that mimics the operational state of a physical system (hardware)(Bilberg & Malik, 2019; Kousi et al., 2021; Li et al., 2021; Lv et al., 2021; Pérez et al., 2020; Schleich et al., 2017; Vlădăreanu et al., 2020). In other words, the digital twin resides on a computer system and it may be regarded as a digital object since it is the digital equivalent of a physical object. In his University of Michigan course in 2002, Professor Grieves (Zong et al., 2021) made the first proposal for digital twin technology. This idea is significant because it recognizes the feedback that exists between the virtual and physical worlds. Its primary uses were to monitor and forecast the spacecraft's early flight condition, as well as to mimic and analyze spacecraft in flight. Over the last 2 decades, this technology has advanced quickly and found widespread use in a variety of different industries, including smart cities, automobiles, ships, power plants, robotics, complicated electromechanical equipment, and medical care to mention a few.

The digital twin concept has played a major role in the convergence of artificial intelligence (AI) (Roy et al., 2019; Sano et al., 2021; Vernon, 2019; Yang et al., 2020) and robotics. Many people mistakenly believe that AI and robots are interchangeable. Robots are often defined as physical machines with sensors and actuators that may or may not need intelligence to carry out certain tasks; artificial intelligence, on the other hand, is a program and does not need physicality. However, as robots are physical beings, advancements in robotics open up new avenues for the integration of AI since these machines can see, act upon, and shape their surroundings as well as engage socially. However, AI gives machines the ability to develop and learn. It makes sense why AI and robots are becoming more and more entwined to yield intelligent robots (X. Zhang, 2021). An intelligent robot is capable of having autonomous interactions with its environment and making decisions.

Machine learning (Afolabi & Akinola, 2024; Guffanti et al., 2024; Nahavandi et al., 2024; Selvarajan et al., 2024; Tan et al., 2024) is the branch of AI that has significantly contributed to the advancement of robotics. Generally, there are three main classifications for machine learning: supervised learning (Adedeji, 2024; De Souza Silva et al., 2024; Zhou et al., 2024), unsupervised learning (Milivojčević et al., 2024; Mukherjee et al., 2024), and reinforcement learning (Löppenberg et al., 2024; Miao & Zhao, 2024; Sun et al., 2024; Tejer et al., 2024). Supervised learning uses annotated data to learn the mapping from input data to ground truth (labels), while unsupervised learning discovers regularities only from input data (Milivojčević et al., 2024). The quality of the training dataset always has a direct impact on how well the supervised and unsupervised techniques perform. However, assembling a high-quality data collection may be difficult, laborious, and reliant on humans, particularly when generating annotations for supervised learning. Reinforcement learning, on the other hand, involves an agent, a collection of states, and a set of actions (Inamdar et al., 2024). Action causes the agent's state to change. Without the need for hand-coded features, this technique teaches agents how to adopt successful strategies—a set of actions—that maximize long-term rewards and deliver the most value over time.

Unlike in supervised learning, no input-output data pair is needed for reinforcement machine learning. Rather, an agent is rewarded for a decision made in a state of the environment. In other words, monitoring of the environment and the design of the reward system are crucial components of this training process. Even while new states might produce rewards, an agent may be punished excessively via the reward system for an action that prompts them to decide to cease exploring their surroundings. On one hand, excessive observation lengthens training time while on the other hand, insufficient sensory input from observations will impede training. Hence, a balance needs to be struck to achieve an acceptable performance.

Deep learning has been deployed in many successful robotic applications (Ge et al., 2024; Hasan et al., 2024; Kok & Chen, 2024; Xu et al., 2024) and neural network designs are used in most deep learning techniques. As a result, another name for it is deep neural networks. To put it simply, deep learning extracts and transforms features via a cascade of many layers of nonlinear processing units. Higher layers learn more sophisticated features derived from lower-layer features, whereas lower layers near the data input learn simpler characteristics (Shinde & Shah, 2018). The architecture creates a strong, hierarchical feature representation. This indicates that deep learning is well suited for both large-scale data analysis and information extraction from disparate data sources. Convolutional Neural Networks (CNNs), Recursive Neural Networks, Deep Belief Networks (DBNs), Direct Deep Reinforcement Learning, Recurrent Neural Networks (RNNs), and Autoencoder (AE) are some of the common deep learning techniques. The relationship between selected fields of AI is illustrated in Figure 1. Recently, the deep reinforcement learning method that combines ideas from deep learning and reinforcement learning has been explored in robotic applications (Aslan et al., 2023; Cai et al., 2023; Okafor et al., 2024; Xia et al., 2024) .

Figure 1. The relationship between selected fields of AI

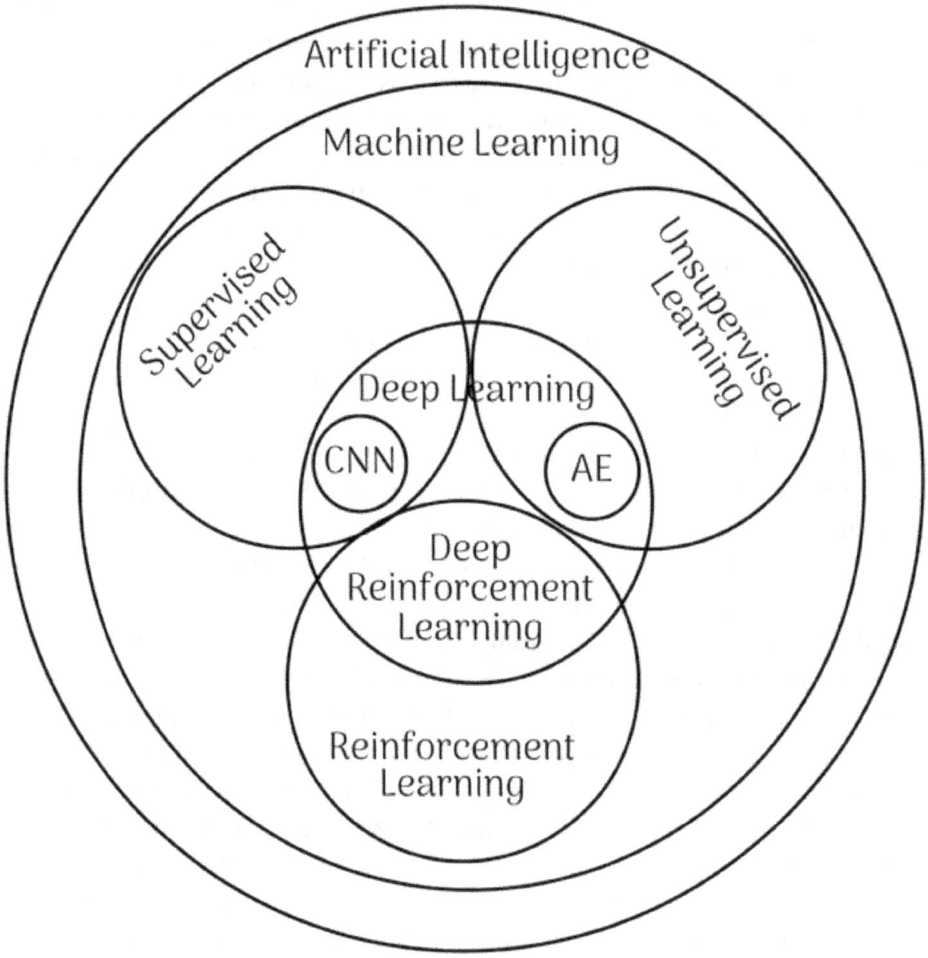

BACKGROUND

The discussion in this chapter covers how a digital object, which is a virtual equivalent of a physical robot, can be given intelligence to perform tasks such as navigation, grasping, object identification, and manipulation. The main focus will be on the development of navigation intelligence and inverse kinematics is considered out of the scope of discussion. This blueprint provides a cost-effective approach to design, test, enhance performance, and modify robot behaviour prior to physical deployment. To achieve this, the digital object can be represented as an agent in an environment in which the environment is made to transition into various states depending on the actions of the agent. These actions are subsets of the actual tasks expected to be performed by the robot, which are sometimes in a strict sequential order and which are ab initio not known to the robot. How to perform the tasks may have to be learned from scratch by the robot through trial and error or it may be transferred to it from preexisting data as a starting point for learning. This process will be explained with the concept of reinforcement learning.

Reinforcement learning

Various applications have been greatly impacted by remarkable research conducted in the field of reinforcement learning (RL) in recent years. Such applications are in healthcare (Ardjmand et al., 2024; R et al., 2024; Ribino et al., 2024; Rüttgers et al., 2024), natural language processing (Raj et al., 2024; X. Zhang & Lapata, 2017; Zheng et al., 2024), self-driving vehicles (Md et al., 2024; Pérez-Gil et al., 2022; Yeom, 2023), gaming (Andersen et al., 2024; Del Rio et al., 2024; H. Liu, 2024; Qi et al., 2023), robotics (Gao et al., 2021; Kumaar & Kochuvila, 2023; D. Liu et al., 2020; Q. Liu et al., 2023)) just to mention a few. Reinforcement learning includes algorithms that strongly rely on states, actions, and rewards. In contrast to conventional supervised and unsupervised learning, this state-based learning paradigm does not normally look for structural inferences in sets of labeled or unlabeled data. In order to discover the best reward-based learning trajectory, reinforcement learning depends on finite state automation and decision procedures. The agent continuously interacts with the environment which responds by presenting new states and rewards that correspond to the actions of the agent (Sutton & Barto, 2018).

Figure 2. State, action, and reward pair of reinforcement learning

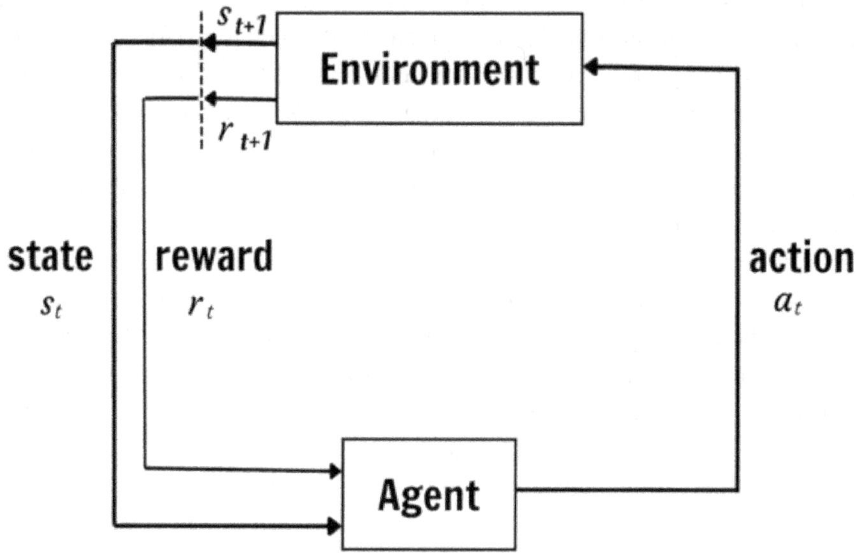

As illustrated in Figure 2, the agent applies an action $a_t \in \mathbb{R}^m$ at each time step t. This action is dependent on the system's state $s_t \in \mathbb{R}^n$. As a consequence, the environment changes states to s_{t+1}, and the agent is rewarded numerically with $r_{t+1} \in \mathbb{R}$. A learning episode occurs when this procedure is repeated for T_s samples. The objective is to train a controller, also known as the policy $u = \pi(s)$, in order to maximize R, which is the cumulative discounted total of rewards given as (Pane et al., 2019):

$$R = \mathbb{E}_\pi\left[r_{t+1} + \gamma r_{t+2} + \gamma^2 r_{t+3} + \cdots\right]$$

The rewards received by the agent are numeric values that the agent attempts to maximize over time. Ideally, it is preferable to have a state signal that summarizes previous experiences of the agent while preserving all pertinent information. Typically, more information is needed for this, although never more than the whole history of all previous experiences. A state signal that is able to keep all relevant information is said to be Markov or to possess the Markov property.

Markov Decision Process

A Markov Decision Process (MDP) may be used to define the continuous control issue (Gangapurwala et al., 2020). The definition of MDP is a tuple $(\mathcal{S}, \mathcal{A}, \mathcal{T}, r, \gamma)$, where $\mathcal{S} = \{s_1, s_2, s_3, \cdots, s_n\}$ is the state space of the observations, $\mathcal{A} = \{a_1, a_2, a_3, \cdots, a_m\}$ is the robot's action space, and T is the set of transition probabilities, in which, $T(s, a, s') = p(s'|s, a)$ is the probability of transitioning to state s' by taking action a on state s, $\gamma \in [0,1)$ is the discount factor, and $r: \mathcal{S} \times \mathcal{A} \rightarrow \mathbb{R}$ indicates the reward function such that $r(s, a)$ is the reward received by taking action a in state s (Silva et al., 2020; Tsai et al., 2021). The action distribution conditioned on the state s and parameterized by parameter θ is specified by a stochastic policy $\pi_\theta: \mathcal{S} \rightarrow \mathcal{A}$. RL aims to find an optimum policy π^* that maximizes the predicted discounted cumulative reward written as (Sutton & Barto, 2018; F. Zhang et al., 2024):

$$R = \max_{\pi_\theta} \mathbb{E}\left[\sum_{t=0}^{\infty} \gamma^t r(s_t)\right]$$

The two common approaches to determining the optimum policy are the model-free policy gradient (PG) learning method (which searches directly for the optimal policy) and value learning method (also known as the Q-value method which employs a value function model). Value learning is slow; it takes |A| times longer than PG learning and looks at every action at every iteration. Furthermore, since the policy is kept the same across iterations, time is further wasted. Therefore, in this chapter, focus will be on the PG learning method.

Policy Gradient Learning

Like many other AI algorithms, RL has some limitations, including memory consumption, computational complexity, and sample complexity. To a large extent, the PG method has shown significant promise in solving these problems. Learning a parameterized policy that chooses an action directly from the state space is the goal of PG approaches. A stochastic gradient approach is used by these methods to obtain an estimate of the policy gradient during training. Equation (3) may be used to estimate the gradient if the cumulative reward is taken into account as an objective function (Schulman et al., 2017; Silva et al., 2020).

$$\hat{g} = \mathbb{E}_t\left[\nabla_\theta \log \pi_\theta(a_t|s_t) \hat{A}_t\right],$$

where $\hat{A}_t$ is an advantage function estimator. In PG algorithms, we essentially gather a few roll-outs from the current policy, estimate an advantage function using the rewards we have received, estimate a policy gradient with respect to the parameters θ, and then update those parameters. The approach is entirely model-free, meaning that the gradient is independent of the dynamics, which is its main benefit. Yet, using such a gradient directly will not provide a suitable policy since the estimate is very noisy and produces disastrous updates that impede learning (Silva et al., 2020).

Policy gradient learning is effective but has a shortcoming of the gradient variance being significantly high. Furthermore, severe local minima may result from the wide variety of parameters in policy gradients. Trust regions may help reduce the possibility of local minima. The trust region search limits the optimization phases to a region in which the true cost function approximation stays valid. We may lessen the risk of a particularly bad update by ensuring that new policies differ as little as possible from the old ones and calculating the Kullback-Leibler (KL) divergence (Kullback & Leibler, 1951) between the proposed and existing policies. Trust Region Policy Optimization (TRPO), which ensures that policy changes are kept to a minimal and that improvements are consistent, has shown robustness. This restricted optimization, however, has limited applicability since it needs the computation of second order gradients. To overcome this, proximal policy optimization (PPO) was developed by Schulman et al. (Schulman et al., 2017), which requires just first-order gradient information to do unconstrained optimisation. PPO uses several stochastic gradient descent epochs for each policy update. Proximal policy optimization has shown better performance in reinforcement learning (RL) experiments, particularly in robotic tasks (Kim & Lee, 2020).

Proximal Policy Optimisation

PPO is a type of PG approach for reinforcement learning which switches between optimizing a "surrogate" objective function by making use of stochastic gradient descent and gathering data by interacting with the environment. By constructing a "clipped" surrogate objective, it possesses the stability and dependability advantages of trust region optimization. The surrogate object is computed as (Gangapurwala et al., 2020; Tsai et al., 2021):

$$\mathscr{L}(\theta) = \mathbb{E}_t\left[\min\left(r_t(\theta)\hat{A}_t, \text{clip}\left(r_t(\theta), 1-\epsilon, 1+\epsilon\right)\hat{A}_t\right)\right],$$

where $\mathbb{E}_t$ is the empirical expectation overtime t, ϵ is a clip hyperparameter and $r_t(\theta)$ represents the probability ratio between the current policy and the previous policy which is computed as (Carvalho Melo & Omena Albuquerque Maximo, 2019; Melo et al., 2021):

$$r_t(\theta) = \frac{\pi_\theta(a_t|s_t)}{\pi_{\theta_{old}}(a_t|s_t)},$$

where π is the stochastic policy and θ is the policy parameter. The minimum of the clipped and unclipped terms is used for the expectation, and the clipped term maintains the ratio $r_t(\theta)$ within the interval $[1 - \epsilon, 1 + \epsilon]$. PPO generates an element-wise minimum between the clipped and unclipped objectives, resulting in a lower limit that optimizes the KL penalty. By eliminating the KL penalty and the necessity for adaptive updates, the algorithm is simplified.

Curriculum Learning

To manage tasks with high variance, RL makes extensive use of the episodically randomized environment (ERE). However, owing of the ERE's sparse rewards and the introduction of difficult tasks at an early learning stage, policy convergence is made difficult and sluggish (Kim & Lee, 2020). By using information gained from earlier, related tasks, deep learning network training may be accelerated. Transfer learning, multitask learning, and curriculum learning (Bengio et al., 2009) are some of the commonly used methods used to expedite training. Curriculum learning begins with a basic task and progresses in task complexity step by step until the desired training requirements are met (Gong et al., 2016). It keeps track of examples that have already been taught. Every lesson (training criteria) generates a new set of weights during training, adding to the previous set.

The benefit of curriculum learning is that, First, it offers an efficient way to do implicit interpolation without the necessity for parameter optimization, which is necessary for traditional interpolation (Shi et al., 2015). Second, fragmentation is addressed. Fragmentation is a risk associated with adaptation models that construct individual component models on subsets of data. Fragmentation is the phenomenon whereby comparatively less data is available to train each component model as more and more are constructed. By using curricular learning for training, the fragmentation problem is elegantly avoided. Every adaptive model may be trained using all of the training data; the sequence in which the data is fed into the model during training determines the outcome.

Simulation Platform

When using reinforcement learning, there are several safety concerns that need to be taken into account, particularly when online training is necessary or the agent interacts with the outside world (such as with robots and self-driving automobiles). The agent may not react appropriately to the current situation before achieving maximum efficacy, which is why safety precautions are necessary. Since the characteristics of the RL model need to be adjusted in real time to reflect the streaming input, RL training presents a challenge in real-world (online training) scenarios. An RL algorithm used for unmanned aerial vehicle (UAV) piloting in real-time online training has a significant chance of malfunctioning or injuring other people. This confirms the safety issues involved in majority of RL algorithm implementations in actual UAVs. In order to train the agent for real-world behaviour, researchers have concentrated on using virtual reality (VR) platforms such as Unity (Juliani et al., 2020) and Python OpenAI Gym (Brockman et al., 2016). Other platforms where reinforcement learning experiments could be performed include DART (Lee et al., 2018), DeepMind Lab (Beattie et al., 2016), PyBullet (Coumans & Bai, n.d.), MuJoCo (Todorov et al., 2012), Isaac (*NVIDIA Isaac Sim*, 2024), Project Malmo (Johnson et al., 2016), RaiSim (Hwangbo et al., 2018), VizDoom (Kempka et al., 2016), GVGAI (Perez-Liebana et al., 2018), and AirSim (Shah et al., 2018).

Unity Simulation Platform

Among the platforms mentioned in the preceding section, the Unity platform stands out for being a General AI Platform since most of the others are either Domain-Specific Platforms or Environment Suites (Juliani et al., 2020). Hence, in theory, this platform may be used to define any AI research setting of potential interest. Although Unity was originally developed for game development (Youssef et al., 2019), it has however, quickly received wide acceptance among AI researchers since the addition of the machine learning-agent (ML-agent) toolkit to the platform. The Unity Machine Learning Agents Toolkit is an open-source application that allows you to create intelligent agents for simulations. Prior to the release of new designs, AI researchers may use these intelligent agents to evaluate different design options, track behaviour, and test builds autonomously. Incorporated in Unity ML-Agent are reinforcement learning algorithms, such as PPO and Soft Actor-Critic (SAC) algorithms. As such, it is an appropriate platform for implementing RL-based designs. Interested readers are directed to the book written by Majumder (2021) for further details.

Unity allows researchers to store and alter the existence of an object in three-dimensional space by using three-dimensional vectors for position and scale, as well as quaternions for rotation. Thus, this offers natural methods for agents to interact in 3D space without having to reimplement complex transformation matrices. Because Unity is enabled with 3D mesh geometries ranging from basic solid forms to sophisticated, textured photorealistic geometries, agents and environments can be implemented in model space with ease (Cheliotis, 2021). Unity supports the training or several agents simultaneously with the same training data which helps cut down on training time. The Apache 2.0 license governs the open-source Unity ML-Agents Toolkit project; ML-Agents may thus be used and modified as required. Researchers can build cognitively, visually, and physically rich AI environments using Unity and the ML-Agents toolbox, which may be used to test and evaluate novel methods and algorithms (Tian et al., 2023).

The Unity ML-agent concurrently employs reinforcement learning and deep learning in its operation. The capacity of deep learning algorithms to learn very complicated functions from vast quantities of training data is one of their primary features. Because of this, they are a logical option for reinforcement learning jobs where a lot of data may be produced, for example, by using a simulator like Unity (Unity Technologies, 2022a). We can learn policies for very complex environments by using Unity to create hundreds of thousands or millions of simulations of the environment (a complex environment is one where an agent sees a large number of observations and has a large number of actions that it may take).

Unity Companion Software

PyTorch and Tensorflow Libraries: The previous deep learning framework of ML-agent (version 1.0) was TensorFlow. However, as from version 2.0, the deep learning framework has transitioned to PyTorch but without breaking backward compatibility with TensorFlow since both run under the Python integrated development environment. Data flow graphs, the fundamental representation of deep learning models, are calculated using the open-source PyTorch library. PyTorch makes training and inference possible on the desktop, server, and mobile devices' CPUs and GPUs. Using the ML-Agents Toolkit to train an agent's behaviour yields a model (.onnx) file that can then be linked to an agent. Unless you create a new algorithm, PyTorch is mostly used in the background (Unity Technologies, 2022b).

Microsoft Visual Studio: Unity's native programming language is the C# (i.e. C-sharp). C# is a well-known and frequently used programming language created by Microsoft for producing Windows and web-based applications. It is therefore common among developers to configure Microsoft Visual Studio as the external editor for Unity. Once Visual Studio is configured as the external editor for Unity, double-clicking a script in the Unity editor will start or switch to Visual Studio and open the selected script (Microsoft, 2021). Unity's codes are written in C# but deep learning neural network frameworks such as TensorFlow and PyTorch operate in an interpreted Python environment. The simplest and most cross-platform friendly method for these two kinds of software to connect is via network ports, even if data is only looped back to the same machine and not transferred across a network (Cheng, 2021).

Tensorboard: Setting specific model attributes, often known as hyperparameters, is one phase in the PyTorch model training process. It could take many tries to find the best values for these hyperparameters. As a result, we use TensorBoard, a visualization tool. During training, it allows the display of some agent properties (such as reward) to help you determine the optimal settings for your Unity environment and build intuitions for the different hyperparameters (Unity Technologies, 2022b).

CASE STUDY

Assuming it is required to develop an intervention robot that responds to sensor readings with as little delay as possible; this can be achieved by training such a robot with as many sensor readings as possible. Further assume the sensor in question is mounted on the robot and the intensity of the sensor reading is dependent on the distance of the robot from the signal source. There are several applications for quick and precise sensor analysis that are pertinent to modern culture. These include monitoring for disasters, identifying and detecting gas and chemical leaks, forest fires, and search and rescue operations. In such cases, the robot would have to navigate from its location through obstructed terrains before arriving at the destination. To simulate this scenario, consider the task of designing a robot that navigates from its position towards a source of gas leakage which is restricted to humans due to potential hazards such an environment could pose to humans. In Unity, such scenario is setup as illustrated in Figures 3 through 5.

In Figure 5, the green object is the robot agent, the red objects are obstacles, the yellow object is the pipe, and the blue region on the pipe signifies a burst on the pipe through which gas leaks. Figures 3 through 5 differ from each other in terms of the number of obstacles such that 1 obstacle is in Figure 3, 10 obstacles are in Figure 4, and 20 obstacles are in Figure 5. It is assumed that the leak can occur randomly at any point on the pipe and the robot has to locate the point of leakage as quickly as possible. While searching, the robot must avoid colliding with the wall and the obstacles in the region of search. This problem is addressed using the deep reinforcement learning capability provided in by the ML-agent toolkit of Unity.

Figure 3. Case study scenario 1: robot navigation problem comprising 1 obstacle.

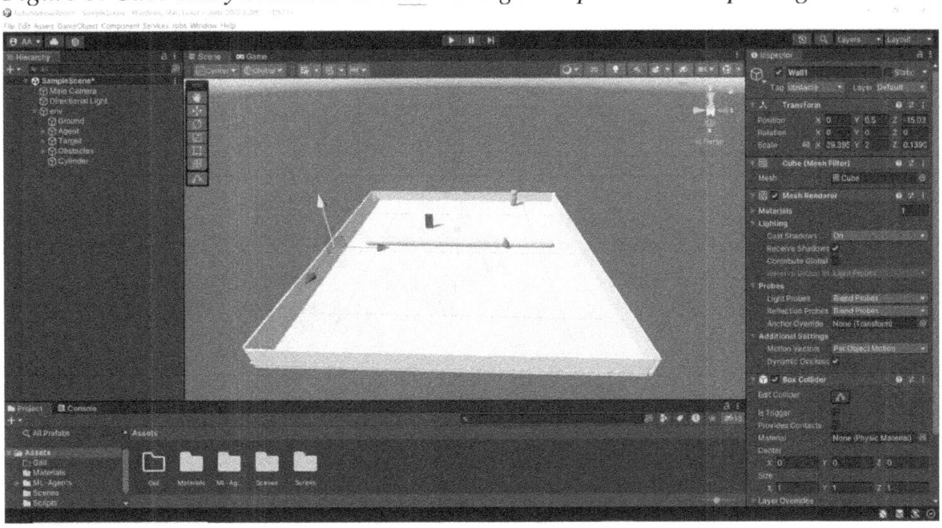

Figure 4. Case study scenario 2: robot navigation problem comprising 10 obstacles.

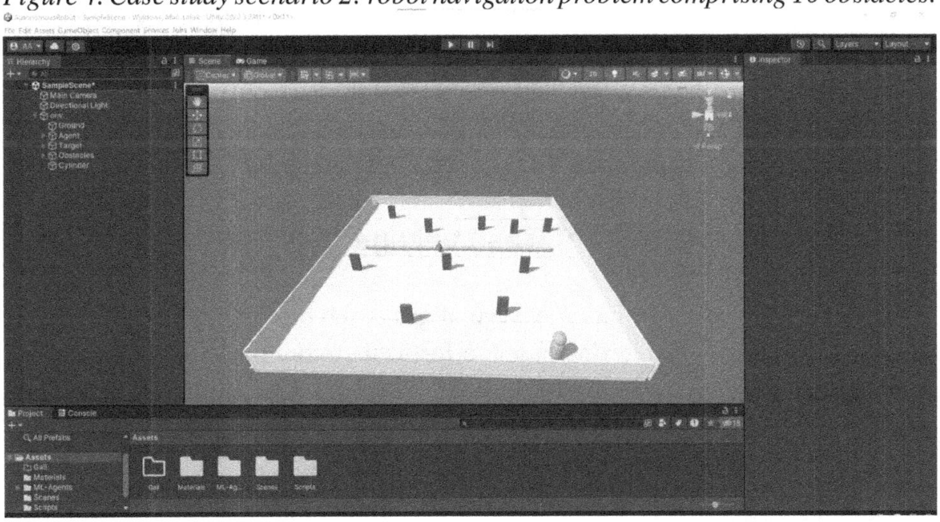

Figure 5. Case study scenario 3: robot navigation problem comprising 20 obstacles

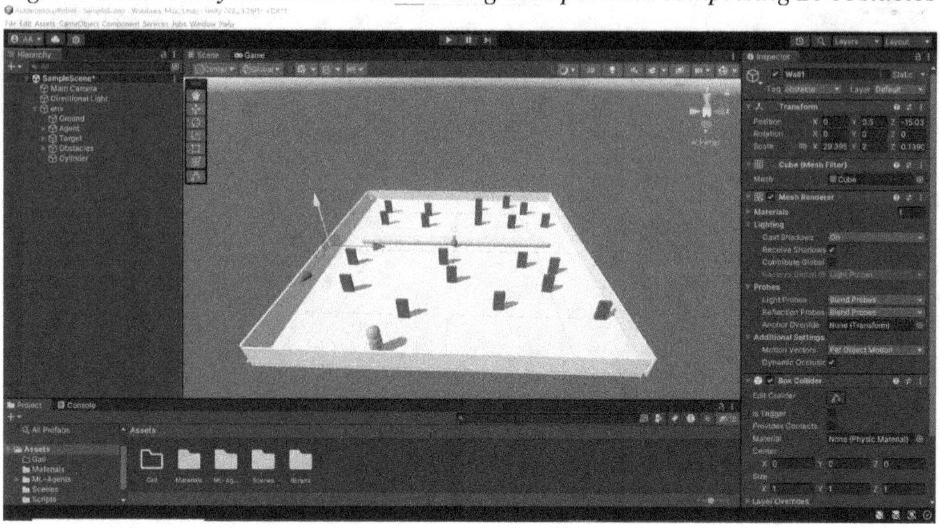

Deployment

Not all the objects in Figures 3 through 5 have fixed positions. The walls surrounding the region, the obstacles, and the gas pipe all have fixed positions. However, the point of leakage of the gas and the location of the robot are constantly changed based on probability distribution functions that are discussed next.

Probability-based Point of Gas Leakage

It is assumed that the point of leakage of gas in the pipe can occur at any point in a real life scenario. In the simulation, effort is therefore made to randomize the point of leakage of gas in the pipe. To achieve this, 3 randomisation approaches are considered which are based on: a) uniform probability distribution; b) beta probability distribution; and c) Gaussian probability distribution.

Uniform Probability Distribution

Consider the pipe shown in Figure 6 in which point A denotes the starting point of pipe and point B denotes the ending point, then the probability density function of a point x defined in the interval [A, B] according to a uniform probability distribution is written as:

$$f(x) = \begin{cases} \frac{1}{B-A}, A \leq x \leq B \\ 0, \text{ otherwise} \end{cases}$$

Figure 6. Random positioning of point of leakage on a pipe based on uniform probability distribution.

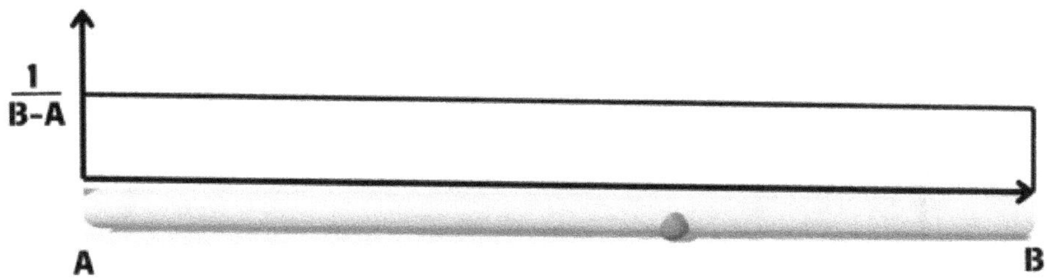

The mean is computed as:

$$\mathbb{E}(X) = \frac{A+B}{2},$$

while the variance is computed as:

$$Var(X) = \frac{(B-A)^2}{12}$$

As can be seen in the probability density graph of Figure 6, there is an equal likelihood of the leak occurring at any point along the stretch of the pipe extending from A to B.

Beta Distribution

Given that α and β are shaping parameters, the probability density function of beta distribution is computed as:

$$f_X(x; A, B, \alpha, \beta) = \frac{(x-A)^{\alpha-1}(B-x)^{\beta-1}}{(B-A)^{\alpha+\beta-1}B(\alpha,\beta)}$$

where $B(\alpha,\beta)$ is the beta function. In this paper, α and β are set to 2. The mean is computed as:

$$\mathbb{E}(X) = A + (B - A) \bullet \frac{\alpha}{\alpha + \beta}$$

and the variance is computed as:

$$Var(X) = (B - A)^2 \bullet \frac{\alpha\beta}{(\alpha + \beta)^2(\alpha + \beta + 1)}$$

Figure 7. Random positioning of the point of leakage on a pipe based on beta probability distribution.

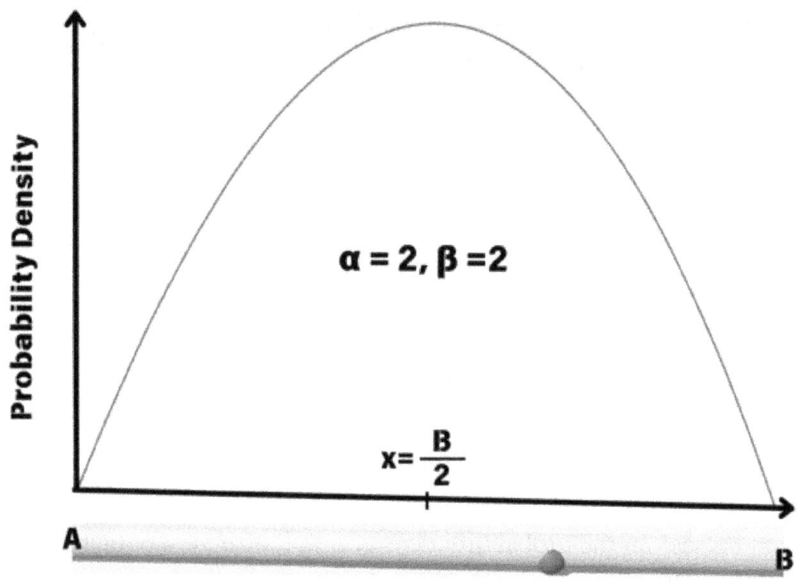

As can be seen in the beta probability density function of Figure 7, the leak is more likely to occur at the centre of the pipe than at any other point along the pipe since the probability density peaks at exactly the middle of the pipe and decreases gently towards the other two ends.

Gaussian Distribution

The probability density function for a Gaussian distribution is computed as:

$$f(x; \mu, \sigma) = \frac{1}{\sigma\sqrt{2\pi}} e^{-\frac{(x-\mu)^2}{2\sigma^2}}$$

where μ is the mean expressed as:

$$\mathbb{E}(X) = \mu$$

and σ is the standard deviation written as:

$$Var(X) = \sigma^2$$

Figure 8. Random positioning of point of leakage on a pipe based on Gaussian probability distribution.

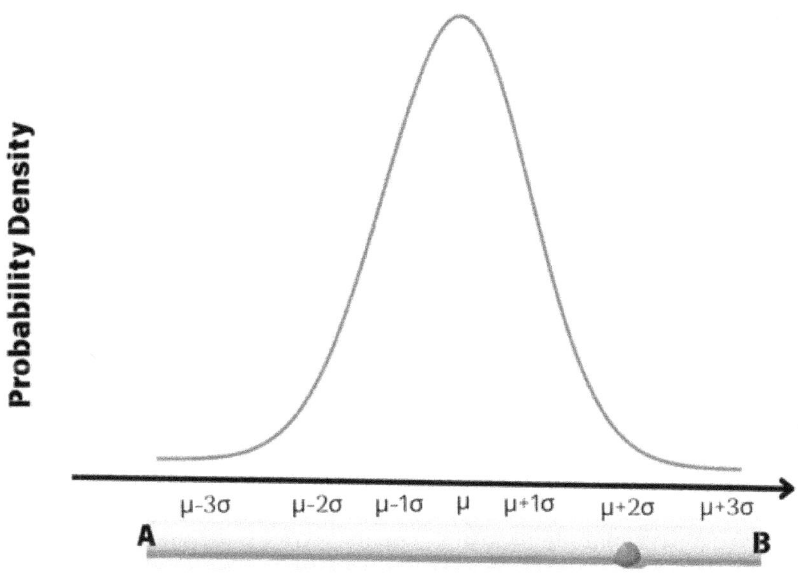

It can be observed in Figure 8 that for the Gaussian distribution, most of the leak events will occur at the centre of the pipe since the centre which is also the mean has the highest probability density value. Furthermore, up to 68.27% occurrences of leakages will are situated in the interval μ-1σ to μ+1σ region of the pipe. Following this interval, the region of the pipe lying in the interval μ-2σ to μ+2σ experiences about 95.45% of the entire leakage events, while the region in the interval μ-3σ to μ+3σ experiences about 99.73% of the entire leakage events.

Probability-based Robot Deployment

At the beginning of every RL episode, it is not only the point of gas leakage that is randomized. The position of the robot is also randomized according to a uniform probability distribution. Firstly, in order to ensure that the robot is always starting at a point far away from the point of leakage, the region of deployment of the robot at the beginning of the search is alternated between the two extreme ends of the space since the pipe where the leakage occurs is permanently situated along the middle line of the space. Secondly, in addition to alternating the region of deployment of the robot, its exact point of deployment within any chosen region is randomized based on a uniform probability distribution. This helps to prevent the robot from learning to start the search only from a single point but from any point.

Setting Up The Reinforcement Learning Environment

In the Unity window, there are a number of entities which are discussed next.

The Agent

According to Jiangyuan et al. (2021), Kempka et al. (2016), Abbass et al. (2023), and Nutonen et al. (2023), the agents in the ML-agents framework are Unity 3D Game Objects. The agent in our situation is a robot. In ML-agents, the agent establishes the state, executes guided actions, and assigns cumulative rewards. There is just one brain linked with the agent. The agent (robot) navigates the surrounding environment by moving one step at a time in a chosen direction while avoiding obstacles and finding the target. In our RL design, each movement incurs a penalty (or negative reward) which is done to ensure that the agent finds the target as soon as possible so as to avoid the persistent penalty. Also, reaching the target earns the agent a positive reward, whereas colliding with an obstacle or a wall results in a negative reward or penalty.

The Brain

Every agent is linked to a single brain, which provides intelligence and dictates behaviour. The brain provides the thinking behind the agent's decisions; it determines what action is best in each scenario. Our brain employs the PPO RL algorithm, which is designed for real-time applications. The ML-agents' PPO algorithm operates in a separate Python process that connects via a socket to the Unity program (Goy, 2020). The set of potential actions (e.g., move one step in the North, South, East, West, North-east, North-west, South-east or South-west direction) and the state-space representation (the contents of the agent's immediate surroundings in the stated directions) are fed into the PPO algorithm, which uses the learned policy to select the action that maximizes the reward.

The PPO algorithm in the ML-agent's architecture consists of a number of processes, including updating the value and policy networks and applying the modified policy to regulate the agent's actions in the environment. The technique makes use of generalized advantage estimation, or GAE (Schulman et al., 2017), to guarantee the stability and convergence of policy changes. Additionally, the clipping parameter limits the amount of pf updates to prevent significant changes that can impede the learning process. The PPO pseudo code with ML-Agents is as follows (Mahmoudi & Ostreika, 2023):

```
Algorithm 1: PPO Algorithm

Initialize policy network with random weights θ

Initialize value network with random weights ϕ

Set learning rate α and clipping parameter ϵ

Set number of training iterations T



for t = 1 to T do:

            Collect batch of experiences using current policy
π_θ

      Compute advantages A using GAE
```

```
        Compute target values V using bootstrapped returns

        Train value network to minimize MSE loss between V and
predicted values

        Compute the surrogate objective Lclip using the current
policy π_θ and

              advantages A

              Compute gradients ∇Lclip with respect to policy
parameters θ

        Clip gradients to avoid large changes

               Update policy using clipped gradients and learn-
ing rate α

         Update the environment with the updated policy

   end for
```

Description of the PPO Algorithm (Mahmoudi & Ostreika, 2023)

1. Initialize policy network with random weights θ: The function that translates observations into actions is called the policy, and it is represented by a neural network which is created with random weights.
2. Initialize value network with random weights ϕ: The value function, or the function that calculates the expected total reward from a state, is represented by a different neural network with random weights.

3. Set the clipping parameter ϵ and learning rate α. The clipping parameter restricts the amount of the parameter updates to avoid too much change at once, while the learning rate controls how much the model weights are changed with each update.
4. Set number of training iterations T: The number of times the algorithm will repeat the training process is specified by setting the number of training iterations, T.
5. Gather a batch of experiences using the current policy π_θ: The agent uses the current policy π_θ to interact with the environment and gather a batch of experiences (state, action, reward, and next state).
6. Calculate advantages A using GAE: The GAE approach is used to estimate the benefit of each policy action, reflecting the degree to which the action exceeded expectations.
7. Determine target values V using bootstrapped returns: For every state-action combination, a target value is determined using the bootstrapped return, which is an estimate of the anticipated future reward from a certain state.
8. Train value network to minimize MSE loss between V and predicted values: Minimize the Mean Squared Error (MSE) loss between the target values and the predicted values by training the value network to perform this task.
9. Use the Advantages A and present policy π_θ to calculate the surrogate objective L_{clip}: The surrogate objective, which is calculated using the Advantages and the existing policy π_θ, is used to estimate how much the policy should be updated.
10. Calculate gradients ∇L_{clip} with respect to policy parameters θ: Backpropagation is used to calculate the surrogate objective's gradients with regard to the policy parameters θ.
11. Clip gradients to prevent big changes: To keep the policy from changing too much at once and to reduce the size of gradients, the gradients are clipped.
12. Use learning rate α and clipped gradients to update the policy: By using learning rate and clipped gradients, the policy is updated to enhance its performance.
13. Apply the updated policy to the environment: The agent uses the updated policy to interact with the environment and gather new experiences. This procedure is repeated for a predetermined number of iterations.

The Academy

The academy serves as a conduit between the brain (logic) and the Python PyTorch (or TensorFlow, as the case may be) implementation of the brain, which programmatically encapsulates the reasoning. The relationship between the mentioned entities is illustrated in Figure 9.

Figure 9. Interaction between the entities of unity 3D ML-agent

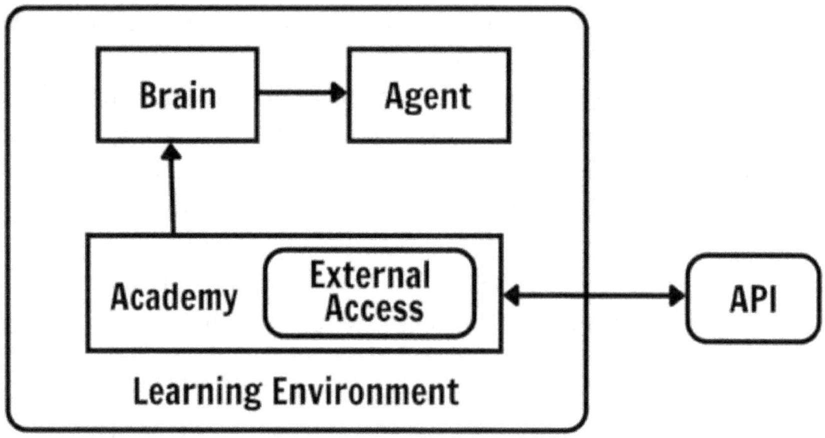

(Tian et al., 2023)

Configuration

Various agent, reward, and environmental configurations were taken into consideration in order to set up the brain and agent. For an implementation to be effective, this process is essential. The agent was penalized with a small negative reward for every step that remained in an episode. Since the aim of the agent is to maximize the cumulative reward, it makes effort to complete each episode in as few steps as possible to reduce the number of times its is penalized. The penalty, P_{delay}, in each step is computed as:

$$P_{delay} = -\mathrm{U}\times\log_{10}\left(E_{length}\right)$$

where U is a small fraction and E_{length} is the number of steps the agent has taken since the commencement of the current episode. E_{length} resets to 1 at the termination of each episode in preparation for the next episode. A reset value of 1 instead of 0 was chosen to avoid taking the logarithm of 0. Furthermore, there are walls and obstacles in the scene which must be avoided by the agent. Therefore, the agent is penalized with a negative reward for colliding with objects in its surroundings. The collision penalty (or negative reward) is computed as:

$$P_{collision} = \begin{cases} -R_{min};\ \text{if } R_{min} < \left(R_{max} - \log_{10}\left(E_{length}\right)\right) \\ -\left(R_{max} - \log_{10}\left(E_{length}\right)\right)\ ;\ \text{otherwise} \end{cases}$$

We carefully formulated the penalty in Eq. (16) to ensure that the penalty due to a collision event that occurs early in the episode is more than late in the episode. This is because the logarithm of E_{length} is subtracted from R_{max} to determine what the penalty is. At the beginning of the episode, E_{length} is usually small, meaning that a small number is subtracted from R_{max} which results in a large result and the negative of this large result becomes a very small number which is the penalty. Hence, early collision leads to a severe penalty. On the other hand, if the collision is much delayed into the later part of the episode, the value of E_{length} is usually large during this period, therefore, subtracting its logarithm from R_{max} results in a much smaller result than the previous case considered. The the penalty is computed as the negative of the small number which implies that the agent is penalized less when a collision is delayed or avoided for as long as possible by the agent. In order not to excessively penalize the agent for an early collision, the maximum penalty that the agent can receive is fixed at $-R_{min}$ as observable in the upper part of Eq. (16).

Just as the agent is penalized, for collision, it is also rewarded for reaching the target. The reward for reaching the target is the complement of the penalty which is computed as Eq. (17):

$$R_{success} = \begin{cases} R_{min}; \text{ if } R_{min} > \left(R_{max} - \log_{10}\left(E_{length}\right)\right) \\ \left(R_{max} - \log_{10}\left(E_{length}\right)\right) \text{ ; otherwise} \end{cases}$$

We carefully formulated the reward in Eq. (17) to promote a quick arrival of the robot at the target since this is the whole essence of the project. In Eq. (17), the logarithm of E_{length} is subtracted from R_{max} to determine what the reward is. At the beginning of the episode, E_{length} is usually small, meaning that a small number is subtracted from R_{max} which results in a large result. This large result is awarded to the agent as a reward. Hence, early arrival at the target location leads to a high reward. On the other hand, if the arrival at the target location is much delayed into the later part of the episode, E_{length} is usually large during this period, therefore, subtracting its logarithm from R_{max} results in a much smaller result than the previous case considered. This ensures that the agent is rewarded less when its arrival at the target is delayed.

Simulation

The robot agent has the mandate of navigating to the position of a gas leak on a pipe as quickly as possible. In this context, the position of the gas leakage is also referred to as the target position. The flowchart in Figure 10 illustrates the processes involved.

At the beginning of each episode, the gas pipe is caused to leak at a random point based on a probability distribution which can either be a uniform distribution, a beta distribution, or a Gaussian distribution. The robot is then deployed at an extreme end of the scene. By applying the PPO algorithm (Algorithm 1), the robot agent explores the scene, and whenever it collides with an obstacle, it gets penalised. If, on the other hand, it arrives at the target location, it gets rewarded. Hence, the ML-agent either fails by colliding with an obstacle, times out, or navigates to the target. Whenever any of these 3 events occur, the current episode ends and a new one begins.

Figure 10. The flowchart of the robot navigation problem

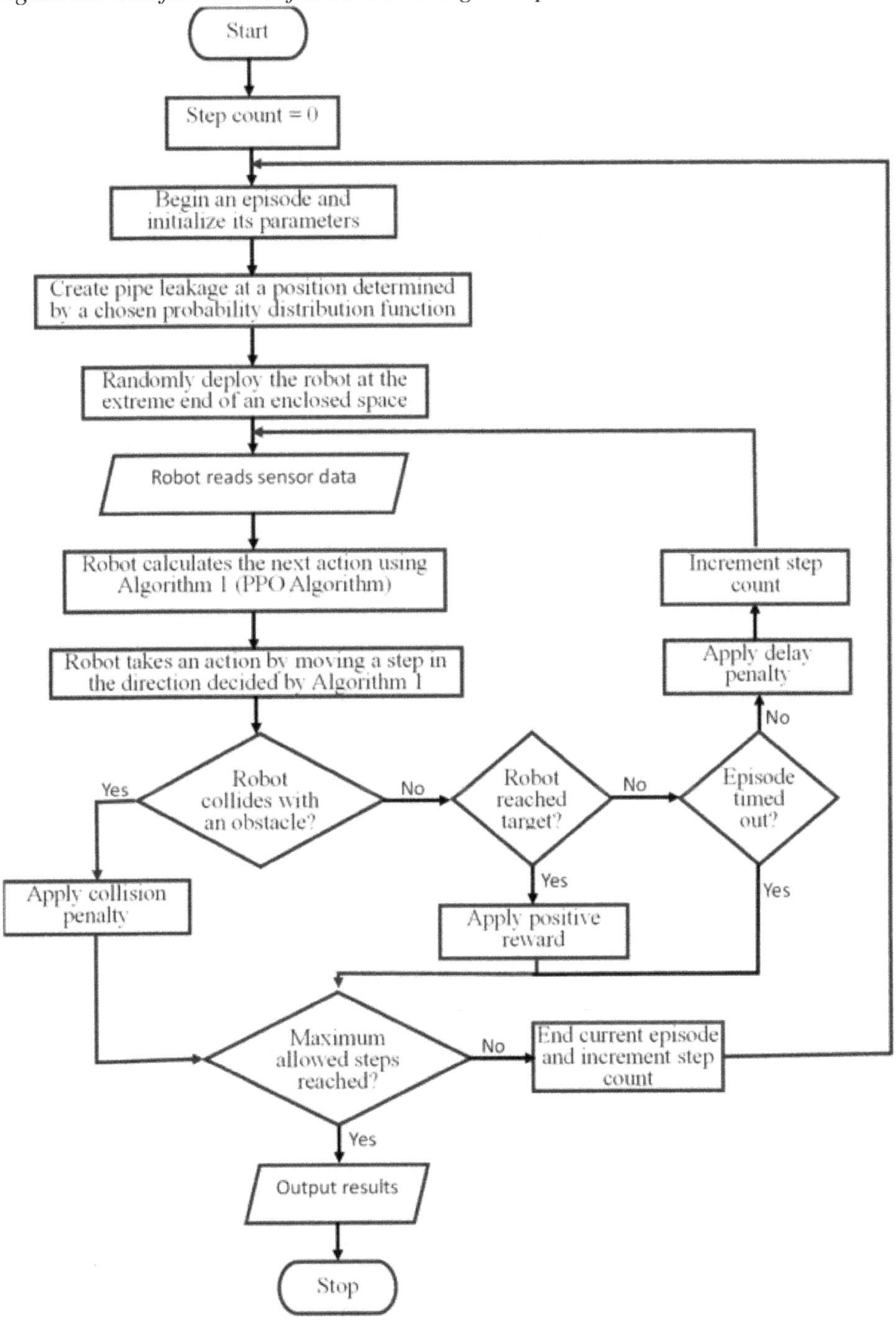

After extensive exploration involving millions of steps, the agent gradually learns and adopts the policy that earns higher rewards and minimum penalties thanks to the PPO algorithm. The careful design of the reward and penalty as well as the selection of appropriate ML-agent hyperparameters are crucial for the success of the learning process. Table 1 provides the set of parameters and corresponding values for the Unity ML-agents that are used for the robot navigation problem. Most of the values in the table have been selected based on personal experience and also by following the recommendations of Unity Technologies (2020) and Goy (2020).

Table 1. Parameters and values

Parameter	**Value**
trainer_type	PPO
max_steps	5,000,000
time_horizon	64
summary_freq	10,000
keep_checkpoints	2
checkpoint_interval	150,000
hyperparameters:	
batch_size	1024
buffer_size	10240
learning_rate	0.0003
Beta	0.005
epsilon	0.2
lambd	0.95
num_epoch	3
network_settings:	
normalize:	true
hidden_units	128
num_layers	2
reward_signals:	
extrinsic:	
gamma	0.99
strength	1.0

The program was written in C# which is the native programming language of Unity. The computer used for the training process was an HP ZBook Studio Computer with an Intel Xeon Processor and running on Windows 10 operating system with 16GB of RAM and an NVIDIA Quadro M1000M GPU. The robot agent was configured using the Anaconda reinforcement learning training framework and Unity software version 2022.3.29f1. The PyTorch model was configured independently in Anaconda and connected to Unity using a socket.

Five million training steps were used to train the brain. Unity creates each episode on its own as a distinct navigation challenge. To test the performance of our robot agent, 3 levels of complexity have been considered for the scene as earlier shown in Figures 3 through 5. The lowest complexity is the case where only 1 obstacle is deployed in the scene (Figure 3). The medium complexity has 10 obstacles (Figure 4) in the scene, while the highest complexity has 20 obstacles (Figure 5) in the scene. Furthermore, the simulation in this chapter has the goal of investigating whether having higher number of gas leakage events in certain regions of the pipe has any influence on the learning process. To achieve this, 3 scenarios have been considered as follows:

a) Uniform distribution scenario (Figure 6) in which a gas leak is equally probable across the length of the gas pipe
b) Beta distribution scenario (Figure 7) where the probability of occurrence of a gas leak is a little higher in certain parts of the gas pipe (e.g., the centre region) than other parts, and
c) Gaussian distribution scenario (Figure 8) where the probability of occurrence of a gas leak is much higher in certain parts of the gas pipe (e.g., the centre region) than the other parts.

It is pertinent to note that the simulation has focussed on the development of navigation intelligence while the inverse kinematics has been abstracted out and considered out of the scope of discussion.

RESULTS AND DISCUSSION

Figures 11 through 13 illustrate graphs of cumulative reward plotted against the total number of steps. It can be seen in Figure 11 that when only one obstacle is in the scene, the number of steps taken before learning the required policy is quite different for each of the 3 probability distributions considered. For example, the agent learned the best policy fastest when the events of gas leakages on the pipe followed the Gaussian distribution pattern. This is because the reward peaks and remains fairly stable at around the 300,000th step. The beta distribution pattern followed at around the 500,000th step, while the uniform distribution learned relatively slowly by learning the policy at around the 750,000th step. This implies that for less complex problems, the probability distribution pattern of events influences the rate at which policies are learned. It is however important to note that once the policy has been learnt in all the 3 instances, the cumulative reward attained by them is the same which implies that they have similar performances once a certain number of steps have been completed.

Figure 11. Cumulative reward plotted against total steps with 1 obstacle in the scene.

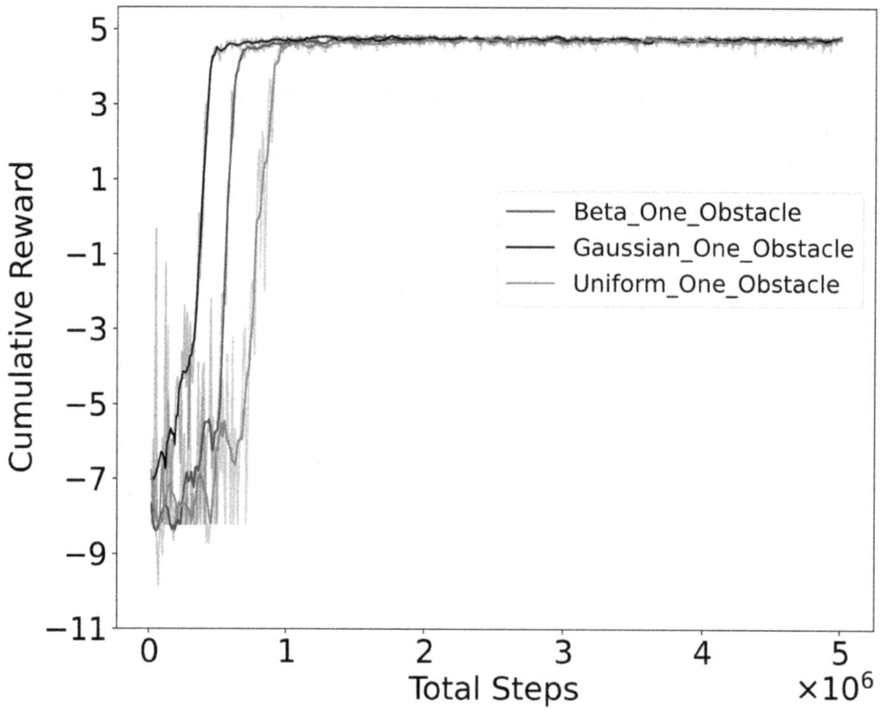

Figure 12. Cumulative reward plotted against total steps with 10 obstacles in the scene.

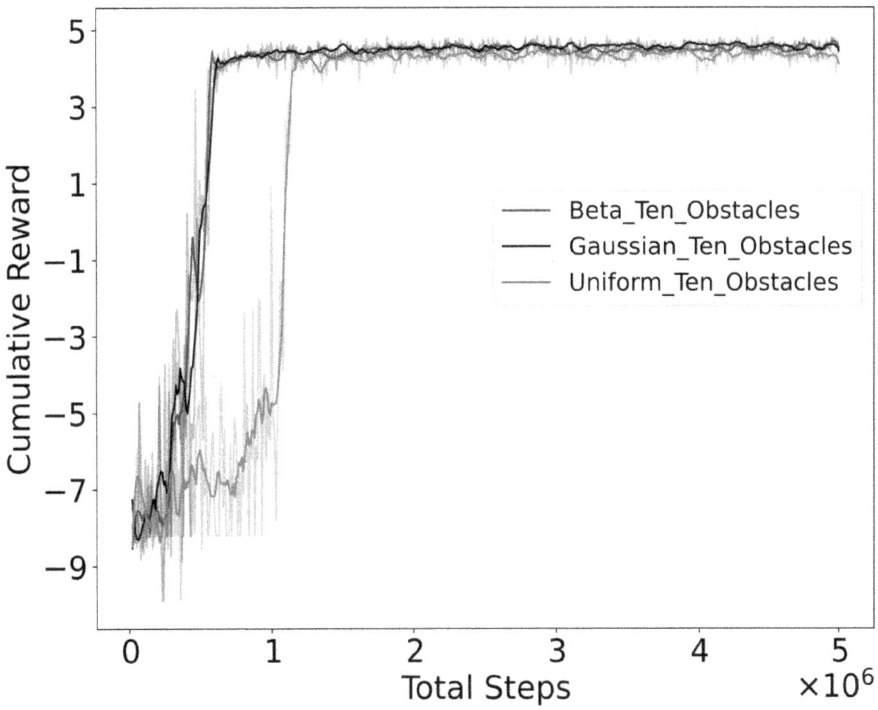

Figure 13. Cumulative reward plotted against total steps with 20 obstacles in the scene.

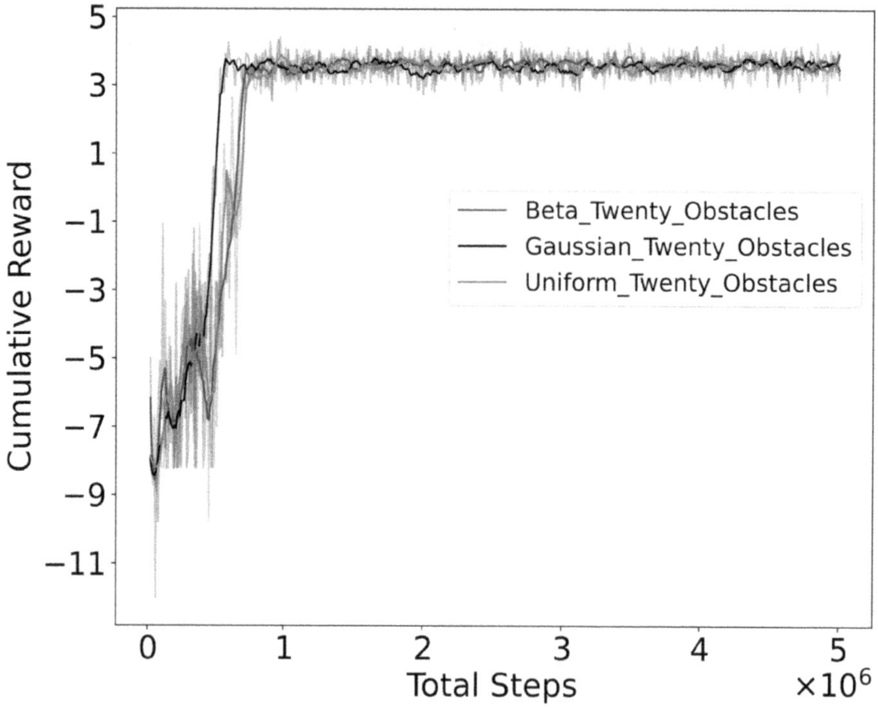

In Figure 12, where the complexity of the problem has increased such that 10 obstacles are now in the scene, the Beta and Gaussian distribution-based events have similar performances, and both outperformed the uniform distribution-based event in terms of the speed at which they learned the required navigation policy. The two continued to have similar performances after learning the policy as they have similar cumulative rewards after the 500,000th step. The uniform distribution-based event on the other hand showed a slightly poorer performance as it has a slightly lower cumulative reward all through the training process.

Figure 13, when compared to the two preceding results, shows an interesting result. It can be seen that when the scene has become complex by increasing the number of obstacles to 20 obstacles, the performance gap between the 3 scenarios (Beta, Gaussian, and uniform distributions) has diminished. All 3 scenarios learned the navigation policy at a speed not too far apart and continued to have similar cumulative rewards afterward.

Figures 14, 15, and 16 illustrate the policy entropy of the cases of 1 obstacle, 10 obstacles, and 20 obstacles in the scene, respectively. On a general note, the entropy indicates how arbitrarily choices are taken by the agent. Throughout the training, this ought to steadily decrease. It can be seen that in the case of 1 scene obstacle in Figure 14, the entropy initially rose and subsequently dropped in all 3 cases that comprise Beta, Gaussian, and Uniform event distributions. In the case of Figures 15 and 16 that have more complex scenes, the entropy rose and afterward maintained fairly stable levels.

Figure 14. Policy entropy plotted against total steps with 1 obstacle in the scene.

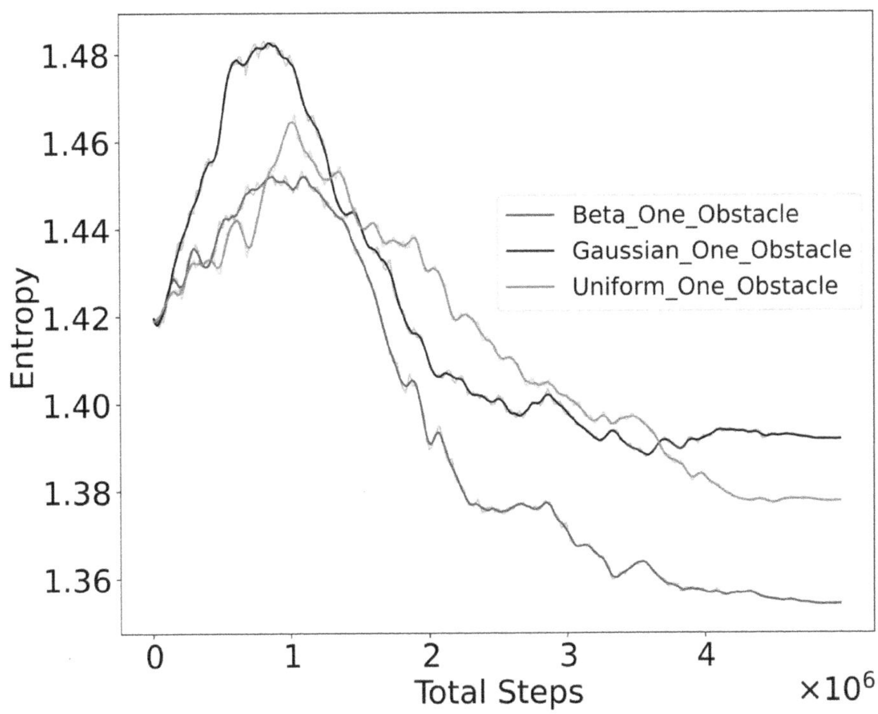

Figure 15. Policy entropy plotted against total steps with 10 obstacles in the scene.

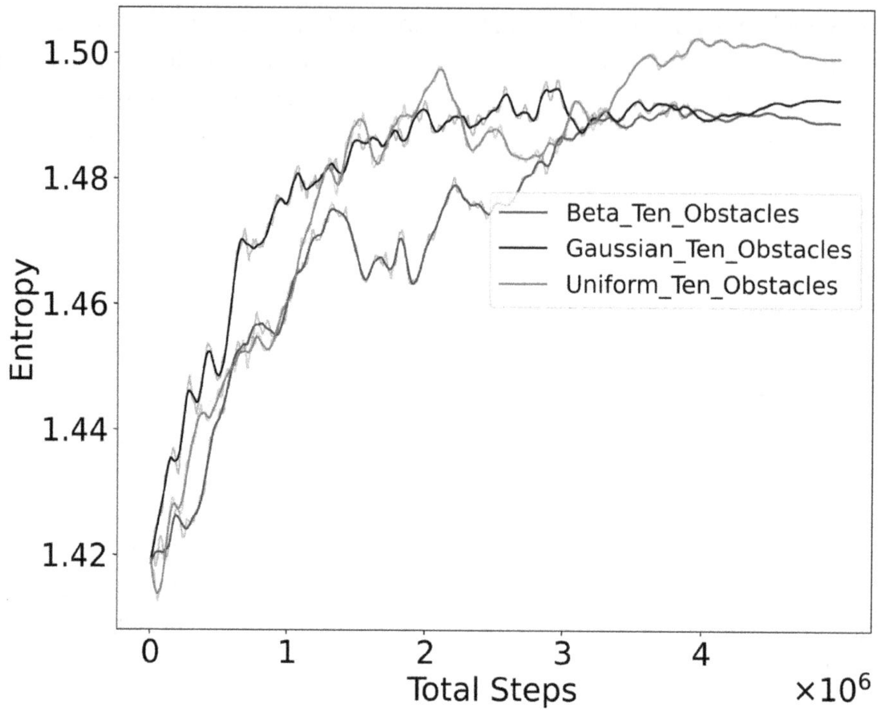

Figure 16. Policy entropy plotted against total steps with 20 obstacles in the scene.

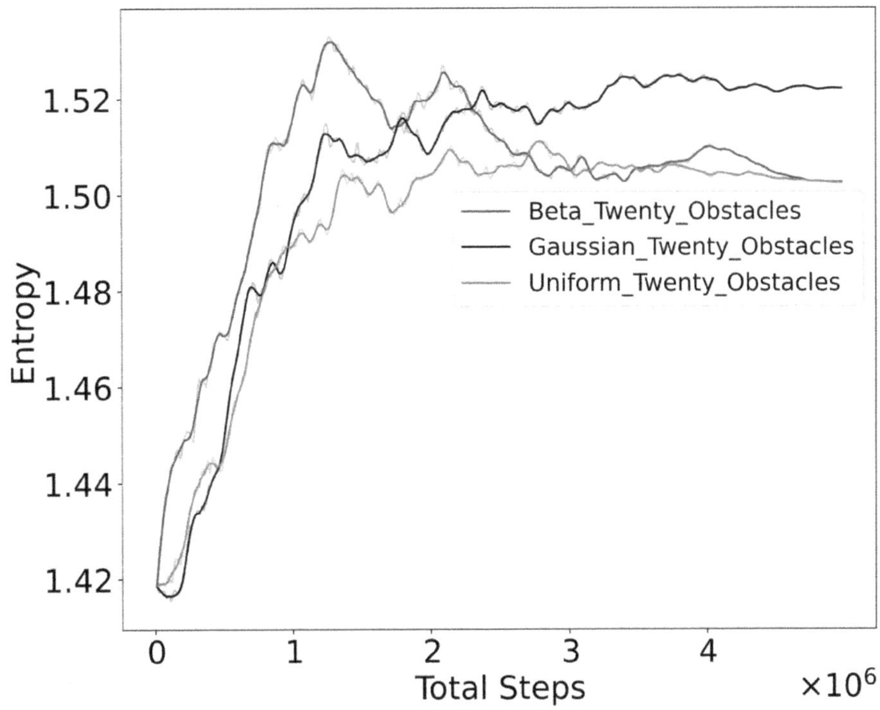

Figures 17, 18, and 19 illustrate the value losses of the cases of 1 obstacle, 10 obstacles, and 20 obstacles in the scene, respectively. Usually, as the reward rises, value losses are expected to rise as well, and as the reward stabilizes, value loss should fall. It can be seen in Figure 17 (which has a simple scene comprising 1 obstacle) that value losses rose sharply and subsequently rapidly dropped to low values in line with expectations. In the case of scenarios with more complex scenes of 10 and 20 scene obstacles, their corresponding value losses shown in Figures 18 and 19, respectively also rose at the beginning of the simulation but did not drop to values as low as seen in Figure 17.

Figure 17. Value loss plotted against total steps with 1 obstacle in the scene.

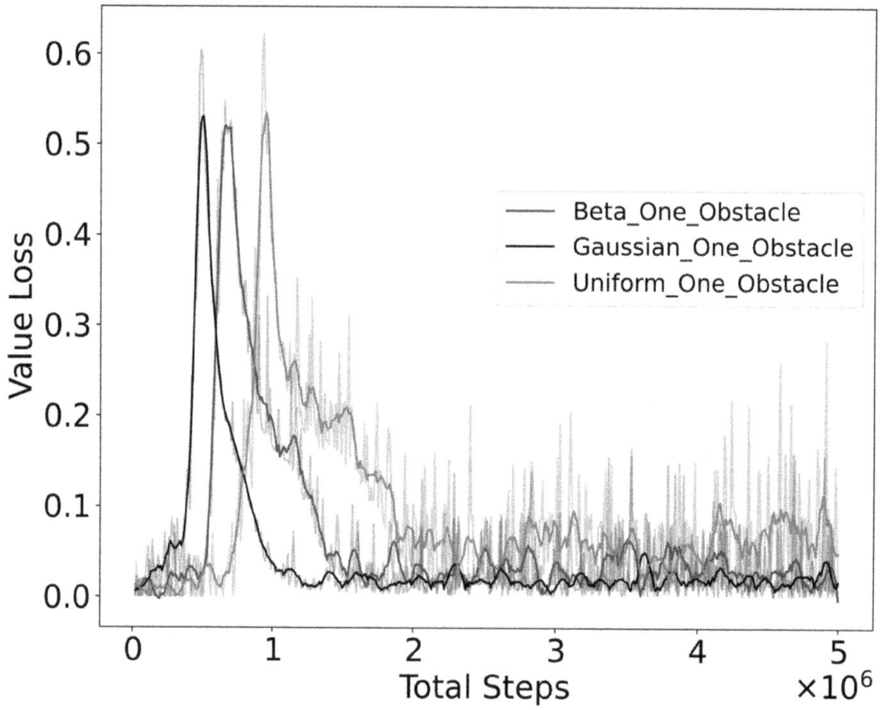

Figure 18. Value loss plotted against total steps with 10 obstacles in the scene.

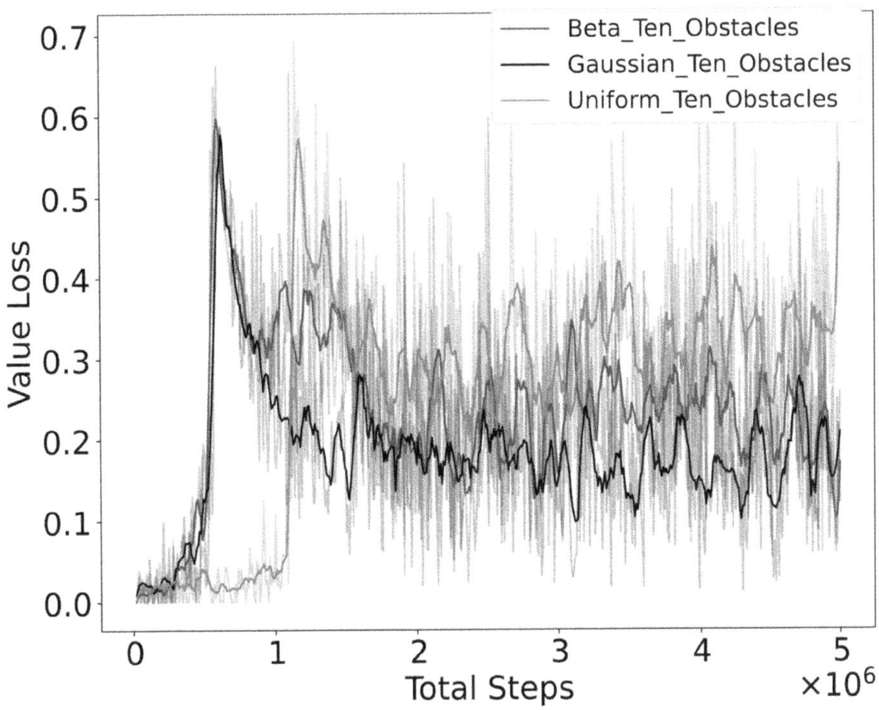

Figure 19. Value loss plotted against total steps with 20 obstacles in the scene.

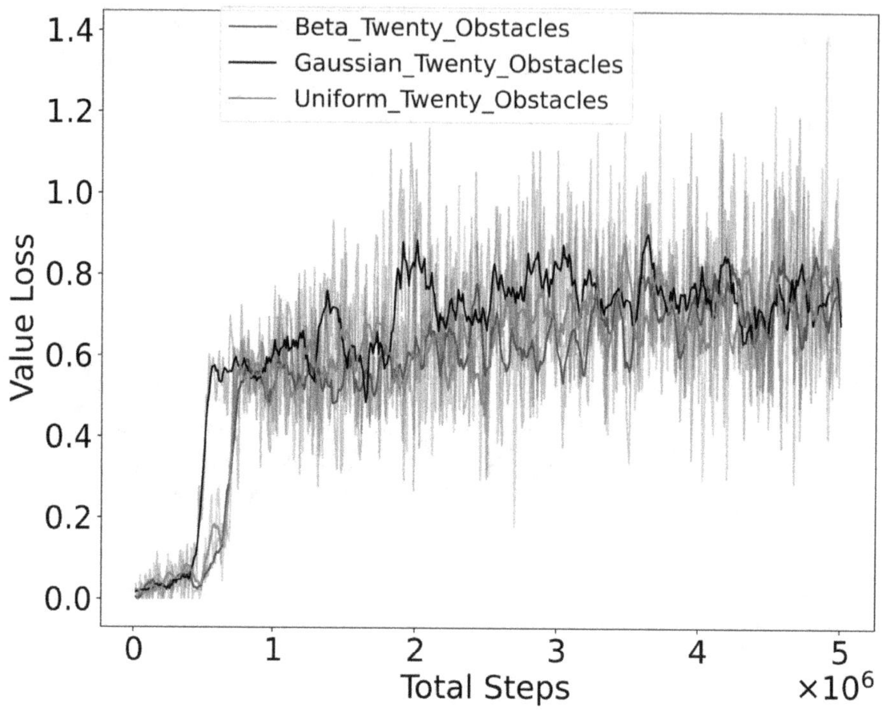

Finally, Figures 20 through 22 illustrate graphs of Episode length plotted against the total steps. Recall that the original goal of the robot agent is to move to the location of the target from wherever it is deployed as quickly as possible before the episode timed out while also avoiding collision with obstacles. A short episode length with a corresponding high cumulative reward indicates that the agent arrived at the target quickly. Therefore, the episode length graph should not be observed in isolation but should be jointly observed with the cumulative reward graphs shown in Figures 11 to 13. This is because a short episode length does not only result from the quick navigation of the agent toward the target but could also be a result of early termination of the episode due to a collision between the agent and an obstacle. However, in the case of a short episode length resulting from a collision, the penalty given to the agent in such an instance makes the cumulative reward to drop. Hence a high cumulative reward and a correspondingly low episode length confirm that the agent arrived at the target within a short time, hence satisfying the agent's goal.

If the episode length graph in Figure 20 is compared with the cumulative reward graph in Figure 10, it can be observed that from the one-millionth step to the five-millionth step, where the episode lengths are observed to be short in Figure 20, the corresponding cumulative reward during the same step period in Figure 11 are observed to be high. This indicates that the goal of the agent has been achieved in these instances since it is an indication of quick arrival of the agent at the gas leakage position. Furthermore, if episode length results in Figures 21 and 22 are compared with the cumulative reward graph in Figures 12 and 13, respectively, the same assertion can be made.

Figure 20. Average episode length plotted against total steps with 1 obstacle in the scene.

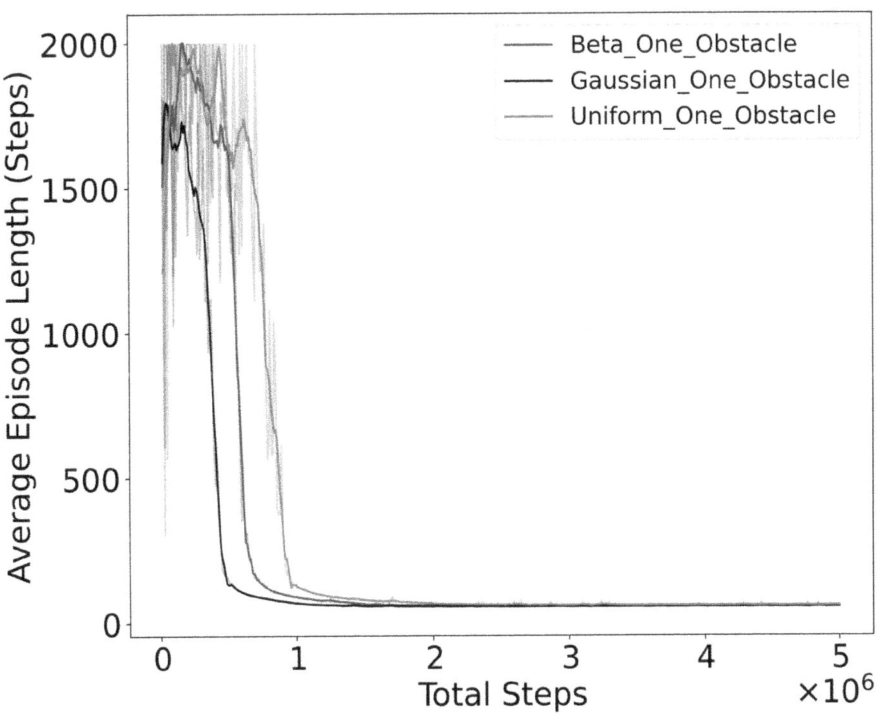

Figure 21. Average episode length plotted against total steps with 10 obstacles in the scene.

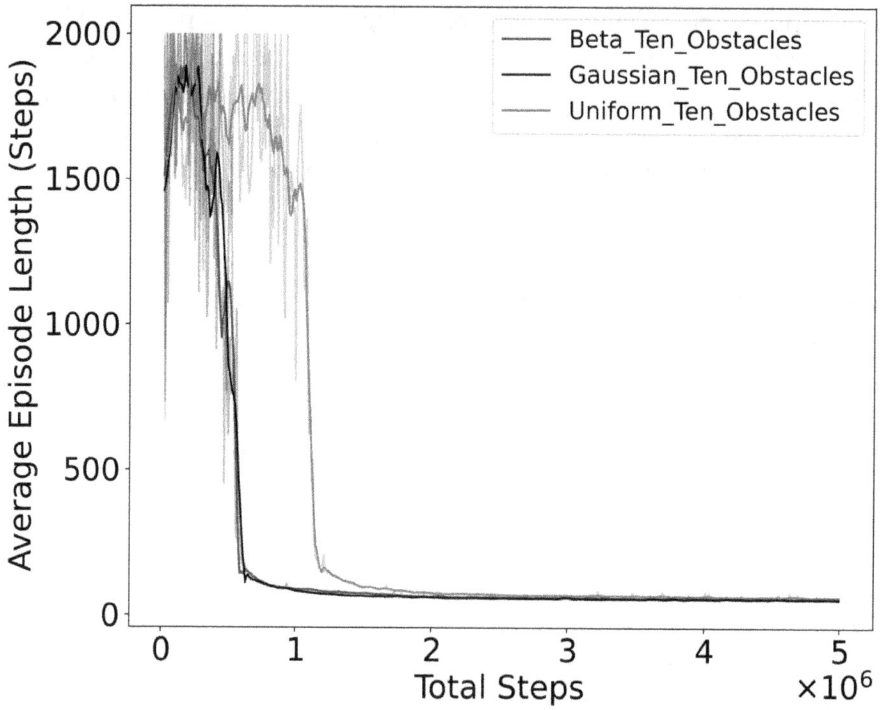

Figure 22. Average episode length plotted against total steps with 20 obstacle in the scene.

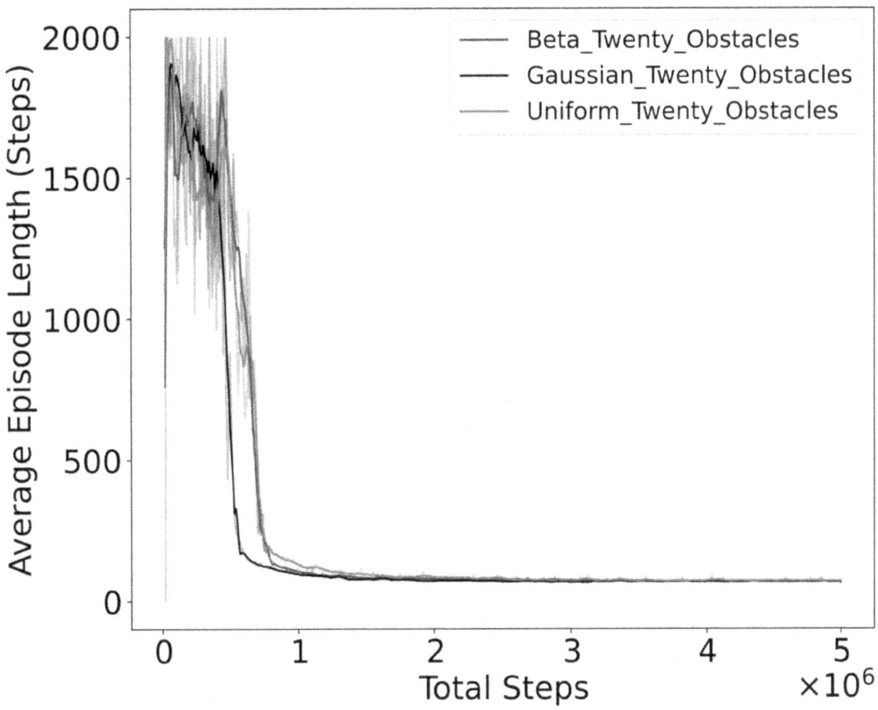

Performing the experiments discussed in this chapter in a simulation environment has the advantage of making it possible to quickly and completely test the system before moving on to a more costly and logistically challenging real-world testing. However, at this point, the robot has already gained the necessary navigation intelligence through simulation since it is able to navigate towards the leakage along the shortest route while avoiding collisions with objects along the way.

The next step after the simulation would be to deploy the robot in a real-world scenario and transfer the behaviour learned in the virtual environment to it for further optimization (Bourdillon et al., 2023).

CONCLUSION

In this chapter, we have discussed the concept of representing a physical system with its digital twin which usually provides a safe and cost-effective avenue to design, test, enhance the performance, and modify the behaviour of physical systems prior to physical deployment. The digital twin can be viewed as the virtual clones of the physical system and specifically, a robot is used as a case study in this chapter. The reinforcement learning (RL) algorithm may be applied to a digital twin to enhance its performance and streamline its behaviour as may be desired. Applying RL has the benefit of being able to handle complex tasks without prior knowledge of the input-output relationship. However, policy convergence can become difficult and sluggish due to the episodically randomized environment, which introduces sparse rewards and challenging tasks at an early learning stage. To address this challenge, the model-free policy gradient learning technique known as proximal policy optimisation (PPO) is sometimes used. PPO uses several stochastic gradient descent epochs for each policy update, which helps to ensure the stability and convergence of policy changes. This approach allows for efficient policy updates without sacrificing performance, making PPO a popular choice for RL applications. A simulation platform known as Unity has incorporated PPO algorithm into its ML-agents toolbox which makes the platform an excellent choice for AI research, most especially research works that involve reinforcement learning.

As a case study, we assumed a situation where it was necessary to train an intervention robot to sense and navigate to the location of a gas pipe leakage while avoiding collision with obstacles positioned along its path. We focussed on the development of navigation intelligence while the inverse kinematics was considered out of the scope of the current discussion and, therefore, abstracted out. The Unity platform was selected and used to train an intervention robot to perform the desired tasks. The simulation was set up to allow the robot to learn these tasks within a maximum of 5 million steps. Simulation experiments showed that the robot learned to perform these tasks, in most cases, before its one-millionth step with the earliest occurring at around the three hundred thousandth step. The simulation described in this chapter are necessary before moving on to the real-world testing, which is more logistically challenging, costly, and sometimes risky. Testing in a simulation environment supports simple and comprehensive evaluation. After determining the system's strengths and limitations in the simulation environment, we may implement it in actual environments and transfer the behaviour learned in the virtual environment to it for further optimization. However, at this stage, the robot has already acquired the essential navigation intelligence via simulation, since it can go to the leakage using the shortest path while avoiding collisions with items along the way.

REFERENCES

Abbass, M. A. B., & Kang, H.-S. (2023). Drone Elevation Control Based on Python-Unity Integrated Framework for Reinforcement Learning Applications. *Drones (Basel), 7*(4), 225. DOI: 10.3390/drones7040225

Adedeji, B. P. (2024). Energy parameter modeling in plug-in hybrid electric vehicles using supervised machine learning approaches. *E-Prime - Advances in Electrical Engineering. Electronics and Energy, 8*, 100584. DOI: 10.1016/j.prime.2024.100584

Afolabi, A. S., & Akinola, O. A. (2024). Network Intrusion Detection Using Knapsack Optimization, Mutual Information Gain, and Machine Learning. *Journal of Electrical and Computer Engineering, 2024*, 1–21. DOI: 10.1155/2024/7302909

Andersen, P.-A., Goodwin, M., & Granmo, O.-C. (2024). Towards safe and sustainable reinforcement learning for real-time strategy games. *Information Sciences, 679*, 120980. DOI: 10.1016/j.ins.2024.120980

Ardjmand, E., Fallahtafti, A., Yazdani, E., Mahmoodi, A., & Young Ii, W. A. (2024). A guided twin delayed deep deterministic reinforcement learning for vaccine allocation in human contact networks. *Applied Soft Computing, 167*, 112322. DOI: 10.1016/j.asoc.2024.112322

Aslan, E., Arserim, M. A., & Uçar, A. (2023). Development of Push-Recovery control system for humanoid robots using deep reinforcement learning. *Ain Shams Engineering Journal, 14*(10), 102167. DOI: 10.1016/j.asej.2023.102167

Beattie, C., Leibo, J. Z., Teplyashin, D., Ward, T., Wainwright, M., Küttler, H., Lefrancq, A., Green, S., Valdés, V., Sadik, A., Schrittwieser, J., Anderson, K., York, S., Cant, M., Cain, A., Bolton, A., Gaffney, S., King, H., Hassabis, D., . . . Petersen, S. (2016). *DeepMind Lab* (Version 2). arXiv. DOI: 10.48550/ARXIV.1612.03801

Bengio, Y., Louradour, J., Collobert, R., & Weston, J. (2009). Curriculum learning. *Proceedings of the 26th Annual International Conference on Machine Learning*, 41–48. DOI: 10.1145/1553374.1553380

Bilberg, A., & Malik, A. A. (2019). Digital twin driven human–robot collaborative assembly. *CIRP Annals, 68*(1), 499–502. DOI: 10.1016/j.cirp.2019.04.011

Bourdillon, A. T., Garg, A., Wang, H., Woo, Y. J., Pavone, M., & Boyd, J. (2023). Integration of Reinforcement Learning in a Virtual Robotic Surgical Simulation. *Surgical Innovation, 30*(1), 94–102. DOI: 10.1177/15533506221095298 PMID: 35503302

Brockman, G., Cheung, V., Pettersson, L., Schneider, J., Schulman, J., Tang, J., & Zaremba, W. (2016). *OpenAI Gym* (arXiv:1606.01540). arXiv. https://doi.org//arXiv.1606.01540DOI: 10.48550

Cai, Z., Feng, Z., Zhou, L., Yang, X., & Xu, T. (2023). Deep-reinforcement-learning-based robot motion strategies for grabbing objects from human hands. *Virtual Reality & Intelligent Hardware*, *5*(5), 407–421. DOI: 10.1016/j.vrih.2022.12.001

Carvalho Melo, L., & Omena Albuquerque Maximo, M. R. (2019). Learning Humanoid Robot Running Skills through Proximal Policy Optimization. *2019 Latin American Robotics Symposium (LARS), 2019 Brazilian Symposium on Robotics (SBR) and 2019 Workshop on Robotics in Education (WRE)*, 37–42. DOI: 10.1109/LARS-SBR-WRE48964.2019.00015

Cheliotis, K. (2021). ABMU: An Agent-Based Modelling Framework for Unity3D. *SoftwareX*, *15*, 100771. DOI: 10.1016/j.softx.2021.100771

Cheng, R. (2021, December 31). Unity-Python Communication for ML-Agents: Good, Bad, and Ugly. *New Screwdriver*. https://newscrewdriver.com/2021/12/31/unity-python-communication-for-ml-agents-good-bad-and-ugly/

Coumans, E., & Bai, Y. (n.d.). *PyBullet Quickstart Guide*. Google Docs. Retrieved 10 October 2024, from https://docs.google.com/document/d/10sXEhzFRSnvFcl3XxNGhnD4N2SedqwdAvK3dsihxVUA/edit?usp=embed_facebook

De Souza Silva, J. L., Mahmoudi, E., Carvalho, R. R. M., & Dos Santos Barros, T. A. (2024). Classification of anomalies in photovoltaic systems using supervised machine learning techniques and real data. *Energy Reports*, *11*, 4642–4656. DOI: 10.1016/j.egyr.2024.04.040

Del Rio, A., Serrano, J., Jimenez, D., Contreras, L. M., & Alvarez, F. (2024). Multisite gaming streaming optimization over virtualized 5G environment using Deep Reinforcement Learning techniques. *Computer Networks*, *244*, 110334. DOI: 10.1016/j.comnet.2024.110334

Gangapurwala, S., Mitchell, A., & Havoutis, I. (2020). Guided Constrained Policy Optimization for Dynamic Quadrupedal Robot Locomotion. *IEEE Robotics and Automation Letters*, *5*(2), 3642–3649. DOI: 10.1109/LRA.2020.2979656

Gao, X., Gao, R., Liang, P., Zhang, Q., Deng, R., & Zhu, W. (2021). A Hybrid Tracking Control Strategy for Nonholonomic Wheeled Mobile Robot Incorporating Deep Reinforcement Learning Approach. *IEEE Access : Practical Innovations, Open Solutions*, *9*, 15592–15602. DOI: 10.1109/ACCESS.2021.3053396

Gayathri, R., Sangeetha, S. K. B., Mathivanan, S. K., Rajadurai, H., Malar, B. A., Mallik, S., & Qin, H. (2024). Enhancing heart disease prediction with reinforcement learning and data augmentation. *Systems and Soft Computing*, *6*, 200129.

Ge, Y., From, P. J., & Xiong, Y. (2024). Multi-view gripper internal sensing for the regression of strawberry ripeness using a mini-convolutional neural network for robotic harvesting. *Computers and Electronics in Agriculture*, *216*, 108474. DOI: 10.1016/j.compag.2023.108474

Gong, C., Tao, D., Maybank, S. J., Liu, W., Kang, G., & Yang, J. (2016). Multi-Modal Curriculum Learning for Semi-Supervised Image Classification. *IEEE Transactions on Image Processing*, *25*(7), 3249–3260. DOI: 10.1109/TIP.2016.2563981 PMID: 27168596

Goy, C. (2020). *Training with Proximal Policy Optimization*. GitHub. https://github.com/yosider/ml-agents-1/blob/master/docs/Training-PPO.md

Guffanti, D., Brunete, A., Hernando, M., Álvarez, D., Rueda, J., & Navarro, E. (2024). Supervised learning for improving the accuracy of robot-mounted 3D camera applied to human gait analysis. *Heliyon*, *10*(4), e26227. DOI: 10.1016/j.heliyon.2024.e26227 PMID: 38404866

Hasan, M., Vasker, N., & Khan, M. S. H. (2024). Real-time Sorting of Broiler Chicken Meat with Robotic arm: XAI-enhanced Deep Learning and LIME Framework for Freshness Detection. *Journal of Agriculture and Food Research*, *18*, 101372. DOI: 10.1016/j.jafr.2024.101372

Hwangbo, J., Lee, J., & Hutter, M. (2018). Per-Contact Iteration Method for Solving Contact Dynamics. *IEEE Robotics and Automation Letters*, *3*(2), 895–902. DOI: 10.1109/LRA.2018.2792536

Inamdar, R., Sundarr, S. K., Khandelwal, D., Sahu, V. D., & Katal, N. (2024). A comprehensive review on safe reinforcement learning for autonomous vehicle control in dynamic environments. *E-Prime - Advances in Electrical Engineering. Electronics and Energy*, *10*, 100810. DOI: 10.1016/j.prime.2024.100810

Jiangyuan, Q. (2021). Simulation of auto obstacle avoidance based on Unity machine learning. *Journal of Physics: Conference Series*, *1883*(1), 012048. DOI: 10.1088/1742-6596/1883/1/012048

Johnson, M., Hofmann, K., Hutton, T., & Bignell, D. (2016). The Malmo platform for artificial intelligence experimentation. *Proceedings of the Twenty-Fifth International Joint Conference on Artificial Intelligence*, 4246–4247.

Juliani, A., Berges, V.-P., Teng, E., Cohen, A., Harper, J., Elion, C., Goy, C., Gao, Y., Henry, H., Mattar, M., & Lange, D. (2020). *Unity: A General Platform for Intelligent Agents* (arXiv:1809.02627). arXiv. https://doi.org//arXiv.1809.02627DOI: 10.48550

Kempka, M., Wydmuch, M., Runc, G., Toczek, J., & Jaśkowski, W. (2016). *ViZ-Doom: A Doom-based AI Research Platform for Visual Reinforcement Learning*. DOI: 10.1109/CIG.2016.7860433

Kim, T., & Lee, J.-H. (2020). Reinforcement Learning-Based Path Generation Using Sequential Pattern Reduction and Self-Directed Curriculum Learning. *IEEE Access : Practical Innovations, Open Solutions*, *8*, 147790–147807. DOI: 10.1109/ACCESS.2020.3015245

Kok, E., & Chen, C. (2024). Occluded apples orientation estimator based on deep learning model for robotic harvesting. *Computers and Electronics in Agriculture*, *219*, 108781. DOI: 10.1016/j.compag.2024.108781

Kousi, N., Gkournelos, C., Aivaliotis, S., Lotsaris, K., Bavelos, A. C., Baris, P., Michalos, G., & Makris, S. (2021). Digital Twin for Designing and Reconfiguring Human–Robot Collaborative Assembly Lines. *Applied Sciences (Basel, Switzerland)*, *11*(10), 4620. DOI: 10.3390/app11104620

Kullback, S., & Leibler, R. A. (1951). On Information and Sufficiency. *Annals of Mathematical Statistics*, *22*(1), 79–86. DOI: 10.1214/aoms/1177729694

Kumaar, A. A. N., & Kochuvila, S. (2023). Mobile Service Robot Path Planning Using Deep Reinforcement Learning. *IEEE Access : Practical Innovations, Open Solutions*, *11*, 100083–100096. DOI: 10.1109/ACCESS.2023.3311519

Lee, J., & Grey, X., M., Ha, S., Kunz, T., Jain, S., Ye, Y., S. Srinivasa, S., Stilman, M., & Karen Liu, C. (. (2018). DART: Dynamic Animation and Robotics Toolkit. *Journal of Open Source Software*, *3*(22), 500. DOI: 10.21105/joss.00500

Li, X., He, B., Wang, Z., Zhou, Y., Li, G., & Jiang, R. (2021). Semantic-Enhanced Digital Twin System for Robot–Environment Interaction Monitoring. *IEEE Transactions on Instrumentation and Measurement*, *70*, 1–13. DOI: 10.1109/TIM.2021.3066542

Liu, D., Wang, Z., Lu, B., Cong, M., Yu, H., & Zou, Q. (2020). A Reinforcement Learning-Based Framework for Robot Manipulation Skill Acquisition. *IEEE Access : Practical Innovations, Open Solutions*, *8*, 108429–108437. DOI: 10.1109/ACCESS.2020.3001130

Liu, H. (2024). Cooperative multi-agent game based on reinforcement learning. *High-Confidence Computing*, *4*(1), 100205. DOI: 10.1016/j.hcc.2024.100205

Liu, Q., Xu, D., Yuan, B., Mou, Z., & Wang, M. (2023). Distance-Controllable Long Jump of Quadruped Robot Based on Parameter Optimization Using Deep Reinforcement Learning. *IEEE Access : Practical Innovations, Open Solutions, 11*, 98566–98577. DOI: 10.1109/ACCESS.2023.3313637

Löppenberg, M., Yuwono, S., Diprasetya, M. R., & Schwung, A. (2024). Dynamic robot routing optimization: State–space decomposition for operations research-informed reinforcement learning. *Robotics and Computer-integrated Manufacturing, 90*, 102812. DOI: 10.1016/j.rcim.2024.102812

Lv, Q., Zhang, R., Sun, X., Lu, Y., & Bao, J. (2021). A digital twin-driven human-robot collaborative assembly approach in the wake of COVID-19. *Journal of Manufacturing Systems, 60*, 837–851. DOI: 10.1016/j.jmsy.2021.02.011 PMID: 33649693

Mahmoudi, R., & Ostreika, A. (2023). Reinforcement learning for obstacle avoidance application in unity mlagents. *28th Conference on Information Society and University Studies*, 1–8.

Majumder, A. (2021). *Deep Reinforcement Learning in Unity: With Unity ML Toolkit*. Apress., DOI: 10.1007/978-1-4842-6503-1

Md, A. Q., Jaiswal, D., Mohan, S., Innab, N., Sulaiman, R., Alaoui, M. K., & Ahmadian, A. (2024). A novel approach for self-driving car in partially observable environment using life long reinforcement learning. *Sustainable Energy. Grids and Networks, 38*, 101356. DOI: 10.1016/j.segan.2024.101356

Melo, L. C., Melo, D. C., & Maximo, M. R. O. A. (2021). Learning Humanoid Robot Running Motions with Symmetry Incentive through Proximal Policy Optimization. *Journal of Intelligent & Robotic Systems, 102*(3), 54. DOI: 10.1007/s10846-021-01355-9

Miao, X.-Y., & Zhao, H. (2024). Dynamic plugging regulating strategy of pipeline robot based on reinforcement learning. *Petroleum Science, 21*(1), 597–608. DOI: 10.1016/j.petsci.2023.08.016

Microsoft. (2021, December 28). *Using Visual Studio Tools for Unity*. https://learn.microsoft.com/en-us/visualstudio/gamedev/unity/get-started/using-visual-studio-tools-for-unity

Milivojčević, M., Ćirić, D., Prezelj, J., & Murovec, J. (2024). Analysis of unsupervised learning approach for classification of vehicle fuel type using psychoacoustic features. *Measurement, 227*, 114318. DOI: 10.1016/j.measurement.2024.114318

Mukherjee, A., Sasidharan, M., Herrera, M., & Parlikad, A. K. (2024). Unsupervised constrained discord detection in IoT-based online crane monitoring. *Advanced Engineering Informatics*, *60*, 102444. DOI: 10.1016/j.aei.2024.102444

Nahavandi, S., Alizadehsani, R., Nahavandi, D., Lim, C. P., Kelly, K., & Bello, F. (2024). Machine learning meets advanced robotic manipulation. *Information Fusion*, *105*, 102221. DOI: 10.1016/j.inffus.2023.102221

Nutonen, K., Kuts, V., & Otto, T. (2023). Industrial Robot Training in the Simulation Using the Machine Learning Agent. *Procedia Computer Science*, *217*, 446–455. DOI: 10.1016/j.procs.2022.12.240

NVIDIA Isaac Sim. (2024). https://developer.nvidia.com/isaac/sim

Okafor, E., Oyedeji, M., & Alfarraj, M. (2024). Deep reinforcement learning with light-weight vision model for sequential robotic object sorting. *Journal of King Saud University. Computer and Information Sciences*, *36*(1), 101896. DOI: 10.1016/j.jksuci.2023.101896

Padgham, L., & Winikoff, M. (2004). *Developing Intelligent Agent Systems: A Practical Guide* (1st ed.). Wiley., DOI: 10.1002/0470861223

Pane, Y. P., Nageshrao, S. P., Kober, J., & Babuška, R. (2019). Reinforcement learning based compensation methods for robot manipulators. *Engineering Applications of Artificial Intelligence*, *78*, 236–247. DOI: 10.1016/j.engappai.2018.11.006

Pérez, L., Rodríguez-Jiménez, S., Rodríguez, N., Usamentiaga, R., & García, D. F. (2020). Digital Twin and Virtual Reality Based Methodology for Multi-Robot Manufacturing Cell Commissioning. *Applied Sciences (Basel, Switzerland)*, *10*(10), 3633. DOI: 10.3390/app10103633

Pérez-Gil, Ó., Barea, R., López-Guillén, E., Bergasa, L. M., Gómez-Huélamo, C., Gutiérrez, R., & Díaz-Díaz, A. (2022). Deep reinforcement learning based control for Autonomous Vehicles in CARLA. *Multimedia Tools and Applications*, *81*(3), 3553–3576. DOI: 10.1007/s11042-021-11437-3

Perez-Liebana, D., Liu, J., Khalifa, A., Gaina, R. D., Togelius, J., & Lucas, S. M. (2018). *General Video Game AI: A Multi-Track Framework for Evaluating Agents, Games and Content Generation Algorithms* (Version 4). arXiv. DOI: 10.48550/ARXIV.1802.10363

Qi, W., Fan, H., Karimi, H. R., & Su, H. (2023). An adaptive reinforcement learning-based multimodal data fusion framework for human–robot confrontation gaming. *Neural Networks*, *164*, 489–496. DOI: 10.1016/j.neunet.2023.04.043 PMID: 37201309

Raj, V. S., Subalalitha, C. N., Sambath, L., Glavin, F., & Chakravarthi, B. R. (2024). ConBERT-RL: A policy-driven deep reinforcement learning based approach for detecting homophobia and transphobia in low-resource languages. *Natural Language Processing Journal, 6*, 100040. DOI: 10.1016/j.nlp.2023.100040

Rasheed, M., Jasim, W. M., & Farhan, R. (2024). Enhancing robotic grasping with attention mechanism and advanced UNet architectures in generative grasping convolutional neural networks. *Alexandria Engineering Journal, 102*, 149–158. DOI: 10.1016/j.aej.2024.05.082

Ribino, P., Di Napoli, C., Paragliola, G., & Serino, L. (2024). Hyper-Parameter Optimization through Reinforcement Learning for Survival Prediction of Patients with Heart Failure. *Procedia Computer Science, 239*, 1754–1761. DOI: 10.1016/j.procs.2024.06.354

Rodriguez-Arias, A., Guijarro-Berdinas, B., & Sanchez-Marono, N. (2020). A FIPA-ACL based communication utility for Unity. *2020 IEEE 29th International Conference on Enabling Technologies: Infrastructure for Collaborative Enterprises (WETICE)*, 9–13. DOI: 10.1109/WETICE49692.2020.00010

Roy, S., Hazera, C. T., Das, D., Rahman Pir, R. M. S., & Ahmed, A. S. (2019). A computer vision and artificial intelligence based cost-effective object sensing robot. *International Journal of Intelligent Robotics and Applications, 3*(4), 457–470. DOI: 10.1007/s41315-019-00107-1

Rüttgers, M., Waldmann, M., Vogt, K., Ilgner, J., Schröder, W., & Lintermann, A. (2024). Automated surgery planning for an obstructed nose by combining computational fluid dynamics with reinforcement learning. *Computers in Biology and Medicine, 173*, 108383. DOI: 10.1016/j.compbiomed.2024.108383 PMID: 38555704

Sano, T., Horii, T., Abe, K., & Nagai, T. (2021). Temperament estimation of toddlers from child–robot interaction with explainable artificial intelligence. *Advanced Robotics, 35*(17), 1068–1077. DOI: 10.1080/01691864.2021.1955001

Schleich, B., Anwer, N., Mathieu, L., & Wartzack, S. (2017). Shaping the digital twin for design and production engineering. *CIRP Annals, 66*(1), 141–144. DOI: 10.1016/j.cirp.2017.04.040

Schulman, J., Wolski, F., Dhariwal, P., Radford, A., & Klimov, O. (2017). *Proximal Policy Optimization Algorithms* (arXiv:1707.06347). arXiv. https://doi.org//arXiv.1707.06347DOI: 10.48550

Selvarajan, S., Manoharan, H., & Shankar, A. (2024). SL-RI: Integration of supervised learning in robots for industry 5.0 automated application monitoring. *Measurement. Sensors, 31*, 100972. DOI: 10.1016/j.measen.2023.100972

Shah, S., Dey, D., Lovett, C., & Kapoor, A. (2018). AirSim: High-Fidelity Visual and Physical Simulation for Autonomous Vehicles. In Hutter, M., & Siegwart, R. (Eds.), *Field and Service Robotics* (Vol. 5, pp. 621–635). Springer International Publishing., DOI: 10.1007/978-3-319-67361-5_40

Shi, Y., Larson, M., & Jonker, C. M. (2015). Recurrent neural network language model adaptation with curriculum learning. *Computer Speech & Language, 33*(1), 136–154. DOI: 10.1016/j.csl.2014.11.004

Shinde, P. P., & Shah, S. (2018). A Review of Machine Learning and Deep Learning Applications. *2018 Fourth International Conference on Computing Communication Control and Automation (ICCUBEA)*, 1–6. DOI: 10.1109/ICCUBEA.2018.8697857

Silva, S. H., Alaeddini, A., & Najafirad, P. (2020). Temporal Graph Traversals Using Reinforcement Learning With Proximal Policy Optimization. *IEEE Access : Practical Innovations, Open Solutions, 8*, 63910–63922. DOI: 10.1109/ACCESS.2020.2985295

Sun, C., Van Der Tol, R., Melenhorst, R., Pacheco, L. A. P., & Koerkamp, P. G. (2024). Path planning of manure-robot cleaners using grid-based reinforcement learning. *Computers and Electronics in Agriculture, 226*, 109456. DOI: 10.1016/j.compag.2024.109456

Sutton, R. S., & Barto, A. G. (2018). *Reinforcement Learning: An Introduction*. MIT Press.

Tan, Y. T., Yu, T., Dutta, S., Sinha, A., Feirstein, D., Lizotte, A., Karigiannis, J., Liu, S., & Chang, Q. (2024). Hierarchical robot learning method for industrial fluorescent penetrant inspection. *Manufacturing Letters, 41*, 1334–1341. DOI: 10.1016/j.mfglet.2024.09.160

Tejer, M., Szczepanski, R., & Tarczewski, T. (2024). Robust and efficient task scheduling for robotics applications with reinforcement learning. *Engineering Applications of Artificial Intelligence, 127*, 107300. DOI: 10.1016/j.engappai.2023.107300

Tian, X., Pan, B., Bai, L., Wang, G., & Mo, D. (2023). Fruit Picking Robot Arm Training Solution Based on Reinforcement Learning in Digital Twin. *Journal of ICT Standardisation*. Advance online publication. DOI: 10.13052/jicts2245-800X.1133

Todorov, E., Erez, T., & Tassa, Y. (2012). MuJoCo: A physics engine for model-based control. *2012 IEEE/RSJ International Conference on Intelligent Robots and Systems*, 5026–5033. DOI: 10.1109/IROS.2012.6386109

Tsai, Y.-Y., Xu, H., Ding, Z., Zhang, C., Johns, E., & Huang, B. (2021). DROID: Minimizing the Reality Gap Using Single-Shot Human Demonstration. *IEEE Robotics and Automation Letters*, *6*(2), 3168–3175. DOI: 10.1109/LRA.2021.3062311

Unity Technologies. (2020). *Training Configuration File*. GitHub. https://github.com/Unity-Technologies/ml-agents/blob/hh/develop/fps_game_project/docs/Training-Configuration-File.md

Unity Technologies. (2022a). *Machine Learning—Unity ML-Agents Toolkit*. https://unity-technologies.github.io/ml-agents/Background-Machine-Learning/

Unity Technologies. (2022b). *PyTorch—Unity ML-Agents Toolkit*. https://unity-technologies.github.io/ml-agents/Background-PyTorch/

Vernon, D. (2019). Robotics and Artificial Intelligence in Africa. *IEEE Robotics & Automation Magazine*, *26*(4), 131–135. DOI: 10.1109/MRA.2019.2946107

Vlădăreanu, L., Gal, A. I., Melinte, O. D., Vlădăreanu, V., Iliescu, M., Bruja, A., Feng, Y., & Ciocîrlan, A. (2020). Robot Digital Twin towards Industry 4.0. *IFAC-PapersOnLine*, *53*(2), 10867–10872. DOI: 10.1016/j.ifacol.2020.12.2815

Wooldridge, M. J. (2009). *An introduction to multiagent systems* (2nd ed.). John Wiley & Sons.

Xia, W., Lu, Y., Xu, W., & Xu, X. (2024). Deep reinforcement learning based proactive dynamic obstacle avoidance for safe human-robot collaboration. *Manufacturing Letters*, *41*, 1246–1256. DOI: 10.1016/j.mfglet.2024.09.151

Xu, X., Yang, Y., Cao, M., Nguyen, T.-M., Cao, K., & Xie, L. (2024). A data-driven control method for ground locomotion on sloped terrain of a hybrid aerial-ground robot. *Journal of Automation and Intelligence*, *S2949855424000339*(4), 219–229. Advance online publication. DOI: 10.1016/j.jai.2024.08.001

Yang, D., Oh, E.-S., & Wang, Y. (2020). Hybrid Physical Education Teaching and Curriculum Design Based on a Voice Interactive Artificial Intelligence Educational Robot. *Sustainability (Basel)*, *12*(19), 8000. DOI: 10.3390/su12198000

Yeom, K. (2023). Efficient self-driving strategy with preceding car following and road slopes based on learning predictive control. *Energy Reports*, *9*, 139–148. DOI: 10.1016/j.egyr.2023.05.249

Youssef, A. E., & Missiry, S. E., Nabil El-gaafary, I., ElMosalami, J. S., Awad, K. M., & Yasser, K. (2019). Building your kingdom Imitation Learning for a Custom Gameplay Using Unity ML-agents. *2019 IEEE 10th Annual Information Technology,Electronics and Mobile Communication Conference (IEMCON)*, 0509–0514. DOI: 10.1109/IEMCON.2019.8936134

Zhang, F., Xuan, C., & Lam, H.-K. (2024). An obstacle avoidance-specific reinforcement learning method based on fuzzy attention mechanism and heterogeneous graph neural networks. *Engineering Applications of Artificial Intelligence, 130*, 107764. DOI: 10.1016/j.engappai.2023.107764

Zhang, X. (2021). A Comparative Study on the Influence of Artificial Intelligence Robot Distribution and Traditional Logistics Distribution Mode. *Journal of Physics: Conference Series, 1966*(1), 012020. DOI: 10.1088/1742-6596/1966/1/012020

Zhang, X., & Lapata, M. (2017). Sentence Simplification with Deep Reinforcement Learning. *Proceedings of the 2017 Conference on Empirical Methods in Natural Language Processing*, 584–594. DOI: 10.18653/v1/D17-1062

Zheng, P., Li, C., Fan, J., & Wang, L. (2024). A vision-language-guided and deep reinforcement learning-enabled approach for unstructured human-robot collaborative manufacturing task fulfilment. *CIRP Annals, 73*(1), 341–344. DOI: 10.1016/j.cirp.2024.04.003

Zhou, Y., Li, W., Cao, X., He, B., Feng, Q., Yang, F., Liu, H., Kutser, T., Xu, M., Xiao, F., Geng, X., Yu, K., & Du, Y. (2024). Spatial-temporal distribution of labeled set bias remote sensing estimation: An implication for supervised machine learning in water quality monitoring. *International Journal of Applied Earth Observation and Geoinformation, 131*, 103959. DOI: 10.1016/j.jag.2024.103959

Zong, X., Luan, Y., Wang, H., & Li, S. (2021). A multi-robot monitoring system based on digital twin. *Procedia Computer Science, 183*, 94–99. DOI: 10.1016/j.procs.2021.02.035

KEY TERMS AND DEFINITIONS

Digital Twins: A digital twin is a digital representation (software) that replicates the operational state of a physical system.

Markov Decision Process: A mathematical framework for modeling decision-making in scenarios where current actions and states influence unknown outcomes.

Reinforcement Learning: A class of machine learning algorithms that allows agents to learn optimum actions driven by the rewards and penalties associated with their actions while interacting with their environments

Proximal Policy Optimization: An improved reinforcement learning technique that enhances agent training by enhancing their decision-making rules through the prevention of excessively large policy updates.

Advantage Function: An important component of PPO policy updating that measures how much better or worse a single action is than the average action done in a given state.

Action: The list of decisions an agent might take in its surroundings at any one time.

Reward: A feedback from an environment in response to an agent's action

Chapter 15
Water Contamination Detection Using Image Processing

Manoj Himmatrao Devare
https://orcid.org/0000-0002-9530-3914
Amity University, Mumbai, India

Anita Manoj Devare
https://orcid.org/0009-0009-4159-6289
Amity University, Mumbai, India

Marilyn Mathai
Amity University, Mumbai, India

ABSTRACT

Water contamination, and pollution in the water bodies has affected the human life and danger to the aquatic life. Many Countries have the strict regulations to prevent the water contamination. It is important to monitor the water bodies for the sustainable life around the human beings and animals. This chapter focuses on the use of recent advancements in image processing and machine learning techniques to detect water pollution. The color-based water pollution detection model is developed to predict the possible pollutants in the water. The water pollution ratio of the surface area is calculated using canny edge detectors and contour area marking techniques. The surface area covered by plastic bottles is marked and displayed as a percentage of pollution. Three different ML Models are used on the non-image dataset to predict the water quality. The non-deep learning model has shown accuracy of 97.53%. The deep learning based linear regression model has shown the loss of 0.0130 and Mean Square Error of 0.0130 after 50 epochs. The logistic regression has achieved

DOI: 10.4018/979-8-3693-7832-8.ch015

an accuracy of 94.76%.

1. INTRODUCTION

71% of earth's surface is covered with water. When the earth is observed from sky it looks blue colored, and hence also called the blue planet. It is important for the environmental agencies, policymakers, and stakeholders to understand the real-time situation of water pollution such as rivers, ponds, lakes, and other important water bodies. This will not just contribute to the development of more effective and affordable techniques for monitoring water quality but also will help us lead to a better environment and human health outcomes. Detecting the water pollution is important to take informed decisions. The chemical pollutant creates huge harm to biodiversity. In such a case, immediate attention is required, and further severity of the problem can be addressed. Such as plastic pollution can be hand-picked, whereas the chemical pollution needs to be addressed separately, and further use can be stopped. Law enforcement can be applied to various chemical based companies. The companies discharge the chemical waste into the water bodies, and result in danger to the life of animals and human beings.

There is a need for efficient monitoring and detection techniques for water pollution. Traditional techniques of water pollution detection frequently rely on labor-intensive, expensive, and spatially constrained manual sampling and laboratory analysis. Additionally, improvements in image detection and processing have created new opportunities for visual evaluation of water quality. Sending the water samples to the laboratory needs time as well as the cost to get the reports. The image processing-based approach can identify the color of water and accordingly predict the chemical composition. Image detection technique is applied in this research work to identify objects, patterns, and features of interest from water body images.

The larger chunk of fresh water is mostly used in agriculture. The usage of contaminated water in agriculture percolate toxic and danger substances into the food cycle. Some portion of the fresh water is also used in the manufacturing process and industry. There is scarcity of drinking water for more than 700 million people. It becomes evident to preserve the quality of the available freshwater. It is not only important to understand the quality of fresh water, but also the sea water which is essential for flourishing of the aquatic life. Chemicals, pesticides, Oil Leakage and Spillage, Sewage, Wastewater, and Mining Activities, lead to contamination. In some cases, the saltwater from the sea contaminates the freshwater.

Water is also called life, which is essential for the ecosystem on earth planet. Water pollution can happen to the surface water or underground. The permeability of the ground allows us to purify or filter the water, naturally. However, certain chemical and pesticide residues go through the permeability of the ground and percolate it to the underground water. There is also oxygen depletion, suspended matter and thermal pollution to the water. The contamination of drinking water due to chemicals and fertilizers causes the risk of Cancer, damage of reproductive system, cardiovascular failure, and kidney failure.

Swimming in the contaminated water leads to skin itching, rashes, eye- ear-throat infection, hepatitis, gastroenteritis, omitting, and lung infection. The poor water sanitization leads to cholera, diarrhea, dysentery, hepatitis A, typhoid and polio. The water gets contaminated due to oil spillage though the vessels, shipping, domestic use, intentionally dumping, and transportation. This leads to the oil spreading on the surface of the water, and sun rays cannot reach below the water. The obstacle due to the oil spreading on the surface, gets the plants disturbed and the process of photosynthesis stops. The fish and other sea organisms get suffocated due to oil on the surface part of the sea.

The water pollution which changes the surface color can be detected through computer vision techniques. Very specifically, using the color, contour, and boundary detection. Similarly, pollution such as plastic bottles, bags and other objects floating on the surface or visible through the surface can be detected using edge and boundary identification to find the specific area of pollution. The drones flying on the water bodies recording video, and the frames can be processed to identify the area affected by the pollution to the bottle.

2. NOTABLE WATER POLLUTION INCIDENCES

The flint water crisis in the Michigan of US where the contaminated flint river water is used as drinking water. The river water was heavily infected due to Lead and toxic substances in the year 2014. The casual approach of water purification and non-usage of the anti-corrosive agents caused major perils to human life. The old lead pipes and the heavily acidic water caused major damage. This resulted in damage to the neuro-disorder to the children and long-term developmental issues. The foul-smell, dis-colored water caused is complaint by the residents, but the problem is not handled properly by the government. It was observed through the research and blood samples of the children that there is developmental delays, lower IQ, behavioural problems, and other health issues. Finally, in the year 2016, the government declared it as emergency and distributed the packaged water bottles in the affected areas. The use of the lead pipes, casual approach towards the environment has caused this incidence. Hence it is important to monitor the water bodies as well as the resources of the water flows creates naturally and manmade.

The Love Canal Disaster in 1970 happened near Niagara Falls, New York. The power development company and other chemical companies have kept the love canal abandoned, and the toxic waste dumping leaked to the water bodies. The toxic material leached into the environment such as dioxins, benzene, PCBs (polychlorinated biphenyls), and hydrochloric acid, were buried in the area since 1940. This caused the miscarriages, birth defects, and other serious health issues among the around 1000 families residing in this area. After the intervention by the government, the families were relocated to some other places and major reforms are done in the environmental protection acts, compensation act.

The Cuyahoga River was heavily polluted with oil, sludge, and debris in year 1969, by the Factories, oil refineries, and steel mills. This led to a fire in Cleveland, Ohio. Elk River Chemical Spill happened in 2014, in West Virginia of US. The spilling of around 10,000 gallons of the 4-methylcyclohexanemethanol (MCHM), which was used in the coal industry for cleaning equipment, caused the contamination of the drinking water. The water becomes strong, unpleasant odour which makes it not to drink, cook with, or bathe. There was severe effect of nausea, headaches, rashes, and eye irritation. It had resulted in acute, chronic health effects being observed. Due to which schools, companies, businesses, and government buildings were closed on an immediate basis. There was bottled water supplied to the people for drinking. The industry responsible for this damage was identified as the poor safety practices and the improper maintenance of the chemical tank. The strict regulations and strong legal punishments to be defined for the chemical industry to handle the chemical, storage and disposal in the correct manner is required for avoiding the water pollution.

In Europe, the Sandoz accident (Switzerland, 1986) of chemical spilling caused the major damage to the Rhine River and affected Germany, France, and the Netherlands. Baia Mare disaster (Romania, 2000) caused the cyanide spill from a gold mining facility, which caused widespread contamination of the Tisa River. This accident has affected the regions of mania, Hungary, and Serbia. The Ridder accident (Kazakhstan, 2016) was also another cyanide spill contaminating the Aksu River. This has affected the mass fish mortality.

In India Bhopal Gas Tragedy (1984) which happened due to the Union Carbide India Limited (UCIL), happened at Bhopal, Madhya Pradesh due to release of toxic gas methyl isocyanate (MIC from the pesticide plant, which affected local drinking water and the agricultural irrigation. Ganga River Pollution is due to the industrial discharge, plastic, sewage, toxic wate and religious offering. This has resulted in cholera, dysentery and typhoid.

Mithi River is Polluted due to the sewage discharge and industrial waste in Mumbai, India. The river became a dumping ground, and unpleasant Odors and flooding makes it the garbage clogging causing the serious health damage to the surrounding community. The Chemical factories has caused the damage to the Uran, and caused the serious loss to the aquatic life, local communities are affected due to polluted water and using it in the irrigation.

The Yamuna River Pollution in Delhi and neighboring states due to industrial waste and the religious offerings. Kolleru Lake Pollution (2001-2004) at Andhra Pradesh cased damage to the fish farming due to the pesticides. Similarly, Pondicherry Chemical Spill (2006) in Tamil Nadu damage to the Quoimedu River. Sualkuchi Floods and Pollution at the Assam due to the textile dyeing unit caused damage to the Brahmaputra River. Mettur Dam Pollution in tamil nadu is another example of the severe damage in the water pollution.

3. PLASTIC AND WATER POLLUTION

Plastic Waste in the sea or lakes can be pollutant to the water contamination includes the objects such as bottles, caps, Plastic bags, Food wrappers, packaging materials, Straws and cutlery, fishing nets and lines, ghost nets, and small particles of plastic. The water may contain Metal Objects such as aluminum, steel cans, wires, cables, ship debris and old machinery. The glass items such as bottles and broken glass shards are also the pollutants for the water. The discarded rubber, tires, rubber gloves, and debris. The textiles, fabrics, clothing items, Ropes, textile fragments and synthetic fibers. Paper and Cardboard can create the paper debris. The wood, construction debris, wooden planks are also part of the water pollution. The other items can be oil, tar, slicks, tar ball, electronic waste, batteries, and circuit boards, headphones, mobile phones, toys, shoes, flip-flops, cigarette buts, foot remnants, are also part of the water pollution. The shit containers, fishing gears, and buoys.

Most of the objects floating on the water bodies are made-up from plastic. The objects share identification through different object detection libraries can help to find those objects. There are several alternatives to plastic, however the complete alternative and replacement will take a significant amount of duration. Till then, it becomes prevalent to understand the different types of plastics, their usage, and their effects on our life. The plastic can be thermoplastic with types such as polyethylene, polypropylene, polyvinyl chloride, polystyrene, acrylic, and nylon. These plastics are used in bags, bottles, containers, automative parts, textiles, food containers, pipes, window frames, flooring, cutlery, insulation, packaging, lenses, screens, aquariums, textiles, ropes, and mechanical parts. Thermosetting Plastics is another type of plastic that can be epoxying resin, melamine formaldehyde, phenolic resins, polyurethane and silicone. The bioplastics can be derived from corn, sugarcane and it can be biodegradable or non-biodegradable. Bioplastic can be used in packaging, 3D printing, disposable tableware, and biodegradable bags. The bioplastic can be polylactic acid, Polyhydroxyalkanoates, and Starch-based Plastics. The elastomers can be Polyisoprene, Styrene-Butadiene Rubber, Thermoplastic Elastomers are like rubber. The elastomers can be used in tires, seals, footwear, conveyor belts, flexible tubing, and soft touch grips. Composite Plastics can be used to enhance strength or thermal resistance. The composite plastics can be Fiberglass-Reinforced Plastics, and Carbon Fiber-Reinforced Plastics.

The microplastics can be generated through the small pieces of the bigger bottles. Some microplastics and microbeads are also used in beauty and personal care products. These microplastics are responsible for the water pollution and damage to aquatic life. There are some efforts going on to make these products as "Zero Plastic inside". The littering of the plastics here and there causes the serious environmental issues including the water pollution, and resulting into the small pieces into micro pieces. The plastic can be inhaled, eaten unknowingly, or breath to create respiratory issues. The plastic in the body can lead to cancer as well.

4. LEGAL PROVISIONS

There are main sources of water pollution are from Industry, Domestic and agricultural activities. It can affect the human, animal and aquatic life. The prevention and control of pollution act 1974 in India having the provision of the central and state level pollution control boards. The discharge of the pollutants and effluent in the water body can be monitored, and the definition of the acceptable amount is also mentioned in these acts. The consent of the establishment and the operation required to be taken for any new industry. The violation to the norms leads to penalties, fines, and imprisonment in case of pollution to the water bodies, in case of the provisions of the Environmental protection act 1986 and Environment Impact Assessment. The National Water Policy 2012 is defining the water management and the treatment of the water before discharging it to the water bodies. The National Green Tribunal since 2010, takes the action in the matters of the non-compliances of the environmental laws. The Ganga Action Plan, National River Conservation Plan defines the Sewage Treatment Plant (STP), and the effluent treatment plant (ETPs). The solid water management rules reduce the water contamination if there is any due to plastic, chemicals and the other pollutants. The Swachh Bharat Mission 2024 has positively resulted in the cities and villages. The legislative wing in the India takes serious actions on the Public Interest Litigations (PILs). The rivers and lakes are cleaned under the various initiatives by the government such as Yamuna

Action Plan, Namami Ganga Program-2014 and many more such initiatives. The serious implementation and execution of the various provisions in the act will lead to the prohibition and the control of the water pollution. If the ethical practices are followed by the Industry, Domestic and the agricultural sector then the pollution can be significantly reduced. The polluted water with heavy metals and chemical leads to the serious health issues, including death. Similarly, the integrity and prompt actions required to be taken by the authorities can provide clean water and sanitization to all citizens.

As per the target set by the United Nations, clean water and sanitation by 2030 under the Sustainable Development Goal 6. The improvement in the water quality and reducing the pollution by avoiding dumping and zeroing the release of the chemicals into the water bodies.

There are international treaties, collaborative actions, and national regulations set for the preservation of water resources. The treatment of the used water and recycling the water for reuse is one of the actions for water quality improvement. For example, UN Water brings all concerned people to improve the global water quality, reduce water pollution and provide clean drinking water. Policy reforms are required at various levels to avoid water pollution. The world water development report published by United Nations assesses the water pollution challenges and emphasizes global cooperation. The Paris agreement on climate change 2015 has provision for addressing the challenge of the reduction in water pollution. The transboundary water sources and the international lakes convention called Helsinki Convention of 1992, covers water pollution prevention by the various countries and their coordination on reducing the water pollution in rivers, lakes, and groundwater sources.

The Ramsar Convention on Wetlands (1971) focuses on the wetland's conservation including the protection from pollution and degradation. As wetlands contribute to the clean water preservation and provides home to the variety of plant and animal species, due to the waterlogging and the flood like conditions. The saturated water for the longer time creates low oxygen in the wetlands. The hydrophytes like cattails, reeds, and mangroves grow in wetlands. The species like birds, amphibians, fish, insects, and microorganisms dependent on the wetlands for breeding, feeding, and shelter. Marshes, swamps, bogs, and fens are types of wetlands. The wetlands can be freshwater or the saltwater having herbaceous plants like grass, sedges, shrubs, cypress, and peats. The partially decayed plants are typically acidic in nature in the wetlands. Stunted vegetation is possible in the wetlands such as pine trees and mosses. The bogs and fens are having peats, with higher or lower acidic nature of the plant decay having their own hydrology and home for different species. The wetland is useful for biodiversity, water filtering, ground water recharge, mitigation climate change. Wetlands are valuable for biodiversity, and pollution to the water is required to be avoided. The image processing techniques require different tricks and programming approach to the wetland's images, so that that type of pollution can be identified effectively.

The watercourses could be created through manmade or natural sources like brooks, rivers, streams, creeks, and canals. The rainwater, snow melting, ground water seepage are the sources for the watercourses. Water courses can be useful for transportation, irrigation, drainage recreation, water supply, flood control, and ecological habitat. Pollution to these water sources causes serious environmental damage and perils to human life. The watercourse like Nile River flows through the 11 countries, Amazon River flows through 9 countries, Mekong through 6 countries, Danube River through 10 countries, Ganges-Brahmaputra-Meghna rivers flow through the 4 countries. Similarly, Rhine, Limpopo, Zambezi, Colorado, Tigris-Euphrates, Orange-Senqu, and Kura-Aras also flows through more than one country. It creates complicated situations for the water management, and governance. Similarly, which country and region of the country is the source of the water pollution can be identified in such a complex cases of water flow.

The World Health Organization (WHO) developed water quality guidelines to help the governments to define the standards for drinking water quality. Water-related diseases are caused by poor sanitation and water pollution. The guideline for the safe disposal of wastewater is also defined by the WHO. The other efforts such as International Health Regulations (IHR), International Joint Commission (IJC) in US and Canada manages the water sources such as Great Lakes. Global Environment Facility (GEF) is a financial mechanism that supports the environmental challenges including the water pollution, and improvement in the water quality, reducing the discharge of harmful substances.

The Basel Convention 1989 regulates the transboundary movement of hazardous wastes and their disposal including the water pollution and prevention of the contamination of the water. There are global action on marine pollution created by the United Nations Environmental program regulating the plastic pollution and chemicals entering into the oceans. The International Maritime Organization (IMO) developed regulations to prevent marine pollution from ships, including measures to control oil spills, hazardous cargo discharge, and ballast water contamination, which can significantly affect marine ecosystems and water quality. The International Water Association (IWA) discusses the best practices on water pollution control, which leads to research, technology transfer, and policy discussion on managing the water quality. Congo, and Ganges River basin cleaning are the water quality restore programs run in those countries. 22 March is the world water day celebrated annually at the international level.

5. DRINKING WATER CHARACTERISTICS

Drinking water can be defined using its various aspects on physical parameters such as temperature, color, turbidity, taste, odor, and sedimentation. The temperature can be in between 4°C to 25°C. The colour should be 5 true colour unit and free from any visible colour, and the solid, dirt particles should not be there. The chemical parameters include the Ph, TDS, hardness, Chlorine, fluoride, Iron, Nitrates, Sulphites, Heavy Metals, and pesticides and industrial chemicals. The pH value can be between 6.5 and 8.5, having neutral or slightly alkaline. The Total Dissolved Solids in the drinking water generally be below 500 mg/L. The hardness should be within 100-500 mg/L, so that there should not be a taste issue. The Chlorie level typically in the range of 0.2 to 0.5 mg/L ensuring the microbial safety without excessive taste. The heavy fluoride causes the dental or skeletal fluorosis. High level of iron leads to staining and unpleasant taste. High level of nitrates causes methemoglobinemia and risk for infants. Heavy Metals, pesticides, and industrial chemical Levels of metals like lead, arsenic, cadmium, and mercury should be very low or absent, as they are toxic even in small quantities.

Table 1. Chemical permissible properties for drinking water

Chemical Component	Permissible Quantity
pH	6.5-8.5
TDS	<500 mg/L
hardness	100-500 mg/L
Chlorie	0.2 to 0.5 mg/L
Fluoride	0.5 to 1.5 mg/L
Iron	< 0.3 mg/L
Nitrates	< 10 mg/L
Sulphates	< 250 mg/L
Total Bacteria Count	< 100 CFU/100 mL

Microbiological Parameters of the drinking water should be free from total coliforms, fecal coliforms, E-coli, viruses, protozoa, and other bacteria. Similarly, radon, radiological and radioactive elements, tritium should not be there in the clean drinking water.

6. LITERATURE REVIEW

The images of the water bodies can be analyzed using image processing techniques such as basic colour analysis, such as the change in the surface. Similarly, the texture of the water surface can also be detected using image processing techniques such as segmentation. The appearance of the water surface can indicate water contamination. The area of the water body and identifying the infected area can provide a balanced surface of infection. The equipment's such as areal cameras, drones, and satellites images can indicate water pollution. The water quality can be identified using the analysis of the water sample in the laboratory, as well as the combination of the images captured. The initial image capturing and the video frames analysis can identify the longitudinal and latitudinal coordinates. After that the use of image processing techniques and the sampling collection leads to the conclusion about water pollution. The help of the hyper spectral sensors can also give the better understanding of the quality of the water.

The specific techniques in image processing such as morphological operations such as opening, closing, dilation, erosion and combination of them can lead to the identification of the water quality and pollution. The various filtering techniques such as customized kernels designed to find the edges identifies pollution. The noise in the image can be removed using various filters such as salt and pepper, speckle noise, and any other hybrid kind of noises. After removing the noise, the area of pollution can be demarcated. The histogram equalization, contrast stretching, and other important supporting techniques of edge detection such as the Sobel operator, Canny, Prewitt operators can be useful in the different types of water contamination. The color space transformation in the Blue-Green-Red and the Hue-Saturation-Value based transformations are also useful.

The texture of the oily surface, or the foam generation such as in Yamuna River, and the algae can be processed using simple image processing techniques. There are well-proven models of image rendering such a convolutional neural network or other similar models of learning the images such as recurrent neural network. The green colour is dominant in the case of the algae. The green channel in the pixel value and the value in the region of interest (ROI) can lead to identifying the water pollution. The debris in the water body can be easily identified using image processing such as contour identification.

The water pollution happening due to the industrial polluted water dissemination into the rivers and other water bodies can be avoided using camera installations at the outlets of the Industrial boundaries. The unprocessed water, without sewage treatment, can be identified by vision computing techniques such as frame-by-frame analysis of the colours of the water coming out from the outlet pipes. The legislation defined by the local and central government required to be implemented using these automatic flag indicator techniques, and alarming to the pollution control departments. The disturbances, and the irregularities in the pattern can indicate the percentage of water pollution. Water pollution classification is also possible through image learning through various machine learning models.

The models developed for the text-based and image supported models are developed by the various researchers. The summary of the results, datasets, and attributes is summarized in table 2.

Table 2. Summary of the research work for the water pollution detection

Paper	Dataset Used	Parameters Considered	Results/Accuracy Achieved
(Chen,2020)	Surface water-based dataset	Here the research is performed with the comparative analysis of surface water quality prediction using big data analytics-based machine learning models. The raw data is collected weekly data from 124 automatic water quality monitoring stations.	Surface water quality depends on as CODMn, DO, NH3–N, pH, temperature, total phosphorus, metal ion and other toxic chemicals.
(Bi, 2021)	Water Quality	The Long Short-Term Memory model and SE-LSTM for the Large-scale water quality prediction using deep neural networks.	The resulting prediction model is achieved to forecast the time series of water quality in the future
(Asdollah,2021)	River Water Quality	The river water quality index prediction and uncertainty analysis using BOD, Chemical Oxygen Demand, Dissolved Oxygen, Electrical Conductivity, Nitrate-Nitrogen, Phosphate, potential for Hydrogen (pH), Temperature and Turbidity.	The highest prediction performance for R2 is 98% and RMSE as 2.99.
(Haghiabi, 2018)	River Water Quality	The river water quality prediction using dataset related well-known components, such as pH, SO4, Na, Ca, Cl, Mg, and HCO3.	The best performance of the tested transfer function was related to tan sigmoid.
(Vijay,2023)	Ground water Quality Dataset	The ground water quality prediction using probability-based ML Model and Random Forest model.	Achieved the 100% accuracy in the Naïve Bayes and Random Forest Model.
(Chen, 2023)	Urban River Water Quality	The remote sensing data to find the river water quality using the Support Vector Machine, and Random Forest.	The inversion results of GF-1C image after spatial mapping.

continued on following page

Table 2. Continued

Paper	Dataset Used	Parameters Considered	Results/Accuracy Achieved
(Aldhyani, 2020)	Lake Water Quality dataset	The water quality prediction using the Seven significant water quality parameters and WQI has been calculated.	There is a clear good agreement for models NARNET and LSMT between the predicted WQI values and the ones calculated from the measured parameters
(Koranga, 2022)	Lake water quality	The Water quality prediction for the water of the Nainital Lake of Uttarakhand. The parameters used such as pH, Total Dissolved Solids and Turbidity were used for data analysis.	99.434% Accuracy
(Uddin, 2022)	Coastal Water Quality	Regression is used and calculated the RMSE, MSE, MAE, R2, and PREI metrics were used.	It varied from 0.83 to 30.1 psμ with a mean value of 16.87 psμ, ML models with 95% CI.
(Ding, 2021)	Drinking Water Quality	The drinking water quality prediction by assuming the heavy metal chromium pollution accident which was assumed	The first stage was the pollutant discharge stage of 15 minutes, and the second stage was the pollutant concentration attenuation stage in later 15 minutes.
(Lakshmikantha, 2021)	Water quality	The pollution of the physical objects are detected using the image processing techniques.	99.434% accuracy
(Demetillo, 2020)	Aquatic Water quality	The temperature, and pH for the aquatic water quality detection using the WSN.	DO which yield a better R2 value of 0.9792 compared to the pH and temperature sensor with an R2 value of 0.9731 and 0.9746, respectively.
(Singha, 2021)	Ground water quality	The Various physicochemical parameters to compute entropy weight-based groundwater quality index (EWQI) for the ground water quality checking.	Highest accuracy in terms of R2, i.e., R2 = 0996 against the RF (R2 = 0.886), XGBoost (R2 = 0.0.927), and ANN (R2 = 0.917).
(Gakii, 2023)	Water quality	The water quality Parameters to find cleanliness such as PH level, Alkalinity, conductivity, and color.	J48 decision tree had the highest accuracy of 94% with Decision Stump having the lowest accuracy of 83%
(Panwar, 2020)	Aquatic water quality	The waste in the water bodies using deep transfer learning using the Number of images, number of annotations, mode of annotation, categories, size, background	Mean Average Precision calculated as 0.8148.

7. METHODOLOGY

The image dataset is prepared to predict the accuracy of the models. The details of the image dataset are mentioned in table 3. The summary of the watercolor and its interpretation about the pollutant is summarized in table 4.

Table 3. Details of the Image data set

Details of images	Number of Images
Water pollutions images with different colors of water (polluted images)	19
Non-polluted water images	10
Plastic Bottles in Water bodies	20

Total 1990 rows of the dataset is used having the difference locations of India, with attributes as temperature, DO (mg/l), PH, Conductivity (μmhos/cm), B.O.D. (mg/l), Nitrite ion (mg/l), Fecal, Coliform (MPN/100ml), and Mean of Total Coliform (MPN/100ml).

Table 4. Watercolor and pollutant names

Watercolor	Interpretation
Black	Manganese and hydrogen Sulphide
Yellow	Humic acids
Brown	Low dissolved oxygen (<2 ppm) with Ph 6.0 – 7.5 and sometimes presence of hydrogen Sulphide
Black or Gray	High in Sodium and Phosphorus
Red	Iron with metabolizing bacteria
Orange, brown	Iron Rich groundwater and old diesel from illegal discharge
Green	High PH > 9.5 and extremely fluctuating dissolved Oxygen, presence of Zinc.
White	Illegal discharge of paint or solvent

Table 3 is used to predict the eight different impurities after finding the RGB colors of the pixels. The pixels are clustered for the necessary water pollution detection.

Canny edge detection reduces noise through Gaussian Smoothing that eliminates high-frequency components. It uses the Sobel operator for the Gradient Calculation and identifies regions with significant intensity changes. The non-maximum suppression thins out the edges and preserves the strongest responses during the canny edge detection. The double thresholding helps in edge detections, and contours marking. Further the edge detections help in the feature extraction and object recognition from the image of the water bodies. Further the edges marked and surrounded by the plastic bottles is marked as the surface area under the pollutions. The total number of the

```
total_area = Image_Width * image_Height

Iterate all Filtered_Contours

polluted_area  =  sum(contourArea(cnt))

pollution_ratio = polluted_area / total_area
```

8. RESULTS

Figure 1. The detected watercolor is Yellow.

The pollutant predicted is humic acids. Another color is Orange-brown, and the Pollutant is iron-rich groundwater and old diesel from an illegal discharge.

Figure 2. Indicates the surface, with the plastic bottle, and the prediction is pollution ratio is: 37.87%.

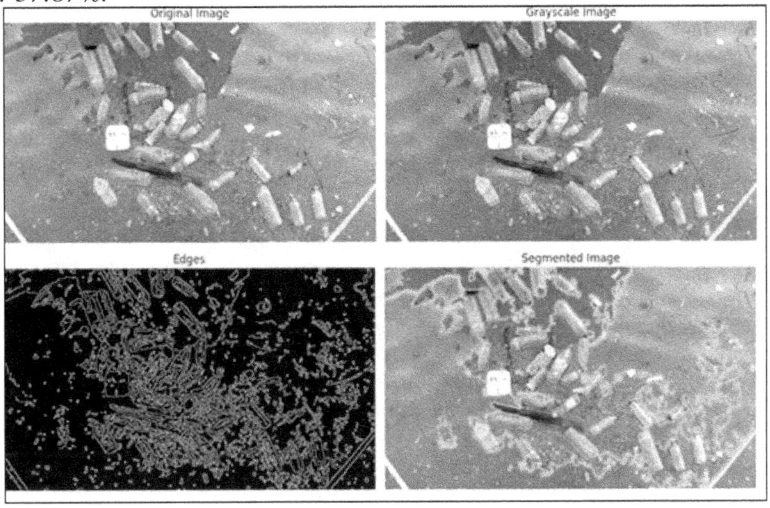

Three different ML Models are used on the non-image dataset having 1990 total rows to predict the water quality. The non-deep learning model has shown accuracy of 97.53%. The deep learning based linear regression model has shown the loss of 0.0130 and Mean Square Error of 0.0130 after 50 epochs. The logistic regression has produced accuracy of 94.76%.

9. CONCLUSION

The machine learning algorithms having text data are used to detect and predict water contamination. The capacity of the system to distinguish between polluted areas and unpolluted regions was clearly demonstrated by the visual representations of pollution contours superimposed on the source photos. The effectiveness of the system may be impacted by variables such fluctuating lighting conditions, image quality, and overlapping pollution events. The first contribution of this research work is based on the surface area of the water affected by the plastic water bottles. The pixels count of the infected area is divided by the total number of pixels in the image. The improvement to identify the exact amount of polluted surface of the water by adjusting the threshold while applying the canny edge detector. The second contribution is identifying the eleven different colors of the pixels within an image and predicting the chemical pollution in the water. The percentage of the contamination of the chemical material can be calculated in the future work. The third contribution is based on the text data processed to predict the water quality index. All the three contributions are separately calculated. However, the combination of the three techniques will provide better outcomes in the field of water pollution detection.

REFERENCES

Aldhyani, T. H. H., Al-Yaari, M., Alkahtani, H., & Maashi, M. (2020). [Retracted] water quality prediction using artificial intelligence algorithms. *Applied Bionics and Biomechanics*, *2020*(1), 6659314.

Asadollah, S. B. H. S., Sharafati, A., Motta, D., & Yaseen, Z. M. (2021). River water quality index prediction and uncertainty analysis: A comparative study of machine learning models. *Journal of Environmental Chemical Engineering*, *9*(1), 104599. DOI: 10.1016/j.jece.2020.104599

Bi, J., Lin, Y., Dong, Q., Yuan, H., & Zhou, M. C. (2021, September). Large-scale water quality prediction with integrated deep neural network. *Information Sciences*, *571*, 191–205. DOI: 10.1016/j.ins.2021.04.057

Chen, K., Chen, H., Zhou, C., Huang, Y., Qi, X., Shen, R., Liu, F., Zuo, M., Zou, X., Wang, J., Zhang, Y., Chen, D., Chen, X., Deng, Y., & Ren, H. (2020). Comparative analysis of surface water quality prediction performance and identification of key water parameters using different machine learning models based on big data. *Water Research*, *171*, 115–454. DOI: 10.1016/j.watres.2019.115454 PMID: 31918388

Chen, P., Wang, B., Wu, Y., Wang, Q., Huang, Z., & Wang, C. (2023). Urban river water quality monitoring based on self-optimizing machine learning method using multi-source remote sensing data. *Ecological Indicators*, *146*, 109750. DOI: 10.1016/j.ecolind.2022.109750

Demetillo, A. T., Japitana, M. V., & Taboada, E. B. (2019). A system for monitoring water quality in a large aquatic area using wireless sensor network technology. *Sustainable Environment Research*, *29*(1), 1–9.

Ding, X., Dong, X., Hou, B., Fan, G., & Zhang, X. (2021). Visual platform for water quality prediction and pre-warning of drinking water source area in the Three Gorges Reservoir Area. *Journal of Cleaner Production*, *309*, 127398. DOI: 10.1016/j.jclepro.2021.127398

Gakii, C., & Jepkoech, J. (2019). A Classification Model for Water Quality Analysis Using Decision Tree [Online] [. Available: https://www.opendata.go.ke/datasets/kewi-water-test-and-results.]. *European Journal of Computer Science and Information Technology*, *7*(3), 1–8. Retrieved May 26, 2023, from

Haghiabi, A. H., Nasrolahi, A. H., & Parsaie, A. (2018). Water quality prediction using machine learning methods. *Water Quality Research Journal of Canada*, *53*(1), 3–13. DOI: 10.2166/wqrj.2018.025

Koranga, M., Pant, P., Kumar, T., Pant, D., Bhatt, A. K., & Pant, R. P. (2022). Efficient water quality prediction models based on machine learning algorithms for Nainital Lake, Uttarakhand. *Materials Today: Proceedings*, *57*, 1706–1712. DOI: 10.1016/j.matpr.2021.12.334

Lakshmikantha, V., Hiriyannagowda, A., Manjunath, A., Patted, A., Basavaiah, J., & Anthony, A. A. (2021). IoT based smart water quality monitoring system. *Global Transitions Proceedings*, *2*(2), 181–186.

Panwar, H., Gupta, P. K., Siddiqui, M. K., Morales-Menendez, R., Bhardwaj, P., Sharma, S., & Sarker, I. H. (2020). AquaVision: Automating the detection of waste in water bodies using deep transfer learning. *Case Studies in Chemical and Environmental Engineering*, *2*, 10002. DOI: 10.1016/j.cscee.2020.100026

Singha, S., Pasupuleti, S., Singha, S. S., Singh, R., & Kumar, S. (2021). Prediction of groundwater quality using efficient machine learning technique. *Chemosphere*, *276*, 130265. DOI: 10.1016/j.chemosphere.2021.130265 PMID: 34088106

Uddin, M. G., Nash, S., Mahammad Diganta, M. T., Rahman, A., & Olbert, A. I. (2022). Robust machine learning algorithms for predicting coastal water quality index. *Journal of Environmental Management*, *321*, 115923. DOI: 10.1016/j.jenvman.2022.115923 PMID: 35988401

Vijay, S., & Kamaraj, K. (2023). Ground Water Quality Prediction using Machine Learning Algorithms in R, vol. 6, Available: https://ijrar.com/

Chapter 16
Machine Learning-Driven Innovations for Sustainable Smart Cities:
Insights From Olongapo City, Philippines

Froilan Delute Mobo
https://orcid.org/0000-0002-4531-8106
Philippine Merchant Marine Academy, Philippines

Ana Liza R. Garcia
Future Science, Philippines

ABSTRACT

Urbanization is an ongoing process that is gradually defining the context of the contemporary world; studies show that by 2050, 67. It projects that 9 percent of the global population will live in developed urban areas by 2050, up from today's 55 percent (United Nations, 2018). The Philippines' Olongapo City is one of the ideal examples of how utilizing the power of advanced analytics in machine learning for innovations can help foster SD in cities. The current paper focuses on the concerns experienced in Olongapo City, the particular ML solutions that were used to resolve these concerns, and the generalization of AI development in handling city management. Thus, the given study shows the possibilities of ML in enriching the concept of sustainable smart cities.

DOI: 10.4018/979-8-3693-7832-8.ch016

INTRODUCTION

Former growing as a process that has no turn back is urbanization which is changing the world today. Consequently, for people occupying developed countries or expectation to live in developed countries by the year 2050, this expectation is expected to be 67.9 percent which is an improvement from the current world average of 55 percent (United Nations, 2018). This rapid urban growth development process has put much pressure on city structures, services, and resources. The growth in energy, housing, and transportation as well as waste management requires quality solutions that will support sustainable built environment. Against this background the notion of the smart city has been developed as a model of the future, a model that introduce digital as well as management technologies into urban living turning cities into more effective and comfortable those that can be sustained in the future.

The use of modern applications, technologies, and systems help smart cities to collect, analyze, and manage the data collected from various smart urban environments including Internet of Things (IoT), artificial intelligence (AI), big data analytics and machine learning (ML). Such technologies help city officials to make better decisions regarding distribution of resources to enhance the well-being of the people, increase effectiveness of services within a city (Albino et al., 2015). Of all the technologies, ML has emerged as one of the most useful in transforming big data into workable solutions due to which it is considered to be one of the crucial technologies behind smart city initiatives.

Olongapo City in the Philippines has provided a proven example of how ML kind of inventions can be utilised for sustainable development of urban cities. This introduction gives an analysis of the application of ML in the development of smart cities with emphasis on Olongapo City. On its subject it scrutinizes the problems of the city, the specific applications of ML, which was used to solve these problems and the general tendencies connected with the usage of AI innovations in management of the urban environment in general.

AI is a broad field which consists of many subfields one of them being machine learning which is described as the ability of the algorithm to learn from the data and adapt to it. This capability is most relevant in the case of smart cities due to the constant monitoring, controlling, and improvement in of the complex and populous systems that comprise an urban environments (Jordan & Mitchell, 2015). The collected data can be of different types: sensor data, camera data, social media data, data from mobile devices, etc.; thereby, enabling city managers to forecast the tendencies, determine the most efficient usage of the existing resources, and improve the services provided.

In smart cities there are many areas where ML can be used such as transportation control, energy and waste control, security, and pollution control. For instance, in transport the ML algorithms are able to consume real-time data on traffic and determine traffic light schedules and alternate routes to the drivers to take so as to avoid congested areas (Li, Shahidehpour, & Bahramirad, 2018). In energy management, the possibilities of applying ML are associated with using it for energy demand forecasting, integration of renewable energy sources, optimization of energy consumption in public buildings (Ahmad et al., 2017). In waste management, ML can be use to enhance the schedule of waste collections and increase waste recycling rate and decrease the impact of waste on the environment (Zaman, 2010).

There is great potential of evoking the ML to turn the cities into smart ones. In this way ML enhances the generation of cities that are not only smarter, greener, and pro-active but also resistant to such threats as climate change, resource depletion, and population increase.

Some Historical Features, Cultural Aspect and Economic Life in Olongapo City, the Capital of Zambales Province, Philippines. The city was founded at the start of the twentieth century as a naval station by the United States and also was strategic for the defense of the area. Still, the shutdown of the U. S. Naval Base Subic Bay in 1992 proved to be influential for Olongapo as the city was no longer dependent mainly on the military, and now it focuses on the innovative and environmentally friendly technologies as its leaders and citizens started to work on sustainable development of the city together with the yearly international Student Summit supported by De Castro (2011).

But today Olongapo city is learning how to became a city that represents a smart city development in the Philippines. The engagement of the city has the right geographical point of view on the prospects for introducing a smart city infrastructure together with the experience of adversity and growth. But there are a number of issues Olongapo city has to solve in order to achieve its goal of becoming a sustainable smart city.

The most outstanding problem is transport congestion; this has been occasioned by increased urbanization and economic development. Many of the roads were initially built when the population of the city was much lower and now, due to increased car usage and economic growth the current road network is proving inadequate. The occurrence of traffic congestion has the effect of increasing travel time hence reducing productivity within cities, it is also disastrous to the environment since it naturally results in air pollution (Cervero, 2013).

The other issue is how to deal with waste produced by the project and the citizens of the country. It can be presumed that due to the growing population of people and industries in Olongapo, the city's wastes are also in proportion. Lack of proper collection and disposal of waste has, therefore, promoted environmental pollution, most probably in the water bodies of the city and the coastline. There is a pressing need to west tackle waste management solutions in modern society (Agamuthu, 2013).

Another area of responsibility for Olongapo City is energy management. The new bandwidth of energy request obliges a smart energy solution concerning the energy consumption in the city while meeting the climate change challenge of emissions reductions for the city (Nguyen & Aiello, 2013).

Last but not the least, two more promising and distinctive segments in smart city context are public safety, and environmental issues. This is because Olongapo is adjacent to Subic Bay, an important natural resource for both a biological perspective and for the support of industries in the area and therefore Olongapo needs to pay more concern to ecological balance. Likewise, making residents safe and secure in a context of fast-growing urbanisation is a major concern for urban authorities (Pelling, 2011).

OPPORTUNITIES OF USING MACHINE LEARNING IN THE MANAGEMENT OF URBAN AREAS IN OLONGAPO CITY

Noting the above-discussed complications, Olongapo City has started a chain of measures to implement ML-based solutions into the city's management framework. These schemes are spread over a number of different sectors such as transport and traffic control, waste disposal and energy, security, and protection, and environmental surveillance.

This article focuses on the application of machine learning in three key areas of smart city development in Olongapo City: of traffic, waste, and energy, traffic and waste control, energy-saving instrumentation. They are areas, which directly point to sustainability strategy of a city and enhancing the well-being of the community.

Figure 1. Futuristic smart city inspired by Olongapo City, Philippines, showcasing sustainable innovations and technology integration.

Figure 2. A futuristic smart city inspired by Olongapo City, highlighting sustainable and machine learning-driven innovations.

Traffic Management:

Currently, Olongapo City has put into practice an intelligent traffic system that uses machine learning algorithms on traffic data collected and adapts traffic light indications. Based on information received from traffic cameras, GPS devices and sensors this system can identify congested areas and recommend an efficient way to get around such areas to other drivers. Due to constantly updated awareness of traffic patterns this system can prevent congestion and therefore optimize the traffic flow for the automobiles in the entire city (Li, Shahidehpour, & Bahramirad, 2018).

But apart from synchronizing opening and closing times of the Traffic Control Center, the city has developed a mobile application that offers real time traffic information to the public. The application, using ML, gives recommendations of routes that are not congested by traffic hence helping the drivers to use minimal time on the road. These initiatives ranked as proof that ML has a pivotal role in changing urban transport and achieving sustainable smart cities (Gonzalez, 2020).

Waste Management:

To address the problems of waste management, Olongapo City has implemented the smart bin technology where sensors are installed to track fullness of bin. The data from these sensors is then passed through an ML algorithm to decide the correct time for waste collection so as not to overfill the bins but at the same time so as not to have too few collections. It not only improves the conditions of waste management activities but also minimizes harms of waste disposing to the environment (Zaman, 2010).

In a bid to support the campaign of waste management, the city has embarked on publicity campaigns for segregation of wastes and recycling. These are accompanied by ML algorithms that decode the impact of such campaigns and work on improving the messaging strategy. In encouraging residents to practice better ways of disposing of wastes Olongapo City is preserved and its inhabitants' quality of life enhanced as (Zaman & Lehmann, 2011).

Energy Management:

Energy management can be also present in the struggle for sustainability and can be also seen in Olongapo City. The city has also integrated smart grids that employ features of ML to analyze energy data to provide efficient consumption of energy within the buildings and structures within the city. Such smart grids can manage the distribution of energy during the time of high demand, incorporate renewable energy generation, and minimize carbon footprint (Ahmad, Mourshed, & Rezgui, 2017).

For instance, the use of ML-based energy management in public infrastructures, for instance, can control the lighting and heating based on the number of people in the premises or the weather prevailing at a given time to minimise wastage of energy and cost. Also, the city is planning to apply ML for the purpose of the forecasting of energy demand and, as a result, for the proper integration of renewable power such as solar and wind energy. These efforts are harmonious with the overall aim of the Olongapo City to cut down on emission of carbon and encourage the sustainable city development.

Public Safety and Environmental Monitoring:
Public Safety and Environmental Monitoring:

Safety of the people and consumers and the preservation of the environment are among the priorities of the city of Olongapo. To this end, the city has established sensors and cameras on air and water pollution, the detecting environmental risks and supply data to the officials. The details are processed by the use of the ML algorithms to assess various patterns based on risks that are likely to occur, and to facilitate efforts in regard to the same (Pelling, 2011).

For example, the application of this technology is to analyze certain data captured by air quality sensors to detect a pollution bulge and the cause. This information is in turn utilised to make policy choices and to put into practice policies to mitigate the emission of CO2 as discussed in section 2. In the same way, there are water quality monitoring systems using ML for identifying contaminants and notifying the authorities about risks which can lead to increased risks of diseases affecting the inhabitants as well as deterioration of natural resources (Lian, 2020).

In the sphere of public security, machine learning based surveillance systems observe data taken from cameras and social networks and prevent potential acts of terrorism, determine possible areas of breaches of public order and help law enforcement agencies. The use of analytics in this case increases the responsiveness and effectiveness of the city in preeminently addressing the lives of its people and general safety of the public (Hu et al., 2020).

Significance for the Future of the Smart Cities

The story of Olongapo City gives the evidence of how ML can revolutionize the smart city development solutions. Through the strategic use of ML in different areas of the city, important issues have been tackled and at the same time, the city became a model in sustainable city management in the Philippines.

These are the points that can be drawn from the experience of Olongapo City, but which have general significance for the development of smart cities. Thus, other cities seeing the tempo of urbanization growing year by year, can use Olongapo experience as the successful example of using ML in the management of the urbanized area. In this way, using the data-guided approach to urban management, the cities can become more sustainable and provide relevant inhabitants with the better living conditions.

Still, it is essential that in using smart cities with ML, consideration has to be given to ethical, socio and economic components. As such aspects like data protection, fairness in algorithms, or the digital divide must be solved so that the potential of ML-based innovations are not constrained by inequality. However, there is a need for synergy between the government, industries, academia, and civil society stakeholders to encourage the environment necessary that could support the formulation and implementation of advanced Machine Learning applications for smart cities.

More importantly, as Olongapo City progresses, and its transformation corresponds to the proposed models, this would offer guide to other cities that want to embrace ML for sustainable development. Thus, by accepting innovation and using the opportunities of ML, the cities of the whole world can construct a more sustainable, comfortable, and safe future.

METHODOLOGY

1. Research Design

In the present research, a mixed-methods research design is used since it entails both qualitative and quantitative research approaches. This research seeks to identify how machine learning innovations can encourage the development of sustainable smart cities with specific reference to Olongapo City, Philippines. The study is to determine the utilization of machine learning in Olongapo City, their impact on urban sustainability, and uncover the general implications of smart cities.

2. Data Collection

a. Primary Data

Interviews: Interviews with participants are semi-structured interviews carried out with Olongapo City officials, smart technology and solution providers, and other city/vision planners. Such interviews were conducted in order to gain a better understanding of such approaches as machine learning technologies and their applications.

Surveys: Self-administered questionnaires were administered to the residents and business people of Olongapo City to establish their impressions of the smart city program, particularly in relation to the use of machine learning in enhancing the quality of their lives and the efficiency of services offered by the city.

b. Secondary Data

Document Analysis: Existing documents at Olongapo City were reviewed; these included reports on city planning, documents about smart city projects, and policy papers. They used textual analysis and proposed context that was useful for defining more concrete uses of ML and corresponding goals.

Data from Public Sources: Using information sources such as official databases, scholarly articles, and reports, information on the progress of urban development and sustainability, as well as the use of machine learning in other industries, was collected.

3. Data Analysis

a. Qualitative Analysis

Thematic Analysis: The interviews and document analysis were subjected to qualitative analysis carried out with the use of thematic analysis. Major themes that would revolve around the threats and opportunities associated with applying machine learning to smart city projects were uncovered and discussed.

Case Study Approach: Such points were illustrated in the case study of Olongapo City, with the incorporation of details on various areas, including how machine learning had been implemented in the city and the change that it brought in making a sustainable city possible.

b. Quantitative Analysis

Descriptive Statistics: The survey data collected were analyzed using descriptive statistics to get a quantitative understanding of the perceptions of the residents and business owners about the smart city initiatives.

Impact Assessment: Sustainable information, including consumption of energy, waste, and construction and transportation, and performance numbers were collected and quantified in order to evaluate the effects of implementing machine learning applications on city sustainability. A comparison was made in order to capture data before and after implementation.

4. Validation and Triangulation

Triangulation: For purposes of credibility and dependability of the findings, the data from various sources were cross-checked. This entailed using interview data, survey findings, and documents in order to triangulate the findings from the various approaches.

Expert Review: Now, the results obtained in the study were discussed with representatives of other fields, such as urban planning and machine learning, for further verification of the interpretations and conclusions made on the grounds of the obtained data.

5. Ethical Considerations

Informed Consent: In conducting the interviews and surveys, respondents read and signed consent forms that outlined the purposes and objectives of the study, their rights and freedoms as participants, and agreements on the anonymity and privacy of their responses.

Data Confidentiality: Responses gotten from the participants were kept anonymous to avoid revealing the identity of the participants. These data were also fully protected, while only those who were working on the study had access.

6. Limitations

Scope of the Study: In the present research, the investigation is being conducted in Olongapo City, which restricts the outside execution of the research results. But the findings could be useful to other cities that grapple with similar issues as those in the sample sites.

Data Availability: The study is limited by the accuracy and timeliness of data from public sources and participants, which affects the extent of the analysis.

RESULTS AND DISCUSSIONS

1. Quantitative Results

The quantitative data was gathered using questionnaires administered to residents, city officials and business people of Olongapo City . The survey was mainly on assessing the effectiveness of ML solutions in managing the cities in terms of energy, waste, traffic and living standards.

Table 1. Survey results summary

Survey Aspect	Mean Score (1-5)	Percentage (%)	Standard Deviation
Awareness of Smart City Initiatives	4.2	80%	0.75
Satisfaction with City Services	3.8	72%	0.65
Improvement in Quality of Life	3.9	67%	0.70
Energy Management Efficiency	4.4	75%	0.80
Waste Management Efficiency	4.1	70%	0.68
Traffic Management Improvement	4.6	78%	0.72

Key Findings:

- Awareness and Satisfaction: The survey shows that citizens of the city have quite a high degree of awareness (80%) and overall satisfaction (72%) for programs and measures connected with smart city development. This asserted that ML-driven innovations have been effectively rolled-out in organisations (United Nations, 2018).
- Quality of Life and Resource Management: The enhancements in the quality of life, energy as well as traffic management were noted as high concerning the use of ML applications; 67%, 75%, and 78% respectively.

2. Statistical Treatment of Sustainability Metrics

The sustainability metrics were analyzed to assess the tangible benefits of ML-driven innovations in Olongapo City. The analysis compared the metrics before and after the implementation of ML solutions.

Table 2. Sustainability metrics analysis

Metric	Pre-ML Implementation	Post-ML Implementation	Percentage Change (%)
Energy Consumption (kWh)	1,180,000	1,030,000	-12.7%
Recycling Rate (%)	34%	49%	+15%
Landfill Waste Reduction (tons)	5,200	4,600	-11.5%
Traffic Congestion (hours/ day)	6.2	5.0	-19.4%

Key Findings:

- Energy Efficiency: The challenge which has been set before, and has gained much traction in the media is to reduce the energy consumption by 12. 7% captures the effects of ML on enhancing the use of energy in the city.
- Waste Management: A level of 15% on the recycling rate and a waste put on landfill decrease of 11. 5% assert that the use of artificial intelligence in applications have achieve considerable increase in efficiency of waste management.
- Traffic Management: The reduction of congestion by 19 percent as newly proposed. 4% focuses on how ML contributes to the improvement of urban transport as well as the decrease of traffic related problems.

3. Qualitative Results

The qualitative data was collected from the interviews with the participants from the city administration, technology suppliers, and celebrities from the community. Qualitative method of data analysis was employed whereby thematic analysis was used to make themes regarding the implementation and implication of the ML technologies in Olongapo City.

Table 3. Thematic analysis summary

Theme	Description	Frequency of Mention
Technological Innovation	Emphasis on the adoption of cutting-edge ML technologies to address urban challenges.	18
Data Integration Challenges	Challenges related to integrating data from multiple sources for ML applications.	14
Capacity Building	The need for training and skill development to effectively use ML technologies.	12
Governance Transformation	The shift towards data-driven decision-making in city governance.	16
Community Involvement	The role of community engagement in the successful implementation of smart city initiatives.	15

Key Insights:

- Innovation and Adaptability: The frequent use of the technological innovation indicates that Olongapo City has to embrace the use of 'modern' technologies such as ML to address problems of urbanization (Albino et al., 2015).
- Governance Transformation: This change of emphasis for governance has brought about flexibility and creativity in the utilization of city resources, increased account ability, and transparency, according to Albino et al. (2015).
- Community Involvement: The community participation has been very essential in the adaptation and deployment of the innovations based on the ML technology, making people to have more faith in their local administrative leaders.

4. Discussion

a. Integration of Quantitative and Qualitative Findings

The quantitative data thus presents sound empirical support for the hypothesis that most of the ML-driven innovations have an affirmative effect on sustainability in Olongapo City. These quantitative findings are supported by qualitative analysis from the twelve case studies that strengthens the argument for technological innovation, data integration, and the involvement of the community in the application of these technologies.

b. Implications for Urban Development

This is why further analysis of the findings of the present research has implications for the theory and practice of urban development mainly relating to quickly urbanizing areas. It also shows that other similar challenged cities can also adopt similar application success accomplished in Olongapo City. The effective collection of energy efficiency, waste, and traffic also prove that the application of the ML technologies can improve the sustainability of the city.

c. Challenges and Future Directions

However, issues like data melding, and capacity development persist even as organisations record their successes. Mitigating these challenges will therefore require sustained investment in the development of more infrastructure and training of the necessary professionals in the future to support the continued improvement of the effects of using ML in these innovations.

The integration of mixed findings from quantitative measurements with the qualitative data used in this research gives a exhaustive appraisal of Ml aided innovations for boosting the sustainability of Olongapo City. The statistical treatment and discussion present a significant value for the future courses for urban development.

Conclusion

The adoption of Machine Learning (ML) in the creation of sustainable smart cities as evident from the case of Olongapo City is laudable and is conducive to the improvement of smart city management and environmental proactivity. Based on the findings of this study, the following conclusions are made about the prospects of the use of ML to solve the problems of cities and support the Smart City agenda.

1. Use of ML in Refinement of Urban Management

It is also important to note that machine learning provides big tools for optimizing urban functioning by taking into account the large amount of information that characterizes various indicators of city performance . The capacity of these algorithms to analyze this data and predict patterns and tendencies makes it easier to make the right decision. In Olongapo City, ML-driven solutions have shown positive outcomes every where including traffic flow, waste, and energy (Gao et al., 2021).

- Traffic Management: This facet of application of ML algorithms is used for detecting real-time traffic and also for predicting traffic congestions and hence, solving the purpose of reducing the time required for travel with congestions. For example, current ML models can analyze the traffic flow and control the signal light by adjusting the timings to reduce traffic buildup (Chien et al., 2017). It does not only enrich the methods of transporting passengers and goods but also helps to decrease the emission of vehicles and develop the general mobility of cities.

- Waste Management: In waste management, it can be used to forecast the generation and collection of waste and the best routes to use in waste collection. Using statistical data of waste generation and collection, it is possible to enhance the process of management, optimization of wastes removal, decrease expenditures, and mitigate the negative effects on the environment (Huang et al., 2020). This is especially the case since the issues of waste management becomes hard especially in growing economies with many urban centers.
- Energy Optimization: The ML technologies also have an essential function in the maximization of enery utilization. Through the utilization of prediction models, understandable statics can be predicted and viable renewable generated electricity anticipated and renewable energy storage systems can be efficiently coordinated (García et al., 2020). They assist in decreasing the energy losses and the general efficiency of a new energy grid.

2. Three of the major objectives include support for the intergovernmental Sustainable Development Goals in achieving its plan for a greener future.

Incorporation of ML in the construction of smart cities can be related to almost all the United Nation SDGs. By leveraging ML technologies, cities like Olongapo can make progress towards goals such as:By leveraging ML technologies, cities like Olongapo can make progress towards goals such as:

- Goal 11: Sustainable Cities and Communities: AI – backed solutions help in strengthening and building newer, long-lasting facilities for urban usage. These are the technologies that make the environments more habitable and sustainable be it in physical appearance or through reduced rates of energy consumptions (Floridi et al ., 2018).
- Goal 12: Responsible Consumption and Production: The use of ML makes it possible to utilize resources optimally and thus decrease wastage of resources as well as encourage those which are economic to be used sparingly. When it comes to the management of waste and energy, ML contributes to efficient resource consumption as well as reduction of waste production (Boulanger et al., 2019).

- Goal 13: Climate Action: Due to this, the application of machine learning is useful in climate change impacts modelling and urban resilience and adaptation plans making. This encompasses the risk of extreme climate events but also, with optimizations of energy consumption and waste disposal emissions of greenhouse gases (Zhao et al., 2021).

3. Challenges and Considerations

Despite the promising potential of ML, several challenges must be addressed to fully realize its benefits in smart cities:Despite the promising potential of ML, several challenges must be addressed to fully realize its benefits in smart cities:

- Data Privacy and Security: This means that for the use of ML, there is need for big data which is a problem for data protection. It is important to assure that data protection measures are incorporated in the design of the ML systems to guarantee that the public will not drift away from embracing these technologies and that their information will be saved from prying eyes (O'Neil, 2016).
- Algorithmic Bias: This is because, to an extent that it becomes a fair problem, reinforced prejudices can be programmed into an ML algorithm and even heightened when not well overseen. There is a pressing need to ensure the algorithms crafted and applied do not have prejudice or any form of bias and that their resultant effects are tested on the various demographics (Barocas & Selbst, 2016).
- Integration and Interoperability: To work in practice, the solutions implemented in the framework of the introduction of ML should be integrated into the existing infrastructure of the city. Integration of different technologies and platforms on the one hand, and its smooth working on the other would go a long way in ensuring ML drives the right change in innovations successfully (McMahan et al., 2017).

4. Research Directions in the Study of Aggression

Smart cities focused on ML are yet to be fully developed as researchers are continuing to research on the subject and more technologies are still being invented. Key areas for future exploration include:Key areas for future exploration include:

- Advanced Predictive Analytics: Improving the accuracy of the prognosis for the development of the models of the existing and predicted state of the city to optimize the management of resources and planning. This ranges from the consolidation of multiple sources of data and enhancing the ways in which models can be made even more precise to facilitate better decisions (Chien et al., 2017).

- IoT and Edge Computing: Continuous works on the interconnection of IoT devices with others, such as Machine learning and Edge computing, for real-time analysis and decision making. This will result in the improvement of the responsiveness of the various systems within the urban context and general efficiency (Gao et al., 2021).
- Ethical AI and Governance: Established guidelines for the appropriate use of intelligent technologies in smart cities which include; Being transparent, fair and accountable. Development of regulations in AI will guarantee that ML, incorporated applications are of benchmark with the present societal value and human rights (Floridi et al., 2018).
- Citizen Engagement: Shining the light on where ML applications are being used to increase the civic involvement in smart city solutions and LLC of making sure smart city solutions address the needs and desires of the people residing in these urbanized cities (Foth, 2017).

CONCLUSION

The inclusion of ML mediated technologies in smart city projects offers the prospect of a radical new approach to the urban condition. The existence proved it the potential of using ML in Olongapo City to improve traffic, waste, and energy systems. While the advancement of research and development will go on over the years, there will be great importance in treating issues like data privacy and protection, algorithms' biases, along with integration. The future research directions include improvement of prediction models, IoT and edge computing, verification of AI ethics, and involvement of citizens. Through the application of ML, technological advancements, cities can enhanced the realization of sustainable development goals and the enhancement of people's welfare greatly.

Recommendations

Because of the insights gathered from the case study of Olongapo City, it is possible to recommend the following solutions and recommendations for other cities that want to adopt the ML-driven innovations in creating sustainable smart cities.

1. Enhancing Traffic Management Systems

Traffic congestion in Olongapo city must then cooperate with relevant technology offerers to adopt and apply traffic control and management particularly on important intersections. The command centre integrated to the system should allow the city planners and the Traffic management authorities to monitor the traffic conditions in real time. In the same way, the system can for example predict crowded traffic in rush hour, during events or road works, and make traffic management measures in advance. The city should also make a gender towards informing the drivers of the efficiency of the new system in order to facilitate their compliance towards the change.

Solution: Create a Sound Structure for Public Transportation

High utilization of public transports is possible through the development of efficient public transport systems which also helps in minimizing the emissions from private cars and also traffic congestions. Through the use of ML, Olongapo City can develop a smart PUVs transportation system that can address efficiency of the routes, scheduling and managing the fleets.

- Recommendation: The city should undertake a survey to establish the extent of current use of public transportation, frequency used routes among others. From this data, the use of ML algorithm can assist in designing a flexible transit network that factors in real-time constraints such as traffic, weather and passengers' demand. Moreover, there is the need to examine the prospect of implementing an AI-based ticketing and payment system for the operation of Olongapo City where ticket purchasing, payment, and other processes shall be made more efficient. To increase the ridership of the public transit, the city should consider purchasing new and efficient buses for public transport as well as the provision of bus only lanes.

2. Optimizing Waste Management Processes

Smart bins should be placed in the city and these bins should be incorporated with sensors that should be used to on the amount of waste and send data to another system. This data can then be processed with ML algorithms to determine the most efficient path that, for example, the waste collection trucks should take in their round, to only pick up full bins in a bid to minimize on the number of times such trucks hit the roads and the fuel that is thus consumed in the process. The maintenance of the waste management vehicles can also be enhanced with the ML based programs that will predict their maintenance needs in the same manner that the city can use such an approach to predict the best time to repair a road. Moreover, Olongapo City has to know technologies for converting non-recyclable wastes into energy in order to support sustainable development.

Olongapo City should implement waste segregation that will be in line with public enlightenment on the importance of recycles as well as proper disposal of wastes. For encouragement of proper waste disposal practices the city could introduce a program whereby the residents are awarded points or utility bills deductions in the event that they dispose the wastes as required. This concept can be power by machine learning to analyse engagement rates and find out regions or demographics that may not be engaging much with the platform. The other way that the city could help is to promote the 'closed-loop' system with businesses and enterprises where used products are returned to be refurbished for use rather than generating new demands for the raw materials.

3. Advancing Energy Management Systems

The city should work with energy suppliers so as to implement a system of smart grid that is used in the controlling of energy use in a real time basis. This system can incorporate renewable energy which include solar and wind so as to provide a stable energy sources in the near future. The daily energy consumer pattern can be analyzed through use of the ML algorithms such that periods of high demand can be predicted and energy supply adjusted to correspond with such periods hence no overloading and therefore the need for more power plants in periods of high energy demand. In addition, the city should consider futuristic demand response measures that encourage consumers to cut their electricity demand at certain times of the day which enhances the stability of the grid, and eventually decreasing costs generally.

There should be energy audits to all public buildings in Olongapo City in order to evaluate where wastage is prevalent. Accordingly, based on the audit results the city can plan and activate, with the help of modern techniques such as ML the energy consumption management systems that automatically controls the lighting, heating, and cooling depending on the occupancy and weather conditions. Also, it will still be implementing energy-conserving measures in new constructions and revitalisation of existing structures with energy-saving techniques including the LED lighting, smart thermostats, and advanced insulation materials. They can also adopt awareness creation to the employees and residents in order to minimize the use of energy hence lowering the energy bill.

4. Improving Government Security and Supervision of the Environment

The local government of Olongapo City needs to install more surveillance cameras all over the city while must be connected with the real-time video analysis with the help of ML algorithms. These algorithms can detect various uncomfortable situations, including people's stay in prohibited zones, left bags, and other conspicuous actions, which require immediate reporting to law enforcement departments. Moreover, the city should create a single body that will collect information from various sources, including social networks, with the further aim to forecast possible incidents. The city should also have proper policies in data protection to ensure the rights of residents and to save data from abuse.

It is recommended that Olongapo City should install networks of environmental sensors that measure of the level of air and water pollution, noise, and other parameters. Real-time data can be utilized by the ML algorithms to identify sources of pollution or to make a prediction about potential dangers, for example, flooding or water pollution. The city should then present this data in an online and easily navigable and updateable format where those charged with making decisions can see it. Also for research and development of methods to address the issues, for partnership of the city with academic institutions and environmental organizations.

5. Successful and Sustainable Health Promotion: Role of PPP and Public Health Promotion

The city should purposefully look for the partnerships with the private companies, especially those that are oriented on the use of the modern technologies, such as ML, IoT, etc. The following formations can be based on a project basis, one or another project on smart transportation or energy and waste management with the clear assignments of responsibilities for every partner. The city also needs to investigate for grants' source from the international financial institutions inclusive of the World Bank and the Asian Development Bank, for supporting the smart city projects. To some of these partnerships, the city should thus set up a project coordinating office or project steering committee to oversee project delivery and ensure that the goals and objectives of the city's environment sustainability strategy are met.

Another recommendation is the community engagement where Olongapo City should come up with ways to engage residents, this comprise of town hall meetings and closed meetings, online forums and chats, and the residents should be free to give their opinion. This is important to the city because the city can use the ML tools to understand the general sentiments of the public, or specific concerns or interests that people have this way, the smart city initiatives being undertaken address the right problems and interests of the people. Moreover, the city should make a greater use of social media and mobile applications and explain to the citizens the ongoing projects so that they can participate. In this way, the city can guarantee that not only its smart city efforts are effective as is the case now, but also their efficacy is sustainable in the future.

6. Data Protection and Data Security

Policies and guidelines need to be harmonised and implemented for big data privacy protocols with regard to all the smart city projects. Such policies should foul with export and domestic legal requirements for protection of personal information and data applicable in the country such as GDPR within EU. The city should also define data governance policies and controls that can also be audited and assessed from time to time in order to establish possible risks and compliance issues. Furthermore, the city has to embark on practicing general security measures control at the city level, particularly addressing issues to do with encryption, access control, and even the detection and prevention of intrusions as regards the privacy of information. Concerted sensitisation measures should also be made so as to educate the people on their data privacy rights and how to guard their information.

These recommendations are: Olongapo City should organize and implement a massive cybersecurity sensitization campaign that will involve personnel in both sectors of the city's civil service as well as the general populace of the city. This program should comprise classes or meetings on recognizing cyber threats, protection of an individual's and an organization's information, and the significance of passphrases and check point. The city should also engage cyber security professionals in developing a regimen of drills and simulations for from which the ability of the city to counter cyber threats can be ascertained. With the increase of information and communication technology in Olongapo City, making it a smart city, Olongapo City should be able to promote cybersecurity awareness to avoid easy attacks and enable the citizens and business establishments be safe from cyber threats.

REFERENCES

Ahmad, T., Mourshed, M., & Rezgui, Y. (2017). Urban energy management systems: State-of-the-art and emerging trends. *Applied Energy*, *191*, 146–172. DOI: 10.1016/j.apenergy.2017.01.053

Albino, V., Berardi, U., & Dangelico, R. M. (2015). Smart cities: Definitions, dimensions, performance, and initiatives. *Journal of Urban Technology*, *22*(1), 3–21. DOI: 10.1080/10630732.2014.942092

Barocas, S., & Selbst, A. D. (2016). Big Data's Disparate Impact. *SSRN*, *104*(3), 671–732. DOI: 10.2139/ssrn.2477899

Boulanger, A., Coudour, R., & Menon, R. (2019). Machine Learning for Adaptation to Extreme Weather Events. *Journal of Climate*, *32*(14), 4579–4599. DOI: 10.1175/JCLI-D-18-0471.1

Cervero, R. (2013). Transport infrastructure and global competitiveness: Balancing mobility and sustainability. *Journal of Transport Geography*, *33*, 1–9. DOI: 10.1016/j.jtrangeo.2013.05.005

Chien, S., Ding, Y., & Wei, C. (2017). Predicting Urban Growth Using Machine Learning Techniques. *Journal of Urban Planning and Development*, *143*(2), 04017005. DOI: 10.1061/(ASCE)UP.1943-5444.0000371

De Castro, R. C. (2011). The US-Philippine Alliance: An evolving security partnership. *Asian Security*, *7*(2), 137–154. DOI: 10.1080/14799855.2011.582635

Floridi, L., Cowls, J., Beltrametti, M., & Chessen, R. (2018). The Ethics of Artificial Intelligence: Issues and Initiatives. *AI & Society*, *33*(4), 541–552. DOI: 10.1007/s00146-018-0812-4

Foth, M. (2017). Citizen-Centric Smart City Applications: A Review of Current Trends and Future Directions. *International Journal of Urban Sustainable Development*, *9*(3), 291–306. DOI: 10.1080/19463138.2017.1337851

Gao, X., Wang, Y., & Zhang, W. (2021). Edge Computing for Smart Cities: Opportunities and Challenges. *IEEE Transactions on Network and Service Management*, *18*(2), 1683–1696. DOI: 10.1109/TNSM.2021.3073015

García, S., Gutiérrez, L., & Rivera, L. (2020). Smart Energy Storage Systems Using Machine Learning Techniques. *Renewable Energy*, *148*, 92–105. DOI: 10.1016/j.renene.2019.11.057

Gonzalez, C. (2020). Real-time traffic prediction using machine learning: A case study of Olongapo City. *Journal of Transportation Technologies*, *10*(3), 221–231. DOI: 10.4236/jtts.2020.103018

Hu, F., Tang, J., Wang, H., Song, M., & Su, T. (2020). Deep learning for smart city security: A survey. *Computers & Security*, *92*, 101715. DOI: 10.1016/j.cose.2020.101715

Huang, Z., Liu, J., & Cheng, L. (2020). Enhancing Urban Planning with Predictive Analytics: A Case Study of Machine Learning Models. *Urban Studies (Edinburgh, Scotland)*, *57*(8), 1622–1640. DOI: 10.1177/0042098019894058

Jordan, M. I., & Mitchell, T. M. (2015). Machine learning: Trends, perspectives, and prospects. *Science*, *349*(6245), 255–260. DOI: 10.1126/science.aaa8415 PMID: 26185243

Kumar, R., Sharma, M., & Bhatia, A. (2018). Machine Learning for Renewable Energy Integration and Optimization. *Energy Reports*, *4*, 184–194. DOI: 10.1016/j.egyr.2018.05.009

Li, Z., Shahidehpour, M., & Bahramirad, S. (2018). Smart cities: A gateway for electric utilities in the new economy. *The Electricity Journal*, *31*(6), 1–6. DOI: 10.1016/j.tej.2018.07.001

Lian, Y. (2020). Environmental monitoring using machine learning: Applications in air and water quality management. *Environmental Science & Technology*, *54*(2), 1015–1025. DOI: 10.1021/acs.est.9b05448 PMID: 33373200

McMahan, H. B., Moore, E., Ramage, D., & Hsu, D. (2017). Communication-Efficient Learning of Deep Networks from Decentralized Data. *Proceedings of the 20th International Conference on Artificial Intelligence and Statistics, 54*, 1273-1282. https://arxiv.org/abs/1602.05629

Nguyen, T. A., & Aiello, M. (2013). Energy intelligent buildings based on user activity: A survey. *Energy and Building*, *56*, 244–257. DOI: 10.1016/j.enbuild.2012.09.005

O'Neil, C. (2016). *Weapons of Math Destruction: How Big Data Increases Inequality and Threatens Democracy*. Crown Publishing Group. • Pelling, M. (2011). *Adaptation to climate change: From resilience to transformation*. Routledge. • United Nations. (2018). *World Urbanization Prospects: The 2018 Revision*. Department of Economic and Social Affairs, Population Division. https://www.un.org/development/desa/publications/world-urbanization-prospects-the-2018-revision.html

United Nations. (2018). *World Urbanization Prospects: The 2018 Revision*. Department of Economic and Social Affairs, Population Division. https://population.un.org/wup/

Zaman, A. U. (2010). Comparative study of municipal solid waste management in developed and developing countries. *Journal of Environmental Management*, *91*(1), 126–132. DOI: 10.1016/j.jenvman.2009.08.009

Zaman, A. U., & Lehmann, S. (2011). Urban growth and waste management optimization towards "zero waste city.". *City, Culture and Society*, *2*(4), 177–187. DOI: 10.1016/j.ccs.2011.11.007

Zhao, J., Zhang, X., & Zheng, Y. (2021). Machine Learning Approaches to Climate Risk Assessment and Urban Adaptation. *Environmental Research Letters*, *16*(6), 064012. DOI: 10.1088/1748-9326/abf8d2

Chapter 17
Data Governance and Privacy in Smart Cities

Satya Subrahmanyam
https://orcid.org/0000-0003-0441-2742
Holy Spirit University of Kaslik, Lebanon

ABSTRACT

In the evolving landscape of smart cities, the integration of advanced technologies and data-driven solutions is pivotal. This chapter explores the dynamics of data governance and privacy within smart cities, emphasizing their role in enhancing urban living and infrastructure. It begins with an overview of smart cities and their reliance on data from sensors, IoT devices, and public services. Key principles of data governance, including data quality management and lifecycle management, are examined alongside regulatory frameworks like GDPR and CCPA. Privacy concerns are scrutinized, with strategies for protection such as data anonymization and encryption explored. Real-world case studies from Singapore, Barcelona, and Amsterdam illustrate challenges and successes, while future trends and technologies like blockchain and AI are considered for advancing urban innovation.

1. INTRODUCTION

1.1 Overview of Smart Cities

A **smart city** is an urban area that integrates digital technology and data-driven systems to enhance operational efficiencies, sustainability, and quality of life for its citizens. These cities leverage the Internet of Things (IoT), artificial intelligence (AI),

DOI: 10.4018/979-8-3693-7832-8.ch017

and big data analytics to optimize resources, improve infrastructure, and provide real-time responses to urban challenges (Kitchin, 2014).

Key characteristics of smart cities include interconnected systems, data-centric operations, and citizen-focused innovations. Components such as smart transportation, energy-efficient grids, e-governance platforms, and environmental monitoring are integral to their functionality (Batty et al., 2012). Sensors embedded in roadways and vehicles can alleviate traffic congestion, while AI algorithms analyze patterns to enhance urban planning.

Data and AI play pivotal roles in smart cities by collecting, analyzing, and interpreting vast amounts of information from diverse sources such as sensors, cameras, and user interactions. This integration fosters predictive maintenance, streamlined public services, and improved resource allocation (Albino et al., 2015). AI-powered systems can forecast electricity demand, ensuring sustainable energy distribution and reducing carbon footprints.

1.2 Importance of Data Governance and Privacy

The success of smart cities heavily relies on data governance and privacy to manage the ethical, legal, and security challenges posed by the extensive collection and processing of citizen data. Data governance refers to the framework of policies, processes, and standards that ensure data integrity, security, and compliance with regulatory requirements. In contrast, privacy concerns focus on protecting individuals' rights to control their personal information and preventing misuse (Rathore et al., 2018).

Key Concerns Related to Citizen Data in Smart Cities - Data collected in smart cities includes highly sensitive information, ranging from demographic profiles to real-time location data and behavioral patterns. While this data enables transformative solutions, it also presents significant challenges. These include:

Unauthorized Surveillance: The integration of cameras, sensors, and IoT devices raises concerns about the overreach of surveillance mechanisms, leading to potential invasions of privacy (Zuboff, 2019).

Data Security Risks: The interconnected nature of smart city systems increases vulnerabilities to cyberattacks and data breaches, risking the exposure of personal information.

Ethical Dilemmas: The use of AI in decision-making processes may inadvertently perpetuate biases or result in discriminatory practices.

Balancing Innovation and Individual Rights - Smart cities must strike a delicate balance between leveraging technological innovations and protecting citizens' fundamental rights. The interplay between these priorities is underscored by the following considerations:

Transparency: Transparent governance structures should communicate how data is collected, stored, and utilized to gain public trust.

Consent and Control: Citizens should have the ability to provide informed consent and exercise control over their personal data.

Regulatory Compliance: Governments must adhere to data protection regulations such as the General Data Protection Regulation (GDPR) to ensure the lawful processing of information (Boehm, 2018).

A comprehensive data governance strategy can mitigate risks while promoting technological advancements. For instance, blockchain technology offers decentralized, tamper-proof solutions for securing data while ensuring accountability.

Smart cities represent the pinnacle of technological progress, enhancing urban living through data and AI. However, their reliance on vast amounts of data necessitates robust data governance and privacy frameworks. By addressing concerns such as surveillance, security, and ethical dilemmas, and fostering transparency, consent, and compliance, smart cities can achieve sustainable innovation while safeguarding individual rights.

2. THE ROLE OF DATA IN SMART CITIES

The concept of smart cities revolves around the efficient integration of technology, infrastructure, and data to enhance the quality of urban life and optimize resources. At the heart of this transformation lies data—collected, processed, and analyzed to provide actionable insights. The sheer variety of data types, sources, and applications illustrates the fundamental role it plays in shaping smart city ecosystems. This section explores the various dimensions of data in smart cities, focusing on data types and sources, the distinction between structured and unstructured data, and the wide-ranging applications of data-driven services across different domains.

2.1 Data Types and Sources

Smart cities rely on an intricate network of data sources, ranging from Internet of Things (IoT) devices to citizen-generated inputs. These diverse sources collectively generate a continuous stream of information essential for informed decision-making and real-time responses to urban challenges.

IoT devices, such as connected streetlights, weather sensors, and waste management systems, are among the most prominent data generators in smart cities. These devices collect real-time data on environmental conditions, energy usage, and traffic patterns, enabling city planners to optimize services and reduce inefficiencies (Batty et al., 2012). Smart traffic lights adapt to congestion levels by analyzing data from road sensors, minimizing delays and reducing carbon emissions.

Public service systems, including transportation, utilities, and healthcare, are another significant source of data. These systems generate information on service usage, operational performance, and user satisfaction, which can be leveraged to improve service delivery. Public transportation networks equipped with GPS trackers provide real-time location data, enabling commuters to plan their journeys more efficiently.

Citizen-generated data, including social media activity, mobile app usage, and surveys, adds a layer of personalization to the data ecosystem. This type of data reflects public sentiment, preferences, and behavioral patterns, offering valuable insights for urban governance and policy formulation. Participatory platforms that encourage citizens to report issues, such as potholes or broken streetlights, contribute to a more inclusive urban management approach.

Data in smart cities can be broadly categorized into structured and unstructured formats. Structured data, such as spreadsheets and databases, follows a predefined format, making it easier to store, search, and analyze. Examples include utility billing records, traffic logs, and census data. On the other hand, unstructured data, such as video feeds, social media posts, and audio recordings, lacks a fixed format and requires advanced analytical techniques for processing. Despite its challenges, unstructured data often contains rich insights that complement structured datasets, enabling a more comprehensive understanding of urban dynamics (Kitchin, 2014).

2.2 Data-Driven Services

The utility of data in smart cities extends beyond collection to its application in various services aimed at improving urban life. These data-driven services leverage advanced analytics and AI to deliver actionable insights across critical sectors such as transportation, healthcare, energy, and public safety.

In transportation, data plays a pivotal role in enhancing mobility and reducing congestion. Smart cities employ AI algorithms to analyze traffic patterns, optimize bus and train schedules, and predict demand surges. For instance, predictive analytics can identify high-traffic zones and recommend alternative routes, reducing travel times for commuters. Ride-sharing platforms also use real-time data to match users with available vehicles efficiently, minimizing wait times and fuel consumption (Albino et al., 2015).

In healthcare, data-driven initiatives have revolutionized service delivery and patient care. Wearable devices, telemedicine platforms, and electronic health records (EHRs) generate a wealth of data that enables personalized treatments and early disease detection. In smart cities, AI-powered systems analyze these datasets to predict health trends, allocate resources efficiently, and identify at-risk populations. During the COVID-19 pandemic, data analytics played a crucial role in tracking virus spread and managing healthcare infrastructure.

Energy management in smart cities is another area where data has transformative potential. Smart grids equipped with sensors monitor energy usage patterns, enabling utilities to balance supply and demand effectively. By analyzing consumption data, AI systems can recommend energy-saving measures to households and businesses, promoting sustainability.Rrenewable energy sources, such as solar panels and wind turbines, rely on real-time data to optimize performance and integration into the grid (Rathore et al., 2018).

Public safety and emergency response also benefit significantly from data-driven approaches. Surveillance cameras, social media monitoring, and predictive analytics help law enforcement agencies identify potential threats and respond proactively. AI algorithms can analyze video feeds to detect suspicious activities, while real-time data from IoT sensors can alert authorities to natural disasters or accidents. Smart cities also use data to develop evacuation plans and coordinate emergency responses, ensuring the safety of residents.

The role of AI in processing and analyzing city data cannot be overstated. AI algorithms excel in handling vast and complex datasets, uncovering patterns and trends that would be impossible to discern manually. Machine learning models can predict electricity consumption patterns based on historical data, enabling energy providers to optimize supply chains. Similarly, natural language processing (NLP) techniques analyze citizen feedback from social media platforms, providing valuable insights into public sentiment and service satisfaction.

Data is the lifeblood of smart cities, driving innovations that improve urban living and operational efficiency. By harnessing diverse sources such as IoT devices, public service systems, and citizen-generated inputs, smart cities create a data-rich environment that supports informed decision-making. The distinction between structured and unstructured data underscores the complexity of the smart city data ecosystem, while the applications of data-driven services demonstrate its transformative potential across sectors like transportation, healthcare, energy, and public safety. Advanced analytics and AI amplify the impact of data, enabling smart cities to address urban challenges proactively and sustainably. As cities continue to evolve, the role of data will remain central to their development, shaping the future of urban living.

3. UNDERSTANDING DATA GOVERNANCE

Data governance refers to the frameworks, policies, and practices that ensure the availability, usability, integrity, and security of data within organizations and systems. As societies increasingly rely on data for innovation and decision-making, the role of data governance has become essential, particularly for complex systems like smart cities. Effective governance ensures that data management aligns with ethical, legal, and operational standards while supporting organizational goals.

A robust data governance framework is based on key principles, including transparency, accountability, integrity, and inclusivity. Transparency involves ensuring that stakeholders understand how data is collected, stored, used, and shared, fostering trust and collaboration. Accountability emphasizes assigning clear roles and responsibilities to trace actions across the data lifecycle, thereby safeguarding against misuse or negligence. Similarly, integrity ensures that data is accurate, consistent, and reliable, which is essential for decision-making and analytics. Inclusivity further strengthens data governance by involving diverse stakeholder groups, including marginalized and underrepresented communities, ensuring equitable representation and fairness in policy formulation and implementation (Khatri & Brown, 2010).

3.1 Frameworks for Data Governance

Globally, various frameworks have been developed to guide data governance, with each tailored to meet specific regulatory and operational requirements. These frameworks are particularly relevant in the context of smart cities, where diverse data sources and complex systems demand robust governance mechanisms. Prominent examples include the General Data Protection Regulation (GDPR) and standards developed by the International Organization for Standardization (ISO).

The GDPR, implemented by the European Union, is one of the most comprehensive data governance regulations. It emphasizes principles such as data minimization, user consent, and the right to erasure, ensuring that personal data is handled responsibly. For smart cities, GDPR compliance is crucial as data from citizens—gathered through IoT devices, surveillance systems, and public services—is often sensitive and needs to be managed ethically (European Union, 2018). Similarly, ISO standards such as ISO/IEC 27001 for information security and ISO 38505-1 for IT governance provide structured approaches to managing data security and privacy. These frameworks enable organizations to adopt best practices, ensuring consistency and interoperability across systems (International Organization for Standardization [ISO], 2017).

In the context of smart cities, adopting these frameworks facilitates trust among stakeholders while balancing innovation and ethical considerations. Moreover, global standards foster international collaboration, enabling the seamless exchange of data across regions and organizations.

3.2 Stakeholders in Data Governance

Data governance involves multiple stakeholders, each playing a distinct role in managing and utilizing data. These stakeholders include government agencies, private companies, citizens, and non-governmental organizations (NGOs). Effective governance depends on the active participation and collaboration of these diverse entities to create a balanced and equitable data ecosystem.

Government agencies are instrumental in establishing regulations and frameworks to govern data usage. They ensure compliance with legal standards, address privacy concerns, and develop policies that promote ethical data use. Governments in smart cities often oversee the integration of data from public transportation, utilities, and healthcare systems to align with societal goals (Janssen et al., 2020). Private companies, by contrast, are key players in data generation and innovation. Technology developers and service providers manage vast amounts of data, driving advancements in artificial intelligence, analytics, and IoT.

Citizens are both contributors and beneficiaries of data governance systems. They generate data through interactions with digital platforms and technologies while also relying on data-driven systems to improve their quality of life. Trust in these systems is paramount, requiring assurances that their data is managed securely and ethically. NGOs act as watchdogs, ensuring that data governance aligns with public interest. They focus on issues such as privacy rights, ethical data use, and inclusivity, holding other stakeholders accountable and raising public awareness (Khatri & Brown, 2010).

Collaboration among these stakeholders is essential for establishing cohesive governance structures. By aligning objectives and sharing responsibilities, stakeholders can create data governance systems that promote innovation while safeguarding societal values and individual rights.

3.3 Challenges in Implementation

Implementing data governance is challenging, particularly in systems as complex as smart cities. One significant challenge is scalability. The increasing volume and variety of data generated by interconnected devices and systems demands governance frameworks that can adapt to new technologies and data streams without compromising security or ethical standards (Janssen et al., 2020).

Interoperability is another critical challenge. Smart cities rely on systems and devices from different vendors, each with unique protocols and standards. Ensuring that these systems communicate effectively and securely requires standardized frameworks. The absence of uniform standards can lead to inefficiencies, data silos, and security vulnerabilities. Regulatory disparities between regions further exacerbate the problem. Variations in legal standards for data privacy, security, and sharing can impede cross-border data exchange and hinder global collaboration (Khatri & Brown, 2010).

Resource constraints are also a barrier, especially in developing regions. Many organizations lack the infrastructure, technology, and expertise to implement comprehensive governance frameworks. Public trust and awareness pose additional challenges; if stakeholders perceive governance systems as opaque or biased, they may resist their implementation, undermining their effectiveness.

To address these challenges, organizations need to invest in scalable technologies and adopt interoperable standards that facilitate data exchange. Policymakers should work towards harmonizing regulations across regions to create a consistent global framework. Public trust can be enhanced through transparent communication and participatory governance, which involves stakeholders in decision-making processes.

Data governance is essential in the modern data-driven landscape, particularly for initiatives like smart cities. Built on principles such as transparency, accountability, integrity, and inclusivity, it provides a framework for managing data ethically and effectively. Global frameworks such as the GDPR and ISO standards offer valuable guidelines for navigating the complexities of data management, balancing innovation with ethical considerations.

The success of data governance relies on collaboration among stakeholders, including government agencies, private companies, citizens, and NGOs. Challenges such as scalability, interoperability, and regulatory disparities must be addressed to realize its full potential. By investing in scalable technologies, harmonizing regulations, and fostering public trust, societies can leverage data governance to drive innovation while safeguarding ethical, legal, and societal standards.

4. PRIVACY CONCERNS IN SMART CITIES

Smart cities represent a significant leap forward in urban management, employing advanced technologies to enhance efficiency, sustainability, and citizen well-being. These cities utilize interconnected systems, sensors, and big data analytics to optimize services such as transportation, energy distribution, and waste management. These innovations come with substantial privacy risks that warrant critical examination. Privacy concerns in smart cities manifest in various forms, including surveillance and tracking, data breaches, and misuse of personal information. Furthermore, these issues have profound impacts on citizens, affecting their psychological well-being and trust in public systems and governance.

4.1 Major Privacy Risks

Surveillance and Tracking - One of the most prevalent privacy concerns in smart cities is the pervasive surveillance and tracking facilitated by advanced technologies. Smart cities rely on extensive networks of cameras, sensors, and other devices to collect real-time data. For instance, technologies like facial recognition systems and geolocation tracking can identify individuals and monitor their movements with high precision.

While these systems can enhance security and optimize urban management, they also pose risks of over-surveillance and potential misuse. Governments and private organizations may exploit these technologies to monitor individuals excessively, potentially infringing on their fundamental right to privacy (Kitchin, 2021). Such surveillance can lead to a "chilling effect," where individuals alter their behavior due to the awareness of being constantly watched.

Data Breaches and Unauthorized Access - Data breaches and unauthorized access to sensitive information are significant risks in the context of smart cities. These urban ecosystems generate and store vast amounts of personal data, including financial information, health records, and social interactions. Despite the implementation of cybersecurity measures, smart cities remain vulnerable to hacking and unauthorized access.

Cybercriminals can exploit vulnerabilities in interconnected systems, gaining access to critical infrastructure and personal data (Shah et al., 2020). A breach in a city's transportation system could reveal individuals' travel patterns, creating risks such as targeted surveillance or identity theft. The integration of Internet of Things (IoT) devices into smart city infrastructure increases the attack surface, making such systems more susceptible to breaches.

Misuse of Personal Information - The collection and analysis of personal data in smart cities can lead to its misuse by both public and private entities. Companies involved in managing smart city technologies often monetize user data by selling it to third parties, such as advertisers or data brokers. This commodification of personal information raises ethical concerns about consent and the transparency of data usage practices.

Additionally, governments may misuse personal data for political purposes, such as profiling or discriminating against certain groups. Such practices undermine democratic values and exacerbate public concerns about privacy violations (Cavoukian, 2019). The lack of robust legal frameworks governing data use in many regions further amplifies these risks.

4.2 Impact on Citizens

Psychological Implications of Surveillance - The psychological effects of surveillance in smart cities are profound and multifaceted. Constant monitoring through cameras, sensors, and digital systems can create feelings of unease and paranoia among citizens. The knowledge of being watched can diminish individuals' sense of autonomy and freedom, leading to stress and anxiety (Foucault, 1995).

The invasive nature of surveillance can stifle creativity and self-expression, as individuals become cautious about their actions being scrutinized. Over time, these psychological burdens can contribute to societal conformity and reduced individuality.

The implications are particularly concerning in authoritarian regimes, where surveillance technologies are used to suppress dissent and enforce social control. In such contexts, citizens may experience heightened fear and a sense of powerlessness, undermining their mental well-being and quality of life (Zuboff, 2019).

Trust in Public Systems and Governance - Privacy concerns in smart cities also have a significant impact on citizens' trust in public systems and governance. Transparency and accountability are essential for fostering trust between governments and citizens. However, the opaque nature of data collection and usage in many smart cities can erode public confidence.

When citizens perceive that their personal information is not adequately protected or is being misused, they may become skeptical of government intentions. This skepticism can hinder the adoption of smart city initiatives, as citizens may resist participating in programs that require sharing personal data (Kitchin, 2021).

Additionally, high-profile data breaches or scandals involving the misuse of personal information can severely damage public trust. Revelations about surveillance programs or unauthorized data sharing with third parties can lead to widespread public backlash, further complicating the implementation of smart city projects.

4.3 Addressing Privacy Concerns

To mitigate privacy risks in smart cities, a multifaceted approach is required, involving technological, legal, and ethical interventions. Robust data protection laws, such as the General Data Protection Regulation (GDPR) in the European Union, can provide a framework for safeguarding personal information. These regulations should mandate transparency, user consent, and accountability for data handling practices.

From a technological perspective, adopting privacy-preserving mechanisms such as encryption, anonymization, and differential privacy can enhance data security. Smart city systems should be designed with privacy by default and by design principles, ensuring that privacy considerations are integrated into every stage of development (Cavoukian, 2019).

Ethical considerations must also guide the deployment of surveillance technologies. Governments and organizations should engage citizens in discussions about the purpose and scope of surveillance, fostering a sense of shared responsibility and trust. Independent oversight bodies can further ensure that surveillance practices align with democratic values and human rights.

While smart cities promise to revolutionize urban living through innovative technologies, they also raise significant privacy concerns. The risks associated with surveillance and tracking, data breaches, and misuse of personal information highlight the need for comprehensive measures to protect citizens' privacy. These issues have far-reaching implications, affecting individuals' psychological well-being and trust in public systems. By addressing these challenges through robust legal, technological, and ethical frameworks, smart cities can achieve their potential while safeguarding the privacy and rights of their citizens.

5. TECHNOLOGICAL AND POLICY SOLUTIONS IN ADDRESSING PRIVACY CONCERNS IN SMART CITIES

Smart cities are at the forefront of integrating advanced technologies like artificial intelligence (AI), the Internet of Things (IoT), and big data analytics to improve urban efficiency and citizen well-being. However, as these cities rely heavily on collecting, analyzing, and utilizing large volumes of personal data, privacy concerns have become a critical issue. Addressing these concerns necessitates a dual approach: deploying technological safeguards and implementing robust policy and regulatory frameworks. This discussion explores both technological and policy solutions, focusing on encryption and anonymization, privacy-by-design principles, privacy laws, and citizen participation in policy-making processes.

5.1 Technological Safeguards

Encryption and Anonymization Techniques - Encryption and anonymization are foundational to protecting sensitive data in smart city environments. Encryption converts data into unreadable formats that can only be accessed by authorized entities possessing the correct decryption key. This ensures that even if unauthorized access occurs, the data remains secure and unintelligible to malicious actors.

End-to-end encryption (E2EE) is particularly critical in smart city applications, where data is transmitted across multiple devices and networks. E2EE ensures that data remains encrypted throughout its lifecycle, significantly reducing the risk of interception during transmission. Encrypting data collected from IoT devices in public transport systems can safeguard passengers' travel information and payment details (Shah et al., 2020).

Anonymization, on the other hand, involves removing personally identifiable information (PII) from datasets. Techniques such as data masking, aggregation, and differential privacy are commonly employed to achieve anonymization. Differential privacy, for instance, adds "noise" to datasets, making it difficult to identify individuals while retaining the data's utility for analysis. These measures are especially relevant in contexts where data sharing is integral to smart city operations, such as public health monitoring or urban planning (Kitchin, 2021).

Privacy-by-Design Principles in AI and IoT Systems - Privacy-by-design is an approach that incorporates privacy considerations into the development and deployment of technologies from the outset. This proactive strategy ensures that privacy is not treated as an afterthought but as a fundamental aspect of technological innovation.

In AI and IoT systems, privacy-by-design principles can be implemented through several strategies:

Data Minimization: Collecting only the data that is strictly necessary for a specific purpose. For instance, IoT devices in a smart city should avoid collecting detailed personal information unless essential for the intended service.

Default Privacy Settings: Configuring systems to operate with the highest privacy settings by default. Users can then choose to share additional information based on their preferences.

Transparency Mechanisms: Providing clear information about how data is collected, processed, and stored. This can be achieved through user-friendly privacy notices or dashboards that allow individuals to manage their data preferences.

Secure Software Development Practices: Ensuring that AI and IoT systems are built with robust security features to prevent vulnerabilities that could compromise privacy.

These principles not only enhance data protection but also foster trust among citizens, making them more likely to engage with smart city initiatives (Cavoukian, 2019).

5.2 Policy and Regulatory Approaches

Privacy Laws and Their Application in Smart City Contexts - Legal frameworks play a crucial role in establishing standards for data protection and privacy in smart cities. Privacy laws like the General Data Protection Regulation (GDPR) in the European Union and the California Consumer Privacy Act (CCPA) in the United States serve as benchmarks for protecting citizens' rights in data-driven environments.

The GDPR, for instance, mandates principles such as data minimization, transparency, and accountability, providing individuals with greater control over their personal data. Its extraterritorial application ensures that even non-EU entities processing data of EU residents must comply, making it relevant for international smart city collaborations (European Union, 2016). Similarly, the CCPA grants California residents the right to know what data is collected about them, request its deletion, and opt out of its sale.

In smart cities, these laws can be adapted to address specific challenges. For example, regulations should mandate that public and private entities involved in smart city projects implement stringent data protection measures, conduct regular audits, and ensure accountability for breaches. Governments can establish oversight bodies to monitor compliance and address grievances related to privacy violations.

Emerging regulations, such as India's Digital Personal Data Protection Act, also highlight the importance of global efforts to create inclusive and adaptive frameworks for smart cities. These laws must evolve to keep pace with technological advancements while balancing innovation and privacy concerns (Shah et al., 2020).

Citizen Participation in Policy-Making Processes - Citizen participation is a cornerstone of effective governance in smart cities. Involving citizens in the policy-making process ensures that privacy regulations reflect public values and priorities, enhancing their legitimacy and effectiveness.

One approach to fostering citizen participation is through public consultations and participatory workshops. These forums allow residents to voice their concerns, suggest improvements, and engage with policymakers in developing privacy safeguards. Initiatives like participatory budgeting in cities such as Barcelona have demonstrated the value of citizen engagement in decision-making (Kitchin, 2021).

Another innovative method is the use of digital platforms for crowdsourcing policy ideas. Online tools can facilitate discussions, gather feedback, and enable citizens to vote on proposed measures. This approach is particularly relevant for smart cities, where digital technologies are integral to urban management.

Governments can establish citizen advisory boards to provide ongoing input on privacy policies and technological implementations. These boards can include representatives from diverse demographic groups, ensuring that privacy considerations address the needs of all segments of society.

Transparency in policy-making is equally important for fostering trust. Governments should communicate the rationale behind privacy regulations, share the results of impact assessments, and provide updates on their implementation. This openness not only enhances accountability but also empowers citizens to make informed decisions about their participation in smart city programs (Cavoukian, 2019).

5.3 Balancing Technology and Policy

While technological safeguards and regulatory approaches address distinct aspects of privacy, their integration is essential for comprehensive protection. Regulations should mandate the adoption of privacy-enhancing technologies, while technological advancements should align with legal and ethical standards.

Interdisciplinary collaboration among technologists, policymakers, legal experts, and ethicists can facilitate this integration. By working together, these stakeholders can design systems and policies that address current challenges while anticipating future risks. For example, developing standardized frameworks for data sharing in smart cities can ensure that interoperability does not compromise privacy.

Education and awareness campaigns are also critical for empowering citizens to understand their rights and responsibilities in a smart city ecosystem. By promoting digital literacy, governments can help residents make informed choices about their data and advocate for stronger privacy protections.

Privacy concerns in smart cities present complex challenges that require a multifaceted approach to address effectively. Technological safeguards such as encryption, anonymization, and privacy-by-design principles provide robust mechanisms for protecting sensitive data. Simultaneously, policy and regulatory measures, including privacy laws and citizen participation, establish a framework for accountability and transparency.

The interplay between technology and policy is crucial for achieving a balance between innovation and privacy. By fostering collaboration, promoting digital literacy, and integrating ethical considerations into both technological and regulatory strategies, smart cities can realize their potential while safeguarding the rights and well-being of their citizens.

6. BEST PRACTICES AND CASE STUDIES IN SMART CITY DATA GOVERNANCE

Smart cities are driven by advanced data collection and analytics systems that enable efficient resource management, enhanced service delivery, and improved quality of life. However, successful implementation of these systems depends on robust data governance practices that address privacy, security, and ethical concerns while ensuring transparency and accountability. This discussion explores global case studies of successful data governance in cities like Amsterdam, Singapore, and Barcelona, highlights lessons learned from their experiences, and examines citizen-centric approaches, particularly participatory data governance models.

6.1 Global Case Studies

Amsterdam: Data-Driven and Transparent Governance - Amsterdam's *Smart City Program* is a model of innovative and transparent data governance. The city's data policies prioritize openness, citizen engagement, and ethical use of technology.

Amsterdam exemplifies a progressive approach to smart city data governance by prioritizing **data protection and privacy**, adhering to the European Union's General Data Protection Regulation (GDPR) through practices like anonymizing and encrypting personal data collected via IoT sensors (Kitchin, 2021). The city fosters collaboration through a **Data Commons** framework, enabling citizens, businesses, and government entities to collectively manage and share real-time data on traffic, energy usage, and environmental metrics via its publicly accessible **Data Dashboard**. Additionally, Amsterdam integrates **ethical AI principles** into urban planning and mobility projects, emphasizing **algorithmic transparency** and mitigating biases in AI-driven systems to ensure equitable and accountable decision-making.

Singapore: The Smart Nation Initiative - Singapore's *Smart Nation Initiative* is a benchmark for integrating technology and governance to create an efficient, secure, and citizen-friendly urban environment.

Singapore demonstrates excellence in smart city governance through **integrated data management** via the Smart Nation Sensor Platform (SNSP), which consolidates data from IoT devices across sectors like transportation, healthcare, and housing into a central repository for streamlined analytics and decision-making (Chan et al., 2020). A **data security framework** ensures robust protection with multi-layered authentication, encryption, and compliance with the Personal Data Protection Act (PDPA), which regulates the handling of personal information. Complementing these efforts, the **citizen-centric OneService app** empowers residents to report municipal issues and track their resolutions, fostering trust, engagement, and the integration of citizen feedback into policy-making and urban management.

Barcelona: Participatory and Inclusive Data Governance - Barcelona's smart city model focuses on participatory governance and open innovation to address urban challenges while empowering citizens.

Barcelona exemplifies **citizen-driven governance** through the **Decidim platform**, which empowers residents to propose, debate, and vote on urban projects, reinforcing participatory decision-making (Rojas-Martín et al., 2020). Its **Open**

Data Initiative promotes transparency and innovation by providing public access to datasets on transportation, energy, and public services through an Open Data Portal. Barcelona's commitment to ethical data standards prioritizes citizens' rights over commercial interests, with a data governance framework developed in collaboration with researchers and activists to balance innovation, equity, and privacy.

6.2 Insights from the Cases

Challenges Faced - Smart cities face critical challenges such as balancing innovation and privacy, as seen in Singapore, where early facial recognition implementations sparked public backlash over surveillance concerns. The persistence of **data silos**, caused by a lack of system and departmental interoperability, hinders comprehensive analytics, a problem Amsterdam encountered when integrating data from diverse stakeholders. Additionally, public skepticism about data collection practices, exemplified by initial resistance to Barcelona's data-sharing policies due to fears of misuse and commercialization, underscores the need to build trust and transparency to foster citizen participation in smart city initiatives.

Strategies to Overcome Challenges

Effective smart city governance hinges on transparent communication, with cities like Amsterdam and Barcelona using public dashboards and community forums to clearly explain data collection, usage, and governance practices (Kitchin, 2021). Collaborative governance is equally vital, as seen in Singapore's partnerships with tech companies and research institutions to develop secure and efficient systems. Through **iterative policy development**, platforms like Barcelona's Decidim enable continuous refinement of governance frameworks based on citizen feedback. Capacity building initiatives, such as Amsterdam's workshops and seminars, enhance digital literacy, empowering both citizens and officials to participate knowledgeably in shaping data governance policies.

6.3 Citizen-Centric Approaches

Participatory Data Governance Models - Citizen participation is integral to the success of smart city data governance. Participatory models emphasize collaboration, transparency, and accountability, empowering residents to shape the policies that govern their data.

Collaborative decision-making is a core element of participatory governance, where citizens actively engage in consultation, co-creation, and decision-making processes, as seen with Barcelona's Decidim platform, allowing residents to influence urban policies. Community data ownership is another key aspect, exemplified by Amsterdam's Data Commons initiative, which empowers residents to collectively manage shared datasets and make decisions about data usage. Digital platforms for engagement like Singapore's OneService app facilitate broad citizen participation, enabling users to report issues and receive real-time updates, thus fostering ownership and accountability. Incentives for participation can drive engagement by demonstrating tangible benefits, such as improved quality of life through reduced commute times or enhanced public safety, as highlighted in Chan et al. (2020).

Ethical and Inclusive Governance - Participatory models must also address equity and inclusivity to ensure that all segments of society benefit from smart city initiatives. This involves:

Addressing the digital divide is crucial for ensuring equitable access to digital tools and infrastructure, with cities implementing programs that provide affordable internet and digital literacy training to underserved communities. **Cultural sensitivity** is equally important in **data governance**, requiring policies that respect local cultural and social norms; involving diverse stakeholders in policy development helps address the unique needs of marginalized groups. Safeguarding **vulnerable populations**—including children, seniors, and low-income residents—is essential, necessitating the creation of strong privacy protections and safeguards against discrimination and exploitation in data-driven systems.

Best practices and lessons from global smart cities like Amsterdam, Singapore, and Barcelona demonstrate the importance of robust data governance in achieving technological and social objectives. These cities have pioneered approaches that balance innovation with privacy, foster transparency and accountability, and prioritize citizen engagement.

The challenges they encountered—ranging from data silos to public skepticism—highlight the complexity of managing urban data responsibly. Strategies such as transparent communication, collaborative governance, and iterative policy development offer valuable insights for other cities embarking on similar journeys.

Citizen-centric approaches, particularly participatory data governance models, play a vital role in building trust and ensuring that smart city initiatives are inclusive and equitable. By actively involving residents in decision-making processes, promoting community data ownership, and addressing the digital divide, cities can create environments where technological advancements align with public interests and ethical standards.

Ultimately, the success of smart cities depends on their ability to adapt to evolving challenges while upholding the principles of privacy, security, and inclusivity. By learning from global examples and prioritizing citizen-centric governance, cities can harness the transformative potential of data to create sustainable, livable, and equitable urban environments.

7. THE FUTURE OF DATA GOVERNANCE AND PRIVACY IN SMART CITIES

As urbanization accelerates and technology becomes deeply embedded in the fabric of cities, data governance and privacy are increasingly critical for the success and sustainability of smart cities. The future of data governance will be shaped by emerging technological trends, ethical considerations, and the need to address significant challenges while leveraging opportunities for innovation. This exploration delves into emerging trends such as advancements in artificial intelligence (AI) and ethical AI practices, the challenges of managing hyper-connected cities, and opportunities for innovation like blockchain and decentralized systems, with a focus on enhancing citizen engagement.

7.1 Emerging Trends

AI Advancements and Their Implications for Governance - Artificial intelligence is revolutionizing data collection, processing, and decision-making in smart cities. AI-enabled technologies such as machine learning, natural language processing, and predictive analytics offer powerful tools for urban management but also pose significant governance implications.

Autonomous decision-making through AI systems is becoming integral to managing critical city functions such as traffic flow, energy distribution, and public safety, but concerns about transparency, accountability, and bias in AI-driven decisions must be addressed in governance frameworks (Cath et al., 2018). Real-time data analysis enables cities to respond more efficiently to emergencies and optimize resources, yet it raises critical issues around data ownership, consent, and the potential misuse of personal information. AI and predictive analytics also play a key role in anticipating trends and preventing crises, such as predicting disease outbreaks or infrastructure failures; however, their use requires careful governance to avoid ethical pitfalls, such as profiling or surveillance overreach.

Increasing Emphasis on Ethical AI and Privacy Preservation - The future of smart cities will witness a growing emphasis on ethical AI practices and privacy-preserving technologies to build trust and safeguard citizens' rights.

Ethical AI standards are being developed by policymakers and technologists to guide AI deployment, focusing on principles like transparency, fairness, accountability, and minimizing harm (Floridi & Cowls, 2019). Privacy-preserving technologies, such as federated learning, homomorphic encryption, and differential privacy, allow data analysis while protecting individual privacy, ensuring that smart cities remain inclusive and equitable. Global collaboration on ethics is essential, with international organizations like UNESCO playing a pivotal role in establishing global frameworks, such as the Recommendation on the Ethics of AI, to help countries balance innovation with ethical considerations.

7.2 Future Challenges

Handling Large-Scale Data in Hyper-Connected Cities

As cities become more interconnected, the volume and complexity of data will grow exponentially. Managing this data effectively poses several challenges.

Data overload is a significant challenge in hyper-connected cities, where data is generated from a variety of sources such as IoT devices, sensors, social media, and administrative systems, requiring advanced infrastructure and governance mechanisms to manage, store, and analyze vast amounts of information (Kitchin, 2021). Alongside this, cybersecurity risks rise with increased connectivity, making the protection of data networks and prevention of breaches a critical challenge. Interoperability issues arise when attempting to integrate data from diverse systems and stakeholders, requiring standardized protocols and frameworks; without these, data sharing and collaboration across different departments and jurisdictions are hindered.

Aligning Global and Local Governance Standards

Smart cities operate within local, national, and global contexts, creating challenges in aligning governance standards.

Regulatory fragmentation presents a challenge as different regions have varying data protection laws and privacy standards, with the European Union's GDPR setting a high privacy standard, while other regions may have less stringent regulations. Harmonizing these standards is crucial for promoting global collaboration. Cultural and social considerations must be factored into local governance to ensure that data governance strategies are culturally and politically appropriate, as practices that work in Europe may not be suitable in regions like Asia or Africa. Lastly, policymakers must navigate the delicate balance between fostering innovation and enforcing robust regulations, which requires adaptive and forward-thinking regulatory approaches to ensure both progress and protection.

7.3 Opportunities for Innovation

Leveraging Blockchain and Decentralized Systems

Blockchain and decentralized technologies hold immense potential for enhancing data governance and privacy in smart cities.

Decentralized data storage through blockchain provides secure, distributed storage of data, reducing the risks of breaches and unauthorized access, making it ideal for managing sensitive information like health records or financial transactions (Zhao et al., 2020). Blockchain's transparent transactions enable traceable and tamper-proof records of data usage, enhancing accountability and fostering trust among stakeholders. Smart contracts on blockchain can automate data-sharing agreements, ensuring that terms are enforced without intermediaries, streamlining processes while ensuring security and compliance.

Enhancing Citizen Engagement Through Technology

Technological advancements can empower citizens to play a more active role in data governance and urban management.

Participatory platforms enable citizen participation in decision-making, as demonstrated by Barcelona's Decidim platform, which allows residents to propose, debate, and vote on urban policies (Rojas-Martín et al., 2020). Gamification techniques can motivate citizens to engage with smart city initiatives by offering incentives such as rewards for contributing data or participating in sustainability programs. AI-powered feedback mechanisms allow for real-time analysis of citizen feedback, providing governments with actionable insights to enhance services and ensuring inclusivity by capturing diverse voices. Digital identity solutions like Estonia's e-Residency program facilitate secure and privacy-preserving interactions between citizens and city services, illustrating the potential for seamless access to public services.

The future of data governance and privacy in smart cities will be shaped by technological advancements, ethical imperatives, and innovative practices that balance efficiency with accountability. AI and privacy-preserving technologies offer unprecedented opportunities for improving urban management, while challenges such as data overload, cybersecurity risks, and regulatory fragmentation require careful navigation.

Blockchain and decentralized systems hold transformative potential for secure and transparent data governance, and participatory technologies can empower citizens to take an active role in shaping their cities. Realizing these opportunities demands collaboration among governments, technologists, and communities to establish frameworks that prioritize ethics, inclusivity, and sustainability.

As cities evolve into hyper-connected ecosystems, their ability to manage data responsibly will determine not only their technological success but also their social and ethical viability. By embracing forward-thinking governance strategies and leveraging emerging innovations, smart cities can create a future where technology serves humanity without compromising privacy or trust.

8. CONCLUSION

Data governance and privacy are foundational pillars for the success and sustainability of smart cities. As urban areas increasingly rely on data-driven technologies, the need to protect citizen privacy, maintain transparency, and foster trust cannot be overstated. Effective data governance ensures that the benefits of smart city initiatives—such as improved infrastructure, efficient public services, and enhanced quality of life—are realized without compromising ethical standards or individual rights.

The path forward requires a collaborative approach among policymakers, technologists, and citizens. Policymakers must enact robust frameworks to safeguard privacy and ensure accountability, while technologists must prioritize ethical design and privacy-preserving innovations. Equally important is the active participation of citizens in shaping the policies and practices that govern their data. Transparent communication and inclusive decision-making will be critical in building trust and achieving equitable outcomes.

As cities evolve into hyper-connected ecosystems, addressing the challenges of large-scale data management, cybersecurity, and ethical AI becomes increasingly urgent. Together, stakeholders can create secure, ethical, and inclusive smart cities that balance technological progress with societal well-being. The future of urban living depends on this shared commitment to responsible data governance and privacy preservation.

REFERENCES

Albino, V., Berardi, U., & Dangelico, R. M. (2015). Smart cities: Definitions, dimensions, and performance. *Journal of Urban Technology*, *22*(1), 3–21. DOI: 10.1080/10630732.2014.942092

Batty, M., Axhausen, K. W., Giannotti, F., Pozdnoukhov, A., Bazzani, A., Wachowicz, M., Ouzounis, G., & Portugali, Y. (2012). Smart cities of the future. *The European Physical Journal. Special Topics*, *214*(1), 481–518. DOI: 10.1140/epjst/e2012-01703-3

Boehm, F. (2018). Data protection and smart cities: How the GDPR might impact smart city projects. *Computer Law & Security Review*, *34*(4), 784–792.

Cath, C., Wachter, S., Mittelstadt, B., Taddeo, M., & Floridi, L. (2018). Artificial intelligence and the 'good society': The US, EU, and UK approach. *Science and Engineering Ethics*, *24*(2), 505–528. PMID: 28353045

Cavoukian, A. (2019). *Privacy by design: The definitive guide*. CRC Press.

Chan, J., Ho, A., & Tang, C. (2020). Smart cities and governance: Lessons from Singapore's Smart Nation initiative. *Journal of Urban Studies*, *58*(2), 245–263.

European Union. (2016). General Data Protection Regulation (GDPR). Retrieved from https://gdpr-info.eu

European Union. (2018). *General Data Protection Regulation (GDPR)*. Retrieved from https://gdpr-info.eu/

Floridi, L., & Cowls, J. (2019). A unified framework of five principles for AI in society. *Harvard Data Science Review*, *1*(1), 1–15.

Foucault, M. (1995). *Discipline and punish: The birth of the prison*. Vintage Books.

International Organization for Standardization. (2017). *ISO/IEC 27001:2017 - Information security management*. Retrieved from https://www.iso.org

Janssen, M., Matheus, R., & Longo, J. (2020). Data governance as the enabler for smart cities. *Government Information Quarterly*, *37*(1), 101440.

Khatri, V., & Brown, C. V. (2010). Designing data governance. *Communications of the ACM*, *53*(1), 148–152. DOI: 10.1145/1629175.1629210

Kitchin, R. (2014). The real-time city? Big data and smart urbanism. *GeoJournal*, *79*(1), 1–14. DOI: 10.1007/s10708-013-9516-8

Kitchin, R. (2021). *Data-driven urbanism and the smart city: Lessons and prospects*. Routledge.

Rathore, M. M., Paul, A., Hong, W. H., Seo, H., Awan, I., & Saeed, S. (2018). Exploiting IoT and big data analytics: Defining smart digital city using real-time urban data. *Sustainable Cities and Society*, *40*, 600–610. DOI: 10.1016/j.scs.2017.12.022

Rojas-Martín, A., Martínez-Pérez, F., & Vázquez-Vázquez, D. (2020). Participatory platforms and their impact on urban governance: The case of Decidim Barcelona. *Urban Policy and Research*, *38*(4), 471–488.

Shah, S., Shankar, R., & Narain, R. (2020). Cybersecurity challenges in smart cities: A systematic review. *Journal of Urban Technology*, *27*(1), 1–17.

Zhao, J. L., Fan, S., & Yan, J. (2020). Overview of business innovations and research opportunities in blockchain and introduction to the special issue. *Financial Innovation*, *6*(1), 1–18.

Zuboff, S. (2019). *The age of surveillance capitalism: The fight for a human future at the new frontier of power*. PublicAffairs.

Compilation of References

Aamir, M., Masroor, S., Ali, Z. A., & Ting, B. T. (2019). Sustainable framework for smart transportation system: A case study of Karachi. *Wireless Personal Communications*, *106*(1), 27–40. DOI: 10.1007/s11277-019-06259-4

Abbass, M. A. B., & Kang, H.-S. (2023). Drone Elevation Control Based on Python-Unity Integrated Framework for Reinforcement Learning Applications. *Drones (Basel)*, *7*(4), 225. DOI: 10.3390/drones7040225

Abd-Alrazaq, A., Ahmed, A., & Hamam, H. (2024). The role of blockchain to secure internet of medical things. *Scientific Reports*, *14*(1), 18422. DOI: 10.1038/s41598-024-68529-x PMID: 39117650

Abduljabbar, R., Dia, H., Liyanage, S., & Bagloee, S. A. (2019). Applications of artificial intelligence in transport: An overview. *Sustainability*, *11*(1), 189.

Abu-Alsaad, H. A., & Al-Taie, R. R. K. (2021). NLP analysis in social media using big data technologies. *Telkomnika*, *19*(6), 1840–1846. DOI: 10.12928/telkomnika.v19i6.19339

Adamopoulou, E., & Moussiades, L. (2020). Chatbots: History, technology, and applications. *Machine Learning with Applications*, *2*, 100006. DOI: 10.1016/j.mlwa.2020.100006

Adedeji, B. P. (2024). Energy parameter modeling in plug-in hybrid electric vehicles using supervised machine learning approaches. *E-Prime - Advances in Electrical Engineering. Electronics and Energy*, *8*, 100584. DOI: 10.1016/j.prime.2024.100584

Adewale, P., Dumont, M. J., & Ngadi, M. (2015). Recent trends of biodiesel production from animal fat wastes and associated production techniques. *Renewable & Sustainable Energy Reviews*, *45*, 574–588. DOI: 10.1016/j.rser.2015.02.039

Aditya, C. R., Deshmukh, C. R., Nayana, D. K., & Vidyavastu, P. G. (2018). Detection and prediction of air pollution using machine learning models. International journal of engineering trends and technology (IJETT), 59(4), 204-207.

Afolabi, A. S., & Akinola, O. A. (2024). Network Intrusion Detection Using Knapsack Optimization, Mutual Information Gain, and Machine Learning. *Journal of Electrical and Computer Engineering*, *2024*, 1–21. DOI: 10.1155/2024/7302909

Agarwal, P. K., Gurjar, J., Agarwal, A. K., & Birla, R. (2015). Application of artificial intelligence for development of intelligent transport system in smart cities. *Journal of Traffic and Transportation Engineering*, *1*(1), 20–30.

Ahangar, M. N., Ahmed, Q. Z., Khan, F. A., & Hafeez, M. (2021). A survey of autonomous vehicles: Enabling communication technologies and challenges. *Sensors (Basel)*, *21*(3), 706.

Ahmadi, G., Tavakkoli-Moghaddam, R., Baboli, A., & Najafi, M. (2022). A decision support model for robust allocation and routing of search and rescue resources after earthquake: A case study. *Operations Research*, *22*(2), 1–43. DOI: 10.1007/s12351-020-00591-5

Ahmad, T., Mourshed, M., & Rezgui, Y. (2017). Urban energy management systems: State-of-the-art and emerging trends. *Applied Energy*, *191*, 146–172. DOI: 10.1016/j.apenergy.2017.01.053

Ahmed, S., Hossain, M., Kaiser, M. S., Noor, M. B., Mahmud, M., & Chakraborty, C. (2021). Artificial intelligence and machine learning for ensuring security in smart cities. In Data-driven mining, learning and analytics for secured smart cities, Springer, Champp. 23-47.

Ahmed, H., Wang, T., & Patel, R. (2018). Hybrid AI approaches for solid waste management and recycling processes in smart cities. *Journal of Environmental Management*, *215*, 67–76. DOI: 10.1016/j.jenvman.2018.02.053

Ahmed, M., Shen, Y., Ahmed, M., Xiao, Z., Cheng, P., Ali, N., Ghaffar, A., & Ali, S. (2022). AQE-Net: A Deep Learning Model for Estimating Air Quality of Karachi City from Mobile Images. *Remote Sensing (Basel)*, *14*(22), 5732. DOI: 10.3390/rs14225732

Akhtar, M., & Moridpour, S. (2021). A review of traffic congestion prediction using artificial intelligence. *Journal of Advanced Transportation*, *2021*, 8878011. Advance online publication. DOI: 10.1155/2021/8878011

Al Kuwaiti, A., Nazer, K., Al-Reedy, A., Al-Shehri, S., Al-Muhanna, A., Subbarayalu, A. V., Al Muhanna, D., & Al-Muhanna, F. A. (2023). A review of the role of artificial intelligence in healthcare. *Journal of Personalized Medicine*, *13*(6), 951. DOI: 10.3390/jpm13060951 PMID: 37373940

Alam, F., Mehmood, R., & Katib, I. (2021). Leveraging AI for disaster preparedness: Opportunities and challenges. *Disaster Management & Prevention*, *15*(2), 203–215.

Alam, F., Ofli, F., & Imran, M. (2020). Descriptive and visual summaries of disaster events using artificial intelligence techniques: Case studies of Hurricanes Harvey, Irma, and Maria. *Behaviour & Information Technology*, *39*(3), 288–318. DOI: 10.1080/0144929X.2019.1610908

Alatoun, K., Matrouk, K., Mohammed, M. A., Nedoma, J., Martinek, R., & Zmij, P. (2022). A novel low-latency and energy-efficient task scheduling framework for internet of medical things in an edge fog cloud system. *Sensors (Basel)*, *22*(14), 5327. DOI: 10.3390/s22145327 PMID: 35891007

Albahri, A., Duhaim, A. M., Fadhel, M. A., Alnoor, A., Baqer, N. S., Alzubaidi, L., Albahri, O., Alamoodi, A., Bai, J., Salhi, A., Santamaría, J., Ouyang, C., Gupta, A., Gu, Y., & Deveci, M. (2023). A systematic review of trustworthy and explainable artificial intelligence in healthcare: Assessment of quality, bias risk, and data fusion. *Information Fusion*, *96*, 156–191. DOI: 10.1016/j.inffus.2023.03.008

Albino, V., Berardi, U., & Dangelico, R. M. (2015). Smart cities: Definitions, dimensions, performance, and initiatives. *Journal of Urban Technology*, *22*(1), 3–21. DOI: 10.1080/10630732.2014.942092

Aldhyani, T. H. H., Al-Yaari, M., Alkahtani, H., & Maashi, M. (2020). [Retracted] water quality prediction using artificial intelligence algorithms. *Applied Bionics and Biomechanics*, *2020*(1), 6659314.

AL-Dosari, K., Hunaiti, Z., & Balachandran, W.AL-Dosari. (2023). Systematic review on civilian drones in safety and security applications. *Drones (Basel)*, *7*(3), 210. DOI: 10.3390/drones7030210

Aldossary, M. (2023). Multi-layer fog-cloud architecture for optimizing the placement of IoT applications in smart cities. *Computers, Materials & Continua*, *75*(1), 633–649. DOI: 10.32604/cmc.2023.035414

Alexander, D. E. (2014). Social media in disaster risk reduction and crisis management. *Science and Engineering Ethics*, *20*(3), 717–733. DOI: 10.1007/s11948-013-9502-z PMID: 24306994

Ali Mohamad, T., Bastone, A., Bernhard, F., & Schiavone, F. (2023). How artificial intelligence impacts the competitive position of healthcare organizations. *Journal of Organizational Change Management, 36*(8), 49–70. DOI: 10.1108/JOCM-03-2023-0057

Aljohani, A. (2023). Predictive Analytics and Machine Learning for Real-Time Supply Chain Risk Mitigation and Agility. *Sustainability (Basel), 15*(20), 15088. DOI: 10.3390/su152015088

Allam, Z., & Dhunny, Z. A. (2019). On big data, artificial intelligence and smart cities. *Cities (London, England), 89*, 80–91. DOI: 10.1016/j.cities.2019.01.032

Allen, R. M., Melgar, D., & Hayes, G. P. (2020). Advances in earthquake early warning. *Annual Review of Earth and Planetary Sciences, 48*(1), 339–366.

Allen, R. M., Melgar, D., & Petersen, G. E. (2019). MyShake: Using smartphones for earthquake early warning and detection. *Science Advances, 5*(3), eaau9825.

Alli, A. A., & Alam, M. M. (2019). SecOFF-FCIoT: Machine learning based secure offloading in Fog-Cloud of things for smart city applications. *Internet of Things : Engineering Cyber Physical Human Systems, 7*, 100070. DOI: 10.1016/j.iot.2019.100070

Alowais, S. A., Alghamdi, S. S., Alsuhebany, N., Alqahtani, T., Alshaya, A. I., Almohareb, S. N., Aldairem, A., Alrashed, M., Bin Saleh, K., Badreldin, H. A., Al Yami, M. S., Al Harbi, S., & Albekairy, A. M. (2023). Revolutionizing healthcare: The role of artificial intelligence in clinical practice. *BMC Medical Education, 23*(1), 689. DOI: 10.1186/s12909-023-04698-z PMID: 37740191

Altieri, A. H., & Gedan, K. B. (2015). Climate change and dead zones. *Global Change Biology, 21*(4), 1395–1406. DOI: 10.1111/gcb.12754 PMID: 25385668

Alvarado, B. J. S., & Solano, P. E. C. (2021). Detecting Disaster Tweets using a Natural Language Processing technique.

Ameer, S., Shah, M. A., Khan, A., Song, H., Maple, C., Islam, S. U., & Asghar, M. N. (2019). Comparative Analysis of Machine Learning Techniques for Predicting Air Quality in Smart Cities. *IEEE Access : Practical Innovations, Open Solutions, 7*, 128325–128338. DOI: 10.1109/ACCESS.2019.2925082

Anandakumar, H., Arulmurugan, R., & Roshini, A. (2019). Intelligent vehicle system problems and future impacts for transport guidelines, in: *Proceedings of the 2019 International Conference on Smart Systems and Inventive Technology (ICSSIT)*, pp. 1–5, https://doi.org/DOI: 10.1109/ICSSIT46314.2019.8987831

Andersen, P.-A., Goodwin, M., & Granmo, O.-C. (2024). Towards safe and sustainable reinforcement learning for real-time strategy games. *Information Sciences*, *679*, 120980. DOI: 10.1016/j.ins.2024.120980

Ardjmand, E., Fallahtafti, A., Yazdani, E., Mahmoodi, A., & Young Ii, W. A. (2024). A guided twin delayed deep deterministic reinforcement learning for vaccine allocation in human contact networks. *Applied Soft Computing*, *167*, 112322. DOI: 10.1016/j.asoc.2024.112322

Arnell, N. W., Lowe, J. A., Challinor, A. J., & Osborn, T. J. (2019). Global and regional impacts of climate change at different levels of global temperature increase. *Climatic Change*, *155*(3), 377–391. DOI: 10.1007/s10584-019-02464-z

Asadollah, S. B. H. S., Sharafati, A., Motta, D., & Yaseen, Z. M. (2021). River water quality index prediction and uncertainty analysis: A comparative study of machine learning models. *Journal of Environmental Chemical Engineering*, *9*(1), 104599. DOI: 10.1016/j.jece.2020.104599

Ashraf, S. (2021). A proactive role of IoT devices in building smart cities. *Internet of Things and Cyber-Physical Systems*, *1*, 8–13. DOI: 10.1016/j.iotcps.2021.08.001

Aslan, E., Arserim, M. A., & Uçar, A. (2023). Development of Push-Recovery control system for humanoid robots using deep reinforcement learning. *Ain Shams Engineering Journal*, *14*(10), 102167. DOI: 10.1016/j.asej.2023.102167

Ayomoh, M. K. O., Oke, S. A., Adedeji, W. O., & Charles-Owaba, O. E. (2008). An approach to tackling the environmental and health impacts of municipal solid waste disposal in developing countries. *Journal of Environmental Management*, *88*(1), 108–114. DOI: 10.1016/j.jenvman.2007.01.040 PMID: 17383077

Babu, C. S., Akshayah, N. S., & Janapriyan, R. (2023). IoT-Based Smart Accident Detection and Alert System. In Handbook of Research on Deep Learning Techniques for Cloud-Based Industrial IoT (pp. 322-337). IGI Global. DOI: 10.4018/978-1-6684-8098-4.ch019

Bai, L., Wang, J., Ma, X., & Lu, H. (2018). Air Pollution Forecasts: An Overview. *International Journal of Environmental Research and Public Health*, *15*(4), 780. DOI: 10.3390/ijerph15040780 PMID: 29673227

Bai, Y., Li, Y., Wang, X., Xie, J., & Li, C. (2016). Air pollutants concentrations forecasting using back propagation neural network based on wavelet decomposition with meteorological conditions. *Atmospheric Pollution Research*, *7*(3), 557–566. DOI: 10.1016/j.apr.2016.01.004

Bajwa, J., Munir, U., Nori, A., & Williams, B. (2021, July). Artificial intelligence in healthcare: Transforming the practice of medicine. *Future Healthcare Journal, 8*(2), e188–e194. DOI: 10.7861/fhj.2021-0095 PMID: 34286183

Balasubramaniam, M., Pawade, A., & Bharambe, K. (2020). A sustainable design approach for the built environment based on the principles of Anthropological circadian rhythms Chronobiology and Chronopharmocology. *Journal of Engineering Research and Application, 10*(02), 27–31.

Barba, C. T., Mateos, M. A., Soto, P. R., Mezher, A. M., & Igartua, M. A. (2012, June). Smart city for VANETs using warning messages, traffic statistics and intelligent traffic lights. In 2012 [IEEE.]. *IEEE Intelligent Vehicles Symposium*, •••, 902–907.

Barocas, S., & Selbst, A. D. (2016). Big Data's Disparate Impact. *SSRN, 104*(3), 671–732. DOI: 10.2139/ssrn.2477899

Basu, M., Bit, S. D., & Ghosh, S. (2022). Utilizing microblogs for optimized real-time resource allocation in post-disaster scenarios. *Social Network Analysis and Mining, 12*(1), 1–20. DOI: 10.1007/s13278-021-00841-0 PMID: 34900021

Basyah, N. A., Syukri, M., Fahmi, I., Ali, I., Rusli, Z., & Putri, E. S. (2023). Disaster Prevention and Management: A Critical Review of The Literature. *Jurnal Penelitian Pendidikan IPA, 9*(11), 1045–1051. DOI: 10.29303/jppipa.v9i11.4486

Batty, M. (2018). Artificial intelligence and smart cities. *Environment and Planning. B, Urban Analytics and City Science, 45*(1), 3–6. DOI: 10.1177/2399808317751169

Batty, M., Axhausen, K. W., Giannotti, F., Pozdnoukhov, A., Bazzani, A., Wachowicz, M., Ouzounis, G., & Portugali, Y. (2012). Smart cities of the future. *The European Physical Journal. Special Topics, 214*(1), 481–518. DOI: 10.1140/epjst/e2012-01703-3

Beattie, C., Leibo, J. Z., Teplyashin, D., Ward, T., Wainwright, M., Küttler, H., Lefrancq, A., Green, S., Valdés, V., Sadik, A., Schrittwieser, J., Anderson, K., York, S., Cant, M., Cain, A., Bolton, A., Gaffney, S., King, H., Hassabis, D., . . . Petersen, S. (2016). *DeepMind Lab* (Version 2). arXiv. DOI: 10.48550/ARXIV.1612.03801

Beigi, G., Hu, X., Maciejewski, R., & Liu, H. (2016). An overview of sentiment analysis in social media and its applications in disaster relief. *Sentiment analysis and ontology engineering: An environment of computational intelligence*, 313-340. https://doi.org/DOI: 10.1007/978-3-319-30319-2_13

Bekkar, A., Hssina, B., Douzi, S., & Douzi, K. (2021). Air-pollution prediction in smart city, deep learning approach. *Journal of Big Data, 8*(1), 1–21. DOI: 10.1186/s40537-021-00548-1 PMID: 34956819

Bengio, Y., Louradour, J., Collobert, R., & Weston, J. (2009). Curriculum learning. *Proceedings of the 26th Annual International Conference on Machine Learning*, 41–48. DOI: 10.1145/1553374.1553380

Bharadiya, J. (2023). Artificial intelligence in transportation systems a critical review. *American Journal of Computing and Engineering*, *6*(1), 34–45. DOI: 10.47672/ajce.1487

Bhardwaj, K. K., Banyal, S., Sharma, D. K., & Al-Numay, W. (2022). Internet of things based smart city design using fog computing and fuzzy logic. *Sustainable Cities and Society*, *79*, 103712. DOI: 10.1016/j.scs.2022.103712

Bhattacharya, S., & Shahnawaz, S. (2021). Using machine learning to predict air quality index in new delhi. arXiv preprint arXiv:2112.05753.

Bidmon, S., Elshiewy, O., Terlutter, R., & Boztug, Y. (2020). What patients value in physicians: Analyzing drivers of patient satisfaction using physician-rating website data. *Journal of Medical Internet Research*, *22*(2), e13830. DOI: 10.2196/13830 PMID: 32012063

Bi, J., Lin, Y., Dong, Q., Yuan, H., & Zhou, M. C. (2021, September). Large-scale water quality prediction with integrated deep neural network. *Information Sciences*, *571*, 191–205. DOI: 10.1016/j.ins.2021.04.057

Bikku, T., Chandrika, P., Kanyadari, A., Prathima, V., & Sai, B. B. (2022). Analysis of disaster tweets using natural language processing. In *Intelligent Computing and Applications:Proceedings of ICDIC 2020* (pp. 491-501). Singapore: Springer Nature Singapore. https://doi.org/DOI: 10.1007/978-981-19-4162-7_46

Bilberg, A., & Malik, A. A. (2019). Digital twin driven human–robot collaborative assembly. *CIRP Annals*, *68*(1), 499–502. DOI: 10.1016/j.cirp.2019.04.011

Boehm, F. (2018). Data protection and smart cities: How the GDPR might impact smart city projects. *Computer Law & Security Review*, *34*(4), 784–792.

Boeken, T., Feydy, J., Lecler, A., Soyer, P., Feydy, A., Barat, M., & Duron, L. (2022). Artificial intelligence in diagnostic and interventional radiology: Where are we now? *Diagnostic and Interventional Imaging*. PMID: 36494290

Boersma, K., Clark, N., & Rizza, C. (2024). Governing the uses of social media and crowdsourcing in crisis and disaster (risk) management. *Risk, Hazards & Crisis in Public Policy*, *15*(2), 94–103. Advance online publication. DOI: 10.1002/rhc3.12310

Bohannon, J. (2015). Credit card study blows holes in anonymity. *Science*, *347*(6221), 468. DOI: 10.1126/science.347.6221.468 PMID: 25635068

Bokhari, S. A., & Myeong, S. (2022). Use of artificial intelligence in smart cities for smart decision-making: A social innovation perspective. *Sustainability (Basel)*, *14*(2), 620. DOI: 10.3390/su14020620

Bonomi, F., Milito, R., Zhu, J., & Addepalli, S. (2012, August). Fog computing and its role in the internet of things. In *Proceedings of the first edition of the MCC workshop on Mobile cloud computing* (pp. 13-16). DOI: 10.1145/2342509.2342513

Boulanger, A., Coudour, R., & Menon, R. (2019). Machine Learning for Adaptation to Extreme Weather Events. *Journal of Climate*, *32*(14), 4579–4599. DOI: 10.1175/JCLI-D-18-0471.1

Bourdillon, A. T., Garg, A., Wang, H., Woo, Y. J., Pavone, M., & Boyd, J. (2023). Integration of Reinforcement Learning in a Virtual Robotic Surgical Simulation. *Surgical Innovation*, *30*(1), 94–102. DOI: 10.1177/15533506221095298 PMID: 35503302

Bouvier, G., & Machin, D. (2020). Critical discourse analysis and the challenges and opportunities of social media. *Critical discourse studies and/in communication*, 39-53. https://doi.org/DOI: 10.1080/15358593.2018.1479881

Bouvier, G. (2019). How journalists source trending social media feeds: A critical discourse perspective on Twitter. *Journalism Studies*, *20*(2), 212–231. DOI: 10.1080/1461670X.2017.1365618

Božić, V. (2023). Artifical intelligence as the reason and the solution of digital divide. Language Education and Technology, 3(2).

Brandão, R., & Arbix, G. (2022). Artificial Intelligence, Ethics and Public Policy—The Use of Facial Recognition Systems in Public Transport in the Largest Brazilian Cities. *Journal of Service Science and Management*, *15*(5), 551–575. Advance online publication. DOI: 10.4236/jssm.2022.155032

Brightwood, S., & Jame, H. (2024). *Data privacy, security, and ethical considerations in AI-powered finance. Article*. Research Gate.

Bryan-Smith, L., Godsall, J., George, F., Egode, K., Dethlefs, N., & Parsons, D. (2023). Real-time social media sentiment analysis for rapid impact assessment of floods. *Computers & Geosciences*, *178*, 105405. DOI: 10.1016/j.cageo.2023.105405

Budd, J., Miller, B. S., Manning, E. M., Lampos, V., Zhuang, M., Edelstein, M., Rees, G., Emery, V. C., Stevens, M. M., Keegan, N., Short, M. J., Pillay, D., Manley, E., Cox, I. J., Heymann, D., Johnson, A. M., & McKendry, R. A. (2020). Digital technologies in the public-health response to COVID-19. *Nature Medicine*, *26*(8), 1183–1192. DOI: 10.1038/s41591-020-1011-4 PMID: 32770165

Busch, C. (2006). Facing the future of biometrics: Demand for safety and security in the public and private sectors is driving research in this rapidly growing field. *EMBO Reports*, *7*(S1), S23–S25.

C. Creß, Z. Bing, and A. C. Knoll. (2023) "Intelligent transportation systems using external infrastructure: A literature survey," IEEE Trans. Intell. Transp. Syst., early acces. .DOI: 10.1109/TITS.2023.3343434

Cadet, E., Osundare, O. S., Ekpobimi, H. O., Samira, Z., & Wondaferew, Y. (2024). AI-powered threat detection in surveillance systems: A real-time data processing framework. Open Access Research Journal of Engineering and Technology, 7(2), 031-045.

Cai, Z., Feng, Z., Zhou, L., Yang, X., & Xu, T. (2023). Deep-reinforcement-learning-based robot motion strategies for grabbing objects from human hands. *Virtual Reality & Intelligent Hardware*, *5*(5), 407–421. DOI: 10.1016/j.vrih.2022.12.001

Carvalho Melo, L., & Omena Albuquerque Maximo, M. R. (2019). Learning Humanoid Robot Running Skills through Proximal Policy Optimization. *2019 Latin American Robotics Symposium (LARS), 2019 Brazilian Symposium on Robotics (SBR) and 2019 Workshop on Robotics in Education (WRE)*, 37–42. DOI: 10.1109/LARS-SBR-WRE48964.2019.00015

Castillo, C. (2016). *Big crisis data: social media in disasters and time-critical situations*. Cambridge University Press. DOI: 10.1017/CBO9781316476840

Cath, C., Wachter, S., Mittelstadt, B., Taddeo, M., & Floridi, L. (2018). Artificial intelligence and the 'good society': The US, EU, and UK approach. *Science and Engineering Ethics*, *24*(2), 505–528. PMID: 28353045

Cavoukian, A. (2019). *Privacy by design: The definitive guide*. CRC Press.

Cembalo, L., Lombardi, A., Pascucci, S., Dentoni, D., Migliore, G., Verneau, F., & Schifani, G. (2015). "Rationally local": Consumer participation in alternative food chains. *Agribusiness*, *31*(3), 330–352. DOI: 10.1002/agr.21419

Cervero, R. (2013). Transport infrastructure and global competitiveness: Balancing mobility and sustainability. *Journal of Transport Geography*, *33*, 1–9. DOI: 10.1016/j.jtrangeo.2013.05.005

Chahine, R., Saab, R., & Mansour, C. (2021). AI-driven supply chain optimization in post-disaster recovery: Lessons from Beirut. *Journal of Humanitarian Logistics and Supply Chain Management*, *11*(2), 237–252.

Chakraborty, S., Joshi, P. K., & Ghosh, A. (2021). AI-driven geospatial analysis for urban flood prediction. *Remote Sensing of Environment, 257*, 112367.

Chandra, R., & Lakshmi, D. (2024). Application of Artificial Intelligence in Disaster Management and Their Challenges. Internet of Things and AI for Natural Disaster Management and Prediction, 1-27. https://doi.org/DOI: 10.4018/979-8-3693-4284-8.ch001

Chan, J., Ho, A., & Tang, C. (2020). Smart cities and governance: Lessons from Singapore's Smart Nation initiative. *Journal of Urban Studies, 58*(2), 245–263.

Chauhan, V., Patel, M., Tanwar, S., Tyagi, S., & Kumar, N. (2020). IoT Enabled real-Time urban transport management system. *Computers & Electrical Engineering, 86*, 106746. DOI: 10.1016/j.compeleceng.2020.106746

Chauncey, S. A., & McKenna, H. P. (2024). by Sarah A. Chauncey 1ORCID andH. Patricia McKenna 2,*ORCID "Creativity and Innovation in Civic Spaces Supported by Cognitive Flexibility When Learning with AI Chatbots in Smart Cities" Published: 16 February 2024. *Urban Science (Basel, Switzerland), 8*(1), 16. DOI: 10.3390/urbansci8010016

Chavhan, S., & Venkataram, P. (2019). Prediction based traffic management in a metropolitan area. *Journal of Traffic and Transportation Engineering*. Advance online publication. DOI: 10.1016/j.jtte.2018.05.003

Cheliotis, K. (2021). ABMU: An Agent-Based Modelling Framework for Unity3D. *SoftwareX, 15*, 100771. DOI: 10.1016/j.softx.2021.100771

Cheng, R. (2021, December 31). Unity-Python Communication for ML-Agents: Good, Bad, and Ugly. *New Screwdriver*. https://newscrewdriver.com/2021/12/31/unity-python-communication-for-ml-agents-good-bad-and-ugly/

Chen, K., Chen, H., Zhou, C., Huang, Y., Qi, X., Shen, R., Liu, F., Zuo, M., Zou, X., Wang, J., Zhang, Y., Chen, D., Chen, X., Deng, Y., & Ren, H. (2020). Comparative analysis of surface water quality prediction performance and identification of key water parameters using different machine learning models based on big data. *Water Research, 171*, 115–454. DOI: 10.1016/j.watres.2019.115454 PMID: 31918388

Chen, P., Wang, B., Wu, Y., Wang, Q., Huang, Z., & Wang, C. (2023). Urban river water quality monitoring based on self-optimizing machine learning method using multi-source remote sensing data. *Ecological Indicators, 146*, 109750. DOI: 10.1016/j.ecolind.2022.109750

Chen, X., Cheng, C., & Yu, X. (2019). Agent-based evacuation modeling for disaster preparedness. *Journal of Urban Planning and Development, 145*(4), 04019012.

Chen, X., Tang, X., & Xu, X. (2023). Digital technology-driven smart society governance mechanism and practice exploration. *Frontiers of Engineering Management, 10*(2), 319–338. DOI: 10.1007/s42524-022-0200-x

Chien, S., Ding, Y., & Wei, C. (2017). Predicting Urban Growth Using Machine Learning Techniques. *Journal of Urban Planning and Development, 143*(2), 04017005. DOI: 10.1061/(ASCE)UP.1943-5444.0000371

Chopra, M., Singh, S. K., Aggarwal, K., & Gupta, A. (2022). Predicting catastrophic events using machine learning models for natural language processing. In *Data mining approaches for big data and sentiment analysis in social media* (pp. 223–243). IGI Global., DOI: 10.4018/978-1-7998-8413-2.ch010

Christophe, E., & Inglada, J. (2009). Open source remote sensing: Increasing the usability of cutting-edge algorithms. *IEEE Geoscience and Remote Sensing Newsletter, 35*(5), 9–15.

Chu, E. W., & Karr, J. R. (2016). Environmental impact: Concept, consequences, measurement. Reference module in life sciences, B978-0.

Chung, S., Kim, J., & Lee, S. (2020). The role of AI in wildfire management: A case study from Australia. *International Journal of Disaster Risk Reduction, 50*, 101739.

Cisco, I. N. C. (2015). Cisco Global Cloud Index 2014–2019. Online: https://bit.Ly/2Kj8FvU.

Cobo, A., Parra, D., & Navón, J. (2015, May). Identifying relevant messages in a twitter-based citizen channel for natural disaster situations. In *Proceedings of the 24th international conference on world wide web* (pp. 1189-1194). https://doi.org/ DOI: 10.1145/2740908.2741719

Coghlan, S. (2022). Robots and the possibility of humanistic care. *International Journal of Social Robotics, 14*(10), 2095–2108. DOI: 10.1007/s12369-021-00804-7 PMID: 34221183

Cohen, J., Kupferschmidt, K., & Servick, K. (2020). AI and the COVID-19 pandemic: Managing global health crises. *Science, 367*(6485), 1418–1420. PMID: 32217710

Coppola, D. (2015). *Introduction to International Disaster Management. Butterworth-Heinemann*. Elsevier.

Coppola, D. P. (2020). *Introduction to international disaster management* (4th ed.). Butterworth-Heinemann.

Coumans, E., & Bai, Y. (n.d.). *PyBullet Quickstart Guide*. Google Docs. Retrieved 10 October 2024, from https://docs.google.com/document/d/10sXEhzFRSnvFcl3XxNGhnD4N2SedqwdAvK3dsihxVUA/edit?usp=embed_facebook

Cromar, K. R., Duncan, B. N., Bartonova, A., Benedict, K., Brauer, M., Habre, R., & Volckens, J. (2019). Air pollution monitoring for health research and patient care. An official American Thoracic Society workshop report. *Annals of the American Thoracic Society*, *16*(10), 1207–1214.

Cui, Y., & Lei, D. (2023). Design of highway intelligent transportation system based on the internet of things and artificial intelligence. *IEEE Access : Practical Innovations, Open Solutions*, *11*, 46653–46664. DOI: 10.1109/ACCESS.2023.3275559

Da Fonseca-Soares, D., Eliziário, S. A., Galvinicio, J. D., & Ramos-Ridao, A. F. (2023). Life-Cycle Greenhouse Gas (GHG) Emissions Calculation for Urban Rail Transit Systems: The Case of Pernambuco Metro. *Applied Sciences (Basel, Switzerland)*, *13*(15), 8965. DOI: 10.3390/app13158965

Dalal, A. K., Piniella, N., Fuller, T. E., Pong, D., Pardo, M., Bessa, N., Yoon, C., Lipsitz, S., & Schnipper, J. L. (2021). Evaluation of electronic health record-integrated digital health tools to engage hospitalized patients in discharge preparation. *Journal of the American Medical Informatics Association : JAMIA*, *28*(4), 704–712. DOI: 10.1093/jamia/ocaa321 PMID: 33463681

Daly, S., & Thom, J. A. (2016, May). Mining and Classifying Image Posts on Social Media to Analyse Fires. In ISCRAM (pp. 1-14).

David Yang, C. Y., & Fisher, D. L. (2021). Safety impacts and benefits of connected and automated vehicles: How real are they? *Journal of Intelligent Transport Systems*, *25*(2), 135–138. DOI: 10.1080/15472450.2021.1872143

Davis, M., & Naumann, S. (2017). Making the case for sustainable urban drainage systems as a nature-based solution to urban flooding. *Nature-Based Solutions to Climate Change Adaptation in Urban Areas: Linkages between Science. Policy & Practice*, •••, 123–137.

De Castro, R. C. (2011). The US-Philippine Alliance: An evolving security partnership. *Asian Security*, *7*(2), 137–154. DOI: 10.1080/14799855.2011.582635

De Souza Silva, J. L., Mahmoudi, E., Carvalho, R. R. M., & Dos Santos Barros, T. A. (2024). Classification of anomalies in photovoltaic systems using supervised machine learning techniques and real data. *Energy Reports*, *11*, 4642–4656. DOI: 10.1016/j.egyr.2024.04.040

Del Rio, A., Serrano, J., Jimenez, D., Contreras, L. M., & Alvarez, F. (2024). Multisite gaming streaming optimization over virtualized 5G environment using Deep Reinforcement Learning techniques. *Computer Networks*, *244*, 110334. DOI: 10.1016/j.comnet.2024.110334

Demetillo, A. T., Japitana, M. V., & Taboada, E. B. (2019). A system for monitoring water quality in a large aquatic area using wireless sensor network technology. *Sustainable Environment Research*, *29*(1), 1–9.

Demetriou, D., Hull, R., Kgoebane-Maseko, M., Lockhat, Z., & Dlamini, Z. (2023). AI-Enhanced Digital Pathology and Radiogenomics in Precision Oncology. In Artificial Intelligence and Precision Oncology: Bridging Cancer Research and Clinical Decision Support (pp. 93-113). Springer.

Deng, Y., Chen, Z., Yao, X., Hassan, S., & Wu, J. (2019). Task scheduling for smart city applications based on multi-server mobile edge computing. *IEEE Access : Practical Innovations, Open Solutions*, *7*, 14410–14421. DOI: 10.1109/ACCESS.2019.2893486

Desikan, K. S., Kotagi, V. J., & Murthy, C. S. R. (2020). Topology control in fog computing enabled IoT networks for smart cities. *Computer Networks*, *176*, 107270. DOI: 10.1016/j.comnet.2020.107270

Devi, M. K., Deepika, R., Pooja, K., & Ramya, N. (2020). Real Time Non-Invasive Continuous Glucose Monitoring Using AI. 2020 International Conference on Power, Energy, Control and Transmission Systems (ICPECTS), Dongari, S., Nisarudeen, M., Devi, J., Irfan, S., Parida, P. K., & Bajpai, A. (2023). Advancing Healthcare through Artificial Intelligence: Innovations at the Intersection of AI and Medicine. Tuijin Jishu/Journal of Propulsion Technology, 44(2).

DeVries, P. M., Wang, K., & Yin, L. (2018). Machine learning for disaster risk management. *Journal of Geophysical Research. Solid Earth*, *123*(9), 7717–7731.

di Vimercati, S. D. C., Genovese, A., Livraga, G., Piuri, V., & Scotti, F. (2013). Privacy and security in environmental monitoring systems: issues and solutions. In *Computer and Information Security Handbook* (pp. 835–853). Morgan Kaufmann. DOI: 10.1016/B978-0-12-394397-2.00047-7

Dijkstra, J., Ellis, J. L., Kebreab, E., Strathe, A. B., López, S., France, J., & Bannink, A. (2012). Ruminal pH regulation and nutritional consequences of low pH. *Animal Feed Science and Technology*, *172*(1-2), 22–33. DOI: 10.1016/j.anifeedsci.2011.12.005

Ding, X., Dong, X., Hou, B., Fan, G., & Zhang, X. (2021). Visual platform for water quality prediction and pre-warning of drinking water source area in the Three Gorges Reservoir Area. *Journal of Cleaner Production*, *309*, 127398. DOI: 10.1016/j.jclepro.2021.127398

Domala, J., Dogra, M., Masrani, V., Fernandes, D., D'souza, K., Fernandes, D., & Carvalho, T. (2020, July). Automated identification of disaster news for crisis management using machine learning and natural language processing. In *2020 International Conference on Electronics and Sustainable Communication Systems (ICESC)* (pp. 503-508). IEEE. https://doi.org/DOI: 10.1109/ICESC48915.2020.9156031

Dong, Y., Guo, S., Liu, J., & Yang, Y. (2019). Energy-efficient fair cooperation fog computing in mobile edge networks for smart city. *IEEE Internet of Things Journal*, *6*(5), 7543–7554. DOI: 10.1109/JIOT.2019.2901532

Ejaz, U., Ramon, W., & Olaoye, G. (2025). The Role of Big Data and AI in Smart Cities and Urban Planning.

El Naqa, I., & Murphy, M. J. (2015). *What is machine learning?* Springer International Publishing.

Elassy, M., Al-Hattab, M., Takruri, M., & Badawi, S. (2024). Intelligent transportation systems for sustainable smart cities. Transportation Engineering, 100252.

Elassy, M., Al-Hattab, M., Takruri, M., & Badawi, S. (2024). Intelligent transportation systems for sustainable smart cities". *Transportation Engineering*, *16*, 100252. DOI: 10.1016/j.treng.2024.100252

Elston, D. M. (2021). The hawthorne effect. *Journal of the American Academy of Dermatology*. Advance online publication. DOI: 10.1016/j.jaad.2021.01.085 PMID: 33810890

Enitan, S., Adejumo, E., Imaralu, J., Adelakun, A., Ladipo, O., & Enitan, C. (2023). Personalized medicine approach to osteoporosis management in women: Integrating genetics, pharmacogenomics, and precision treatments. *Clinical Research Communications*, *6*(3), 18. DOI: 10.53388/CRC2023018

Erbeyoğlu, G., & Bilge, Ü. (2020). A robust disaster preparedness model for effective and fair disaster response. *European Journal of Operational Research*, *280*(2), 479–494. DOI: 10.1016/j.ejor.2019.07.029

Eubanks, V. (2018). *Automating inequality: How high-tech tools profile, police, and punish the poor*. St. Martin's Press.

European Union. (2016). General Data Protection Regulation (GDPR). Retrieved from https://gdpr-info.eu

European Union. (2018). *General Data Protection Regulation (GDPR)*. Retrieved from https://gdpr-info.eu/

Fakhruddin, B., Clark, H., Robinson, L., & Hieber-Girardet, L. (2020). Should I stay or should I go now? Why risk communication is the critical component in disaster risk reduction. *Progress in Disaster Science*, *8*, 100139. DOI: 10.1016/j.pdisas.2020.100139 PMID: 34977532

Fanni, S. C., Febi, M., Aghakhanyan, G., & Neri, E. (2023). Natural language processing. In *Introduction to Artificial Intelligence* (pp. 87–99). Springer International Publishing., DOI: 10.1007/978-3-031-25928-9_5

Feng, Y., Brenner, C., & Sester, M. (2020). Flood severity mapping from Volunteered Geographic Information by interpreting water level from images containing people: A case study of Hurricane Harvey. *ISPRS Journal of Photogrammetry and Remote Sensing*, *169*, 301–319. DOI: 10.1016/j.isprsjprs.2020.09.011

Ferrag, M. A., Shu, L., Yang, X., Derhab, A., & Maglaras, L. (2020). Security and Privacy for Green IoT-Based Agriculture: Review, Blockchain Solutions, and Challenges. *IEEE Access : Practical Innovations, Open Solutions*, *8*, 32031–32053. DOI: 10.1109/ACCESS.2020.2973178

Figueiredo, L., Jesus, I., Machado, J. T., Ferreira, J. R., & De Carvalho, J. M. (2001). "Towards the development of intelligent transportation systems," in Proc. IEEE Intell. Transp. Syst. Proc., pp. 1206–1211. DOI: DOI: 10.1109/ITSC.2001.948835

Finnerty, S., Piazza, J., & Levine, M. (2024). Scientists' identities shape engagement with environmental activism. *Communications Earth & Environment*, *5*(1), 240. DOI: 10.1038/s43247-024-01412-9

Flores-Salgado, B., Gonzalez-Ambriz, S. J., Martínez-García-Moreno, C. A., & Beltrán, J. (2024). IoT-based system for campus community security. *Internet of Things : Engineering Cyber Physical Human Systems*, *26*, 101179. DOI: 10.1016/j.iot.2024.101179

Floridi, L., & Cowls, J. (2019). A unified framework of five principles for AI in society. *Harvard Data Science Review*, *1*(1), 1–15.

Floridi, L., Cowls, J., Beltrametti, M., & Chessen, R. (2018). The Ethics of Artificial Intelligence: Issues and Initiatives. *AI & Society*, *33*(4), 541–552. DOI: 10.1007/s00146-018-0812-4

Fontes, C., Al Haddad, C., Antoniou, C., & Lütge, C. (2024). Assessing the collective challenges of AI: An applied framework focused on people centeredness and public participation. *Urban Governance*, *4*(4), 245–254.

Foresti, R., Rossi, S., Magnani, M., Bianco, C. G. L., & Delmonte, N. (2020). Smart society and artificial intelligence: Big data scheduling and the global standard method applied to smart maintenance. *Engineering (Beijing)*, *6*(7), 835–846. DOI: 10.1016/j.eng.2019.11.014

Foth, M. (2017). Citizen-Centric Smart City Applications: A Review of Current Trends and Future Directions. *International Journal of Urban Sustainable Development*, *9*(3), 291–306. DOI: 10.1080/19463138.2017.1337851

Foucault, M. (1995). *Discipline and punish: The birth of the prison*. Vintage Books.

Freeman, B. S., Taylor, G., Gharabaghi, B., & Thé, J. (2018). Forecasting air quality time series using deep learning. *Journal of the Air & Waste Management Association*, *68*(8), 866–886. DOI: 10.1080/10962247.2018.1459956 PMID: 29652217

Gakii, C., & Jepkoech, J. (2019). A Classification Model for Water Quality Analysis Using Decision Tree [Online] [. Available: https://www.opendata.go.ke/datasets/kewi-water-test-and-results.]. *European Journal of Computer Science and Information Technology*, *7*(3), 1–8. Retrieved May 26, 2023, from

Galea, S., Merchant, R. M., & Lurie, N. (2020). The mental health impact of the COVID-19 pandemic: Applications of AI in psychological support. *Journal of the American Medical Association*, *324*(3), 225–226. PMID: 32530455

Gangapurwala, S., Mitchell, A., & Havoutis, I. (2020). Guided Constrained Policy Optimization for Dynamic Quadrupedal Robot Locomotion. *IEEE Robotics and Automation Letters*, *5*(2), 3642–3649. DOI: 10.1109/LRA.2020.2979656

Gao, H., Barbier, G., & Goolsby, R. (2011). Harnessing the crowdsourcing power of social media for disaster relief. *IEEE Intelligent Systems*, *26*(3), 10–14. DOI: 10.1109/MIS.2011.52

Gao, X., Gao, R., Liang, P., Zhang, Q., Deng, R., & Zhu, W. (2021). A Hybrid Tracking Control Strategy for Nonholonomic Wheeled Mobile Robot Incorporating Deep Reinforcement Learning Approach. *IEEE Access : Practical Innovations, Open Solutions*, *9*, 15592–15602. DOI: 10.1109/ACCESS.2021.3053396

Gao, X., Wang, Y., & Zhang, W. (2021). Edge Computing for Smart Cities: Opportunities and Challenges. *IEEE Transactions on Network and Service Management*, *18*(2), 1683–1696. DOI: 10.1109/TNSM.2021.3073015

García, S., Gutiérrez, L., & Rivera, L. (2020). Smart Energy Storage Systems Using Machine Learning Techniques. *Renewable Energy*, *148*, 92–105. DOI: 10.1016/j.renene.2019.11.057

Gayathri, R., Sangeetha, S. K. B., Mathivanan, S. K., Rajadurai, H., Malar, B. A., Mallik, S., & Qin, H. (2024). Enhancing heart disease prediction with reinforcement learning and data augmentation. *Systems and Soft Computing*, *6*, 200129.

Gevaert, C. M., Carman, M., Rosman, B., Georgiadou, Y., & Soden, R. (2021). Fairness and accountability of AI in disaster risk management: Opportunities and challenges. *Patterns (New York, N.Y.)*, *2*(11), 100363. Advance online publication. DOI: 10.1016/j.patter.2021.100363 PMID: 34820647

Ge, Y., From, P. J., & Xiong, Y. (2024). Multi-view gripper internal sensing for the regression of strawberry ripeness using a mini-convolutional neural network for robotic harvesting. *Computers and Electronics in Agriculture*, *216*, 108474. DOI: 10.1016/j.compag.2023.108474

Ghosh, A., Parveen, S., & Das, R. (2020). AI-powered logistics for disaster management: Lessons from case studies. *Disaster Prevention and Management*, *29*(3), 409–422.

Gialampoukidis, I., Andreadis, S., Vrochidis, S., & Kompatsiaris, I. (2021, July). Multimodal data fusion of social media and satellite images for emergency response and decision-making. In *2021 IEEE International Geoscience and Remote Sensing Symposium IGARSS* (pp. 228-231). IEEE. https://doi.org/DOI: 10.1109/IGARSS47720.2021.9554176

Glantz, V., Phattharapornjaroen, P., Carlström, E., & Khorram-Manesh, A. (2020). Regional flexible surge capacity—A flexible response system. *Sustainability (Basel)*, *12*(15), 5984. DOI: 10.3390/su12155984

Gnana, M. A. (2023). Indian Air Quality Prediction and Analysis Using Machine Learning, Available: http://www.ripublication.com

Goldblum, M., Tsipras, D., Xie, C., Chen, X., Schwarzschild, A., Song, D., Madry, A., Li, B., & Goldstein, T. (2022). Dataset security for machine learning: Data poisoning, backdoor attacks, and defenses. *IEEE Transactions on Pattern Analysis and Machine Intelligence*, *45*(2), 1563–1580. DOI: 10.1109/TPAMI.2022.3162397 PMID: 35333711

Golubchikov, O., & Thornbush, M. (2020). Artificial intelligence and robotics in smart city strategies and planned smart development. Smart Cities, 3(4).

Gomez, A., & Nicoletti, R. (2020). Real-time hazard mapping for disaster risk reduction. *International Journal of Disaster Risk Reduction*, *49*, 101685.

Gong, C., Tao, D., Maybank, S. J., Liu, W., Kang, G., & Yang, J. (2016). Multi-Modal Curriculum Learning for Semi-Supervised Image Classification. *IEEE Transactions on Image Processing*, *25*(7), 3249–3260. DOI: 10.1109/TIP.2016.2563981 PMID: 27168596

Gonzalez, C. (2020). Real-time traffic prediction using machine learning: A case study of Olongapo City. *Journal of Transportation Technologies*, *10*(3), 221–231. DOI: 10.4236/jtts.2020.103018

Goy, C. (2020). *Training with Proximal Policy Optimization*. GitHub. https://github.com/yosider/ml-agents-1/blob/master/docs/Training-PPO.md

Granier, K., Oltz, K., Ingram, R., & Segal, D. (2023). Getting the Seal of Approval: A Critical Literature Review of the Evidence for the Use of the PARO Robotic Companion Seal with Older Adults with Cognitive Impairment in Long-Term Care. *Journal of Aging and Long-Term Care*, *6*(2), 57–79.

Guerrero-Ibañez, J., Contreras-Castillo, J., & Zeadally, S. (2021). Deep learning support for intelligent transportation systems. *Transactions on Emerging Telecommunications Technologies*, *32*(3), e4169. Advance online publication. DOI: 10.1002/ett.4169

Guffanti, D., Brunete, A., Hernando, M., Álvarez, D., Rueda, J., & Navarro, E. (2024). Supervised learning for improving the accuracy of robot-mounted 3D camera applied to human gait analysis. *Heliyon*, *10*(4), e26227. DOI: 10.1016/j.heliyon.2024.e26227 PMID: 38404866

Gunjal, S. G., & Kamalapurkar, S. (2023). Air Pollution Prediction Using Machine Learning Supervised Learning Approach, Available: www.ijstr.org

Guntur, S. R., Gorrepati, R. R., & Dirisala, V. R. (2019). Robotics in healthcare: an internet of medical robotic things (IoMRT) perspective. In *Machine learning in bio-signal analysis and diagnostic imaging* (pp. 293–318). Elsevier. DOI: 10.1016/B978-0-12-816086-2.00012-6

Guo, B., Ding, Y., Yao, L., Liang, Y., & Yu, Z. (2020). The future of false information detection on social media: New perspectives and trends. *ACM Computing Surveys*, *53*(4), 1–36. DOI: 10.1145/3393880

Gupta, R., & Singh, A. (2020). Real-time monitoring of industrial emissions using artificial neural networks. *Environmental Pollution*, *258*, 113743. DOI: 10.1016/j.envpol.2019.113743

Gupta, S., Kumar, S., & Singh, P. (2016). Damage assessment using AI: A case study of the 2015 Nepal earthquake. *Natural Hazards*, *84*(2), 1249–1267.

Gu, Y., Qian, Z., & Chen, F. (2016). From Twitter to detector: Real-time traffic incident detection using social media data. *Transportation Research Part C, Emerging Technologies*, *67*, 321–342. DOI: 10.1016/j.trc.2016.02.011

HaCohen-Kerner, Y., Miller, D., & Yigal, Y.HaCohen-Kerner. (2020). The influence of preprocessing on text classification using a bag-of-words representation. *PLoS One*, *15*(5), e0232525. DOI: 10.1371/journal.pone.0232525 PMID: 32357164

Haghiabi, A. H., Nasrolahi, A. H., & Parsaie, A. (2018). Water quality prediction using machine learning methods. *Water Quality Research Journal of Canada*, *53*(1), 3–13. DOI: 10.2166/wqrj.2018.025

Hao, H., & Wang, Y. (2020). Leveraging multimodal social media data for rapid disaster damage assessment. *International Journal of Disaster Risk Reduction*, *51*, 101760. DOI: 10.1016/j.ijdrr.2020.101760

Hartono, D., Yulianto, E., & Wibisono, A. (2019). AI applications in mental health support: Lessons from Sulawesi earthquake recovery. *International Journal of Disaster Risk Reduction*, *33*, 113–119.

Hasan, M., Vasker, N., & Khan, M. S. H. (2024). Real-time Sorting of Broiler Chicken Meat with Robotic arm: XAI-enhanced Deep Learning and LIME Framework for Freshness Detection. *Journal of Agriculture and Food Research*, *18*, 101372. DOI: 10.1016/j.jafr.2024.101372

Hassan, S. Z., Ahmad, K., Hicks, S., Halvorsen, P., Al-Fuqaha, A., Conci, N., & Riegler, M. (2022). Visual sentiment analysis from disaster images in social media. *Sensors (Basel)*, *22*(10), 3628. DOI: 10.3390/s22103628 PMID: 35632034

Hayes, J. L., Britt, B. C., Evans, W., Rush, S. W., Towery, N. A., & Adamson, A. C. (2021). Can social media listening platforms' artificial intelligence be trusted? Examining the accuracy of Crimson Hexagon's (now Brandwatch Consumer Research's) AI-Driven analyses. *Journal of Advertising*, *50*(1), 81–91. DOI: 10.1080/00913367.2020.1809576

Hayes, P., & Kelly, S. (2018). Distributed morality, privacy, and social media in natural disaster response. *Technology in Society*, *54*, 155–167. DOI: 10.1016/j.techsoc.2018.05.003

Hecht, R., Dong, Z., & Khwaja, A. (2020). Collaborative platforms for disaster management: The role of open data. *Journal of Urban Technology*, *27*(1), 23–42.

Hecker, N., & Domres, B. D. (2018). The German emergency and disaster medicine and management system—history and present. *Chinese Journal of Traumatology = Zhonghua Chuang Shang Za Zhi*, *21*(2), 64–72. DOI: 10.1016/j.cjtee.2017.09.003 PMID: 29622286

Herath, H. M. K. K. M. B., & Mittal, M. (2022). Adoption of artificial intelligence in smart cities: A comprehensive review. *International Journal of Information Management Data Insights*, *2*(1), 2667–0968. DOI: 10.1016/j.jjimei.2022.100076

Hickok, M. (2021). Lessons learned from AI ethics principles for future actions. *AI and Ethics*, *1*(1), 41–47. DOI: 10.1007/s43681-020-00008-1

Holzinger, A., Langs, G., Denk, H., Zatloukal, K., & Müller, H. (2019). Causability and explainability of artificial intelligence in medicine. *Wiley Interdisciplinary Reviews. Data Mining and Knowledge Discovery*, *9*(4), e1312. DOI: 10.1002/widm.1312 PMID: 32089788

Hopko, S., Wang, J., & Mehta, R. (2022). Human factors considerations and metrics in shared space human-robot collaboration: A systematic review. *Frontiers in Robotics and AI*, *9*, 799522. DOI: 10.3389/frobt.2022.799522 PMID: 35187093

Hosseini, S. R., Scaioni, M., & Marani, M. (2018). On the influence of global warming on Atlantic hurricane frequency. *The International Archives of the Photogrammetry, Remote Sensing and Spatial Information Sciences*, *42*(3), 527–532. DOI: 10.5194/isprs-archives-XLII-3-527-2018

Hosseini, S., Barker, K., & Ramirez-Marquez, J. E. (2016). A review of definitions and measures of system resilience. *Reliability Engineering & System Safety*, *145*, 47–61. DOI: 10.1016/j.ress.2015.08.006

Huang, L., Wu, J., & Yan, L. (2015). Defining and measuring urban sustainability: A review of indicators. *Landscape Ecology*, *30*(7), 1175–1193. DOI: 10.1007/s10980-015-0208-2

Huang, Z., Liu, J., & Cheng, L. (2020). Enhancing Urban Planning with Predictive Analytics: A Case Study of Machine Learning Models. *Urban Studies (Edinburgh, Scotland)*, *57*(8), 1622–1640. DOI: 10.1177/0042098019894058

Hu, F., Tang, J., Wang, H., Song, M., & Su, T. (2020). Deep learning for smart city security: A survey. *Computers & Security*, *92*, 101715. DOI: 10.1016/j.cose.2020.101715

Hughes, A. L., & Palen, L. (2009). Twitter adoption and use in mass convergence and emergency events. *International Journal of Emergency Management*, *6*(3-4), 248–260. DOI: 10.1504/IJEM.2009.031564

Hwangbo, J., Lee, J., & Hutter, M. (2018). Per-Contact Iteration Method for Solving Contact Dynamics. *IEEE Robotics and Automation Letters*, *3*(2), 895–902. DOI: 10.1109/LRA.2018.2792536

Iglesias, C. A., & Moreno, A. (2019). Sentiment analysis for social media. *Applied Sciences (Basel, Switzerland)*, *9*(23), 5037. DOI: 10.3390/app9235037

Inamdar, R., Sundarr, S. K., Khandelwal, D., Sahu, V. D., & Katal, N. (2024). A comprehensive review on safe reinforcement learning for autonomous vehicle control in dynamic environments. *E-Prime - Advances in Electrical Engineering. Electronics and Energy*, *10*, 100810. DOI: 10.1016/j.prime.2024.100810

Ingram, G. K. (1998). Patterns of metropolitan development: What have we learned? *Urban Studies (Edinburgh, Scotland)*, *35*(7), 1019–1035. DOI: 10.1080/0042098984466

International Organization for Standardization. (2017). *ISO/IEC 27001:2017 - Information security management*. Retrieved from https://www.iso.org

IPCC. (2021). Climate change 2021: The physical science basis. *Intergovernmental Panel on Climate Change*. Retrieved from https://www.ipcc.ch/report/ar6/wg1/

Istepanian, R. S. (2022). Mobile health (m-Health) in retrospect: The known unknowns. *International Journal of Environmental Research and Public Health*, *19*(7), 3747. DOI: 10.3390/ijerph19073747 PMID: 35409431

Jafari, M., Kavousi-Fard, A., Chen, T., & Karimi, M. (2023). A review on digital twin technology in smart grid, transportation system and smart city: Challenges and future. *IEEE Access : Practical Innovations, Open Solutions*, *11*, 17471–17484. DOI: 10.1109/ACCESS.2023.3241588

Jagatheesaperumal, S. K., Bibri, S. E., Huang, J., Rajapandian, J., & Parthiban, B. (2024). Artificial intelligence of things for smart cities: Advanced solutions for enhancing transportation safety. *Computational Urban Science*, *4*(1), 10.

Jain, P., Gyanchandani, M., & Khare, N. (2016). Big data privacy: A technological perspective and review. *Journal of Big Data*, *3*(1), 25. DOI: 10.1186/s40537-016-0059-y

Janssen, M., Matheus, R., & Longo, J. (2020). Data governance as the enabler for smart cities. *Government Information Quarterly*, *37*(1), 101440.

Javaid, M., Haleem, A., Singh, R. P., & Suman, R. (2023). Towards insighting cybersecurity for healthcare domains: A comprehensive review of recent practices and trends. Cyber Security and Applications, 100016.

Jevinger, Å., Zhao, C., Persson, J. A., & Davidsson, P. (2024). Artificial intelligence for improving public transport: A mapping study. *Public Transport (Berlin)*, *16*(1), 99–158. DOI: 10.1007/s12469-023-00334-7

Jiang, L., Wang, H., & Zhou, J. (2020). AI applications for smart disaster management in the era of big data. *International Journal of Disaster Risk Reduction*, *46*, 101469.

Jiangyuan, Q. (2021). Simulation of auto obstacle avoidance based on Unity machine learning. *Journal of Physics: Conference Series*, *1883*(1), 012048. DOI: 10.1088/1742-6596/1883/1/012048

John-Otumu, A. M., Rahman, M. M., Nwokonkwo, O. C., & Onuoha, M. C. (2022). AI-Based Techniques for Online Social Media Network Sentiment Analysis: A Methodical Review. *International Journal of Computer and Information Engineering*, *16*(12), 555–560.

Johnson, M., Hofmann, K., Hutton, T., & Bignell, D. (2016). The Malmo platform for artificial intelligence experimentation. *Proceedings of the Twenty-Fifth International Joint Conference on Artificial Intelligence*, 4246–4247.

Jones, M. W., Peters, G. P., Gasser, T., Andrew, R. M., Schwingshackl, C., Gütschow, J., & Le Quéré, C. (2023). National contributions to climate change due to historical emissions of carbon dioxide, methane, and nitrous oxide since 1850. *Scientific Data*, *10*(1), 155. DOI: 10.1038/s41597-023-02041-1 PMID: 36991071

Jordan, M. I., & Mitchell, T. M. (2015). Machine learning: Trends, perspectives, and prospects. *Science*, *349*(6245), 255–260. DOI: 10.1126/science.aaa8415 PMID: 26185243

Junaid, S. B., Imam, A. A., Balogun, A. O., De Silva, L. C., Surakat, Y. A., Kumar, G., Abdulkarim, M., Shuaibu, A. N., Garba, A., Sahalu, Y., Mohammed, A., Mohammed, T. Y., Abdulkadir, B. A., Abba, A. A., Kakumi, N. A. I., & Mahamad, S. (2022, October 3). Recent Advancements in Emerging Technologies for Healthcare Management Systems: A Survey. *Healthcare (Basel)*, *10*(10), 1940. DOI: 10.3390/healthcare10101940 PMID: 36292387

Jung, J.-K., & Shin, J. (2018). A Hybrid Approach to Geotweets. In *Thinking Big Data in Geography. New Regimes, New Research* (pp. 91–122). University of Nebraska Press., Available at https://www.jstor.org/stable/j.ctt21h4z6m.10 DOI: 10.2307/j.ctt21h4z6m.10

Kamruzzaman, A., Ismat, S., Brickley, J. C., Liu, A., & Thakur, K. (2022, December). A comprehensive review of endpoint security: Threats and defenses. In *2022 International Conference on Cyber Warfare and Security (ICCWS)* (pp. 1-7). IEEE. https://doi.org/DOI: 10.1109/ICCWS56285.2022.9998470

Kankanamge, N., Yigitcanlar, T., & Goonetilleke, A. (2020). How engaging are disaster management related social media channels? The case of Australian state emergency organisations. *International Journal of Disaster Risk Reduction*, *48*, 101571. DOI: 10.1016/j.ijdrr.2020.101571

Kankanamge, N., Yigitcanlar, T., Goonetilleke, A., & Kamruzzaman, M. (2019). Can volunteer crowdsourcing reduce disaster risk? A systematic review of the literature. *International Journal of Disaster Risk Reduction*, *35*, 101097. DOI: 10.1016/j.ijdrr.2019.101097

Kankanamge, N., Yigitcanlar, T., Goonetilleke, A., & Kamruzzaman, M. (2020a). Determining disaster severity through social media analysis: Testing the methodology with South East Queensland Flood tweets. *International Journal of Disaster Risk Reduction*, *42*, 101360. DOI: 10.1016/j.ijdrr.2019.101360

Kapucu, N., Arslan, T., & Collins, M. L. (2010). Examining intergovernmental and interorganizational response to catastrophic disasters: Toward a network-centered approach. *Administration & Society*, *42*(2), 222–247. DOI: 10.1177/0095399710362517

Karimiziarani, M. (2023). Social media analytics in disaster response: A comprehensive review. *arXiv preprint arXiv:2307.04046*. https://doi.org//arXiv.2307.04046DOI: 10.48550

Karimiziarani, M., & Moradkhani, H. (2023). Social response and Disaster management: Insights from twitter data Assimilation on Hurricane Ian. *International Journal of Disaster Risk Reduction*, *95*, 103865. DOI: 10.1016/j.ijdrr.2023.103865

Kastrati, Z., Ahmedi, L., Kurti, A., Kadriu, F., Murtezaj, D., & Gashi, F. (2021). A deep learning sentiment analyser for social media comments in low-resource languages. *Electronics (Basel)*, *10*(10), 1133. DOI: 10.3390/electronics10101133

Kataria, A., & Puri, V. (2022). AI- and IoT-based hybrid model for air quality prediction in a smart city with network assistance. *IET Networks*, *11*(6), 221–233. DOI: 10.1049/ntw2.12053

Kaur, M., & Saini, M. (2024). Role of Artificial Intelligence in the crime prediction and pattern analysis studies published over the last decade: A scientometric analysis. *Artificial Intelligence Review*, *57*(8), 202. DOI: 10.1007/s10462-024-10823-1

Kemavuthanon, K., & Uchida, O. (2020). Classification of social media messages posted at the time of disaster. In *Information Technology in Disaster Risk Reduction: 4th IFIP TC 5 DCITDRR International Conference, ITDRR 2019, Kyiv, Ukraine, October 9–10, 2019, Revised Selected Papers 4* (pp. 212-226). Springer International Publishing. https://doi.org/DOI: 10.1007/978-3-030-48939-7_18

Kempka, M., Wydmuch, M., Runc, G., Toczek, J., & Jaśkowski, W. (2016). *ViZ-Doom: A Doom-based AI Research Platform for Visual Reinforcement Learning*. DOI: 10.1109/CIG.2016.7860433

Khatoon, S., Asif, A., Hasan, M. M., & Alshamari, M. (2022). Social media-based intelligence for disaster response and management in smart cities. In *Artificial Intelligence, Machine Learning, and Optimization Tools for Smart Cities: Designing for Sustainability* (pp. 211–235). Springer International Publishing., DOI: 10.1007/978-3-030-84459-2_11

Khatoon, S., Romman, L. A., & Hasan, M. M.Lamis Abu Romman. (2020). Domain independent automatic labeling system for large-scale social data using Lexicon and web-based augmentation. *Information Technology and Control*, *49*(1), 36–54. DOI: 10.5755/j01.itc.49.1.23769

Khatri, V., & Brown, C. V. (2010). Designing data governance. *Communications of the ACM*, *53*(1), 148–152. DOI: 10.1145/1629175.1629210

Khurana, D., Koli, A., Khatter, K., & Singh, S. (2023). Natural language processing: State of the art, current trends and challenges. *Multimedia Tools and Applications*, *82*(3), 3713–3744. DOI: 10.1007/s11042-022-13428-4 PMID: 35855771

Kim, S., Park, J., & Choi, H. (2019). Optimizing urban traffic flow using reinforcement learning to reduce noise pollution. *Transportation Research Part D, Transport and Environment*, *67*, 672–684. DOI: 10.1016/j.trd.2019.01.009

Kim, T., & Lee, J.-H. (2020). Reinforcement Learning-Based Path Generation Using Sequential Pattern Reduction and Self-Directed Curriculum Learning. *IEEE Access : Practical Innovations, Open Solutions*, *8*, 147790–147807. DOI: 10.1109/ACCESS.2020.3015245

Kirwan, C. G., & Zhiyong, F. (2020). *Smart cities and artificial intelligence: Convergent systems for planning, design, and operations*. Elsevier.

Kitazawa, K., & Hale, S. A. (2021). Social media and early warning systems for natural disasters: A case study of Typhoon Etau in Japan. *International Journal of Disaster Risk Reduction*, *52*, 101926. DOI: 10.1016/j.ijdrr.2020.101926

Kitchin, R. (2014). The real-time city? Big data and smart urbanism. *GeoJournal, 79*(1), 1–14. DOI: 10.1007/s10708-013-9516-8

Kitchin, R. (2021). *Data-driven urbanism and the smart city: Lessons and prospects*. Routledge.

Kok, E., & Chen, C. (2024). Occluded apples orientation estimator based on deep learning model for robotic harvesting. *Computers and Electronics in Agriculture, 219*, 108781. DOI: 10.1016/j.compag.2024.108781

Koranga, M., Pant, P., Kumar, T., Pant, D., Bhatt, A. K., & Pant, R. P. (2022). Efficient water quality prediction models based on machine learning algorithms for Nainital Lake, Uttarakhand. *Materials Today: Proceedings, 57*, 1706–1712. DOI: 10.1016/j.matpr.2021.12.334

Kothandaraman, D., ... Intelligent Forecasting of Air Quality and Pollution Prediction Using Machine Learning, *Adsorption Science and Technology*, vol. 2022, DOI: 10.1155/2022/5086622

Kousi, N., Gkournelos, C., Aivaliotis, S., Lotsaris, K., Bavelos, A. C., Baris, P., Michalos, G., & Makris, S. (2021). Digital Twin for Designing and Reconfiguring Human–Robot Collaborative Assembly Lines. *Applied Sciences (Basel, Switzerland), 11*(10), 4620. DOI: 10.3390/app11104620

Kouyoumdjian, P., Mansour, J., Assi, C., Caton, J., Lustig, S., & Coulomb, R. (2020). Current concepts in robotic total hip arthroplasty. *SICOT-J, 6*, 6. DOI: 10.1051/sicotj/2020041 PMID: 33258445

Kshetri, N. (2021). Blockchain's roles in meeting key supply chain management objectives. *International Journal of Information Management, 57*, 102145.

Kullback, S., & Leibler, R. A. (1951). On Information and Sufficiency. *Annals of Mathematical Statistics, 22*(1), 79–86. DOI: 10.1214/aoms/1177729694

Kumaar, A. A. N., & Kochuvila, S. (2023). Mobile Service Robot Path Planning Using Deep Reinforcement Learning. *IEEE Access : Practical Innovations, Open Solutions, 11*, 100083–100096. DOI: 10.1109/ACCESS.2023.3311519

Kumar, K., & Pande, B. P. (2022). Air pollution prediction with machine learning: A case study of Indian cities. *International Journal of Environmental Science and Technology*. Advance online publication. DOI: 10.1007/s13762-022-04241-5 PMID: 35603096

Kumar, R. (2021). Managing Business in the Digital Era–The use of IT and Analytics for Process Transformation. *Journal of Decision Systems*, *30*(4), 410–413. DOI: 10.1080/12460125.2021.1925397

Kumar, R., Sharma, M., & Bhatia, A. (2018). Machine Learning for Renewable Energy Integration and Optimization. *Energy Reports*, *4*, 184–194. DOI: 10.1016/j.egyr.2018.05.009

Kushwah, V. S., Goyal, S. K., & Sharma, A. (2020). Maximize resource utilization using aco in cloud computing environment for load balancing. In Soft Computing: Theories and Applications [Springer Singapore.]. *Proceedings of SoCTA*, *2018*, 583–590.

Lakshmi Shankar Iyer. (2021). *AI enabled applications towards intelligent transportation. 2666-691. Transportation Engineering 5 (2021) 100083*. Elsevier Ltd., DOI: 10.1016/j.treng.2021.100083

Lakshmikantha, V., Hiriyannagowda, A., Manjunath, A., Patted, A., Basavaiah, J., & Anthony, A. A. (2021). IoT based smart water quality monitoring system. *Global Transitions Proceedings*, *2*(2), 181–186.

Lakshminarayanan, V., Ravikumar, A., Sriraman, H., Alla, S., & Chattu, V. K. (2023). Health care equity through intelligent edge computing and augmented reality/virtual reality: A systematic review. *Journal of Multidisciplinary Healthcare*, *16*, 2839–2859. DOI: 10.2147/JMDH.S419923 PMID: 37753339

Lamssaggad, A., Benamar, N., Hafid, A. S., & Msahli, M. (2021). A survey on the current security landscape of intelligent transportation systems. *IEEE Access : Practical Innovations, Open Solutions*, *9*, 9180–9208. DOI: 10.1109/ACCESS.2021.3050038

Lawton, G. (2023). AI transparency: What is it and why do we need it. TechTarget. *Retrieved*, (October), 13.

Lee, D., & Yoon, S. N. (2021). Application of artificial intelligence-based technologies in the healthcare industry: Opportunities and challenges. *International Journal of Environmental Research and Public Health*, *18*(1), 271. DOI: 10.3390/ijerph18010271 PMID: 33401373

Lee, I. (2018). Social media analytics for enterprises: Typology, methods, and processes. *Business Horizons*, *61*(2), 199–210. DOI: 10.1016/j.bushor.2017.11.002

Lee, J., & Grey, X., M., Ha, S., Kunz, T., Jain, S., Ye, Y., S. Srinivasa, S., Stilman, M., & Karen Liu, C. (. (2018). DART: Dynamic Animation and Robotics Toolkit. *Journal of Open Source Software*, *3*(22), 500. DOI: 10.21105/joss.00500

Lee, Y., Bradford, B., & Posch, K. (2024). The Effectiveness of Big Data-Driven Predictive Policing: Systematic Review. *Justice Evaluation Journal*, *7*(2), 127–160. DOI: 10.1080/24751979.2024.2371781

Lei, T. M. T., Siu, S. W. I., Monjardino, J., Mendes, L., & Ferreira, F. (2022). Using Machine Learning Methods to Forecast Air Quality: A Case Study in Macao. *Atmosphere (Basel)*, *13*(9), 1412. Advance online publication. DOI: 10.3390/atmos13091412

Lian, Y. (2020). Environmental monitoring using machine learning: Applications in air and water quality management. *Environmental Science & Technology*, *54*(2), 1015–1025. DOI: 10.1021/acs.est.9b05448 PMID: 33373200

Lin, X., Wang, Y., & Zhang, H. (2021). The application of AI and robotics in disaster response: A review. *Disaster Management & Prevention*, *10*(3), 267–280.

Liu, Q., Wei, Y., Leng, S., & Chen, Y. (2017, October). Task scheduling in fog enabled Internet of Things for smart cities. In 2017 IEEE 17th International conference on communication technology (ICCT) (pp. 975-980). IEEE. DOI: 10.1109/ICCT.2017.8359780

Liu, D., Wang, Z., Lu, B., Cong, M., Yu, H., & Zou, Q. (2020). A Reinforcement Learning-Based Framework for Robot Manipulation Skill Acquisition. *IEEE Access : Practical Innovations, Open Solutions*, *8*, 108429–108437. DOI: 10.1109/ACCESS.2020.3001130

Liu, H. (2024). Cooperative multi-agent game based on reinforcement learning. *High-Confidence Computing*, *4*(1), 100205. DOI: 10.1016/j.hcc.2024.100205

Liu, Q., Xu, D., Yuan, B., Mou, Z., & Wang, M. (2023). Distance-Controllable Long Jump of Quadruped Robot Based on Parameter Optimization Using Deep Reinforcement Learning. *IEEE Access : Practical Innovations, Open Solutions*, *11*, 98566–98577. DOI: 10.1109/ACCESS.2023.3313637

Li, X., He, B., Wang, Z., Zhou, Y., Li, G., & Jiang, R. (2021). Semantic-Enhanced Digital Twin System for Robot–Environment Interaction Monitoring. *IEEE Transactions on Instrumentation and Measurement*, *70*, 1–13. DOI: 10.1109/TIM.2021.3066542

Li, Y., & Liu, Q. (2021). A comprehensive review study of cyber-attacks and cyber security; Emerging trends and recent developments. *Energy Reports*, *7*, 8176–8186. DOI: 10.1016/j.egyr.2021.08.126

Li, Z., Shahidehpour, M., & Bahramirad, S. (2018). Smart cities: A gateway for electric utilities in the new economy. *The Electricity Journal*, *31*(6), 1–6. DOI: 10.1016/j.tej.2018.07.001

Loomis, J. J., & Dziedzic, M. (2018). Evaluating EIA systems' effectiveness: A state of the art. *Environmental Impact Assessment Review*, *68*, 29–37. DOI: 10.1016/j.eiar.2017.10.005

Löppenberg, M., Yuwono, S., Diprasetya, M. R., & Schwung, A. (2024). Dynamic robot routing optimization: State–space decomposition for operations research-informed reinforcement learning. *Robotics and Computer-integrated Manufacturing*, *90*, 102812. DOI: 10.1016/j.rcim.2024.102812

Luckey, D., Fritz, H., Legatiuk, D., Dragos, K., & Smarsly, K. (2020). Artificial intelligence techniques for smart city applications. In *International Conference on Computing in Civil and Building Engineering* (pp. 3-15). Springer, Cham.

Lv, Q., Zhang, R., Sun, X., Lu, Y., & Bao, J. (2021). A digital twin-driven human-robot collaborative assembly approach in the wake of COVID-19. *Journal of Manufacturing Systems*, *60*, 837–851. DOI: 10.1016/j.jmsy.2021.02.011 PMID: 33649693

Lv, Z., Zhang, S., & Xiu, W. (2021). Solving the security problem of intelligent transportation systems with deep learning. *IEEE Transactions on Intelligent Transportation Systems*, *22*(7), 4281–4290. DOI: 10.1109/TITS.2020.2980864

Ly, H. B., Le, L. M., Phi, L. V., Phan, V. H., Tran, V. Q., Pham, B. T., Le, T. T., & Derrible, S. (2019). Development of an AI model to measure traffic air pollution from multisensor and weather data. *Sensors (Basel)*, *19*(22), 4941. DOI: 10.3390/s19224941 PMID: 31766187

Ma, Y., Wang, Z., Yang, H., & Yang, L. (2020). Artificial intelligence applications in the development of autonomous vehicles: a survey. IEEE. Page(s): 315 - 329. ISSN: 2329-9266. DOI: DOI: 10.1109/JAS.2020.1003021

Mahmoudi, R., & Ostreika, A. (2023). Reinforcement learning for obstacle avoidance application in unity mlagents. *28th Conference on Information Society and University Studies*, 1–8.

Majumder, A. (2021). *Deep Reinforcement Learning in Unity: With Unity ML Toolkit*. Apress., DOI: 10.1007/978-1-4842-6503-1

Maleki Varnosfaderani, S., & Forouzanfar, M. (2024, March 29). The Role of AI in Hospitals and Clinics: Transforming Healthcare in the 21st Century. *Bioengineering (Basel, Switzerland)*, *11*(4), 337. DOI: 10.3390/bioengineering11040337 PMID: 38671759

Malik, A., Onyema, E. M., Dalal, S., Lilhore, U. K., Anand, D., Sharma, A., & Simaiya, S. (2023). Forecasting students' adaptability in online entrepreneurship education using modified ensemble machine learning model. *Array (New York, N.Y.)*, *19*, 100303. DOI: 10.1016/j.array.2023.100303

Mangones, A. (n.d.). Social Media in Disasters. Accessed 11 July 2024. https://preparecenter.org/topic/social-media-disasters/

Manikandan, G., Bhuvaneswari, G., & Joel, M. R. (2023, August). Artificial Intelligence to the Assessment, Monitoring, and Forecasting of Drought in Developing Countries. In *2023 International Conference on Circuit Power and Computing Technologies (ICCPCT)* (pp. 886-892). IEEE. DOI: 10.1109/ICCPCT58313.2023.10245072

Manisalidis, I., Stavropoulou, E., Stavropoulos, A., & Bezirtzoglou, E. (2020). Environmental and Health Impacts of Air Pollution: A Review. *Frontiers in Public Health*, *8*, 14. DOI: 10.3389/fpubh.2020.00014 PMID: 32154200

Manoharan, G., Razak, A., Rao, B. S., Singh, R., Ashtikar, S. P., & Nivedha, M. (2024). Navigating the Crescendo of Challenges in Harnessing Artificial Intelligence for Disaster Management. In *Predicting Natural Disasters With AI and Machine Learning* (pp. 64–94). IGI Global., DOI: 10.4018/979-8-3693-2280-2.ch003

Mao, Y., & Lee, S. (2019, August). Deep convolutional neural network for air quality prediction. [). IOP Publishing.]. *Journal of Physics: Conference Series*, *1302*(3), 032046. DOI: 10.1088/1742-6596/1302/3/032046

Marchand, R. C., Sodhi, N., Khlopas, A., Sultan, A. A., Harwin, S. F., Malkani, A. L., & Mont, M. A. (2017). Patient satisfaction outcomes after robotic arm-assisted total knee arthroplasty: A short-term evaluation. *The Journal of Knee Surgery*, *30*(09), 849–853. DOI: 10.1055/s-0037-1607450 PMID: 29029352

Marogna, M., Spadolini, I., Massolo, A., Canonica, G. W., & Passalacqua, G. (2010). Long-lasting effects of sublingual immunotherapy according to its duration: A 15-year prospective study. *The Journal of Allergy and Clinical Immunology*, *126*(5), 969–975. DOI: 10.1016/j.jaci.2010.08.030 PMID: 20934206

Maroju, R. G., Choudhari, S. G., Shaikh, M. K., Borkar, S. K., & Mendhe, H. (2023). Role of telemedicine and digital technology in public health in India: A narrative review. *Cureus*, *15*(3). Advance online publication. DOI: 10.7759/cureus.35986 PMID: 37050980

Martí, P., Serrano-Estrada, L., & Nolasco-Cirugeda, A. (2019). Social media data: Challenges, opportunities and limitations in urban studies. *Computers, Environment and Urban Systems*, *74*, 161–174. DOI: 10.1016/j.compenvurbsys.2018.11.001

Maselli, D. J., Bhatt, S. P., Anzueto, A., Bowler, R. P., DeMeo, D. L., Diaz, A. A., Dransfield, M. T., Fawzy, A., Foreman, M. G., Hanania, N. A., Hersh, C. P., Kim, V., Kinney, G. L., Putcha, N., Wan, E. S., Wells, J. M., Westney, G. E., Young, K. A., Silverman, E. K., & Make, B. J. (2019). Clinical epidemiology of COPD: Insights from 10 years of the COPDGene study. *Chest, 156*(2), 228–238. DOI: 10.1016/j.chest.2019.04.135 PMID: 31154041

Matsuoka, M., Nojima, N., & Yamaguchi, S. (2012). AI-driven generative design in post-tsunami reconstruction. *Engineering Structures*, *44*, 214–223.

Mattia, G. P., & Beraldi, R. (2022, March). On real-time scheduling in Fog computing: A Reinforcement Learning algorithm with application to smart cities. In 2022 IEEE International conference on pervasive computing and communications workshops and other affiliated events (PerCom Workshops) (pp. 187-193). IEEE. DOI: 10.1109/PerComWorkshops53856.2022.9767498

Mbunge, E., & Muchemwa, B. (2022). Towards emotive sensory Web in virtual health care: Trends, technologies, challenges and ethical issues. *Sensors International*, *3*, 100134. DOI: 10.1016/j.sintl.2021.100134

Mbunge, E., Muchemwa, B., & Batani, J. (2021). Sensors and healthcare 5.0: Transformative shift in virtual care through emerging digital health technologies. *Global Health Journal (Amsterdam, Netherlands)*, *5*(4), 169–177. DOI: 10.1016/j.glohj.2021.11.008

McLain, R., Poe, M., Biedenweg, K., Cerveny, L., Besser, D., & Blahna, D. (2013). Making sense of human ecology mapping: An overview of approaches to integrating socio-spatial data into environmental planning. *Human Ecology: an Interdisciplinary Journal*, *41*(5), 651–665. DOI: 10.1007/s10745-013-9573-0

McMahan, H. B., Moore, E., Ramage, D., & Hsu, D. (2017). Communication-Efficient Learning of Deep Networks from Decentralized Data. *Proceedings of the 20th International Conference on Artificial Intelligence and Statistics, 54*, 1273-1282. https://arxiv.org/abs/1602.05629

McMahon, T. A., Rohr, J. R., & Bernal, X. E. (2017). Light and noise pollution interact to disrupt interspecific interactions. *Ecology*, *98*(5), 1290–1299. DOI: 10.1002/ecy.1770 PMID: 28170099

Md, A. Q., Jaiswal, D., Mohan, S., Innab, N., Sulaiman, R., Alaoui, M. K., & Ahmadian, A. (2024). A novel approach for self-driving car in partially observable environment using life long reinforcement learning. *Sustainable Energy. Grids and Networks*, *38*, 101356. DOI: 10.1016/j.segan.2024.101356

Mehmet Tuğrul, K. (2023). *Drone Technologies and Applications*. IntechOpen., DOI: 10.5772/intechopen.1001987

Mehrabi, N., Morstatter, F., Saxena, N., Lerman, K., & Galstyan, A. (2021). A survey on bias and fairness in machine learning. *ACM Computing Surveys*, *54*(6), 1–35. DOI: 10.1145/3457607

Meier, P. (2012). Ushahidi and the promise of crowdsourcing in crisis response. *International Journal of Information Systems for Crisis Response and Management*, *4*(1), 22–30.

Meier, P. (2015). *Digital humanitarians: how big data is changing the face of humanitarian response*. Crc Press. DOI: 10.1201/b18023

Melo, L. C., Melo, D. C., & Maximo, M. R. O. A. (2021). Learning Humanoid Robot Running Motions with Symmetry Incentive through Proximal Policy Optimization. *Journal of Intelligent & Robotic Systems*, *102*(3), 54. DOI: 10.1007/s10846-021-01355-9

Messeri, L., & Crockett, M. J. (2024). Artificial intelligence and illusions of understanding in scientific research. *Nature*, *627*(8002), 49–58. DOI: 10.1038/s41586-024-07146-0 PMID: 38448693

Miao, X.-Y., & Zhao, H. (2024). Dynamic plugging regulating strategy of pipeline robot based on reinforcement learning. *Petroleum Science*, *21*(1), 597–608. DOI: 10.1016/j.petsci.2023.08.016

Michael, C. (2020). Leveraging Intelligent Transportation Systems and Smart Vehicles Using Crowdsourcing: An Overview. MDPI. *Smart Cities*, *3*(2), 341–360. DOI: 10.3390/smartcities3020018

Microsoft. (2018). *Seeing AI: Bringing independence to visually impaired users*. Microsoft Newsroom.

Microsoft. (2021, December 28). *Using Visual Studio Tools for Unity*. https://learn.microsoft.com/en-us/visualstudio/gamedev/unity/get-started/using-visual-studio-tools-for-unity

Miles, J. C., & Walker, A. J. (2006). "The potential application of artificial intelligence in transport," IEE Proc. Intell. Transp. Syst., vol. 153, no. 3, pp. 183–198, 2006. DOI: DOI: 10.1049/ip-its:20060014

Milivojčević, M., Ćirić, D., Prezelj, J., & Murovec, J. (2024). Analysis of unsupervised learning approach for classification of vehicle fuel type using psychoacoustic features. *Measurement*, *227*, 114318. DOI: 10.1016/j.measurement.2024.114318

Minopoulos, G. M., Memos, V. A., Stergiou, K. D., Stergiou, C. L., & Psannis, K. E. (2023). A Medical Image Visualization Technique Assisted with AI-Based Haptic Feedback for Robotic Surgery and Healthcare. *Applied Sciences (Basel, Switzerland)*, *13*(6), 3592. DOI: 10.3390/app13063592

Mohsin, A. H. (2022). Optimize routing protocol overheads in MANETs: challenges and solutions: a review paper. *Wireless Personal Communications*, *126*(4), 2871–2910. DOI: 10.1007/s11277-022-09843-3

Morley, J., Floridi, L., Kinsey, L., & Elhalal, A. (2020). Ethical guidelines for COVID-19 tracing apps. *Nature Electronics*, *3*(10), 559–562. PMID: 32467596

Morley, J., Machado, C. C., Burr, C., Cowls, J., Joshi, I., Taddeo, M., & Floridi, L. (2020). The ethics of AI in health care: A mapping review. *Social Science & Medicine*, *260*, 113172. DOI: 10.1016/j.socscimed.2020.113172 PMID: 32702587

Mukherjee, A., Sasidharan, M., Herrera, M., & Parlikad, A. K. (2024). Unsupervised constrained discord detection in IoT-based online crane monitoring. *Advanced Engineering Informatics*, *60*, 102444. DOI: 10.1016/j.aei.2024.102444

Munir, A., Aved, A., & Blasch, E. (2022). Situational awareness: Techniques, challenges, and prospects. *AI*, *3*(1), 55–77. DOI: 10.3390/ai3010005

Myagmar-Ochir, Y., & Kim, W. (2023). A Survey of Video Surveillance Systems in Smart City. *Electronics (Basel)*, *12*(17), 3567. DOI: 10.3390/electronics12173567

Naeem, M., Jamal, T., Diaz-Martinez, J., Butt, S. A., Montesano, N., Tariq, M. I., . . . De-La-Hoz-Valdiris, E. (2022). Trends and future perspective challenges in big data. In *Advances in Intelligent Data Analysis and Applications:Proceeding of the Sixth Euro-China Conference on Intelligent Data Analysis and Applications,15–18 October 2019,Arad, Romania* (pp. 309-325). Springer Singapore. https://doi.org/ DOI: 10.1007/978-981-16-5036-9_30

Nagarajan, S. M., Deverajan, G. G., Chatterjee, P., Alnumay, W., & Ghosh, U. (2021). Effective task scheduling algorithm with deep learning for Internet of Health Things (IoHT) in sustainable smart cities. *Sustainable Cities and Society*, *71*, 102945. DOI: 10.1016/j.scs.2021.102945

Nagrecha, K.. (2022). *Sensor-Based Air Pollution Prediction Using Deep CNN-LSTM CSCI-ISAI, 2022*. Short Paper., DOI: 10.1109/CSCI51800.2020.00127

Nahavandi, S., Alizadehsani, R., Nahavandi, D., Lim, C. P., Kelly, K., & Bello, F. (2024). Machine learning meets advanced robotic manipulation. *Information Fusion*, *105*, 102221. DOI: 10.1016/j.inffus.2023.102221

Naranjo, P. G. V., Pooranian, Z., Shojafar, M., Conti, M., & Buyya, R. (2019). FOCAN: A Fog-supported smart city network architecture for management of applications in the Internet of Everything environments. *Journal of Parallel and Distributed Computing*, *132*, 274–283. DOI: 10.1016/j.jpdc.2018.07.003

Nazer, T. H., Morstatter, F., Dani, H., & Liu, H. (2016, August). Finding requests in social media for disaster relief. In *2016 IEEE/ACM International Conference on Advances in Social Networks Analysis and Mining (ASONAM)* (pp. 1410-1413). IEEE. https://doi.org/DOI: 10.1109/ASONAM.2016.7752432

Newman, B., Joseph, K., Chauhan, A., Seale, H., Li, J., Manias, E., Walton, M., Mears, S., Jones, B., & Harrison, R. (2021). Do patient engagement interventions work for all patients? A systematic review and realist synthesis of interventions to enhance patient safety. *Health Expectations*, *24*(6), 1905–1923. DOI: 10.1111/hex.13343 PMID: 34432339

Nguyen, T. A., & Aiello, M. (2013). Energy intelligent buildings based on user activity: A survey. *Energy and Building*, *56*, 244–257. DOI: 10.1016/j.enbuild.2012.09.005

Nicholas, J. (2019). Schork "ARTIFICIAL INTELLIGENCE AND PERSONALIZED MEDICINE" Published in final edited form as. *Cancer Treatment and Research*, *178*, 265–283. DOI: 10.1007/978-3-030-16391-4_11

Nicholson, E., Fulton, E. A., Brooks, T. M., Blanchard, R., Leadley, P., Metzger, J. P., Mokany, K., Stevenson, S., Wintle, B. A., Woolley, S. N. C., Barnes, M., Watson, J. E. M., & Ferrier, S. (2019). Scenarios and models to support global conservation targets. *Trends in Ecology & Evolution*, *34*(1), 57–68. DOI: 10.1016/j.tree.2018.10.006 PMID: 30514580

Nikpour, M., Yousefi, P. B., Jafarzadeh, H., Danesh, K., Shomali, R., Asadi, S., & Ahmadi, M. (2024). Intelligent Energy Management in Smart Cities: Leveraging IoT and Machine Learning for Optimizing Complex Networks and Systems. *Journal of Network and Computer Applications*, •••, 104089.

Njoku, J. N., Nwakanma, C. I., Amaizu, G. C., & Kim, D.-S. (2023). Prospects and challenges of metaverse application in data-driven intelligent transportation systems. *IET Intelligent Transport Systems*, *17*(1), 1–21. DOI: 10.1049/itr2.12252

Nunavath, V., & Goodwin, M. (2018, December). The role of artificial intelligence in social media big data analytics for disaster management-initial results of a systematic literature review. In *2018 5th International Conference on information and communication technologies for disaster management (ICT-DM)* (pp. 1-4). IEEE. https://doi.org/DOI: 10.1109/ICT-DM.2018.8636388

Nutonen, K., Kuts, V., & Otto, T. (2023). Industrial Robot Training in the Simulation Using the Machine Learning Agent. *Procedia Computer Science*, *217*, 446–455. DOI: 10.1016/j.procs.2022.12.240

NVIDIA Isaac Sim. (2024). https://developer.nvidia.com/isaac/sim

O'Neil, C. (2016). *Weapons of Math Destruction: How Big Data Increases Inequality and Threatens Democracy*. Crown Publishing Group. • Pelling, M. (2011). *Adaptation to climate change: From resilience to transformation*. Routledge. • United Nations. (2018). *World Urbanization Prospects: The 2018 Revision*. Department of Economic and Social Affairs, Population Division. https://www.un.org/development/desa/publications/world-urbanization-prospects-the-2018-revision.html

Okafor, E., Oyedeji, M., & Alfarraj, M. (2024). Deep reinforcement learning with light-weight vision model for sequential robotic object sorting. *Journal of King Saud University. Computer and Information Sciences*, *36*(1), 101896. DOI: 10.1016/j.jksuci.2023.101896

Okonta, D. E., & Vukovic, V. (2024). Smart cities software applications for sustainability and resilience. *Heliyon*, *10*(12), e32654. DOI: 10.1016/j.heliyon.2024.e32654 PMID: 39183850

Oladimeji, D., Gupta, K., Kose, N. A., Gundogan, K., Ge, L., & Liang, F. (2023). Smart transportation: An overview of technologies and applications. *Sensors (Basel)*, *23*(8), 3880. DOI: 10.3390/s23083880 PMID: 37112221

Olaniyi, O. O., Okunleye, O. J., & Olabanji, S. O. (2023). Advancing data-driven decision-making in smart cities through big data analytics: A comprehensive review of existing literature. *Current Journal of Applied Science and Technology*, *42*(25), 10–18.

Olawade, D. B., Wada, O. Z., Ige, A. O., Egbewole, B. I., Olojo, A., & Oladapo, B. I. (2024). Artificial intelligence in environmental monitoring: Advancements, challenges, and future directions. *Hygiene and Environmental Health Advances*, *12*, 100114. DOI: 10.1016/j.heha.2024.100114

Olawumi, M. A., & Oladapo, B. I. (2025). AI-driven predictive models for sustainability. *Journal of Environmental Management*, *373*, 123472. DOI: 10.1016/j.jenvman.2024.123472 PMID: 39612794

Olayode, O. I., Tartibu, L. K., & Okwu, M. O. (2020). Application of Artificial Intelligence in Traffic Control System of Non-autonomous Vehicles at Signalized Road Intersection. *Procedia CIRP*, *91*, 194–200. DOI: 10.1016/j.procir.2020.02.167

Olteanu, A., Vieweg, S., & Castillo, C. (2015, February). What to expect when the unexpected happens: Social media communications across crises. In Proceedings of the 18th ACM conference on computer supported cooperative work & social computing (pp. 994-1009). https://doi.org/DOI: 10.1145/2675133.2675242

Olugbade, S., Ojo, S., Imoize, A. L., Isabona, J., & Alaba, M. O. (2022). A review of artificial intelligence and machine learning for incident detectors in road transport systems. *Mathematical & Computational Applications*, *27*(5), 77. DOI: 10.3390/mca27050077

Oruma, S. O., Ayele, Y. Z., Sechi, F., & Rødsethol, H. (2023, September 24). Security Aspects of Social Robots in Public Spaces: A Systematic Mapping Study. *Sensors (Basel)*, *23*(19), 8056. DOI: 10.3390/s23198056 PMID: 37836888

Padgham, L., & Winikoff, M. (2004). *Developing Intelligent Agent Systems: A Practical Guide* (1st ed.). Wiley., DOI: 10.1002/0470861223

Paluch, S., & Wirtz, J. (2020). Artificial intelligence and robots in the service encounter. Journal of service management research.

Panchal, R., Mathew, S., & Baweja, A. (2021). AI-powered training simulations for emergency response. *Simulation in Healthcare*, *16*(5), 320–329.

Panchamukhi, M., Ghosh, D., & Kumar, S. (2021). Flood prediction using AI: Case study from India. *Journal of Hydrology (Amsterdam)*, *593*, 125908.

Pane, Y. P., Nageshrao, S. P., Kober, J., & Babuška, R. (2019). Reinforcement learning based compensation methods for robot manipulators. *Engineering Applications of Artificial Intelligence*, *78*, 236–247. DOI: 10.1016/j.engappai.2018.11.006

Panwar, H., Gupta, P. K., Siddiqui, M. K., Morales-Menendez, R., Bhardwaj, P., Sharma, S., & Sarker, I. H. (2020). AquaVision: Automating the detection of waste in water bodies using deep transfer learning. *Case Studies in Chemical and Environmental Engineering*, *2*, 10002. DOI: 10.1016/j.cscee.2020.100026

Patel, V., Chesmore, A., Legner, C. M., & Pandey, S. (2022). Trends in workplace wearable technologies and connected-worker solutions for next-generation occupational safety, health, and productivity. *Advanced Intelligent Systems*, *4*(1), 2100099. DOI: 10.1002/aisy.202100099

Pechinger, M., Schröer, G., Bogenberger, K., & Markgraf, C. (2023). Roadside infrastructure support for urban automated driving. *IEEE Transactions on Intelligent Transportation Systems*, *24*(10), 10643–10652. DOI: 10.1109/TITS.2023.3277138

Pérez-Gil, Ó., Barea, R., López-Guillén, E., Bergasa, L. M., Gómez-Huélamo, C., Gutiérrez, R., & Díaz-Díaz, A. (2022). Deep reinforcement learning based control for Autonomous Vehicles in CARLA. *Multimedia Tools and Applications*, *81*(3), 3553–3576. DOI: 10.1007/s11042-021-11437-3

Pérez, L., Rodríguez-Jiménez, S., Rodríguez, N., Usamentiaga, R., & García, D. F. (2020). Digital Twin and Virtual Reality Based Methodology for Multi-Robot Manufacturing Cell Commissioning. *Applied Sciences (Basel, Switzerland)*, *10*(10), 3633. DOI: 10.3390/app10103633

Perez-Liebana, D., Liu, J., Khalifa, A., Gaina, R. D., Togelius, J., & Lucas, S. M. (2018). *General Video Game AI: A Multi-Track Framework for Evaluating Agents, Games and Content Generation Algorithms* (Version 4). arXiv. DOI: 10.48550/ARXIV.1802.10363

Perry, R. W., & Lindell, M. K. (2003). Preparedness for emergency response: Guidelines for the emergency planning process. *Disasters*, *27*(4), 336–350. DOI: 10.1111/j.0361-3666.2003.00237.x PMID: 14725091

Persis, J., & Ben Amar, A. (2023, February 1). Predictive modeling and analysis of air quality - Visualizing before and during COVID-19 scenarios. *Journal of Environmental Management*, *327*, 116911. DOI: 10.1016/j.jenvman.2022.116911 PMID: 36470187

Pool, J., Smith, N., Dodds, H., Lockey, S., Curtis, C., Rinta-Kahila, T., & Gillespie, N. (2023). An AI-Enabled Community Safety Service: Stakeholder Benefits and Vulnerabilities.

Pradhan, A., Mohapatra, P., & Nayak, B. (2021). AI-driven supply chain optimization in disaster response. *Journal of Operations Research*, *45*(2), 123–135.

Pratomo, A. B., Mokodenseho, S., & Aziz, A. M. (2023). Data encryption and anonymization techniques for enhanced information system security and privacy. *West Science Information System and Technology*, *1*(01), 1–9. DOI: 10.58812/wsist.v1i01.176

Profiroiu, C. M., Bodislav, D. A., Burlacu, S., & Rădulescu, C. V. (2020). Challenges of sustainable urban development in the context of population growth. *European Journal of Sustainable Development*, *9*(3), 51–51. DOI: 10.14207/ejsd.2020.v9n3p51

Qayyum, T., Trabelsi, Z., Malik, A. W., & Hayawi, K. (2021). Multi-level resource sharing framework using collaborative fog environment for smart cities. *IEEE Access : Practical Innovations, Open Solutions*, *9*, 21859–21869. DOI: 10.1109/ACCESS.2021.3054420

Qin, Y., Xu, Z., Wang, X., & Skare, M. (2024). Artificial Intelligence and Economic Development: An Evolutionary Investigation and Systematic Review. *Journal of the Knowledge Economy*, *15*(1), 1736–1770. DOI: 10.1007/s13132-023-01183-2

Qi, W., Fan, H., Karimi, H. R., & Su, H. (2023). An adaptive reinforcement learning-based multimodal data fusion framework for human–robot confrontation gaming. *Neural Networks*, *164*, 489–496. DOI: 10.1016/j.neunet.2023.04.043 PMID: 37201309

Qu, Y., Wu, P. F., & Wang, X. (2009, January). Online community response to major disaster: A study of Tianya forum in the 2008 Sichuan earthquake. In 2009 42nd Hawaii International Conference on System Sciences (pp. 1-11). IEEE. https://doi.org/DOI: 10.1109/HICSS.2009.330

Rajput, R. P. (2022). Air Pollution Prediction using Machine Learning, *International Research Journal of Engineering and Technology*, Available: www.irjet.net

Raj, V. S., Subalalitha, C. N., Sambath, L., Glavin, F., & Chakravarthi, B. R. (2024). ConBERT-RL: A policy-driven deep reinforcement learning based approach for detecting homophobia and transphobia in low-resource languages. *Natural Language Processing Journal*, *6*, 100040. DOI: 10.1016/j.nlp.2023.100040

Ramachandran, R., Arthi, D., & Babu, A., & RS, A. S. (2024, April). A Meta-Analytical Review on Microplastic Pollution in the Indian Ocean. In *2024 International Conference on Science Technology Engineering and Management (ICSTEM)* (pp. 1-7). IEEE. DOI: 10.1109/ICSTEM61137.2024.10561208

Rampérez, V., Soriano, J., & Lizcano, D. (2018). A multidomain standards-based fog computing architecture for smart cities. *Wireless Communications and Mobile Computing*, *2018*(1), 4019858. DOI: 10.1155/2018/4019858

Rana, R., Singh, P., & Gupta, S. (2021). Flood prediction and response using AI and IoT: Case study of Kerala floods. *International Journal of Hydrology*, *4*(3), 201–209.

Rasheed, M., Jasim, W. M., & Farhan, R. (2024). Enhancing robotic grasping with attention mechanism and advanced UNet architectures in generative grasping convolutional neural networks. *Alexandria Engineering Journal*, *102*, 149–158. DOI: 10.1016/j.aej.2024.05.082

Rasp, S., Dueben, P. D., Scher, S., Weyn, J. A., Mouatadid, S., & Thuerey, N. (2020). WeatherBench: A benchmark dataset for data-driven weather forecasting. *Journal of Advances in Modeling Earth Systems, 12*(11), e2020MS002203.

Rathore, M. M., Paul, A., Hong, W. H., Seo, H., Awan, I., & Saeed, S. (2018). Exploiting IoT and big data analytics: Defining smart digital city using real-time urban data. *Sustainable Cities and Society*, *40*, 600–610. DOI: 10.1016/j.scs.2017.12.022

Razavi, M., Hamidkhani, M., & Sadeghi, R. (2019). *Smart traffic light scheduling in smart city using image and video processing*. IEEE Xplore., DOI: 10.1109/IICITA.2019.8808836

Reddy, K. H. K., Goswami, R. S., Roy, D. S., & Senior Member, I. E. E. E. (2023). A futuristic green service computing approach for smart city: A fog layered intelligent service management model for smart transport system. *Computer Communications*, *212*, 151–160. DOI: 10.1016/j.comcom.2023.08.001

Reece, A. G., & Youssef, N. (2018). AI-driven evacuation planning during Hurricane Irma. *Disaster Medicine and Public Health Preparedness*, *12*(5), 565–570.

Reuter, C., Kaufhold, M.-A., Spahr, F., Spielhofer, T., & Hahne, A. S. (2020). Emergency Service Staff and Social Media – A Comparative Empirical Study of the Attitude By Emergency Services Staff in Europe in 2014 and 2017. *International Journal of Disaster Risk Reduction*, *46*, 101516. DOI: 10.1016/j.ijdrr.2020.101516

Reynard, D., & Shirgaokar, M. (2019). Harnessing the power of machine learning: Can Twitter data be useful in guiding resource allocation decisions during a natural disaster? *Transportation Research Part D, Transport and Environment*, *77*, 449–463. DOI: 10.1016/j.trd.2019.03.002

Ribino, P., Di Napoli, C., Paragliola, G., & Serino, L. (2024). Hyper-Parameter Optimization through Reinforcement Learning for Survival Prediction of Patients with Heart Failure. *Procedia Computer Science*, *239*, 1754–1761. DOI: 10.1016/j.procs.2024.06.354

Rodriguez-Arias, A., Guijarro-Berdinas, B., & Sanchez-Marono, N. (2020). A FIPA-ACL based communication utility for Unity. *2020 IEEE 29th International Conference on Enabling Technologies: Infrastructure for Collaborative Enterprises (WETICE)*, 9–13. DOI: 10.1109/WETICE49692.2020.00010

Rojas-Martín, A., Martínez-Pérez, F., & Vázquez-Vázquez, D. (2020). Participatory platforms and their impact on urban governance: The case of Decidim Barcelona. *Urban Policy and Research*, *38*(4), 471–488.

Roy, S., Hazera, C. T., Das, D., Rahman Pir, R. M. S., & Ahmed, A. S. (2019). A computer vision and artificial intelligence based cost-effective object sensing robot. *International Journal of Intelligent Robotics and Applications*, *3*(4), 457–470. DOI: 10.1007/s41315-019-00107-1

Rubinger, L., Gazendam, A., Ekhtiari, S., & Bhandari, M. (2023). Machine learning and artificial intelligence in research and healthcare. *Injury*, *54*, S69–S73. DOI: 10.1016/j.injury.2022.01.046 PMID: 35135685

Rüttgers, M., Waldmann, M., Vogt, K., Ilgner, J., Schröder, W., & Lintermann, A. (2024). Automated surgery planning for an obstructed nose by combining computational fluid dynamics with reinforcement learning. *Computers in Biology and Medicine*, *173*, 108383. DOI: 10.1016/j.compbiomed.2024.108383 PMID: 38555704

Saha, O., & Dasgupta, P. (2018). A comprehensive survey of recent trends in cloud robotics architectures and applications. *Robotics (Basel, Switzerland)*, *7*(3), 47. DOI: 10.3390/robotics7030047

Sambolek, S., & Ivasic-Kos, M. (2021). Automatic person detection in search and rescue operations using deep CNN detectors. *IEEE Access : Practical Innovations, Open Solutions*, *9*, 37905–37922. DOI: 10.1109/ACCESS.2021.3063681

Sano, T., Horii, T., Abe, K., & Nagai, T. (2021). Temperament estimation of toddlers from child–robot interaction with explainable artificial intelligence. *Advanced Robotics*, *35*(17), 1068–1077. DOI: 10.1080/01691864.2021.1955001

Saravanan, P., Saravanan, V., Rajeshkannan, R., Arnica, G., Rajasimman, M., Gurunathan, B., & Pugazhendhi, A. (2024). Comprehensive review on toxic heavy metals in the aquatic system: Sources, identification, treatment strategies, and health risk assessment. *Environmental Research*, *258*, 119440. DOI: 10.1016/j.envres.2024.119440 PMID: 38906448

Saroj, A., & Pal, S. (2020). Use of Social Media in Crisis Management: A Survey. *International Journal of Disaster Risk Reduction*, *48*, 101584. DOI: 10.1016/j.ijdrr.2020.101584

Sathianarayanan, M., Hsu, P. H., & Chang, C. C. (2024). Extracting disaster location identification from social media images using deep learning. *International Journal of Disaster Risk Reduction*, *104*, 104352. DOI: 10.1016/j.ijdrr.2024.104352

Sayadi, A. R., Asadpour, M., Shabani, Z., & Sayadi, M. (2012). Pharmaceutical pollution of the eco-system and its detrimental effects on public health. *Majallah-i Ilmi-i Danishgah-i Ulum-i Pizishki-i Rafsanjan*, *11*(3), 269–284.

Sayed, A., Himeur, Y., Bensaali, F., & Amira, A. (2022). Aya SayedAya SayedYassine HimeurYassine HimeurFaycal BensaaliFaycal BensaaliAbbes AmiraAbbes Amira " Artificial intelligence with IoT for energy efficiency in buildings" In book. *Emerging Real-World Applications of Internet of Things*, (September), 233–252. Advance online publication. DOI: 10.1201/9781003304203-12

Schleich, B., Anwer, N., Mathieu, L., & Wartzack, S. (2017). Shaping the digital twin for design and production engineering. *CIRP Annals*, *66*(1), 141–144. DOI: 10.1016/j.cirp.2017.04.040

Schmid, D. (2023). Laboratory Studies on Aqueous Absorption and High Temperature Chemistry of NOx and SOx in Thermal Conversion of Biomass Waste.

Schmidt, A., Wolbers, J., Ferguson, J., & Boersma, K. (2018). Are You Ready-2Help? Conceptualizing the Management of Online and Onsite Volunteer Convergence. *Journal of Contingencies and Crisis Management, 26*(3), 338–349. DOI: 10.1111/1468-5973.12200

Schweitzer, L. (2014). Planning and social media: A case study of public transit and stigma on Twitter. *Journal of the American Planning Association, 80*(3), 218–238. DOI: 10.1080/01944363.2014.980439

Selvarajan, S., Manoharan, H., & Shankar, A. (2024). SL-RI: Integration of supervised learning in robots for industry 5.0 automated application monitoring. *Measurement. Sensors, 31*, 100972. DOI: 10.1016/j.measen.2023.100972

Sepasgozar, S. S., & Pierre, S. (2022). Fed-ntp: A federated learning algorithm for network traffic prediction in vanet. *IEEE Access : Practical Innovations, Open Solutions, 10*, 119607–119616. DOI: 10.1109/ACCESS.2022.3221970

Seung, B. S., & Dhananjay, S. (2018). *Smart Town Traffic Management System Using LoRa and Machine Learning Mechanism By ReSENSE Lab Hankuk University of Foreign Studies*. IEEE.

Seuwou, P., Banissi, E., & Ubakanma, G. (2020). In Farsi, M., Daneshkhah, A., Hosseinian-Far, A., & Jahankhani, H. (Eds.), *"The future of mobility with connected and autonomous vehicles in smart cities," in Digital Twin Technologies and Smart Cities (Internet of Things)* (pp. 37–52). Springer., https://link.springer.com/chapter/10.1007/978-3-030-18732-3_3

Shahabuddin, M., Uddin, M. N., Chowdhury, J. I., Ahmed, S. F., Uddin, M. N., Mofijur, M., & Uddin, M. A. (2023). A review of the recent development, challenges, and opportunities of electronic waste (e-waste). *International Journal of Environmental Science and Technology, 20*(4), 4513–4520. DOI: 10.1007/s13762-022-04274-w

Shahbazi, Z., & Byun, Y. C. (2021). Blockchain-based event detection and trust verification using natural language processing and machine learning. *IEEE Access : Practical Innovations, Open Solutions, 10*, 5790–5800. DOI: 10.1109/ACCESS.2021.3139586

Shah, S., Dey, D., Lovett, C., & Kapoor, A. (2018). AirSim: High-Fidelity Visual and Physical Simulation for Autonomous Vehicles. In Hutter, M., & Siegwart, R. (Eds.), *Field and Service Robotics* (Vol. 5, pp. 621–635). Springer International Publishing., DOI: 10.1007/978-3-319-67361-5_40

Shah, S., Shankar, R., & Narain, R. (2020). Cybersecurity challenges in smart cities: A systematic review. *Journal of Urban Technology*, *27*(1), 1–17.

Shinde, P. P., & Shah, S. (2018). A Review of Machine Learning and Deep Learning Applications. *2018 Fourth International Conference on Computing Communication Control and Automation (ICCUBEA)*, 1–6. DOI: 10.1109/ICCUBEA.2018.8697857

Shi, Y., Larson, M., & Jonker, C. M. (2015). Recurrent neural network language model adaptation with curriculum learning. *Computer Speech & Language*, *33*(1), 136–154. DOI: 10.1016/j.csl.2014.11.004

Shrimali, B., & Patel, H. B. (2022). Blockchain state-of-the-art: Architecture, use cases, consensus, challenges and opportunities. *Journal of King Saud University. Computer and Information Sciences*, *34*(9), 6793–6807. DOI: 10.1016/j.jksuci.2021.08.005

Shuja, J., Alanazi, E., Alasmari, M., & Alashaikh, A. (2020). Role of AI in pandemic response: Case study of IBM Watson Assistant during COVID-19. *Healthcare Informatics Research*, *26*(4), 256–263.

Silva, S. H., Alaeddini, A., & Najafirad, P. (2020). Temporal Graph Traversals Using Reinforcement Learning With Proximal Policy Optimization. *IEEE Access : Practical Innovations, Open Solutions*, *8*, 63910–63922. DOI: 10.1109/ACCESS.2020.2985295

Silvera-Tawil, D. (2024). Robotics in Healthcare: A Survey. *SN Computer Science*, *5*(1), 189. DOI: 10.1007/s42979-023-02551-0

Singh, Col Ravinder, & Manoharan, G. (2024). "Strengthening Resilience: AI and Machine Learning in Emergency Decision-Making for Natural Disasters." In *Internet of Things and AI for Natural Disaster Management and Prediction*, pp. 249-278. IGI Global. https://doi.org/DOI: 10.4018/979-8-3693-4284-8.ch012

Singh, R., Manoharan, G., & Singh, S. (2024). Strategic Deployment of AI and Drones Enhancing Disaster Management in Natural Disasters. AI and IoT for Proactive Disaster Management, 172-203. https://doi.org/DOI: 10.4018/979-8-3693-3896-4.ch009

Singh, S. P., & Singh, M. K. (2020). Soil pollution and human health. Plant responses to soil pollution, 205-220.

Singha, S., Pasupuleti, S., Singha, S. S., Singh, R., & Kumar, S. (2021). Prediction of groundwater quality using efficient machine learning technique. *Chemosphere*, *276*, 130265. DOI: 10.1016/j.chemosphere.2021.130265 PMID: 34088106

Smith, H., Roberts, A., & Johnson, M. (2020). FireGuard: AI for wildfire detection and citizen alerts. *Journal of Environmental Management, 275*, 111238.

Smith, J. (2023). Rise of the Machines: Emerging Trends in Robotics. *International Journal of Research and Review Techniques, 2*(3), 1–8.

Smith, J., Brown, P., & Lee, Y. (2022). Predicting air pollution levels using machine learning techniques: A case study on PM2.5. *Atmospheric Environment, 257*, 118073. DOI: 10.1016/j.atmosenv.2021.118073

Solangi, Y. A., Alyamani, R., & Ali, S. (2024). Exploring the influence of digital technology innovation on air quality: Insights from developed and developing economies. *Sustainable Futures : An Applied Journal of Technology, Environment and Society, 8*, 100342. DOI: 10.1016/j.sftr.2024.100342

Soni, H. K. (2024). 14 Social Media Skirmish. Text and Social Media Analytics for Fake News and Hate Speech Detection, 248.

Son, T. H., Weedon, Z., Yigitcanlar, T., Sanchez, T., Corchado, J. M., & Mehmood, R. (2023). Zack Weedon [a], Tan Yigitcanlar [a], Thomas Sanchez [b], Juan M. Corchado [c], Rashid Mehmood [d] "Algorithmic urban planning for smart and sustainable development: Systematic review of the literature". *Sustainable Cities and Society, 94*(July), 104562. DOI: 10.1016/j.scs.2023.104562

Soriano, G. P., Yasuhara, Y., Ito, H., Matsumoto, K., Osaka, K., Kai, Y., Locsin, R., Schoenhofer, S., & Tanioka, T. (2022). Robots and robotics in nursing. Healthcare, Stasevych, M., & Zvarych, V. (2023). Innovative Robotic Technologies and Artificial Intelligence in Pharmacy and Medicine: Paving the Way for the Future of Health Care—A Review. *Big Data and Cognitive Computing, 7*(3), 147.

Soundararajan, G., Chidambaranathan, B., Rajendran, A. K., Venugopal, D., & Devarajan, Y. (2024). Plastic pyrolytic oils as renewable fuel: Improving its physical properties and ignition patterns by waste renewable source—an experimental analysis. *Environmental Science and Pollution Research International, 31*(18), 26497–26509. DOI: 10.1007/s11356-024-32668-5 PMID: 38446296

Srivastava, S., Bisht, A., & Narayan, N. (2017). Safety and security in smart cities using artificial intelligence—A review. In *2017 7th International Conference on Cloud Computing, Data Science & Engineering-Confluence*, IEEEpp. 130-133.

Stahl, B. C., Andreou, A., Brey, P., Hatzakis, T., Kirichenko, A., Macnish, K., & Wright, D. (2021). Artificial intelligence for human flourishing–Beyond principles for machine learning. *Journal of Business Research, 124*, 374–388.

Starkey, J. R., Chowdhury, M. A., & Ayres, N. (2021). Leveraging artificial intelligence for disaster management: A review of current applications and challenges. *Artificial Intelligence Review*, *54*(3), 1863–1894.

Stieglitz, S., Mirbabaie, M., Ross, B., & Neuberger, C. (2018). Social media analytics–Challenges in topic discovery, data collection, and data preparation. *International Journal of Information Management*, *39*, 156–168. DOI: 10.1016/j.ijinfomgt.2017.12.002

Sufi, F. K. (2022). AI-Social Disaster: An AI-based software for identifying and analyzing natural disasters from social media. *Software Impacts*, *13*, 100319. DOI: 10.1016/j.simpa.2022.100319

Sufi, F. K., & Khalil, I. (2022). Automated disaster monitoring from social media posts using AI-based location intelligence and sentiment analysis. *IEEE Transactions on Computational Social Systems*. Advance online publication. DOI: 10.1109/TCSS.2022.3157142

Sun, C., Van Der Tol, R., Melenhorst, R., Pacheco, L. A. P., & Koerkamp, P. G. (2024). Path planning of manure-robot cleaners using grid-based reinforcement learning. *Computers and Electronics in Agriculture*, *226*, 109456. DOI: 10.1016/j.compag.2024.109456

Suryati, I., Khair, H., & Gusrianti, D. (2019). Distribution analysis of nitrogen dioxide (NO2) and ozone (O3) in Medan city with Geographic Information System (GIS). In *MATEC Web of Conferences* (Vol. 276, p. 06013). EDP Sciences.

Sutarlie, L., Ow, S. Y., & Su, X. (2017). Nanomaterials-based biosensors for detection of microorganisms and microbial toxins. *Biotechnology Journal*, *12*(4).

Sutton, R. S., & Barto, A. G. (2018). *Reinforcement Learning: An Introduction*. MIT Press.

Tabernik, D., & Skocaj, D. (2020). Deep learning for large-scale traffic-sign detection and recognition. *IEEE Transactions on Intelligent Transportation Systems*, *21*(4), 1427–1440. DOI: 10.1109/TITS.2019.2913588

Tahir, F., & Khan, M. (2023). *Big Data: the Fuel for Machine Learning and AI Advancement* (No. 10951). EasyChair.

Tanev, H., Zavarella, V., & Steinberger, J. (2017, May). Monitoring disaster impact: detecting micro-events and eyewitness reports in mainstream and social media. In ISCRAM.

Tang, B., Suman, R., & Watson, J. (2020). AI-enhanced hurricane forecasting: A review. *Climate Dynamics*, *54*(2), 231–248.

Tang, C., Wei, X., Zhu, C., Wang, Y., & Jia, W. (2020). Mobile vehicles as fog nodes for latency optimization in smart cities. *IEEE Transactions on Vehicular Technology*, *69*(9), 9364–9375. DOI: 10.1109/TVT.2020.2970763

Tan, J., Lee, C., & Low, Y. (2022). Smart cities and disaster resilience: The role of AI. *Journal of Urban Technology*, *29*(2), 45–62.

Tan, Y. T., Yu, T., Dutta, S., Sinha, A., Feirstein, D., Lizotte, A., Karigiannis, J., Liu, S., & Chang, Q. (2024). Hierarchical robot learning method for industrial fluorescent penetrant inspection. *Manufacturing Letters*, *41*, 1334–1341. DOI: 10.1016/j.mfglet.2024.09.160

Tao, Q., Liu, F., Li, Y., & Sidorov, D. (2019). Air Pollution Forecasting Using a Deep Learning Model Based on 1D Convnets and Bidirectional GRU. *IEEE Access : Practical Innovations, Open Solutions*, *7*, 76690–76698. DOI: 10.1109/ACCESS.2019.2921578

Tariq, A., Gill, A. Y., & Hussain, H. K. (2023). Evaluating the Potential of Artificial Intelligence in Orthopedic Surgery for Value-based Healthcare. *International Journal of Multidisciplinary Sciences and Arts*, *2*(1), 27–35. DOI: 10.47709/ijmdsa.v2i1.2394

Tejer, M., Szczepanski, R., & Tarczewski, T. (2024). Robust and efficient task scheduling for robotics applications with reinforcement learning. *Engineering Applications of Artificial Intelligence*, *127*, 107300. DOI: 10.1016/j.engappai.2023.107300

Tian, X., Pan, B., Bai, L., Wang, G., & Mo, D. (2023). Fruit Picking Robot Arm Training Solution Based on Reinforcement Learning in Digital Twin. *Journal of ICT Standardisation*. Advance online publication. DOI: 10.13052/jicts2245-800X.1133

Todorov, E., Erez, T., & Tassa, Y. (2012). MuJoCo: A physics engine for model-based control. *2012 IEEE/RSJ International Conference on Intelligent Robots and Systems*, 5026–5033. DOI: 10.1109/IROS.2012.6386109

Tomaszewski, B., & Judex, M. (2020). Decision-support systems for emergency management using AI: Trends and insights. *ISPRS International Journal of Geo-Information*, *9*(4), 246.

Tong, W., Hussain, A., Bo, W. X., & Maharjan, S. (2019). Artificial intelligence for vehicle-to-everything: A survey. *IEEE Access : Practical Innovations, Open Solutions*, *7*, 10823–10843.

Tounsi, A., & Temimi, M. (2023). A systematic review of natural language processing applications for hydrometeorological hazards assessment. *Natural Hazards*, *116*(3), 2819–2870. DOI: 10.1007/s11069-023-05842-0 PMID: 36776702

Tsai, Y.-Y., Xu, H., Ding, Z., Zhang, C., Johns, E., & Huang, B. (2021). DROID: Minimizing the Reality Gap Using Single-Shot Human Demonstration. *IEEE Robotics and Automation Letters*, *6*(2), 3168–3175. DOI: 10.1109/LRA.2021.3062311

Tsoy, D., Tirasawasdichai, T., & Kurpayanidi, K. I. (2021). Role of social media in shaping public risk perception during COVID-19 pandemic: A theoretical review. *International Journal of Management Science and Business Administration*, *7*(2), 35–41. DOI: 10.18775/ijmsba.1849-5664-5419.2014.72.1005

Uddin, M. G., Nash, S., Mahammad Diganta, M. T., Rahman, A., & Olbert, A. I. (2022). Robust machine learning algorithms for predicting coastal water quality index. *Journal of Environmental Management*, *321*, 115923. DOI: 10.1016/j.jenvman.2022.115923 PMID: 35988401

Ullah, A., Anwar, S. M., Li, J., Nadeem, L., Mahmood, T., Rehman, A., & Saba, T. (2024). Smart cities: The role of Internet of Things and machine learning in realizing a data-centric smart environment. *Complex & Intelligent Systems*, *10*(1), 1607–1637. DOI: 10.1007/s40747-023-01175-4

Unger, J., & Wodak, R., & KhosraviNik, M. (2016). Critical discourse studies and social media data. *Qualitative Research*, •••, 277–293.

United Nations. (2018). *World Urbanization Prospects: The 2018 Revision*. Department of Economic and Social Affairs, Population Division. https://population.un.org/wup/

Unity Technologies. (2020). *Training Configuration File*. GitHub. https://github.com/Unity-Technologies/ml-agents/blob/hh/develop/fps_game_project/docs/Training-Configuration-File.md

Unity Technologies. (2022a). *Machine Learning—Unity ML-Agents Toolkit*. https://unity-technologies.github.io/ml-agents/Background-Machine-Learning/

Unity Technologies. (2022b). *PyTorch—Unity ML-Agents Toolkit*. https://unity-technologies.github.io/ml-agents/Background-PyTorch/

Ushakov, D., Dudukalov, E., Shmatko, L., & Shatila, K. (2022). Artificial Intelligence as a factor of public transportations system development. *Transportation Research Procedia*, *63*, 2401–2408. DOI: 10.1016/j.trpro.2022.06.276

Vani, R., Thendral, N., Kavitha, J. C., & Bhavani, N. P. G. (2018). Intelligent traffic control system with priority to emergency vehicles, IOP Conf. Ser. Mater. Sci. Eng. 455 (2018) 012023, https://doi.org/DOI: 10.1088/1757-899X/455/1/012023

Varsha, V. R., Naganandini, S., & Hariharan, C. (2024). Utilizing AI and machine learning for natural disaster management: predicting natural disasters with AI and machine learning. In *Internet of Things and AI for Natural Disaster Management and Prediction* (pp. 279–304). IGI Global., DOI: 10.4018/979-8-3693-4284-8.ch013

Venkataramanan, V., Kavitha, G., Joel, M. R., & Lenin, J. (2023, January). Forest fire detection and temperature monitoring alert using iot and machine learning algorithm. In *2023 5th International Conference on Smart Systems and Inventive Technology (ICSSIT)* (pp. 1150-1156). IEEE. DOI: 10.1109/ICSSIT55814.2023.10061086

Vernon, D. (2019). Robotics and Artificial Intelligence in Africa. *IEEE Robotics & Automation Magazine*, *26*(4), 131–135. DOI: 10.1109/MRA.2019.2946107

Veselov, G., Tselykh, A., Sharma, A., & Huang, R. (2021). Applications of Artificial Intelligence in Evolution of Smart Cities and Societies. *Informatica, 45*(5). *EAI Endorsed Transactions on Smart Cities*, *6*(3), e5.

Vijay, S., & Kamaraj, K. (2023). Ground Water Quality Prediction using Machine Learning Algorithms in R, vol. 6, Available: https://ijrar.com/

Vinuesa, R., Azizpour, H., & Leite, I.. (2020). The role of AI in achieving sustainable development goals. *Nature Communications*, *11*(1), 233. DOI: 10.1038/s41467-019-14108-y PMID: 31932590

Vlădăreanu, L., Gal, A. I., Melinte, O. D., Vlădăreanu, V., Iliescu, M., Bruja, A., Feng, Y., & Ciocîrlan, A. (2020). Robot Digital Twin towards Industry 4.0. *IFAC-PapersOnLine*, *53*(2), 10867–10872. DOI: 10.1016/j.ifacol.2020.12.2815

Voda, A. I., & Radu, L. D. (2019). How can artificial intelligence respond to smart cities challenges? In *Smart Cities: Issues and Challenges,* Elsevierpp. 199-216. DOI: 10.1016/B978-0-12-816639-0.00012-0

Voda, A. I., & Radu, L. D. (2018). Artificial intelligence and the future of smart cities. *BRAIN.Broad Research in Artificial Intelligence and Neuroscience*, *9*(2), 110–127.

Voigt, P., & Von dem Bussche, A. (2017). *The EU General Data Protection Regulation (GDPR): A Practical Guide*. Springer. DOI: 10.1007/978-3-319-57959-7

Vongkusolkit, J., & Huang, Q. (2021). Situational awareness extraction: A comprehensive review of social media data classification during natural hazards. *Annals of GIS*, *27*(1), 5–28. DOI: 10.1080/19475683.2020.1817146

Walters, M., & Kalinova, E. (2021). Virtualized care systems, medical artificial intelligence, and real-time clinical monitoring in COVID-19 diagnosis, screening, surveillance, and prevention. *American Journal of Medical Research (New York, N.Y.)*, *8*(2), 37–50. DOI: 10.22381/ajmr8220213

Wang, Z., Hale, S., Adelani, D. I., Grabowicz, P., Hartman, T., Flöck, F., & Jurgens, D. (2019, May). Demographic inference and representative population estimates from multilingual social media data. In *The world wide web conference* (pp. 2056-2067). https://doi.org/DOI: 10.1145/3308558.3313684

Wang, P., Yu, R., Gao, N., Lin, C., & Liu, Y. (2020). Task-driven data offloading for fog-enabled urban IoT services. *IEEE Internet of Things Journal*, *8*(9), 7562–7574. DOI: 10.1109/JIOT.2020.3039467

Wang, Q., & Liu, Y. (2023). Blockchain for Public Safety: A Survey of Techniques and Applications. *Journal of Safety Science and Resilience = An Quan Ke Xue Yu Ren Xing (Ying Wen)*, *4*(4), 389–395. DOI: 10.1016/j.jnlssr.2023.09.001

Wang, X., & Liu, Y. (2019). Social media data analysis for disaster response: Applications of AI during Hurricane Harvey. *Natural Hazards*, *99*(1), 333–350.

Wang, Y., Hao, H., & Platt, L. S. (2021). Examining risk and crisis communications of government agencies and stakeholders during early-stages of COVID-19 on Twitter. *Computers in Human Behavior*, *114*, 106568. DOI: 10.1016/j.chb.2020.106568 PMID: 32982038

Wang, Y., Shafik, W., Seong, J. T., Al Mutairi, A., Mustafa, M. S., & Mouhamed, M. R. (2023). Service delay and optimization of the energy efficiency of a system in fog-enabled smart cities. *Alexandria Engineering Journal*, *84*, 112–125. DOI: 10.1016/j.aej.2023.10.034

Wang, Z., Luo, N., & Zhou, P. (2020). GuardHealth: Blockchain empowered secure data management and Graph Convolutional Network enabled anomaly detection in smart healthcare. *Journal of Parallel and Distributed Computing*, *142*, 1–12. DOI: 10.1016/j.jpdc.2020.03.004

Wilbur, M., Sivagnanam, A., Ayman, A., Samaranayeke, S., Dubey, A., & Laszka, A. (2023). Artificial intelligence for smart transportation. arXiv preprint arXiv:2308.07457.

Williamson, S. M., & Prybutok, V. (2024). Balancing privacy and progress: A review of privacy challenges, systemic oversight, and patient perceptions in AI-driven healthcare. *Applied Sciences (Basel, Switzerland)*, *14*(2), 675. DOI: 10.3390/app14020675

Winston, P. H. (1992). *Artificial intelligence*. Addison-Wesley Longman Publishing Co., Inc. Hamet, P., & Tremblay, J. (2017). Artificial intelligence in medicine. *Metabolism: Clinical and Experimental, 69*, S36–S40.

Wooldridge, M. J. (2009). *An introduction to multiagent systems* (2nd ed.). John Wiley & Sons.

World Health Organization. (2021). *WHO global air quality guidelines: particulate matter (PM2. 5 and PM10), ozone, nitrogen dioxide, sulfur dioxide and carbon monoxide*. World Health Organization.

World Meteorological Organization. (2021). State of the global climate. Retrieved from https://public.wmo.int/en/resources/state-of-the-global-climate

Wu, C., Beroza, G. C., & Allen, R. M. (2021). Deep learning for earthquake prediction: Progress and prospects. *Geophysical Research Letters, 48*(6), e2020GL092100.

Wukich, C. (2020). GETTING MORE FROM: SOCIAL MEDIA for Pandemic and Disaster Management: In times of crisis, the use of social media is key for risk communication and community engagement. *Public Management, 102*(11), 17–22.

Xia, W., Lu, Y., Xu, W., & Xu, X. (2024). Deep reinforcement learning based proactive dynamic obstacle avoidance for safe human-robot collaboration. *Manufacturing Letters, 41*, 1246–1256. DOI: 10.1016/j.mfglet.2024.09.151

Xing, H., Torabi, A., Ding, L., Gao, H., Deng, Z., Mushahwar, V. K., & Tavakoli, M. (2021). An admittance-controlled wheeled mobile manipulator for mobility assistance: Human–robot interaction estimation and redundancy resolution for enhanced force exertion ability. *Mechatronics, 74*, 102497. DOI: 10.1016/j.mechatronics.2021.102497

Xu, H., Jia, Y., Sun, Z., Su, J., Liu, Q. S., Zhou, Q., & Jiang, G. (2022). Environmental pollution, a hidden culprit for health issues. *Eco-Environment & Health, 1*(1), 31–45. DOI: 10.1016/j.eehl.2022.04.003 PMID: 38078200

Xu, Q. A., Chang, V., & Jayne, C. (2022). A systematic review of social media-based sentiment analysis: Emerging trends and challenges. *Decision Analytics Journal, 3*, 100073. DOI: 10.1016/j.dajour.2022.100073

Xu, X., Yang, Y., Cao, M., Nguyen, T.-M., Cao, K., & Xie, L. (2024). A data-driven control method for ground locomotion on sloped terrain of a hybrid aerial-ground robot. *Journal of Automation and Intelligence, S2949855424000339*(4), 219–229. Advance online publication. DOI: 10.1016/j.jai.2024.08.001

Yang, D., Oh, E.-S., & Wang, Y. (2020). Hybrid Physical Education Teaching and Curriculum Design Based on a Voice Interactive Artificial Intelligence Educational Robot. *Sustainability (Basel), 12*(19), 8000. DOI: 10.3390/su12198000

Yanuargi, B., Utami, E., & Parikesit, A. A. (2024, February). Location-Based Service Insights: A Comprehensive Review of Data Mining Objects. In *2024 IEEE International Conference on Artificial Intelligence and Mechatronics Systems (AIMS)* (pp. 1-6). IEEE. https://doi.org/DOI: 10.1109/AIMS61812.2024.10513296

Yeom, K. (2023). Efficient self-driving strategy with preceding car following and road slopes based on learning predictive control. *Energy Reports, 9*, 139–148. DOI: 10.1016/j.egyr.2023.05.249

Youssef, A. E., & Missiry, S. E., Nabil El-gaafary, I., ElMosalami, J. S., Awad, K. M., & Yasser, K. (2019). Building your kingdom Imitation Learning for a Custom Gameplay Using Unity ML-agents. *2019 IEEE 10th Annual Information Technology,Electronics and Mobile Communication Conference (IEMCON)*, 0509–0514. DOI: 10.1109/IEMCON.2019.8936134

Yue, L., Chen, W., Li, X., Zuo, W., & Yin, M. (2019). A survey of sentiment analysis in social media. *Knowledge and Information Systems, 60*(2), 617–663. DOI: 10.1007/s10115-018-1236-4

Zade, H., Shah, K., Rangarajan, V., Kshirsagar, P., Imran, M., & Starbird, K. (2018). From situational awareness to actionability: Towards improving the utility of social media data for crisis response. Proceedings of the ACM on human-computer interaction, 2(CSCW), 1-18. https://doi.org/DOI: 10.1145/3274464

Zaman, A. U. (2010). Comparative study of municipal solid waste management in developed and developing countries. *Journal of Environmental Management, 91*(1), 126–132. DOI: 10.1016/j.jenvman.2009.08.009

Zaman, A. U., & Lehmann, S. (2011). Urban growth and waste management optimization towards "zero waste city.". *City, Culture and Society, 2*(4), 177–187. DOI: 10.1016/j.ccs.2011.11.007

Zeng, D., Cao, Z., & Neill, D. B. (2021). Artificial intelligence–enabled public health surveillance—from local detection to global epidemic monitoring and control. In *Artificial intelligence in medicine* (pp. 437–453). Academic Press. DOI: 10.1016/B978-0-12-821259-2.00022-3

Zhang, W., Xu, M., & Jiang, Q. (2018). Opinion mining and sentiment analysis in social media: Challenges and applications. In *HCI in Business, Government, and Organizations: 5th International Conference, HCIBGO 2018, Held as Part of HCI International 2018, Las Vegas, NV, USA,July 15-20, 2018,Proceedings 5* (pp. 536-548). Springer International Publishing. https://doi.org/DOI: 10.1007/978-3-319-91716-0_43

Zhang, C. (2020). Design and application of fog computing and Internet of Things service platform for smart city. *Future Generation Computer Systems, 112*, 630–640. DOI: 10.1016/j.future.2020.06.016

Zhang, F., Xuan, C., & Lam, H.-K. (2024). An obstacle avoidance-specific reinforcement learning method based on fuzzy attention mechanism and heterogeneous graph neural networks. *Engineering Applications of Artificial Intelligence, 130*, 107764. DOI: 10.1016/j.engappai.2023.107764

Zhang, H., & Zheng, J. (2021). The application analysis of medical chatbots and virtual assistant. *Front. Soc. Sci. Technol, 3*, 11–16.

Zhang, X. (2021). A Comparative Study on the Influence of Artificial Intelligence Robot Distribution and Traditional Logistics Distribution Mode. *Journal of Physics: Conference Series, 1966*(1), 012020. DOI: 10.1088/1742-6596/1966/1/012020

Zhang, X., & Lapata, M. (2017). Sentence Simplification with Deep Reinforcement Learning. *Proceedings of the 2017 Conference on Empirical Methods in Natural Language Processing*, 584–594. DOI: 10.18653/v1/D17-1062

Zhao, J. L., Fan, S., & Yan, J. (2020). Overview of business innovations and research opportunities in blockchain and introduction to the special issue. *Financial Innovation, 6*(1), 1–18.

Zhao, J., Zhang, X., & Zheng, Y. (2021). Machine Learning Approaches to Climate Risk Assessment and Urban Adaptation. *Environmental Research Letters, 16*(6), 064012. DOI: 10.1088/1748-9326/abf8d2

Zhao, L., & Li, X. (2021). Deep learning for water quality analysis: A comprehensive study. *Water Research, 196*, 116983. DOI: 10.1016/j.watres.2021.116983

Zhao, R., Gu, X., Xue, B., Zhang, J., & Ren, W. (2018). Short period PM2.5 prediction based on multivariate linear regression model. *PLoS One, 13*(7), e0201011. DOI: 10.1371/journal.pone.0201011 PMID: 30048475

Zheng, H., Wang, J., & Gao, X. (2020). Machine learning for disaster prediction: Current trends and future directions. *Applied AI Review, 12*(4), 327–345.

Zheng, P., Li, C., Fan, J., & Wang, L. (2024). A vision-language-guided and deep reinforcement learning-enabled approach for unstructured human-robot collaborative manufacturing task fulfilment. *CIRP Annals*, *73*(1), 341–344. DOI: 10.1016/j.cirp.2024.04.003

Zhou, Y., Li, W., Cao, X., He, B., Feng, Q., Yang, F., Liu, H., Kutser, T., Xu, M., Xiao, F., Geng, X., Yu, K., & Du, Y. (2024). Spatial-temporal distribution of labeled set bias remote sensing estimation: An implication for supervised machine learning in water quality monitoring. *International Journal of Applied Earth Observation and Geoinformation*, *131*, 103959. DOI: 10.1016/j.jag.2024.103959

Zhu, C. (2025, January). Artificial Intelligence Applications in Everyday Life. *Applied and Computational Engineering*, *121*(1), 191–197. DOI: 10.54254/2755-2721/2025.20074

Zhu, D., Cai, C., Yang, T., & Zhou, X. (2018). A Machine Learning Approach for Air Quality Prediction: Model Regularization and Optimization. *Big Data and Cognitive Computing*, *2*(1), 5. DOI: 10.3390/bdcc2010005

Zhu, X., Yao, Y., & Wu, H. (2018). Integrating drone and satellite data using AI for disaster recovery: Case study of Hurricane Maria. *Remote Sensing*, *10*(6), 875.

Zhu, X., Zhou, Z., & Wang, Y. (2018). Leveraging AI-powered drones in disaster response: Case study from the Nepal earthquake. *Journal of Humanitarian Logistics and Supply Chain Management*, *8*(3), 400–420.

Zong, X., Luan, Y., Wang, H., & Li, S. (2021). A multi-robot monitoring system based on digital twin. *Procedia Computer Science*, *183*, 94–99. DOI: 10.1016/j.procs.2021.02.035

Zuboff, S. (2019). *The age of surveillance capitalism: The fight for a human future at the new frontier of power*. PublicAffairs.

About the Contributors

Ashok Sharma is having 21 Years of Teaching Experiences in Higher Education and He has worked in Various Reputed Institution of Higher Learning in India in different capacity. His area of Interest is Machine Learning, Cloud Computing and Data Science. He is certified in Beidou Technology from Shanghai Jio Tong University, Shanghai, Leveraging Technology for Effective Teaching in the Classroom and Beyond from International Institute of Information Technology, Bangalore, Internet of Things and Introduction to Big Data from University of California San Diego Machine Learning, High-dimensional Statistics and Inference for the New Generation" from Abdus Salam International Centre for Theoretical Physics (ICTP), Trieste Italy Digital Education from Shanghai Jio Tong University, Shanghai Deep Reinforcement Learning from IIT Ropar Brain and Computing from IIT Delhi He has attended 40+ DST/AICTE sponsored Training in different Technologies and have 40+ Research Articles in SCI/SCIE/Scopus indexed Journals with 10 Patent and Four Copyright, has developed MooCs in 4 Quadrant of 15 Courses, Running online Courses on Virtual Platform like Moodle,MoodleCloud,Canvas and Blackboard LMS. 5 PhD has been awarded and 4 Scholars are working under his guidance in the area of Cloud Computing, Data Scienceand Cognitive Behaviour Analysis. Dr. Ashok has completed Three DST SERB Sponosred Project and submitted 4 Projects in various agencies. and received National Award for Excellence in Innovative Teaching 2021 by Government of Haryana . He is presently holding position of Assistant Professor in Department of Computer Science and IT, BhaderwahCampus, University of Jammu, Jammu, India

Vibhakar Mansotra is presently the senior most Professor and Head working in the Department of Computer Science and IT, University of Jammu. He holds MSc and MPhil in Physics from University of Jammu and MTech from Computer from IIT Delhi. He has Completed his PhD in Computer Science from University of Jammu. He is having more that 30 year's experience in teaching and research. He was awarded BEST Teacher in IT by Amar Ujala, B-School Excellence –Awards held at Bombay 0n 23rd Nov. 2012. Best Professor in IT Award by LOKMAT National Educational Leadership- Awards – held At Bombay on 13th Feb. 2015.He has also remained as Head of the Department, Dean of the faculty of mathematical Sciences and Director, of the Centre for IT, University of Jammu. In addition to these administrative positions he has also remained convener/chairman of various academic bodies like Departmental Research Committee (DRC), Board of Studies in Computer Science's, Departmental Affairs Committee (DAC), Computer Purchase Committee of the University and member of a number of other academic bodies of the University. He has also remained member of the University Council, the highest executive body of the University. His area of interest include Data Mining/Machine Learning, Information Retrieval Computer Networks/ Security. He has to his credit more than 100 Publications in International/National Journal and in Proceedings of (International/National) Conferences and has also attended many seminars and conferences. PhD awarded 8 and in progress 6 .He has been active supervisor for more than 25 students of MTech dissertation in different areas of computer science and IT.He is on Panel of various executive committee of different organisation like UGC, AICTE and NBA and in addition he is on the panel of selection committee and research evaluation in various universities in India.

Parveen Singh Associate Professor, Department of Computer Science, Cluster University Jammu. Completed PhD (2015-2019) on UGC Teacher fellowship, as full time research Scholar at University of Jammu, J&K, worked in the Area of Data mining, on the topic "Analytic Study of Data Mining based model for public Health Care Management". Strong math background and 6+ years of experience in using predictive modeling, data processing, and data mining algorithms to solve challenging medical problems. Involved in Python open source community and passionate about deep reinforcement learning. Recently awarded (April 2021) DST (Department of science and technology) project titled "Creating a Dashboard of Survey on Usage of ICT and learning Management System during Covid-19 Pandemic in colleges and Universities in UT of Jammu and Kashmir".

***

Akindele Segun Afolabi is a Senior Lecturer at the Department of Electrical and Electronics Engineering, University of Ilorin. He received the Bachelor's and Master's Degrees in Electrical Engineering from the University of Ilorin, Nigeria, and the Ph.D. Degree in Computer Science and Systems Engineering from Kobe University, Japan. He was the recipient of the prestigious Japanese Government MEXT Scholarship Award from 2009 to 2012. Dr. Afolabi is a registered engineer

(R.Engr.) with the Council for the Regulation of Engineering in Nigeria (COREN). He has several scholarly publications in journals and conference proceedings, some of which are indexed in Scopus/ISI. He currently serves as a Section Editor with the Nigerian Journal of Technological Development (NJTD), focusing on electrical and electronics engineering, computer engineering, applied mathematics, and computer science. His research interests include machine intelligence, cloud/fog and high-performance computing, wireless network densification and IP convergence, VANET, and D2D communications.

Olubunmi Adewale Akinola received the Bachelor, Masters, and Ph.D. Degrees in Electrical Engineering in 1991, 2001, and 2016, respectively. He is currently with the Federal University of Agriculture, Abeokuta, Nigeria. He was the recipient of a plethora of researchbased awards issued by OMICS group – USA, NUC – Nigeria just to mention a few. He is a member of the Nigerian Society of Engineers and a registered Engineer with the Council for the Regulation of Engineering in Nigeria (COREN). His research interest includes Artificial Intelligence, IoT, D2D communications, MANETS, Automation and Electronic System Design & Applications.

Safaa Najah Saud Al-Humairi is an esteemed Associate Professor at Management and Science University, serving as the Program Coordinator and Researcher Coordinator. With over 15 years of experience in bio-engineering design and manufacturing, he has made significant contributions in the field, particularly in sensor design and implementation over the last 10 years. Throughout his career, Dr. Safaa has been an avid researcher, dedicated to expanding knowledge and pushing the boundaries of technology. His extensive body of work includes the publication of more than 120 research articles in highly esteemed and impactful journals, earning him recognition and respect within the academic community. In addition to his research achievements, Dr. Safaa has garnered numerous accolades for his innovative contributions. He has been honoured with special gold, silver, and bronze medals in various national and international engineering and technology exhibitions. These awards testify to his exceptional creativity, problem-solving skills, and ability to implement groundbreaking ideas. Recognized for his expertise, Dr. Safaa actively contributes to the academic community as an editor and reviewer for several renowned journals and publishers. His involvement in these crucial roles demonstrates his commitment to maintaining high standards of research and advancing the field of engineering. Dr. Safaa's multifaceted career reflects his passion for engineering design, manufacturing, and research. Through his exceptional skills, relentless pursuit of knowledge, and unwavering dedication, he continues to shape the future of the field, inspiring fellow researchers and aspiring engineers alike.

Anita Devare has completed her MSc and PhD in Mathematics. Her major interest is in Applied Mathematics. Her research area includes the mathematical modeling of the resources allocation in computing infrastructure.

Manoj Devare received BSc & MSc degree from North Maharashtra University and PhD in Computer Science from Bharati Vidyapeeth University, India. He is working as Associate Professor at Amity Institute of Information Technology, Amity University Mumbai. He has 17 years of teaching and research experience in Computer Science. His PhD thesis was based on the Congestion Controlling in Homogeneous and Heterogeneous Computer Networks. Dr. Manoj won the "Best Paper Award", in ICSCI 2008. He has served as Post Doctorate Fellow at Centre of Excellence on HPC, Uni. of Calabria, Italy under young researcher scheme. He has been developed Desktop Cloud system. His research deals with IoT, Cloud, Machine Learning and innovative applications of those technologies to scientific problems. He has 02 Patents pending; he edited 05 book chapters, 09 Int. Journal papers, 15 conference Papers. He has delivered 08 national and international keynote speeches. He is connected with review process of reputed international journal papers, edited chapters from the reputed journals like Elsevier's FGCS, Springer's review system, Symbiosis International Journal.

Devavarapu Sreenivasarao is an Assistant Professor in Computer Science and Enginerring at Sreenidhi Insitute of Science and Technology, Hderabad. He is an academician and researcher. He has published various number of research papers and book chapters, books etc. His research area includes Digital Image Processing, Machine Learning, and Deep Learning, Alogortithms and Analysis.

M. Robinson Joel received the Doctorate Ph.D degree in Computer and Information Technology from the Manonmaniam Sundaranar University, Tirunelveli in March 2019. He completed his M.Tech and MCA from the same university year 2008 and 2002 respectively. He is currently working as an Associate Professor in the Department of Computer Science and Engineering at KCG College of Technology, Chennai. He has 16 years of teaching experience.

Diksha Joshi (Dani) is an Assistant Professor in the Department of Computer Engineering at MPSTME, with over 20 years of academic experience. She holds a Ph.D. in Computer Science and Engineering from Guru Gobind Singh Inderprastha University, New Delhi .in 2017, along with an M.Tech and M.Sc in the same field. Her specialization lies in accessibility. Key topics of her research include web accessibility, IoT, machine learning, and usability evaluation.

|Fouzia Sulthana K - Contributing Author|Assistant Professor in Rajalakshmi Institute of technology . Interested in writing and reviewing Book chapters and articles.

K. Ishwarya, M.Tech., Ph.D is presently working as Assistant Professor in the Department of Computing Technologies, School of Computing at SRM Institute of Science and Technology at Kattankulathur, Chennai. She has more than 8 years of teaching and research experience. She completed her Doctorate in Computer Science and Engineering from SRM Institute of Science and Technology, Kattankulathur, Chennai in the year of 2024. She completed her Master's Degree in Software Engineering from B.S. Abdur Rahman University, Chennai in the year of 2014 and Bachelor's Degree in Computer Science and Engineering at Anna University Chennai, in the year of 2012. Her main area of interest includes pattern recognition, image processing, machine learning, IOT and Big data analytics. She has published several papers in well known peer-reviewed journals and has a professional membership in IAENG (International Association of Engineers).

Anju M I received B.Tech degree in Electronics and Communication Engineering from Cochin University of Science and Technology, Kerala, India in 2006, M.E.degree in VLSI Design from Karunya University, Coimbatore, Tamil Nadu in 2008 and Ph.D. degree from Anna University, Chennai, India in 2023. She is currently working as Assistant Professor in the Department of Electronics and Communication Engineering at SRM Institute of Science and Technology, Vadapalani Campus, Chennai, India. Her research interests include Device Modeling, FPGA Implementation, Low- Power VLSI systems, and VLSI Architectures for Image processing..

Geetha Manoharan is currently working in Telangana as an assistant professor at SR University. She is the university-level PhD program coordinator and has also been given the additional responsibility of In Charge Director of Publications and Patents under the Research Division at SR University. Under her tutelage, students are inspired to reach their full potential in all areas of their education and beyond through experiential learning. It creates an atmosphere conducive to the growth of students into independent thinkers and avid readers. She has more than ten years of experience across the board in the business world, academia,and the academy. She has a keen interest in the study of organizational behavior and management. More than forty articles and books have been published in scholarly venues such as UGC-refereed, SCOPUS, Web of Science, and Springer. Over the past six-plus years, she has participated in varied research and student exchange programs at both the national and international levels. A total of five of her collaborative innovations in this area have already been published and patented. Emotional intelligence, selfefficacy, and work-life balance are among her specialties. She organizes programs for academic organizations. She belongs to several professional organizations, including the CMA and the CPC. The TIPS GLOBAL Institute of Coimbatore has recognized her twice (in 2017 and 2018) for her outstanding academic performance.

Marilyn Mathai has completed her Masters in Computer Application in Year 2023. She is IT enthusiast and interested in application of AI techniques to solve the societal and governance issues.

Chandresh Kumar Maurya, is currently working as an assistant professor at the Indian Institute of Technology Indore, India since July 2020. During his Ph.D. at IIT Roorkee, India, he worked on Anomaly Detection in Big Data. His Ph.D. was funded by the prestigious Prime Minister Fellowship for Doctoral Research. Post-Ph.D, he joined IBM Research India as a research scientist working primarily in Natural Language Processing. He worked there for two years and subsequently moved to Budapest, Hungary and joined ELTE University as a research assistant professor. He had a short stint at NIT Delhi before joining IIT Indore in July 2020. He has also worked with Microsoft India R&D and Bosch Research Center, Bangalore. Dr. Chandresh is passionate about building practical and theoretical models and algorithms for multimodal data (Text+Image+Video+Speech). Why we need to build such a system is that we perceive and interact with our environment through many sensory organs such as eyes, ears, mouth, etc. He has published in top CS venues such as LREC-COLING, IEEE Transactions on Big data, Neurocomputing, Information Sciences, etc., and served as a reviewer for EMNLP, NAACL, ECML-PKDD, Interspeech, etc. He is a member of IEEE and IEEE SPS.

Froilan Mobo He is a Doctor of Public Administration graduate from the Urdaneta City University Class of 2016 and a graduate of the 2nd Doctorate Degree (Ph.D.) in Development Education program at the Central Luzon State University, Nueva Ecija, Philippines, Class of 2022. On March 11, 2024, Dr. Mobo was accredited and reclassified by the Commission on Higher Education (CHED) to the position of Professor II in the Philippine Merchant Marine Academy (PMMA), and this allowed him to work with different international research institutions, such as the Director and Research Consultant of the IKSAD Research Institute, Turkey. At present, he is in the process of finishing his 3rd master's degree, leading to social studies education at Bicol University. Recently, Dr. Mobo passed Batch 3—Certified Research Professional—and ranked in the top 5 in the National Examination.

Variza Negi is an Assistant Professor in the STME Department at NMIMS, Navi-Mumbai. She received her B. Tech. degree in 2008 from PTU, Jalandhar and

M.E. degree in 2013 from NITTTR, Chandigarh. She is currently pursing PhD from NMIMS, Mumbai. Her main research interests are Cloud Computing, Fog Computing, Algorithms, Evolutionary algorithms.

Aparna Nishad has completed her MCA degree from Amity University Mumbai. She has interest in Geographical Information System and applications.

Bhupendra Panchal is pursuing his doctorate from Devi Ahilya Vishwavidyalaya, Indore. He has completed M.Tech. in Computer Technology & Application from National Institute of Technical Teacher`s Training & Research, Bhopal (in 2014). His bachelor is in Information Technology from University RGPV, Bhopal (in 2011). He has an academic experience of 9 years and has worked at renowned Institutes. He has published 3 Indian patents, one research paper (SCI indexed) and four book chapters (Scopus Indexed). He has 9 publications, in International/National journals with high impact factor and has 3 publications in various International/National Conferences. Mr. Panchal has been awarded by SRIJAN as a best faculty for DBMS and he has also been certified as AWS trainer. His research areas are in Computer Networking, Database Management, Cloud Computing, and Machine Learning. He has attended many National/International workshops, seminars, conferences etc. He has organized three workshops and attended various Faculty Development Programs. Mr. Panchal has been completed various training and learning certification from renowned organization.

Rajneesh Patel is an Assistant Professor in Vit Bhopal University.

Pranshu Pranjal is an Assistant Professor in Vit Bhopal University.

Arunadevi R Accomplished Assistant Professor with over a decade of experience in the field of Computer Science and Engineering. Played a pivotal role in both academic and administrative capacities, serving as an Exam Cell Coordinator for Anna University exams, as well as contributing significantly to the NAAC and NBA accreditation processes. Teaching experience spans coaching and tutoring students across various computer science subjects, preparing course materials, setting exam questionnaires, conducting regular exams, and evaluating students' performance. Additionally, actively involved in several key institutional programs, including the AICTE accreditation, admission campaigning, and ERP management. Professionally, served at multiple esteemed institutions, in including Prince Shri Venkateshwara Padmavathy Engineering College, SMK Fomra Institute of Technology, PRIST University, and IGCETW Chengalpattu. She holds a Master's degree in Computer Science from Anna University with a CGPA of 8.2. Contributed to the academic community by presenting several research papers at national and international conferences. My work has been published in reputed journals and IEEE conferences, covering topics like machine learning, cloud computing, network security, and artificial intelligence. Expertise in subjects such as Service Oriented Architecture, Object-Oriented Analysis and Design, and Human-Computer Interaction, among others, highlights the deep knowledge and passion for the field.

Kavitha Rajakumari Has published 21 papers in international and national conferences and Scopus indexed journals. Has presented papers in London (IEEE Conference) and in Singapore.

Akshatha Reddy is a student at Sreenidhi Instittue of science and technolgy and working in various aspects of research areas including publications, book chapters etc.

Shaik Khasim Saheb is an Associate Professor in Computer Science and Enginerring at Sreenidhi Insitute of Science and Technology, Hderabad. He is an academician and researcher. He has published various number of research papers and book chapters, books etc. His research area includes Digital Image Processing, Machine Learning, and Deep Learning.

Sumit S. Shevtekar is a Technocrat and Dedicated Research Scholar, currently doing his Research - PhD in Computer Science and Engineering (CSE) Department at the Indian Institute of Technology (IIT) Indore. He holds a Bachelor's in Computer Engineering (B.E.) and a Master's in Computer Engineering (M.E.) from PREC, SIT Lonavala, Pune University. He is working as an Assistant Professor at Pune Institute of Computer Technology (PICT) Pune, India since Jan 2008. Sumit's research interests span a broad range of cutting-edge technologies, including Artificial Intelligence (AI), Machine Learning (ML), Deep Learning (DL), Two-Wheeler Safety, Road Safety, Cloud Computing, Web Technologies, and Blockchain Technology. Additionally, he is passionate about development of innovative products, ideas, and innovative technological solutions. His academic and research endeavors reflect a commitment to leveraging these technologies to address real-world challenges and contribute to advancements in the field. Sumit's diverse expertise and focused approach position him as a promising and impactful Technocrat and Researcher in Computer Science and Engineering.

Col Ravinder Singh was commissioned in the Indian Army in June 1989 into Artillery Regiment and he is a serving officer with 35 years of service. An alumnus of National Defence Academy and Indian Military Academy, he has a vast military experience in various terrains. He holds a Master of Science in (Technology) Weapon Systems from Pune University and also qualified in Disaster Management from Gujarat Institute of Disaster Management, Ahmedabad. He also holds a Post Graduate Diploma in Mass Communication and Journalism from National Institute of Mass Communication and Journalism, Ahmedabad He conducts lectures on Disaster Management at Gujarat Institute of Disaster Management, Colleges, schools and for Associate NCC officers and NCC cadets. He is also holding a degree in MBA from ICFAI University. He has also completed Post Graduate Diploma in Disaster Management from IGNOU and currently he is research scholar with SR University.

Samrath Singh is a student currently pursuing a Bachelor's degree in Computer Science and Engineering. With a fervent passion for innovation and technology, Samrath has actively participated in several competitions to showcase his talents and contribute to societal betterment. One of his notable achievements is his participation in the esteemed IEEE Yesist Junior track, an international event that celebrates innovation and creativity. Here, he demonstrated his compassion and technical acumen by developing Ultrasonic Obstacle Detecting Goggles tailored specifically for the visually impaired. His groundbreaking project not only showcased his technical skills but also highlighted his commitment to making a positive impact on the lives of others. For this innovative solution, Samrath received honorable recognition, earning acclaim for his dedication and ingenuity. In addition to his international endeavors, Samrath has also made significant contributions at the local level. He participated in the Inter APS Science Competition, where his innovative spirit shone once again. His project, a wireless firecracker igniter, captured the attention of the judges and earned him the prestigious first prize. His ability to combine technical expertise with creative problem-solving underscores his potential to effect meaningful change in the world. Through his participation in various competitions and projects, Samrath Singh exemplifies the qualities of a forward-thinking innovator, driven by a desire to make a positive difference in society. As he continues his academic journey in Computer Science and Engineering, Samrath remains committed to leveraging technology for the betterment of humanity.

Simranjot Singh is a dynamic and creative individual with a solid foundation in media studies, complemented by a minor in Psychology. Her experience in digital marketing, advertising, and communication have honed her ability to develop engaging narratives, conduct thorough research, and collaborate effectively within teams. During her internship she has conducted in-depth research for a documentary, performed competition analysis and collaborated with renowned brands while working with Planning Department of a renowned advertising agency. She has completed various training programs, including courses in digital advertising, journalism, and marketing. I am also well-versed with social media platforms and up-to-date with current trends.

Satya Subrahmanyam is a distinguished academic leader, researcher, and institutional strategist with over 27 years of experience in higher education, leadership, and research management. He holds two PhDs and a Postdoctoral qualification from the Polytechnic Institute of Leiria, Portugal. Currently serving as Professor and Dean (Research) at Holy Spirit University of Kaslik (USEK), Lebanon, he spearheads research initiatives that enhance academic excellence and institutional reputation. He played a pivotal role in the development of the Catholic University in Erbil, Kurdistan, where he established new departments, led research programs, and collaborated on international educational projects. As a founding member and Managing Partner of Vignan Institute of Technology and Management, India, he contributed to its transformation into a premier institution. With expertise in AI-driven business strategies, HR analytics, and leadership in technology adoption, he has published extensively, guided PhD research, and led training programs in corporate and academic settings.

T. Venkat Narayana Rao is a professor and hod of CSE-IoT is an academician and researcher. Hir has published various number of research papers and book chapters, books etc. His research area includes Image Processing, Cloud Computing, Information Security.

Index

Symbols

A

B

C

D

E

F

G

H

I

L

M

N

O

P

R

S

T

U

V

W

www.ingramcontent.com/pod-product-compliance
Lightning Source LLC
LaVergne TN
LVHW080351011026
849161LV00009B/2268